Zanzibar

Pemba • Mafia

the Bradt Travel Guide

Chris McIntyre & Susan McIntyre

edition
7

www.bradtguides.com

Bradt Travel Guides Ltd, UK
The Globe Pequot Press Inc, USA

Mnemba Island Marine Conservation Area
page 236

Mnarani Natural Aquarium
page 219

Pemba Island
Chake Chake

Zanzibar Island
(Unguja)
Zanzibar Town

DAR ES SALAAM

Mafia Island
Kilindoni

TANZANIA

Selous
Game
Reserve

Tanga

Pemba
Channel

Panza Island

Tumbatu
Island

INDIAN
OCEAN

Bradt

0   80km
0   50 miles

INDIAN OCEAN

Mnemba Island

Muyuni Beach

Mvuleni

Mvuleni Ruins

Ras Nungwi

Nungwi

Kendwa

Fukuchani Ruins

Matemwe

Pwani Mchangani

Kiwengwa

Pongwe

Uroa

Ras Uroa

Mchangani

Kiboje

Kizimbani

Chuini

Mahonda

Ndagaa

Kinyasini

Chaani

Mkwajuni

Kivunge

Donge

Bumbwini

Makoba

Mangapwani

Mkokotoni

Tumbatu Island

Gomani

Shirazi Ruins

Bradt

INDIAN OCEAN

Zanzibar
Don't miss…

Wildlife
Kirk's red colobus
Procolobus kirkii
(AZ) page 53

Diving & snorkelling
Diver on wall
(FJ) page 103

Beaches
Beach at sunset
(AZ) page 73

**Zanzibar
Stone Town**
and House of Wonders
(AZ) page 167

Culture
Artist at work
(AZ) page 42

top   **Leaf fish** (FJ)
above left   **Soft coral** (RCC)
above right   **Spotted eagle ray** (RCC)
below   **Coral grouper** (RCC)

top Salender's toby (FJ)

above Juvenile angelfish and big eye (FJ)

right Flat worm (FJ)

below Black snapper (FJ)

above **Leaving a sandbar, Mafia Island** (CM) page 343
below left **Learning how to make rope from coconut fibre** (CM) page 51
below right **Basket weaver** (AZ)

Authors and Contributors

Chris McIntyre went to Africa in 1987, after reading physics at Queen's College, Oxford. He taught with VSO in Zimbabwe for almost three years and travelled extensively, before co-authoring the UK's first guide to Namibia and Botswana for Bradt Travel Guides. He now writes the Bradt guides to Namibia, Botswana and Zambia, and updates them with months of travel and research every year.

Chris is also the managing director of Expert Africa – a leading African tour operator. When not travelling, he works with his specialist team to organise individual trips and honeymoons to southern and eastern Africa – including the islands of Zanzibar and Mafia.

He is a Fellow of the Royal Geographical Society, and occasionally writes and photographs for the media. Based in West London, he lives with his wife, Susan McIntyre, and can be contacted by email on chris.mcintyre@expertafrica.com.

Susan McIntyre spent her formative years living in Zambia and Saudi Arabia, which gave her a tremendous enthusiasm for travel. After returning to the UK to attend university, Susan spent a further year globetrotting before joining the travel industry in a professional capacity in 1999. Having created communications' strategies for tourist boards, hotels and tour operators, Susan sought a career focusing on African travel, the area about which she is most passionate. She has acted as a consultant for Expert Africa and has coordinated media campaigns for a number of southern Africa's finest independent safari camps and boutique hotels.

Susan spends several months each year in Africa with Chris McIntyre, and many more encouraging the press and public to visit; she can be contacted by email on susie@themcintyres.co.uk.

MAJOR CONTRIBUTORS

Philip Briggs provided the original base information for the *Southern Tanzania Safaris* chapter and additional facts and figures. He is the author of the Bradt guides to Tanzania, Uganda, Ethiopia, Malawi, Mozambique and Ghana, as well as their *East African Wildlife*, and co-author of their guide to Rwanda. He also contributes regular travel and wildlife features to *Travel Africa*, *Africa Geographic* and *Africa Birds & Birding* magazines.

Sarah Chanter wrote the original *History* section and many of the historical items for early editions of this book. She has a keen interest in the history and culture of Zanzibar, has worked as a teacher in Kenya, and has travelled extensively throughout east and southern Africa.

Said el-Gheithy lives and works in both Zanzibar and London. As director of the Centre for African Language Learning (London) and the Princess Salme Institute (Zanzibar/London), he kindly provided information for the *Language* and *History* sections in previous editions of this book.

David Else is a professional travel writer. He first reached Zanzibar in 1985, sailing by dhow from Dar es Salaam. Over the next two decades (and using more comfortable transport) he visited Zanzibar regularly and wrote the first five editions of this guidebook. David now lives in the north of England – a long way indeed from a tropical coastline.

Jeff Fleisher is an archaeological researcher in the Department of Anthropology at the University of Virginia, and provided valuable information for the historical and cultural sections of this book.

Tricia and Bob Hayne researched and provided much of the current section on Pemba. Formerly editorial director of Bradt Travel Guides, Tricia is now a freelance travel writer, and a member of the British Guild of Travel Writers. She and Bob have also helped to update Chris's guides to Namibia, Botswana and Zambia.

Penny Hooper was responsible for much of the current *Mafia Archipelago* chapter. She taught in China, and travelled throughout southeast Asia and South America, before reading English and European Literature at Warwick University. Since then she's fallen in love with Africa, and led many tours through Morocco, Djibouti and South Africa.

Dudley Iles is a keen ornithologist and conservationist, and provided information on the wildlife of Zanzibar. From 1993 to 1995 he worked for the Commission for Lands and Environment in Zanzibar, helping to set up environmental clubs and train conservation officers.

Christine Osborne wrote the original text on which this book's *Mafia Archipelago* chapter was based. Born in Australia, she has travelled widely through Africa and the Indian Ocean islands as a writer and photographer. Christine now runs the multi-faith and travel image libraries www.worldreligions.co.uk and www.copix.co.uk. She is a member of the British Guild of Travel Writers.

Gemma Pitcher is a travel writer who has lived and worked on Zanzibar, and travelled widely throughout eastern and southern Africa. She provided content for the early editions of this book; some of the text originally appeared in *Zanzibar Style* which was written by Gemma, and is reproduced with permission.

Dr Matthew Richmond is a marine science and fisheries expert who has lived and worked on Zanzibar and around the western Indian Ocean since 1989. Matt is involved in numerous marine education and biodiversity projects in the region, is the author of *A Guide to the Seashores of Eastern Africa and the Western Indian Ocean Islands*, and provided the text on marine wildlife for this book.

AUTHORS' STORY

Holidays in Africa have long concentrated on game-rich safaris on the mainland. Visitors since Livingstone have travelled from across the globe for great wildlife spectacles set in vast tracts of wilderness, sometimes accompanied by strange and fascinating traditional cultures. Many find themselves bitten by the Africa bug, returning as frequently as possible, but it is only recently that Africa's islands have been viewed as final destinations their own right.

For us, the transition from bush to beach followed a similar pattern. We have both lived in southern Africa, Chris teaching in rural Zimbabwe and pioneering Bradt's travel guides to Namibia, Botswana and Zambia; Susie spending a happy childhood in Zambia. Our early experiences were concentrated in the heart of Africa; any travel focused heavily on the national parks and wildlife wonders of neighbouring countries.

Years later and still hooked on the continent, Chris used his experience to establish Expert Africa, a UK-based tour operator. Slowly, an opportunity became clear to offer exotic beach hideaways: relaxing ends to more traditional safaris. Keen to understand the options, we explored all the archipelagos from southern Mozambique to Tanzania's Pemba. Our first trip took us to Zanzibar and its idyllic neighbour, Mafia – we were enchanted! So when the opportunity arose to take on the Bradt guide to these islands, we leapt at the chance to research in more depth, and get a deeper understanding of these islands.

Now, as we sign off our second edition of this guide, we're pleased to have been able to completely overhaul some sections of this guidebook and extensively update many others. We remain humbled by the helpful individuals we've encountered, amazed at the marine life in the turquoise seas, and also concerned by some of the less responsible developments that we've seen. We hope that this guide my help ethical travellers to contribute towards a better future for these striking islands.

PUBLISHER'S FOREWORD   *Hilary Bradt*

The first Bradt travel guide was written in 1974 by George and Hilary Bradt on a river barge floating down a tributary of the Amazon. In the 1980s and '90s the focus shifted away from hiking to broader-based guides covering new destinations – usually the first to be published about these places. In the 21st century Bradt continues to publish such ground-breaking guides, as well as others to established holiday destinations, incorporating in-depth information on culture and natural history with the nuts and bolts of where to stay and what to see.

Bradt authors support responsible travel, and provide advice not only on minimum impact but also on how to give something back through local charities. In this way a true synergy is achieved between the traveller and local communities.

My association with Zanzibar goes back to 1976 when the newly 'Africanised' and socialist government of the island was hostile to foreign visitors. I have since returned many times as lecturer on board expedition ships and have relished the changes I have seen. The beaches are still superb, and while Stone Town still has the intimacy and total otherness that I loved, the buildings have been renovated and tourists now receive a warm welcome. On my last visit I escaped my group and wandered the narrow streets away from the tourist centre, stopping to watch a small child play with a toy car made from wire and bottle tops. His father, seeing my interest, came forward with a broad grin and asked me to photograph the two of them. That brief encounter epitomised all that I love about Zanzibar.

Chris McIntyre's talent at knowing what Bradt readers are looking for has made him one of our most praised writers on Africa. Once again, he and Susan McIntyre have extensively revised one of our most successful guides, bringing their inside knowledge to an ever-widening audience of travellers to Zanzibar.

Seventh edition February 2009 First published 1993

Bradt Travel Guides Ltd
23 High Street, Chalfont St Peter, Bucks SL9 9QE, England; www.bradtguides.com
Published in the USA by The Globe Pequot Press Inc, 246 Goose Lane,
PO Box 480, Guilford, Connecticut 06475-0480

Text copyright © 2009 Chris McIntyre   Maps copyright © 2009 Bradt Travel Guides Ltd
Illustrations © 2009 individual photographers and artists (see below)

British Library Cataloguing in Publication Data
A catalogue record for this book is available from the British Library
ISBN-13: 978 1 84162 254 5

Photographs Russell & Cindy Campbell (RCC, russandcindy@oceansense.net), Eleanor Dunkels (ED), Tricia Hayne (TH), Keith Hern (KH), Farhat Jah (FJ), Chris McIntyre (CM), Susan McIntyre (SM), Ariadne Van Zandbergen (AZ)
Front cover Sailing dhow, Kiwengwa beach (Yadid Levy/Alamy)
Back cover Colourful Zanzibar painting (AZ), Artist at work (AZ)
Title page Detail of dhow (AZ), Girl at traditional Zanzibar door (AZ), Fabric stall, Stone Town (KH)
Illustrations Annabel Milne, Carole Vincer   **Maps** Malcolm Barnes

Typeset from the authors' disc by Wakewing
Printed and bound in India by Nutech Photolithographers, New Delhi

Acknowledgements

Susan and Chris McIntyre have extensively updated and rewritten the guide for this seventh edition. However, thanks are due to the many people who have helped with advice, information and contributions throughout the book's many years of life.

Some are already listed as major contributors (pages II–III) and others are named in the text. Of the rest, special thanks go to Peter Bennett, who helped research and gather information for four early editions of this book. Further help has come from many others, including Javed Jafferji, John da Silva, Balkishna Gorolay, who greatly benefited our history section, and Fiona Clark and Jim Boggs, for input on wildlife and culture. For wildlife contributions, particular thanks to Rob Wild, Dr Nadia Corp, Lorna Slade and Dr Per Berggren. Thanks also to Toufiq Juma Toufiq, Ali Addurahim, and Ali Khamis Mohammed for local insights; and to Adria LaViolette for historical, archaeological and anthropological input. Hildegard Kiel and Yusuf Mahmoud helped with the music and dance section, whilst Haji Hafidh and Robert Pasiani of Eco+Culture gave great insight into community tourism initiatives and practical help with local transport details.

For this seventh edition we're very grateful also to all those who have so willingly offered information, insight and a place to rest our heads: Salim Abdullah, Dr Per Berggren, Anthony Chege, Jonathan Cheres, Christian Chilcott, Nicola Colangelo, Dorthe Davidsen Langås, Nigel Firman, Chris Goodwin, Elies Hagedoorn, Keith Horan, Bas Hochstenbach, Christian Chilcott, Tammy Holter, Guyonne James, Ralph Kruidering, Frida Lanshammar, Kassim Mande, Elly M'langa, Dr Aviti J Mmochi, Hashir Mohammed, Mohammed Naushad Mohammed, Flo Montgomery, Mustafa Mukame, Sam Mundia, Ali Mwinyi, Thomas Norberg, Julian O'Leary, Alison Oliver, Sue and Andrew Page, Illa Peters, Stefanie Schoetz, Paul Shepherd, Abdul Simai, Puneet Singh, Sylvie and Torgeir Vaage, Jean de Villiers, Tom and Gloria Zimmermann and Edwin van Zwam.

THE NEXT EDITION

Our readers play a vital role in updating books for the next edition. If you have found changes, or new and exciting places, or have a story to share, do write. Email the authors on chris@expertafrica.com or susie@themcintyres.co.uk, or write to: 'Zanzibar', Bradt Travel Guides Ltd, 23 High Street, Chalfont St Peter, Bucks SL9 9QE, UK; ☎ +44 (0)1753 893444; e info@bradtguides.com; www.bradtguides.com.

Contents

TANZANIA

LIST OF MAPS

Introduction

Zanzibar is one of those magical, evocative African names, like Timbuktu, Casablanca or Kilimanjaro. For many travellers, the name alone is reason enough to come. Yet although expectations run high, awareness of the reality on Zanzibar and its neighbouring islands is often rather hazy.

Like many visitors, we discovered the islands relatively recently. We both had friends who had sailed from mainland Tanzania to Zanzibar decades ago, and returned eulogising about the intoxicating aroma of spices, the amazing beaches, and just how cheap it was – but somehow neither of us made it there.

When we eventually visited at the start of the new millennium, stylish lodges were flourishing alongside backpackers' beach hideaways, and flights around the islands were becoming easier. On that first trip we also discovered Mafia – a smaller and quieter archipelago to the south, with fewer visitors and spectacular diving.

It's now close to nine years and many trips since our first encounters, and a tremendous amount of change has taken place: both good and bad. It remains impossible not to be enchanted as you approach from the air, looking down on sparkling turquoise waters, darkened only by patch reefs, and punctuated by the billowing triangular white sails of passing dhows. We still always smile as we step off the plane, to be enveloped by Zanzibar's exotic blend of warmth, humidity and aromatic spices.

For many, the islands offer a quintessential Indian Ocean experience: palm-lined stretches of powder-white coral sand line the coast for miles, while below the waves, reef fish flit amongst colourful coral gardens, overshadowed only by the occasional pelagic looming out of the blue. From the turtles that nest here, to the whale sharks seen annually off Mafia, there is always something unexpected awaiting the diver and snorkeller. On land, too, these islands can enthral. Kirk's red colobus monkeys can be seen in the forest, Arabian architecture provides an exotic urban backdrop, and village life remains steeped in tradition. Yet, despite the stunning raw material and depth of culture, aspects of Zanzibar have the potential to disappoint.

Development along huge swathes of Zanzibar's coastline, by both foreign and local investors, has been astonishingly fast, and much of it is lamentable. In general, there appears to be scant regard for environmental impact and a disturbing lack of real community development. The islands are also handicapped by a largely autonomous government which, at best, has combined inefficiency at regulating development with ineffectiveness at providing even the most basic of public services. At worst, and in stark contrast to the more positive situation in Tanzania, it seems to conform to the most negative stereotypes of African governance.

Despite these issues, we have found much to hearten us on recent research trips, mostly due to a sprinkling of dedicated, forward-thinking individuals who are determined not to give up on the islands and their people. A handful of interesting, ethically run hotels and lodges do exist, even if they need to be carefully sought out in advance of visiting. (Planning well will invariably improve your overall island experience.) For those who want to escape to simple, small lodges with great diving and snorkelling, the lodges on Mafia are firm personal favourites and less visited simply because the island is less well known. On Zanzibar, Fumba Beach Lodge in the southwest is trail-blazing a new part of the island in some style; the top-end Matemwe Bungalows continues to impress; and Casa del Mar in Jambiani has also adopted some excellent community initiatives. Meanwhile, trail-blazing models of responsible tourism, like Chumbe Island and Mafia's Chole Mjini, continue to force the pace.

Away from hotels and lodges, opportunities for visitors to enrich their holidays whilst also making a positive impact on the people, range from original and high-quality souvenir shopping, which also happens to be fair trade, to local village restaurants with impressively high standards of cuisine, and the eclectic island tours run by Eco+Culture, who are dedicated to funding community development. We love these primarily because they're all very good indeed – but also because these initiatives are responsible in their approach. If you take time to look beyond the gaze of most visitors, and vote with your feet to support them, you might find your trip taken to a whole new level.

While researching this latest edition, we arranged to meet with Mr Kassim Mande, founder and leader of the Jambiani Village Cultural Tour. A kind and knowledgeable Zanzibari, he is totally dedicated to his community and their surroundings. With Kassim to guide us, we met and talked to ordinary, hard-working Jambiani residents: nursery children and teachers, young boys climbing for coconuts, women preparing seaweed for sale, the revered traditional healer and local restaurateurs. As we were welcomed into humble homes and learnt about daily life, it became patently clear why Kassim is so passionate and dedicated to educating tourists about Zanzibari village life and generating funds to improve the lives of his community.

Jambiani has a proud history and a deep culture. Kassim is determined that both must be protected, but he is equally resolute that it should have a happy, prosperous future. He believes that, by encouraging visitors and community members to engage with each other and understand local sensitivities, he can start to break down some of the negative barriers which have arisen from a lack of knowledge and respect, and in doing so bring in some much-needed cash to their economy.

Kassim's enthusiasm and warmth is infectious, his mission commendable, and the generosity we encountered humbling. This was one of our favourite days on Zanzibar, quite simply because it offered one of the archipelago's most genuine and accessible opportunities to interact with local Zanzibaris.

The message is clear: don't discount the less well-known areas of Zanzibar, Pemba Island or the Mafia Archipelago. And for some of the best experiences, get off the beaten track, ideally with knowledgeable residents. Your choices will make a difference not only to your stay, but also to the communities that you encounter.

These islands already receive more than 140,000 visitors each year; fewer than one in every fifty will have a copy of this guide. We hope it helps you to get there, to choose the right places to stay, and to make the most of your time on the islands. But more than that, we hope that it will open your eyes to some of the more off-beat and responsible travel opportunities on the islands, and give you the confidence to venture off on your own, away from the lodges that we've so carefully described, to explore and to meet people like Mr Kassim Mande – for their sake, as well as for the good of your holiday.

Part One

GENERAL INFORMATION

Islands Zanzibar Island (Unguja), Pemba Island, and surrounding islands

Location About 40km off the coast of east Africa, in the Indian Ocean, about 6°S of Equator

Size Zanzibar 1,660km², Pemba 985km²

Climate Wet season mid March to end May; short rains November; rest of year generally dry. Average temperature 26–28°C

Status Separate state within United Republic of Tanzania, governed by Revolutionary Council and House of Representatives

Population 1,070,000 (2004 estimate)

Life expectancy 48

Main town Zanzibar Town, population 205,870 (2002)

Economy Fishing, agriculture, tourism

Languages Swahili (official), also Arabic

Religion Islam

Currency Tanzanian shilling (TSh)

Exchange rate £1 = TSh2,157, US$1 = TSh1,166, €1 = TSh1,722 (August 2008)

International telephone code +255

Time GMT +3

Electrical voltage 230v 50Hz; round or square three-pin 'British-style' plugs

Weights and measures Metric

Flag The new flag, inaugurated in 2005, consists of three horizontal stripes in green, black and blue, and features an inset of the United Republic of Tanzania flag.

National anthem *Mungu ibariki Afrika* (God Bless Africa)

Public holidays 1 January, 12 January, 26 April, 1 May, 7 July, 9 December, 25 December (see also pages 102–3)

History, Politics and Economy

HISTORY *Sarah Chanter, with additional contributions by Jeff Fleisher*

The monsoons that blow across the Indian Ocean have allowed contact between Persia, Arabia, India and the coast of east Africa (including the islands of Zanzibar) for over 2,000 years. The first European arrivals were Portuguese 'navigators' looking for a trade route to India. They reached Zanzibar at the end of the 15th century and established a trading station here and at other points on the east African coast.

At the end of the 17th century the Portuguese were ousted by the Omani Arabs. During this period, Zanzibar became a major slaving centre. In 1840, the Omani sultan Said moved his court from Muscat to Zanzibar, and the island became an Arab state and an important centre of trade and politics in the region. Many European explorers, including Livingstone and Stanley, began their expeditions into the interior of Africa from Zanzibar during the second half of the 19th century.

Zanzibar was a British protectorate from 1890 until 1963, when the state gained independence. In 1964, the sultan and the government were overthrown in a revolution. In the same year, Zanzibar and the newly independent country of Tanganyika combined to form the United Republic of Tanzania.

FIRST INHABITANTS AND EARLY VISITORS The first human beings, *Homo erectus*, evolved in the East African Rift Valley, within 1,000 miles of Zanzibar, about 1.5 million years ago. They migrated throughout Africa and later Asia and beyond, becoming hunter-gatherers. Near rivers and coasts these people developed fishing techniques, and it is possible that Zanzibar's first human inhabitants were fishermen who crossed from the African mainland in dugout canoes sometime during the 1st millennium BC.

At around the same time, or even earlier, the east African coast (including the islands of Zanzibar) may have received visitors from many parts of the ancient world, such as Mesopotamia (present-day Iraq) and Egypt. The Egyptian pharaohs sent expeditions to the land they called Punt (present-day Somalia) in around 3000BC and again in 1492BC; these possibly continued southwards down the east African coast. This theory is supported by carvings on temple walls at Luxor showing sailing boats with slaves unloading gold, ivory tusks, leopard skins and trees of frankincense.

Other visitors may have included Phoenicians, a seafaring people from the eastern shores of the Mediterranean. Around 600BC, a Phoenician fleet sailed south along the coast, past Zanzibar, and is believed to have circumnavigated Africa before returning to the Mediterranean three years later.

By the 1st century AD, Greek and Roman ships were sailing from the Red Sea down the east African coast, searching for valuable trade goods such as tortoiseshell, ebony and ivory. Around AD60, a Greek merchant from Alexandria wrote a guide for

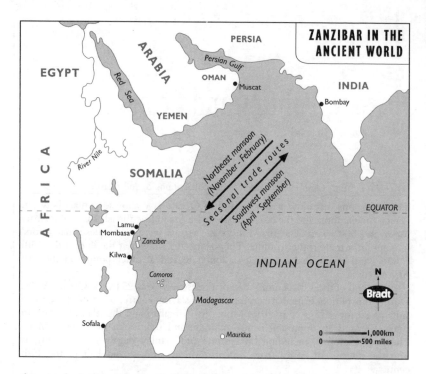

The map shows:

PERSIA

ARABIA

Persian Gulf

EGYPT

OMAN

Muscat

Red Sea

ZANZIBAR IN THE ANCIENT WORLD

INDIA

Bombay

YEMEN

River Nile

SOMALIA

AFRICA

Northeast monsoon (November – February)

Seasonal trade routes

Southwest monsoon (April – September)

EQUATOR

Lamu
Mombasa
Zanzibar
Kilwa

Comoros

INDIAN OCEAN

N

Bradt

Madagascar

Sofala

Mauritius

0 — 1,000km
0 — 500 miles

ships in the Indian Ocean called *The Periplus of the Erythaean Sea*. This is the first recorded eyewitness account of the east African coast, and describes 'the Island of Menouthesias' (most likely the present-day island of Unguja, also called Zanzibar Island) as 'flat and wooded' with 'many rivers' and 'small sewn boats used for fishing'. Another Alexandrine Greek, Claudius Ptolemaeus (usually called Ptolemy), also mentioned Menouthesias in his book *Geographike*, written about AD150.

At about the same time, it is thought that Arab and Persian trading ships from the Persian Gulf were also sailing down the coast of east Africa. They sailed south on the northeast monsoon between November and February, carrying beads and cloth, and even Chinese porcelain that had come via India. Then, between March and September, after the winds changed direction, they returned north on the southwest monsoon, carrying the same tortoiseshell, ebony and ivory that had attracted the Greeks and Romans, plus mangrove poles for timber and other goods. The Arabs and Persians traded with the local inhabitants but they remained visitors and, at this stage, did not settle.

During the 3rd and 4th centuries AD, other groups of migrating peoples started to arrive on the east coast of Africa. These people were Bantu (the name comes from the term used to define their group of languages); they originated from the area around present-day Cameroon in the centre of the continent, then spread throughout eastern and southern Africa. On the east African coast, they established settlements, which slowly grew into towns, and eventually became the major trading cities such as Kilwa, Lamu and Mombasa on the mainland, and Unguja Ukuu on the island of Unguja (Zanzibar Island). These coastal settlers traded with the Arabs, exporting ivory, rhino-horn, tortoiseshell and palm oil, and importing metal tools and weapons, wine and wheat.

The Arab traders called the east African coast Zinj el Barr, meaning 'land of the black people', from where the modern name Zanzibar is derived. 'Zinj' comes from *zang*, the Persian word for 'black', and *barr* is the Arabic word for 'land'. The Arabs may also have derived the word from *Zayn za'l barr*, meaning 'fair is this land'. Zanzibar remained the name of the whole coast, including the islands of Unguja and Pemba (which together make up the present-day state of Zanzibar), until the late 15th century.

EARLY ARAB SETTLERS The 7th century AD saw the rise of Islam in Arabia. At the same time wars in this area, and subsequent unrest in Persia, caused a small number of people from these regions to escape to the east African coast, where they settled permanently, bringing the new Islamic religion with them.

There are several accounts of emigrations from Arabia to east Africa. (The history of this period is largely based on stories handed down by word of mouth through generations, which are difficult to separate from myth and legend.) One story tells of two Arab chiefs from Oman who arrived in east Africa with their families around the end of the 7th century, and settled on the island of Pate, near Lamu. Another story tells of an emigration from Shiraz, in Persia, some time between the 8th and 10th centuries. The Sultan of Shiraz and his six sons migrated with their followers in seven boats. One of the sons stopped at Pemba, while others settled in Mombasa and Kilwa. The 9th-century Arab tale of Sinbad the Sailor, one of the stories in *The Arabian Nights*, was most probably inspired by accounts of journeys by Arab sailors to east Africa and southeast Asia.

THE RISE OF THE SWAHILI During the second half of the first millennium, the coastal Bantu people developed a language and culture (in fact, a whole civilisation) which became known as Swahili. This name came from the Arabic word *sahil*, meaning 'coast'. Their language, Kiswahili, although Bantu in origin, contained many Arabic words. It also included some Persian words, mainly nautical terms. There was some intermarriage, and the Swahili adopted many Arab customs and traditions, including the Islamic religion. On Unguja (Zanzibar Island), Shirazi settlers are believed to have married into the family of the island's Swahili king. Several centuries later, the Mwinyi Mkuu ('the great lord'), the traditional ruler of Unguja, continued to claim descent from a Shirazi prince.

By the 7th century, the Swahili people were trading regularly with Arab and Persian merchants. In the same way, Swahili dhows (traditional ships based on an Arab design) also became involved in the trade and sailed regularly to and from the Persian Gulf, carrying gold, ivory, rhino-horn, leopard skins, tortoiseshell, and ambergris from whales. African slaves were also carried to the Persian Gulf, probably to work in the marshlands of Mesopotamia.

Over the following centuries the trade between Africa and Arabia increased, as did trading links between east Africa and Asia. Ivory was exported to India, and later China, while Indian cloth and Chinese porcelain and silk were imported to Arabia and Zanzibar. At around this time, Indonesian sailors from Java and Sumatra are thought to have reached east Africa and Madagascar, possibly introducing coconuts and bananas.

From this period (7th to 10th centuries) archaeologists have discovered a very distinctive kind of local pottery, known as Tana Tradition, which looks the same at sites along the whole east African coast, from northern Kenya to southern Tanzania, and out to the Comoros Islands. The similarity of this pottery over such a large area shows how closely linked the people of the coast were, and also shows – for the first time – a sense of commonality and shared experience. Imported ceramics, called Sassian Islamic, from the Persian Gulf, have also been discovered.

Archaeological, linguistic and historical research conducted since the early 1980s has also led to a shift in the way that the early history of the coast is interpreted, rejecting some of the ideas put forward by scholars working during the 1950s, 1960s and 1970s. In essence, this research suggests that at its core – its foundation – Swahili culture and history are African phenomena. Until recently, archaeologists had proposed that the large towns of the east African coast (such as Kilwa, Lamu, Mombasa and Unguja Ukuu) had been built by Persian or Arab settlers, and the local Bantu people had then intermarried and 'Africanised' the Arabs, thus resulting in the Swahili people. But, through extensive excavations at many of these towns, it is now known that they were founded by people from the interior of Africa and, instead of simply starting as grand towns, were actually built up slowly over time by these same people.

Unquestionably, the links to the Indian Ocean trade were some of the most important for these towns, but there is little evidence of large-scale migrations from Arabia or Persia to the coast of east Africa until the middle of the second millennium.

ZANZIBAR ENTERS THE SECOND MILLENNIUM On Unguja, one of the earliest remaining examples of permanent settlement from Persia is a mosque at Kizimkazi, on the southern part of the island. It contains an inscription dated AH500 (Anno Hegirae), which corresponds to the Christian year AD1107, making this the oldest-known Islamic building on the east African coast. From the end of the 12th century, Omani immigrants also settled in Pemba. At around the same time, the settlement that was to become Zanzibar Town also began to grow.

As the trade between Africa, Arabia and the rest of the Indian Ocean continued to expand, Zanzibar became an increasingly powerful and important commercial centre. Major imports included cotton cloth, porcelain and copper from Dabhol, a port on the west coast of India, and exports included iron from Sofala (in present-day Mozambique). By the 13th century, Zanzibar was minting its own coins, and stone buildings were starting to replace more basic mud dwellings. In 1295, the Venetian traveller Marco Polo wrote of Zanzibar: 'The people have a king … elephants in plenty … and whales in large numbers', although he never visited the island. Other writers of the time noted that the kings and queens of Zanzibar and Pemba dressed in fine silks and cottons, wore gold jewellery, and lived in stone houses decorated with Persian carpets and Chinese porcelain.

Many Chinese imports had come to Zanzibar via India, but in the early 15th century the ports on the coast of east Africa were trading directly with China. Gold, ivory and rhino-horn were transported to the East, as well as a small number of slaves. In 1414, a dhow from the city of Malindi (in present-day Kenya) carried a giraffe to China, as a present for the emperor. The trade came to an abrupt end in 1443 when the new Ming emperor banned Chinese merchants from going abroad, but the demand for ivory remained, supplied by Arab dhows via markets in India.

By the mid 15th century, the islands of Zanzibar, along with Mombasa, Malindi, Lamu and Kilwa, formed a chain of thriving Swahili Islamic city states, each with its own sultan, spread along the east African coast. These cities had close trading links with Arabia, Persia, India and southeast Asia. Commerce between Africa and the Indian Ocean had become very profitable, and it seems that the sultans of Zanzibar and the other city states were more than happy for their territories to remain as gateways or conduits for it. At the end of the 15th century, though, the situation was severely disrupted by the arrival of the Portuguese on the coast of east Africa.

PORTUGUESE RULE By the mid 15th century, Prince Henry 'the Navigator' of Portugal was encouraging voyages of exploration around the African coast. He hoped to find a sea route to the east, as well as the Christian kingdom of the legendary Pester John (or 'Priest-king') of Abyssinia. With the rise of the Ottoman

Empire in 1453, all goods from the East, including the increasingly valuable spices, now reached Portugal via potentially hostile Muslim countries.

In 1487, Prince Henry's successor, King John II, dispatched two expeditions to the East led by Bartholomew Dias and Pedro da Covilhan: one by sea around the southern tip of Africa, the other overland through Egypt. In 1497, another Portuguese navigator, Vasco da Gama, encouraged by the reports of Dias and da Covilhan, rounded the Cape of Good Hope and sailed northwards up the coast of east Africa, on the way to India. He passed Zanzibar and landed at Mombasa, where he received a hostile reception from the sultan. But he got a warm welcome in Malindi, an old enemy of Mombasa. Da Gama built a pillar of friendship on the shore at Malindi and employed an Omani navigator called Ahmed bin Majid to guide him across the Indian Ocean. On his return from India in 1499 he moored for a day off Unguja.

More Portuguese ships followed in the wake of da Covilhan and da Gama. They needed safe provisioning and repair bases for their voyages to and from the Far East, and so garrisons were established in the harbours of Unguja, Pemba and Mombasa.

Any early friendship was soon forgotten when the Portuguese took control of Unguja in 1503. A ship commanded by Rui Lorenco Ravasco moored off the southern end of the island while Portuguese sailors captured over 20 Swahili dhows and shot about 35 islanders. The Mwinyi Mkuu (ruler of Zanzibar) was forced to become a subject of Portugal, and agreed to allow Portuguese ships free access to Zanzibar. Additionally, he was required to pay an annual tribute to the Portuguese crown.

Portuguese domination of the region continued. In 1505, they took control of Mombasa, and in 1506, Pemba. Between 1507 and 1511, the Portuguese also occupied territories in the Arabian Gulf, including Muscat and the island of Hormuz.

By 1510, Unguja's tribute had fallen short and the people of Pemba had also become hostile to the Portuguese. Under Duarte de Lemos, the Portuguese looted and set fire to settlements on Unguja, then plundered the town of Pujini in Pemba. They soon regained both islands and by 1525 the whole east African coast, from Lamu to Sofala, was under Portuguese control. Gold, ivory, ebony and slaves from the interior were carried to Portuguese colonies in India or back to Portugal. Iron ore and garnets from Sofala, and coconut fibre and gum-copal (a tree resin) from the islands were also exported. Cloth, beads, porcelain and metal tools were imported to the east African coast from Oman and Portugal.

Around 1560 the Portuguese built a church and small trading settlement on a western peninsula of Unguja. This was to become Zanzibar Town. But although the Portuguese occupied Unguja, and forced the local people to trade under their supervision, the islanders continued to pay allegiance to the Mwinyi Mkuu, their own king.

Portugal was not the only European power with interests in the Indian Ocean. In November 1591, the *Edward Bonaventura*, captained by Sir James Lancaster, became the first English ship to call at Zanzibar. It was supplied with fresh food and water by the Mwinyi Mkuu. Soon, more European ships were calling at Zanzibar on their way to and from the Indian subcontinent and islands of the East Indies.

John Henderson, a Scottish sailor from one English ship, was reportedly held captive on Zanzibar in 1625. He later escaped, but not until he had fallen in love with a Zanzibari princess who escaped with him back to Scotland. Today, their portraits are in the collection of the Scottish National Portrait Gallery in Edinburgh.

THE PORTUGUESE LEGACY

Zanzibar was occupied by the Portuguese in the 16th and 17th centuries. They introduced many new foods, brought from their colonies in other parts of the world, and the Swahili words used for these today are borrowed directly from the Portuguese language: cassava or manioc is *muhogo* in Swahili (from the Portuguese *mandioca*) and the cashew nut is *mbibo*, from *bibo*, both plants originally grown in Brazil. Avocado is *mpea* and guava is *mpera*, both from the Portuguese word *pera*. The Portuguese also introduced the use of dung (Swahili: *mboleo*, Portuguese: *boleo*) for cultivation, and the iron nail (Swahili: *parafujo*, Portuguese: *parafuso*) for boatbuilding.

Source: A History of East Africa by Oliver Roland and Matthew Gervase, Oxford University Press, 1963

With the advent of English ships in the Indian Ocean, the Portuguese needed to strengthen their position on the coast. In 1594, they built a fort at Chake Chake in Pemba, and from 1593 to 1595, Fort Jesus in Mombasa was constructed. Settlers arrived from Portugal, and a Portuguese garrison was established in Fort Jesus, brutally suppressing the local population. Mombasa became known as *Mvita*, 'the place of war', and the Portuguese governor as *Afriti*, 'the devil'.

Despite these fortifications, however, the Portuguese position in east Africa began to weaken. In Arabia, Hormuz was regained by the Persians in 1622, and in January 1650, Muscat was regained by the Omani Arabs. Following this victory, the Sultan of Oman's navy sailed to Zanzibar to help the Mwinyi Mkuu, Queen Mwana Mwema. The Omanis raided the Portuguese settlement on Unguja, killing many people and imprisoning about 400 in the church. They also attacked and burnt the Portuguese settlement on Pemba. By 1668, virtually the entire coastal area was in Omani hands. The only garrisons still held by the Portuguese were at Fort Jesus in Mombasa, and on the western peninsula of Unguja.

In 1682, the Portuguese persuaded the Queen of Pemba, who was living in Goa, to return, but this attempt to install a friendly ruler in Pemba was frustrated when her own subjects drove her out. The last Portuguese inhabitants were expelled in 1695.

By this time, Queen Mwana Mwema of Unguja had been succeeded by her son, Yusuf. After his death, towards the end of the 17th century, the island was divided between his two children, Bakari and Fatuma. King Bakari ruled the southern part of the island, with Kizimkazi as his capital, while his sister, Queen Fatuma, ruled the northern part. Fatuma supported the Portuguese, so her capital was built near the garrison on the western peninsula which later became the site of Zanzibar Town.

When the Omani fleet arrived at Mombasa and laid siege to Fort Jesus in March 1696, Queen Fatuma sent three dhows full of food to help the Portuguese defenders. The dhows were captured and burnt by the Omanis, who then attacked Zanzibar itself, forcing Queen Fatuma and her followers to flee into the interior of the island.

The siege of Mombasa lasted until December 1698, when the Omani forces took Fort Jesus and installed an Omani governor. Once again, the Omanis attacked Zanzibar. They drove out the last of the Portuguese settlers, captured Queen Fatuma and took her to Oman, where she spent the next 12 years in exile before returning to resume her rule. While she was away, her son Hassan took the title Mwinyi Mkuu, but paid allegiance to Oman.

Thus the Portuguese were finally ousted from the whole east African coast, and the Omanis were firmly in control of the entire region as far south as present-day Mozambique (which remained in Portuguese hands until 1972).

OMANI RULE

Early sultans and the rise of the slave trade
From 1698, the Sultan of Oman ruled the islands of Zanzibar from Muscat, his capital, through appointed governors and occasional armed raids to put down minor rebellions. To consolidate his grip on the islands, a fort was built in Zanzibar Town, on the site of the Portuguese church, and by 1710 about 50 Omani soldiers were garrisoned there.

By this time, Oman had become a major trading nation. One of its major exports was dates, and the expansion of date plantations created a demand for cheap slave labour. The rules of Islam forbade the enslavement of Muslims, so Africans were imported in large numbers, many of them transported through Zanzibar. It is estimated that there were about 5,000 African slaves in Oman at the beginning of the 18th century, with about 500 new slaves arriving each year. Although most slaves were used on the plantations, others were employed as domestic workers or concubines, and some were re-exported to Persia or India.

In 1744, in Oman, the ruling Yaa'rubi dynasty (which had been in power since 1624) came to an end after a long civil war. It was succeeded by the new Busaidi dynasty led by Ahmed bin Said al Busaidi, an Omani merchant and shipowner. Ahmed was made Sultan of Oman and the east African coast; one of his first moves was to install a new governor in Zanzibar.

At this time, the governors of the east African city states paid allegiance to Oman, but in practice they enjoyed a great deal of autonomy. Zanzibar, Pemba, Lamu and Kilwa were all ruled by members of the Busaidi family, but Mombasa was controlled by a rival Omani family, the Mazrui. In 1746, the Mazruis declared Mombasa independent of Oman, and overthrew the Busaidi force on Pemba. In 1753, they tried to capture Zanzibar, but the governor here remained loyal to Oman and repelled the attack.

During this period, the Mwinyi Mkuu, King Hassan, had died and been succeeded by his son, named Sultan, who in turn was succeeded by his son Ahmed, and then by his grandson Hassan II.

Zanzibar was now a major commercial centre and had also become very important strategically. From the middle of the 18th century there was a flourishing trade in slaves from Zanzibar and Kilwa to the Mascarenes (present-day Mauritius and Réunion). By the 1770s, these numbered about 3,000 slaves a year. In the same period Dutch ships came to Zanzibar in search of slaves to work on plantations in the East Indies.

Until this time African slave traders had brought captured slaves to the coast, but by the end of the 18th century the demand for slaves had increased to such an extent that Arab and Swahili traders from the coast and islands were penetrating the African interior. By the 1770s, caravan traders had already travelled inland as far as Lake Nyasa (present-day Lake Malawi). (For more details, see box, *The east African slave trade*, pages 172–3.)

Sultan bin Ahmed and British involvement
In Oman a new sultan, Sultan bin Ahmed, came to power in 1792. He needed a strong ally to help him combat the Mazrui of Mombasa and also to keep the Persians out of Oman. He found this ally in Britain, by this time a powerful maritime nation with an empire expanding all over the world. In the late 18th century, Britain was at war with France and knew that the French emperor, Napoleon Bonaparte, was planning to march through

Persia and capture Muscat, on his way to invade India. In 1798, Britain and Oman agreed a Treaty of Commerce and Navigation. Sultan bin Ahmed pledged himself to British interests in India, and his territories became out of bounds to the French. He allowed the British East India Company to establish a trading station in the Persian Gulf, and a British consul was posted to Muscat.

As well as defeating Bonaparte, the British had another motive for the treaty with Oman: they wanted to put pressure on the sultan to end slavery, which had been declared illegal in England in 1772. At this time, the trade from Africa to Oman was still buoyant.

At the same time, Zanzibar's position as an important trade centre was bolstered further when the supply of ivory from Mozambique to India collapsed because of excessive Portuguese export duties. The traders simply shipped their ivory through Zanzibar instead.

Sultan Said and the birth of the spice trade In 1804, Sultan bin Ahmed of Oman was killed in battle, and his sons Salim and Said (aged 15 and 13) jointly inherited his kingdom with their cousin Bedr acting as regent. Two years later the young Said killed Bedr, who he believed was plotting to kill him; in 1806, he was proclaimed Sultan of Oman and the east African coast.

Said ruled his kingdom from Muscat and did not visit his African territories for several years. He maintained good relations with Britain because, like his father, he hoped for British help against the Persians and the Mazruis. During this period, wars and drought had drained Oman's economy, and many Omani merchants migrated to Zanzibar to participate in coastal trading and the caravans to the interior.

Meanwhile, in Europe, a campaign led by William Wilberforce resulted in the abolition of the slave trade within the British Empire in 1807. The USA passed a law against slave trading in 1808; the French and Germans did the same a few years later.

In east Africa, however, about 8,000 slaves were brought from the mainland to Zanzibar every year, many of them carrying ivory. The resultant surplus of slaves was addressed in 1812, when a Muscat-born Arab called Saleh bin Haramil al Abray introduced clove trees into Zanzibar from the island of Bourbon (now Réunion). The slaves were diverted to work on clove plantations and demand increased once again.

As the demand for slaves and ivory continued to expand, Arab traders from the coast pushed further inland. In 1820, they established a trading centre at Kazeh (near present-day Tabora, in Tanzania), over 800km (500 miles) from the coast. From Kazeh, trade routes branched north to the shores of present-day Lake Victoria, northwest to Buganda (now Uganda), and southwest to the southern end of Lake Tanganyika. (See map, *Zanzibar and the slave trade*, opposite.)

Early British anti-slaving attempts To combat this expansion in slavery the British consul in Muscat continued to put pressure on Sultan Said to end the slave trade. In September 1822, Said signed an anti-slavery treaty with the British captain Fairfax Moresby which prohibited slave transport south and east of the 'Moresby line' drawn from Cape Delgado, the southern limit of the sultan's domain in Africa, to Diu Head on the coast of India (see map, *Zanzibar and the slave trade*, opposite).

This treaty meant that the transport of slaves from Zanzibar to the Mascarenes and India was banned, but still permitted between Zanzibar and Oman. The sultan was also banned from selling slaves to Christians, which included the French for their Indian Ocean islands. British warships gained the right to confiscate any dhows found carrying slaves in forbidden waters. Ironically, British prohibition of the slave trade to the Mascarenes only led to an increased development of the slave

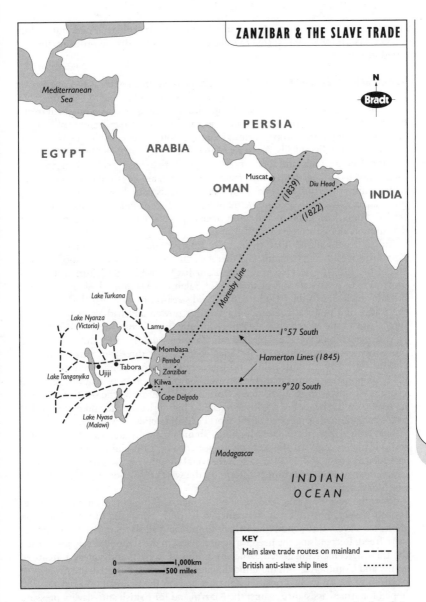

ZANZIBAR & THE SLAVE TRADE

Mediterranean Sea

EGYPT

ARABIA

PERSIA

OMAN

Muscat

(1839)

(1822)

Diu Head

INDIA

Moresby Line

Lake Turkana

Lake Nyanza (Victoria)

Lamu

Mombasa

Pemba

Zanzibar

Kilwa

1°57 South

Hamerton Lines (1845)

9°20 South

Tabora

Ujiji

Lake Tanganyika

Lake Nyasa (Malawi)

Cape Delgado

Madagascar

INDIAN OCEAN

KEY

Main slave trade routes on mainland ————

British anti-slave ship lines ··········

0   1,000km
0   500 miles

trade in Zanzibar itself. Sultan Said lost the revenue he would have received as duty on all slaves sold, so to make up the shortfall he encouraged the development of more clove plantations.

Meanwhile, Sultan Said continued to attempt to oust the Mazrui Sultan of Mombasa. In 1823, the sultan asked for British protection against Oman. Captain William Owen of HMS *Leven* saw that he could use this local dispute to Britain's advantage: he sailed to Muscat and informed Sultan Said that he intended to grant the Mazrui request for British protection unless Said agreed to end the slave trade. Said refused to do this, so Owen declared Mombasa a British protectorate, along with the coastline from Malindi to Pangani, on condition that the Mazrui sultan agreed to abolish the slave trade. The sultan agreed, but within a few years, the Mazrui reverted to slave trading, and the British protectorate was lifted in July 1826.

Sultan Said in Zanzibar In 1827, Sultan Said sailed from Muscat to Zanzibar to inspect his far-flung territory. Here he met one Edmund Roberts, an American merchant from Portsmouth, New Hampshire, who suggested a commercial treaty between Said and America. Soon Zanzibar was supplying large amounts of ivory to America and western Europe. African ivory was soft and easy to carve into combs, piano keys and billiard balls. Asian ivory, in contrast, was hard and brittle. (So great was the American demand for ivory in the 1830s that a town called Ivoryton was established in Connecticut, with a factory making piano keys and billiard balls out of ivory imported from Zanzibar.) The Americans also purchased animal hides and gum-copal, a tree resin used in the manufacture of varnish. In return, cotton cloth (called 'Amerikani'), guns and gunpowder were imported into Zanzibar for distribution along the coast and to Arabia.

Sultan Said realised that trade with Europe and America would increase Zanzibar's wealth and strength, and thereby consolidate his own position, so at the end of the 1820s he decided to develop Zanzibar's clove industry further. His first move was to confiscate the plantations of Saleh bin Haramil al Abray, who had introduced cloves to the island in 1812. Said's reason for this was that Saleh was the leader of a political faction competing for power, and had also continued to send slaves to the Mascarenes after the Moresby treaty had made this illegal.

Vast plantations were established on Zanzibar and Pemba, and the islands' prosperity soon grew dramatically. Said decreed that three clove trees must be planted for every coconut palm, and that any landowner failing to do so would have his property confiscated. He became the owner of 45 plantations scattered over the islands, with about 50 slaves working as labourers on the smaller plots and up to 500 on the larger ones. Cloves fetched a high price abroad and by the end of Said's reign Zanzibar was one of the world's leading clove producers.

Said valued Zanzibar's large harbour, abundant freshwater supply and fertile soil. He also recognised the strategic importance of a Busaidi power base on the east African coast, and decided to spend several months on the island each year. A large house was built for him at Mtoni, on the west coast of the island about 5km north of Zanzibar Town.

Over the next few years, Said came under increased pressure from the British to abolish slavery. This call was strengthened in 1833, when the Emancipation Act abolished slavery throughout the British Empire and all slaves in British territories were freed. Recognising the need for strong allies, in the same year Said formalised the trade agreement suggested earlier by Edmund Roberts and signed a Treaty of Amity and Commerce with the United States of America. This gave the Americans freedom to set up trading posts at Zanzibar and on the mainland. In return, Said hoped for armed assistance against the Mazrui and for British anti-slavery pressure to ease. In 1837, Said finally managed to oust the Mazrui from Mombasa and install his own garrison of soldiers in Fort Jesus. His presence along the coast of east Africa was finally complete.

Links between Zanzibar and America became increasingly cordial, and a consul, Richard Waters, was appointed in March 1837. Said presented him with a horse and a boat, and Waters was often the sultan's guest at Mtoni Palace. In November 1839, Said sent his trading ship *El-Sultani* to America. The ship arrived in New York in May 1840, the first Arab boat ever to visit an American port, and returned to Zanzibar with a cargo of arms and ammunition, china, beads and 'Amerikani' cloth.

Zanzibar becomes the capital of Oman In December 1840, Sultan Said established his capital in Zanzibar, transferring it 3,000 miles from Muscat. He made this move at a time when Zanzibar's prosperity was increasing rapidly, and Oman's was in decline. Said also believed that the dual powerbase of Zanzibar and Oman would help safeguard his territories on the African mainland and maintain his dominance over Indian Ocean trade. Many of Oman's most influential merchants were already based in Zanzibar, and more followed him in the move from Muscat.

Said's title was now Sultan of Zanzibar and Oman. He ruled Zanzibar directly while his eldest surviving son, Thuwaini, remained in Muscat as Governor of Oman. Zanzibar's own king, the Mwinyi Mkuu, presided over local matters but Said's government took control of trade and international affairs. Zanzibar Town began to expand: when Said had first arrived in the 1820s the buildings were mostly huts of mud thatched with coconut fronds, but by the 1850s many impressive stone buildings had been constructed by the new immigrants from Oman.

Said was also followed to Zanzibar by Captain Atkins Hamerton, who had originally been installed in Muscat to act as British consul. In December 1841, he became the first British consul in Zanzibar. France also established diplomatic relations with Zanzibar: a French consulate was opened in 1844.

Meanwhile, despite the restrictions imposed by the Moresby Treaty, the slave trade continued to expand. In 1841, Arab traders had established a trading colony at Ujiji on Lake Tanganyika, almost 1,600km (1,000 miles) from the coast, and in 1843 the first Arab caravans had reached Buganda (now Uganda) on the shores of present-day Lake Victoria. By the end of the 1840s, Arab traders had gone even further, reaching the Upper Congo (now eastern DRC), the Central Highland area around Mount Kenya, the Rift Valley lakes of Baringo and Turkana, and southern Ethiopia. About 13,000 slaves a year were arriving in Zanzibar from the mainland (see map, *Zanzibar and the slave trade*, page 11).

Britain's opposition to the slave trade Sultan Said became increasingly concerned that British attempts to abolish the slave trade would weaken his power in the region. In 1842, he sent his envoy Ali bin Nasur to London on the ship *El-Sultani* to plead his case. Said's gifts for Queen Victoria included emeralds, cashmere shawls, pearl necklaces and ten Arab horses.

In reply, the British government told the Zanzibari ruler that it wished to abolish the slave trade to Arabia, Oman, Persia and the Red Sea. To soften the blow Queen Victoria gave Said a state coach and a silver-gilt tea service. (The state coach arrived in pieces and had to be assembled. It was still unused a year later, as Zanzibar had no roads. The tea service was considered too ornate to use and was taken to the British consulate for safe keeping.)

Britain continued putting restrictions on the slave trade. In October 1845, Said was virtually forced by Captain Hamerton to sign another anti-slavery treaty, which allowed slave transport only between lines of latitude 1° 57' S and 9° 20' S (between Lamu and Kilwa, the northern and southern limits of Said's dominions on the coast). This meant slaves could still be imported into Zanzibar but could no longer be exported to Oman.

Ships from the British navy were employed to help enforce the treaty by capturing any dhows carrying slaves. When a dhow was captured, it was set on fire and the slaves were taken to Aden, India, or a free-slave community on the mainland coast, such as English Point in Mombasa. However, with only four ships to patrol a huge area of sea, the British navy found it hard to enforce the treaty, so the slave dhows continued to sail. Ships from France, Germany, Spain,

Portugal and America also continued to carry slaves, as there were still huge profits to be made. And on the mainland slave traders continued to push further into the interior.

Early European explorers In the 1840s, European missionaries and explorers began to venture into the east African interior. In Britain, an Association for Promoting the Discovery of the Interior Parts of Africa had been formed as early as 1788, and had since merged with the Royal Geographical Society (RGS). In the following years it would play a leading role in the search for the source of the River Nile.

Zanzibar became the usual starting point for journeys into the interior. Here, the European missionaries and explorers paid their respects to Sultan Said, who 'owned' most of the land they would pass through. They equipped their expeditions with supplies and porters, before sailing to Bagamoyo on the mainland. Many explorers followed the established slaving routes into the interior, often employing slave traders to act as guides.

In 1844, the English Church Missionary Society, unable to find any British recruits, sent the German Johann Krapf to east Africa in an early attempt to convert the local people to Christianity. He was joined by his missionary colleague, Johann Rebmann, who arrived in Zanzibar two years later. They travelled widely across the areas now known as southern Kenya and northern Tanzania. In May 1848, Rebmann became the first European to see Kilimanjaro and in December 1849 Krapf was the first European to see Mount Kenya (see map, *Exploration in east Africa*, page 15).

Meanwhile on Zanzibar the slave trade continued. By the 1850s, about 14,000 to 15,000 slaves a year were being imported into Zanzibar from the mainland, providing Sultan Said with a large income from duties. Zanzibar traders pushed even deeper into the interior, reaching what is now northern Zambia. In 1852, a caravan reached Benguela (in present-day Angola) having completely traversed the continent from east to west, while the following year another group reached Linyanti, in the present-day Caprivi Strip of Namibia.

Through the slave caravans Said had become the nominal ruler of a vast commercial empire stretching along the coast from Mozambique to the Somali ports, and inland to the Great Lakes of Nyasa (Malawi), Tanganyika, Nyanza (Victoria) and Turkana. By the end of his reign Zanzibar's empire covered about 2.5 million km² (1 million square miles), or 10% of the African continent, including the whole of present-day Tanzania, plus sizeable parts of Malawi, Zambia, the DRC, Uganda and Kenya. The Arabs had a saying: 'When the flute plays in Zanzibar, they dance on the lakes.' But it was an empire in name only and Said never attempted to conquer or develop the area.

The end of Said's reign Sultan Said made periodic visits to Muscat, leaving his son Khaled as Governor of Zanzibar in his absence. Khaled had a predilection for French goods and called his principal country estate Marseilles, after the French Mediterranean port. When Khaled died of tuberculosis in November 1854, an order came from Said in Muscat appointing another son, the 20-year-old Majid, as governor.

In September 1856, Said sailed for Zanzibar again in his boat *Kitorie*. He travelled with his family, including his son Barghash, now 19 years old. Said ordered some loose planks of wood to be loaded onto the ship, saying that if anyone should die on board, the body must not be buried at sea according to Muslim custom, but embalmed and taken to Zanzibar in a coffin. Said seemed to know it was he who was about to die: he began to suffer severe pains from an old

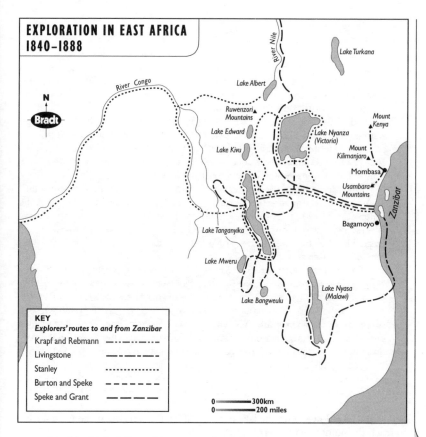

EXPLORATION IN EAST AFRICA 1840–1888

Bradt

N

River Congo

River Nile

Lake Turkana

Lake Albert

Ruwenzori Mountains

Lake Edward

Lake Kivu

Lake Nyanza (Victoria)

Mount Kenya

Mount Kilimanjaro

Mombasa

Usambara Mountains

Zanzibar

Lake Tanganyika

Bagamoyo

Lake Mweru

Lake Nyasa (Malawi)

Lake Bangweulu

KEY
Explorers' routes to and from Zanzibar

Krapf and Rebmann —··—··—··—

Livingstone —— ·· —— ·· ——

Stanley ················

Burton and Speke — — — — —

Speke and Grant —— —— ——

0 ———— 300km
0 ———— 200 miles

wound in his thigh followed by an attack of dysentery. On 19 October 1856, he died on board the ship. He was 65 years old.

Barghash put his father's body in the coffin and took command of the fleet. He knew his elder brother Majid would succeed his father as the new Sultan of Zanzibar, but he also realised that Majid would be unaware of their father's death. On the night of his arrival at Zanzibar, Barghash came ashore secretly and tried to take control of the palace at Mtoni and the Fort in Zanzibar Town, but he was unable to muster enough supporters and his attempt was thwarted.

On 28 October 1856, Majid bin Said was proclaimed Sultan of Zanzibar. A ship was sent to Oman with the news, but Said's eldest son Thuwaini refused to acknowledge Majid as sultan, believing that he was the legitimate successor. Majid agreed to pay Thuwaini 40,000 Maria Theresa dollars annually as compensation, but after a year the payment ceased.

Later European explorers By this time, the reports of early explorers like Rebmann and Krapf encouraged the British Royal Geographical Society to send an expedition to east Africa to search for the source of the White Nile. The leaders were Lieutenant (later Sir) Richard Francis Burton and Lieutenant John Hanning Speke.

In December 1856, on the last day of mourning for Sultan Said, Burton and Speke arrived in Zanzibar. They sailed for Bagamoyo and followed the slave route towards Lake Tanganyika, which they hoped was the source of the Nile. When they arrived, in January 1858, local Arab traders told them that a river at the northern

In October 1859, Barghash was plotting to overthrow his brother, Majid, who was Sultan of Zanzibar. Barghash was living in a house in Zanzibar Town, close to the palace of Beit el Sahel, with his sister Meyye and 11-year-old brother Abdil Aziz. Two more sisters, Salme and Khole, and two of his nieces, the princesses Shembua and Farashuu, all supported Barghash and wanted Majid overthrown.

Majid, aware that his brother was plotting against him, arranged to have their houses watched and ordered Barghash's house to be blockaded. Several hundred soldiers were posted outside the front of the house with strict orders to shoot any suspicious person and cut off all communications. But Barghash had plenty of provisions, and his fellow conspirators smuggled water to him through the back of the house.

Meanwhile, at the fortified plantation of Marseilles (so named by another brother, Khaled, who had a predilection for all things French), in the centre of the island, the conspirators stored arms, ammunition and food supplies in preparation for a siege. Princess Salme played an important part in the preparations because she could write, and prepared secret messages to be carried between the other conspirators. She later referred to herself as 'secretary to the alliance of rebels'.

At midnight on 8 October 1859, Salme and Khole went to Barghash's house with a large escort including Shembua and Farashuu. Bluffing their way past the soldiers on duty (Arab women did not normally speak to strange men), they were allowed to pay the prisoner a short visit. They brought women's robes and veils and Barghash wrapped himself in a voluminous black robe, which left only his eyes free. The tallest women walked alongside him to make his height less conspicuous, and the guards on the door made way respectfully for the royal party when they left the building.

Once outside the town Barghash threw off his disguise and headed for Marseilles with his supporters, while his sisters returned to Zanzibar Town. Majid soon heard

end of the lake flowed into the lake (not out of it). Burton and Speke were unable to reach the point where the river met the lake.

Bitterly disappointed, they began to return eastwards to Zanzibar. Burton became ill, and was forced to stop, so Speke struck out northwards on his own, and became the first European to see the great *nyanza* (meaning 'lake') which he named Lake Victoria, certain it was the source of the White Nile – although he was unable to prove it at the time. Speke and Burton returned to Zanzibar in March 1859, and then separately to London.

To verify his theory, Speke returned to Zanzibar in 1860 with the Scottish explorer James Grant. Together they travelled inland to Lake Victoria, and this time found a great river emptying Lake Victoria at a waterfall, which they named the Ripon Falls after an earlier president of the Royal Geographical Society. Although they were still unable to prove without doubt that this river was the Nile, it was the closest any explorer had got to settling the great geographical question of the age.

The division of Oman and Zanzibar Meanwhile, back on Zanzibar, a power struggle was developing between the Omani rulers. Sultan Thuwaini of Oman planned to overthrow Sultan Majid of Zanzibar, as his promised tribute had not been paid. In February 1859, Thuwaini sailed southwards but was intercepted by a British cruiser at the eastern tip of Arabia. The British government wanted to keep control of the sea route to India, and did not want a civil war to develop in this area. Captain Hamerton, the British consul, had died, but Thuwaini was persuaded to submit his claims to the arbitration of Lord Canning, the Governor-General of India. Thuwaini agreed and returned to Muscat.

news of Barghash's escape, and mustered 5,000 soldiers, while the British consul, Sir Christopher Rigby, provided nine soldiers and a gun from the British warship HMS *Assaye*.

Majid marched to Marseilles and started to bombard the house, but Barghash's supporters emerged from their fortifications, and fought off Majid's troops until sunset. Several hundred lives were lost. Majid retreated for the night but, as he and his army slept, Barghash and his supporters slipped back into town. On the morning of 16 October, Majid re-advanced on Marseilles and smashed open the gates, only to find it abandoned.

By this time, Barghash had returned to his house. Realising that his plans were thwarted, he remained concealed, refusing even to go to the window. Rigby arranged for HMS *Assaye* to be anchored just offshore, and a detachment of marines landed and marched to the front of Barghash's house, calling on Barghash to surrender. When there was no answer, the marines started to fire their guns at the front of the house. Khole, calling from her house across the street, persuaded her brother to surrender. Contemporary reports describe how cries of *Aman!* ('Peace!') were heard from inside the house and how, after the firing had stopped, Rigby rapped on the door with his walking stick and demanded immediate surrender. When Barghash emerged, Rigby arrested him and put him on board the *Assaye*. He was taken to India, where he lived in exile for two years. Abdil Aziz insisted on accompanying his elder brother and stayed in India after Barghash's return in 1861.

Princess Salme was rejected by her family, and in 1866 met a German trader called Heinrich Ruete. They became lovers and moved to Germany, where Salme changed her name to Emily and later wrote a book about her life at the court of Zanzibar. (For more details see box, *Princess Salme*, pages 186–7.)

But Majid was in danger from another member of the family. His brother Barghash was still plotting to overthrow him and proclaim himself Sultan of Zanzibar. Majid learnt of the plot but Barghash escaped to the Marseilles plantation. He was finally captured and exiled to India for two years. (For more details see *The escape to Marseilles* box above.)

In April 1861, Lord Canning declared that Oman and Zanzibar should be completely separate states. The annual tribute from Zanzibar to Oman was reinstated and in March 1862 Britain and France signed an Anglo-French declaration which recognised Majid as Sultan of Zanzibar and his territories as an independent sovereignty.

Although the Mwinyi Mkuu still lived in the palace at Dunga, his power was now negligible. Hassan II was succeeded by Mohammed, who died in 1865, aged 80. He was succeeded by his son, Ahmed, who died of smallpox in March 1873, leaving no male heir. The line of the Mwinyi Mkuu of Zanzibar had come to an end, and its passing was hardly noticed.

In 1866, in Oman, Thuwaini was murdered in his sleep by his son, Salim, who succeeded him. Majid discontinued the payment of the tribute on the grounds that Salim was a usurper, and Oman withdrew into isolation. (This isolation lasted for over 100 years, until the accession of Sultan Qaboos bin Said in 1970.)

DAVID LIVINGSTONE AND 'STINKIBAR' In 1866, the Scottish missionary and explorer David Livingstone arrived in Zanzibar. He had already travelled across much of central and southern Africa, and written at great length about the horrors of the slave trade. He wanted to introduce what he regarded as essential elements of civilisation – commerce and Christianity – to Africa as a way of defeating the slave trade. He had also been asked by the Royal Geographical Society to clarify the pattern of the watersheds in the area of Lake Nyasa and Lake Tanganyika and their relation to the source of the White Nile – still an unsolved problem for the geographers of the day.

By this period, Zanzibar's increasing trade and growing population had created its own problems and Livingstone did not enjoy his stay:

> No-one can truly enjoy good health here. The stench from … two square miles of exposed sea-beach, which is the general depository of the filth of the town, is quite horrible. At night, it is so gross and crass, one might cut a slice and manure the garden with it. It might be called 'Stinkibar' rather than Zanzibar.

During the same period, other European visitors arriving by ship claimed they could smell Zanzibar before they could see it. In the town itself, the freshwater springs were not particularly fresh. Dr James Christie, an English physician who arrived in Zanzibar in 1869, reported that the springs consisted of the 'diluted drainage of dunghills and graveyards'. Not surprisingly, this led to frequent bouts of dysentery and epidemics of smallpox and cholera. Malaria and bilharzia were also problems. Cholera epidemics had occurred in 1821 and 1836, and smallpox in 1858. Later cholera epidemics in 1858 and 1869–70 killed one-sixth of the population of Zanzibar Town, and 35,000 people throughout the island.

At this time, slavery had still not been abolished on Zanzibar. In the early 1860s, an average 15,000 slaves a year were being imported into Zanzibar from mainland Africa, and by 1866 this had grown to 20,000 a year. The slave population had reached its peak and clove production entered a phase of overproduction and stagnation, so prices dropped.

As a result of the declining profitability of clove production, there was a greater interest in the production of coconut and sesame seed oils, mainly for export to France. There was also a revival of sugar production, and rubber plantations were established along the coast.

LIVINGSTONE, STANLEY AND THE RELIEF EXPEDITIONS David Livingstone had

left Zanzibar in March 1866. Lack of news in the outside world led to speculation on his whereabouts, and in January 1871 the American journalist Henry Morton Stanley arrived in Zanzibar, having been commissioned by the *New York Herald* to search for the 'lost explorer'. In November the same year Stanley arrived at Ujiji, where he found Livingstone and greeted him with the now immortal phrase, 'Doctor Livingstone, I presume?' (For more details on the explorations of Livingstone see boxes *David Livingstone*, page 174, and *Henry Morton Stanley*, opposite.)

After Stanley had found Livingstone, and returned alone to Zanzibar, Livingstone stayed at Kazeh until August 1872, then set off southwards on another expedition to find the source of the Nile, which he thought would take no more than a few months. (He had already been in the interior for six years at this stage.)

Meanwhile the RGS in London was unaware of Stanley's 'find' so in February 1872 the Livingstone Search and Relief Expedition, led by Lieutenant Llewellyn Dawson, was dispatched to Zanzibar in the steamship *Abydos*. Two months later, the expedition arrived in Zanzibar, where their ship was caught in the freak hurricane of 14 April. Every ship and dhow in the harbour was driven ashore except the *Abydos*. The town was wrecked, many people were killed, and over two-thirds of the coconut and clove trees on the island were uprooted.

A few weeks after the hurricane, in May 1872, Stanley arrived at Bagamoyo, where he met Dawson and told him that Livingstone was safe and would be

The man known to the world as Henry Morton Stanley was born John Rowland on 29 January 1841 at Denbigh in Wales. He spent nine years in a workhouse and two years as a farmhand, before joining a ship from Liverpool to New Orleans, which he reached in 1858. In New Orleans he was adopted by his employer, a cotton merchant, from whom he took his new name, Henry Stanley. 'Morton' was added later.

By 1869, Stanley was a correspondent for the *New York Herald*. The manager of the newspaper, James Gordon Bennett, dispatched him to Africa with orders to cover the inauguration of the Suez Canal, and then find Livingstone if he was alive, or bring back his bones if he was dead.

Stanley arrived in Zanzibar on 6 January 1871. He borrowed a top hat from the American consul, John Francis Webb, and went to visit Sultan Barghash who gave him letters of recommendation to show his agents in the interior. Stanley set off from Zanzibar in March that year, just two days before the start of the rainy season. His provisions included American cloth, beads of glass, coral and china for trading, plus two silver goblets and a bottle of champagne for the day he met Livingstone.

Stanley finally met Livingstone at Ujiji, on the eastern shore of Lake Tanganyika, on 10 November 1871. According to Stanley's own description of the meeting, Stanley took off his hat, held out his hand, and said, 'Doctor Livingstone, I presume?' When Livingstone answered, 'Yes,' Stanley continued with, 'I thank God that I have been permitted to see you,' to which Livingstone gravely replied, 'I feel thankful that I am here to welcome you.'

After these traditional English niceties, and the seemingly mundane phrase that was to dog Stanley for the rest of his life, Stanley and Livingstone travelled in the area together for some time, but Livingstone was still determined to discover the source of the Nile and pressed on southwards alone. Stanley returned to Zanzibar on 7 May 1872, before travelling to London.

Two years later, Stanley gave up journalism to return to Africa as an explorer. He reached Zanzibar again in September 1874, and left for the mainland in November the same year. On this expedition he rounded the southern shore of Lake Victoria, went through Buganda (now Uganda), and followed the Congo River (through present-day DRC) to the Atlantic Ocean, which he reached on 12 August 1877, thus crossing Africa in 999 days.

From 1879 to 1884, Stanley returned to the Congo for King Léopold II of Belgium. He established and governed the Congo Free State (which was to become Zaire, now renamed the Democratic Republic of Congo), and the town of Stanleyville (now Kisangani) was named after him.

After another expedition from 1887 to 1889, Stanley returned to Britain a celebrity. He was married in Westminster Abbey in 1890, elected to parliament as a Liberal Unionist for North Lambeth in 1895, and knighted in 1899. He died in London on 10 May 1904.

arriving after a few more months. Dawson cancelled the Search and Relief Expedition and returned to London. But by the end of 1872 Livingstone had still not arrived back at Zanzibar as expected, so in February 1873 a second Relief Expedition, led by Lieutenant Verney Lovett Cameron, set out from Zanzibar to find him.

Unknown to Cameron, and the rest of the world, Livingstone had grown ill, with a recurrence of dysentery. On 2 May 1873, he died in the village of Chitambo, near Lake Bangweulu (in present-day Zambia), 800km (500 miles) south of Ujiji, and even further from the actual source of the Nile. Two of his companions carried his body back towards Zanzibar. In August 1873, they reached Kazeh, where they met Cameron.

Cameron decided to march on to Ujiji which he reached in February 1874 and where he found Livingstone's papers. From Ujiji, Cameron continued westwards, eventually reaching the Atlantic coast in November 1875, thereby becoming the first European to travel across this part of Africa from east to west.

SULTAN BARGHASH AND JOHN KIRK By this time, on Zanzibar, Sultan Majid had died, aged 36. His only child was a daughter so his brother Barghash (who had twice already tried to seize the throne and had returned to Zanzibar from exile in India in 1861) finally succeeded to the throne, and was proclaimed sultan on 7 October 1870. In the same year, Dr John Kirk (who had originally come to Zanzibar as a medical officer on Livingstone's expedition) was made acting British consul.

After the hurricane of April 1872, Sultan Barghash had announced plans to grow new plantations, and the slave trade picked up once again. By late 1872, around 16,000 slaves had been imported into Zanzibar. (The hurricane hit only the southern tip of Pemba, leaving most of the clove trees on that island untouched. By the 1880s Pemba was producing about 80% of the total clove harvest from Zanzibar and Pemba.)

At the same time, the anti-slavery movement continued to grow, fuelled in America by the publication of *Uncle Tom's Cabin*. In January 1873, Sir Bartle Frere, a special envoy from Queen Victoria, arrived in Zanzibar to negotiate a treaty which he hoped would finally put an end to the Arab slave trade. Sultan Barghash was naturally reluctant to end slavery and Frere sailed for England at the beginning of March 1873 without a treaty. Almost immediately the British navy began a blockade of every slave port on the mainland. The number of slaves passing through the Customs House in Zanzibar Town between January and March dropped to 21, compared with 4,000 in the same period the previous year.

In June 1873, Sir John Kirk informed Sultan Barghash that a total blockade of Zanzibar Island was imminent. Reluctantly Barghash signed the Anglo-Zanzibari treaty which provided for the complete abolition of the slave trade in Barghash's territories, the closing of all slave markets and the protection of all liberated slaves. Transport of slaves was forbidden, and slaves could no longer be exported from mainland Africa to Zanzibar and Pemba, except for domestic purposes.

The large slave market in Zanzibar Town was closed immediately. The site was bought by missionaries of the Universities' Mission to Central Africa (UMCA), and work started on the cathedral which can still be seen in Zanzibar Town today (see *Chapter 6*, pages 171–3).

One of the main effects of the treaty, now that slavery was illegal, was to push up the price of slaves and the trade continued in a clandestine manner. Through the 1870s smugglers were estimated to be exporting between 10,000 and 12,000 slaves a year.

In 1875, Kirk brought Sultan Barghash an official invitation to visit Britain to ratify the Anglo-Zanzibari treaty. In June the same year Barghash and Kirk arrived in London where Barghash received the Freedom of the City at the Guildhall and attended a state banquet at Mansion House. While Barghash was in London, his sister Salme had come from Germany (see box, *Princess Salme*, pages 186–7) hoping to be reconciled with her brother, but Barghash refused to meet her. After four weeks of intensive sightseeing and entertainment, Barghash and his party returned to Zanzibar via Paris and Marseilles, arriving home in September.

For the British, Zanzibar was no longer a distant, obscure island, and links between the two countries became even more firmly established. In 1869, the Suez Canal had opened, making the sea voyage between Britain and the coast of east Africa much shorter and simpler. In 1872, the British India Steamship Navigation Company started a monthly mail service between Zanzibar and Aden. It brought the first scheduled passenger and cargo service to Zanzibar, which allowed merchandise to be exported quickly. Communication was again improved in 1879, when the Eastern Telegraph Company completed their cable from Zanzibar to Europe via Aden, and a telegraphic link with Europe was established.

Inspired by his visit to Europe, Barghash decided to make many changes on Zanzibar. Advised by John Kirk (now firmly installed as the power behind the throne), he appointed Lieutenant William Lloyd Mathews (see box, *William Lloyd Mathews*, page 193) to reorganise his army and enforce his sovereignty over the interior.

During his exile in India, Barghash had seen the opulent wealth of the Indian palaces and he tried to emulate them on Zanzibar. Many luxurious palaces were built, including Chukwani, to the south of Zanzibar Town, and Maruhubi Palace, to the north, for his harem. Another palace, in the town, became known as the Beit al Ajaib, or House of Wonders, as it was the first building on Zanzibar to have electric lighting. In all his palaces, Barghash upgraded the dinner services from silver to gold. Divan coverings of goat and camel hair were replaced by silks and taffetas, and French carpets covered the floors.

Barghash introduced Zanzibar's first clean water system to replace supplies from local wells and rainwater: aqueducts and conduits brought pure water from a spring at Bububu into Zanzibar Town, a distance of some 6km. Other developments introduced by Barghash included a police force, an ice-making factory, electric street lighting, and telephones to connect his city and country palaces. Barghash also built and improved the roads on the island, and every year he provided one of his private steamships for Muslims wishing to make the pilgrimage to Mecca.

THE SCRAMBLE FOR AFRICA In 1884, Dr Karl Peters, founder of the Society for German Colonisation, arrived in Zanzibar, then sailed for the mainland where he made 'treaties of eternal friendship' with the local African chiefs in return for large areas of land. By the time he reached Kilimanjaro he had annexed more than 6,000km² (2,500 square miles) of land, which were still nominally under the control of Sultan Barghash.

Britain was concerned at the presence of a rival European power on its patch, but was distracted by events elsewhere. In January 1885, Khartoum, the capital of Anglo-Egyptian Sudan, fell to the forces of the Mahdi. The British general Gordon was killed and the British governor of Equatoria Province, south of Khartoum, was cut off. (Ironically, the governor was actually a German called Eduard Schnitzer, although he had adopted the name Emin Pasha and was working for the British.)

Otto von Bismarck, the German chancellor, saw the Mahdi's victory as a sign of Britain's weakness and believed that Germany could consolidate its claims in east Africa without British opposition. In February the same year the General Act of Berlin, signed by Kaiser Wilhelm of Germany, officially proclaimed a German protectorate over the territories annexed by Karl Peters. Sultan Barghash was only formally told about his loss of land in April of the same year. He hoped for support from the British, but Britain did not want to make an enemy of Germany, and so declined.

In June 1885, the Germans claimed another protectorate over Witu and the mouth of the Tana River, near Lamu, and in August the same year five ships of the

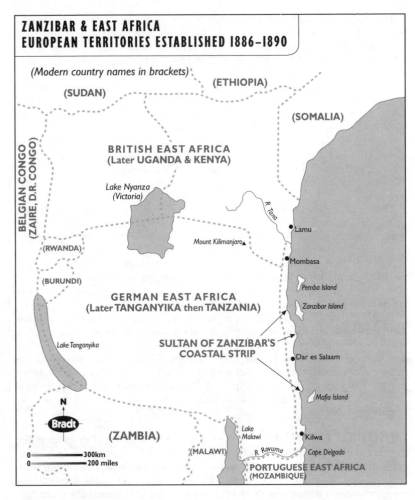

ZANZIBAR & EAST AFRICA
EUROPEAN TERRITORIES ESTABLISHED 1886–1890

(Modern country names in brackets)

(ETHIOPIA)

(SUDAN)

(SOMALIA)

BELGIAN CONGO
(ZAIRE, D.R. CONGO)

BRITISH EAST AFRICA
(Later UGANDA & KENYA)

Lake Nyanza
(Victoria)

R Tana

Lamu

Mount Kilimanjaro▲

(RWANDA)

Mombasa

Pemba Island

(BURUNDI)

GERMAN EAST AFRICA
(Later TANGANYIKA then TANZANIA)

Zanzibar Island

SULTAN OF ZANZIBAR'S
COASTAL STRIP

Lake Tanganyika

Dar es Salaam

Mafia Island

N

Bradt

(ZAMBIA)

Lake
Malawi

Kilwa

0 ━━━ 300km
0 ━━━ 200 miles

(MALAWI)

R Rovuma

Cape Delgado

PORTUGUESE EAST AFRICA
(MOZAMBIQUE)

German navy, commanded by Carl Paschen, arrived in Zanzibar harbour. Paschen demanded that Sultan Barghash recognise the German protectorates. Kirk, on the recommendations of the British government, persuaded Barghash to submit.

A few days after the arrival of the German fleet, another German ship entered the harbour, carrying Barghash's sister Salme (who had eloped to Germany in 1866). She was with her son Said-Rudolph, now 16 years old, and two other children. On Kirk's advice, Barghash tolerated Salme's presence. Barghash sent his formal recognition of the German protectorate to Carl Paschen and two months later, the British government arranged for a joint commission between Britain, Germany and France to establish their own boundaries in the mainland territories that were still officially under the control of the Sultan of Zanzibar.

After lengthy discussions the first Anglo-German agreement was signed in late 1886. Barghash's lands were reduced to Zanzibar, Pemba, Mafia, Lamu and a ten-mile (16km) wide coastal strip stretching around 1,200km (about 750 miles) from the Tana River, near Lamu, to the Rovuma River, near Cape Delgado. The rest of the mainland, east of Lake Victoria and Lake Tanganyika, was divided between Britain and Germany. Britain took the northern portion, between the Tana and

Umba rivers, which became British East Africa, later Kenya. Germany took the southern portion, between the Umba and Rovuma rivers. This became German East Africa, later Tanganyika (see map, *Zanzibar and east Africa*, opposite).

Given no option, Barghash agreed to this treaty in December 1886 and the French government signed it a few days later. In June 1887, Barghash leased the northern section of his coastal strip (between the Tana and Umba rivers) to the British East African Association (BEAA), which had been formed by William Mackinnon in May the same year. Meanwhile the Germans and Portuguese met in Barghash's absence to discuss their own border, and Portugal gained more of Barghash's land in the south.

In February 1888, Barghash sailed to Muscat, to recuperate from tuberculosis and elephantiasis at the healing Bushire Springs on the Persian coast. He returned to Zanzibar on 26 March, but died five hours after his arrival, aged 51.

On 29 March 1888, Barghash's brother Khalifa bin Said was proclaimed sultan. In April the same year, the British East African Association became the Imperial British East Africa Company (IBEA), with its capital at Mombasa, which was beginning to take Zanzibar's place as the commercial centre for Africa.

A BRITISH PROTECTORATE In September 1889, Khalifa signed an agreement with the British government agreeing to abolish slavery in his territories. Anybody who entered the sultan's realms, and any children born, would be free. Britain and Germany were awarded a permanent right to search for slaves in Zanzibar's waters. As a sign of Britain's appreciation, Khalifa was knighted, but less than a month later he died, aged 36.

Khalifa's brother, Ali bin Said, was the fourth and last of Said's sons to become Sultan of Zanzibar. On 1 August 1890, Ali signed an anti-slavery treaty forbidding the purchase and sale of slaves. With the end of the slave trade, the only viable export from the interior was ivory, by now a rapidly waning asset.

Meanwhile, in the interior Karl Peters entered Uganda in February 1890 and claimed the territory for Germany, just ahead of Sir Frederick Jackson from England. The British politician Lord Robert Salisbury realised that control of the Upper Nile could lead indirectly to the control of the Suez Canal and thus the trade route to India. Germany was persuaded to renounce any claims over Uganda in return for British support of the Kaiser against the major European powers of the day, France and Russia.

By the second Anglo-German agreement (the Treaty of Zanzibar) of 1 July 1890, Germany agreed to recognise a British protectorate over the Sultanate of Zanzibar, and to abandon any claim to Witu and the country inland as far as the Upper Nile. Germany also abandoned any claim to the west of Lake Nyasa but, in return, gained sovereignty over the coast of German East Africa, later to become Tanganyika. The British–German border was continued westwards across Lake Victoria to the boundary of the Belgian territory of Congo, thus securing Uganda for Britain. The British coastal strip (which still belonged to the Sultan of Zanzibar) was removed from the control of the British East Africa Company and administered by the British East Africa Protectorate, later to become Kenya and Uganda.

In exchange for the thousands of square miles of east African territory, including the islands of Zanzibar (Unguja and Pemba) which it gave up to British control, Germany gained Heligoland, a strategically important small island off the German coast which lay near the mouth of the Kiel Canal.

In 1891, a constitutional government was established in Zanzibar, with General Sir Lloyd Mathews as first minister. But although Zanzibar enjoyed the status of a British protectorate, the island's importance as a commercial centre was declining further in favour of Mombasa.

The British now controlled Zanzibar, so when Sultan Ali died in March 1893, without making a will, they proclaimed Hamad, son of Thuwaini (the former sultan of Oman), as sultan.

During Hamad's reign, in November 1895, Zanzibar issued its first stamps (from about 1875 the island had been using Indian stamps with 'Zanzibar' overprinted). Then a newspaper, the *Gazette for Zanzibar and East Africa*, was produced. It was followed by others in English, Arabic, Swahili and Urdu.

THE LAST YEARS OF THE 19TH CENTURY When Sultan Hamad died in August 1896, the British recommended his cousin Hamoud as sultan. But Barghash's son, Khaled, who had already tried to seize power from Hamad, made a second attempt at snatching the throne. He was briefly successful this time but was ousted by the British, after 'the shortest war in history' (see box, *The shortest war in history*, page 26).

On 27 August 1896, Hamoud was conducted into the Customs House and proclaimed Sultan of Zanzibar, amidst the salute of the ships. The new sultan supported the British government and on 5 April 1897 he signed a treaty to abolish the legal status of slavery in Zanzibar and Pemba. Shortly after this Queen Victoria awarded him the Grand Cross of the Most Distinguished Order of St Michael and St George. Hamoud sent his son Ali to school at Harrow in England where he represented his father at the coronation of King Edward VII.

Sultan Hamoud died on 18 July 1902 and the British proclaimed the 18-year-old Ali as the new sultan. From his school days he spoke English fluently, and continued to travel in Europe during his reign. In May 1911, Ali attended the coronation of King George V in England. While in Europe his health deteriorated and he abdicated in December 1911. He spent the last seven years of his life in Europe, and died in Paris in December 1918. Khalifa bin Harub, a cousin of Ali, became Sultan Khalifa II on 16 December 1911.

ZANZIBAR ENTERS THE 20TH CENTURY Sultan Khalifa bin Harub proved to be a moderate but influential ruler, and proceeded to guide Zanzibar through the first half of the turbulent 20th century with skill and diplomacy.

Soon after Khalifa gained power, changes were made to the British way of overseeing their interests in Zanzibar. In July 1913, responsibility for Zanzibar was transferred from the Foreign Office to the Colonial Office. The post of British consul became British Resident, subject to the control of the Governor of the British East Africa Protectorate. At the same time a Protectorate Council was established. This was an advisory body with the sultan as president and the British Resident as vice-president.

During World War I the German and British armies, with conscripted African soldiers, were involved in several campaigns on the mainland. The war did not affect Zanzibar directly except for one incident when the British ship *Pegasus* was bombarded and sunk by the German ship *Königsberg* in Zanzibar Town harbour. (Graves marking the bodies of sailors killed in this incident can still be seen on Grave Island.)

Towards the end of the war, in 1917, the British army drove the Germans out of their territory and marched into Dar es Salaam. Khaled, who had tried to seize the throne of Zanzibar during 'the shortest war' in 1896, was still there and was captured. He was exiled to the Seychelles, then allowed to return to Mombasa in 1925 where he lived quietly until 1927.

After the war, the German East African territory was administered by Britain under a League of Nations mandate and called Tanganyika. Later, in 1920, the British East Africa Protectorate became known as the Kenya Colony.

In 1925, the British Resident on Zanzibar was made directly responsible to the Colonial Office in London, and a new Legislative Council was established. The ten-mile (16km) wide strip of land along the coast of Kenya, including Mombasa, which had been leased to Kenya in 1895 was still technically 'owned' by the Sultan of Zanzibar and the new Kenyan government continued to pay the lease of £11,000 per year.

During World War II, Zanzibar was not involved in any military action. The war's main effect was to interrupt the supply of rice, a staple food for the Asian and African people, that had until then been imported from Burma.

THE ROAD TO INDEPENDENCE After World War II Britain gradually allowed the local people of Zanzibar to become involved in the islands' government. Several local political parties were formed and Zanzibar's first elections were held in July 1957. The Afro-Shirazi Union (which later became the Afro-Shirazi Party – ASP) defeated the Zanzibar Nationalist Party (ZNP). Broadly speaking, the ASP was dominated by Africans, the ZNP by Arabs.

In October 1960, Sultan Khalifa died, after ruling for 49 years, and was succeeded by his only son, Abdullah. In November the same year Zanzibar was granted a new constitution which allowed for the elections of the members of the Legislative Council. Elections took place in January 1961, producing no clear result, and again in June 1961, but these were marked by serious inter-racial rioting. Nevertheless the ZNP, along with the aligned Zanzibar and Pemba People's Party, won 13 of the seats on the council, while the ASP won ten.

Britain realised that internal self-government for Zanzibar was inevitable, and this was finally granted in June 1963. In July that year Sultan Abdullah died. Throughout his short reign he had suffered from severe pains in his legs, which were eventually amputated. Abdullah was succeeded by his eldest son Jamshid.

On 10 December 1963, Zanzibar became an independent sultanate, and the coastal strip was finally ceded to Kenya, which became independent two days later. Zanzibar was made a full member of the British Commonwealth and on 16 December became a member of the United Nations. But the new sultanate was short-lived: on 12 January 1964, the Zanzibari government was overthrown in a violent revolution.

REVOLUTIONARY ZANZIBAR The leader of Zanzibar's revolution was a Ugandan called John Okello who had been living in Pemba. The local African population supported Okello with great enthusiasm, and went on a rampage through the islands, during which more than 17,000 Arabs and Indians were killed in one night. The leader of the Afro-Shirazi Party, Sheik Abied Amani Karume, was installed as president of the newly proclaimed People's Republic of Zanzibar, which included the islands of Unguja and Pemba.

Karume and other prominent ASP members formed the Revolutionary Government of Zanzibar (Serikali ya Mapinduzi ya Zanzibar, or SMZ). Most of Zanzibar's Asian and Indian people left the islands; their property was confiscated and their land nationalised. (On the mainland Sultan Jamshid was given temporary asylum in Dar es Salaam, then went to Britain where he lived in exile.)

Meanwhile, Tanganyika had also become independent in December 1961, with Julius Nyerere elected as president the following year. Nyerere had known and supported Karume since the mid 1950s but the Zanzibar Revolution created problems in Tanganyika, inspiring an attempted coup in Dar es Salaam only a few days later. (To suppress this coup Nyerere received help from Britain in the form of a battalion of commandos.)

Once Nyerere had regained control he approached Karume to discuss a political union, and on 24 April 1964 the two countries joined to form the United Republic

THE SHORTEST WAR IN HISTORY

Sultan Hamad died on 25 August 1896 while the British consul, Arthur Hardinge, was on leave in England. The acting British consul, Basil Cave, recommended that Hamoud (Hamad's cousin) be appointed sultan, but when Cave and Sir Lloyd Mathews reached the palace of Beit el Sahel in Zanzibar Town they found the doors barred. Khaled, the son of Barghash (and another cousin of Hamoud), had arrived before them with about 60 armed men, entered the palace by climbing through a broken window, and been quickly joined by more than 2,000 supporters.

Khaled proclaimed himself sultan, and raised the red flag of Zanzibar on the palace roof. But Basil Cave refused to recognise his claim: British ships in the harbour landed guards of marines, which were posted at the British consulate (where the British women sought refuge), the Customs House, and elsewhere around the town. Many foreigners gathered on the roof of the English Club, where they had a clear view of the harbour and the palace.

On the morning of 26 August the three British ships were reinforced by the timely arrival of two others, and the following day, at dawn, the British fleet under Rear-Admiral Harry Holdsworth Rawson delivered an ultimatum: Khaled was to surrender, disarm, evacuate the palace and be at the Customs House by 09.00, or the British ships would open fire. At 08.00 Khaled sent an envoy to Cave, asking for a chance to discuss peace, but his request was refused.

The palace clock struck three (09.00 British time) and at 09.02 the bombardment started. In half an hour Beit el Sahel and the adjoining palace of Beit el Hukm were badly damaged. The lighthouse outside the palace was in flames and the nearby House of Wonders was also hit a few times. Many of Khaled's supporters had fled, leaving 500 dead and wounded lying about the palace grounds.

At 09.40 Khaled surrendered. He lowered the flag, the firing ceased and the war was over. This dispute over the succession is listed in the *Guinness Book of Records* as the shortest war in history.

Khaled escaped through the narrow streets and fled to the German consulate, where he was given asylum. As the steps of the consulate led onto the beach, Khaled was able to board the German warship *Seeadler* without risking arrest. Khaled was taken to Dar es Salaam where he lived in exile. He died in Mombasa in 1927, aged 53.

of Tanganyika and Zanzibar. In October the same year the country was renamed Tanzania (from 'Tan' in Tanganyika and 'Zan' in Zanzibar). Nyerere became the president of the new state while Karume became vice-president. The SMZ was to control all local affairs on the islands of Unguja and Pemba, while foreign affairs would be handled by the Tanzanian government.

(During the negotiations John Okello had gone to the mainland to meet Nyerere. On his return to Zanzibar in March 1964 he was sent back to Dar es Salaam. He made no further public appearances.)

Despite the so-called union Karume kept Zanzibar separate from the rest of Tanzania in many respects. The clove plantations on Unguja and Pemba were developed and the earnings from exports continued to increase, but this revenue was not shared with mainland Tanzania.

After the revolution almost all the European and Asian residents had left Zanzibar. To fill the vacuum caused by the departure of these skilled people Karume attracted technical and military assistance from Cuba, China and the then Eastern bloc countries of East Germany, Bulgaria and the Soviet Union. Engineers from East Germany designed and built new blocks of flats in Zanzibar

Town, and in 'new towns' elsewhere on the islands of Unguja and Pemba. In 1970, Karume's government was accused of human rights violations against political opponents.

On 7 April 1972, Karume was assassinated while playing cards in the ASP headquarters in Zanzibar Town. Aboud Jumbe Mwinyi, who had been a member of the ASP since before independence, became the new leader of the Revolutionary Government. Mwinyi was less hardline than Karume and introduced several reforms. He was also more sympathetic towards Nyerere and mainland Tanzania. In February 1977, the ASP united with Nyerere's party, the Tanzania African National Union (TANU), to form the Chama Cha Mapinduzi (Party of the Revolution).

After this unification, both leaders began to relax some of their policies on nationalised industries and state financial control. Relations with some Western nations, including Britain, slowly improved. In July 1979, as a sign that Tanzania was regaining some international respect, Queen Elizabeth II visited Zanzibar. Then, in 1980, the first presidential elections took place, and Aboud Jumbe Mwinyi was officially elected as President of Zanzibar.

POLITICS AND RECENT HISTORY

Zanzibar is a semi-autonomous state within the United Republic of Tanzania. It is governed by its own Revolutionary Council and 50-strong House of Representatives, whose members are elected or appointed for five-year terms. The President of Zanzibar is also the Vice-president of Tanzania.

Zanzibar has seen many changes on the political front since the early 1990s. Along with the rest of Tanzania, Zanzibar ceased to be a one-party state in 1992. For the first time in almost 20 years Chama Cha Mapinduzi (CCM) was faced with several new opposition groups, which quickly coalesced into parties. The Civic United Front (CUF), led by Seif Sherif Hamad from Pemba, became the major opposition party for Zanzibar. Elections were planned for October 1995, as all parties agreed that a gradual transition to a multi-party political system would be beneficial. Salmin Amour remained as Zanzibar's president and CCM leader, while on the mainland the CCM chose a new president, Benjamin Mkapa, in July 1995. This followed the resignation of Julius Nyerere, the 'father of the nation', who had ruled since independence, although he remained an important figure behind the scenes.

Elections were duly held in Zanzibar on 22 October 1995, a week before the mainland vote. It was a simple two-horse race between Salmin Amour and Seif Sherif Hamad for President of Zanzibar, and between CCM and CUF candidates in the islands' parliament. There was a very high turnout (over 95% of registered voters) and voting passed peacefully, but the counting took three days for just over 300,000 votes.

Although the ruling party's control of the government structure gave it an in-built advantage, it soon transpired that the CUF was polling strongly. Complaints by the CCM that the election process was flawed were withdrawn when it transpired that Amour had won with 50.2% of the vote, but then the CUF picked up the claim of unfair procedures. International observers agreed that there was evidence of serious irregularities, but the nominally independent Zanzibar Electoral Commission refused to hold a recount or to compare their figures with some of those recorded by the UN. On the mainland, a divided opposition and an even more shambolic election, not to mention the possibility of vote-rigging, meant that the CCM and President Mkapa stayed in power. The CUF brought a high-profile legal case against the CCM on the grounds that the results and the whole election process were not representative of the wishes of the people, but this was bogged down in the courts and finally dismissed in 1998.

In the lead-up to elections in late 2000, Amour rocked the boat by announcing he would stand for a third (and unconstitutional) term as president. The instant response among the people of Zanzibar was a sharp swing in support for the CUF. An equally quick response from CCM high command meant Amour was relieved of his post, and Amani Karume, son of President Karume who had been assassinated in the 1960s, was ushered in as Zanzibar's new CCM leader and presidential candidate.

At a grassroots level, there was still considerable support for the CUF, but the strong Pemba following this party enjoyed meant that ostensibly political differences stood in danger of degenerating into inter-island (or 'tribal') conflicts. This sense of grievance also translated into separatist aspirations; since the end of the 1990s, the desire of many Zanzibaris to be independent of mainland Tanzania has been stronger than it has been for many years. The urge for separation is also partly due to the death in 1999 of Julius Nyerere.

When elections were held in October 2000, President Mkapa and the CCM romped home with huge and increased majorities. The people of mainland Tanzania seemed happy (in fact, many seemed indifferent) about the result, and international observers agreed that voting had been free and fair. On Zanzibar, however, it was a different story. In the period leading up to the election, fist-fights erupted on several occasions between CUF and CCM supporters, local party offices were attacked or burned, and CUF demonstrations were broken up by the police and army. On election day, things were so bad in 16 constituencies that the whole process was cancelled, and a re-run vote arranged for 5 November. CUF demonstrations turned into violent protests, especially in Zanzibar Town, to be met with police tear gas, rubber bullets and even live ammunition. In disgust, the CUF pulled out of the election process, leaving the November re-runs to be easily won by CCM candidates. In response, the CUF announced its continued boycott of procedures in the House of Representatives.

In one of his first moves as newly elected president of Zanzibar, Amani Karume called for peace and reconciliation between the two sides, which he backed up by releasing from prison the group of CUF leaders who'd been held on charges of treason since 1998. Hopes for peace were dashed shortly afterwards when a series of bombs exploded in Zanzibar. The trouble simmered on, with more CUF street protests in January 2001. This time the police used even stronger tactics to break things up: in a single day, between 20 and 70 demonstrators were shot, one policeman was killed, and many more were injured. The events were reported in media around the world, the USA and the donor nations of Europe expressed concern, and aid money which had been frozen following the discrepancies of the 1995 election remained firmly out of reach.

In March 2001, at the direct behest of President Mkapa, leaders from the CCM and the CUF tentatively started to discuss their differences, and in October that year, after a long series of negotiations, the two sides signed an accord to end their dispute over the election results. By 2002, the islands had returned to their traditional calm and peaceful atmosphere, and Zanzibar was fully open for business once again.

In the elections of October 2005, the CCM and the CUF were once again vying for power, with rallies held across the island throughout the summer of 2005. Although there seemed to be little in the way of party manifestos, and despite claims by the CUF of vote-rigging and other irregularities, this time the election passed off comparatively peacefully. With a 90% turnout of the electorate, the CCM retained control, with the CUF polling 46% of the total votes, and Amani Karume retaining the presidency which he still holds today. Tensions remain between the parties and their supporters, with the CUF claiming in both 2000 and 2005 that election victory had been stolen from them and the Zanzibar Electoral Commission citing many irregularities in the voting. Sporadic negotiations to agree on power-sharing terms and secure a peaceful resolution have taken place ever since. However, in April 2008 a major setback stalled the process completely: the CCM called for a referendum to approve a contentious power-sharing agreement resulting in the CUF abandoning the negotiations altogether. The political future remains slightly murky with the poor rural population suffering from the lack of real commitment to bettering their future.

ECONOMY

For the people of Zanzibar, fishing and farming are the main economic activities. From the beginning of the 19th century to the mid 1970s Zanzibar exported a large proportion of the world's supply of cloves, and the islands' economy was based largely on this commodity. Some diversification has occurred since then as the world market price for cloves fell dramatically in the 1980s, but cloves are still a major export, along with coconut products and other spices. In recent years, seaweed has also become an important export commodity. The potential for tourism to be a major earner of foreign currency has been recognised and has been developing apace for the last decade.

In 2006, Tanzania, and by association Zanzibar, was one of the 32 countries worldwide designated for HIPC (Heavily Indebted Poor Countries) debt relief. Their debt wiped, with the African Development Bank cancelling a balance in excess of US$640 million, the economy gained new buoyancy. According to accountancy powerhouse PricewaterhouseCoopers, approximately 20% of government revenue was spent in paying external debt prior to HIPC; whilst afterwards less than 8% of revenue will be spent on debt service leading up to 2010. Under the HIPC, resources saved from debt service are allocated to key anti-poverty programmes, including education, health and infrastructure. With fewer draining economic pressures, the people of Zanzibar should benefit. It remains to be seen whether the Zanzibari government can follow the successful lead of its mainland counterpart.

SEAWEED FARMING In 1989, seaweed farming was introduced on the east coast of Unguja (Zanzibar Island) and has since become a vital source of income for coastal villagers. The seaweed is planted and tended on beach areas between the high- and low-water marks (see box, *Sustainable seaweed farming*, pages 262–3). It is harvested and dried, collected in Zanzibar Town, and then exported to several countries in Europe and Asia for use as a food thickener or stabiliser. Seaweed is now a valuable addition to Zanzibar's traditional exports of coconuts, cloves and other spices (see boxes, *Coconuts*, page 51, and *Cloves*, page 52).

Despite the success with seaweed, exports are limited, and Zanzibar imports many basic foodstuffs, including rice (from Pakistan, Thailand, Vietnam, Indonesia, India, China and the USA), maize (from mainland Tanzania), cooking oil (from Kenya, Tanzania, Singapore and Dubai), sugar (from Brazil), plus wheat and flour (from France, Germany and the USA). Other imports include mineral water (from the Gulf States) and beer (from Denmark).

TOURISM Whilst tourism remains relatively marginal to life in Pemba and Mafia, it has grown rapidly on Zanzibar Island over the last 20 years. Investment here has been significant and some of the wealth has stayed on the islands, but as well as providing opportunities, this has created many new problems.

The earliest peoples on Zanzibar are thought to have been hunter-gatherers who made little impact on the natural vegetation. However, the first Bantu settlers, who probably arrived some time in the 3rd or 4th centuries AD, started to clear patches of natural forest to plant crops such as millet and sorghum.

At some stage, plants such as bananas, coconut palms and yams were introduced, possibly by peoples from Madagascar who in turn had originally migrated from the islands of Indonesia. As these crops became more popular, more indigenous forest was cleared.

In the 16th century, Portuguese traders established bases along the east African coast, including those on Zanzibar and Pemba, and introduced plants such as cassava and maize from their colonies in South America. More forest was felled as local people cleared the land required to grow these crops.

After the Omani Arabs gained control of the islands in the early 18th century, and the trade in ivory and slaves expanded, Zanzibar became an important import and export centre. Cassava was used for feeding the vast numbers of slaves who passed through the island's infamous market. Another major export at this time was copra (produced from coconuts) which meant more land was cleared for coconut palm plantations.

At the turn of the 19th century, cloves were introduced from other islands in the Indian Ocean, and they soon became a major export crop. Other spices, such as vanilla and cardamom, were also grown and yet more forest was cleared for plantations.

Throughout the 19th century, the powerful nations of Europe put pressure on the sultans of Zanzibar to restrict the trade in slaves. As this was reduced, the trade in cloves and other spices became even more important. During the colonial period, plantations continued to be developed and the natural forest continued to be reduced. A department of forestry was established to exploit the forests' timber supplies, but apparently it was not until the 1950s that it came to the attention of the Forestry Department that there was very little indigenous forest left on the island of Zanzibar. The largest remaining area, Jozani Forest, to the southeast of Zanzibar Town, was purchased from an Arab landowner by the department and the felling of trees was restricted. In 1960, Jozani was declared a protected nature reserve and in 2004 it became the heart of Zanzibar's first national park: Jozani-Chwaka Bay National Park.

Jobs in the tourism sector have developed skills in many islanders, and there is a class of local entrepreneurs who wouldn't have existed without tourism. Popular festivals have been introduced, several traditional handicraft techniques have been restored, and some villagers, especially women, have had the chance to earn income and better their lifestyle as a direct result of growing tourism.

The benefits are easy to find, but the tourism boom has not been universally good. Pragmatic observers agree that it's not tourism which is the problem per se; it's the sensitivity and sustainability of the individual tourism developments. It's all about how responsible the tourism enterprises are with the resources and culture of the islands. This issue of 'responsible tourism' is moving up the agenda, as evidenced by the rise of consciously responsible lodges like Chumbe Island and Mafia's Chole Mjini. However, there's a long way to go before all of the hotels and lodges match the high standards set by these.

Officially, the government recognises this problem, and back in 1992 introduced a National Environmental Policy for Zanzibar. This stressed that the quality of life of the Zanzibaris should not be harmed by the destruction of their environment, and that cultural and biological diversity should be preserved. In the words of President Salmin Amour, 'unchecked development could soon become unsustainable for our people and our small islands'. Sadly, in spite of the policies and well-intentioned sentiment, the speed and scale of the current growth in tourism developments continues unabated, and the local population is increasingly questioning its benefits.

There are signs that some of the more ethical elements of the tour operator community are starting to take these issues seriously. In 2008, the independent UK-based charity Tourism Concern (*www.tourismconcern.org.uk*) conducted a review of tourism on Zanzibar on behalf of the UK members of its Ethical Tour Operators Group (ETOG). This involved analysing and inspecting some of the hotels most popularly featured and spending time with island-based industry bodies, local and international NGOs, tourists, community groups and local residents. ETOG started this project to establish the most critical issues affecting tourism businesses and communities, and to highlight examples of best practice. Armed with this information, ETOG's members aim to find a practical way to raise ethical standards.

This is a positive step by a few overseas tour operators, but to have a substantial impact on Zanzibar's tourism issues requires the Zanzibari government to engage fully in the issue, and to work for long-term sustainability. Sadly, there is currently no sign of this happening. The government is doing little in the way of fairly regulating the pace of development, or trying to upgrade the island's basic water supplies, communications, rubbish collections or other island infrastructure. Despite this, as visitors, we should do our best to act responsibly towards Zanzibar's environment and cultures, and to travel as responsibly as possible.

Visitor numbers and the tourism economy The Zanzibar Commission for Tourism was founded in 1987 to promote Zanzibar as a tourist destination, and in 1992 the Zanzibar Investment Promotion Agency was created to encourage overseas investment, particularly in tourism projects. Buoyed by their presence, the first half of the 1990s saw a dramatic rise in the development of tourism, but the last few years have seen a truly staggering increase.

In 1995, over 56,000 visitors were arriving in Zanzibar each year; earnings derived from the tourism sector are said to have contributed an estimated US$1,971 million to the economy. (See the Tanzanian government website, www.tanzania.go.tz/zanzibar, although we are unsure how these stats were derived, as this means that each visitor effectively contributes over US$35,000!)

By the end of 2005, numbers had exceeded 100,000 visitors per year for the first time, and by 2008 official tourism figures were sitting at 140,000 arrivals, with real figures estimating visitor numbers to be closer to 160,000. This discrepancy lies in the fact that official figures only include those arriving directly from abroad and not tourists coming in from Dar es Salaam or from safaris on the Tanzanian mainland. In descending order, the majority of visitors come from Italy, the UK, Germany, the Netherlands and the US, all lured by images of pristine beaches, swaying palms and exotic island life. Tourist arrivals to Pemba and the Mafia Archipelago remain insignificant by comparison.

The government recently announced a target of half a million tourists to Zanzibar annually by 2013. In a similar vein, the Zanzibar Commission for Tourism's projection figures currently estimate close to 450,000 annual visitors by 2020. While far below the figures recorded by larger countries like Kenya, these ever-increasing visitor numbers clearly show that Zanzibar's tourism industry has changed gear since the early 1980s. If the projected growth is achieved, it is hard to see how the islands will cope, socially or environmentally, with what would equate to about a 700% increase in visitors in 25 years.

Tourism currently represents about 22% of Zanzibar's gross domestic product (GDP) and 77% of foreign direct investment (FDI), which contrasts with cloves, which account for around 45% of GDP. Whilst export earnings from this traditional commodity fall (see box *Cloves*, page 52), the income from tourism is rising to plug the gap. Some observers expect tourism to be Zanzibar's largest generator of foreign exchange within a decade.

National tourism policies The Zanzibari government's current policies and development plans consistently emphasise tourism which benefits the local population, protects and conserves the natural environment and maximises local employment and locally produced goods and services. All very admirable aims, but in reality, few of these guiding principles seem to be translated into laws to regulate development.

Large developments, often European all-inclusive resorts, seem to be being built on every available plot of land on the north and east coasts, container-loads of goods are continually imported from China, and in most hotels significant numbers of employees are from mainland Tanzania and overseas. It is hard not to reach the conclusion that the government is doing its people a gross disservice by only paying lip service to these issues.

In spite of this, there are some stalwart hoteliers and tour operators doing the utmost to be socially and environmentally aware; throughout this book we have highlighted their achievements and ambitions, so that travellers can vote with their feet.

Issue awareness With huge question marks hanging over the sustainability of the current level of tourism to Zanzibar, and the islands' leaders exhibiting only myopia on many of the issues, alarm bells are ringing for responsible travellers. Being aware of what the issues are is a crucial step towards travelling responsibly, and some of the main issues include the following:

Fresh water depletion Fresh water is very precious on low-lying islands like these, and there is mounting evidence of ground water depletion: water levels in wells used by villagers for generations have dropped and, in a few areas, old wells that were once fresh are now becoming brackish.

Zanzibar Town draws its water from a freshwater aquifer flowing under the centre of the island; a pipe network pumps water to the main coastal communities outside the capital. The demand from hotels is rising, sometimes leaving the volume of piped fresh water for the villagers as both inadequate and unreliable. Some communities have sunk wells to directly access the ground water, as have some hotels (whilst others ferry their water in by truck), but the pressure on this critical resource is growing. One survey claimed that, on average, tourists use 180 litres of water per day (this of course includes all use – washing, laundry, hotel cleaning, etc) compared with the average local Zanzibari's consumption of less than 40 litres.

Nungwi and Kendwa are at the end of the pipe network, and here the problem is most acute. Villagers are increasingly experiencing serious problems getting access to fresh water. With the island's mushrooming hotels drawing more water from the pipe, in addition to all the communities along its route north, there is rarely much water left by the time it gets to Nungwi. This has led to conflict between the villagers and the hotels and, with further development underway and no real solution in place, things are set to get increasingly difficult.

Rubbish Rubbish is a major problem on Zanzibar Island. There is minimal municipal waste collection, and that which does exist focuses almost exclusively on Zanzibar Town. At the end of 2006, the statement from the governmental Environment Department declared that 'out of about 200 tonnes of solid waste produced daily in Stone Town, the Zanzibar Municipal Council workers are only able to collect about 60 tonnes'. This situation is visibly worsening every year with little state investment or significant effort to manage the problem.

The main problem, however, is that there is only a single stinking landfill site for the whole of Zanzibar Island to use. This is totally inadequate. The result is that much rubbish is dumped around the island, or at sea, by both local residents and irresponsible hotels and tourists. It's often noted that, as much of the island is made of coral rock, digging more landfill sites may not be easy, but despite this there are a number of active rock quarries around the island.

Several of the better hotels now have efficient waste management plans, some pay for an official collection and hope the waste is not dumped before it reaches the landfill site, some investment comes from overseas governments, and in Jambiani and Kendwa small NGOs and concerned residents are trying hard to address the problem on a local level, but with large-scale developments mushrooming, a formal government strategy and serious financial backing is critical to curb the problem.

Social vices Most local people on Zanzibar regard tourism as a broadly positive industry in terms of its potential to earn money. However, increasingly there is resentment felt about the behaviour of tourists. You only need to watch bikini-clad women walking through a village, or see beer bottles piled high at a beach barbecue, to realise how inconsiderate some visitors are to local values.

Unsurprisingly, as with many traditional, reserved communities faced with a dramatic influx of international tourists, cultural erosion can also be observed on Zanzibar. As a predominantly (95%) Muslim country, alcohol and drugs have had little place in society in the past. Now, with the Western influence of tourists and growing wealth from ad hoc guiding, souvenir selling and prostitution, exposure and addiction to both is starting to become a problem among young local men, especially in Stone Town and Nungwi. This often evolves to cause problems like opportunist theft for money, and it increases village tensions with traditional elders appalled at the behaviour of the youths.

Similarly, prostitution is another fairly recent island issue, both within the tourist and local communities. Female sex workers are now travelling from the mainland in search of tourist dollars, local men are offering their services to foreign girls in beach bars, and local women are selling their bodies to other villagers flush with new-found wealth.

Many hotels and NGOs are acutely aware of these tensions and are working hard, directly or through local charities, to address social and environmental issues in their area. Many more in the tourism sector appear oblivious to the issues.

Overfishing There is growing concern about overfishing, particularly for crab, lobster, squid and octopus, to supply restaurants catering for tourists. Fishermen on all coasts are reporting difficulties in finding fish big enough to sell and, in spite of legal restrictions, fishing on the coral reef is increasing as a direct result. A secondary consequence of the voracious tourist appetite for fresh seafood has been to inflate the price of fish and shellfish beyond the means of many local villagers. Demand in some areas is making the ingredients for traditional meals, such as octopus, too expensive for purchase by the fishing communities from where they come.

Construction materials For years, beach sand, coral rock and native trees have been used for construction, leading to accelerated coastal erosion. As just one example, mangrove poles are a particularly good construction material; they are very strong, often straight and highly resistant to termites (see box, *Mangrove forest depletion*, page 252). However, these have seldom been sustainably harvested. This has depleted Zanzibar's original mangrove forests, which are vital to the marine ecosystems – as a nursery for many small fish – as well as a buffer for the coast against the ocean.

2

People and Culture

PEOPLE

POPULATION AND SETTLEMENT The population of Zanzibar was 984,625 in 2002, the date of the last census, with an annual growth rate of 3.1%. This growth remained fairly steady for some years though the general feeling of Zanzibari residents today is that recent years have seen a more significant increase. Of the total residents, around two-thirds of the people (622,459) live on Zanzibar Island (Unguja), with the greatest proportion settled in the densely populated west. Zanzibar's largest settlement is Zanzibar Town (sometimes called Zanzibar City), on Zanzibar Island, with 205,870 inhabitants. Other towns on Zanzibar Island include Chaani, Bambi, Mahonda and Makunduchi, but these are small by comparison. Outside these towns, most people live in small, traditional villages and are engaged in farming, fishing or tourism-related industries.

On Pemba the overall settlement pattern is similar. The largest town is Chake Chake, with a population of 19,283; other smaller towns are Wete and Mkoani. Mafia's total population was 40,801 in 2002.

There is considerable disparity in the standard of living between the inhabitants of Mafia, Pemba and Unguja and between urban and rural populations, which are split roughly equally. The average annual income of just US$250 hides the fact that about half the population lives below the poverty line on less than US$1 per day. Despite a reasonable standard of primary healthcare and education, infant mortality is still 83 in 1,000 live births, and it is estimated that malnutrition affects one in three of the islands' people; life expectancy at birth is 48. While the incidence of HIV/AIDS is considerably less in Zanzibar than in Tanzania as a whole (0.6% of the population, as against the national average of around 8%), it is a growing problem. The Zanzibar AIDS Commission reports that women show prevalence rates that are five times higher than their male counterparts and that understanding of infection transmission is still poor in many communities. In late 2006, the government unanimously adopted its first National HIV/AIDS Policy with plans for a door-to-door awareness campaign, HIV prevention education in school curricula and the promotion of condom use (the screening of visitors for HIV on arrival was omitted). This is clearly a positive step, but sadly the simultaneous increase in drug and alcohol usage, the rise in prostitution, and mounting numbers of mainland Tanzanians seeking work on the island, is still likely to increase the infection rate.

ORIGINS It is thought that Zanzibar's original inhabitants came from the African mainland around 3,000 to 4,000 years ago, although this is not certain and no descendants of these early people remain, having been completely absorbed by later arrivals.

Over the last 2,000 years, the records have become a little clearer. Historians know that Bantu-speaking people migrated from central Africa and settled across east and southern Africa during the 1st millennium AD. (For more details see *Chapter 1, History*.) Those who settled on the east African coast and offshore islands, including Zanzibar, came into contact with Arab traders who had sailed southwards from the Red Sea region. The Bantu adopted some customs of the Arabs and gradually established a language and culture which became known as Swahili.

From the 10th century, small groups of immigrants from Shiraz (Persia) also settled at various places along the east African coast, and especially in Zanzibar, and mingled with the local people. Over the following centuries, small groups of Arab and Persian peoples continued to settle here and intermarried with the Swahili and Shirazi. The largest influx occurred in the 18th and 19th centuries, when Omani Arabs settled on Zanzibar as rulers and landowners, forming an elite group. At about the same time, Indian settlers formed a merchant class.

Today, most of the people in Zanzibar are Shirazi or Swahili, although clear distinctions are not always possible. They fall into three groups: the Wahadimu (mainly in the southern and central parts of Zanzibar Island), the Watumbatu (on Tumbatu Island and in the northern part of Zanzibar Island), and the Wapemba (on Pemba Island), although again distinctions are hard to draw, and in fact, often not made by the people of Zanzibar themselves. The islands' long history of receiving (if not always welcoming) immigrants from Africa and Arabia has created a more relaxed attitude to matters of tribe or clan than is found in some parts of Africa.

Zanzibar is also home to groups of people of African origin who are descendants of freed slaves, dating from the 18th and 19th centuries. In more recent times, a large number of Africans have immigrated from mainland Tanzania. Additionally, some Arabs who were expelled after the 1964 Revolution have returned to Zanzibar.

Other people on Zanzibar include small populations from Goa, India and Pakistan, mainly involved in trade or tourism, and a growing number of European expatriates and volunteers, many working in the tour industry, with others employed as teachers, doctors and engineers.

LANGUAGE with thanks to Said el-Gheithy

The indigenous language spoken throughout Zanzibar is Swahili (called Kiswahili locally). This language is also spoken as a first language by Swahili people along the east African coast, particularly in Kenya and mainland Tanzania, and as a second or third language by many other people throughout east Africa (including Kenya, Tanzania and Uganda, and in parts of several other countries such as Rwanda, Mozambique and Congo), making Swahili the common tongue of the region. Although there are many forms and dialects found in different areas, visitors with a basic grasp of Swahili will be understood anywhere.

Swahili is an African language, and includes many words and phrases of Arabic origin, plus words from other languages such as Persian, English and Portuguese. Over the centuries Swahili has developed into a rich language, lending itself especially to poetry. Zanzibar is regarded as the home of Swahili – it is spoken in its purest form here and in pockets on the coast of Tanzania and Kenya. In fact in these areas, tradition dictates that ordinary conversation should approximate the elegance of poetry. Generally, as you travel further inland on the east African mainland, the Swahili becomes increasingly more basic and simplified.

For visitors, English and several other European languages, such as French and Italian, are spoken in Zanzibar Town and most tourist areas. However, if you get off the beaten track a few words of Swahili will be useful to ask directions, to greet people or even to begin a simple conversation. Even in the tourist areas, using a few

Swahili words (for example, to ask the price of a souvenir, or order a meal in a restaurant) can add to the enjoyment of your visit. Arabic is also spoken. For basic words and phrases, see *Appendix 1, Language.*

RELIGION

Most of the people in Zanzibar are Muslims (followers of the Islamic faith) and all towns and villages on Zanzibar Island and Pemba have mosques. Visitors to Zanzibar Town cannot fail to hear the evocative sound of the muezzins calling people to prayer from the minarets, especially for the evening session at sunset. And visitors cannot fail to notice the effects of the holy month of Ramadan, when most people fast during the day, and the pace of life slows down considerably (see also *Public holidays*, pages 102–3). There are also small populations of Christians and Hindus.

ISLAM Islam was founded by the Prophet Muhammad, who was born around AD570 in Arabia. He received messages from God during solitary vigils on Mount Hira, outside his home town of Mecca. When driven out of Mecca by his enemies, he migrated to Medina. Here, at the age of about 53, he started to convert the world to Islam, and his message spread rapidly through the Arab world and beyond.

Muhammad died in AD632, but fired by evangelist zeal Arab Muslims had conquered all of northern Africa by the early 8th century, and introduced the new religion there. By AD1100, Islam had spread from Arabia and the Horn of Africa along the east African coast, through the current countries of Kenya and Tanzania, all the way down to Sofala (in present-day Mozambique). Today, Islam is the dominant religion of these coastal areas, which include the islands of Zanzibar.

The five main tenets of Islam are prayer (five times a day), testimony of the faith, fasting (the period of Ramadan), almsgiving, and the pilgrimage to Mecca (the Hajj). The Muslim calendar dates from the Hejira, the flight of Muhammad from Mecca to Medina, which corresponds to 16 July AD622 in the Christian calendar. The Muslim year consists of 12 lunar months of 29 or 30 days each, making 354 days. Eleven times in every cycle of 30 years a day is added to the year. This means that Muslim festivals fall 11 or 12 days earlier every year, according to the Western calendar.

OTHER RELIGIONS There are small populations of Christians and Hindus living on the islands. The two most notable churches are the Anglican Cathedral Church of Christ and the Catholic Church of St Joseph in Zanzibar Town; Hindu temples are also present to serve the local community.

Alongside the established world faiths, traditional African beliefs are still held by most local people, and there is often considerable cross-over between aspects of Islam and local customs. (See box, *The Shetani of Zanzibar*, overleaf for more details.)

CULTURE

ARTS AND CRAFTS
Music and dance As you wander around Zanzibar Town, you will hear calls to prayer from the many mosques as well as the sounds of American rap music and Jamaican reggae. Around the next corner, however, you are also likely to hear film music from India or the latest chart-toppers from Egypt and the Gulf States. Thankfully the islands have not entirely lost their own cultural traditions, and

Gemma Pitcher

Throughout the centuries Zanzibar Island (Unguja) and, to a greater extent, Pemba Island have been famous as centres of traditional religion and witchcraft, alongside their better-known role as centres of the spice and slave trades. Today the cult of the *shetani* (meaning a spirit or spirits, the word is singular or plural) is still going strong in Zanzibar and Pemba – a dark undercurrent unseen and unknown by the majority of visitors.

According to local traditional beliefs, shetani are creatures from another world, living on earth alongside animals and humans, but invisible most of the time and generally ill-intentioned. Many of the ebony carvings on sale in Zanzibar's curio shops depict the various forms a shetani can take – for example, a hunched and hideously twisted old woman, a man–dog hybrid, or a young girl with the legs of a donkey.

There is no real way, say the locals, of protecting yourself from the possibility of being haunted or attacked by a shetani. The best thing is simply to keep out of their way and try to make sure they keep out of yours – for example by hanging a piece of paper, inscribed with special Arabic verses, from the ceiling of the house. Almost every home or shop in Zanzibar has one of these brown, mottled scraps, attached to a roof beam by a piece of cotton.

Should the worst happen in spite of these precautions and a shetani decide to take up residence in your home – or even, in the worst-case scenario, your body – the only thing to do is to visit a *mganga* (sorcerer). To be a mganga is a trade that generally runs in families, with secrets and charms passed on from father to son or mother to daughter. *Waganga* (the plural of mganga) meet periodically in large numbers to discuss their business (patients must pay handsomely for their services) and initiate new recruits. A committee of elderly, experienced practitioners will vet a younger, untested mganga before declaring him or her fit to practise.

Each mganga is in contact with ten or so shetani, who can be instructed to drive out other shetani from someone who is possessed, or to work their power in favour of the customer. The waganga are also herbalists, preparing healing medicines where spirit possession is not indicated, or combining both physical and occult treatment in severe cases.

But there are some shetani, goes the current thinking, which even a mganga cannot control. The latest and most famous of these was (or is) Popo Bawa – a phenomenon of far greater significance than just a run-of-the-mill shetani, which gripped Zanzibar's population in a wave of mass hysteria in 1995.

Popo Bawa (the name comes from the Swahili words for 'bat' and 'wing') began on the island of Pemba, where he terrorised the local population to such an extent that they

equally popular in Zanzibar are local musical forms, in particular the style known as *taarab*.

Taarab Zanzibar has been at the crossroads of trade routes for thousands of years as peoples of Africa, India, Iran, China and other parts of Asia and the Arab world have all played their parts in influencing the music, architecture, food and culture of the region. In its origins, taarab was court music, played in the palace of Sultan Barghash. The sounds of Arabic musical traditions and those from India, Indonesia and other countries of the 'Dhow region' (the Indian Ocean basin) are clearly distinguishable even today, mingling to form a unique flavour and providing the frame for the Swahili poetry which makes up the heart of taarab music.

Currently, two major taarab groups exist in Zanzibar: Nadi Ikhwan Safaa and Mila na Utamaduni (also called Culture Musical Club, or just Culture). Of the two, Culture are the more professional and have become quite well known called upon their most powerful sorcerers to drive him across the sea to Zanzibar. There the reign of terror of the 'shetani-above-all-shetani' continued.

The experiences of those who claimed to be visited by the demon were terrifying. They awoke in the middle of the night to find themselves paralysed and with the feeling of being suffocated. They then saw a squat, winged figure, around 1m tall, or slightly smaller, and with a single eye in the middle of its forehead, approaching the bed. Helpless, they were powerless to move or cry out as the demon raped them, men and women alike. Only when Popo Bawa had departed were they able to raise the alarm.

During the height of the Popo Bawa hysteria, people took to the rooftops and village squares, following a rumour that safety could only be had by those who slept outside, in a group. Despite precautions like these, tales of the demon's progress around the island spread, until the government was forced to broadcast announcements on the radio pleading for calm. Despite this, a helpless, mentally handicapped young man was beaten to death by a mob that had become convinced he was the demon. This seemed to be the climax of the whole affair – after that, the hysteria abated somewhat and Popo Bawa retreated. He is widely expected to return, however, and when local people talk of him, it's with a nervous laugh.

American psychologists came to Zanzibar to study the events and write papers, and stated that the case of Popo Bawa is simply a Zanzibari version of a phenomenon known as a 'waking dream'. One of the characteristics of such a dream is a feeling of being weighted down or even paralysed. Other characteristics include extreme vividness of the dream and bizarre or terrifying content. It is this same phenomenon that is used by sceptics in the USA to explain the stories of those who claim to have been abducted by aliens.

Nevertheless, to the people of Zanzibar, Popo Bawa was very real and proof that shetani exist. Of course, they are not all as horrific as Popo Bawa; the lesser shetani come in all shapes, sizes and colours – beautiful Arabic women, hideous Ethiopian hags, or tall, handsome white men. Shetani can be forced to work for humans, but it's a risky business. Some successful businessmen are said to keep a whole room of shetani in their houses to promote material success and make mischief on their adversaries. But the price of such supernatural intervention is high – a goat, a chicken or a cow must be sacrificed regularly and its blood sprinkled in the four corners of the room. If this sacrifice is not faithfully and regularly made, the shetani will take a terrible substitute – it will demand instead one of its master's male children...

internationally, not only through CD releases such as *Spices of Zanzibar* or the more recent *Bashraf* albums, but also because they have successfully toured Belgium, France, Germany, Switzerland, the United Arab Emirates, Réunion and many other countries. Nadi Ikhwan Safaa, affectionately known by local people as Malindi Music Club, are Zanzibar's oldest group, who trace their roots back to 1905. The group plays a style of taarab in which the distant Middle Eastern origins are still very much to the fore.

Different theories abound about the real origins of taarab in Zanzibar. Legend has it that in the 1870s Sultan Barghash sent a Zanzibari to Cairo to learn to play the *qanun*, a kind of zither, common to the Arab-speaking world. Among the first singers to record taarab music in the Swahili language was the legendary Siti binti Saad, who was taken to India by a film director. Siti stopped performing in the 1940s, but her records – solo and in duet with Sheikh Mbaruk – continued to be issued on 78rpm throughout the 1950s and are still much in demand. Besides the qanun, other instruments that came to feature in the taarab groups (or orchestras) include the oud, violins, *ney*, accordion, cello and a variety of percussion. Hence much of the traditional taarab music sounds like a more Africanised version of some of the great Egyptian popular classical orchestras that played alongside singers like Oum Kulthoum, who is still played on Radio Zanzibar to this day.

The best way to experience taarab is at a local concert, but visitors to Zanzibar are also welcome at the orchestras' rehearsals in Malindi or at Vuga Clubhouse in the evening. What Andy Morgan (*Roots* magazine) says in an article on Zanzibari music definitely holds true: 'There's hardly anything in the whole of Africa as uplifting as the swelling sounds of a full taarab orchestra in full sail.'

Kidumbak The suburb of Ng'ambo – the 'other side' of Zanzibar Town, where the lower-class living areas spread out and where poorer families and more recent arrivals to the city live – is the home of *kidumbak*. This music style, which is less refined and more upbeat than taarab, could be located musically somewhere between Stone Town big-orchestra taarab and the rural *ngoma* music. It is most often performed at weddings and other celebrations and is closely related to taarab. In fact, contemporary kidumbak often makes use of the latest taarab hit songs and is sometimes called *kitaarab*, which means 'a diminutive type of taarab' or 'derived from taarab'. Historical evidence suggests that Swahili taarab was originally performed in a very similar way to kidumbak and only later changed to resemble court orchestra music.

The kidumbak ensemble consists of a single melodic instrument, customarily a violin (played in frantic fiddle-style), a *sanduku*, or tea-chest-bass, two small clay drums (*ki-dumbak*), which form the rhythmic core of every such ensemble, and other rhythm instruments, such as *cherewa*, a kind of maracas manufactured from coconut shells filled with seeds, or *mkwasa*, short wooden sticks played like claves. In contrast to taarab, kidumbak is much more rhythmic and the lyrics more drastic than the poetic settings of the taarab songs, often criticising other people's social behaviour. At wedding performances, the singer has to be able to string together a well-timed medley of ngoma songs, and she or he must have the ability to compose lyrics on the spot. At a Zanzibari wedding, one kidumbak set usually lasts for an hour; as one song joins the next, the intensity heats up, with the main attraction being the interplay between the music and song of the players and the dancing and chorus response of the wedding guests.

Beni This brass band music originated around the end the 19th century as a mockery of colonial-style military bands. It was soon incorporated in the competitive song-and-dance exchanges so popular on the Swahili coast and spread from there all over east Africa. *Beni* (from the English 'band') is a popular wedding entertainment with a strong focus on rhythm and dance, and audience participation.

Beni borrows choruses from the latest taarab hits and arranges them in extended medleys with the female wedding audience joining in for the chorus and as dancers. It is funny music, vivacious, raucous and lively. If you can imagine a deranged military marching band playing as loud as possible on half-broken trumpets, trombones, drums – only vaguely in tune with each other, but having a great time – then you will get the idea!

In Zanzibar, beni is performed both as a street parade and, stationary, for a wedding dance. The band Beni ya Kingi usually kicks off the opening parade for the Festival of the Dhow Countries (see *Festivals*, pages 46–7), which winds its way slowly through the narrow streets of Stone Town before reaching Forodhani Gardens at the waterfront with a great crowd which then turns into a wild and lively party.

Ngoma Ngoma, literally translated, means 'drum' and is a term used to encompass all local African traditional forms of dancing, drumming and singing. There are literally hundreds of different ngoma styles throughout Tanzania, variations often being so slight that untrained eyes and ears can hardly notice the difference. A number of these originate from Zanzibar and Pemba and all are spectacular to watch. The often-elaborate native costumes emphasise the unity of the dancers' steps and the rhythm section which usually consists of several handmade drums and percussion instruments (such as oil tins beaten with a stick). *Ngoma ya kibati* from Pemba, for example, consists of a very rapid declamatory style of singing which is an improvised dialogue to drum accompaniment with singers/dancers coming in for a chorus every so often. Even if you can't follow a single word of the firework-like exchange between the two main singers, *kibati* is hilariously funny; if you understand all the references and hints implied, it is of course even more so. Another example is *msewe*, supporting the rhythm section, and named after the material which is strapped to the ankles of the male dancers.

Each ngoma style has its own special costume. In *kyaso*, men dance dressed in shirts and *kikois* (special woven cloth from the east African coast) with a long, narrow stick in their hand, all movements beautifully co-ordinated. In *ndege*, women in colourful dresses all hold bright umbrellas, moving forwards with slightly rotating steps and movements of the hips. In *bomu*, the women dress up like men and in other funny costumes and dance around in a circle.

The variations are endless and performances are never dull. According to Abdalla R Mdoe, choreographer for Imani Ngoma Troupe, a privately initiated performance ensemble that specialises in all kinds of ngoma, three different types can be differentiated: ceremonial ngomas, which are performed at weddings, circumcision and other festivities; ritual ngomas (eg: *kisomali* to cure a sick person, or *pungwa* to avert evil); and religious ngomas, which in Zanzibar are closely related to the Muslim festivities of Zikri, Duffu, Maulidi and Hom.

Modern taarab Undoubtedly a pop-phenomenon (and therefore ephemeral) is a modern style of taarab, called *rusha roho*, which translates literally 'to make the spirit fly' and has some untranslatable meaning approximating to 'upsetting someone' or 'making the other one jealous'. Modern taarab is also the first style of taarab that's designed to be danced to, and features direct lyrics, bypassing the unwritten laws of lyrical subtlety of the older groups. Much of modern taarab music is composed and played on keyboards, increasing portability; hence the group is much smaller in number than 'real taarab' orchestras and therefore more readily available to tour and play shows throughout the region. This fact has led to enormous popularity in Zanzibar, boosted by the prolific output of cassette recordings, which, though not up to European studio quality standards, still outsell tapes by any other artist local or international.

Visual arts

Tingatinga paintings Among the visual arts, by far the best-known contemporary Zanzibari style is Tingatinga (or tinga-tinga). Paintings in this distinctive style can be found for sale at souvenir stalls and shops all over Zanzibar, as well as at tourist centres on the Tanzanian mainland, and in Kenya. The subjects of Tingatinga paintings are usually African animals, especially elephants, leopards, hippos, crocodiles and gazelles, as well as guineafowl, hornbills and other birds. The main characteristics of the style include images which are both simplified and fantastical, bold colours, solid outlines and the frequent use of dots and small circles in the design.

The style was founded by Edward Saidi Tingatinga, who was born in southern Tanzania in 1937 and came to Dar es Salaam looking for work in the 1950s. After doing various jobs, in the early 1960s Tingatinga became unemployed and looked around for a way to earn money. At that time, carvers and sculptors, notably Makonde people, were producing some indigenous work, but most local painters favoured pictures based on European representational styles or Congolese styles from central Africa. (In fact, in the 1950s and 1960s many painters from Congo and Zaire (now the DRC) came to Kenya and Tanzania to sell their work to tourists and well-off residents.) Legend has it that Saidi Tingatinga decided he could do what the Congolese artists did – paint pictures and sell them for money.

With no training, he produced pictures that were initially simple and straightforward. Subjects were the animals and people he remembered from his home in southern Tanzania. He used just four or five different colours (actually house paint – and the only colours available) and painted on wooden boards. But despite this humble beginning, Tingatinga quickly sold his early paintings, mainly to local European residents who admired the original, 'naïve' style.

Within a few months, Tingatinga's paintings were in high demand. He couldn't keep up with the orders which flooded in, so he employed several fellow painters to help him produce more. There was no concept of copyright, and Tingatinga encouraged his colleagues to base their works on his style. As their success grew, soon the artists were able to afford to use bright enamel paints (the type used for touching up paintwork on cars and bicycles) and painted on canvas so tourists could take home pictures more easily. By the end of the 1960s, Tingatinga painting had become recognised as truly original contemporary African art.

In 1972, Saidi Tingatinga died, but the artists he'd encouraged formed a group named in his honour, and continued to produce and sell works in his style. Today, demand from tourists is still high, and vast numbers of Tingatinga artists produce paintings on cloth, wooden boards and other objects such as trays, plates and model wooden cars. There's even an aeroplane at Zanzibar Airport with its tail decorated in Tingatinga style.

With so many Tingatinga paintings available in Zanzibar and around east Africa, the quality of the work varies considerably; many pictures for sale in the streets have been bashed out quickly with little care or attention to detail. But if you search hard among the dross, or visit a shop where the trader has an interest in stocking better-quality stuff, you can often find real works of art (and still at reasonable prices) which do justice to the memory of Saidi Tingatinga – the founder of a fascinating, entertaining and quintessentially African style.

ZANZIBAR DOORS

Around Zanzibar and particularly in Stone Town, you'll come across massive, carved and decorated doorways, some on imposing frontages and others tucked incongruously down narrow alleys.

When a house was built in Zanzibar, the door was traditionally the first part to be erected. The greater the wealth and status of the house's owner, the larger and more elaborately carved his front door. Symbolic designs and quotations from the Koran were added to exert a benign influence: a kind of hand-crafted insurance policy. Waves of the sea climbing up the doorpost represent the livelihood of the Arab merchant to whom the house belonged, while frankincense and date-palms symbolise wealth and plenty. From a darker side of history, chains carved at the side indicate that slaves were held in the house. Some designs are thought to pre-date the Koran: the stylised lotuses could relate to Egyptian fertility symbols, and the fish may possibly represent the protective Syrian goddess Atargatis or the ancient Egyptian fish-god.

Many doors are studded with brass spikes and bosses, which may stem from the Indian practice of studding doors of medieval castles with sharp iron spikes to prevent their being battered in by war elephants. In AD915, an Arab traveller recorded that Zanzibar Island abounded in elephants, and around 1295 Marco Polo wrote that Zanzibar had 'elephants in plenty'. But they must have been extinct long before the Arabs built houses in Stone Town, and the studs and bosses seen today are purely decorative.

The oldest carved door in Zanzibar, which dates from 1694, is now the front door of the Peace Memorial Museum.

Gemma Pitcher

Baraza benches, often simply called *barazas*, have been a focal point of community life in Zanzibar for centuries. These thick benches of solid stone are built into the walls around courtyards or flank the heavy doors of distinctive Arab-style townhouses. The houses which line the long, narrow streets of Stone Town often have barazas outside – and you will also see barazas on the verandas outside traditional Swahili homes, while in the villages a palm-leaf shelter, flanked by wooden seats, fulfils the same function.

Barazas evolved as a way for Islamic men to receive visitors in their homes without compromising the privacy of their womenfolk. Coffee and sweetmeats would be served on the baraza to anyone who arrived, with only the closest friends or family members being invited into the house. The Omani sultans held public meetings, also known as barazas, outside their palaces to receive petitioners or give visiting dignitaries a public audience.

Today, barazas are still a meeting point for all sections of Zanzibari society. Every urban baraza area is lined with people lolling on the warm, smooth cement benches, gossiping, playing games of *bao* or cards, drinking sweet, thick Arabic coffee or simply idling away a long afternoon with a nap. Draughts boards are scratched in chalk on the stone surfaces, ladies sit comfortably to plait each other's hair, and for traders with no market stall of their own, a baraza provides a flat surface on which to pile their tiny pyramids of oranges, tomatoes and mangoes.

In the rainy season, when torrents of water, sometimes laced with rubbish, make walking down the streets of Stone Town uncomfortable and even hazardous, the barazas outside the houses provide a useful elevated pavement, and pedestrians jump from one to the next in an attempt to keep their feet dry.

The baraza as an architectural feature is an idea that seems to have caught on in a big way among the designers of Zanzibar's smarter hotels; almost every courtyard, nook and cranny – and even bathroom – now boasts its own baraza bench, often whitewashed to match the coral walls or inlaid with mosaic tiles.

Traditional games Stroll casually around any village or town on the islands of Zanzibar, and eventually you'll be sure to come across two hunched, intent figures seated on a baraza bench – their grunts of satisfaction or derision accompanied by the click of counters on wood. Sometimes a crowd of spectators will have gathered, pointing and shouting garbled instructions. Look closer and you'll make out the object of all this excitement – a flat wooden board, 32 little round holes and a lot of brown polished seeds. This is *bao* – Zanzibar's favourite pastime.

Games of bao – the name simply means 'wood' in Swahili – can go on for hours or even days at a time. Experienced players develop little flourishes, scattering the counters (known as *kete* – usually seeds, or pebbles or shells) expertly into holes or slapping handfuls down triumphantly at the end of a turn. Bao is played, under various different names and with many rule variations, across Africa, western India and the Caribbean. Swahili people are proud of their version, known as 'king' bao, and claim it as the original and purest form of the game. Tournaments are held periodically in Zanzibar and on the coast of the mainland – as in chess, one grandmaster eventually emerges.

The object of the game is simple: to secure as many of your opponent's counters as possible. Bao masters (usually old men) are said to be able to think strategically five to seven moves ahead, a level comparable to professional chess players.

Children learn bao as soon as they can count, scratching little holes in the ground in lieu of a board and using chips of wood or stones as counters.

The African love of carving has produced a proliferation of bao boards of many different sizes, shapes and forms – the board can be represented as resting on the

DHOWS OF THE SWAHILI COAST

Philip Briggs

The word 'dhow', commonly applied by Europeans to any traditional seafaring vessel used off the coast of east Africa, is generally assumed to be Arabic in origin. There is, however, no historical evidence to back up this notion, nor does it appear to be an established Swahili name for any specific type of boat. Caroline Sassoon, writing in *Tanganyika Notes & Records* in 1970, suggests that the word 'dhow' is a corruption of *não*, used by the first Portuguese navigators in the Indian Ocean to refer to any small local seafaring vessel, or of the Swahili *kidau*, a specific type of small boat.

The largest traditional sailing vessel in wide use off the coast of east Africa is the *jahazi*, which measures up to 20m long and whose large billowing sails are a characteristic sight off Zanzibar and other traditional ports. With a capacity of about 100 passengers, the jahazi is used mainly for transporting cargo and passengers over relatively long distances or in open water, for instance between Dar es Salaam and Zanzibar. Minor modifications in the Portuguese and Omani eras notwithstanding, the design of the modern jahazi is pretty much identical to that of similar seafaring vessels used in medieval times and before. The name *jahazi* is generally applied to boats with cutaway bows and square sterns built on Zanzibar and nearby parts of the mainland. Similar boats built in Lamu and nearby ports in Kenya are called *jalbut* (possibly derived from the English 'jolly boat' or Indian *gallevat*) and have a vertical bow and wineglass-shaped stern. Smaller but essentially similar in design, the *mashua* measures up to 10m long, has a capacity of about 25 passengers, and is mostly used for fishing close to the shore or as local transport.

The most rudimentary and smallest type of boat used on the Swahili Coast is the *mtumbwi*, which is basically a dugout canoe made by hollowing out the trunk of a large tree – the mango tree is favoured today – and used for fishing in mangrove creeks and other still-water environments. The *mtumbwi* is certainly the oldest type of boat used in east Africa, and its simple design probably replicates that of the very first boats crafted by humans. A more elaborate and distinctive variation on the mtumbwi is the *ngalawa*, a 5–6m-long dugout supported by a narrow outrigger on each side, making it sufficiently stable to be propelled by a sail. The ngalawa is generally used for fishing close to shore as well as for transporting passengers across protected channels such as the one between Mafia and Chole islands in the Mafia Archipelago.

The largest traditional boats of the Indian Ocean, the ocean-going dhows that were once used to transport cargo between east Africa, Asia and Arabia, have become increasingly scarce in recent decades due to the advent of foreign ships and other, faster modes of intercontinental transport. Several distinct types of ocean-going dhow are recognised, ranging from the 60-ton *sambuk* from Persia to 250-ton boats originating from India. Oddly, one of the larger of these vessels, the Indian *dengiya*, is thought to be the root of the English word 'dinghy'. Although a few large dhows still ply the old maritime trade routes of the Indian Ocean, they are now powered almost exclusively with motors rather than by sails.

There's an excellent small exhibition on boats in the Pemba Museum in Chake Chake, and in the House of Wonders in Zanzibar Town. Don't miss the fascinating examples of traditional 'stitched dhows', with their timbers 'sewn' tightly together.

back of a mythical beast, grows human heads from either end, or is smoothed into the shape of a fish. Bao boards make excellent souvenirs and are sold in almost every curio shop, often along with a badly photocopied set of printed instructions that are guaranteed to bamboozle even a maths professor. Far better to find a friendly local to teach you – the game is actually surprisingly simple to pick up.

Keram is the second most popular game in Zanzibar, and probably first arrived here from India. It's a fast-paced, raucous game played on a piece of wood carefully shaped into a small, square snooker table with cloth pockets at each corner. The game is similar to pool, with nine black disks, nine white disks, one red 'queen' disk and one larger white striker. Players flick the striker from their side of the board in an effort to get their own-colour disks into the pockets. Boards are kept smooth and speedy by liberal applications of talcum powder.

Bao and keram, like their Western equivalents chess and pool, have very different characters. While bao is traditionally a daytime game, played in shady village squares by elderly, dignified men, keram is popularly played at night in bars, often in the midst of a noisy and tipsy crowd of jack-the-lads.

FESTIVALS

Festival of the Dhow Countries
Without a doubt, the highlight of Zanzibar's artistic and cultural calendar is the Festival of the Dhow Countries – a 16-day event usually held in early July every year, and touted as east Africa's premier cultural event and among the most significant cultural events in all of Africa. The 'dhow countries' are those of Africa and the Indian Ocean basin, and so include east and southern Africa, northern east Africa, west and central Africa, the Horn of Africa, Arabia, Iraq, Iran, the subcontinent of India, Madagascar and the Indian Ocean islands, plus what the organisers call 'their global diaspora'.

The festival has grown from strength to strength since its humble beginnings at the Zanzibar International Film Festival (ZIFF) back in 1998, and now includes theatre, performances of traditional and contemporary music and dance, plus exhibitions of paintings, sculptures, craftwork and photography. However, the central part of this event is still the film festival, with its large, interesting and eclectic mix of films from all the dhow countries and places further afield. Several film-makers are also present, there are prestigious awards for new films (short and long features, and documentaries) and the festival also includes workshops, talks and discussions, as well as an energetic series of entertainments called the Children's Panorama.

On the more serious side, film- and media-related workshops have included Women Film-makers, Making Current Affairs Programmes for African Audiences, Constructing African History in the Cinema, and Creative Journalism.

The main venue for the festival is the open-air theatre at the Arab Fort, with films and performances on the main stage of the amphitheatre and live music in the adjoining Mambo Club, while other events are held at the Palace Museum, the House of Wonders and the Old Dispensary (Stone Town Cultural Centre). The Old Customs House, which became the home of the Dhow Countries Music Academy in 2002, is the venue for musical masterclasses. There's also a series of free shows in Forodhani Gardens, just outside the Fort.

Many events are free and admission charges are kept to a minimum (around US$0.50 for Tanzanian residents, US$5 for non-residents) to encourage local participation. The festival's directors have always aimed to deliver an event which is accessible to the local population; pricing them out would fail their objective. There's also an ambitious (but highly successful) programme of 'Village Events', which transports a selection of everything the festival offers in Zanzibar Town (film, music, theatre, women's workshops, children's shows, etc) out to the rural areas of Unguja and Pemba islands. The Festival of the Dhow Countries' organisers are keen to promote July as 'culture month' on Zanzibar, and this is undoubtedly an excellent time to visit the islands, although of course it's likely to be busy at this time. You can get more information from ZIFF, the festival organisers, who are based at the Old Fort in Zanzibar Stone Town (m *0777 411499;* e *ziff@ziff.or.tz; www.ziff.or.tz*).

Mwaka Kogwa In a very different vein, the festival of Mwaka Kogwa is held every year in several villages around Zanzibar, but most famously and most flamboyantly at the village of Makunduchi, in the south of Zanzibar Island. The traditional festival originated in Persia and celebrates the arrival of the New Year according to the Shirazi calendar. This one-day festival normally occurs during July, but it would be better to check the dates locally as changes are possible. (For more details on the festival itself see box, *The Mwaka Kogwa festival at Makunduchi*, page 285.)

3

Natural Environment

PHYSICAL ENVIRONMENT

This place, for the goodness of the harbour and watering and plentiful refreshing
with fish, and for sending sorts of fruits of the country, as cows ... and oxen
and hens, is carefully to be sought for by such of all ships as shall hereafter pass
that way.

James Lancaster, captain of the *Edward Bonaventure*,
first English ship to visit Zanzibar (1592)

LOCATION AND SIZE Zanzibar consists of two large islands, plus several smaller
ones, about 40km off the coast of east Africa, in the Indian Ocean, about 6° S of the
Equator. The two large islands are Unguja (usually called Zanzibar Island) and
Pemba. Zanzibar Island is about 85km long and between 20km and 30km wide,
with an area of 1,660km². The smaller Pemba Island, at around 985km², is some
67km long and between 15km and 20km wide.

The islands are generally flat and low lying, surrounded by coasts of rocky inlets
or sandy beaches, with lagoons and mangrove swamps, and coral reefs beyond the
shoreline. The western and central parts of Zanzibar Island have some low hills,
where the highest point is about 120m above sea level. Pemba Island has a central
ridge, cut by several small valleys, and appears more hilly than Zanzibar Island,
although the highest point on Pemba is only 95m above sea level.

CLIMATE

February 19th. We anchored off Zanzibar at dawn. A day of fierce heat. The island is
said to enjoy a cool season. I have never struck it. An hour's stroll ashore sufficed to
revive old memories, then I retired to the ship for a cold bath and an afternoon under
the electric fans.

Evelyn Waugh, *Tourist in Africa* (1959)

The climate of Zanzibar is dominated by the movements of the Indian Ocean
monsoons, and characterised by wet and dry seasons. The northeast monsoon
winds (known locally as the *kaskazi*) blow from November/December to
February/March, and the southwest monsoon winds (the *kusi*) blow from June to
September/October. The main rains (the *masika*) fall from mid-March to the end
of May, and there is a short rainy season (the *vuli*) in November.

Throughout the year, humidity is generally quite high (less so in the rainy
season), although this can be relieved by winds and sea breezes. Temperatures do
not vary greatly throughout the year, with daytime averages around 26°C (80°F) on
Zanzibar Island from June to October, and around 28°C from December to
February, although in this latter period the humidity is often higher, so
temperatures feel hotter. Pemba tends to be cooler and gets slightly more rain than
Zanzibar Island.

Unlike on the African mainland, there are no large wild animals on Zanzibar. Forest areas are inhabited by monkeys and small antelopes, while civets and various species of mongoose are found all over the islands. Birdlife is varied and interesting, with over 200 species being recorded, although bird populations are not as high as in other parts of the east African region. The marine wildlife, in the coral reefs that surround the islands, is particularly rich.

FLORA The islands of Pemba and Unguja (usually called Zanzibar Island) were originally forested, but human habitation has resulted in widespread clearing, although a few isolated pockets of indigenous forest remain. Formed about 27 million years ago and seven million years ago respectively, both islands were originally coral reefs which became exposed as sea levels dropped, so the main rock type is a coralline limestone, known locally as 'coral rag'.

On the eastern side of Zanzibar Island, and in parts of the northern and southern areas, the landscape is very flat where coralline rock is exposed or covered by a thin layer of a calcareous sandstone soil, which supports low scrubby bush, known as coral rag thicket, quite dense in some areas. The western and central parts of the island are slightly more undulating, with a deeper soil cover: red, iron-rich and more fertile. Additionally, the western sides receive more rain than the eastern sides of the islands. Thus the western parts of Zanzibar Island were once covered in forest, similar in most respects to the low coastal forest which existed on the east African mainland, but today very little of Zanzibar's indigenous natural forest remains, as it has mostly been cleared and used for agriculture. Local people grow crops on a subsistence basis, and this area is also where most of Zanzibar Island's commercial farms and spice and fruit plantations have been established.

The only significant areas of natural forest remaining in Zanzibar are at Jozani, a forest reserve on the south-central part of Zanzibar Island, and at Ngezi, a forest reserve in the north of Pemba Island, although smaller patches do exist elsewhere. The water table around Jozani is particularly high (during the rainy season the water can be over 1m above the ground) and the trees are mainly moisture-loving species.

Trees and deforestation Despite the establishment of forest reserves such as Jozani and Ngezi, Zanzibar's forests continue to be cut down at an unsustainable rate. Timber is used for boatbuilding and furniture-making, and as fuel, both for domestic purposes and to burn coral to produce lime for building construction. (This last use has grown particularly quickly as the number of hotels in Zanzibar has increased.)

Mangrove wood from coastal areas is also being cut at an unsustainable rate. Forestry Department figures show that in 1992 about ten million poles were cut in Chwaka Bay Forest, compared with 2.5 million in 1990. This wood is used for fuel and furniture, and in the construction and repair of buildings, but unfortunately the cutting of poles in the mangrove swamps leads to beach erosion and the destruction of habitats for fish and other marine life.

To replace some of the disappearing forest, through the 1990s, the Zanzibar Forestry Department planted acacia, casuarina and eucalyptus trees in Unguja and Pemba, as well as orange, coffee and cinnamon plants in Pemba. Another scheme, called the Zanzibar Cash Crop Farming System Project (ZCCFSP), discouraged farmers from cutting clove trees for firewood. All logging, and even the removal of dead wood, has officially been stopped in the Jozani and Ngezi reserves, although how carefully this new rule will be policed remains to be seen.

COCONUTS

Coconuts are the second most important crop on Zanzibar after cloves. They grow on a certain species of palm tree which is generally planted where clove trees cannot survive, although as diversification is encouraged it is not uncommon today to see coconut palms and clove trees on the same plantation.

Coconuts are picked throughout the year, and large quantities are consumed locally as food, with the milk used for cooking. The pickers skilfully climb up the palm trunks using only a short loop of rope, then drop the nuts to the ground. The outer husks of the coconuts are removed by striking them on a sharp stick or metal bar fixed in the ground.

Coconut products – mainly the 'kernel' (the white edible parts) – are also exported. The process involves splitting the coconuts in two and leaving them to dry so that the white fleshy kernels can be easily removed from the shells. The kernels are then dried for a few more days in the sun or in a special kiln. Gangs of workers separating the husks and kernels, and small coconut kilns, can be seen in the plantation areas outside Zanzibar Town.

When the kernels are properly dried, the resulting substance is called 'copra', which is widely used in the food industry as a flavouring, or for decoration. Copra is also processed into an oil that is used in some foods and in the production of soap, candles and hair oils. In the days before aerosol foam, copra was particularly good for making shaving soap as it helped produce a good lather.

The coconut husks are not wasted: they are buried under sand on the beach for several months, which helps to soften the fibres and make them separate from the rest of the husk. They are periodically dug up and beaten on rocks to help this process, and then buried again for another few months. The fibre is called 'coir', and is used for mats and rope-making. In the areas outside the towns you will often see local women working with coir in this way.

A new project outside Zanzibar Town is engaged in the use of timber from coconut palm trees, which are found all over Zanzibar and Pemba islands. Traditionally, palm has not been used as a timber because it is very hard to cut or plane. However, modern high-quality joinery tools mean coconut wood can now be turned into beautiful furniture and fittings such as doors and window frames. The aim of the project is to use the local palm trees after they have come to the end of their natural fruit-producing life. By using this local source of timber, it is hoped that other trees will not be cut down or imported to Zanzibar from the mainland. Several of the hotels and tour companies around Zanzibar are now using coconut-wood items.

Other trees occurring on Zanzibar include mango (*mwembe*), which is used for its fruit and as timber for boatbuilding, kapok (*capoc*), and *Bombax rhodographalon*, which is used in light construction, and also produces a substance similar to cotton, traditionally used to make stuffing for mattresses and pillows. Other fruit-producing trees, grown in plantations or singly around local villages include guava, breadfruit, orange and pomegranate.

Spice trees and food plants The main crops grown in Zanzibar are coconuts and cloves. Bananas, citrus fruits and other spices are also grown commercially. As well as the famous clove trees, other spice plants found on Zanzibar and Pemba include black pepper, cinnamon, cardamom, jasmine, chilli and henna, whose small leaves are dried, ground and mixed with lemon to give the paste familiar to Eastern beauticians. The main crops grown by local people for their own consumption

CLOVES

Cloves are the buds of a tree which, when dried, produce a unique flavour and aroma that is beloved of chefs the world over. The name comes from the French word *clou* meaning 'nail', which the buds resemble.

Cloves were introduced to Zanzibar from the end of the 18th century from the French colonies of the Seychelles, Ile de France (now Mauritius) and Réunion, where they had earlier been introduced from the Moluccas in Indonesia by French sailors. Sultan Said (sultan from 1804 to 1856) recognised their value and encouraged the setting up of plantations on Zanzibar and Pemba. When the plantations were established, it was found that growing conditions on Pemba Island were superior to those on Zanzibar, and the bulk of the clove crop actually came from there.

At the height of the clove trade, in the second half of the 19th century and the early 20th century, the islands of Zanzibar produced more than 90% of the world's supply of cloves, and the power and wealth of Zanzibar were based largely on this trade. Today, about 75% of the islands' total produce comes from Pemba.

Clove trees (*Eugenia aromatica* or *Eugenia caryophyllata*) grow to a height of around 10–15m and can produce crops for over 50 years. In the first eight years of growth the buds are left to turn into colourful pink flowers. When a tree reaches maturity, however, the buds are painstakingly picked by hand before they open, when they are still white, then separated from their stems. Buds and stems are dried in the sun on palm-leaf mats or on a special stone platform called a *sakufu*, during which time they turn brown. During the harvest season, between July and January, with a break during the November rainy season, the scent of cloves is carried on the breeze right across Pemba in particular, where you can often see sacks of cloves being loaded at Mkoani for shipping to Zanzibar Island. Here, they are offloaded at the port, or on the beach near the Tembo Hotel, and carried by truck to the nearby distillery.

All cloves in Zanzibar have to be sold to the government, which buys at fixed rates, then sells on at market rates to the users and producers. So important is the crop that, on Pemba, vehicles have to stop as they pass police checkpoints to give the opportunity for vehicles to be checked for smuggled cloves. Sometimes, however, the government rates paid to the clove growers are so low that a harvest is not economically viable, and the cloves are left on the trees. As a result, some plantations have been completely abandoned in recent years, creating anger and resentment among the local farmers.

Most of the cloves that are harvested are processed into oil at the distillery on Zanzibar Island. This oil is used mainly as a flavouring device in foods such as cakes, pickles, cooked meats and ready-made mixes. It is also used in some antiseptic solutions, such as mouthwashes, and in mild painkillers for toothache. Its other major use is in cosmetics, where it gives a sweet-spicy note to many different kinds of perfumes.

The best-quality dried buds are kept separate and used whole in cooking, pickling or the making of spiced wines and liqueurs. These buds are also distilled into a high-grade oil for use in particularly fine perfumes. In the cosmetics industry the oil from good Zanzibar clove buds is reckoned to be the best in the world.

Today, Zanzibar is still a major exporter of cloves and clove products, representing about 70% of foreign-exchange earnings – although these are highly dependent on the fluctuating world market price. Agriculture's contribution to Zanzibar's gross domestic product (GDP) currently stands at around 34%, although this has been falling over recent years.

include maize, cassava, yams, bananas and pumpkins (see box, *History of Zanzibari agriculture*, page 30).

MAMMALS As described above, much of Zanzibar's indigenous forested area has been cleared, so natural habitats for all wild animals are severely restricted. Probably the best places to see indigenous mammals are the Jozani Forest Reserve on Zanzibar Island and the Ngezi Forest Reserve on Pemba.

In this section, scientific names of species are given according to information provided by the Jozani Forest Reserve and Ngezi Forest Reserve. Other authorities disagree on some classifications and nomenclature, especially regarding subspecies, but this is unlikely to be important for most visitors.

The Jozani Forest Reserve is well known for its population of **red colobus monkeys** (see colour section, pages 4–5). This animal is found elsewhere in Africa, but those on Zanzibar form a distinct species, called Zanzibar red colobus or Kirk's red colobus (*Procolobus kirkii*), endemic to the island and one of the rarest primates in Africa.

Although hard to see in the forest canopy, one group of red colobus in Jozani is partly habituated to human presence, so you are quite likely to spot some if you visit. These monkeys are mainly reddish-brown in colour, with a darker back and 'cap', and a paler forehead patch, but their most striking and unusual feature is the male's white crest on the forehead. On closer inspection, particularly of facial areas, you will notice that each monkey has slightly different coat patterns and colourings.

In Jozani and some other patches of forest you are likely to see the **blue monkey**, also called Sykes's monkey, the mitis monkey or the Zanzibar white-throated guenon (*Cercopithecus mitis albgularis*), which on Zanzibar is bluish-grey, or even a greenish-grey, with a distinct white throat-patch. Although the two types of monkey compete for some food items, they are often seen foraging peacefully in mixed groups. The Swahili word for monkey is *kima*. On Zanzibar, the blue monkey is more commonly given this name. When distinguishing between the two, the blue monkey is called *kima mweusi*, and the red colobus *kima punju* – 'poison monkey' (probably because the colobus has a stronger smell than other monkeys, and is reputed to have an evil influence on trees where it feeds).

Blue monkey

A local subspecies of **vervet monkey** (*Cercopithecus aethiops nesiotes*) occurs on Pemba, but it is thought not on Zanzibar Island. This monkey is smaller than the red colobus and the blue monkey, generally greyish with a dark, rusty-brown back and black feet.

Other mammals found on Zanzibar, mainly in forested areas, include **bush pig** (*Potamochoerus porcus*), although its numbers are reported to be greatly reduced; **Zanzibar tree hyrax** (*Dendrohyrax arboreus neumanni*), a rodent-like animal the size of a rabbit (this subspecies is endemic), with hoofed feet and rounded ears, and a loud piercing scream when threatened; **Ader's duiker** (*Cephalophus adersi*), a species of small antelope found only on Zanzibar and, until recently, the Kenyan coast; and **Zanzibar suni** (*Nesotragus moschatu moschatus*), another endemic subspecies of antelope which is even smaller than the duiker. The endemic Pemba **blue duiker** (*Cephalophus monticola pembae*) occurs at Ngezi Forest. All these animals are nocturnal or extremely shy and are unlikely to be seen.

Ader's duiker

The Zanzibar leopard (*Panthera pardus adersi*), is a local subspecies. Two different types have been recorded: the *kisutu*, which is similar to the mainland leopard, but with a more compact spot pattern and lighter background; and the *konge*, which is larger than the kisutu with dark fur and faint spot pattern.

Leopard tend to be shy, and mainly active at night. Perhaps because of their elusive, nocturnal habits, they have traditionally been considered unlucky by local people, and are often associated with witchcraft, so have been actively hunted. They are also hunted because they are seen as vermin by farmers, and for their skins which can be sold to dealers. The leopard has been further pushed to the edge of extinction by an ever-growing loss of suitable habitat, as forest areas are cleared, and by a loss of prey, as Zanzibar's small antelopes are also hunted unsustainably.

By the 1980s, the leopard was believed to be extinct in Zanzibar, but in 1994 an American researcher called Scott Marshall found evidence of three leopards on Unguja (Zanzibar Island), including prints, droppings and a suspected den near Chwaka. In his report, Marshall suggested that these leopards were trapped and 'domesticated' at a young age, to be used in ceremonies by local witchdoctors or traditional healers. He also suggested that there may be several more leopards similarly kept in captivity at other villages in Zanzibar, although this assumption was based on local anecdotal evidence, rather than on positive sightings.

However, in 1998, the South African wildlife experts Chris and Tilde Stuart published a report describing their exhaustive methods to locate any signs of leopard on Zanzibar Island, and concluded that none existed in a wild state. They also looked into the possibility of a few 'kept' leopards remaining in existence but found no hard evidence. They further concluded that even if a small number of 'kept' leopards were being held in secret, there was no hope at all for long-term survival of this species on Zanzibar.

Leopard (*Panthera pardus adersi*), or *chui* in Swahili, have been recorded in Jozani, and elsewhere in Zanzibar. Again, this is an endemic subspecies, smaller than the mainland version and with finer markings, and also very unlikely to be sighted. Recent studies have concluded that this animal is now extinct on Zanzibar. (For more details see box, *Leopards in Zanzibar*, above.)

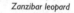

Zanzibar leopard

The small-eared **greater galago** or **bushbaby** (*Otolemur garnettii*) and the Zanzibar **lesser galago** (*Galagoides zanzibaricus*) both occur on Zanzibar, the latter listed as vulnerable by the IUCN. The **small-eared galago** (*komba* in Swahili) is about the size of a rabbit, generally brown, with very distinctive large ears and eyes, and a large bushy tail. The **Zanzibar galago** (*komba ndogo*) also has large eyes and ears, but it is smaller (about half the size of the greater galago) and grey in colour. Both animals are nocturnal, especially active at dawn and dusk, and have distinctive cries – sometimes like a child crying (hence their name), other times loud and shrill, and positively spine-chilling. They are known to be inquisitive and will forage around huts and villages at night. They are attracted to bowls of locally brewed palm wine, and often get captured when intoxicated and incapable of escape. A local saying, *mlevi kama komba*, means 'as drunk as a bushbaby'!

Also found in Zanzibar is the **African civet** (*Viverra civetta schwarzi*, orngawa in Swahili); it looks like a very large cat with a stocky body, thick tail, and black, white and grey markings which form rough stripes. The **Javan civet** (*Viverricula indica rasse*) occurs on Pemba and Unguja, probably introduced by southeast Asian traders.

Smaller mammals include the **Zanzibar slender mongoose** (*Herpestes sanguineus rufescens*), most often seen running across roads with its tail vertical, and the **bushy-tailed mongoose** (*Bdeogale crassicauda tenuis*) – rarely seen anywhere. The **marsh mongoose** (*Atilax paludinosus rubescens*) occurs only on Pemba and may be seen at Ngezi Forest. The banded mongoose is a non-indigenous species, introduced to Zanzibar Island.

Populations of rats, mice and shrews (plus 14 species of bat) occur on both Zanzibar and Pemba islands. Those worthy of note include the **Zanzibar four-toed elephant shrew** (*Petrodromus tetradactylus zanzibaricus*) with distinctive long slender legs and a trunk-like snout for eating insects, and the **Pemba flying fox** (*Pteropus voeltzkowi*), a large fruit bat with distinctive rufous colouring and fox-like face, found only on Pemba Island. (For more details, see page 309.)

REPTILES, AMPHIBIANS AND INVERTEBRATES Of all the reptiles on Zanzibar, undoubtedly the easiest to spot is the **giant tortoise** (*Geochelone gigantea*) that inhabit Prison Island, a few kilometres offshore from Zanzibar Town. They were introduced here from the island of Aldabra, in the Seychelles archipelago, in the 18th century.

If you visit Jozani, you'll probably see some of the forest's population of tiny black and gold **frogs**. In the rainy season, when the ground floods, you'll see their tadpoles too. **Chameleons** can also be seen in Jozani and other parts of the island. Like the mongoose they are often seen crossing roads, but often very slowly, and very precariously. Other reptiles include **snakes** (rarely seen) and **geckos** (frequently seen on the inside walls of buildings – particularly the budget hotels in Zanzibar Town – although this is no cause for worry as they're small, timid and harmless).

The long black **millipedes** which you'll see on paths, especially after rains, are also harmless, and will curl up in a ball if you disturb them. Smaller still, though much more dangerous, is the **mosquito**. These are relatively common on Zanzibar, so see *Chapter 4, Malaria prevention*, pages 82–4 before you arrive.

One of the best places to see some of Zanzibar's reptiles (among other animals) is at the Zanzibar Land Animals Park (ZALA) a few kilometres west of Jozani Forest on the road to Kizimkazi. (For more details see page 299.)

BIRDS Dudley Iles
Zanzibar is not noted as a major birdwatching area, but over 200 species of bird have been recorded on the islands of the archipelago. The avifauna of Zanzibar includes the resident birds, plus visitors – migrants and seabirds. For any keen birdwatcher travelling on the east African mainland, polishing off the holiday with at least a few days in Zanzibar can make the trip-list even more impressive – the islands boast several species and races which are unique. Even for the more casual birdwatcher, Zanzibar provides some fine opportunities. Knowing the name of the bird that flew over the beach, or sings from a bush in your hotel garden, will make your time in Zanzibar even more rewarding and enjoyable.

Overview Like the majority of offshore islands, Unguja and Pemba have a smaller avifauna than the mainland of east Africa. Unguja can claim about 220 species, and Pemba slightly fewer. Of these, about 35 have been added since 1994, an indication

THE INDIAN HOUSE CROW

From information provided by Dudley Iles, updated by Helen de Jode, Zanzibar Ecotourism Association

The Indian house crow (Corvus splendens) was introduced to Zanzibar in 1891. The bird is a scavenger and 50 crows were sent by the Indian government to help clear domestic waste building up in Stone Town at the time. Although the Indian house crow did consume some of this rubbish, it is by nature an aggressive bird and it began to attack many of the island's small birds and their eggs. As early as 1917 it was realised that the crows had become a pest, and they were subject to various control efforts including trapping, shooting and poisoning, but to little effect. By the 1940s, the Indian house crow had spread throughout Zanzibar Island, and by the 1970s its population had increased to such an extent in Zanzibar Town that many small bird species were rarely seen.

The crow population continued to grow and by 1990 their impact on the indigenous bird population was considerable, with the town becoming virtually devoid of all other species. In addition the Indian house crow was affecting agricultural and livestock production: feeding on germinating maize, sorghum and soft fruits, eating young chicks and ducklings and attacking calves and sometimes even cattle.

Between 1990 and 1995, the Finnish International Development Agency funded a control programme organised by wildlife expert Tony Archer and a team from the Zanzibar Commission for Lands and Environment. They used firstly a Malaysian-designed crow trap, and later a poison which was developed in the USA to control starlings as agricultural pests. The trapping and poisoning strategies were combined with a bounty on the collection of Indian house crow eggs and chicks during the breeding season. According to a report issued by Tony Archer, almost 45,000 crows were killed between 1993 and 1995. An estimated 95% of the crow population was killed in Stone Town and 75% across the island as a whole, allowing the small bird populations to return.

Unfortunately, since 1995, as funding dried up, there has been little continued effort to control the numbers of crows in Zanzibar. Increasing amounts of rubbish generated by a growing human population in Zanzibar Town, and a growth in tourism in coastal areas, are partly to blame for the rise in the number of crows. Current levels are having a serious impact on the indigenous bird population and are becoming an environmental health hazard.

In Dar es Salaam, where a similar crow problem exists, the Wildlife Conservation Society of Tanzania (WCST) has succeeded in killing over 43,000 crows using crow traps paid for by hotel owners and with some limited funding from the Canadian Fund for Local Initiatives.

In Zanzibar, a small voluntary organisation, registered as the Zanzibar Ecotourism Association, or ZEA (e ecotourism-znz@twiga.com), has since 1999 been encouraging hotels to become part of a similar sustainable programme for Zanzibar, but lacks financial support. Under ZEA co-ordination several hotels and individuals around Unguja have now established their own crow traps, but many more are needed if the island is to be rid of the Indian house crow.

of increasing tourist interest and observations. On Zanzibar, visitors are able to make a larger contribution to natural history records than on the mainland, since there have been fewer observers until recently.

Although Unguja and Pemba are similar in size, geography and position, they provide an interesting avifauna comparison. Unguja has woodpeckers, shrikes, cuckoo-shrikes and bulbuls, while Pemba has none of these. But Pemba has its own species of green pigeon, scops owl, white-eye and sunbird found nowhere else in the world.

As well as the resident birds, migrants from Eurasia, the Middle East and southern Africa pass through or remain to winter on the islands. Those from the north arrive in September/October and leave again in February/March. For European visitors it is a delight to see a familiar spotted flycatcher in the hotel garden, or hear the sound of a curlew calling from the shore at low tide.

Habitats The main bird habitats on Zanzibar, and some of the species found there, are described below. If the name of a bird is singular (eg: golden weaver), it refers to one species. If the name is plural (eg: bee-eaters, kingfishers), it refers to several species of the same or similar genus.

Parks and gardens Perhaps surprisingly, some of the best places to see birds are the parks and public gardens of Zanzibar Town, or the gardens of the many hotels situated along the coasts of Unguja and Pemba. The seed- and fruit-bearing trees, and the insects they attract, in turn attract many mannikins, warblers, coucals, sunbirds and swifts.

A bird you cannot miss in towns and around the big hotels on the coast is the Indian house crow – see the box opposite for more information.

Farmland The more fertile areas of Zanzibar, mostly the centre and west of Unguja and much of Pemba, are occupied by the majority of the rural population. Over the centuries natural coastal scrub and forest have been cleared and turned over to agriculture, either for small-scale subsistence farming, or for commercial plantations growing fruit and spices. The plentiful supplies of seeds, fruits and insects here attract many birds, including the beautiful long-tailed paradise flycatcher and parties of golden weaver (the only widespread weaver in Zanzibar). You may also see green wood-hoopoe, crested guineafowl (although these are now rare) and the diminutive emerald-spotted wood dove.

The telegraph wires along the roads provide vantage points for lilac-breasted roller and occasionally for the rufous-coloured broad-billed roller, and in winter for the blue-cheeked bee-eater.

Lesser-striped swallow hunt for flying insects over the countryside, and visit pools to collect mud for nest building. In areas where there are coconut palms you will see palm swift.

Freshwater ponds and grasslands Some farming areas consist of grassland, grazed by cattle, and often flooded after rain. Some of these wet areas are used to grow rice. Here you will see black-winged bishop, a small bright red weaver, plus herons and egrets, especially cattle egret, and maybe even a goshawk or harrier.

Where undisturbed, ponds and marshes support breeding jacana (or lilytrotter) and black crake, and possibly Allen's gallinule. You may also see small parties of pygmy goose, white-faced whistling duck and occasionally the rare white-backed duck. In winter months, purple heron and yellow wagtails (from Eurasia) feed in the rushes along pond edges.

Other birds seen in these areas include little grebe, red-billed teal and moorhen.

Bush Many areas of Zanzibar, especially the north and east of Unguja (Zanzibar Island), are not fertile and have not been cleared. They are covered in low scrubby vegetation called coral rag bush. It grows on well-drained rock which was once a coral reef, but was exposed when sea levels dropped many millions of years ago.

The poor vegetation here does not attract great numbers of birds, but a few exciting species can be seen, especially in the early morning or late evening, including the pale-eyed sombre bulbul, eastern bearded scrub robin, crowned hornbill and collared sunbird. You might also see birds of prey such as African goshawk or black kite, plus rollers and shrikes. With luck a Gabon nightjar may rise suddenly from near your feet.

Forests and woodland Only a small percentage of Zanzibar's indigenous forest remains, following centuries of clearing for farms and plantations. The main areas are Jozani Forest on Unguja and Ngezi Forest and Kiyuu Forest on Pemba, characterised by tall trees with buttressed roots and a convergent canopy, interspersed with ferns and smaller bushes. Masingini Forest near Bububu north of Zanzibar Town can also be rewarding. The forest birds of Zanzibar are shy and hard to spot, but your chances are better in the early morning, when you might see Fischer's turaco, wood owl, crested guineafowl or tambourine dove, plus swifts, hornbills, woodpeckers and weavers.

In patches of woodland, on the edge of areas which have been cleared for farming, you may see more weavers, plus coucals, sunbirds, flycatchers and bulbuls.

Mangroves Mangroves occur on small offshore islands or around estuaries, in or near areas which are covered by water at high tide. Individual mangroves can grow to 5m in height, and close together, which creates a forest-like atmosphere. (The mangrove vegetation of Zanzibar is discussed in *The seas and shores of Zanzibar,* page 61.) This habitat is rich in marine life, which is exploited by humans as well as resident and migrant shore birds including herons and kingfishers. Other species you are likely to see include mouse-coloured sunbird and blue-cheeked bee-eater.

Seashore and sandbars Naturally, as a group of islands, Zanzibar is surrounded by seashores, made up of beaches, low cliffs, creeks and tidal coral-mud flats. On the beaches you will find various wading birds, including plovers, whimbrels and sandpipers; many of these will be familiar to European naturalists, as Zanzibar becomes an increasingly important wintering ground for these northern species.

Also look out for the greater sand plover (which comes from central Asia) and the striking crab plover, which breeds along the Somali coast. Another notable shore bird is the dimorphic heron, which feeds along the tide line: about 49% of these birds is mouse grey, and another 49% is pure white, while the rest show intermediate plumages. Perhaps the most striking seashore bird is the African fish eagle, which may be seen in some areas.

On the numerous sandbars off the west coast of Zanzibar you can see more waders, plus flocks of terns, gulls and cormorants. The sooty gull often seen here is a visitor from the Red Sea.

Open sea Some birds spend most of their time at sea, in (or above) deeper water, and rarely come to the shore. You will see these only if you are out on a boat, possibly diving or fishing, or crossing to Zanzibar Town on a ship from Pemba or Dar es Salaam. Oceanic birds are rare, but you may occasionally see frigatebirds or a roseate tern, or a masked booby from the breeding colony on Latham Island, south of Zanzibar.

Birdwatching areas There are many places where you can watch birds on Zanzibar, and we list just a few recommended areas here.

Victoria Gardens Also known as The People's Gardens (see page 176), this small park in Zanzibar Town has flowers and flowering trees and attracts a good range of birds. Here you might see scarlet-breasted sunbird, the Indian race of house sparrow, bronze mannikin, black-and-white mannikin, and the neat but skulking green-backed camaroptera, a complex name for Zanzibar's only widespread resident warbler. Overhead, parties of little swift hawk for insects.

Mbweni Ruins Hotel garden On the outskirts of Zanzibar Town (see page 181), this good hotel has a beautiful garden, and is an excellent birdwatching area. You don't have to be a guest to come here for lunch and a walk around their nature trail. At least 50 species have been recorded here by the hotel management who are very knowledgeable on local wildlife, and can advise on good birdwatching places on Zanzibar. The hotel's dining veranda overlooks a beach, where many shore birds, including oystercatchers, whimbrels, sooty gull and lesser crested tern, await the retreat of the tide. Nearby is an area of mangrove. In the hotel gardens you'll see bronze mannikin, mangrove kingfisher, little swift and scarlet-chested sunbird, plus Eurasian golden oriole and blue-cheeked bee-eater in winter. During the heat of the day, the hotel pond is beloved by black-breasted glossy starling, dark-capped bulbul (more widely known as common, black-eyed or yellow-vented bulbul), golden weaver and as many as 50 Java sparrows (introduced around 1857, but now resident).

Bwawani Marsh Situated near the port, on the edge of Zanzibar Town, this is the largest reed swamp on Unguja, although it was formed by accident when the Bwawani Hotel was built. Some 20% of Unguja's birds have been recorded here including a few, like the hottentot teal and purple gallinule, which have not been recorded elsewhere on the island.

Other species to look out for are lesser swamp warbler, Allen's gallinule, jacana, wood sandpiper, night heron, purple heron and the African race of the little bittern. The best viewing spots are on the Bububu road and on the smaller road leading to the hotel. Unfortunately, the swamp has become a dumping ground for local rubbish. Beware!

Jozani Forest A good area for keen birders, particularly if you visit early or late in the day, is Jozani Forest Reserve, although the birds here typically hide themselves in the undergrowth or high canopies. The area south of Jozani Forest itself, on the other side of the main road, where the semi-habituated monkeys are found, is also good for birding. (For more details, see page 298.) Birds occurring here include the olive sunbird, the little greenbul (a racial endemic), dark-backed weaver, paradise flycatcher, east coast batis (a neat black-and-white flycatcher), crowned hornbill and cardinal woodpecker. Local specials include the east coast akalat and Fischer's turaco. At dawn or dusk you may also see African wood owl.

In the nearby mangrove forest, where a walkway has been constructed, you can see mangrove kingfisher, mouse-coloured sunbird and maybe tropical boubou.

Chwaka Bay This is the largest and most complex area of mud and sand on Zanzibar. It is an important area for local fishing, seaweed production, and for wintering shore birds, most notably the crab plover. Much of the east coast, from Chwaka to Nungwe, can offer good birdwatching along the shore – and even beyond the reef at low tide. Birds occurring here include waders, terns and gulls, plus herons such as the green-backed heron and dimorphic heron.

Matemwe This is a small village about halfway between Chwaka and Nungwi – with typical east coast conditions. There is a wide beach here, backed by palm groves and coral rag bush, and each habitat attracts typical species. The Matemwe Bungalows' gardens are typical of many carefully planted and well-watered lodge gardens; they attract sombre greenbul, collared sunbird and paradise flycatcher, among others.

Chumbe Island This small island lies off the west coast, within easy reach of Zanzibar Town. About 63 bird species have been recorded here since 1992, but these are mostly sea and shore birds. The resident land birds are limited to about six common species, including African reed warbler, and most notably the small colony of mouse-coloured sunbird. Perhaps Chumbe's main avian interest lies in the vagrants which occasionally appear, such as a wood warbler (only the third recorded sighting in all Tanzania) and, in 1999, a peregrine falcon. In 1994, around 750 pairs of roseate tern bred on two islets off Chumbe but, although some 500 young were reared, the birds have not returned. House crows, fish eagles, rats (now eliminated) and bad weather were the probable reasons for their staying away.

Misali and Panza islands Misali Island lies close to Pemba Island while Panza Island lies off Unguja. Each has coastal forest and typical shore habitats. Like all small islands they are limited in bird species but are attractive for migrants. Misali is noted for a small population of Fischer's turaco, while on Panza brown-necked parrot occur. Panza also has large colonies of fruit bat and white-winged bat which attract bat hawks.

Ngezi Forest On Pemba Island, Ngezi Forest is a good birding destination. Birds recorded here include palm-nut vulture, African goshawk, and four endemics: Pemba scops owl, Pemba white-eye, Pemba green pigeon and Pemba violet-breasted sunbird. Ngezi is also home to a good population of fruit bats.

THE SEAS AND SHORES OF ZANZIBAR Matt Richmond PhD

For anyone visiting the islands of Zanzibar, Mafia Island or the coast of mainland Tanzania, the diversity of marine life in the surrounding shallow waters may not be immediately obvious. However, the main marine habitats (mangroves, coral reefs and seagrass beds) are part of an extremely diverse, productive and vitally important marine ecosystem. Other marine habitats are the beaches and cliffs fringing the shore, and the vast areas of open water. The species of plants and animals which make up these habitats around Zanzibar and off mainland Tanzania are mostly the same as those found elsewhere in the western Indian Ocean (eg: Mozambique, Madagascar, Mauritius and the Seychelles), though slightly different from those in similar habitats as far away as southeast Asia, Australia and the South Pacific islands. Some species of fish and other creatures do, however, span this entire Indo-Pacific region.

MARINE HABITATS

Beaches and cliffs Around the main islands of Zanzibar (that is, Unguja and Pemba), many shores are fringed by either coconut-lined coral-sand beaches, where ghost crabs scamper, or rocky limestone cliffs – remains of ancient reefs once below the sea (over 100,000 million years ago), then exposed as sea levels dropped, now undercut and battered by high-tide waves. The cliffs provide a home to the brilliant red-yellow grapsid rock crabs and the bizarre eight-plated chiton snail, plus numerous other small snails, rock oysters and rock-skipper fish.

Mangroves In sheltered bays and inlets, where wave action is reduced, mangrove stands and forests are commonplace. Mangrove trees are specially adapted to survive in the sea, and all ten species found in the western Indian Ocean occur in Zanzibar. At high tide mangroves attract numerous species of fish, crabs and shrimps which depend on the forests as nursery grounds for their young. At low tide, red-clawed fiddler crabs carry out their formal challenges when not sifting the mud for food, while mud-skippers flip from pool to pool, or from branch to branch when the tide is in. One of the best places to experience these fascinating marine forests is the mangrove boardwalk at Jozani Forest – especially when the tide is in. You can also snorkel around a mangrove forest on Misali Island, off Pemba, or in many other inlets around the main islands.

Seagrass beds and lagoons The intertidal areas or zones lie between the high- and low-tide marks. Where beaches slope sharply, this is a narrow strip. Where old coral beds slope imperceptibly and are almost flat, this area may extend 2km or more. Intertidal zones provide a habitat for thousands of molluscs, crabs, sea-cucumbers, seaweeds and several species of seagrasses, which are themselves food for fish at high tide.

Seagrass Thalassodendron ciliatum

Seagrass Cymodocea rotundata

Along the east coast of Unguja (and the east coasts of the other islands and the mainland) shallow lagoons occur, extending to the reef crest. The lagoons support assorted coral, seagrass and seaweed communities and often great selections of starfish and beautiful nudibranch (sea hares and their relatives).

Blue starfish

Coral reefs Corals are not plants, but animals belonging to the *Coelenterata* group (which also includes sea anemones and jellyfish). Corals exist in clean, clear, shallow, warm water, and so are found only in tropical regions. A coral begins life as a soft, many-tentacled 'polyp' around 1mm in size, and then produces a hard calcium carbonate skeleton around itself for protection. These types of coral are called **hard corals**. A coral colony develops from a single polyp

Crown-of-thorns starfish feeding on brain coral

by a process called 'budding' (where a new polyp grows out of an existing one). When polyps die, their hard skeletons remain, and the colony expands as new polyps form on the skeletons of old dead polyps. In this way colonies grow, and the growth rate varies from about 1cm to 5cm per year depending on species, depth and water conditions. Groups of colonies together make up the coral reefs found fringing the islands. Different types of hard coral form their colonies in different shapes; the commonly known varieties include stag-horn coral, plate coral, mushroom coral, table corals and brain corals – all abundant in shallow water.

Staghorn coral

Coral also uses a form of sexual reproduction where sperm and eggs are mixed (either internally with a coral embryo or larvae later being released, or by 'spawning' where eggs and sperm are released by polyps to mix in the water). In both ways the corals can colonise new areas.

Within the polyps exist microscopic algae-type organisms called *zooxanthellae*, which trap the sunlight needed to power the chemical reactions which produce the coral's hard calcium skeleton. It is the *zooxanthellae* which give the coral its colour – usually pink or pale brown in a variety of shades – as the coral polyps themselves are virtually transparent. Thus when coral is picked, and taken out of the water, the corals and the *zooxanthellae* die and lose colour, leaving only the pale 'bleached' chalky-white skeletons.

During daylight hours, the coral colonies use sunlight in much the same way as plants do, but at night-time on a reef, most hard coral species are busy, with polyps extending their tentacles to catch planktonic foods.

Soft corals, on the other hand, do not have a hard external skeleton and do not form reefs. They are far more colourful than hard corals, although they also require light to build the tiny crystal fibres embedded in their soft pink, lilac or cream-coloured tissues. The daytime feeding of the eight-tentacled polyps, a feature of this group, is clearly visible on soft corals which can, in places, dominate underwater scenes.

On the east coasts of Unguja and Pemba typical fringing reefs are marked by a continuous line of surf resulting from Indian Ocean swells. At low tide the reef crest dries out revealing pink algal-rock and boulders – the coral itself usually only becoming prolific on the seaward slope below 5m. On Unguja, the coral-covered reef slopes dip down to about 20m, after which a fairly bare sandy seabed continues down a further 4km to the ocean bottom. On the more sheltered west coasts of the Zanzibar Channel smaller, isolated patch reefs with sandbars, and island reefs (around Chapwani, Changuu, Bawe and Chumbi islands), provide coral gardens in the relatively shallow waters. In contrast, parts of the reef around Pemba Island drop down over 50m or more offering spectacular vertical coral walls. Some of the most dramatic dive sites along the Tanzanian coast are found on the steep slopes of Pemba Island.

On any of these coral reefs you will immediately note the amazing variety of colourful fish of all sizes and shapes, incredible in their patterns and forms: butterflyfish, parrotfish, surgeonfish, damselfish, emperors, goatfish, pufferfish, angelfish, triggerfish, groupers and grunts to name a few. Most of these typical coral reef fish are territorial and reside over small areas of reef, rarely leaving their patch and aggressively protecting it from others of

Emperor fish

Grouper

their own species. Some, like the butterflyfish, pair up for life and occupy a patch the size of a tennis court; others, such as the blue-lined yellow snappers, roam around the reefs in schools of a few hundred.

Because of the rich diversity of life forms, coral reefs have been compared to tropical rainforests. With Zanzibar's waters containing more than 700 fish species associated with coral reefs, over 100 species of hard corals, 150-odd species of seaweed and 300-plus species of seashells, to mention just a few of the more obvious sea creatures, the comparison is certainly a valid one. Then there are sponges, anemones, brittlestars, sea cucumbers, sea-squirts, feather-stars and crustaceans, all forming a seemingly chaotic, mind-boggling complexity which has fascinated scientists since Darwin's time.

The loss of the microscopic *zooxanthellae* from the coral, resulting in bleaching, was a major feature of the reefs around Zanzibar and elsewhere in the tropics in 1998, as the region experienced increased seawater temperatures (up to 32°C) associated with a severe, and much-publicised, shift in global climate conditions called El Niño. Although coral bleaching had occurred in the past, this event was on a scale not witnessed before. Much coral (both hard and soft) bleached and failed to regain its *zooxanthellae*. Within about five months vast areas of previously rich and diverse coral communities died. In many reef areas since then, new, small colonies have begun to emerge from settlement of coral larvae, and the coral component of these reefs is beginning to return to that prior to 1998. In other areas, total recovery to pre-1998 conditions may take decades or centuries. For reasons that are still unclear, much more coral around Pemba eventually died, whereas on Unguja corals recovered after bleaching.

Open waters The open waters, though mostly empty at first glance, can be very busy at times. They are home to vast schools of small, plankton-feeding, pelagic fish species such as sardines, silver-sides and Indian mackerel, continuously on the move and relentlessly pursued by larger pelagic fish, like skipjack, yellowfin tuna, kingfish, sailfish and marlin. Out at sea, in the Pemba Channel or off the east coast, flocks of hundreds of white terns identify tuna feeding frenzies as they dart into the shoals of small pelagic fish forced up to the surface by the tuna below.

Sailfish

Yellowfin tuna

Also feeding out at sea for most of their lives are turtles, coming into shallow waters when looking for a mate. Green and hawksbill turtles are the most common. (For more details, see pages 66–9.)

Both the friendly bottlenose dolphin and the less bold humpback dolphin can be seen in small groups, or pods, quite close to the shore (see box, *The Kizimkazi dolphins*, page 292). Around Unguja there appear to be a few pods of ten–15 members, each with its own territory. One area where they are commonly seen is off Kizimkazi in southwest Unguja (viewing is easily arranged with a local boat), or around Mnemba Island in the northeast, or, with a bit of luck, even off Zanzibar Town. (Watching dolphins is especially enjoyable if you're also sipping a cool beer on the Africa House Hotel terrace at sunset.) At Kizimkazi and Mnemba it's also sometimes possible to see groups of hundreds of spinner dolphins, providing an unforgettable memory.

Less common are whales, though humpback whales have been spotted several times around October–November in the Zanzibar Channel and off Nungwi in the north, leading their recently born young back to the summer feeding grounds in Antarctica.

TIDES AND WEATHER Tides, the daily rise and fall of sea level, are a noticeable feature along the east coast of Africa. They are dictated mostly by the moon (and to a lesser extent the sun) and there are two main types. The smaller tides, known as neap tides, occur during the half-moon phases and result in a tidal range (the difference between high and low water) of only 1.5m. From this period onwards the tidal range increases, until a full or new moon (ie: every two weeks), when spring tides occur. These result in the largest tidal range, of about 4m between high tide and low tide. Spring tide low water always occurs at around 10.00–11.00, for about three days, twice every lunar cycle (at full moon and new moon). Through the rest of the lunar cycle, the time of each tide changes from one day to the next

3

by an average of 50 minutes (about 30 minutes during spring). So if high tide is at 15.00 on one day it will be about 15.50 on the following day.

During spring low tides the low-water mark can be a couple of kilometres out and these days are ideal for walking out on the inter-tidal flats and reef crest to explore the kaleidoscope of life. Take care to avoid trampling on living coral and on sea urchins or blue-spotted stingrays. Good footwear (trainers, plastic sandals or neoprene booties) is strongly recommended. Even the tiniest cut or graze can flare up into a nasty tropical ulcer which will keep you out of the sea for days recovering. Be aware, also, of the speed with which the tide comes in and don't be caught out on the reef crest of the east coast with the incoming tide around your waist – you'll have an exhausting swim back to the beach if you do. And remember, tidal currents are strongest during spring tides so be careful not to swim too far out, or into tidal channels.

Needle spine urchin

Prevailing weather also greatly influences sea conditions and travellers should be aware of the main seasons. (These are described in more detail in *Chapter 4*, *When to visit*, page 71.)

LOCAL PEOPLE AND MARINE LIFE It won't take you long to realise that a great number of Zanzibaris are dependent on the surrounding seas and shallows for their variety of foods. Various fishing methods are used to catch this vital source of protein which contributes over 70% of the needs of the local population. On dark new-moon nights in the Zanzibar Channel, sardine boats with lights attract and net vast shoals; on the same nights gill-netting boats, with 15cm-mesh nets, are after the large pelagic species (tuna, kingfish and billfish) in the southern Pemba Channel, operating mostly from Nungwi. Conventional hook-and-line fishing and passive fish-trapping using baited basket-traps (*madema*) are still practised all around the islands.

Kingfish

Octopus

During the low spring tides thousands of women and children collect octopus, shells, sea-cucumbers and moray eels from the intertidal flats, whilst other women tend to their seaweed (*mwani*) farm patches in the lagoons on the east coast. The lines of sticks protruding out of the water at low tide can't be missed. (For more details see box, *Sustainable seaweed farming*, pages 262–3.)

Mangroves are also harvested: the wood has been used for building poles for centuries, because of its resistance to rotting and insect infestation. However, the rapid increase in demand over the last few years, with overcutting in places, has led to deterioration of the forests and the marine life which relies on them. Recently, the felling of planted casuarina (Australian pine, though not actually a true pine) has produced, so far, acceptable insect-resistant poles, easing some of the pressure on the mangroves.

CONSERVATION Owing to the rapid increase in population (at present doubling every 20 years), the availability of new fishing materials, the development of a number of destructive fishing methods and the inability of the government to enforce fisheries regulations, the delicate balance of life in the shallow seas (and therefore this vital source of food) is beginning to be destroyed. Spear-fishing is on the increase and because of its effectiveness can quickly strip the reefs of the larger fish, and even of small species such as butterflyfish. Not only does it reduce fish numbers and make them wary of snorkellers, such as around the shallow reefs close to Zanzibar Town or in the lagoon on the east, but by removing these vital predators the balance within the ecosystem is being lost. Netting around reefs, and the type of fishing known locally as *kigumi*, where corals are broken deliberately to force fish out into the surrounding net, are also practised and extremely destructive. Dynamite-fishing is also very destructive, but mostly restricted to the mainland coast. Also restricted to the mainland and Mafia coasts, fortunately for Zanzibar, is the collecting of shallow live coral (mainly of the genus *Porites*) for baking on open kilns into lime. On Unguja at least, quarried coral rock is used instead.

Careless anchoring of boats on coral reefs can also, over a short time, cause considerable localised damage. In 1994, a project funded by the Dutch embassy of Dar es Salaam through the Institute of Marine Sciences established, in conjunction with the tourist boat operators who use the reefs, 15 permanent moorings for the islands and reefs close to Zanzibar Town, thus reducing tourism-related damage. Although these have since deteriorated and are no longer functional, the project did serve to increase the awareness of the importance and needs of living coral reefs, and in general boat operators around Zanzibar Town are careful when dropping anchor, attempting to set it in sand or rubble. Perhaps in the future the shallow coral gardens around Bawe Island and the sandbanks off Stone Town will come under some form of management to conserve their productivity and attractiveness to visitors. The main threat to these shallow coral reefs, some of which have superb hard coral communities, remain the *kigumi* fishermen.

The local demand for marine curios (shells, dead coral and turtle products) has increased with the growing number of tourists, further adding to the overexploitation of the marine resources. The collection of large, colourful, attractive mollusc shells like the giant triton (*Charonia tritonis*) and the bull-mouth helmet shell (*Cypraecassis rufa*) have secondary effects which are not that obvious. These feed on the crown-of-thorns starfish (*Acanthaster planci*) and sea-urchins respectively. Absence of the molluscs again upsets the balance, and populations of these echinoderms can increase alarmingly, furthering the destruction of the coral reefs. Collection of live hard corals is, of course, extremely damaging to the reef ecosystem. A colony the size of a football can take over 20 years to grow and the implications of mass removal for sale to tourists or export need no further explanation. Don't buy the stuff!

crimson-red

Giant triton shell

Bull-mouth helmet shell

Some steps are being taken to try and address the problems. With the involvement of donor organisations, and conservation bodies such as the Worldwide Fund for Nature, private enterprise, the Institute of Marine Sciences, and the Zanzibar authorities (Department of Fisheries, Commission of Environment and Department of Tourism), plans to create marine protected areas have made some progress. On Pemba the only marine protected area is Misali Island Conservation Area which involves local fishermen in conservation and charges fees to visiting divers and snorkellers. On Unguja, a few miles south of Zanzibar Town, Chumbe Island Coral Park (CHICOP), a private investment, includes a protected forest and coral reef on its western shores. Chumbe (see pages

304–6) can be visited for a day, or you can stay overnight, and funds generated contribute to raising awareness of marine issues through the educational centre used by local school pupils. Further south the Menai Bay Conservation Area brings fisheries and mangrove issues to local community groups supported by the government in an attempt to manage the resources for the long term. The only other marine protected area is a zone 200m wide around Mnemba Island, an exclusive private island resort off the northeast coast. However, the spectacular turquoise waters around Mnemba Island extend beyond this boundary and the 20km of fringing reefs are accessible to divers and snorkellers from several beach hotels operating from the north and east coasts of Unguja.

Tourism development, now a rapidly growing industry, also has a role to play in marine conservation. By acknowledging that the marine resources on which it depends are finite and also vital to the neighbouring coastal villages, and by attempting to come up with methods which assist all the users, tourism can contribute to a healthy future for all concerned. Survival of both may be in the balance.

So, when bobbing around over a coral garden, or simply sitting on the seabed, 10m down, watching the coral reef world around you, or wading through the dark mud in a mangrove forest, think about it … and enjoy it. There's a whole lot going on: between individuals, between species, between habitats and between the ecosystem and the people who use it. This section has touched on some of the more salient issues and examples of life in the seas and on the shores of Zanzibar. Many more exist to be discovered and pondered upon; while doing so, the following are a few points to remember:

- Don't touch living coral. There's no need to and it is more sensitive than it looks. Be careful when reef walking and snorkelling or diving. Be aware of what your flippers are doing and avoid landing on coral when entering into the water. Maintain good buoyancy control at all times.
- Help prevent anchor damage. Insist on the use of permanent moorings, if available, or anchor only in sand.
- Don't buy shells, turtle products or corals.
- Spread the word. Explain what you now know about the local marine ecosystems to other visitors and locals.

SEA TURTLES *Original text by Fiona Clark, updated by Lorna Slade, ecologist, Zanzibar Sea Turtle Survival Project*
Five types of sea turtle occur in the western Indian Ocean: the **green turtle** (*Chelonia mydas*), the **hawksbill turtle** (*Eretmochelys imbricata*), the **loggerhead turtle** (*Caretta caretta*), the **Olive Ridley turtle** (*Lepidochelys olivacea*) and the **leatherback turtle** (*Dermochhelys coriacea*). All are endangered species. The most commonly found turtle in Zanzibar is the green turtle, followed by the hawksbill. Both nest in Zanzibar. Leatherback and loggerhead are sometimes seen, but don't nest. There have been no records for the Olive Ridley since 1975.

Zanzibar is not a major turtle nesting site, but appears to be a feeding ground for sea turtles from other areas; nesting is more prolific on Pemba. Conservationists have recovered tags from captured turtles showing that green turtles come to Zanzibar from Aldabra Island, in the Seychelles, and from Europa and Tromelin islands. Loggerheads that nest in KwaZulu-Natal (South Africa) also feed in Tanzania – one loggerhead was captured in Tanzania just 66 days after being tagged in South Africa.

The current turtle scene The IOSEA (Indian Ocean and South-East Asian) Marine Turtle policy is an intergovernmental agreement that aims to protect, conserve, replenish and recover marine turtles through partnership organisations. According to its 2008 country report on Tanzania, there remain a number of challenges to sea turtles, including illegal harvesting, limited knowledge of genetics and population dynamics, and other inherent threatening factors. All this in spite of a number of protection and conservation initiatives being spearheaded by the government in collaboration with local communities, NGOs, the National Turtle Committee and development partners.

Zanzibar's turtle conservation work has so far centred on working with communities to raise general awareness about surveillance, nesting activities, monitoring, beach cleaning and potential ecotourism benefits. This community education and involvement is critical but it must be matched with workable solutions to help the traditional fishing industry better adapt to the necessary conservation goals.

The number of turtles caught in the nets of bottom trawlers has declined steadily from the mid 1990s, though it remains at approximately 70-80 turtles annually at present. (Many of these survive capture only to be later slaughtered for their shells.) In addition, almost 600 turtles annually become trapped in the long, curtain-like gill nets used in traditional fishing methods (85% of fish in Tanzanian waters are caught in this way). Illegal and unregulated turtle fishing also continues with dynamite-fishing, the use of spear guns and lethal entanglement in monofilament fishing lines. The future is not entirely bleak though. A dedicated government committee has been formed to address all of these problems and there are a number of techniques and devices which can yet be employed to protect the turtles. We must only hope that adequate financial and human resources will back up the new policies and protect these graceful sea creatures.

The bad news The sea turtle population is decreasing in Zanzibar. This is bad because turtles are part of a food web which includes sea-grasses, sponges, jellyfish and tiger sharks, and also because living turtles are attractive to tourists and (like dolphins) can sometimes be a way for local people to earn money.

The number of nesting sites has been reduced dramatically, and turtles are hunted and trapped by more efficient means than previously. Local fishermen tell how, 20 or 30 years ago, some beaches would contain 100 or more turtle nests every year. But these days the same beaches contain only two or three nests. Places where nests can still be found include Mnemba Island, the beaches north of Matemwe Bungalows, and around Kizimkazi. Pemba is home to the most important nesting beaches; turtles nest on Misali Island, at Ras Kiuyu and on the beaches near Ngezi Forest – especially Vumawimbi. Unfortunately, except for the island sites, few of these nests are successful: many eggs are taken by people, while others are lost to the sea when erosion has formed steps on some beaches forcing turtles to nest in places that are vulnerable to the high tide.

The burgeoning tourist industry also has its costs. In the last ten years many hotels have been built on turtle-nesting beaches. Buildings often extend right to the beach, vegetation is cleared and the beach lit up at night, disturbing any turtles coming up to nest and disorientating any hatchlings. For example, Kiwengwa Beach on the east coast of Unguja (Zanzibar Island) is now wall-to-wall hotel with no space or peace for turtles.

Turtle-hunting in Zanzibar only became illegal in October 1993. Although penalties are quite severe (a large fine, or two years in prison, or both) enforcement of the new law is unlikely. The Fisheries Department is under-resourced and has many other problems to deal with (such as dynamite-fishing).

Turtles are usually captured with gill nets, which are set on the seabed, while others are caught with spear guns. They are brought ashore and have their flippers and shell removed, often while still alive. The number of turtles caught increased dramatically in the 1960s when gill nets, snorkelling gear and spear guns were introduced. Some local fishermen claim that their increased catch proves the population is increasing too, but the same fishermen also agree that nesting turtles have all but disappeared. Uroa on the east coast of Unguja is a renowned area for turtle-hunting and the beach sometimes looks like a turtle graveyard.

In March 1996, there were two incidents of poisoning in Pemba through the consumption of turtle meat, resulting in the deaths of 37 people. Hawksbill turtles, in particular, are known on occasion to harbour toxins thought to originate from toxic algae in the food chain. These toxins do not harm the turtle, but have disastrous effects on any humans eating the meat. These unfortunate incidents helped reduce turtle slaughter, but apparently only for a short while.

The good news Since 1992, there have been several small-scale turtle-protection projects run with volunteer help through the government of Zanzibar's Department of the Environment. These include the following:

- A Swahili-language education package for schools and other youth groups, emphasising the plight of sea turtles, and their need to be protected. A poster carrying the same message has also been produced both in English, aimed at visitors, and in Swahili, aimed at locals.
- A nest protection scheme, run by Matemwe Bungalows, a hotel on the east coast. Local villagers are paid a small fee if they report an intact nest, and a further bonus for each successful hatching. To avoid the problems of beach erosion, some nests are moved to safer sites.
- A survey and protection scheme carried out by the management of the exclusive lodge on the private Mnemba Island. This is an ideal site for turtles, with safe beaches (no local fishermen are allowed to land) and deep-water access.
- A nest protection and monitoring scheme on the protected Misali Island, off Pemba, now a marine conservation area, patrolled by local rangers and still one of the best turtle-nesting areas in Zanzibar.
- Community education and involvement in nest-recording and monitoring in both Pemba and Unguja, including the successful production of an educational drama and video, has played a key role in reducing threats to turtles. Through active inclusion of local community members in conservation activities, the role of turtle security has become a source of employment and social status, reinforcing the benefits of protecting the creatures.
- There are plans afoot to try and introduce the use of Turtle Excluder Devices (TED) in the country's fisheries legislation. In essence, the TED is a metal grid of bars that attaches to trawling nets and allows larger animals, like turtles and sharks, to escape whilst still keeping prawns, shrimp and the like inside. With a hatch opening at either the top or the bottom, the heavy weight of the sea turtles, sharks and larger fish cause the hatch to open on impact, providing them with an escape route. The success of the TED has varied around the world, but it is a start at further regulating fishing methods, and may help a few more adult turtles to escape in the future.
- In areas where turtle mortality is critically high, through animal and egg poaching, cash rewards for conservation have been used. This is clearly not financially sustainable and has had mixed results in the archipelago. On Zanzibar Island, incentive-driven conservation has proven to be counter-productive in obtaining committed public participation; however, on Mafia

modest incentives have been highly effective in involving local communities and in protecting nests. This is a short-term solution though and it is generally agreed that generating revenue to fund turtle conservation through turtle tourism and park entry fees is a far more positive and sustainable method. Mnarani Aquarium below is one successful example.

- Mnarani Aquarium (see pages 219–20) in Nungwi is a local conservation initiative to protect turtles and educate villagers and tourists. Managed by a group of local fishermen, in a large tidal-fed rock pool, the water has been stocked with several species of fish and around ten green and hawksbill turtles. The Department of the Environment has allowed this group (only) to keep a maximum of eight turtles for educational purposes and any excess brought in by fishermen are periodically tagged and released. Although generally keeping turtles in captivity is not to be encouraged, in this case the local community benefit, and the educational value to locals (school children are allowed in free) and tourists is judged to be worth it. The aquarium does not keep mature female turtles.
- Both green and hawksbill turtles are now being tagged for monitoring on Pemba and Mafia islands, with the latter project also undertaking genetic studies.

Turtle-shell products Zanzibar used to be a major centre for turtle-shell, usually called 'tortoiseshell', and at the height of the trade (the early 20th century) some 3,300kg were exported every year from the islands and nearby mainland coast. Demand dropped, but has recently been revived by the growth of tourism. A survey showed that the amount of turtle-shell jewellery went up five times between early 1993 and late 1994. Less than half the tourists who bought turtle-shell items knew what it was, or that turtles were endangered. However, local conservationists and aware tourists complained to such a degree that many shops now refuse to stock turtle-shell products. Tourists are asked by conservation organisations to boycott any shops that continue to sell turtle products.

Local police and customs officials are now also aware that turtle-shell products are illegal. Tourists buying whole shells from hawkers should be aware that conservationists and hoteliers will report them to the police for possession of turtle shells, and if caught they will be reprimanded and the shell confiscated.

Local perspectives Lest we get too self-righteous about all this, we should perhaps remember that Zanzibar is a poor country and that a large sea turtle is worth about a month's wages for an office worker, and considerably more than that to a fisherman or farmer. Turtle meat is also held traditionally to have healing properties. Stopping the local people from catching turtles will inevitably make some of them poorer, yet if the turtle-hunting continues there will soon be none left anyway. But many Zanzibaris can't afford the luxury of thinking ahead. Life is hand to mouth and the 'If I don't catch it someone else will' attitude is of course understandable.

Having said that, there does need to be a halt to turtle killing as populations are in danger of extinction. In addition to finding alternative food and income sources for local communities, it is also essential that continued education, improved law enforcement and government protection for important nesting beaches are maintained, to ensure that the turtle has a place in Zanzibar's future.

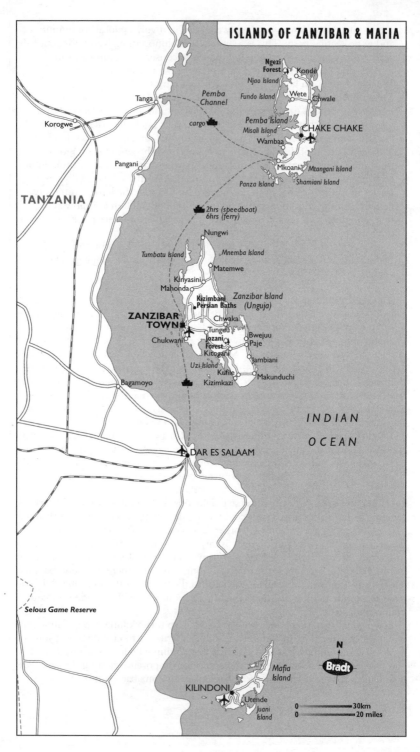

ISLANDS OF ZANZIBAR & MAFIA

Korogwe

Tanga

TANZANIA

Pangani

Pemba Channel

cargo

Pemba Island

Ngezi Forest Konde

Njao Island

Fundo Island Wete Chwale

Misali Island **CHAKE CHAKE**

Wambaa

Mkoani *Mtangani Island*

Panza Island *Shamiani Island*

2hrs (speedboat)
6hrs (ferry)

Nungwi

Tumbatu Island *Mnemba Island*

Matemwe

Kinyasini
Mahonda

Kizimbani Persian Baths *Zanzibar Island (Unguja)*

ZANZIBAR TOWN Chwaka

Tunguu

Chukwani **Jozani Forest** Bwejuu
Kitogani Paje

Uzi Island Jambiani

Kufile
Kizimkazi Makunduchi

Bagamoyo

INDIAN

OCEAN

DAR ES SALAAM

Selous Game Reserve

N

Bradt

Mafia Island

KILINDONI

Utende
Juani Island

0   30km
0   20 miles

4

Planning and Preparation

Truly prepossessing was our first view … of Zanzibar. Earth, sea and sky all seemed wrapped in a soft and sensuous repose … The sea of purest sapphire… lay basking … under a blaze of sunshine.

Richard Burton, British explorer (1856)

WHEN TO VISIT

The best time to visit these islands is during the dry seasons: December to February and June to October. See *Climate*, page 49, for more details, but generally speaking, from December to February any wind comes from the northeast, so beaches on the southern and western parts of the islands are more sheltered. Conversely, from June to October it tends to come from the southwest, so northern and eastern coasts are best. Ultimately, however, these islands are at the mercy of the ocean, and their weather patterns can be unpredictable at any time of year. Even during the 'dry' seasons, afternoon showers are not unknown, although they tend to be short and pleasantly cooling. (For more details, see box, *Climate chart*, below.)

It is also possible to visit the islands during the rainy season. Then there are fewer visitors and you are more likely to get good bargains from lodges and hotels (the ones that remain open) and trips. The rain can be heavy, but is not usually constant; the sunsets can be particularly magnificent; and pineapples are in season! Travel can be more difficult at this time, with roads damaged and buses delayed, but you'll get there eventually.

At holiday times, such as Christmas and Easter, the islands are popular with expatriate workers from Dar es Salaam and Nairobi as well as overseas visitors. Expect full flights and higher hotel rates. Conversely, during the Islamic fasting period of Ramadan (see pages 102–3), many restaurants and shops are closed during the day, and life runs at a generally slower pace.

If you're going scuba diving or game fishing, see box, *Zanzibar diving and fishing seasons*, page 106. If local festivals appeal, then see pages 46–7. Sports fans may like to tie in their visit with the Zanzibar International Marathon, held every year in early November.

CLIMATE CHART

	Jan	Feb	Mar	Apr	May	Jun	Jul	Aug	Sep	Oct	Nov	Dec
Temp (°C): av min	25	25	24	23	22	20	19	19	19	21	22	24
av max	31	31	31	30	29	29	28	28	28	29	30	31
Hrs of sun/day	8	8	7	5	6	8	7	8	8	8	8	8
Rainfall (mm)	80	70	140	390	250	60	45	40	50	90	220	160
Av days of rain	7	6	12	19	14	4	5	6	6	7	14	12

Read this book's introduction to understand why we think the real highlights of these islands are often away from the resorts and obvious places – and in the unscheduled interactions with the local people that you meet, and the unspoilt areas you stumble across whilst exploring. That said, we recognise that a little initial direction can help to make the best of a trip so we'll try to give you a few pointers here.

WHERE TO STAY The choice of places to stay is endless – but a few really stand out. Top of the list, and most budgets, is **Mnemba Island** (pages 236–8). It's very expensive, but it's also exceedingly good, and remains the best by far in the archipelago. We approached it fully expecting to comment that it was overpriced, but the reality is that it is in a different league from the other places in this guide. It's very polished, yet also very simple; the ultimate in barefoot luxury.

For small, high-quality beach lodges with more reasonable price tags, our top tips would be the trio of spacious villas at **Matemwe Retreat** (pages 231–2); its more relaxed sister property, **Matemwe Bungalows** (pages 232–3); **Ras Nungwi Beach Hotel** (page 210) in Nungwi; **Shooting Star** (pages 242–3) in Pwani Mchangani; and **Fumba Beach Lodge** (pages 301–2) in the quiet southwest of Zanzibar. All offer consistently high levels of service, individually styled accommodation and access to stunning beaches and watersports.

Whilst looking at these, compare them with the three main lodges on Mafia Island: **Pole Pole** (pages 343–4), **Kinasi** (page 344) and **Chole Mjini** (page 345). Mafia doesn't offer the extensive beaches of Zanzibar, but it's much quieter and in many ways gives a great deal of exclusivity for your money, with the added bonus of some superb diving and snorkelling. It's a great favourite of ours, and very undervalued.

For small, secluded beach retreats which cost even less, have a look at **Mchanga Beach Lodge** (page 238), **Pongwe Beach Hotel** (page 246) and **Echo Beach** (page 270). Or for a more village-centred experience, but still on the beach, **Kikadini Villas** (page 281) in the heart of Jambiani is exceptional value for a lovely place.

Budget travellers might want to check out **Sunset Bungalows** (pages 222–3) in Kendwa, which offers good-value bungalows on the beach, the delightful **Bellevue Bungalows** (pages 267–8) on the Michamvi Peninsula, which has neat rooms, good food and a thoroughly chilled vibe, or **Keys Bungalows** (page 233) and **Nyota Beach Bunglows** (page 235), both in Matemwe. Meanwhile, **Santa Maria Coral Reef** (pages 246–8) is a small and simple place in a coconut grove beside a sweeping bay; it's proof that you can still find magical places to match tight budgets.

If you're looking specifically at the busy Nungwi area, then at the top end, **Z Hotel** (pages 202–3) claims 'boutique on the beach', and has tried hard to raise the hospitality bar in the area. The mid-range **Flame Tree Cottages** (pages 206–7) offers a more laid-back, great-value place to stay a few minutes' walk from the buzzing heart of town, and a little further away **Mnarani Beach Cottages** (pages 208–9) is very friendly and reasonably priced, with one of Zanzibar Island's best views.

If you're taking a family, lack mobility, or are simply seeking the extensive facilities of a larger resort, then look first at the new **Fairmont Zanzibar** (pages 235–6) in Matemwe. It's extremely well managed and the facilities and beach location are excellent. Alternatively, the contemporary **Zamani Zanzibar Kempinski** (page 241) in Pwani Mchangani is unlike anything else on the island;

whilst **La Gemma dell'Est** (page 224) in Kendwa is also worth considering. We feel all of these are a step above most of the island's other big resort offerings.

For something completely different, those interested in ecology or conservation shouldn't miss a few days at **Chumbe Island** (page 306) for a terrific all-round experience!

The best hotels in Stone Town change quite fast, as new ones start up and often raise the bar, but currently **Beyt al Chai** (page 138), alongside newcomers **Al Johari** (pages 138–9) and **Zanzibar Palace** (page 140) are our pick of the finest upmarket, boutique guesthouses. The large and efficient **Serena Inn** (pages 134–5) remains the undisputed best hotel in town, whilst for something less expensive, but still with a pool, **Dhow Palace** (page 141) is a good choice. Slightly cheaper in price, but brimming with character, **Zanzibar Coffee House** (page 142) is excellent, as is the **Clove Hotel** (page 141).

For backpackers and the budget-conscious, **Malindi Guesthouse** (pages 144–5) by the port, **Victoria House** (page 142) on the northern side of The People's Gardens, and the newly renovated **St Monica's Hostel** should be top of the list.

If you are keen to stay by the beach just outside Zanzibar Town, **Mtoni Marine** is idyllic and excellent for families, whilst **Maruhubi Beach Villas** has some good sea-view rooms. **Mbweni Ruins Hotel** (page 181), just south of town, is also a reliably good option.

THINGS TO SEE AND DO Whilst lazing on the beach can be very relaxing, if this is the limit of your activities then you will miss out on a lot. At least accept the offer of a local beach masseuse if there is one; they can be surprisingly good.

A highlight of many trips to Zanzibar and Mafia is the **diving**, which is good at many places around these islands. The best diving spots would certainly include the reef around Mnemba Island (pages 236–7), and those around Mafia (pages 347–9). The less aquatic might prefer to go **snorkelling**, and if so they should add Chumbe Island to this short list of reefs. Chumbe has world-class, pristine coral, and no scuba diving is allowed there. Chumbe's also worth visiting for its guided **forest and inter-tidal walks** (page 306), which are both attractions in their own right, especially for nocturnal sightings of huge coconut crabs.

A sunset dhow cruise can be magical and romantic, but better still is a **dhow trip to a remote sandbar**: lie on a deserted beach, snorkel on the reef, eat fresh seafood and look out to nothing but tropical ocean. The upmarket lodges on Mafia (pages 343–6) all arrange these trips from Chole Bay, whilst on Zanzibar Island, Fumba Beach Lodge (pages 301–2), Unguja Lodge (page 289) and ethical operator Eco+Culture (page 303) all run similar trips in the Menai Bay Conservation Area.

If you're in the Nungwi area, then do wander along to see the turtles at the **Mnarani Natural Aquarium** (pages 219–20). It's a great conservation project and a rare chance to see hatchling turtles at very close quarters.

More generally, any trip to Zanzibar Island should include a **spice tour**: ask around to make sure you will have a knowledgeable guide. The trip idea may seem clichéd, but plucking everyday spices from what seems like a tangled bit of unruly forest can be fascinating. For something slightly different, combine the spices with some Zanzibari history on the **Princess Salme tour** (page 184). Starting at Mtoni Palace, the day trip takes in the palace ruins, a traditional coffee ceremony, the Kidichi plantations and a delicious Swahili lunch, and even helps fund the palace conservation initiatives.

For animal and wildlife lovers, visit the colobus monkey colony in **Jozani-Chwaka Bay National Park** (pages 294–8), and maybe even drop into the new **Zanzibar Butterfly Centre** (pages 298–9) next door. Meanwhile, those in search of a much more original, albeit less predictable, experience should consider visiting the community beside **Ufufuma Forest** (pages 251–4).

For some genuine community insight and interaction, the **Jambiani Village Tour** (pages 284–5) is really very good. Tailored to the particular interests of the visitor, it offers some hands-on entertainment and enlightening insights into the lives of the rural population, and ensures a percentage of the tour is reinvested into necessary village development.

No trip to Zanzibar is really complete without a night or two in **Stone Town**. Whilst here, take a walk around the narrow alleys, venture into the amazing market on Creek Road, and treat yourself to a rooftop meal on a balmy evening. For more insight, most of the local tour operators can arrange guides for half- and full-day excursions.

WHERE TO EAT If you enjoy good food, then Zanzibar can be a great place to visit – though choose your lodges carefully. Most of the top lodges have good food and you can expect to eat well; but only a few stand out. The costly **Ras Nungwi Beach Hotel** (page 210) and new restaurant at Stone Town's **Beyt al Chai** come right at the top of the chart for cuisine. **Pongwe Beach Hotel** (page 246), **Kikadini Villas** (page 281) and **Mtoni Marine** (pages 291–2) all pride themselves on fine food, and actually deliver it.

They share this with the vastly cheaper, superb village cuisine served in **Okala Restaurant's** (page 283) implausibly simple *makuti banda*. For tasty tapas try **Bellevue Bungalows** or for fabulous fish, consistently praised by guests, **Hakuna Matata Beach Lodge**, beside Chuini Palace (page 188).

For up-to-date advice on Stone Town's best restaurants, we'd always suggest that you ask someone locally. Things change fast in this game and our recommendations here are likely to be out of date sooner than they're printed. However, favourites must include the reliable Terrace at the **Serena Inn** (pages 134–5), **Rendezvous Les Spices** (page 150) for really delicious, fresh Indian dishes, and **Nyambani** or **Two Tables** for authentic Zanzibari dinners.

i TOURIST INFORMATION

Tanzania Tourist Board IPS Bldg, Dar es Salaam, Tanzania; ☏ +255 022 2111244; e safari@ ud.co.tz; www.tanzaniatouristboard.com

Tanzania Trade Centre (UK) 3 Stratford Pl, London WIC IAS; ☏ +44 207 758 8070; e info@ tanzatrade.co.uk; www.tanzatrade.co.uk/contactus

ORGANISED TOURS

If you're staying on a low budget (eg: US$20-per-night bungalows) or want to travel without a fixed schedule, then it'll be best to arrange your own

READING UP BEFORE YOU GO

An important part of your preparation for a visit is learning about the history, geography and culture of Zanzibar before you arrive. If textbooks and encyclopaedias put you off, read a few novels or travelogues to get yourself in the mood, or dip into some of the early explorers' accounts (see the books listed in *Appendix 2, Further Information*, pages 376–81). Also, scan the foreign pages of newspapers, or magazines specialising in developing countries, to familiarise yourself with politics and current affairs. You should certainly try to learn a few phrases of Swahili. All this will make your trip much more rewarding.

accommodation and flights, booking things as you go or a few days in advance during high season – then you can just travel where and when the mood takes you.

The advantages of such a trip hinge on the freedom that you have to make and change your arrangements, as well as from the increased choice of lower-budget options available to you. The disadvantages mainly arise from the problems you may have when places are full, and you are forced to spend time and energy finding somewhere different to stay.

However, if you're planning to book your trip in advance, and you want to stay in more comfortable places (eg: US$75 per night or more), then you will probably find it easier, and also cheaper, to arrange your trip through a specialist tour operator. Few tour operators will deal with low-budget accommodation.

A few tour operators offer scheduled trips to Zanzibar (ie: you join a group on fixed dates and with a pre-determined itinerary). However, most will work on a tailor-made basis (ie: they design a trip for you, around your dates and what you want to do).

The main advantage of such trips is that using a specialist, you have their experience and knowledge of the island, and its various options, at your command. You should discuss your preferences with them in detail, and then a good tour operator will be able to plan a trip that will suit you well – discussing all the pros and cons of the various choices, and answering all your questions, along the way. Hence you're much more likely to get a trip that will really suit you well!

A very good secondary reason is if you're visiting top-end lodges and camps, then it will almost certainly be cheaper to book your trip through a good specialist than it would be to arrange the trip for yourself. And, of course, you pay one price upfront which includes most things (flights, transfers, accommodation, etc), so you simply sit back, relax and enjoy the trip, knowing you don't need to worry about the logistics of it.

The main disadvantage of using a tour operator is the fixed itinerary: you cannot change your plans on a whim (or at least not without a cost), say to spend more or less time at a particular place.

The best way to find a trip that suits your own interest and pocket is to phone a knowledgeable tour operator direct. (For a list of tour operators, see pages 76–7.) Ask for their brochure, study their website, and then discuss your ideas with them. You'll often find tour operators advertising in the Sunday travel supplements of major newspapers and specialist travel magazines.

TOUR OPERATORS Finding a good tour operator for a trip to Zanzibar and the islands isn't always easy. Endless operators can send you, but you will get the best trip if you work with one who really knows the area and has visited all of the islands and lodges.

Don't let anyone convince you that there are only half-a-dozen decent beach lodges here: it's simply not true. If the operator that you're speaking to doesn't know most of the places in this book and offer a wide choice to suit you – then use one that does.

Here I (Chris McIntyre) must admit a personal interest in the tour-operating business. I run the specialist UK tour operator Expert Africa (✆ *020 8232 9777;* e *info@expertafrica.com; www.expertafrica.com*). We organise trips to Tanzania and its islands for travellers from all over the world. Booking your trip with us will always cost you the same as, or less than, booking the safari camps and beach lodges directly.

We advise our travellers from personal experience, and then allow them to make up their own minds. None of our team works on commission – so unlike many companies, we'll never push you into buying anything. Similarly, we have no financial ties to anywhere in Africa, so can offer truly independent advice on the full range of the choices available. Our only aim in advising you is to arrive at a trip that suits you perfectly.

Our trips are completely flexible, and they start at about US$2,500/£1,250 per person for a week, including flights from London, transfers, accommodation and most meals. I believe that Expert Africa has the best-value programme to Zanzibar and the islands – and the most extensive and comprehensive website; I'll happily send you a detailed colour brochure and start to help you plan your trip. However, for a fair comparison, some of the specialist African tour operators who also feature Zanzibar and the islands include:

In the UK

Aardvark Safaris RBL Hse, Ordnance Rd, Tidworth, Hants SP9 7QD; ✆ 01980 849160; e mail@aardvarksafaris.com; www.aardvarksafaris.com. Small, reliable upmarket safari specialist to Africa & Madagascar.

Abercrombie and Kent St George's Hse, Ambrose St, Cheltenham, Glos GL50 3LG; ✆ 0845 618 2200; www.abercrombiekent.co.uk. Worldwide holidays for groups & individuals to upmarket destinations with upmarket price tags.

Acacia Expeditions 23a Craven Terrace, London W2 3QH; ✆ 020 7706 4700; www.acacia-africa.com. Adventure holidays & overland/camping safaris throughout Africa.

Africa Travel Resource Westcott Rd, Dorking, Surrey RH4 3NB; ✆ 01306 880770; www.africatravelresource.com. Web-based tour operator selling its own Zanzibar favourites.

Cazenove and Loyd 9 Imperial Studios, 3–11 Imperial Rd, London SW6 2AG; ✆ 020 7384 2332; www.caz-loyd.com. Top-end tailor-made specialists to Africa, the Indian Ocean islands, Latin America & the Indian subcontinent.

Expert Africa 9/10 Upper Sq, Old Isleworth, Middx TW7 7BJ; ✆ 020 8232 9777; www.expertafrica.com. Specialist team including Chris McIntyre, this book's co-author, offering a wide range of unbiased tailor-made choices.

Gane and Marshall Aldenham, 2 Deer Park Lane, Tavistock, Devon PL19 9HD; ✆ 01822 600600; e holidays@ganeandmarshall.com; www.ganeandmarshall.co.uk. Worldwide operator with a Zanzibar programme.

Hartley Safaris The Old Chapel, Chapel Lane, Hackthorn, Lincs LN2 3PN; ✆ 01673 861600; www.hartleys-safaris.co.uk. Long-established tailor-made specialists to east & southern Africa & the Indian Ocean islands.

Imagine Africa 1a Salcott Rd, London SW11 6DQ; ✆ 020 7622 5114; e info@imagineafrica.co.uk; www.imagineafrica.co.uk. Relatively new tour operator offering all Africa plus the Indian Ocean.

Natural High 5 Chaldicott Barns, Semley, Shaftesbury, Dorset SP7 9AW; e (via website); www.naturalhighsafaris.com. Relatively new tailor-made specialists to Africa, run by old African hands, majoring on Tanzania.

Okavango Tours and Safaris Marlborough Hse, 298 Regents Park Rd, London N3 2TJ; ✆ 020 8343 3283; e info@okavango.com; www.okavango.com. Tailor-made specialists to Africa & the Indian Ocean islands, with a good knowledge of Tanzania.

Pulse Africa ✆ 020 8995 5909; www.pulseafrica.com. Specialist operator featuring Egypt, Gabon & southern & east Africa, including Zanzibar.

Rainbow Tours 305 Upper St, London N1 2TU; ✆ 020 7226 1004; e info@rainbowtours.co.uk; www.rainbowtours.co.uk. Established specialists to South Africa, with a northern Tanzania programme & extensions to the islands.

Safari Consultants Africa Hse, 2 Cornard Mills, Cornard Tye, Great Cornard, Suffolk CO10 0GW; ✆ 01787 888590; www.safari-consultants.co.uk. Long-established tailor-made specialists to east & southern Africa, & the Indian Ocean islands, with a very good knowledge.

Scott Dunn World Fovant Mews, 12 Noyna Rd, London SW17 7PH; ✆ 020 8682 5070; e africa@scottdunn.com; www.scottdunn.com. Worldwide coverage (everywhere except North America), with a tailor-made programme to Tanzania.

Simply Tanzania 54 Cotesbach Rd, London, E5 9QJ; ✆ 020 8986 0615. For many years this was a tiny but responsible operator which was particularly knowledgeable about the more obscure areas of the mainland. As we go to press, the news is that they have ceased trading.

Steppes Travel (formerly Art of Travel) 51 Castle St, Cirencester, Glos GL7 1QD; ✆ 01285 650011; e africa@steppestravel.co.uk; www.steppestravel.co.uk. Upmarket tailor-made specialists to Latin America, Asia, Africa & the Indian Ocean islands, including Tanzania.

Tim Best Travel 4 Cromwell Pl, London SW7 2JE; ☎ 020 7591 0300; e info@timbesttravel.com; www.timbesttravel.com. Upmarket holidays to Africa, the Indian Ocean islands & Latin America, including Tanzania.

Tribes Travel 12 The Business Centre, Earl Soham, Woodbridge, Suffolk IP13 7SA; ☎ 01728 685971; www.tribes.co.uk. Small, highly responsible operator, particularly strong on cultural trips, offering holidays worldwide on fair-trade principles.

Zanzibar Travel Reynards Hse, Selkirk Gdns, Cheltenham, Glos GL52 5LY; ☎ 01242 222027; e info@zanzibartravel.co.uk; www.zanzibartravel.co.uk. Small tailor-made operator concentrating on Kenya, Tanzania & Tanzania's islands.

In France
Wild Spirit Safari ☎ +33 1 45 74 11 14; +33 1 47 49 91 50; e infos@wild-spirit-safari.com; www.wild-spirit-safari.com. Kenya & Tanzania specialists offering add-on trips to Zanzibar, with offices in Paris & Arusha (Tanzania).

Zanzibar Voyage ☎ +33 1 53 34 92 71; e contact@zanzibar-voyage.com; www.zanzibar-voyage.com. Paris-based Zanzibar specialist with a good range of hotels & Tanzanian safari add-ons.

In South Africa
Unusual Destinations ☎ +27 11 706 1991; e info@unusualdestinations.com; www.unusualdestinations.com. Respected trips to east Africa & the Indian Ocean islands.

Zanzibar Bazaar ☎ +27 0860 110 325; e info@zanzibarislands.travel; www.zanzibarislands.travel. Beach breaks & safaris in Kenya, Tanzania & the eastern Indian Ocean.

Dive specialists If you're looking for a pure diving trip, perhaps including a live-aboard (see pages 216–17, 218 and 318), then you should consider one of the UK's specialist diving operators:

Dive Tours 46 Watergate St, Chester CH1 2LA; ☎ 01244 401177; e info@divetours.co.uk; www.divetours.co.uk

Dive Worldwide Long Barn South, Sutton Manor Farm, Bishop's Sutton, Alresford, Hants SO24 0AA; ☎ 0845 130 6980; e info@diveworldwide.com; www.diveworldwide.com

Planet Dive (formerly Scubasnacks Diving) 11 Jew St, Brighton BN1 1UT; ☎ 0870 749 1959; e enquiry@planetdive.co.uk; www.planetdive.co.uk

VISAS AND RED TAPE

Most foreigners entering the country need a visa for Tanzania or a visitor's pass, depending on their own nationality. Currently, most visas can be obtained on arrival in Tanzania – although the airport queues can be long and so it's often best to get them in advance. A visa will often take several weeks to issue, so apply well in advance of your trip. The charge for issuing a single-entry visa ranges from US$20 to US$100, depending on your nationality. At the time of writing, it is US$75 for UK citizens and US$100 for US passport holders, but do check the latest charges with your local embassy. Visa applications by researchers and journalists will need to be cleared by the Commission for Science and Technology (COSTECH) before being granted.

If you are planning to come via Nairobi or Mombasa, you may also need a visa or visitor's pass for Kenya. You may also need a return ticket out of Tanzania or Kenya, or be required to show that you have sufficient funds to cover your stay. (For other currency matters, see pages 96–8.)

Whether you first arrive in Dar or Zanzibar, you will be asked how long you want to stay. Up to three months is usually not a problem, and you'll receive a stamp in your passport. If you haven't obtained a visa in advance, this can be done upon arrival, though it must be paid for in hard currency cash.

Tanzanian regulations, which also cover Zanzibar, forbid the import or export of Tanzanian shillings worth more than US$100 without a permit. Similarly, if you wish to import or export more than US$10,000 in foreign currency, you should also seek advice from your local Tanzanian embassy or high commission.

There is no longer any legal requirement for a yellow fever vaccination certificate, unless you have come from a country where yellow fever is endemic. That said, the vaccination is strongly advised (see page 81). In theory you might also be asked for a cholera-exemption certificate; in practice we've never experienced this.

If you intend hiring a car or motorbike, then it's best to bring an International Driving Permit (IDP), which is easy to obtain from your national motoring association (in Britain contact the AA or RAC), and also a few spare passport-size photos. Entry regulations do change, so double-check the above with your nearest Tanzanian embassy, high commission or tourist office before you leave.

Ⓔ EMBASSIES AND CONSULATES

TANZANIAN EMBASSIES ABROAD

UK 3 Stratford Pl, Bond St, London WIC IAS; \f 020 7569 1470; www.tanzania-online.gov.uk. You can download a visa application form from this website, & send it off to the high commission along with your passport, the visa fee (currently £38 for a single-entry visa), 2 passport photos, & a SAE for return. The process takes up to 10 days by post. If you want to visit the high commission in London in person, you need to pay in cash; cards, cheques or postal orders are not accepted.
US 2139 R St, NW, Washington, DC 20008; \ +1 202 939 6125; www.tanzaniaembassy-us.org

Belgium 363 Av Louise, 11050 Brussels; \ +32 2 640 6500; e tanzania@skynet.be; http://tanzania.visahq.com/embassy/Belgium/
Canada 50 Range Rd, Ottawa, Ontario KIN 8J4; \ +1 613 232 1500/1509;
f +1 613 232 5184; www.vec.ca
Germany Botschaft der Vereinigte Republik von Tansania, Eschenallee 11 Charlottenburg, Westend, 14050 Berlin; \ +49 30 303 0800; f +49 030 303 08020; www.tanzania-gov.de
South Africa 822 George Av, Arcadia, Pretoria; \ +27 12 342 4371; f +27 12 430 4383; www.tanzania.org.za

FOREIGN CONSULATES IN ZANZIBAR Most countries have embassies or high commissions in Dar es Salaam or Nairobi, but a couple, including Britain and Germany, also have limited diplomatic representation on Zanzibar:

UK British Consular Correspondent, Mr Carl Salisbury; ZanAir Limited; \ 024 2233670; e reservations@zanair.com

Germany Honorary Consul, Mrs Angelika Sepetu, Kiembe Samaki Kijijini, Zanzibar; \ 024 2233691 (am)/024 2234062 or m 0777 410045 (pm); e sepetu_family@yahoo.com; www.daressalam.diplo.de

Consulates are generally unable to assist with visas or with simple problems such as illness or theft of belongings, but they will try to help in more serious cases such as wrongful arrest or imprisonment.

If you lose your passport, you can get an Emergency Travel Document from the Ministry of the Interior in Zanzibar. This will allow you to leave Zanzibar, and either go directly back to your own country, or reach Dar where most countries have representation and you should be able to get a replacement.

GETTING TO ZANZIBAR

✈ **BY AIR** Most visitors to these islands fly first to Dar es Salaam, on mainland Tanzania, and then take a short regional service to Zanzibar. Small Tanzanian carriers (particularly Coastal Airways and ZanAir – see page 116) offer a frequent schedule of flights that hop back and to across the Zanzibar Channel, and this is by far the quickest and easiest way to reach the islands from mainland Tanzania.

There are a handful of direct flights between Zanzibar and Nairobi, in Kenya, with Kenya Airways; these are very convenient when combining Zanzibar with a safari itinerary in Kenya. There are also direct flights between Europe and Zanzibar, but currently all of these are charter flights run by mass-market tour operators based in Italy, France and Spain.

From Europe
Scheduled flights The main international scheduled airlines serving Tanzania are:

Air Tanzania www.airtanzania.com. To Dar from Johannesburg daily, with good connections to Zanzibar.
British Airways www.ba.com. From London to Dar direct, 3 flights a week.
Emirates www.emirates.com. From most major European cities, via Dubai, to Dar daily.
Ethiopian Airlines www.flyethiopian.com. From Addis Ababa daily except Thu, with connections to most European & several American cities.

Kenya Airways www.kenya-airways.com. At least 2 flights daily between Nairobi & Dar, plus 2 between Nairobi & Zanzibar, with good connections to Europe & around Africa.
KLM www.klm.com. From Amsterdam to Dar daily, via Kilimanjaro International Airport.
South African Airlines www.flysaa.com. To Dar from Johannesburg daily, plus direct flights between Johannesburg & Zanzibar 3 times a week.

Britain is one of the cheapest places in Europe to buy scheduled flights to Zanzibar, Dar, Mombasa or Nairobi. Specialist African agencies can also arrange regional flights to/from Zanzibar, and whole trips, including safari-and-beach combinations. The cheapest direct flights from London to Zanzibar start from around £400 (US$700) in the low season, and rise to around £750 (US$1,300) in the high season – plus an additional amount for airport and departure taxes, and fuel surcharges, which is currently about £300. The relatively high level of taxes and surcharges is a direct reflection of the current state of the price of aviation fuel – and hence of the world price for oil.

The best deals are usually found by buying a long time (9–12 months) in advance; tickets for travel in the near future almost always command a premium. To buy just flights, you should talk to the 'seat-only' travel agents. To find them, look through the advertisements in the travel supplements of the Sunday newspapers. Be prepared to shop around, and to find that many of the bargain fares offered in ads are unavailable when you phone.

Flights bought as part of a whole trip which includes accommodation (known as 'Inclusive Tour fares', or 'IT fares' in the trade) will usually be the lowest. To buy an IT fare as part of a whole trip, seek out a tour operator who specialises in Africa, perhaps starting with the list of specialist tour operators, on pages 76–7.

Charter flights For visitors from mainland Europe, another option to consider may be holiday charter flights. Increasing numbers of charter flights from Europe (and particularly Italy, France and Spain) fly direct to Zanzibar; currently there are none from the UK. These are usually sold only as part of a week or two-week package visiting one of Zanzibar's larger 'resorts'. However, if the planes are not full then tour operators will sometimes sell 'flight only' deals, which are good value. Again, see adverts in national newspapers.

From the USA There are no direct flights to any of the islands, or even to Dar es Salaam, from the USA. You must fly to Europe or another African capital, such as Johannesburg or Nairobi, and then connect through to Dar es Salaam or Zanzibar.

From Kenya Kenya Airways and Precision Air fly between Nairobi and Zanzibar daily, often code-sharing. Currently, there are daily flights at 08.00 (Precision), 12.30 (Kenya Airways) and 19.00 (Precision), taking approximately 90 minutes. In addition, there is a flight at 10.30 on Fridays and Sundays, and a 17.00 flight on Saturdays.

The fare is about US$250 one-way, including taxes. Agents in Nairobi or Mombasa can arrange these flights. More details of airlines are given in *Chapter 6, Local services*, page 159.

From South Africa and elsewhere From South Africa, Air Tanzania and South African Airways run a code-share flight between Johannesburg and Dar es Salaam daily, departing at 13.50 and arriving in Dar at 18.30. There is a connection to Zanzibar (at no extra cost if you book through Air Tanzania). South African Airways has also started daily direct flights between Johannesburg and Dar, departing at 09.50 (arriving 14.35), and two additional flights on Sundays and Fridays at 14.55 (arriving 19.25).

If you want to reach Zanzibar from somewhere else in the world other than the countries mentioned above, it is usual to fly to Europe, Nairobi or the Gulf States and pick up a connecting flight from there. For example, from many parts of Asia you could fly on Gulf Air to Muscat then take another plane to Dar es Salaam.

Departure taxes There is a departure tax in US dollars (currently US$20) when flying out of a mainland Tanzanian or Zanzibar airport on an international flight. This is payable in US dollars, either in cash or, increasingly, it is included in the cost of pre-paid airline tickets. If you do need to pay in cash, then travellers' cheques, other currencies and even Tanzanian shillings are not accepted for this; you must have US dollars cash. You can change whatever you have into US dollars at an airport bureau de change, but often the exchange rates given are very poor. However you carry your money, it's always worth carrying some dollars in cash to cover costs like this. For domestic flights, the airport tax is US$5.

Before you pay anything, especially if you've come to Zanzibar on an international return flight, check that the departure tax isn't already included in your ticket price (even better, check what taxes are included when you buy your ticket). If you are flying to Dar to pick up an international flight, you need only pay the international departure tax once (probably at Dar), although you will still pay the domestic departure tax for your flight out of Zanzibar.

Even ship passengers cannot escape departure taxes! Tourists leaving by boat from Zanzibar are charged a US$5 'seaport departure service charge'. This also is payable in dollars only, but many of the ship companies include this tax in the ticket price. Check this carefully to avoid paying twice.

BY SEA

From Kenya We're not aware of any passenger ships currently running between Zanzibar and Mombasa. Dhows taking tourists from Kenya to Zanzibar Island are very rare; they're more frequent between Mombasa and Pemba (see page 310) but do read the warnings in *Chapter 5*, page 117 carefully before deciding on this form of transport. If you ask around in the old port area of Mombasa you can usually find a boat going about twice a week to Wete or Mkoani on Pemba, although times and days are variable. A one-way trip costs about US$10 to US$15, payable in Kenyan shillings or hard currency.

From mainland Tanzania Several large passenger ships run daily between Dar es Salaam, Zanzibar and Pemba, and less frequently to other points on the mainland. (For details of these see *Chapter 5*, pages 116–18.)

BEFORE YOU GO

Travel insurance Visitors to Zambia must take out a comprehensive **medical insurance policy** to cover them for emergencies, including the cost of evacuation to another country within the region. Such policies come with an emergency number (often on a reverse-charge/call-collect basis). You would be wise to memorise this – or indelibly tattoo it in as many places as possible on your baggage. Note that many policies exclude diving as an activity, so do check this.

Personal effects insurance is also a sensible precaution, but check the policy's fine print before you leave home. Often, in even the best policies, you will find a limit per item, or per claim – which can be well below the cost of a replacement. If you need to list your valuables separately, then do so comprehensively. Check that receipts are not required for claims if you do not have them, and that the excess that you have to pay on every claim is reasonable.

Annual travel policies can be excellent value if you travel a lot, and some of the larger credit-card companies offer good deals. However, often it is better to get your valuables named and insured for travel using your home contents insurance. These year-round policies will try harder to settle your claim fairly as they want your business in the long term.

Immunisations Having a full set of immunisations takes time, normally at least six weeks, although some protection can be had by visiting your doctor as late as a few days before you travel. Ideally, see your doctor or travel clinic (see pages 84–6) early on to establish an inoculation timetable.

Legal requirements Officially a **yellow fever** vaccination certificate is required only on entry from another country with a risk of yellow fever. However, since December 2007 the Zanzibar authorities have been asking for proof of vaccination from those arriving from Tanzania – which effectively incorporates most visitors. The risks of yellow fever in parts of east Africa are low and the decision whether to have the vaccine or not will need to be discussed with a doctor. An official yellow fever certificate will be issued by the medical centre proving your inoculation, but be aware that the certificate is not valid until ten days after your vaccination, although it then lasts for ten years. If you are coming from a yellow fever area, you must carry your vaccination certificate with you. You may not always be required to produce it when you enter the country, but it's important to be prepared. If the vaccine is contraindicated or it is considered that the risk of vaccination outweighs the risk of disease, then you are advised to carry a formal exemption certificate, which can be obtained from a travel clinic.

Recommended precautions Vaccinations for typhoid, tetanus, diphtheria, polio and hepatitis A are generally recommended. Most travellers are advised to have immunisation against **hepatitis A** with a vaccine such as Havrix Monodose or Avaxim. One dose of vaccine lasts for one year and can be boosted to give protection for up to 20 years. The course of two injections costs about £100 but may be available in the UK on the NHS, and can be used even close to the time of departure. The newer **typhoid** vaccines last for three years and are about 85% effective. They should be encouraged unless the traveller is leaving within a few days, for a trip of a week or less, when the vaccine would not be effective in time.

Meningitis vaccine (containing strains ACW and Y) is also recommended, especially for trips of more than four weeks, or for shorter trips if you are working with children (see *Meningitis*, page 92).

Dr Jane Wilson-Howarth

Long-haul air travel increases the risk of deep vein thrombosis (DVT). Although recent research has suggested that many of us develop clots when immobilised, most resolve without us ever having been aware of them. In certain susceptible individuals, though, clots form on clots and when large ones break away and lodge in the lungs this is dangerous. Fortunately this happens in a tiny minority of passengers.

Studies have shown that flights of over five and a half hours are significant, and that people who take lots of shorter flights over a short space of time can also form clots. People at highest risk are:

- Those who have had a clot before – unless they are now taking warfarin
- People over 80 years of age
- Anyone who has recently undergone a major operation or surgery for varicose veins
- Someone who has had a hip or knee replacement in the last three months
- Cancer sufferers
- Those who have ever had a stroke
- People with heart disease
- Those with a close blood relative who has had a clot

Those with a slightly increased risk are:

- People over 40
- Women who are pregnant or have had a baby in the last couple of weeks
- People taking female hormones, the combined contraceptive pill or other oestrogen therapy
- Heavy smokers
- Those who have very severe varicose veins
- The very obese
- People who are very tall (over 6ft/1.8m) or short (under 5ft/1.5m)

Immunisation against **cholera** is not generally recommended for Zanzibar and exemption certificates are no longer required. Vaccinations for **rabies** are advised for travellers visiting more remote areas (see *Rabies*, pages 92–3). **Hepatitis B** vaccination should be considered for longer trips (two months or more) or for those working in situations where the chance of contact with blood is increased, or with children. Three injections are preferred and can be given over a 21-day period (Engerix only for those aged 16 or over) prior to travel. Longer schedules are preferred if you go to your doctor in plenty of time. A BCG vaccination against **tuberculosis** (TB) may be advised for trips of two months or more if you have not had one before, although this recommendation is becoming less common. Ideally, then, you should visit your own doctor or a specialist travel clinic (see pages 84–6) to discuss your requirements about eight weeks before you plan to travel.

Malaria Malaria is the most dangerous disease in Africa, and the greatest risk to the traveller. It occurs throughout Zanzibar, all the year round, so it is essential that you take all possible precautions against it.

Malaria prevention Prophylaxis regimes aim to infuse your bloodstream with drugs that inhibit and kill the malaria parasites which are injected into you by a biting mosquito. This is why you must start to take the drugs *before* you arrive

A deep vein thrombosis is a blood clot that forms in the deep leg veins. This is very different from irritating but harmless superficial phlebitis. DVT causes swelling and redness of one leg, usually with heat and pain in one calf and sometimes the thigh. A DVT is only dangerous if a clot breaks away and travels to the lungs (pulmonary embolus). Symptoms of a pulmonary embolus (PE) include chest pain that is worse on breathing in deeply, shortness of breath, and sometimes coughing up small amounts of blood. The symptoms commonly start three to ten days after a long flight. Anyone who thinks that they might have a DVT needs to see a doctor immediately who will arrange a scan. Warfarin tablets (to thin the blood) are then taken for at least six months.

PREVENTION OF DVT Several conditions make the problem more likely. Immobility is the key, and factors like reduced oxygen in cabin air and dehydration may also contribute. To reduce the risk of thrombosis on a long journey:

EXERCISE BEFORE AND AFTER THE FLIGHT
- Keep mobile before and during the flight; move around every couple of hours
- Drink plenty of water or juices during the flight
- Avoid taking sleeping pills and excessive tea, coffee and alcohol
- Perform exercises that mimic walking and tense the calf muscles
- Consider wearing flight socks or support stockings (see www.legshealth.com)
- Ideally take a meal each week of oily fish (mackerel, trout, salmon, sardines, etc) ahead of your departure. This reduces the blood's ability to clot and thus DVT risk. It may even be worth just taking a meal of oily fish 24 hours before departure if this is more practical.

If you think you are at increased risk of a clot, ask your doctor if it is safe to travel.

in a malarial area – so that they are established in your bloodstream from day one. Unfortunately, malaria parasites continually adapt to the drugs used to combat them, so the recommended regimes must adapt and change in order to remain effective. None is 100% effective, and all require time to kill the parasites – so unless there is a medical indication for stopping, it is important to complete the course after leaving the area as directed (usually one to four weeks depending on the regime). Falciparum (cerebral) malaria is the most common in Africa, and usually fatal if untreated, so it is worth your while trying to avoid it.

Seek current advice on the best antimalarials to take: usually mefloquine, Malarone or doxycycline. If mefloquine (Lariam) is suggested, start this two and a half weeks (three doses) before departure to check that it suits you; stop it immediately if it seems to cause depression or anxiety, visual or hearing disturbances, severe headaches, fits or changes in heart rhythm. Side effects such as nightmares or dizziness are not medical reasons for stopping unless they are sufficiently debilitating or annoying. Anyone who has been treated for depression or psychiatric problems, has diabetes controlled by oral therapy or who is epileptic (or who has suffered fits in the past) or has a close blood relative who is epileptic, should probably avoid mefloquine.

In the past doctors were nervous about prescribing mefloquine to pregnant women, but experience has shown that it is relatively safe and certainly safer than the risk of malaria. That said, there are other issues, so if you are travelling to Zanzibar while pregnant, seek expert advice before departure.

Malarone (proguanil and atovaquone) is as effective as mefloquine. It has the advantage of having few side effects and need only be continued for one week after returning. However, it is expensive and because of this tends to be reserved for shorter trips. Malarone may not be suitable for everybody, so take advice from a doctor. The licence in the UK has been extended for up to three months' use and a paediatric form of tablet is also available, prescribed on a weight basis.

A third alternative is the antibiotic doxycycline (100mg daily). Like Malarone it can be started one to two days before arrival. Unlike mefloquine, it may also be used in travellers with epilepsy, although certain anti-epileptic medication may make it less effective. In perhaps 1–3% of people there is the possibility of allergic skin reactions developing in sunlight; the drug should be stopped if this happens. Women using the oral contraceptive should use an additional method of protection for the first four weeks when using doxycycline. It is also unsuitable in pregnancy or for children under 12 years.

Chloroquine and proguanil are no longer considered to be effective enough for Zanzibar but may be considered as a last resort if nothing else is deemed suitable.

All tablets should be taken with or after the evening meal, washed down with plenty of fluid and, with the exception of Malarone (see above), continued for four weeks after leaving.

Despite all these precautions, it is important to be aware that no anti-malarial drug is 100% protective, although those on prophylactics who are unlucky enough to catch malaria are less likely to get rapidly into serious trouble. In addition to taking anti-malarials, it is therefore important to avoid mosquito bites between dusk and dawn (see *Avoiding insect bites*, pages 89–90).

There is unfortunately the occasional traveller who prefers to 'acquire resistance' to malaria rather than take preventative tablets, or who takes homeopathic prophylactics thinking these are effective against killer disease. Homeopathy theory dictates treating like with like so there is no place for prophylaxis or immunisation in a well person; bone fide homeopaths do not advocate it. Travellers to Africa cannot acquire any effective resistance to malaria, and those who don't make use of prophylactic drugs risk their life in a manner that is both foolish and unnecessary.

Medical kit Pharmacies in the main towns in Zanzibar generally have good supplies of medicines, but away from these you will find very little, so it's wise to take a small personal medical kit (see page 95).

Travel clinics and health information A full list of current travel clinic websites worldwide is available from the International Society of Travel Medicine on www.istm.org. For other journey preparation information, consult www.tripprep.com. Information about various medications may be found on www.emedicine.com. For information on malaria prevention, see www.preventingmalaria.info.

UK

Berkeley Travel Clinic 32 Berkeley St, London W1J 8EL (near Green Park tube station); ✆ 020 7629 6233 **Cambridge Travel Clinic** 48a Mill Rd, Cambridge CB1 2AS; ✆ 01223 367362; e enquiries@ travelcliniccambridge.co.uk; www.travelcliniccambridge.co.uk; ⊕ 12.00–19.00 Tue–Fri, 10.00–16.00 Sat.

Edinburgh Travel Clinic Regional Infectious Diseases Unit, Ward 41 OPD, Western General Hospital, Crewe Rd South, Edinburgh EH4 2UX; ✆ 0131 537 2822; www.mvm.ed.ac.uk. Travel helpline (✆ 0906 589 0380) ⊕ 09.00–12.00 Mon–Fri. Provides inoculations & antimalarial prophylaxis, & advises on travel-related health risks.

Fleet Street Travel Clinic 29 Fleet St, London EC4Y 1AA; tel: 020 7353 5678; www.fleetstreetclinic.com. Vaccinations, travel products & latest advice.

Hospital for Tropical Diseases Travel Clinic Mortimer Market Bldg, Capper St (off Tottenham Ct Rd), London WC1E 6AU; ☎ 020 7388 9600; www.thehtd.org. Offers consultations & advice, & is able to provide all necessary drugs & vaccines for travellers. Runs a healthline (☎ 0906 133 7733) for country-specific information & health hazards. Also stocks nets, water-purification equipment & personal protection measures.

Interhealth Worldwide Partnership Hse, 157 Waterloo Rd, London SE1 8US; ☎ 020 7902 9000; www.interhealth.org.uk. Competitively priced, one-stop travel health service. All profits go to their affiliated company, InterHealth, which provides healthcare for overseas workers on Christian projects.

Liverpool School of Medicine Pembroke Pl, Liverpool L3 5QA; ☎ 0151 708 9393; f 0151 705 3370; www.liv.ac.uk/lstm

MASTA (Medical Advisory Service for Travellers Abroad) Moorfield Rd, Yeadon, Leeds, West Yorkshire LS19 7BN; ☎ 0113 238 7500; www.masta-travel-health.com. Provides travel health advice, antimalarials & vaccinations. There are over 25 MASTA pre-travel

clinics in Britain; call or check online for the nearest. Clinics also sell mosquito nets, medical kits, insect protection & travel hygiene products.

NHS travel website www.fitfortravel.scot.nhs.uk. Provides country-by-country advice on immunisation & malaria, plus details of recent developments, & a list of relevant health organisations.

Nomad Travel Store/Clinic 3–4 Wellington Terrace, Turnpike Lane, London N8 0PX; ☎ 020 8889 7014; travel-health line (office hours only) ☎ 0906 863 3414; e sales@nomadtravel.co.uk; www.nomadtravel.co.uk. Also at 40 Bernard St, London WC1N 1LJ; ☎ 020 7833 4114; 52 Grosvenor Gdns, London SW1W 0AG; ☎ 020 7823 5823; & 43 Queens Rd, Bristol BS8 1QH; ☎ 0117 922 6567. For health advice, equipment such as mosquito nets & other anti-bug devices, & an excellent range of adventure travel gear. Clinic also in Southampton.

Trailfinders Travel Clinic 194 Kensington High St, London W8 7RG; ☎ 020 7938 3999; www.trailfinders.com/travelessentials/travelclinic.htm

Travelpharm The Travelpharm website www.travelpharm.com offers up-to-date guidance on travel-related health & has a range of medications available through their online mini pharmacy.

Irish Republic

Tropical Medical Bureau Grafton St Medical Centre, Grafton Bldgs, 34 Grafton St, Dublin 2; ☎ 1 671 9200; www.tmb.ie. A useful website specific to

tropical destinations. Also check website for other bureaux locations throughout Ireland.

USA

Centers for Disease Control 1600 Clifton Rd, Atlanta, GA 30333; ☎ 800 311 3435; travellers' health hotline (fax service) 888 232 3299; www.cdc.gov/travel. The central source of travel information in the USA. The invaluable *Health Information for International Travel*, published annually, is available from the Division of Quarantine at this address.

Connaught Laboratories Pasteur Merieux Connaught, Route 611, PO Box 187, Swiftwater, PA 18370; ☎ 800 822 2463. They will send a free list of specialist tropical-medicine physicians in your state.

IAMAT (International Association for Medical Assistance to Travelers) 1623 Military Rd, 279, Niagara Falls, NY 14304-1745; ☎ 716 754 4883; e info@iamat.org; www.iamat.org. A non-profit organisation that provides lists of English-speaking doctors abroad.

International Medicine Center 915 Gessner Rd, Suite 525, Houston, TX 77024; ☎ 713 550 2000; www.traveldoc.com

Canada

IAMAT Suite 1, 1287 St Clair Av W, Toronto, Ontario M6E 1B8; ☎ 416 652 0137; www.iamat.org

TMVC Suite 314, 1030 W Georgia St, Vancouver, BC V6E 2Y3; ☎ 888 288 8682; www.tmvc.com. Private clinic with several outlets in Canada.

Australia, New Zealand, Singapore

IAMAT PO Box 5049, Christchurch 5, New Zealand; www.iamat.org

TMVC ☎ 1300 65 88 44; www.tmvc.com.au. Clinics in Australia, New Zealand & Singapore, including:

Gordon Rattray www.able-travel.com

Zanzibar might sound like the last place you'd want to venture to if you have difficulties walking. Wheelchairs and sandy beaches don't agree, and its island status provides more logistical problems, forcing you to ask if the getting there is actually worth it.

It is. A Zanzibar experience is unique, and with some preparation, patience, and the innate helpfulness of the local people, you will be surprised by just how possible it is.

GETTING THERE AND AWAY The ferries from Dar es Salaam are not an easy option. Boarding on Zanzibar is via a gangplank, which is steep at low tide and can be difficult even for able-bodied people with luggage. On board there are various decks with stairways between them and there are no facilities to make mobility easier.

A quicker, more comfortable and more practical (albeit more expensive) option is to fly. The airport staff cope very well with disabled passengers, although you will need to be manually lifted in and out of the small 13-seater planes which are used for many flights from Dar to Zanzibar. Zanzibar airport has standard bathroom facilities only.

LOCAL OPERATORS Sama Tours (page 126) and Fernandes Tours (page 125) are particularly open to requests from less-mobile travellers. Sama Tours have a guide/driver who is also an experienced personal assistant.

TRANSPORT Buses and *dala-dalas* (small converted trucks) have no facilities for wheelchairs. Help will always be available, but be aware that they may run only as far as the dirt track leading to some coastal resorts, leaving you to walk a short distance. Taxis might be your easiest way of getting around, and drivers are usually happy to assist with transfers, but you must be assertive and explain clearly what help you need. It is always advisable for people prone to skin damage to sit on their wheelchair cushion in the vehicle as it may be old, meaning the seating won't give as much support as it once did.

ACCOMMODATION At the time of writing, Zanzibar has only one 'fully accessible' hotel, the Fairmont Zanzibar (see pages 235–6). Although most buildings' entrances are at least one step up from street level, the majority are ground floor and might be construed as being 'accessible', depending on your abilities. Unless you are going to

---

Auckland Canterbury Arcade, 170 Queen St, Auckland; ☎ 9 373 3531
Brisbane 75a Astor Terrace, Spring Hill, QLD 4000; ☎ 7 3815 6900

South Africa and Namibia
SAA-Netcare Travel Clinics Sanlam Bldg, 19 Fredman Drive, Sandton, P Bag X34, Benmore, JHB, Gauteng, 2010; www.travelclinic.co.za. Clinics throughout South Africa.

Switzerland
IAMAT 57 Chemin des Voirets, 1212 Grand Lancy, Geneva; www.iamat.org

Melbourne 393 Little Bourke St, 2nd floor, Melbourne, VIC 3000; ☎ 3 9602 5788
Sydney Dymocks Bldg, 7th floor, 428 George St, Sydney, NSW 2000; ☎ 2 9221 7133

TMVC NHC Health Centre, Cnr Beyers Naude & Waugh Northcliff; PO Box 48499, Roosevelt Park, 2129 (postal address); ☎ 011 888 7488; www.tmvc.com.au. Consult website for details of other clinics in South Africa & Namibia.

have the time and energy to look for accommodation on arrival, the best advice is to research your options in advance. Specialist tour operators will normally take time to listen to your needs or, if you prefer, many hotels can be found directly on the internet. If photos aren't available, the owners are easily contacted and can describe their facilities by email. Bradt's forthcoming guidebook, *Access Africa* (see *Further Information*, page 380), includes a section on Zanzibar, where access in properties all round the island is described.

RESTAURANTS Many eateries are on the ground floor, with one or two steps at the entrance. The proprietors will want your custom, so if you fancy eating there, you can be sure they will quickly organise a couple of waiters to help you in.

HEALTH Doctors will know about 'everyday' illnesses, but you must understand and be able to explain your own particular medical requirements. If possible, take all necessary medication and equipment with you and pack this in your hand luggage during flights in case your main luggage gets lost. Zanzibar is humid, so feels hot all year. If this is a problem for you, a plant-spray bottle is an ideal cooling aid.

SECURITY The advice given elsewhere in this book (see page 93) applies to all travellers, but it is worthwhile remembering that, as a disabled person, you might appear more vulnerable. My experience, however, is that the converse is true; Zanzibaris will sooner help and protect someone who is obviously less able, than take advantage of the situation.

ACTIVITIES The streets around Stone Town are generally smooth and step-free, and many of the highlights are ground floor with only one or two steps. Where ancient stairways do exist, help is easily found. Several spice farms are on level ground, and if you cannot follow the tour group then guides are usually happy to bring the spices to you – even in your vehicle – and explain their uses. Inform your guide or tour company in advance of your capabilities and they will make an appropriate itinerary.

Beaches will always be naturally difficult for wheelchair users. I've still not heard of anyone on Zanzibar using a beach wheelchair (with massive tyres to ride on soft sand), but I have no doubt this will come. Until then, we'll need to be content with sipping a cool drink in the shade with a good book. Is that so bad?

IN ZANZIBAR When travelling around Zanzibar or east Africa, the different climatic and social conditions mean visitors are exposed to diseases not normally encountered at home. Although you will have received all the vaccinations recommended in the *Before you go* section, this does not mean you will be free of all illness during your travels: certain precautions still have to be taken.

You should read a good book on travel medicine (see *Appendix 2, Further Information*, page 380) and be aware of the causes, symptoms and treatments of the more serious diseases. But don't let these colourful descriptions put you off – with a little care and attention most of these illnesses can be avoided.

Hospitals and pharmacies If you need medical attention, there are several **hospitals and medical centres** in Zanzibar Town. **Pharmacies** in Zanzibar Town have a basic range of medicines, but specific brands are often unavailable, so bring with you all that you will need. For details, see pages 161–2.

Staying healthy Visitors using the better hotels, lodges and camps are unlikely to encounter any serious health problems.

The major dangers in Zanzibar (and Tanzania as a whole) are car accidents (especially likely if you drive at night) and sunburn. Both can also be very serious, yet both are within the power of the visitor to avoid.

The following is general advice, applicable to travelling anywhere, including Zanzibar.

Food and storage Throughout the world, most health problems encountered by travellers are contracted by eating contaminated food or drinking unclean water. If you are staying in safari camps or lodges, or eating in restaurants, then you are unlikely to have problems in Zanzibar.

However, if you are backpacking and cooking for yourself, or relying on local food, then you need to take more care. Tins, packets and fresh green vegetables (when you can find them) are least likely to cause problems – provided that clean water has been used in preparing the meal. In Zanzibar's hot climate, keeping meat or animal products unrefrigerated for more than a few hours is asking for trouble.

Water purification It is less common to get sick from drinking contaminated water, but it happens, so try to drink from safe sources. At good hotels, clean drinking water will always be available. You can now buy bottled water widely throughout these islands, although if you venture very far from the beaten track, then supplies are not always reliable so carry bottles with you.

When buying bottled water, check the seal as it is not unknown for discarded bottles to be filled with tap water and sold again. That said, don't become nervous and avoid drinking altogether; such scams are very rare. It is vital to keep up your liquid intake in the hot climate to avoid dehydration.

If heading far from civilisation, then prepare to purify your own water with tablets (or iodine solution), which are available from outdoor/camping shops. Bring these with you; you may not be able to buy them in Zanzibar. These will work more effectively if you filter out any larger, suspended particles from the water before adding them. Several manufacturers in Europe and USA produce filter pumps designed to do this whole process quickly and easily.

Heat and sun Heatstroke, heat exhaustion and sunburn are often problems for travellers to Zanzibar, despite being easy to prevent. To avoid them, you need to remember that your body is under stress and make allowances for it. First, take things gently; you are on holiday, after all. Next, keep your fluid and salt levels high: lots of water and soft drinks, but go easy on the caffeine and alcohol. Third, dress to keep cool with loose-fitting, thin garments – preferably of cotton, linen or silk. Finally, beware of the sun. Hats and long-sleeved shirts are essential. If you must expose your skin to the sun, then use sun blocks and high-factor sunscreens (the sun is so strong that you will still get a tan). Be especially careful of exposure in the middle of the day and of sun reflected off water, and wear a T-shirt and lots of waterproof suncream (at least SPF15) when swimming. The glare and the dust can be hard on the eyes, too, so bring UV-protecting sunglasses and, perhaps, a soothing eyebath.

Prickly heat A fine pimply rash on the trunk is likely to be heat rash; cool showers, dabbing dry and talc will help. Treat the problem by slowing down to a relaxed schedule, wearing only loose, baggy, 100%-cotton clothes and sleeping naked under a fan; if it's bad you may need to check into an air-conditioned hotel room for a while.

Skin infections Any mosquito bite or small nick in the skin gives an opportunity for bacteria to foil the body's usually excellent defences; it will surprise many travellers how quickly skin infections start in warm humid climates and it is essential to clean and cover even the slightest wound. Creams are not as effective as a good drying antiseptic such as dilute iodine, potassium permanganate (a few crystals in half a cup of water) or crystal (or gentian) violet. One of these should be available in most towns. If the wound starts to throb, or becomes red and the redness starts to spread, or the wound oozes, and especially if you develop a fever, antibiotics will probably be needed: flucloxacillin (250mg four times a day) or cloxacillin (500mg four times a day). For those allergic to penicillin, erythromycin (500mg twice a day) for five days should help. See a doctor if the symptoms do not start to improve within 48 hours.

Fungal infections also get a hold easily in hot, moist climates so wear 100%-cotton socks and underwear and shower frequently. An itchy rash in the groin or flaking between the toes is likely to be a fungal infection. This needs treatment with an antifungal cream such as Canesten (clotrimazole); if this is not available try Whitfield's ointment (compound benzoic acid ointment) or crystal violet (although this will turn you purple!).

Avoiding insect bites The most dangerous biting insects in parts of Zanzibar are mosquitoes, because they can transmit malaria, yellow fever and a host of other diseases. As antimalarial drugs do not provide complete protection, you should take steps to avoid being bitten by a mosquito: wear long-sleeved shirts and long trousers, covering wrists and ankles in the evening when mosquitoes are active. Most hotels have mosquito nets and these should always be used. In cheaper hotels some nets may be broken, so a needle and thread for quick repairs is useful. Or carry your own (see *What to take*, pages 93–5). The nets should also be impregnated with permethrin – if in doubt carry an impregnation kit bought before you leave. Sleeping in a stream of moving air, such as under a fan, or in an air-conditioned room, will help to reduce your chances of being bitten.

Insect sprays and mosquito coils, which burn slowly through the night, can be bought in shops in Zanzibar Town, but the tubes of repellent to rub on your skin which tend to be very effective (eg: the excellent Repel range containing 50% DEET) are not available. DEET (diethyltoluamide) is the active ingredient in many repellents, and the current guidance is to use one containing around 50–55%. It is also fine to use for children and pregnant women. You need to reapply the repellent about every six hours and again if you have been in water. It will dissolve some plastics and synthetic materials, and may irritate sensitive skin. Because of this, many people use concentrated DEET to impregnate materials, rather than applying it to themselves. An alternative to this is to use Bug Guards – wrist and ankle bands containing 100% DEET in capsule form. The capsules break on movement, but the chemical never touches the skin. One pack contains four bands, which when used, last for two weeks. Mosquito nets, socks and even cravats can be impregnated and used to deter insects from biting. Eating large quantities of garlic, or cream of tartar, or taking yeast tablets, are said to deter some biting insects, although the evidence is anecdotal – and the garlic may affect your social life.

Mosquitoes and many other insects are attracted to light. If you are camping, never put a lamp near the opening of your tent, or you will have a swarm of biters waiting to join you when you retire. In hotel rooms, be aware that the longer your light is on, the greater the number of insects will be sharing your accommodation.

Aside from avoiding mosquito bites between dusk and dawn, which will protect you from a range of nasty insect-borne viruses, as well as malaria (see pages 90–1), it is important to take precautions against other insect bites. During the day it is wise to wear long, loose (preferably 100%-cotton) clothes if you are pushing through scrubby country.

Jiggers, or **sandfleas**, can be best avoided by wearing shoes. They latch on if you walk barefoot in contaminated places, and set up home under the skin of the foot, usually at the side of a toenail where they cause a painful, boil-like swelling. They need picking out by a local expert.

DISEASES AND WHEN TO SEE A DOCTOR

Travellers' diarrhoea There are almost as many names for this as there are travellers' tales on the subject. Firstly, do resist the temptation to reach for the medical kit as soon as your stomach turns a little fluid. Most cases of travellers' diarrhoea will resolve themselves within 24–48 hours with no treatment at all. To speed up this process of acclimatisation, eat well but simply: avoid fats in favour of starches, and keep your fluid intake high. Bananas and papaya fruit are often claimed to be helpful. If you urgently need to stop the symptoms, for a long journey for example, then Lomotil, Imodium or another of the commercial anti-diarrhoea preparations will do the trick. They stop the symptoms, by paralysing the bowel, but will not cure the problem. They should be used only as a last resort and never if you have bad abdominal cramps with the diarrhoea.

If the diarrhoea persists for more than two days, or the stools contain blood, pus or slime, and/or you have a fever, you must seek medical advice. There are as many possible treatments as there are causes, and a proper diagnosis involves microscopic analysis of a stool sample, so go straight to your nearest hospital. The most important thing, especially in Zanzibar's climate, is to keep your fluid intake up. If it is not possible to reach medical help quickly then a dose of norfloxacin or ciprofloxacin repeated twice a day until reaching medical help may be appropriate (if you are planning to take an antibiotic with you, note that both norfloxacin and ciprofloxacin are available only on prescription in the UK). If the diarrhoea is greasy and bulky and is accompanied by sulphurous (eggy) burps the likely cause is giardia. This is best treated with tinidazole (four x 500mg in one dose, repeated seven days later if symptoms persist).

The body's absorption of fluids is assisted by adding small amounts of dissolved sugars, salts and minerals to the water. Sachets of oral rehydration salts give the perfect biochemical mix you need to replace what is pouring out of your bottom but they do not taste so nice. Any dilute mixture of sugar and salt in water will do you good so, if you like Coke or orange squash, drink that with a three-finger pinch of salt added to each glass. The ideal ratio is eight level teaspoons of sugar and one level teaspoon of salt dissolved in one litre of water. Palm syrup or honey make good substitutes for sugar, and including fresh citrus juice will not only improve the taste of these solutions, but also add valuable potassium.

Drink two large glasses after every bowel action, and more if you are thirsty. If you are not eating you need to drink three litres a day *plus* whatever you are sweating *and* the equivalent of what's going into the toilet. If you feel like eating, take a bland diet; heavy greasy foods will give you cramps.

If you are likely to be more than a few days from qualified medical help, then come equipped with a good health manual and the selection of antibiotics which it recommends. *Bugs, Bites & Bowels* by Dr Jane Wilson-Howarth (see *Appendix 2*, page 380) is excellent for this purpose.

Malaria You can still catch malaria even if you are taking anti-malarial drugs so you should do everything possible to avoid mosquito bites. Untreated malaria is likely to be fatal, but even strains resistant to prophylaxis respond well to prompt treatment. Because of this, your immediate priority upon displaying possible malaria symptoms – including a rapid rise in temperature (over 38°C), and any combination of a headache, flu-like aches and pains, a general sense of disorientation, and possibly even nausea and diarrhoea – is to establish whether you have malaria, ideally by visiting a clinic.

A definite diagnosis of malaria is normally possible only by examining a blood sample under the microscope. It is best to get the problem properly diagnosed if possible, so don't treat yourself if you can easily reach a hospital first. Even if you test negative, it would be wise to stay within reach of a laboratory until the symptoms clear up, and to test again after a day or two if they don't. It's worth noting that if you have a fever and the malaria test is negative, you may have typhoid or paratyphoid, which should also receive immediate treatment.

If (and only if) medical help is unavailable, then self-treatment is fairly safe, except for people who are pregnant or under 12 years of age. Should you be travelling to remote areas, you would be wise to carry a course of treatment to cure malaria, and a rapid test kit. With malaria, it is normal enough to go from feeling healthy to having a high fever in the space of a few hours (and it is possible to die from falciparum malaria within 24 hours of the first symptoms). In such circumstances, assume that you have malaria and act accordingly – whatever risks are attached to taking an unnecessary cure are outweighed by the dangers of untreated malaria.

There is some division about the best treatment for malaria, but either Malarone or Coarthemeter are the current treatments of choice. Discuss your trip with a specialist at home or in Zanzibar.

Dengue fever This mosquito-borne disease – and other similar arboviruses – may mimic malaria but there is no prophylactic medication available to deal with it. The mosquitoes that carry this virus bite during the daytime, so it is worth applying repellent if you see any mosquitoes around. Symptoms include strong headaches, rashes, excruciating joint and muscle pains and high fever. Dengue fever lasts only for a week or so and is not usually fatal. Complete rest and paracetamol are the usual treatment. Plenty of fluids also help. Some patients are given an intravenous drip to keep them from dehydrating. It is especially important to protect yourself if you have had dengue fever before. A second infection with a different strain can result in the potentially fatal dengue haemorrhagic fever.

Bilharzia or schistosomiasis Bilharzia is an insidious disease, contracted by coming into contact with contaminated water. It is caused by parasitic worms which live part of their lives in freshwater snails, and part of their lives in human bladders or intestines. A common indication of an infection is a localised itchy rash – where the parasites have burrowed through the skin – and later symptoms of a more advanced infection may include passing bloody urine. Bilharzia is readily treated by medication, and only serious if it remains untreated.

The only way to avoid infection completely is to stay away from any bodies of fresh water. More pragmatic advice is to avoid slow-moving or sluggish water, and ask local opinion on the bilharzia risk, as not all water is contaminated. Generally bilharzia snails do not inhabit fast-flowing water, and hence rivers are free of it. However, dams and standing water, especially in populated areas, are usually heavily contaminated. If you think you have been infected, don't worry about it – just get a test done on your return at least six weeks after your last possible exposure.

Avoiding bilharzia If you are bathing, swimming, paddling or wading in fresh water which you think may carry a bilharzia risk, try to get out of the water within ten minutes.

- Avoid bathing or paddling on shores within 200m of villages or places where people use the water a great deal, especially reedy shores or where there is lots of water weed.
- Dry off thoroughly with a towel; rub vigorously.
- If your bathing water comes from a risky source try to ensure that the water is taken from the lake in the early morning and stored snail-free, otherwise it should be filtered or Dettol or Cresol added.
- Bathing early in the morning is safer than bathing in the last half of the day.
- Cover yourself with DEET insect repellent before swimming: it may offer some protection.

Sexually transmitted diseases AIDS is spread in exactly the same way in Africa as it is at home, through body secretions, blood and blood products. The same goes for the dangerous hepatitis B. Both can be spread through sex.

Remember that the risks of sexually transmitted disease are high, whether you sleep with fellow travellers or locals. About 80% of HIV infections in British heterosexuals is acquired abroad. If you must indulge, use condoms or femidoms, which help reduce the risk of transmission. If you do have unprotected sex, visit a clinic as soon as possible; this should be within 24 hours, or no later than 72 hours, for post-exposure prophylaxis. And if you notice any genital ulcers or discharge, get treatment promptly.

Meningitis This is a particularly nasty disease as it can kill within hours of the first symptoms appearing. The telltale symptoms are a combination of a blinding headache (light sensitivity), a blotchy rash and a high fever. Immunisation (see page 81) protects against the most serious bacterial form of meningitis. Although other forms of meningitis (usually viral) exist, there are no vaccines for these. Local papers normally report localised outbreaks. A severe headache and fever should make you get to a doctor immediately. There are also other causes of headache and fever, one of which is typhoid, which occurs in travellers to Zanzibar. Seek medical help if you are ill for more than a few days.

Rabies Rabies is contracted when broken skin comes into contact with saliva from an infected animal. The disease is almost always fatal when fully developed, but fortunately there are excellent post-exposure vaccines. It is possible, albeit expensive, to be immunised against rabies before you travel. You are advised to take this if you intend working with animals or you are travelling for four weeks or more to remote areas. Rabies is rarely a problem for visitors, but the small risk is further minimised by avoiding small mammals. This is especially true of any animals acting strangely. Both mad dogs in town and friendly jackals in the bush should be given a very wide berth, as should ground squirrels.

If you are bitten, scratched or licked over an open wound, clean and disinfect the wound thoroughly by scrubbing it with soap under running water for five minutes, and then flood it with local spirit or diluted iodine. This helps stop the rabies virus entering the body and will guard against wound infections, including tetanus.

Seek help immediately, ideally within 24 hours, though it is never too late, as the incubation period for rabies can be very long. Those who have not been immunised will need a full course of injections. The vast majority of travel health advisors, including WHO, recommend rabies immunoglobulin (RIG), but this product is expensive (around US$800) and may be hard to come by – another reason why pre-exposure vaccination should be encouraged. Tell the doctor if you have had pre-exposure vaccine, as this should change the treatment you receive. The later stages of the disease are horrendous – spasms, personality changes and hydrophobia (fear of water). Death from rabies is probably one of the worst ways to go.

CRIME AND SAFETY

As in most countries, crime in these islands is gradually on the increase. Similarly, problems tend to occur more in the cities than in the rural areas. Perhaps inevitably, the juxtaposition of relatively wealthy tourists and a high density of relatively poor local people causes envy and leads to the occasional crime.

Zanzibar Town is notorious for opportunist pickpockets, and occasionally tourists do have bags and cameras snatched while walking around the narrow streets of the Old Town. (For more specific details on places to be careful, see *Chapter 6, Zanzibar Town*.) There have also been robberies on some of the beaches around Zanzibar Town; it is better not to go there alone, especially at night. The authors have yet to hear of any crime problems on Mafia Island – but then this is a small, rural island with a low population density.

You can reduce the chances of having anything stolen by not displaying your wealth. Don't bring valuable jewellery to these islands; leave it at home. Keep your valuables secure, out of sight and preferably back in the safe at your hotel. Keep most of your money there too, and do not peel off notes from a huge wad for every small purchase. Wandering around the town with a camera or personal stereo casually slung over your shoulder is insensitive and simply asking for trouble. A simple, dull-looking bag is much safer than something smart or fashionable.

Theft from hotel rooms is unusual. Most hotels have safes, where valuables can be stored, although reports of stuff disappearing from the safes of more basic budget hotels are not unknown. (For more details, see *Chapter 6, Zanzibar Town*, page 134.)

In contrast to the comments above, there have been several very serious incidents in recent years where an organised, armed gang attacks and robs a remote beach lodge or resort. These incidents are thankfully rare – but they do happen. In response, some of the more upmarket resorts now have armed security teams or armed policemen patrolling at night. Whist these cannot guarantee the safety of visitors, it does give some reassurance that such serious crime is being tackled by the Zanzibari police.

TERRORISM On 7 August 1998, al-Qaeda bombed the US embassies in Nairobi and Dar es Salaam; they killed about 224 people (of whom only 12 were Americans) and injured more than 5,000. Ever since then, some travellers have looked nervously towards east Africa, citing Islamic influences, porous borders, long coastlines, and a relative availability of arms as reasons to be wary of terrorism there.

The truth is that there are large Islamic communities on the islands, especially on Pemba and Zanzibar. These communities probably have their extremist elements, very much like the extremists who live in communities in the UK, Europe and the USA. So whilst Zanzibar (and, to a lesser extent, Pemba) has many factors which add up to the British Foreign and Commonwealth Office rating it as having a 'high threat from terrorism', at the time of writing nobody has been injured in any terrorist attacks there.

WHAT TO TAKE

CLOTHING You are unlikely to experience great extremes of temperature on Zanzibar, although days can be very warm and some nights chilly. Clothing should be light and loose-fitting for daytime, and you may need something slightly more substantial for evenings. Even in the dry seasons, a rain jacket is a good idea (though you may not need it). Umbrellas (should you need them) are available locally. You'll need a good pair of shoes for sightseeing, and a pair of sandals for relaxing. A hat to keep off sun and rain completes the outfit.

Plastic beach shoes, rafting sandals, or something similar to avoid the spiky sea-urchins, are useful for walking out into the sea across old coral beds. (Remember, though, never to tread on live coral. In a few seconds you can break off chunks which will take several decades to re-grow.)

Dress codes are very relaxed, even in the smartest hotels and restaurants, so you won't need black tie or ball gown. However, it's important to be sensitive towards local customs. When wandering around towns and villages you should be aware of local Muslim sensibilities: dress modestly and do not expose too much bare flesh. Remember that a woman walking around a Zanzibar town with bare shoulders and a short skirt, or a man without a shirt, is as unacceptable as someone parading naked in your local high street.

Of course, tourists don't need to don robes, veils and turbans, but around town it is important for women to have knees and shoulders covered. This is recommended for men, too. Therefore, for men and women, long trousers are better than shorts, although baggy surf-shorts or culottes are acceptable. Many women find skirts more comfortable than trousers. For men and women, long-sleeved shirts and blouses are better than vests and skimpy T-shirts. For the beach, normal swimming gear is fine, although going into local fishing villages in briefs or bikinis shows a complete lack of sensitivity.

EQUIPMENT If you're planning to base yourself in one place during your stay, or if your transfers are pre-arranged, then carrying your stuff in a suitcase or kitbag is absolutely fine. However, if you're likely to have to carry your own luggage, particularly if you're travelling around and visiting the islands as part of a longer trip, then it is usually easier to carry all your clothing and equipment in a rucksack.

Most rucksacks have internal frames, whilst some turn neatly into travel bags, with a zipped flap to enclose the straps and waist-belt. Both are fine, although if the straps can be zipped away then they are less likely to be damaged on bus roof-racks or airport carousels.

If you're staying in the cheaper hotels, sheets are not always very clean, so a light sheet sleeping bag is useful. It's unlikely you'll need a full sleeping bag; if you do hit the islands in a cold snap, most smaller hotels provide blankets. The better hotels and lodges have good facilities including towels and clean bed linen.

To avoid getting malaria, it is important to protect yourself from mosquitoes. Most hotels provide nets over the beds, but in the smaller cheaper hotels these are often in bad condition and riddled with holes. Either take your own mosquito net (visit a good camping shop before you travel), or take a needle and cotton to make running repairs. For added protection, bring a roll-on insect repellent and use mosquito coils (available locally) in your room at night. Remember: it takes only one mosquito to give you malaria.

Free-camping, outside an organised campsite, is illegal on the islands and there are no official campsites, so it is not worth bringing a tent. Fortunately, basic beach hotels and hostels can be very cheap.

All but the cheapest hotels provide towels. Personal items to bring include toiletries, lipsalve, sun protection cream and sunglasses. Soap, toothpaste and some medicines can be bought locally if you run out. Suncream is available in some hotel shops, but it's expensive, so it's advisable to bring all you need. Equally, condoms can be extremely difficult to buy on the islands, so bring your own supply if you are likely to need them.

A *kanga*, the traditional coloured wrap worn by local women, makes an ideal souvenir. You can wear it, use it as a beach mat on the coast or a sheet to cover bare mattresses if you're in cheap hotels, and then hang it on your wall, throw it over your sofa or turn it into cushion covers when you get home. A kanga normally comes as a large rectangle which the women then cut into two pieces, each about a metre square. One half is worn as a wrap-over skirt and the other is worn as a headscarf (a knot is usually tied in one corner and used for keeping money in). Prices for a kanga, from the market or a local cloth shop, start at about US$5.

On Zanzibar, and elsewhere on the coast, men traditionally wear a *kikoi*, a wrap-around 'kilt' of woven cotton, usually striped and thicker than a kanga. Once again, a kikoi also has many practical travel uses before you take it home to use as a seat cover. Prices start at US$8.

If you want to combine African and Western clothing, you could even have a local tailor make up a shirt or pair of baggy shorts from a kikoi. For more ideas see the excellent little book *101 Uses for a Kanga*, by David Bygott, available in Zanzibar bookshops.

You'll almost certainly bring a camera; make sure you bring spare batteries and enough film, if you use it (although basic print film can be bought in Zanzibar Town, and from some hotels and beach lodges). For more information on cameras and photography, see box, *Photographic tips*, pages 96–7.

A **first-aid and medical kit** is recommended, but what you need depends on your type of holiday, the amount of travel, and how far you plan to get off the beaten track. Whatever, you should include the basics:

* sticking plasters (some waterproof)
* antiseptic wipes and cream
* antihistamine tablets and cream (good for insect bites)
* tubigrip bandages
* aspirin or paracetamol
* anti-diarrhoea pills
* adequate supplies of any personal medication you may need

More elaborate medicines, if you need them, are available from the private hospitals in Zanzibar (see page 162). A few travellers also carry an 'anti-AIDS' kit (a pack of needles, syringes and other items which come into contact with blood) for use in an emergency. Your doctor or a vaccination centre can provide more information.

If you're staying in the smaller, cheaper hotels, the following items will be useful:

* **Torch/flashlight** Power cuts are frequent. Most of the larger hotels and more upmarket places have generators, but some do not; some places only have power for a few hours at night, if at all.
* **Water bottle and purification tablets** If you're heading into the most remote areas, then water supplies may not always be drinkable.
* **Universal sink plug** Plugs always seem to be missing from the more basic hotels.

Finally, if you're keen on snorkelling or diving, it is worth taking your own **mask, snorkel** and **fins**. Hiring these is usually easy and cheap, but hired kit often fits poorly, spoiling the whole experience.

Planning and Preparation **WHAT TO TAKE**

4

Ariadne Van Zandbergen

Zanzibar doesn't offer the possibilities for wildlife photography that exist on mainland Tanzania (although the red colobus monkeys at Jozani Forest can be an excellent subject), but the Swahili culture combined with the idyllic Indian Ocean beach scenes create some stunning photographic opportunities.

EQUIPMENT Although with some thought and an eye for composition you can take reasonable photos with a 'point-and-shoot' camera, you need an SLR camera if you are at all serious about photography. Modern SLRs tend to be very clever, with automatic programmes for almost every possible situation, but remember that these programmes are limited in the sense that the camera cannot think, but only make calculations. Every starting amateur photographer should read a photographic manual for beginners and get to grips with such basics as the relationship between aperture and shutter speed.

Always buy the best lens you can afford. The lens determines the quality of your photo more than the camera body. Fixed fast lenses are ideal, but very costly. A zoom lens makes it easier to change composition without changing lenses the whole time. If you carry only one lens, a 28–70mm (digital 17–55mm) or similar zoom should be ideal. For a second lens, a lightweight 80–200mm or 70–300mm (digital 55–200mm) or similar will be excellent for candid shots and varying your composition. Wildlife photography will be very frustrating if you don't have at least a 300mm lens. For a small loss of quality, tele-converters are a cheap and compact way to increase magnification: a 300 lens with a 1.4x converter becomes 420mm, and with a 2x it becomes 600mm. Note, however, that 1.4x and 2x tele-converters reduce the speed of your lens by 1.4 and 2 stops respectively.

For wildlife photography from a safari vehicle, a solid beanbag, which you can make yourself very cheaply, will be necessary to avoid blurred images, and is more useful than a tripod. A clamp with a tripod head screwed on to it can be attached to the vehicle as well. Modern dedicated flash units are easy to use; aside from the obvious need to flash when you photograph at night, you can improve a lot of photos in difficult 'high contrast' or very dull light with some fill-in flash. It pays to have a proper flash unit as opposed to a built-in camera flash.

DIGITAL/FILM Digital photography is now the preference of most amateur and professional photographers, with the resolution of digital cameras improving the whole time. For ordinary prints a six-megapixel camera is fine. For better results and the possibility to enlarge images and for professional reproduction, higher resolution is available up to 16 megapixels.

Memory space is important. The number of pictures you can fit on a memory card depends on the quality you choose. Calculate in advance how many pictures you can fit on a card and either take enough cards to last for your trip, or take a storage drive onto which you can download the content. A laptop gives the advantage that you can see your

$ MONEY AND BANKING

CURRENCY Tanzania's unit of currency, used throughout these islands, is the Tanzania shilling (TSh). However, as non-Tanzanians have to pay for some items, such as flights, ferry tickets and hotels, in foreign currency, the US dollar has effectively become an unofficial second currency. The prices of many other items, such as tours or rental cars, are also often quoted in dollars, although these may be paid in TSh at the current rate. Increasingly, all of the watersports and dive pictures properly at the end of each day and edit and delete rejects, but a storage device is lighter and less bulky. These drives come in different capacities up to 80GB.

Bear in mind that digital camera batteries, computers and other storage devices need charging, so make sure you have all the chargers, cables and converters with you. Most hotels have charging points, but do enquire about this in advance. When camping you might have to rely on charging from the car battery; a spare battery is invaluable.

If you are shooting film, 100 to 200 ISO print film and 50 to 100 ISO slide film are ideal. Low ISO film is slow but fine grained and gives the best colour saturation, but will need more light, so support in the form of a tripod or monopod is important. You can also bring a few 'fast' 400 ISO films for low-light situations where a tripod or flash is no option.

DUST AND HEAT Dust and heat are often a problem. Keep your equipment in a sealed bag, stow films in an airtight container (eg: a small cooler bag) and avoid exposing equipment and film to the sun. Digital cameras are prone to collecting dust particles on the sensor which results in spots on the image. The dirt mostly enters the camera when changing lenses, so be careful when doing this. To some extent photos can be 'cleaned' up afterwards in Photoshop, but this is time-consuming. You can have your camera sensor professionally cleaned, or you can do this yourself with special brushes and swabs made for the purpose, but note that touching the sensor might cause damage and should only be done with the greatest care.

LIGHT The most striking outdoor photographs are often taken during the hour or two of 'golden light' after dawn and before sunset. Shooting in low light may enforce the use of very low shutter speeds, in which case a tripod will be required to avoid camera shake.

With careful handling, side lighting and back lighting can produce stunning effects, especially in soft light and at sunrise or sunset. Generally, however, it is best to shoot with the sun behind you. When photographing animals or people in the harsh midday sun, images taken in light but even shade are likely to be more effective than those taken in direct sunlight or patchy shade, since the latter conditions create too much contrast.

PROTOCOL In some countries, it is unacceptable to photograph local people without permission, and many people will refuse to pose or will ask for a donation. In such circumstances, don't try to sneak photographs as you might get yourself into trouble. Even the most willing subject will often pose stiffly when a camera is pointed at them; relax them by making a joke, and take a few shots in quick succession to improve the odds of capturing a natural pose.

Ariadne Van Zandbergen is a professional travel and wildlife photographer specialising in Africa. She runs the Africa Image Library. For photo requests, visit www.africaimagelibrary.co.za or contact her on ariadne@hixnet.co.za.

operators on the islands are quoting prices in euros, and this trend may well spread to the hotels in years to come. (Although if the dollar starts to strengthen relative to the euro, then most will probably switch back to quoting in dollars again!)

Prices in TSh, and exchange rates against hard currencies, are likely to vary considerably in the future, but prices in US dollars tend to remain more constant. As much as is possible, we have tried to quote in US dollars in this book to allow for sensible cross-comparisons.

In November 2008, the rate of exchange was as follows:

£1 = TSh 1,840
US$1 = TSh 1,233
€1 = TSh 1,542

For visitors to the islands, the most convenient currency to use is US dollars. Ideally, it should be carried in cash, in a mix of high and low denominations; this is handy as it can be used almost anywhere. Although travellers' cheques are a more secure form of money to carry (as they can be replaced if stolen), here they attract very poor rates of exchange and are simply not accepted by some hotels. Hence unless you're bringing a great deal, cash is much easier to carry.

CHANGING MONEY On the islands, the easiest place to change money is Zanzibar Town, where there are banks and many bureaux de change (see *Chapter 6*, pages 159–60). It is also possible to change money in Chake Chake on Pemba (see page 315). Around Zanzibar Island, money can also be changed at most large and medium-sized hotels – although often the rates are poor. Several tour companies are also licensed to change money. For those travelling via Dar es Salaam Airport, there are a couple of convenient bureaux de change just outside the international terminal; the domestic terminal has no change facility.

Both banks and bureaux de change offer tourists free-floating market rates; there is no black market in currency in Tanzania. Generally, the banks offer better rates for travellers' cheques and the private bureaux offer better rates for cash, particularly for large denomination bills. The bureaux also tend to have a faster service. Banks and bureaux accept most foreign currencies, but staff are most familiar with US dollars and euros, and these get relatively better rates than other currencies.

Try not to change more than you will need into Tanzanian shillings (TSh); it can be difficult to get a good rate when changing this back. When calculating the amount of money you need to change into TSh, remember that under Tanzanian law, visitors from overseas must pay for many items, such as the larger hotels, car hire and air tickets, in foreign currency (usually US dollars). Most other large purchases, like boat trips and costly souvenirs, can also be paid for with US dollars.

CREDIT CARDS You can use your credit card (or debit card) at most larger souvenir shops, travel agents, and better hotels and lodges (even just to settle the bill for 'extras'); however, you may be charged as much as a 10–15% handling fee. This will seem unreasonable, until you talk to owners of businesses about their difficulties in dealing with the banks in Zanzibar, then you'll understand!

There are a couple of Automated Teller Machines (ATMs) in Stone Town, and we'd be surprised if these don't gradually multiply with time. In theory, drawing cash may also be possible through larger hotels or tour companies, but again, expect high commissions. (More information on using credit cards is given in *Payments and reservations*, page 101.) For Visa cardholders there's an assistance point at the office of Coastal Travels and Mtoni Marine, near the Serena Inn in Zanzibar Town. This is not a bank or bureau, though: it issues only relatively small amounts of cash against a card in cases of emergency, and the exchange rates are still poor compared with cash or travellers' cheques.

COSTS AND BUDGETING The cost of a visit to the islands depends very much on your standard of travel. Zanzibar Town has the most choice and, in many ways, the lowest prices for the quality that you get.

At the bottom end, the very cheapest hotels cost between US$10 and US$25 per person per night and will be extremely basic. If you have meals in local eating-houses and small restaurants (snacks US$2–3; curry US$4–5; grilled seafood

US$4–9; pizza US$5–8), supplemented by lunches of fruit and bread from the market, plus tea or soft drinks (US$1–3) or the occasional alcoholic sundowner (US$3–4), then your food and drink budget will be around US$15–20 a day.

Hotels in the expansive middle range cost between about US$75 and US$150 for a double, and meals in smarter restaurants cost the equivalent of around US$15 per person. Towards the top of the range, good-quality hotels are US$150–300 for a double, with meals in the best establishments from around US$25 per person.

Outside Zanzibar Town, most places are beach lodges. The cheapest of these, supplying little more than a (sometimes clean) room, will again be around US$20–30 per person per night. Pay between about US$40 and US$75 per person per night and you can find clean and pleasant places by the dozen. US$75–150 per person per night buys you somewhere smart – usually places that need booking in advance, whilst you can pay up to US$1,250 per person sharing for the exclusive delights of Mnemba – but then this is one of Africa's top lodges.

You also need to take into account the costs of getting around. Buses are very cheap, costing the equivalent of only a few dollars to cross the island. For independent travel, you can hire bicycles for around US$5 per day, motor-scooters for US$25 or cars from around US$40.

Organised tours of the spice plantations, Jozani Forest or boat trips out to the smaller islands start from about US$25 per person for a small group. If you want a vehicle or boat to yourself, this can go up to about US$75 for a day's outing. Snorkelling trips are around US$30 whilst a single dive to local reefs starts at US$35; both activities command a supplement if conducted on the reefs off Mnemba Island, which ranges from US$15 to US$60. PADI Open Water dive certification courses range from US$350 to US$600; centres are now obliged to sell the teaching material (around US$50) for these courses, but this is not always included in the price. Game-fishing trips are notoriously costly with a half day coming in at around US$500. Entry to most of the historical sites and ruins on the island is free, as is lying on the beach!

ACCOMMODATION

For visitors to Zanzibar, the accommodation and food available are amongst the most important aspects of a visit. This section describes briefly what you can expect, but these things do change with time and you should be ready for this.

Aside from style, throughout the guide, the accommodation listings have been sub-divided into six price brackets to help you choose something best suited to your budget. The price code is based on the cost of a standard double room.

Hotels offering full-board (FB) or all-inclusive stays have details of their rates at the time of going to print, to help with budget planning.

HOTELS AND GUESTHOUSES

Zanzibar Town At the upper end of the range, Zanzibar Town's only large, international-standard hotel is the Serena Inn, part of a chain with other properties in Tanzania and Kenya. Double rooms cost around US$265. There is currently nothing in Stone Town of the same quality and size, although several grand old buildings have been renovated and opened as smaller, boutique hotels. They combine good quality with local flavour

HOTEL PRICE CODES

Based on double room per night

Exclusive	♛	US$300
Luxury	$$$$$	US$200–300
Upmarket	$$$$	US$100–200
Mid range	$$$	US$50–100
Budget	$$	US$25–50
Shoestring	$	Below US$25

and often some style, although they lack some of the extensive facilities of the Serena. Prices range from US$125 to US$200 for a double room.

Zanzibar Town has a wide choice of mid-range hotels, costing between US$50 and US$120 for a double, where rooms are en suite, clean and comfortable, but are unlikely to be air conditioned.

At the lower end of the price range there are many small hotels and guesthouses which offer a basic room for US$10–20 per person. Rooms may not be spotless, and are not usually en suite, but these are generally popular with budget travellers.

All hotels in Zanzibar include breakfast in the room price, unless otherwise stated.

Zanzibar Island Around Zanzibar Island, away from Zanzibar Town, nearly all the hotels and guesthouses are built on, or very near, idyllic tropical beaches, complete with palm trees, white sand and warm blue waters. Some travellers come here for a couple of days, just to relax; others linger for weeks. Places to stay range from large hotels and resorts with many facilities, through small but comfortable lodges and bungalows, to very basic local-style guesthouses.

At the top end are a dozen or so fairly stylish, **smaller beach lodges** which cater to individual visitors, usually on pre-arranged trips. Typically they'll have between about ten and 30 rooms. Staying here you can expect good food, very comfortable accommodation and a fairly exclusive atmosphere. Expect to pay around US$75–150 per person per night for somewhere smart – or considerably more in the case of Mnemba.

Next there are a number of **large beach resorts**, with upwards of 50 rooms each. These are generally used by pre-booked package tourists who fly in and spend most or all of their time on Zanzibar within the resort. Some focus so clearly on packages bought overseas (typically in Italy) that their rates are in euros, and they do not even accept 'walk-in' guests.

At the **budget end of the market**, US$10–60 will give you a night at one of a diverse range of places. These have little in common except that they normally deal largely with walk-in guests. (At the better places, reservations are recommended during the busy season.) There's a huge choice, ranging from places that are aspiring to be the next exclusive beach lodge, down to basic bungalows beside a beach where even if you did succeed in reserving a room (if they had a phone, and if it was working), it would be a very unusual thing to do.

As the number of tourists visiting Zanzibar continues to grow, the number of places on Zanzibar's coast – and the range of places – increases also. Expect to find more new places when you arrive, and expect a few old places to have disappeared or been renamed.

Pemba and Mafia Visitor numbers to Pemba and Mafia are absolutely minuscule compared with Zanzibar; these islands therefore have far less choice than Zanzibar. Mafia's clutch of small beach lodges represent particularly good value if you value a fairly high degree of exclusivity, without wanting anything that is too luxurious or expensive. Pemba has only two real beach lodges, both very different.

SELF-CATERING Cooking for yourself is not common at all. A few budget hotels and guesthouses might allow you to use the kitchen, but this would be very unusual. For places that do allow self-catering, this is always noted in our listings. Perhaps the obvious candidates are Flame Tree Cottages and Mnarani Beach Cottages, both in Nungwi, the Zi Villa properties in Matemwe, or Kipepeo Lodge in Jambiani.

CAMPING Informal camping on Zanzibar is illegal and, as yet, there are no official campsites in the islands. Camping is permitted in the grounds of some budget hotels on the coast, but this is far from usual as the hotels are so cheap anyway.

PAYMENTS AND RESERVATIONS Officially, all non-Tanzanian visitors must pay hotel bills in foreign currency, usually US dollars, so all prices are quoted in this currency. Residents and citizens are sometimes charged lower rates (typically 50–80% of the visitor rate), and can usually pay in Tanzanian shillings (TSh). In many places foreigners can also pay in TSh – at the current rate of exchange so it makes no difference to the price – but dollars are usually easier to carry and deal with. Smaller hotels often accept only cash. Larger and smarter hotels (typically over the 'US$50 per night' bracket) will usually accept credit cards, and sometimes accept US dollar travellers' cheques – although many will add a surcharge of 5–15% for the privilege. To avoid surprises, always check a hotel's policy on payments before reserving a room.

Hotels and lodges which remain open during the low season (March to early June) often have substantially lower prices then. Conversely, many places will charge additional premiums (over and above their normal high-season rates) for accommodation over Christmas and the New Year. At any time of year, rates may be negotiable if you're in a small group (six people or more), or plan to stay for a long time (more than about five or six nights); this is especially true of the smaller, lower-budget lodges and hotels.

If you intend staying in budget hotels and lodges, then it is usually possible simply to arrive and get a room on the spot; there's normally lots of choice. However, the smartest hotels and lodges on these islands are generally the busiest, and for them advance reservations are always wise. Unless you book at least three to four months in advance, it can be difficult to secure consecutive free nights available at any of the island's top 15 or so beach lodges between July and October.

Communications by phone, fax and email are all possible, but allow between three and five weeks for a reply by normal mail!

✖ EATING AND DRINKING

RESTAURANTS In **Zanzibar Town** there are several good restaurants catering specifically for visitors, specialising in local dishes, seafood or curries; meals usually cost between US$7 and US$20 per person. There are also smarter restaurants, where prices are a little higher.

Zanzibar Town also has restaurants where meals and snacks are less elaborate and prices are around US$5. There are also some small eating-houses catering mainly for local people where you can eat for around US$2. They usually only have one or two types of food available, such as stew and rice, but they also serve chapattis, samosas and other snacks.

Outside Zanzibar Town, in the smaller towns and villages on Zanzibar, Pemba and Mafia, there are relatively few places to eat. Local people tend to eat in their own houses and there are not enough tourists around yet to create a substantial market for cafés and restaurants. On the coast, hotels and guesthouses usually have restaurants attached, where food and service generally

RESTAURANT PRICE CODES

Average price of main meal

Gastronomic	$$$$$	US$15+
Creative cooking	$$$$	US$10–15
Mid range	$$$	US$5–10
Cheap & cheerful	$$	US$3–5
Rock bottom	$	US$1–3

Between December and March is the main mango time on Zanzibar, and the markets are full of these tasty green-to-yellow fruits. From March to mid-June it's the wet season (*Masika*), when pineapples are plentiful, and July to September is when oranges are in abundance.

reflect the overall standard of the accommodation. A few small restaurants have opened by the most popular beaches, catering for the growing influx of visitors.

You have to try hard to really splash out on food in Zanzibar but throughout this book listed restaurants are accompanied with a price code to give an indication of expense.

CAFÉS AND BARS In Zanzibar Town, many places serve drinks as well as food, although at busy times you may be required to buy a meal rather than have a drink on its own. You can buy international and Tanzanian brands of fizzy drink, plus local and imported beers. Prices vary greatly according to where you drink: a bottle of Coke from a shop or small backstreet café costs US$0.50, and may cost four times this in a smarter café or restaurant. A bottle of local beer (including Safari, Tusker or Kilimanjaro) costs US$1.50 in a local bar, and at least double this in smarter places.

At larger hotels and restaurants in Zanzibar Town or on the coast you can also buy imported beers, wines (mostly from South Africa) and spirits.

SELF-CATERING If you plan to provide for yourself, in Zanzibar Town there are several shops selling locally produced bread and cakes, plus a reasonable choice of food in tins and packets imported from Kenya and beyond. Zanzibar Town has a market that's good for fruit and vegetables, plus fresh meat and fish if you have a means of cooking it. Other towns have small markets where you can buy meat, fish, fruit and vegetables, and shops with a limited but adequate supply of tinned food.

PUBLIC HOLIDAYS

The islands share most public holidays with the rest of Tanzania. Offices and businesses are usually closed on these days, although some tour companies remain open. Public holidays include:

12 January	Mapinduzi (Revolution) Day
26 April	Union Day
1 May	Workers' Day
7 July	Peasants' and Farmers' Day (called *Saba Saba* – Seven Seven)
9 December	Independence Day

Christmas Day, New Year's Day and Easter are also public holidays, although many tour companies stay open, and celebrations are low key on this largely Muslim island.

The Muslim feasts of Idd il Fitri – the end of Ramadan – and Idd il Maulidi (also called Maulidi ya Mfunguo Sita) – Muhammad's birthday – are celebrated by many people and are effectively public holidays. Dates of these holidays depend on the lunar calendar, and fall 11 or 12 days earlier every year. Approximate dates for Ramadan for the next few years are as follows:

2009	21 August–19 September
2010	11 August–8 September
2011	1 August–29 August

On Revolution Day (12 January), don't be surprised if you hear gunfire (live) from the army barracks or even heavy anti-aircraft artillery fire (also live) from warships moored off Zanzibar Town, particularly at night (when the tracer makes a nice arc through the sky). It's just the military celebrating – not another revolution!

WATERSPORTS

These islands have some superb destinations for divers, fishermen (and women) and watersports enthusiasts, and even if you're only a casual snorkeller or angler, there's plenty to attract you. Some diving and fishing companies are based in Zanzibar Town, but most operate from the coastal hotels around the islands. (For details on the best seasons for diving and fishing, see box, *Zanzibar diving and fishing seasons*, page 106.)

DIVING Diving is an important element of an increasing number of people's trips, so here are some general comments on the various areas for diving around the islands. See individual sections for more details.

Dive sites The seas around these islands offer some of the best diving conditions in the Indian Ocean. As well as coral reefs, the marine life is also a major attraction. All around the islands you'll find coral and colourful reef fish, while encounters with larger fish such as groupers, barracudas, sharks, rays and mantas, plus turtles, dolphins and even whales, are possible at the better dive sites.

Off the west coast of Zanzibar Island, and within easy reach of Zanzibar Town, are numerous small islands, sandbanks and reefs where divers can experience good corals with slopes and drop-offs. There are also some good sites for experienced divers, including a couple of wrecks. (There are no wrecks on the east coast.)

Off the north coast and northern part of the east coast are many more reefs. There's also Mnemba Island (sometimes more fancifully termed Mnemba Atoll). This tiny island stands on the edge of a much larger circular coral reef upon which you'll find some of the finest dive sites of this stretch of the east African coast. These days it is popular though, and so you'll find many dive boats floating above different sites on this reef; all come from around Nungwi and Zanzibar's northeast coast. Tumbatu Island also has some good reefs, used by one or two of the operations in Kendwa and Nungwi.

One long barrier reef runs along virtually the whole of the **east coast of Zanzibar Island**. Although this is seldom quite as colourful as the Mnemba reef, it does offer good variation between its different sites, and many are good. You are much more likely to be on your own here, especially towards the south, than anywhere around the northern tip of Zanzibar.

Southwest Zanzibar has long been ignored with few divers being able to dive here, but the relatively new dive centres at Fumba Beach Lodge (pages 301–2) and Unguja Lodge (page 289) are changing this. On the evidence so far, the diving here is a match for anywhere around Zanzibar, with the possible exception of some of the best Mnemba reefs. However, with usually no other divers or boats around, the whole experience here is arguably much better.

Pemba Island, and the numerous smaller islands nearby, has some spectacular diving spots. A number of Pemba's wall and drift dives are notable for variable and strong currents, and so are really more suitable for very experienced divers – hence the island is a favourite amongst live-aboard operations.

Mafia Island, by contrast, has a real mix. Inside Chole Bay is generally sheltered and shallow; an ideal place for novice divers to learn with some lovely, gentle diving. Outside the bay is more dramatic fare, capable of surprising even experienced divers with big ocean fish and breathtaking sights, including a particularly spectacular ocean-facing coral wall. The corals here probably aren't generally as lush as Mnemba's – but larger fish are much more common.

Dive companies The main diving seasons are outlined in the box, *Zanzibar diving and fishing* seasons, page 106, but it's worth noting that at any time of year the east coast areas are exposed to the Indian Ocean swell, while the west coast tends to be more sheltered.

The diving operators on the island are detailed within the individual chapters of this book, under the relevant area section. Prices for dives vary slightly between them, but of the main, and arguably best, centres, there is little between them. Pricing is increasingly in euros, with good reductions available for multi-dive packages.

Diving is a dangerous sport and some of the better operators will insist on divers doing a formal refresher course if they have not been underwater within the previous six months. Treat this as a valuable reintroduction, and a testament that the dive centre takes safety seriously; it's a sensible precaution.

Nearly all the dive centres on the islands are based at hotels and beach lodges, and can be contacted either directly or through the hotel/lodge. With the exception of Mnemba, you do not need to be staying at a hotel to use the dive centre facilities, although some places give a discount to guests. The individual dive operations are listed in the relevant areas in which they operate, but there are a few centres on Zanzibar Island (as well as on Pemba and Mafia) that are worthy of mention for appearing to us (we're divers, although we're not specialist dive-centre inspectors) to offer high-quality trips, and for displaying a responsible attitude towards safety.

On Zanzibar Island, listed clockwise by location from Zanzibar Town, our pick from the sub-aqua scene: the largest of the dive chains, **One Ocean** with centres in Stone Town as well as at Matemwe Beach Bungalows, Bluebay Beach Resort, Ocean Paradise and Unguja Resort; **Scuba Do Diving** in the heart of Kendwa beach; long-established **East Africa Diving & Watersport Centre** on Nungwi's West Beach; **Zanzibar Watersports** at Ras Nungwi Beach Hotel and Paradise Bungalows in Nungwi; **Mnemba Island Lodge Dive Centre** for guest use only; **Rising Sun Dive Centre** at Breezes Beach Club and Royal Zanzibar, with especially good underwater photography knowledge; and finally, a relative newcomer, **Fumba Beach Lodge Dive Centre** in the island's southwest.

Courses Most – but not all – of Zanzibar's dive operators are affiliated to PADI, and offer at least the introductory courses. Of these, the most popular is Discover Scuba which, for around $95 per person, incorporates a theory session, usually based in a pool, followed by a boat dive to around 40ft (12m). The course may be completed in half a day, but is sometimes spread out over a day with a break for lunch.

The first of PADI's certification courses is the Open Water, which includes tuition in both diving theory and practical skills, and four open-water dives. Prices for this start at around US$500, rising to over US$700. The equivalent Open Water referral (where the classroom element has been completed in advance) comes in at nearer US$400. PADI (*www.padi.com*) has recently introduced PADI eLearning, a new way in which prospective divers can take the Open Water course.

PADI International recognises that there can be issues with some unlicensed dive centres and instructors passing themselves off as registered centres, particularly in remote locations. Their advice to all divers is 'don't take anything at face value – certificates, flags and branding can be forged and obtained outside official channels'. In a bid to combat these unscrupulous operations and individuals, PADI has recently set up a searchable database of licensed members and resorts so that divers can access reliable, up-to-date information (*www.padi.com/english/common/search/dcnr*). It is equally possible to search by location for instructors and companies that are under investigation or have been suspended. It may be wise to check both before donning any sub-aqua kit.

With all dive centres, PADI registered or not, divers are well advised to talk with the staff (and management where possible) to ascertain their commitment to providing a quality service. Are they eager to listen? Do they understand the kind of dive experience sought? Are they willing, perhaps even eager, to prove their credentials? Are they willing to demonstrate the quality of their equipment before requiring a commitment to hire or dive with it? Can they demonstrate that the air in the cylinders is from a reputable source, and is recently certified as clean (air quality should be sampled and checked quarterly)? Is there a sense of pride among the staff that they are working for a trustworthy and reputable company?

There are many operations on Zanzibar, Pemba and Mafia offering safe, enjoyable diving, with well-maintained modern equipment, clean air and a keen eye on customer service, but asking questions and getting a feel for an operation is critical before taking the decision to venture underwater.

Applicants nominate a dive operator, then complete all the paperwork online while still at home. They then print out the results, and take them down to their chosen operator, who will conduct the practical part of the course, and pose an 18-question review. While costs are the same as for taking the course in the more traditional way, the benefits are significant in terms of convenience at home, as well as time saved when on holiday. Rates for the Advanced course, which incorporates five dives, are slightly lower than those for the Open Water, which is a prerequisite.

As a rule, all these 'entry' courses include equipment; for more advanced courses, equipment hire may incur an additional charge.

Nitrox diving is gaining popularity for the extended bottom time it can give at shallow depths. By adjusting the mix of air in a tank to 32/68 oxygen/nitrogen (the norm is 21/79), divers can dive to a maximum of 30m (100ft) but can stay at that depth for up to 30 minutes on a first dive. On 50/50 oxygen/nitrogen, divers are limited to 9–12m (30–40 ft) but bottom time is increased by up to 50%. Nitrox certification is offered by only a handful of companies on Zanzibar. It takes two days for an initial course, and costs around US$300.

SNORKELLING Most of the dive centres mentioned above will also cater for snorkellers, by hiring out snorkels and fins. You'll have to take a boat from virtually all the lodges and hotels throughout the islands in order to reach decent reefs for snorkelling. Some places will offer excursions of an hour, at other places snorkelling is a half-day trip and you'll share the boat with divers.

Off the west coast of Zanzibar Island, Chumbe Island stands out as having some of the best-preserved and most easily accessible coral in the region; it really is in pristine condition, outshining any of the coral gardens known elsewhere near the islands.

ZANZIBAR DIVING AND FISHING SEASONS

If you are coming to Zanzibar specifically for scuba diving, there are some points you need to know. Diving is possible at any time of year, and divers visit different parts of the archipelago according to conditions. Having said that, most people avoid the main rainy season from March/April to May, even though during this period there can be some very good days. The weather is especially changeable at this time, and in less than an hour can switch from beautifully calm and sunny conditions to a full-blown tropical rainstorm, reducing visibility on the surface to a few hundred metres and churning up the water.

Generally speaking, from June/July to October, when the winds come from the south, the northern coasts of Zanzibar Island and Pemba Island are better, although during August some days can offer perfect conditions, while on other days the sea may be rough. September to December is usually the calmest time, and from November to February/March, the southern coasts are preferred, as the winds come from the north. Pemba enjoys some of its best visibility of the year in February.

At any time of year the western sides are more sheltered, while the eastern sides (the ocean side) are more prone to swells and rough days. As in many other parts of the world, the weather and sea conditions on Zanzibar are unpredictable and there's always a chance of a bad day during the 'good' times, and perfect conditions at the heart of the 'bad' times.

If you're seriously into game fishing, the best time is from August to March, although conditions are also reasonable from July to September. August to November boasts excellent sport fishing for yellowfin tuna, sailfish and marlin. Marlin are even more prevalent between November and March during the billfish season, when striped marlin are positively prolific (schools of up to ten recorded) and blue and black marlin are common.

Off the northeast coast, the house reef close to the shore on the western side of Mnemba Island is used by many lodges from Nungwi and the northeast coast. Residents of Mnemba have the relaxing luxury of being able to walk into the water rather than sail for several hours to get there, but they share the same reef. Further south, on **Zanzibar's southeast coast**, snorkelling is along the main barrier reef.

The **southwest of Zanzibar** has been explored relatively little compared with most of Zanzibar's other areas, although it's perhaps worth noting that the team from Safari Blue (see pages 303–4) and Eco+Culture (see page 303) offer snorkelling on the tiny islands south of Fumba.

The place most often used for snorkelling off **Pemba** is known as Misali Island. After a speedboat ride here from Fundu Lagoon, you can snorkel from the beach (often while the boat takes divers elsewhere to dive). Live-aboards obviously have more scope, although they tend to concentrate on the diving rather than snorkelling.

From the lodges on **Mafia Island**, snorkelling is usually an hour or two's gentle dhow ride away. The reefs around the mouth of Chole Bay are interesting and quite tidal; the sandbanks exposed by the ocean around low tide are idyllic – magical empty places to laze around, beachcomb and snorkel from the beach.

FISHING The waters around Zanzibar and Pemba islands offer some of the best fishing in the world, especially the Pemba Channel, between Zanzibar and Pemba islands, or around Mafia Island, south of Zanzibar. Big-game fish include barracuda, kingfish, sailfish, billfish, wahoo, dorado and blue marlin.

Fishing companies There are several fishing companies based on Zanzibar: some are experienced and reputable, others seem less so. When making bookings or enquiries you should ask about the equipment they use: What type is it? How suitable is it for big-game fishing? How old is it? How often is it serviced? Ask about safety equipment too: Are the boats fitted with radios? Do they carry spare outboard motors, life jackets and so on? You may also feel it important to assess their 'catch and release' ethos; with numbers of big-game fish dwindling, 'catch and release' really should be the norm.

A few of the dive centres listed above can also organise fishing trips on request, or Mtoni Marine (pages 191–2) can also put you in touch with game-fishing operators on the north and east coasts. Serious game-fishermen may be best starting their enquiries with **Zanzibar Watersports**, **Fishing Zanzibar** and **Game Fish Lodge**, all in Nungwi (pages 217–18).

⛴ SHOPPING

If you're looking for souvenirs, collectables or gifts to take home, then the islands have a lot to offer. Most of the shops and stalls are in Zanzibar Town (see *Chapter 6, Shopping*, pages 155–9), but you can also buy things at many of the lodges and hotels elsewhere. The villages do not tend to have much in the way of curios visibly displayed as in other African countries.

Zanzibar Town market is particularly good for the aromatic spices that make Zanzibar so famous. Wander around the Old Town to find endless shops and stalls selling wooden carvings; paintings in the Tingatinga (see pages 42–3) style and others; jewellery in stone, gold and silver; models or mobiles made from coconut shells; and a plethora of other souvenirs. Carved boxes inlaid with shells, or decorated with hammered brass, are very popular.

Several curio shops sell antiques and original hand-crafted pieces; very many more sell genuine junk. Some antiques have been brought to the islands by Arab or Indian traders in the last couple of centuries; virtually all are now reproductions. The Zanzibar clocks, originally used by Zanzibari merchants, are unique. Carpets, rugs and mats, made in the Persian or Arab style, are easy to carry home. Traditional Zanzibar furniture, such as tables, beds and wardrobes decorated with stained glass and mirrors, can be found but these are less easy to get back!

Some shops still sell shells and coral, taken from the reefs and beaches around the islands. They wouldn't do this if thoughtless visitors didn't buy them. This trade encourages people to catch and collect live molluscs, and to break off live coral. Reefs take decades to grow, and if you buy these items, then you are helping to degrade, and eventually destroy, the islands' fascinating marine life.

You may also see turtle shells, or items made from turtle-shell such as bracelets or earrings. Again, turtles are an endangered species in Zanzibar and you should not buy these things. (For more details, see *Sea turtles*, pages 66–9.) Similarly, in this part of the world anything made from ivory is likely to have come from a poached elephant: avoid it. All of the above marine objects are illegal to export, so beware if you do try to take anything through the airport.

✉ MEDIA AND COMMUNICATIONS

MEDIA Unlike mainland Tanzania's vibrant media scene, Zanzibar's independent press has had a rough ride. In November 2003, *Dira*, the island's first post-revolution, independent newspaper, was forced to cease publication after the Zanzibar government alleged that it had violated registration procedures and professional ethics. The popular private paper had been previously almost bankrupted by a huge libel fine of TSh660 million (about US$500,000) following the publication of 'false and harmful' reports about the Zanzibar President's family: namely two articles that accused his children of using their father's influence to buy up state-owned companies.

Following this, a period ensued where, in spite of international pressure to allow free expression, the media scene was wholly government-run; private broadcasters and newspaper publishers were banned. Then, at the end of 2005, 13 new private publications were granted licences, including four newspapers: *Zanzibar Wiki Hii*, *Marhaba*, *ZIFF* and *Fahari*. However, it must be noted that their content is far from independent and impartial. State-operated TV Zanzibar and its radio counterpart, Voice of Tanzania-Zanzibar, still dominate, and continue to act as a channel for government opinion, with little, if any, room for political criticism of those in power. The current media environment may be private but it is far from independent.

International media rights organisation Reporters Without Borders, who campaign for global press freedom and the right to be informed, maintain that there is 'no press freedom in Zanzibar'. They note that: 'The government on the semi-autonomous island [of Zanzibar] often attacks the independent press, accusing it of being "a threat to national unity" at the first sign of criticism.'

However, many locals can in fact receive mainland (independent) broadcast channels and satellite television is increasingly widespread. The BBC World Service is also available on FM in both Zanzibar and Pemba.

Looking to the future, it is possible that the combination of allowing a private press to operate, and the creation of a revised Freedom of Information Act, will eventually lead to increased press freedom on the islands.

POST Most towns and large villages on these islands have post offices, but it's best to send all your mail from Zanzibar Town. The main poste restante service for Zanzibar is also in Zanzibar Town (see page 160). The post service is reliable, with letters taking about a week to ten days to reach destinations in Europe and North America (Australia takes a bit longer). Letters to destinations inside Tanzania cost about US$0.20, while postcards to countries outside Africa are about US$0.50 (slightly more for letters).

TELEPHONE AND FAX The best place on the islands for calling from a landline is the public call office, next to the old post office in Zanzibar Town. There are several private phone bureaux around here also. International calls to Europe or the USA cost between US$2.50 and US$5 per minute, depending on where you go. Note that most places charge per full minute; go over by one second and you might as well speak for the next 59. (More details are given in *Chapter 6, Zanzibar Town*, pages 160–1.) Elsewhere on the islands the better hotels and lodges will usually allow guests to make international calls, although rates are high.

There are now a handful of mobile phone (cell phone) networks and increasingly good signal coverage of the islands. These work around most larger towns and main arteries, and increasingly in more isolated spots too. You'll get a signal in most parts of Zanzibar Island; in the busier areas of Pemba Island and Mafia; and even in the lodges on Mafia Island, and the exclusive Mnemba Island.

If you're bringing a mobile phone from home, those with GSM capability should work here; check with your own service provider before you depart.

INTERNET Most of the phone bureaux in Zanzibar Town also offer internet services, and there are an ever-increasing number of dedicated internet bureaux. More details and specific locations are given in *Chapter 6, Zanzibar Town*, page 161.

ZANZIBAR TELECOMMUNICATIONS

Changes to telephone codes are a frequent occurrence in Tanzania, Zanzibar and the other archipelago islands. Every effort has been made to ensure this book is accurate; however, further numeric variations are inevitable in the future. The key dialling codes and most significant recent changes are detailed here.

CALLS TO ZANZIBAR The area code for all of Zanzibar (Zanzibar Island and Pemba Island) is 024, if you are calling from elsewhere in Tanzania, Kenya or Uganda. For calls from other countries, individual numbers must be prefixed with the international code for Tanzania +255, then 24 for Zanzibar (minus the first 0).

CALLS WITHIN ZANZIBAR Calling within Zanzibar, you simply dial the number you want, without the 024 area code. Some literature will be out of date, so note that individual numbers on Zanzibar Island and Pemba all changed in January 2000 – becoming six digits instead of five – and then altered again in 2002, when they increased to seven digits.

For emergency calls dial 112 (replacing 999), and for directory enquiries dial 118 (replacing 991).

CALLS FROM ZANZIBAR Phoning out of Zanzibar to mainland Tanzania, Kenya or Uganda you will need the city or area code (see changes below), followed by the individual number. For all other countries, it is necessary to dial the international access code (000), plus the country code (eg: 1 for USA, 44 for Britain, 27 for South Africa), followed by the city or area code (minus the first 0), then the individual number.

Area codes on the Tanzanian mainland that have changed include:

Area	Old code	New code	Area	Old code	New code
Dar es Salaam	051	022	Mtwara	059	023
Tanga	053	027	Dodoma	061	026
Arusha	057	027	Tabora	062	026
Kilimanjaro	055	027	Mwanza	068	028

MOBILE TELEPHONE NUMBERS Zanzibari mobile phones used to have six-digit numbers, but in 2006 this changed with the introduction of seven-digit numbers and new operator codes. The 'new' codes follow the pattern below ('x' indicates an additional digit), and are essential prefixes wherever you're phoning from.

Service provider	Old format	New format
Celtel	+255 748 000000	+255 78 000000x
Celtel	+255 749 000000	+255 78 000000x
MIC	+255 741 000000	+255 71 000000x
Vodacom	+255 744 000000	+255 74 000000x
Vodacom	+255 745 000000	+255 74 000000x
Zantel	+255 747 000000	+255 77 000000x

⏱ BUSINESS HOURS

Most shops and travel company offices in Zanzibar Town are open every day, although some close on Fridays, the Muslim holy day, or on Sundays, the official day off. Normal business hours are from between 08.00 and 09.00 until noon, then from 13.00 or 14.00 until 17.00 or 18.00. Some private shops and tour agencies take a longer break at midday and stay open later in the evening. In the low season, some souvenir shops stay closed, while others open mornings only. Government offices and banks are closed on Saturdays and Sundays; post offices are closed Saturday afternoons and Sundays. Opening hours on Pemba and Mafia are similar, but less predictable.

TRAVELLING RESPONSIBLY

CULTURAL ETIQUETTE

- Dress and act sensitively: locals consider revealing clothing or public displays of affection offensive. Keep swimwear for the beach, and in towns or villages keep your upper legs and shoulders covered. Sporting bare chests or bikini tops as you stroll around the market is the height of rudeness and arrogance.
- Support locally owned, small-scale shops and businesses. This is the best way for your money to benefit the grassroots economy.
- Buy locally made crafts, but avoid wildlife products, such as ivory, skins, coral, shells from turtles or any other kind of marine animal, and even wooden carvings, unless the material comes from a sustainable renewable source.
- Always ask permission before photographing local people. And accept refusals.
- Non-Muslims should not enter mosques without permission.
- During the holy month of Ramadan, local people fast, and you can show understanding for this tradition by not eating or drinking in public places. (Eating in tourist restaurants is fine.)

GIVING SOMETHING BACK Shopping in some of the fair-trade shops listed on pages 156–7, booking through an ethical tour operator, and donating money to lodge-sponsored community projects are all ways in which visitors to Zanzibar are able to actively contribute to the social and environmental development of the island and its poorest communities. For those who would like to take that a step further, we have listed a few local NGOs (Non-Governmental Organizations) on the island which seem to be doing excellent charity and development work, and very much need sustained support.

During our research, we visited and contacted a number of possible NGOs, but we know from experience that they're not always good at responding to enquiries – perhaps partly due to the pressures that they're under, and partly due to the limitations of their communications. A few stood out for not only doing some great work, but also for having a clear mission, good leadership and relatively easy communication channels. We have listed them here for travellers keen to 'give something back' in a real sense when they visit or return from a trip to Zanzibar.

Hands Across Borders Society (HABS) PO Box 210, Jambiani or c/o Dr Stan Marcus, 3831 Blenkinsop Rd, Victoria, BC V8P 3P6, Canada; ✆ +1 250 721 9009; e habszanzibar@yahoo.ca; www.handsacrossborderssociety.org. HABS was established in 1999 in British Columbia. Its main priority is to provide complementary health & education services to communities in need within the developing world, including from its excellent base in Jambiani on Zanzibar Island. In addition to providing complementary healthcare services &

education to the villagers at its Chiropractic Wellness Centre, HABS is also involved in assisting & funding a number of other village projects & amenities, with the most recent construction of the Jambiani Tourism Institute where they hope to train local people to help them secure employment in the burgeoning hotel scene.

Healthcare practitioners are welcome to volunteer here for placements of 1 month & over, financial contributions are gratefully received to fund everything from electricity to supplies, & unlike

STUFF YOUR RUCKSACK – AND MAKE A DIFFERENCE

www.stuffyourrucksack.com is a website set up by TV's Kate Humble which enables travellers to give direct help to small charities, schools or other organisations in the country they are visiting.   Maybe a local school needs books, a map or pencils, or an orphanage needs children's clothes or toys – all things that can easily be 'stuffed in a rucksack' before departure. The charities get exactly what they need and travellers have the chance to meet local people and see how and where their gifts will be used.

The website describes organisations that need your help and lists the items they most need. Check what's needed in Zanzibar, contact the organisation to say you're coming and bring not only the much-needed goods but an extra dimension to your travels and the knowledge that in a small way you have made a difference.

www.stuffyourrucksack.com
Responsible tourism in action

many charities, the Jambiani base is happy to receive material donations from walk-in visitors. The most useful supplies to donate are orthopaedic supports, straps, bandages, Deep Cold & antibiotic creams.

Health Improvement Project: Zanzibar (HIPZ) Rosehill, Broomfield, Bridgwater, Somerset TA5 2EL, England; ⚄ 01823 451 510; e team@makunduchi.com; www.makunduchiproject.com. Registered as a charity in 2006, HIPZ is an ambitious healthcare development scheme, being spearheaded by 2 British consultant surgeons. It aims to establish a unique public/private partnership with the Zanzibar Government to improve healthcare in Zanzibar, through fundraising & professional support. Their current flagship project is to renovate, equip & run the district hospital in Makunduchi (southern Zanzibar), where many of the 60,000 locals currently have little or no access to healthcare. Makunduchi Hospital is 1 of only 2 District Hospitals on Zanzibar, but its facilities have been neglected for years. HIPZ plans to build a new hospital, train local staff, provide medical & IT equipment, offer high standards of clinical care, & to expand medical services to include everything from A&E to maternity & dental care. The hope is that the hospital will become a model for the introduction of similar facilities across the island, & that a sustainable, locally managed facility can vastly improve access to high-quality community healthcare.

SOS Children's Village Zanzibar St Andrew's Hse, 59 St Andrew's St, Cambridge CB2 3BZ; ⚄ 01223 365589; e info@sos-uk.org.uk; www.soschildrensvillages.org.uk. The Zanzibar SOS Children's Village was built in 1988, in a residential district near the airport. 11 family houses are now home to 120 orphaned & abandoned children, providing them with a safe place to live, a 'mother', love & care. The construction of a nursery school, primary & secondary school, healthcare centre, sports fields & mosque, have led the village to become a real neighbourhood centre, serving the local community as well as the orphans. Away from the village, 3 youth houses are home to older children & young people taking their first steps towards independence. The orphanage is doing excellent work but it relies on the continued charity of many people: for financial donations to fund school books, desks, a generator, construction & renovation; gifts from footballs to pens; & child sponsorship. If you are interested in helping, they have a clear website which can accept donations & arrange child sponsorship. They're trying to provide as normal an environment as possible for their children & this understandably precludes impromptu visits from curious visitors, although existing sponsors are warmly welcomed.

Umoja wa Walemavu Zanzibar (UWZ) – Organisation of People with Disabilities in Zanzibar ⚄ 024 2233719; e uwz@zanzinet.com; www.uwz.or.tz. Established in 1985, UWZ is a cross-disability organisation operating on Pemba & Unguja (Zanzibar Island). Their aim is to assist disabled people within the community in practical ways as well as championing their human rights. The group's stated vision: a society in which people with disabilities have equal rights, opportunities, respect & dignity. They are actively involved in training on disabled rights, policy & legislation, in addition to community work to provide support, rehabilitation, skills training (eg: sign language) & education to people with disabilities & their local communities.

Zanzibar Action Project (ZAP) The Old Buck, Church Lane, Sedgeford, Norfolk PE36 5NA, UK; ℄ 01485 570905; e (via website); www.zanzibaraction.co.uk. ZAP is a small UK-based charity, run by its founders Pat & Janie Preece. Dividing their time between England & Zanzibar, their aim with ZAP is to work in close partnership with the local community to provide sustainable medical, educational & vocational aid, concentrating on the area around Jambiani. It's a very community-driven organisation striving to ensure over 80% of its funding goes directly to diverse projects in the village. Current ZAP projects include a scheme to provide basic drugs, equipment & healthcare education to the local government clinic; enabling volunteer teachers & retired doctors from the UK to work with the community on 3-month placements; running English, sewing & IT classes for women & teenagers; providing porridge for the nursery school; sponsoring vocational training for young people, & most recently securing a £5,000 grant to construct a much-needed concrete water tank.

Part Two

THE GUIDE

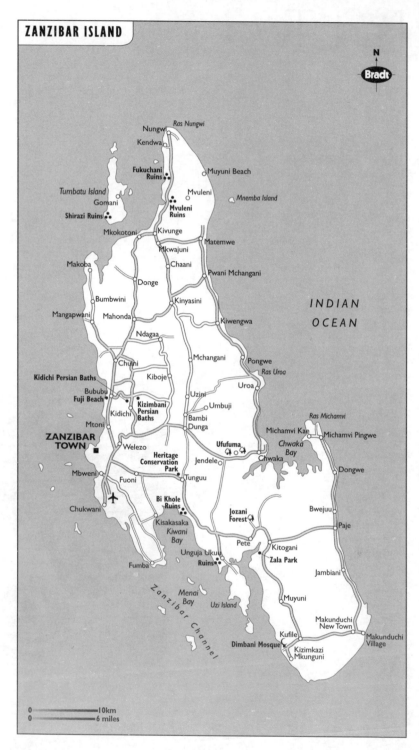

ZANZIBAR ISLAND

N

Bradt

Ras Nungwi

Nungwi
Kendwa

Fukuchani
Ruins

Muyuni Beach

Mvuleni

Mnemba Island

Tumbatu Island
Gomani

Mvuleni
Ruins

Shirazi Ruins

Mkokotoni
Kivunge

Matemwe

Mkwajuni

Makoba

Chaani

Pwani Mchangani

Donge

Bumbwini

Kinyasini

INDIAN
OCEAN

Mangapwani
Mahonda

Ndagaa

Kiwengwa

Chuini

Mchangani

Pongwe

Ras Uroa

Kidichi Persian Baths

Kiboje

Bububu
Fuji Beach

Kizimbani
Persian
Baths

Uroa

Uzini

Kidichi

Umbuji

Mtoni

Bambi
Dunga

ZANZIBAR
TOWN

Welezo

Ufufuma

Michamvi Kae

Ras Michamvi

Michamvi Pingwe

*Chwaka
Bay*

Heritage
Conservation
Park

Jendele

Chwaka

Dongwe

Mbweni

Fuoni

Tunguu

Chukwani

Bi Khole
Ruins

Bwejuu

Jozani
Forest

Paje

Kisakasaka
*Kiwani
Bay*

Pete

Kitogani

Fumba

Unguja Ukuu
Ruins

Zala Park

Jambiani

*Menai
Bay*

Uzi Island

Muyuni

Zanzibar Channel

Makunduchi
New Town

Kufile

Makunduchi
Village

Dimbani Mosque

Kizimkazi
Mkunguni

0 ————— 10km
0 ————— 6 miles

114

5

Zanzibar Island Essentials

GETTING TO ZANZIBAR

International flights to Tanzania are covered in *Chapter 4*, pages 78–80. From mainland Tanzania, there are two main ways of reaching Zanzibar: plane or boat.

The gruelling and slightly cheaper option is by sea, using one of several boat services that cross daily between Zanzibar and Dar es Salaam. However, the vast majority of people arrive by air on one of the many reasonably priced, direct daily flights from Dar es Salaam, Arusha or Kilimanjaro International Airport (the last named lies roughly midway along the 80km road connecting the towns of Arusha and Moshi). Light aircraft flights (often via Dar) also link Zanzibar to Pemba and Mafia, as well as the more popular national parks and game reserves in northern and southern Tanzania.

ZANZIBAR'S PORT AND AIRPORT Zanzibar's main port is beside Zanzibar Town; its airport is about 7km inland from the capital. The island's customs and immigration officials used to have a reputation for toughness and corruption; today they're by and large polite, if somewhat disorganised. In any case, most people arriving from Europe, Kenya or elsewhere will fly via Dar es Salaam and clear Tanzanian customs and immigration there.

If you are arriving or leaving Zanzibar on a large international flight (as is the case with most charters to Europe), then you may well be required to queue outside for some time under the beating African sun. Queues are long, slow and muddled, so come with a cool hat, some water and lots of patience.

If you have arranged a tailor-made trip with a good tour company, then they will usually arrange for a member of staff to guide you through the arrival and check-in process and will often help you to circumvent any long queues for charter planes.

BY AIR Dar es Salaam's domestic terminal is a short drive from the international terminal. If you already have a connection to Zanzibar booked then you will be met at the international terminal and transferred in a small minibus. If you haven't arranged anything, take a taxi for a few dollars. There is no bureau de change here, but a small souvenir shop has a good range of books. Here – and for all internal flights – you will be asked to pay a departure tax of US$6 – made up of US$5 'safety tax', and a further US$1 port tax.

Scheduled flights There are a number of scheduled flights from Dar es Salaam to Zanzibar, and although airfares vary slightly you'll be looking at around US$80 one-way from Dar es Salaam. Flights between Zanzibar and Pemba are US$105; Zanzibar and Mafia around US$160; Zanzibar to Selous are US$200; to Ruaha US$360; and up to Arusha (gateway to the parks of the northern circuit) US$250.

The main carriers on these routes are:

Air Tanzania (ATC) ATC Bldg, Ohio St, Dar es Salaam; ☎ 022 2118411/2; e bookings@ airtanzania.com; www.airtanzania.com. Flies daily between Dar es Salaam & Zanzibar, with same-day connection to flights to & from Johannesburg.

Coastal Aviation 107 Upanga Rd, Dar es Salaam; ☎ 022 2117959 or 022 2842700/1 (Dar Airport) or 024 2233112, m 0713 670815 (Zanzibar Airport); e safari@coastal.cc; www.coastal.cc. A reliable small operator with a good reputation & strong network of scheduled flights connecting Zanzibar daily to Dar es Salaam, Arusha, Tanga, Pemba, Selous Game Reserve, Ruaha National Park, Mwanza, Serengeti, Ngorongoro & Manyara. In addition to Dar, they have an office beside the Serena Hotel in Zanzibar's Kelele Sq.

Precision Air Flight Services Nyerere/Pugu Rd, Dar es Salaam; ☎ 022 2860701; m 0748 834800

(Dar) or ☎ 024 2234521 (Zanzibar); e pwznz@ precisionairtz.com/contactcentre@precisionairtz.com; www.precisionairtz.com. This company has a few daily flights between Zanzibar & Dar, as well as connections to several other destinations in east Africa. There is an office in Dar as well as the desk at the Mazsons Hotel in Zanzibar.

ZanAir Limited Main office: Malawi Rd, Zanzibar Town; ☎ 024 2233670/3768; branch office, Zanzibar Airport; ☎ 024 2233670; e reservations@ zanair.com; www.zanair.com. This is based on Zanzibar – with offices in Zanzibar Town & at the airport. There are 7 flights from Dar es Salaam to Zanzibar daily, & these usually tie in with the timetables of long-haul flights to/from Europe. There are also connecting flights to Selous, Arusha (7 per day) & Pemba (14 per day).

Private charter flights If you're in a hurry, or need to connect to another flight at a difficult time, then you can charter your own aircraft to get from Zanzibar to almost anywhere in east Africa. The charter planes are small, from three to eight seats, and best arranged well in advance. Private charters can be arranged with Precision, Coastal or ZanAir (listed above).

If you're on Zanzibar Island and need to fly to the mainland, more details on air services are given in *Chapter 6*, pages 115–16.

BY SEA Several large passenger ships run daily between Dar es Salaam, Zanzibar and Pemba, and – more rarely – to other points on the mainland. As the number of flights between Dar and Zanzibar has increased, and their airfares have become more competitive, the number of passenger boat services has declined.

Ships that are used by occasional tourists are listed below. In both Dar es Salaam and Zanzibar Town, all the ship booking offices are at the main passenger port, very near the city centre. Schedules and prices are chalked up on boards outside each office and you can easily buy tickets on the spot. Reservations are not essential but if at all possible you should buy a ticket in advance (a few hours to a couple of days) to make sure. Non-Tanzanians usually have to pay in US dollars and prices are quoted in this currency; Tanzanian residents enjoy cheaper rates, and can pay in Tanzanian shillings.

Note that all non-Tanzanian passengers leaving Dar must pay a port departure tax of US$5. The departure tax office is near the ship booking offices, and tickets are carefully checked before you board. Most of the shipping companies include this charge in the ticket price, so check very carefully whether this is included to avoid paying again unnecessarily at the port tax office.

In Zanzibar particularly, many touts and hustlers hang around the boat ticket offices, encouraging you to go to one company instead of another. This can be disconcerting, and as an alternative you can buy your ticket through one of the tour companies listed on pages 125–7. This will often save time and hassle, and it usually does not cost you any more money (the tour company gets a commission from the shipping company). Some tour companies do charge extra for this service, however, so check before you make arrangements. At Dar es Salaam, there are fewer hustlers, but still it's best to decline assistance politely.

BOAT TICKET SCAMS

Some shoestring travellers have been approached by baggage porters at the ferry port, and been tempted into buying ferry tickets at the (cheaper) residents' rate, rather than the foreigners' rate. The porter offers to buy the ticket for you, then accompanies you onto the boat, explaining to 'their friend' the ticket collector about your temporary residential status. Then, once you're on board, the porter asks for (or demands) a tip – which is often more than the foreigners' ticket price. If you resist, you get reported to the no-longer-friendly ticket collector, who demands that you pay a costly fine. Resist that, and they'll call the police, who will no doubt be keen to extract their own, even more costly, fine. So you end up paying the porter more than the normal ferry price, and feeling cheap and embarrassed into the bargain. Now it's our turn for a tip: always pay the correct fare.

Travellers at the port have also reported problems from over-zealous porters. If you drive into the port by taxi, you might want to ask your taxi driver to carry your bags for an extra tip, simply to avoid hassle.

Traditional dhows do still run between Dar es Salaam, Zanzibar and the ports along the Swahili coast, but – following a spate of incidents in which tourists drowned – the government has imposed strict safety standards on any dhows wanting to carry tourists. (They need to have radios, life jackets, and various other fairly standard pieces of marine safety equipment – which are notably lacking from most dhows!)

We advise strongly against travelling illegally on any dhow unless the captain is very clearly aware of these regulations, and working within them. Not only is it illegal, but many 'normal' working dhows are dangerously overloaded, and quite frightening and unpleasant vessels in which to cross a busy stretch of open ocean.

Passenger ships and ferries The main passenger ships used by visitors between Dar es Salaam and Zanzibar are:

Aziza I and Aziza II Pride of the fleet is *Aziza I*, which together with *Aziza II*, sails daily between Dar & Zanzibar, leaving at the same times as the MV *Flying Horse*. Going the other way it's an overnight trip. The journey time is 5–8hrs. *Fares: Dar–Zanzibar US$20, Zanzibar–Dar US$20, Zanzibar–Pemba US$20*

Fast Ferries (*Sea Express I* and *Sea Express II*) m 0754 278692 (Zanzibar), ◢ 022 2137049 (Dar); e fastferries@cats-net.com; www.fastferriestz.com. *Sea Express I* is a large hydrofoil, with a capacity of 150 passengers, which travels between Dar & Zanzibar once daily in each direction. The journey takes 2–2.5hrs. Departures from Dar are at midday, arriving Zanzibar around 14.30; departing Zanzibar at 16.00 to arrive back in Dar approximately 18.30. This boat looks significantly more attractive than some that ply the waters, though it is sometimes reported to be unsteady in rough seas, & seasick bags are not provided! There is limited deck space but comfortable airline-style seating is provided inside.

Sea Express II, the company's newest vessel, commenced operations between Dar, Zanzibar Island & Pemba in Nov 2005. Travelling in a circuit between the ports, it's worth checking locally for the current schedule. At the time of writing, Fast Ferries were departing Zanzibar at midday for the 3hr crossing to Pemba on Mon, Wed & Sat; for the return from Pemba to Zanzibar, boats were departing at 08.30 on Thu. Journeys from Dar to Zanzibar depart 07.30 & 09.00, arriving 2–3hrs later.

The office for Fast Ferries is on the right at the far end of the parade between the port gates & the water. One-way fares for non-residents: *Dar–Zanzibar US$40; Zanzibar–Pemba US$45; Dar–Pemba US$65; child fares reduced by 50% on the Dar–Zanzibar route*

Mapinduzi ◢ 024 2230302/2857. Zanzibar Shipping Corporation (ZSC), the state-owned line, runs the *Mapinduzi* ('Revolution'), an old cargo–passenger ship, between Dar & Zanzibar, & also between Zanzibar & Pemba, & Dar & Mtwara on the southern coast of mainland Tanzania. These services are used by local people because they are cheap, & some travellers on a tight budget also travel this way. Although the boats are slow, the cabins are quite airy & comfortable, & this is a pleasant way to travel if you're in no hurry. The official schedule follows a 2-week pattern, although it is notoriously unreliable. *Fares: on the deck, around US$5; shared cabin US$10; private cabin US$12*

Mega Speed Liners (MV Sepideh) m 0774 447333/0777 303308; **e** megaspeed@zanzinet.com. This nippy service run by Mega Speed Liners operates between Dar es Salaam & Zanzibar also continues on to Pemba, taking around 2hrs for each leg. On Mon, Thu & Sat, the ferry starts its circuit in Dar es Salaam at 07.15, arriving in Zanzibar around 09.00, before heading on to Pemba at 09.30. The boat then returns from Pemba to Zanzibar at 12.30, & back to Dar at 16.00. On Tue, Wed & Sun, the MV *Sepideh* departs Dar for Zanzibar at 07.30 & returns again at 16.00; Pemba boats depart Zanzibar at 10.00 & return at 12.30 on these days. There is no service to Pemba on Fri or Sun. The booking office is in a small booth to the left as you enter the port gates. *Fares: Zanzibar–Dar US$35; Zanzibar–Pemba US$44*

MV Flying Horse 022 2124507 (Dar); **m** 0784 472497/606177 (Zanzibar); **e** asc@raha.com. This large catamaran, run by the African Shipping Corporation, has a capacity of more than 400 passengers. The daytime service from Dar to Zanzibar departs at 12.30 daily & arrives at 15.30. The return trip from Zanzibar departs at 21.00 daily, but does not arrive in Dar until 06.00 the following day. The boat runs deliberately slowly, stopping at sea for a time, on this overnight journey so passengers don't have to disembark in the middle of the night. The seating areas have AC & an 'in-flight' video is usually shown. The ship also has a small bar & restaurant. It's possible to travel on the deck, which has a few seats & an awning to keep off the sun, but little else. Some travellers view this as a very pleasant way to travel, especially when leaving Zanzibar port at sunset, & for budget travellers it is a good way to save on a night's accommodation. In Zanzibar, the booking office is the first on the left inside the port gates. *Fares: US$20pp inc a mattress for overnight*

Sea Bus I and Sea Bus II 024 2231655 (Zanzibar)/022 2123324 (Dar); **m** 0777 334347; **e** azam@cats-net.com; www.azam-marine.com. Highly recommended, these are 2 large Australian-built high-speed boats, owned by Azam Marine both running once daily in either direction between Zanzibar & Dar es Salaam, taking about 2hrs to make the crossing. *Sea Bus I* departs from Dar at 10.30 & starts the return trip from Zanzibar at 13.00. *Sea Bus II* departs from Zanzibar at 10.00 & starts the return trip from Dar at 16.00. *Fares: first-class tickets US$40; second class US$35; children US$20*

Seagull Sea Transport 024 2236315 Another daily Dar connection, *Seagull* departs Dar at midday for a 3hr crossing to Zanzibar, though word on the street implies this boat more usually arrives between 17.00 & 19.00. It returns to Dar at 21.00, arriving at 06.00 the following morning, in similar vein to the MV *Flying Horse. Fares: US$20pp*

Sea Star Services Ltd 024 2234768; **m** 0777 411505. This large catamaran is also among the most efficient services between Dar es Salaam & Zanzibar. With a grand-looking green marble booking office at the port (relative to the beach hut-style office occupied by others), tickets can be bought for the once-daily departure to Dar es Salaam. *Sea Star* departs Zanzibar for Dar at 07.00 for a 2hr crossing. *Fares: first class US$35; second class US$45*

GETTING AROUND ZANZIBAR ISLAND

You can travel around Zanzibar Island in several different ways: by hire car, motorbike, scooter, bicycle, tourist minibus, *dala-dala*, bus, taxi, organised tour, walking, hitchhiking, or a combination of all of these. Outside Zanzibar Town, the main roads are often tarred, whilst the rest are dirt or graded gravel. All are highly variable in quality, from smooth, newly resurfaced tar to appallingly rutted gravel, where travel can be slow and uncomfortable. As in the rest of east and southern Africa, traffic drives on the left in Zanzibar. In many ways, the greatest risk on the road is the other drivers: be very aware.

HIRED VEHICLES

Car hire Car hire is possible on Zanzibar Island, although whether it's wise for most visitors is a real question. Driving standards are not good on the islands and roads are often in poor condition, so accidents are frequent. We do not recommend visitors to hire cars here, but if you choose to then exercise great caution. You should never drive at night; it can be exceedingly dangerous.

If you do want a car, it's probably best arranged through one of the tour companies (see *Tour companies*, pages 125–7). A few have their own vehicles, while others will make arrangements on your behalf. Rates vary but are generally between US$50 and US$60 per day for a small car (eg: a Suzuki 'jeep') and around US$100 per day for a larger car (eg: a Toyota Land Cruiser). However, quality is more variable than price, and standards on Zanzibar are often low; check your car very carefully for defects and even go for a short test drive before accepting it. The price usually includes unlimited distance, but you pay for the fuel.

Insurance is normally included in the rental, although some companies are vague about this. It's always important to check your exact legal position should you be unfortunate enough to have an accident involving another car or person. Get this in writing. A deposit and proof of identity are usually asked for. Make sure you have a valid International Driving Licence or local driving permit (see *Driving licences*, pages 122–3).

Motorbike and scooter hire It is possible to hire motorbikes (almost all are Honda 125cc or 250cc trail bikes or similar) or scooters (mostly Vespas and Piaggios) from many of the tour companies (see pages 125–7). Prices vary, but are generally around US$25–30 per day for a scooter, US$35–40 per day for a motorbike.

For a cheaper deal, try Nasor Aly Mussa's Scooter Service, usually shortened to Fundi Nasor, a small garage just off New Mkunazini Road in Zanzibar Town, near the Anglican Cathedral. As with cars, you should take your scooter for a test drive to make sure everything works before agreeing to hire.

Some tourists to Zanzibar hire scooters, imagining them to be similar to Greek island-style mopeds. However, scooters have larger engines and are harder to handle than mopeds, and there have been a number of accidents and injuries. You should not hire a scooter if you have never ridden one before; the dirt tracks and pot-holed roads of Zanzibar are not ideal places to start learning.

Check beforehand that your travel insurance policy covers you for using this type of transport, as not all do.

Bicycle hire For getting around Zanzibar Town, or going further afield around the island, fit and adventurous visitors will find bicycles ideal. Most bikes are heavy steel Chinese-built roadsters, so you shouldn't plan on covering too many miles (it's too hot to cycle fast anyway). You can also hire mountain bikes, but most of these are pretty basic all-steel models, and only slightly lighter than the Chinese roadsters. They do have gears though, which makes them easier to ride.

Bikes can be hired through several of the tour companies listed (see pages 125–7). Daily rates start at US$10 for the Chinese roadsters, and US$15 for mountain bikes. Take your bike for a short test ride before hiring to make sure everything works. Unless you plan extensive off-road forays, make sure your tyres are pumped up fairly hard, especially on the mountain bikes where semi-flat fat tyres can make for hard going. Your bike should come with a puncture outfit and pump, but if it doesn't these can be bought from the bicycle *fundi* (mechanic) in the market in Zanzibar Town.

Roads can be rough, but are generally flat, and traffic is very light once you get away from Zanzibar Town. If you get tired, you can put your bike on top of a bus or *dala-dala* and come home the easy way.

Keen cyclists might like to contact Mreh Tours (see page 126) – the only company as far as we know to offer specific cycle tours of Zanzibar.

Taxis The saloon car taxis which are available around Zanzibar Town can be hired to take you further afield, but some drivers do not like to go off the tar roads as the rocky dirt roads are liable to damage the undersides of their beloved vehicles (the minibuses have higher clearance, or at least the drivers seem not to worry).

A short ride through town will cost just over US$3, a trip further afield to Mbweni Ruins or Mtoni Marine Centre around US$7–10 (one-way), and an airport transfer to/from Zanzibar Town US$10–15. A taxi to Jozani Forest is US$20–25 one-way, or around US$30–35 return, possibly more if you plan to spend all day in the forest. To Nungwi or Bwejuu is around US$40–50 one-way. If you're going this far, then it's probably best to arrange for a proper minibus and guide to take you.

Tourist minibuses On Zanzibar Island, most travellers will get between Zanzibar Town and one of the beaches using a minibus. These can be arranged by the *papaasi* (touts) (see box, *Guides and the 'papaasi'*, page 132) who lurk at budget hotels looking for custom. A ride in one of these vehicles can cost as little as US$5, although often the *papaasi* will have their own favourite beach places, which pay them a commission for each visitor who stays; make sure you are very clear about your destination, the timings and the cost before getting on board.

If haggling with the *papaasi* is not for you, then most local travel agents can arrange a reliable private minibus from Zanzibar Town to any beach lodge for about US$50 per vehicle. For most people this is the preferred way to get around.

Alternatively, if you know which lodge you want to go to, call them and ask them to arrange a minibus for you; they will often do this through a reliable travel agent with whom they work and at a reasonable rate.

BUS TIMETABLE

The bus route numbers, destinations and frequencies are:

Route	To	Buses/day	First	Last
NORTH				
1	Mkokotoni (occasionally continuing to Nungwi)	15	05.30	20.00
2	Bumbwini and Makoba, via Mangapwani	3	05.30	18.00
14	Nungwi, via Mahonda, Kinyasini and Chaani	7	07.00	18.00
NORTHEAST				
6	Chwaka (some continue to Uroa and Pongwe)	5	07.00	16.00
13	Uroa	5	08.00	16.00
15	Kiwengwa	5	08.00	18.00
16	Matemwe	6	07.00	18.00
SOUTHEAST				
9	Paje, sometimes to Bwejuu and Jambiani	7	06.00	17.00
10	Makunduchi, via Tunguu, Pete and Munyuni	4	07.00	16.00
SOUTHWEST				
7	Fumba, via Kombeni	4	06.00	16.00
8	Unguja Ukuu	4	06.00	16.00
CENTRAL				
3	Kidichi and Kizimbani, via Welezo	7	06.00	18.00
4	Mchangani, via Dunga, Bambi and Uzini	5	06.00	17.00
5	Ndagaa, via Kiboje	4	06.00	16.00
11	Fuoni, via Tungu and Binguni	10	07.00	18.00
12	Dunga, then north to Bambi	5	07.00	17.00

DALA-DALA TIMETABLE

No	Departs	To	Buses/day	First	Last
AROUND ZNZ TOWN					
502	Darajani	Bububu, via Maruhubi and Mtoni	Lots	06.00	21.00
505	Darajani	Airport (U/Ndege)	Lots	06.00	21.00
510	Darajani	Mwana Kwerekwe (M/Kwerekwe)	Lots	06.00	21.00
511	Darajani	Kidichi Spice (K/Spice), via Kidichi Persian baths	Lots	06.00	21.00
NORTH					
101	Creek Road	Mkokotoni	15	05.30	21.00
102	Darajani	Bumbwini, via Mangapwani	5	10.00	16.00
116	Creek Road	Nungwi	25	05.30	21.00
121	Darajani	Donge and Mahonda	5	10.00	18.00
NORTHEAST					
117	Creek Road	Kiwengwa, some continue to Pwani Mchangani	9	06.00	19.00
118	Creek Road	Matemwe	10	06.00	19.00
206	Darajani or Mwembe Ladu	Chwaka, via Dunga Palace	10	06.00	18.00
209	Mwembe Ladu	Pongwe	3	07.00	16.00
214	Mwembe Ladu	Uroa, via Dunga Palace	7	06.00	18.00
SOUTHEAST					
309	Darajani or Mwana Kwerekwe	Jambiani, via Jozani	5	07.30	16.00
310	Darajani	Makunduchi, via Jozani	10	06.30	21.00
324	Darajani	Bwejuu, via Jozani, Paje & Kae Michamvi	Lots	09.00	14.00
SOUTHWEST					
308	Mwembe Ladu or Mwana Kwerekwe	Unguja Ukuu	4	08.00	15.00
336	Darajani or Mwana Kwerekwe	Kibondeni	Lots	06.00	20.00
326	Darajani or Mwana Kwerekwe	Kizimkazi, via Zala Park	5	07.00	16.00

If you have pre-arranged your trip, then you'll probably be met at the airport by a driver with a vehicle who will transfer you to your chosen lodge. Sometimes it's easy to incorporate a visit to a spice farm on the way, as part of these transfers.

PUBLIC TRANSPORT

Buses It is possible to reach many parts of Zanzibar Island by public bus, although few visitors use their services. (Most use tourist minibuses or *dala-dalas*.) All buses leave from Darajani Bus Station, on Creek Road in Zanzibar Town. Fares are very cheap: for example, it costs only a few dollars to travel half the length of the island between Zanzibar Town and Bwejuu. Note, however, that prices can rise suddenly if there is a fuel shortage.

On most routes, especially the longer ones, there is only one bus each day. They usually leave Zanzibar Town around midday to take people back to their villages after visiting the market. They reach their destinations in the evening, and 'sleep' there before returning to Zanzibar Town very early in the morning (between 02.00 and 04.00) in time for the start of that day's market. Some of the longer journeys can be very slow. For example, Zanzibar Town to Nungwi takes three to five hours, Zanzibar Town to Makunduchi between four and eight hours.

Buses do not always go to their final destination. For example, bus No 1 (the route for Nungwi) may only go as far as Mkokotoni. Therefore, always check that the bus is going to the destination you think it should be.

Some of the bus routes listed above are also covered by public minibuses or *dala-dalas*, which fill the gaps in the bus service 'timetables'. These are usually slightly more expensive than the buses, but also tend to be quicker.

Public minibuses and *dala-dalas* For independent travellers, local minibuses and small converted trucks called *dala-dalas* cover many routes around Zanzibar Island. On Pemba, minibuses and *dala-dalas* link Chake Chake to the towns of Wete and Mkoani, and also serve outlying villages. Minibuses and *dala-dalas* are faster than buses, and are gradually replacing them on the roads. Fares are cheap: typically about US$0.50 around Zanzibar Town and a few dollars to cross the island.

Buses and *dala-dalas* from outlying villages heading for Zanzibar Town tend to leave very early in the morning but, apart from that, there are no truly fixed timetables: most vehicles simply leave when they're full. At any bus or *dala-dala* station, don't expect an information board: you will need to ask around to find the transport you need. Be aware that the last buses to some coastal villages will leave Zanzibar Town by mid afternoon.

Dala-dala journeys are invariably an experience, with time to interact with local people, but comfort is limited. Seating is on hard timber benches along the sides of the vehicle, and it's quite likely that parcels and packages of all shapes and sizes will be packed in around you.

In spite of their erratic appearance, *dala-dalas* do have standardised route numbers, destinations and frequencies. There are three main terminals in Zanzibar Town: Darajani Bus Station on Creek Road (opposite the market), Mwembe Ladu and Mwana Kwerekwe. The latter two stations are a few kilometres from town and are best accessed by a short hop on a *dala-dala* from Darajani.

The most useful *dala-dala* routes and times are listed in the box on page 121; the name in brackets is the destination as written on the front of the vehicle.

Hitchhiking Hitching around Zanzibar Island is possible, but traffic can be light so you will need patience. However, a combination of public transport, walking and hitching is sometimes the only way to travel – and simply a matter of taking the first vehicle which will give you a lift. You should usually expect to pay a few dollars for a lift.

PRACTICALITIES
Driving licences Unlike mainland Tanzania, you need an International Driving Permit (IDP) or a 'local driving permit' to drive either cars or motorcycles legally on Zanzibar.

An IDP is easy to obtain from your national motoring association – eg: in Britain contact the AA (*www.theaa.com*), or the RAC (*www.rac.co.uk*), provided that you have a standard driving licence at home. If applying by post, the process takes time so order one well in advance of your trip. In the UK, it is also possible to apply for an IDP in person at major post offices.

The alternative is a local driving permit, which can be issued for you in Zanzibar. The rental company can usually organise this for you with minimal fuss for about US$10.

It is essential that you have either this or an IDP if you drive a car or a motorcycle on the islands; your own national driving licence is not enough. Enforcing this, the traffic police on Zanzibar routinely stop any tourist they see behind a wheel. (There are several checkpoints on the roads between Zanzibar Town and the north and east coasts.) If you do not have either an IDP or a local driving permit then you'll have repeatedly to pay small bribes or a heftier official fine.

Beware of eager tour companies who are keen to rent you a car and say that IDPs are not essential. Also watch out for a scam where local *papaasi* rent you a motorbike claiming that an IDP is not needed, before informing the police, who then find and fine you.

Petrol and diesel Petrol is available (usually, but not with total reliability) in Zanzibar Town, Kinyasini, Chwaka, on the road to Nungwi, and at Kitogani, near the junction where the road turns off to Paje.

Petrol costs are increasing on the island as in the rest of the world, with fuel roughly 50% more expensive than three years ago. Currently it's about US$1.70 per litre for petrol and diesel (TSh2,050 per litre for diesel; TSh1,990 for petrol). Occasional fuel shortages in outlying parts of the island mean it is generally worth filling up in Zanzibar Town, though in an emergency it is normally possible to locate 'black market' fuel at about 20% above the standard pump price.

Maps The most up-to-date area maps you will find are likely to be within this book. We spend a great deal of time plotting all of the listings and roads using GPS co-ordinates and tracks that we generate whilst researching. Many of the larger, more colourful maps available are sadly out of date as development on Zanzibar far outstrips the time between reprints. However, for those keen to get hold of some larger island maps than we are able to include here, there are a few possibilities.

A straightforward tourist map of Zanzibar Town and Zanzibar Island is available from the Zanzibar Tourist Corporation offices, and from some bookshops and hotels in the town. It costs around US$2. Better than this is the attractive hand-drawn map of Zanzibar Stone Town and Zanzibar Island produced by local artist Giovanni, which is widely available. The Zanzibar Island map on the reverse is at a scale of about 1:100,000. This is part of a wider series of maps, including many of the national parks and mountains of mainland Tanzania.

The *Gallery Map of Zanzibar* is available in the bookshop of the same name. The map of Zanzibar Island is not as easy to read as the Giovanni map, but the map of Stone Town is clear and useful.

A map called *Pemba: The Clove Island* is available in some book and gift shops, and is well researched, again at a scale of 1:100,000. There are two versions however: one from 1992, and a better one from 1995. The date is on the back cover.

Most commercially produced maps of Tanzania also include Zanzibar. One of the best is the *Tanzania Travellers Map* published by Macmillan, which shows the mainland at a scale of 1:2,000,000 and has more detailed maps of Zanzibar Island (1:500,000) and Pemba Island (1:830,000) on the back, although even these contain a few errors.

Good-quality maps of Zanzibar and Pemba islands (produced by the British Directorate of Overseas Surveys at scales of 1:50,000 and 1:10,000) are available in Zanzibar Town from the Map Office in the Commission of Lands and Planning, part of the Ministry of Environment, near the People's Bank of Zanzibar and the Fort. Maps cost about US$2.

ORGANISED TOURS

In Zanzibar Town, it seems that every other shop or office is a tour company, and it's always easy to find someone to arrange and organise tours within Zanzibar. The problem is finding a good tour company. This section is designed to help you locate something suitable for your needs and budget.

The most popular tours organised from Zanzibar Town are boat excursions to Prison Island and the trips around the plantations called 'spice tours' (see box, *Spices and spice tours*, pages 126–7). Most companies also arrange tours to Jozani-Chwaka Bay National Park to see the colobus monkeys (pages 294–8), trips to Kizimkazi to see the dolphins (page 292), and visits to old palaces and other ruins in the Zanzibar Town area (pages 179–96) or elsewhere on the island. You can also usually arrange transport to the beaches on the north or east coasts and other parts of Zanzibar with a tour company.

Many companies can also make hotel and ship reservations, flight bookings, car-hire arrangements, and so on. Check the arrangement before organising this: some make no charge for the service (instead getting commission from the transport company or hotel), whilst others charge a small fee. Watch out for those charging a hefty fee for the service, which can sometimes be no more than a couple of phone calls on your behalf.

Tour prices are usually quoted in US dollars (although they can be paid for in TSh or other currencies), and tend to vary considerably between the different companies. A lot depends on the quality you're looking for. At one end of the scale, budget outfits offer cheap and cheerful tours, where you'll be sharing a basic minibus or *dala-dala* with several other tourists, the quality or knowledge of your guide may be poor, and their social and environmental ethics highly questionable. At the other end of the scale, you can arrange a private tour for just a couple of people, in a good-quality vehicle, often with air conditioning, and a knowledgeable, responsible guide. Good companies can provide guides who speak English, French, German, Italian and some other languages.

This is not to knock the cheaper outfits: many tourists go on budget tours and have an excellent time. In the same way, some of the so-called upmarket companies may rest on their laurels a bit and not be up to scratch. It is therefore worth comparing a few tour companies before finally arranging your tour, and when comparing prices it is also very important to compare exactly what you get for your money. Your best source of recommendations (good or bad) is always other tourists and travellers, so talk to some of them if you can before signing up for anything. All the companies listed here have been recommended by the authors or readers of previous editions of this book.

To get an idea of prices, companies running tours which you share with (four–eight) other people offer the following rates:

City Tour	US$15–20	**Prison Island Tour**	US$20–25
Dolphin Tour	US$30–45	**Spice Tour**	US$20–25
Jozani Forest Tour	US$20–25		

All these rates are per person, but for the tour only, and do not include extras like entrance fees (ie: for the Palace Museum this is US$2, for Prison Island US$4, for Jozani Forest US$4).

If you want a private tour, with a mid-range or top-quality tour company, the rates are more likely to be around US$15–30 more expensive per person, for a minimum of two passengers, and usually include all entrance fees, although you should check this when booking or comparing prices.

While in Zanzibar you can also use tour companies to set you up with tours to Pemba, the Tanzanian mainland, Kenya and even further afield. In recent years there's been significant growth in the number of companies offering fly-in safaris to the national parks of Selous and Ruaha in southern Tanzania. Logistically it's easier to get there than to the northern parks of Serengeti and Ngorongoro, although many companies offer this option, too.

All tour companies have to be licensed by the government of Zanzibar and, if you have a reason to be dissatisfied, you can complain to the Ministry of Tourism who may take action against the company on your behalf. In reality, there's little control but it's still best to use only registered companies. If you decide to use unofficial operators, take care. We heard of a group of travellers who arranged things with a company which turned out to be bogus, and were then attacked and robbed when their minibus was on a remote stretch of road. The whole thing appeared to be a scam set up between the driver and the robbers, but don't let it worry you too much – it was an isolated event.

Most of the companies listed here can arrange tours on the spot (or with a day's notice), but you can also make prior arrangements by phoning, faxing or emailing in advance.

TOUR COMPANIES Recommended tour companies based in Zanzibar Town include the following (listed alphabetically):

Eco+Culture Tours ℡ 024 2233731; m 0777 410873; e ecoculture@gmx.net; www.ecoculture-zanzibar.org. Relatively new on the scene, this tour company (situated on Hurumzi St opposite 236 Hurumzi Hotel) is deliberately not trying to do what all the other companies do. For example, instead of the ubiquitous 'standard' spice tour, it takes guests to plantations & gardens guided by a local herbalist, & as well as a visit to Jozani Forest, walks in the community forest at Ufufuma are arranged. Well-guided, insightful village tours are another great option – a genuine opportunity to meet local people in the company of respected local guides. Trips are slightly more expensive than those arranged by some other tour companies but they are refreshingly different, ethically minded & very well guided. A percentage of all tour revenue is returned into funding solid community projects, telling of the organisation's origins as an NGO. Robert & Haji in the Zanzibar office are gentle & very friendly, & we highly recommend them as an island operator. See also page 285.
Fernandes Tours & Safaris ℡ 024 2230666; m 0777 413352/474344; e fts@zanlink.com; www.fernandestoursznz.com. This small, friendly & well-connected company on Vuga Rd used to work mainly with incoming tour groups from Britain, South Africa & elsewhere, but is now branching out to provide good-quality tailor-made trips around Zanzibar for groups & individuals in the mid-range price bracket. You can arrange things on the spot, or in advance.
Fisherman Tours & Travel ℡ 024 2238791/2; m 0777 440044/441144/412677; e reservations@fishermantours.com;

www.fishermantours.com. This well-established & experienced company on Vuga Rd has skilled & efficient staff, & caters for overseas tour groups, as well as individuals & small parties, offering a complete guide & escort service. They have their own fleet of vehicles, & most drivers are equipped with mobile phones. Other services include the organisation of wildlife safaris on mainland Tanzania, as well as the usual tours around Zanzibar, plus car hire, hotel bookings, ground transfers & so on. In the past, Fisherman Tours received quality awards from business organisations in Europe & America, & do (fairly) consistently deliver a good service. The office is near Air Tanzania & they have full credit-card facilities.
Gallery Tours & Safaris ℡ 024 2232088; m 0777 853824; e info@gallerytours.net; www.gallerytours.net. In 2007, Gallery Tours & Safaris was opened by local businessman Javed Jafferji, owner of Gallery Bookshop & author of several coffee-table books on the Swahili coast. Positioned as a high-end tour operation, it is hoping to raise the standard of guiding, vehicles & customer service found amongst the ground handlers. Catering for both groups & individuals, the team here is geared up to deal with everything from standard spice tours to weddings.

In conjunction with Zanzibar Serena Inn, Gallery Tours also owns The Original Dhow Safaris company. Its fleet of 3 traditional dhows depart every sundown from the Serena Hotel for a luxury sundowner trip, complete with a well-stocked bar & tasty canapés. This trip must be booked at least 1 full day in advance & is highly recommended as a pre-dinner holiday treat.

Madeira Tours & Safaris PO Box 251, Zanzibar; 024 2230406; m 0744 297486; e madeira@ zanlink.com/madeira@zanzinet.com. All the usual tours are offered by this switched-on & efficient company situated opposite Baghani House & Dhow Palace Hotel, plus air ticket reservations, safaris on the mainland, & car, motorbike & bicycle hire.

Mreh Tours 024 2233476; e mrehtours@ zanzinet.com. This company offers all the usual tours, & is especially keen on bicycle hire & tours by bike. One itinerary is a 9-day cycling trip around the island (no doddle even on Zanzibar's flat roads, as the bikes are the traditional steel Chinese models, not tip-top lightweight jobs), though shorter, more manageable variations are possible. Costs are around US$50 a day including bike, food, drink & back-up vehicle. Basically, if you have the slightest interest in cycling, call in at their office on Baghani St, near the Chavda Hotel, & discuss the options with Saleh Mreh Salum, the energetic & friendly owner.

Sama Tours m 0713 608576/0777 430385; e samatours@zitec.org; www.samatours.com. As well as spice tours, boat trips & all the usual services, the friendly & helpful team at Sama Tours on Gizenga St (behind the House of Wonders) arranges cultural tours, giving visitors an opportunity to meet local people:

recommended by clients as a great opportunity for photos. Guides speak English, French, German & Italian. Sama Tours also offers 'special' spice tours, organised by one of the knowledgeable, multi-lingual owners, Salim Abdullah. Sama Tours caters for both groups (anything from cruise ships to overland trucks) & individuals seeking tailor-made tours, airport & port collection, hotels, excursions, transfers, car hire, & so on. Prices depend on the length of the tour, the services required & the number in the group.

Sun N Fun Safaris 024 2237381/7665; m 0741 600206; e zanzibarsun@hotmail.com. In the same building on the waterfront as Sea View Indian Restaurant, & with the same enthusiastic management, this company can set you up with absolutely anything, usually at a very reasonable price. It runs tours of Zanzibar Town & the island, provides transfer services to the airport or east coast, & can help with general tourist information on the island & beyond. It can also assist with visas, car & bike hire, boat trips, flight tickets & bus tickets, in Zanzibar & on the mainland. The office sells postcards, stamps (it has a mailbox), maps & souvenirs of the 'I love Zanzibar' variety.

Suna Tours 024 2237344. Suna is run by the formidable Naila Majid Jiddawi, a former Zanzibari MP & bastion of Zanzibar tourism promotion. The

SPICES AND SPICE TOURS

Gemma Pitcher

Sooner or later every visitor to Zanzibar Island (Unguja) will be offered a 'spice tour' – a trip to the farmlands just outside Stone Town to see aromatic plants and herbs growing wild or cultivated in kitchen gardens. Even if you decline a tour, the array of spices on offer in the souvenir shops or heaped in baskets in the local markets will tell you that spice is central to Zanzibar's history and economy.

The history of spices in Zanzibar begins early in the 16th century, when the 'spice race' between the major European powers to control the lucrative trading routes to the Far East was at its height. Portuguese traders gained a toe-hold on Zanzibar as part of their plan to rule the coast of east Africa and imported various plants, including spices, from their colonies in South America and India. Some land was cleared for plantations, but the Portuguese never really developed their presence on Zanzibar beyond a military one.

It was left to the Omani Arabs, who ruled Zanzibar from the early 19th century, to develop Zanzibar economically as a spice-producing entity. Sultan Seyyid Said, the first Omani sultan to govern Zanzibar, quickly realised the potential of his new dominion, with its hot climate and regular rainfall, as a location for spice farming. With the demise of the slave trade in the late 19th century, spices became Zanzibar's main source of income.

When the era of the sultans ended and the long arm of the British Empire reached Zanzibar, the island's new colonial administrators encouraged the farming of spices and other useful plants, bringing European scientists to establish experimental agricultural company represents some mid-range hotels on the east coast & can assist with reservations for any other hotel on the coast, as well as arranging transport, good-quality spice tours & trips to the islands. The company office is in a small white building at the end of Forodhani Gardens, near the Arab Fort, & the staff here are very happy to provide general tourist information, even if you don't take one of their tours.

Tropical Tours ☎ 024 2230868; m 0777 413454; e tropicalts@hotmail.com. From a small but highly efficient office, this straightforward & friendly budget company has been recommended by several travellers, & offers the usual range of tours (a spice tour, dolphins, Jozani Forest, Nungwi & Prison Island trips), plus car hire, & ferry & air ticket reservations. It's on Kenyatta Rd, opposite Mazsons Hotel.

ZanTours ☎ 024 2233042/3116; m 0777 417279; e zantoursinfo@zitec.org; www.zantours.com. This company confidently entered the tourist scene in 1997 & is now the largest operator on Zanzibar. It has a large office in the Malindi area, efficient staff, a fleet of clean vehicles & an impressive range of tours, transfers, excursions & safaris. They cater for groups of any size (from several hundred to just a few) including individuals wanting tailor-made services. You can walk in & they'll set something up on the spot, although most of their clients arrange things in advance by email. ZanTours is closely allied to ZanAir (see page 116) & some tours utilise their fleet of planes. One of their most popular tours is a short fly-in excursion from Zanzibar direct to the Selous National Park in southern Tanzania, which many other agents sell. (For more details see *Chapter 14*, page 262.)

Zanzibar Excursions ☎/f 024 2237281; m 0777 433036/0713 591064; e info@ zanzibarexcursions.com; www.zanzibarexcursions.com. Situated in the Old Fort, this responsive & long-serving company offers a wide selection of tours around the island, as well as organising vehicle hire, transfers, hotel reservations, air tickets, & safaris to the mainland.

Zenith Tours ☎ 024 2232320; m 0777 413084/0774 413084; e info@zenithtours.com; www.zenithtours.com. This very professional & efficient organisation, situated behind the Old Fort, offers transfers, accommodation & excursions in the mid-range price bracket, including safaris to the mainland. They are also linked to World Unite, a German-based international volunteering organisation, & have an office in Dar es Salaam in the Clocktower Bldg on Uhuru St. Their website details tour & travel information in 4 European languages for those wishing to plan in advance.

stations and government farms such as those at Kizimbani and Kindichi. Today these areas still contain spice plantations controlled by the modern Tanzanian government.

But spices in Zanzibar today are by no means simply the preserve of governments keen to produce cash-rich export products or a useful tourist attraction. For the ordinary people of Zanzibar, spices and useful plants are a vital part of everyday life and a rich element in the island's strong and vibrant culture. The spices grown in village kitchen-gardens give their flavour to the distinctive cuisine of Zanzibar, provide innumerable cures for everyday ailments, and yield the dyes and cosmetic products needed to celebrate weddings and festivals.

A spice tour is probably the best way of seeing the countryside around Stone Town and meeting rural communities. Guides take you on a walking tour of the villages and plantations at Kizimbani or Kindichi, picking bunches of leaves, fruit and twigs from bushes and inviting you to smell or taste them to guess what they are. Pretty much all the ingredients of the average kitchen spice rack are represented – cinnamon, turmeric, ginger, garlic, chillies, black pepper, nutmeg and vanilla among many others. Local children follow you all the way round, making baskets of palm leaves and filling them with flowers to give to you. At lunchtime, you'll stop in a local house for a meal of pilau rice and curry, followed by sweet Arabic coffee and perhaps a slice of lemongrass cake. Many spice tours include a visit to the Persian baths built by Sultan Said for his harem, and stop at Fuji or Mangapwani beaches just outside Stone Town for a swim on the way back.

All in all, even if horticulture isn't one of your interests, a spice tour is still an excellent way of gaining an insight into one of the most important aspects of rural life in Zanzibar.

INDEPENDENT GUIDES If you prefer not to use a tour company, it is possible to arrange a tour of the spice plantations, a boat trip to the islands or transport to the east coast with an independent guide. Many double as taxi drivers; in fact many are taxi drivers first, and guides second. One driver, a Mr Mitu, has been doing these tours for many years and has been recommended by many visitors, although sometimes he subcontracts work to other drivers. These days he's so popular that instead of Mr Mitu in his taxi you might find yourself joining a large group touring the island in a fleet of minibuses. He's even got his own office (↘ *024 2234636;* m *0777 418098*) – a tiny room tucked away behind the old Ciné Afrique with the walls covered in photos. Mr Mitu's tours leave from outside the Ciné Afrique every morning at 09.30, returning about 15.00, cost around US$15 per person and are still highly recommended by those who have been.

There are several other taxi drivers who also organise their own spice tours. Most will undercut the tour companies (about US$35 for the car seems average), although you may not get the same degree of information that you'd get with a specialist guide.

You are almost certain to meet some of the local independent 'guides' who are in fact just hustlers (see box, *Guides and the 'papaasi'*, page 132) who tout for business outside hotels and restaurants, or along the streets of Stone Town. For spice tours, *papaasi* prices are often cheaper than those offered by regular companies; but the tours are usually shorter, the vehicles out of condition, and without a proper guide, which usually makes the whole thing pointless unless you are a fairly skilled botanist.

For short boat trips, it doesn't usually make much difference if you go with the *papaasi* or a regular company, although if you deal with the *papaasi* be aware that safety equipment is likely to be inadequate, if available at all, and if things go wrong, it is very difficult to complain or get your money back.

6

Zanzibar Town

> The streets are, as they should be under such a sky, deep and winding alleys, hardly twenty feet broad, and travellers compare them to the threads of a tangled skein.
>
> Richard Burton, British explorer (1857)

Zanzibar Town, sometimes called Zanzibar City, is situated about halfway along the west coast of Zanzibar Island. It has a population estimated at 205,870 in the 2002 national census, which makes it by far the largest settlement on the Zanzibar Archipelago, and the sixth largest in Tanzania. During the colonial period, before the development of towns such as Dar es Salaam, Nairobi and Mombasa, Zanzibar Town was the largest settlement in the whole of east Africa.

Zanzibar Town is divided into two sections by Creek Road, though the creek itself has now been reclaimed. On the west side is the 'heart' of Zanzibar Town: the evocative old quarter, usually called Stone Town. This is the more interesting section for visitors: many of the buildings here were constructed during the 19th century (although some date from before this time), when Zanzibar was a major trading centre and at the height of its power. The trade created wealth which in turn led to the construction of palaces, mosques and many fine houses. Discovering the architectural gems hidden along the tortuous maze of narrow streets and alleyways that wind through Stone Town is part of the island's magic and mystery for many visitors. Aside from the souvenir Tingatinga paintings and beaded jewellery, it's a scene virtually unchanged since the mid 19th century, when it was described by Burton in this chapter's epigraph.

On the east side of Creek Road is Michenzani, or the 'New City', though this part of town used to be called Ng'ambo (literally 'the other side') and is still often referred to by its unofficial name. It's a sprawling area of mainly single-storey houses, local shops and offices, covering a much wider area than Stone Town. This used to be where the poorer African and Swahili people lived, while wealthier Arabs, Indians and Europeans lived in Stone Town. To a large extent this rich–poor division still exists today. Some attempt has been made to 'modernise' this area: at the centre of Michenzani are some dreary, uninviting blocks of flats (apartment buildings) which were built in the late 1960s by East German engineers as part of an international aid scheme. Few visitors go to this eastern part of Zanzibar Town, as there is little in the way of 'sights', though a visit here certainly helps to broaden your understanding: you'll realise that beside Stone Town is a city where thousands of real people live and work in less exotic, but no less authentic, surroundings.

The best way to explore Stone Town is on foot, but the maze of lanes and alleys can be very disorientating. To help you get your bearings, it is useful to think of Stone Town as a triangle, bounded on two sides by sea, and along the third by Creek Road (see map, *Zanzibar Stone Town*, pages 130–1). If you get lost, it is always possible to aim in one direction until you reach the outer edge of the town where you should find a landmark.

ZANZIBAR STONE TOWN
Landmarks, Travel & Transport, Shops & Services

Old Dhow Harbour

New Port ships to Dar es Salaam

Bwawani Marsh

KEY
one-way street
Road viable by car
Other roads
Built up area
Parks
Marshland
For Accommodation, Restaurants, Bars & Cafés see pages 136–7

Main road northwards out of town to Livingstone House, Mtoni, Maruhubi Palace & Bububu

to Michenzani Flats, Amaani Stadium & east coast

MALAWI ROAD

small boats to islands

MALINDI STREET

ZANZIBAR NEW TOWN (NG'AMBO)

FORODHANI ROAD

MIZINGANI ROAD

KIPONDA STREET

HURUMZI STREET

CHANGA BAZAAR

Forodhani Gardens

small boats to islands

THARIA STREET

GIZENGA ST

CATHEDRAL STREET

SULTAN AHMED MUGHEIRI RD

NEW MKUNAZINI RD

KARUME ROAD

Jamhuri Gardens

KENYATTA ROAD

SHANGANI RD

BAGHANI STREET

SOKO MOHOGO STREET

MKUNAZINI STREET

CREEK ROAD

VUGA ROAD

VICTORIA RD

KAUNDA ROAD

People's Gardens (Victoria Gardens)

MAPINDUZI ROAD

Mnazi Mmoja Sports Ground

N
Bradt

0 ——————— 300m
0 ——————— 300yds

Mbweni Ruins Hotel, Island View Hotel, Airport

130

KEY TO ZANZIBAR STONE TOWN
Landmarks, Travel & Transport, Shops & Services

LANDMARKS & ATTRACTIONS
A   Clove Distillery
B   Fish Market
C   Port Gates
D   Ciné Afrique (closed)
E   Old Dispensary
      (Stone Town Cultural Centre)
F   Ijumaa Mosque
G   The Big Tree
H   Old Customs House
I   Palace Museum
J   Aga Khan Mosque
K   Hindu Temple
L   House of Wonders
M   Old Arab Fort
N   Orphanage
O   Anglican Cathedral
P   Hamamni Baths
Q   Old British Embassay
R   St Joseph's Catholic Cathedral
S   Mrembo Traditional Spa
T   Tippu Tip's House
U   State University of Zanzibar
V   High Court
W   Museum Annexe
X   Zanzibar Milestone
Y   Peace Memorial Museum
Z   State House

TRANSPORT & TOUR OPERATORS
1   Shipping company ticket offices
2   Mitu Tours
7   Zan Tours and ZanAir
8   New Passenger Terminal
10   Sun N Fun Tours
13   Taxi rank
15   Eco+Culture
16   Taxi rank
20   Bus & *dala-dala* station
24   Sama Tours
27   Gallery Tours
29   Bahari Dive Centre
32   One Ocean Dive Centre
40   Air Tanzania
42   Mreh Tours
43   Kenya Airlines
43   Precision Air

44   Tropical Tours
45   Madeira Tours
47   Coastal Travel & Aviation
49   Fernandes Tours
49   Fisherman Tours

SHOPS
12   Vodacom shop
17   Pharmacy
18   Masumo Bookshop
19   Market
21   Shamshuddin Cash & Carry
      Supermarket
23   Moto
25   Keramica shop
26   Sasik
28   Zawadi Chest
31   Gallery Bookshop
35   Upendo
37   Supermarket
38   Zanzibar Gallery
41   Memories of Zanzibar

LOCAL SERVICES
3   Petrol station (Gapco)
4   Malindi Bureau de Change
5   Star Bureau de Change
6   Police station (main)
9   Zanzibar Tourism Corporation (ZTC)
11   Petrol station (Gapco)
14   Palace Internet Café
22   Microwaves Internet
30   People's Bank of Zanzibar
33   National Bank of Commerce
34   Too Short Internet Café
36   People's Bank of Zanzibar
      (Foreign Exchange)
39   Post Office & Telephone Centre
46   Zanzibar Medical & Diagnostic Centre
48   Kiswahili Language Institute
50   Afya Medical Hospital
51   Dr Mehta's Hospital
52   Zanzibar Medical Group
53   Mnazi Mmoja Hospital

Zanzibar Town

6

GUIDES AND THE 'PAPAASI'

Nearly all tourists who come to Zanzibar Town use the services of a guide at some stage during their visit. If you come on a trip arranged from outside Zanzibar, this will sometimes include the services of a guide. Even if you arrange something simple through a tour company in Zanzibar, like a trip to the spice plantations, the price usually includes a guide to show you around. Guides from reputable companies have to be registered with the Tourism Commission, and will carry identity cards.

There are also many other guides in Zanzibar who are not registered. Most of these are not really guides at all, but touts and hustlers who make their money showing tourists to hotels and souvenir shops, arranging transport or getting groups together to share boat rides. These touts are known locally as beach-boys or papaasi – literally meaning 'ticks', ie: parasites or irritating blood-suckers.

When a ship comes into Zanzibar from Dar es Salaam, there is usually a group of papaasi on the dockside. Some can be quite aggressive, but a few are not too unpleasant and will help you find a place to stay (which may be useful, as the labyrinth of alleys in Stone Town is disorientating at first). Tell them exactly what you want in terms of standard and price. In theory, it should not cost you any more money and could save you a lot of walking.

However, in practice, this plan does not always work so well. The papaasi will usually expect a commission from the hotel, for bringing them a guest. Some hotels pay more commission than others, and some do not pay at all, so the papaasi will only take you to the places where they get a decent cut. Hence their hotel recommendations are usually far from impartial – they'll usually take you to the hotel which they know will offer them the largest commission.

We have heard from several travellers who arrived on Zanzibar, aiming to stay in a certain hotel only to be told by the welcome party of papaasi that it was 'full', 'closed' or even 'burnt down'. If you're in any doubt, it is best to be polite but firm (or simply ignore them completely), and find your own hotel. Even better, make a phone call or send an email to reserve a room in advance; some hotels even give discounts for advance bookings.

After arranging your hotel, most papaasi will want to be your 'guide', offering to show you around the sights or souvenir shops of Stone Town, find companions for dive trips or boat excursions, or arrange transport to the east coast. Use these services if you need them but be prepared to pay if necessary. Always be aware that the owners of the souvenir shops, boats and dive centres will usually pay commission to the papaasi, a charge which will, of course, be effectively passed on to you.

Some papaasi are outright crooks, and involved in robberies and other crimes like drug dealing. Others are con-men, and some travellers have been stung arranging budget hire cars where a papaasi has taken a deposit then simply disappeared. Changing money is another potentially expensive operation, where initially tempting good rates precede sleight-of-hand tricks or simply snatch-and-run theft. Budget travellers have also reported having drugs planted on them by papaasi they befriended, who then reported them to the police; any fines (official or unofficial) paid out included a kickback to the informant.

If you deal only with reputable tour companies (whether low or high budget) you'll have none of these problems. Although trustworthy guides have identity cards, some papaasi have managed to get some too (they could be fakes, or simply stolen – it's hard to tell). This of course is confusing for tourists. There is a need for legitimate guides on Zanzibar, who can help tourists without hassling them, and it is hoped that the government department responsible for tourism will apply itself to this matter in the near future.

Although many of the thoroughfares in Stone Town are too narrow for cars, when walking you should watch out for bikes and scooters being ridden around at breakneck speed! It's also useful to realise that paths wide enough for cars are usually called roads while narrower ones are generally referred to as streets. Hence, you can drive along New Mkunazini Road or Kenyatta Road, but to visit a place on Kiponda Street or Mkunazini Street you have to walk. When looking for hotels or places of interest, you should also note that most areas of Stone Town are named after the main street in that area: the area being referred to as Kiponda Street or Malindi Street, instead of simply Kiponda or Malindi. This can be confusing, as you may not be on the street of that name. But don't worry: at least you're near!

TRAVEL AROUND ZANZIBAR TOWN

Most visitors and locals get around the town on foot, and in Stone Town this is the best and often the only way, but there are other means of transport available.

TAXI Private taxis for hire wait at taxi ranks around town; they do not usually cruise for business, although if you see a taxi in the street it is always possible to flag it down. The main taxi ranks are near the Gapco petrol station on Creek Road, outside the ZanAir office just east of the Port Gates, beside the House of Wonders, in front of the Serena Inn, and at the northern end of Kenyatta Road.

There are no meters. Wherever you go, you should agree the fare with the driver before starting your journey. A short ride through town costs US$1.50 to US$2. All the way across town costs US$3 to US$4. A longer ride, from town out to Mtoni Marine Centre or Mbweni Ruins Hotel will be about US$5. From town to the airport is around US$10, and it should be the same the other way, but from the airport into town, taxi drivers may quote fares of US$20 or higher.

One last thing to remember: if there is a petrol shortage, as periodically happens, taxi fares automatically go up.

DALA-DALA Converted small lorries with two rows of wooden seats at the back, called *dala-dalas* (or *dalas* for short), carry passengers on local runs around town and to outlying suburbs. There are several routes, all starting at the Darajani Bus Station on Creek Road. The most useful routes for visitors are detailed in *Chapter 5*, page 121.

BICYCLE For getting around Zanzibar Town and the surrounding area, a bike is very handy. Bikes can be hired from several of the tour companies listed in this chapter (see also *Chapter 5*, page 119). They are either sturdy steel Chinese-made models, or more modern-looking (though almost as heavy) mountain bikes. Prices for Chinese bikes are about US$10 per day. Mountain bikes are US$15 per day. A deposit of around US$50 may be required.

CAR AND MOTORBIKE A car or motorbike is not really necessary or practical for getting around Zanzibar Town as distances are short and parking is often difficult. There are no international car-hire companies on the island, however, both can be hired from various tour companies listed in *Chapter 5*, page 119. Prices vary, but are generally around US$25 to US$30 per day for a scooter, US$35 to US$40 per day for a motorbike, between US$50 and US$60 per day for a small car (eg: Suzuki 'Jeep') and around US$100 per day for a larger 4x4 (eg: a Toyota Land Cruiser). Petrol costs about US$1.70 per litre, with diesel now slightly more expensive.

There follows a selection of places to stay in and around Zanzibar Town. It's not exhaustive, as new places continually open and existing ones change name, location and ownership; however, it is as comprehensive as we could make it, and it does aim to highlight the best accommodation in each price bracket.

If you are coming from the airport (or elsewhere on the island) by taxi, and don't have a reservation, be firm about which hotel you want to go to, otherwise the driver will most likely take you to wherever offers him the best commission, not you the best quality or value. Do also remember that many hotels in the older part of Zanzibar Town cannot be reached by vehicle because of the narrow maze of lanes, and you may have to walk a few hundred metres through the streets to reach your hotel. If the driver shows you the way, and this is advisable if you haven't been before, then he'll probably help with your luggage, in which case it's usual to give a fair tip for this extra service.

Much of the accommodation is in, or very near, Stone Town, which is the best area for atmosphere and ease of getting around. Several of the places do not have exact street addresses, or if they do these are not used. Also, many lanes and house numbers, even if they exist, are unmarked. For ease, we have tried hard to mark the lanes, landmarks and all listed properties on the Zanzibar Stone Town maps, pages 136–7.

For details of price categories, see page 99.

EXCLUSIVE

⌂ **Zanzibar Serena Inn** (51 rooms) ✆ 024 2232306; e zserena@zanzinet.com; www.serenahotels.com. Part of the renowned Serena chain, which has lodges all over east Africa, this large, impressive hotel is in the Shangani area of Stone Town, overlooking the sea. Converted from 2 historic buildings, & restored at great expense (see box, *The Serena Inn*, opposite), the staff here are consistently excellent, in part due to the hotel's very good training scheme, & will actively go out of their way to engage & assist. On a practical level, every room is en suite with AC & boasts all the in-room & public facilities visitors expect of an international-class hotel, including a large inviting swimming pool overlooking the sea, 2 excellent restaurants (or a porter escort to the public food market), a coffee shop, Wi-Fi, satellite TV & reasonably priced, in-house massage treatments. If you happen not to be on holiday here, there's a

SAFETY IN AND AROUND ZANZIBAR TOWN

Theft from hotel rooms is very unusual, but we'd always recommend that you pack away your things into a locked bag when you leave your room for any length of time, and that you store any valuables (passport, air tickets, money, etc) in the hotel's safe, preferably within a sealed, lockable bag or pouch, to prevent tampering when it's out of your hands. This is really not such an issue at hotels in the middle and upper price ranges, because many offer individual safe deposit boxes, either at reception or in the rooms, and several of the budget hotels in Zanzibar Town now run an organised system with a book for guests to write in exactly what they leave.

More serious robberies (sometimes with violence) have occurred on some of the beaches in and around Zanzibar Town. You should not walk here alone, particularly after dark. Other notorious parts of town include the port, and the area around the old Garage Club on Shangani Road by Wings Fast Food, especially late at night when drunken youths wander the streets looking for kicks (just as they do in many other parts of the world). Another time to be wary is the hour or two just after sunset during the period of Ramadan, when everybody is inside breaking their fast, and the streets are absolutely deserted.

THE SERENA INN

The Zanzibar Serena Inn is in the Shangani part of Stone Town. The main building was originally the External Communications ('Extelcoms') headquarters, built in the early 20th century by the British colonial administration. The next-door house is much older and was originally known as the Chinese Doctor's Residence. The explorer David Livingstone stayed here before one of his journeys to the African mainland. It later became the private home of the British consul.

The Extelcoms building had been empty for many years, and the Chinese Doctor's Residence had fallen into a bad state of repair, before restoration began. Their conversion into today's Serena Inn hotel was sensitively handled, the design reflecting Zanzibar's Indian, Arabic and colonial heritage. The regeneration was completed in 1997, and the architects and local craftsmen must be congratulated on the quality of their work and the retention of the building's original character. The walls of the hotel are decorated with historic prints and contemporary paintings, but perhaps the most interesting 'decorations' are the old telecommunications equipment that was discovered in the basement. Abandoned and forgotten by the colonial staff 100 years before, most of the apparatus was handmade in wood and brass. Several items have now been restored to their original condition.

The Serena's restoration goes beyond façades and decorations. It is the first hotel in Zanzibar to install a sewage plant, so that waste discharges are treated to international standards. (Most other waste from Stone Town gets pumped out to sea in its raw state.) Although dumping sewage at sea, in whatever state, is never an ideal solution, the hotel owners should be congratulated for this positive step.

business centre with fax, photocopying & email services (although rates are high) & conference facilities. In addition to its standard rooms, the hotel also has state, executive, honeymoon & business rooms. It is possible that in the next couple of years, the Serena will expand into the neighbouring property to generate an additional 20–30 rooms & a larger conference facility, though no firm plans are yet agreed. Generous discounts are available in the low season & sometimes also during quiet midweek periods; it's also worth noting that here, like many of the hotels at the top end of the market, cheaper rates are often available if you book through an overseas tour operator rather than direct. ♛

LUXURY

⌂ **236 Hurumzi** (16 rooms) m 0777 423266; e 236hurumzibookings@zanlink.com; www.emerson-green.com. An offshoot of the defunct Emerson's House, & formerly Emerson & Green Hotel until its namesake owners parted company, 236 Hurumzi is a Stone Town institution. The hotel itself sprawls across 2 venerable buildings dating from 1840–70, one of which was originally the home of Tharia Topan, a prominent Ismaili Indian merchant who also built the Old Dispensary (see page 166), & Zanzibar Coffee House (see page 142). The house has been completely restored & tastefully decorated with antique Zanzibari furniture & carpets, & has a distinctly bohemian atmosphere. Each of the 16 rooms is different in character, including the open-sided Pavilion Room, the vast Crystal Room with its intricately carved balcony & the airy island South Room – reached by a small bridge! Each room, very deliberately, has no phone, no TV & no fridge. Some rooms have AC, others rely on natural cooling – shutters, shades, deep balconies & a sea breeze. B/fast is taken in the hotel's Tower Top Restaurant, the second-highest building in Zanzibar Town, with some of the finest skyline views to boot. Daily dinners (US$30pp) with traditional entertainment are also served here – frequently to diners coming with high expectations & leaving with disappointment at the quality of the food & service. Still, its location & marketing do well & reservations for rooftop dinners remain essential for hotel residents & others. (For more restaurant details, see pages 147–8). $$$$–$$$$$

⌂ **Africa House Hotel** (15 rooms) m 0777 432340; e info@theafricahouse.com; www.theafricahouse-zanzibar.com. Reopened in 2003 following extensive restoration, this sea-facing hotel

ZANZIBAR STONE TOWN
Accommodation, Restaurants, Bars & Cafés

Old Dhow Harbour

New Port ships to Dar es Salaam

KEY
one-way street
Road viable by car
Other roads
Built up area
Parks
Marshland
For Landmarks, Travel & Transport,
Shops & Services see pages 130–1

Bwawani Marsh

MALAWI   ROAD

Main road northwards out of town to Livingstone House, Mtoni, Maruhubi Palace & Bububu

to Michenzani Flats, Amaani Stadium & east coast

small boats to islands

MALINDI STREET

ZANZIBAR NEW TOWN (NG'AMBO)

MIZINGANI ROAD

Forodhani Road

KIPONDA STREET

Forodhani Gardens

HURUMZI STREET

CHANGA BAZAAR

THARIA STREET

CREEK   ROAD

small boats to islands

SHANGANI RD

GIZENGA ST

CATHEDRAL STREET

SOKO MOHOGO STREET

SULTAN AHMED MUGHEIRI RD

NEW-MKUNAZINI-RD

KARUME ROAD

Jamhuri Gardens

KENYATTA ROAD

BAGHANI STREET

MKUNAZINI STREET

VUGA   ROAD

MAPINDUZI-ROAD

CREEK ROAD

People's Gardens (Victoria Gardens)

VICTORIA-RD

KAUNDA ROAD

Mnazi Mmoja Sports Ground

113

N

Bradt

0   300m
0   300yds

Mbweni Ruins Hotel, Island View Hotel, Airport

136

HOTELS & GUESTHOUSES

1 Bwawani Hotel
2 Malindi Guesthouse
3 Bandari Lodge
4 Princess Salme Inn
5 Warere Town House
6 Hotel Marine
7 Malindi Lodge
8 Mzuri Guest House
9 Safari Lodge
10 Narrow Street Hotel
11 Pyramid Hotel
12 Kokoni Hotel
13 Zanzibar Palace Hotel
14 Kiponda Hotel
15 Asmini Palace
16 Annex II Narrow Street Hotel
17 The Swahili House
18 236 Hurumzi
19 Zanzibar Coffee House
20 Clove Hotel
21 Riverman Hotel
22 St Monica's Hostel
23 Karibu Inn
24 Coco de Mer Hotel
25 Tembo Hotel
26 Abuso Inn
27 Shangani Hotel
28 Jambo Guesthouse
29 Chavda Hotel
30 Beyt al Chai
31 Flamingo Guest House
32 Zanzibar Serena Inn
33 Mazsons Hotel
34 Manch Lodge
35 Ahlan Palace Hotel
36 Haven Hotel
37 Dhow Palace Hotel
38 Baghani House Hotel
39 Zanzibar Hotel
40 Florida Guest House
41 Al Johari
42 Mauwani Inn
43 Africa House Hotel
44 Victoria House
45 Garden Lodge

RESTAURANTS, BARS & CAFÉS

A Passing Show Restaurant
B Mercury's Bar & Restaurant
C Sea View Indian Restaurant
D Pal
E Kidude
F Tunda Café
G Clove Restaurant
H Kaya Tea Room
I Monsoon Restaurant
J Buni Café
K Livingstone Beach Restaurant
L Radha Food House
M Archipelago Restaurant
N Dharma Lounge
O Wings Fast Food
P Barracuda Restaurant
P Fany's Green Restaurant
Q Green Garden Restaurant
R Nyumbani Restaurant
S New Happy Club 2000
T Pagoda Chinese Restaurant
U La Fenice
V Amore Mio Restaurant
W Casablanca Restaurant
X Camlur's Restaurant
Y Rendezvous Les Spices
Z Sambusa Two Tables Restaurant
18 Two Top Restaurant
   (236 Hurumzi)
19 Zanzibar Coffee House Café
   (Zanzibar Coffee House)
30 Beyt al Chai Restaurant
   (Beyt al Chai)
32 Baharia Restaurant
   (Zanizbar Serena Inn)
41 Fusion
   (Al Johari)
44 Bustani
   (Victoria House)

ranks among the most popular places to stay in Zanzibar Town. Situated along the Shangani waterfront, Africa House served as the English Club from 1888 until the end of the colonial era, but is perhaps best known for its expansive balcony bar, which remains an ever-popular sundowner venue offering a winning combination of reasonably priced (albeit not cheap) cocktails, a cracking ocean view & tasty bar food. It also displays some interesting 'before & after' photographs documenting the building's history & restoration. Aside from its celebrated meeting point, the spacious en-suite rooms are a mix of stylish traditional décor & modern facilities (satellite TV, AC & minibar). The tiled floors may seem incongruous with the antique beds but the rooms are cool, clean & functional, & a particularly good low-season deal. $$$$–$$$$$

⌂ **Beyt al Chai** (6 rooms) m 0777 444111; e reservations@stonetowninn.com; www.stonetowninn.com. Behind thick walls & antique shuttered windows, Beyt al Chai is a relaxed & peaceful haven. Standing across Kelele Sq from the Serena, it was originally built by an Arab merchant & its name, literally meaning 'house of tea', bears testament to its past use as a place where the local nobility came to indulge in the house speciality, spiced tea. Until its opening as a boutique hotel in 2005, the building had always been someone's home, & its friendly Zanzibari team continues to offer relaxed hospitality & home comforts. There are 6 en-suite rooms – 5 dbls, 1 twin – spread over 3 floors & each with an individual name & style. The rooms are large & full of character with high ceilings, authentic Zanzibari furniture & vibrant silk & organza fabrics covering the windows & beds. Although all lovely, the 3 room categories – Sultan, Prince & Princess – are distinguished largely by the size & opulence of the rooms, with the latter also having no view over the square. On the first floor, a large landing area leads out onto a small courtyard, whilst inside, the front corner of the house boasts a bright & airy lounge filled with stylish antique furniture covered in sumptuous, azure & gold-thread cushions. An honesty bar (local & imported alcohol), self-service stereo, & views into the square & sea beyond, make this a wonderfully chilled place to read, write, chat, snooze & watch the world go by. More recently, a fabulous restaurant has been added on the ground floor, serving b/fasts, light lunches & delicious dinners to guests & city visitors. It's unquestionably one of Zanzibar Town's current culinary hot-spots, & though prices are relatively high, the quality of food & tempting wine list make it good value for money. $$$$–$$$$$

UPMARKET

⌂ **Ahlan Palace Hotel** (7 rooms) ☏ 024 2231435; m 0773 441551; e ahlan@zanlink.com; www.ahlanpalace.com. Opened in early 2008, the Ahlan Palace is a small hotel owned by Mohammed Nensi & his gentle wife Zuwena. They are a lovely couple who are genuinely committed to providing a very personal guest experience & have tried very hard to produce a pleasant city base. All named after gemstones, & accordingly colour co-ordinated, their 7 rooms are light, bright & spotlessly clean. Each has a telephone, cable TV, AC & a couple have internet access. 2 of the rooms, Prenight & Emerald, even enjoy views across the Zanzibar Hotel's lush gardens from their balconies. The Dhow Restaurant, appropriately named for the large boat in its interior, prepares fresh, made-to-order dishes of Indian & Arab origin which are worth the wait required to prepare them. Zuwena is also a trained aromatherapist & offers beauty & massage treatments for men & women (including good-value packages) in the Ahlan Palace Spa. Both hotel guests & interested visitors are welcome to make appointments at the spa. $$$

⌂ **Al Johari** (15 rooms) ☏ 024 2236779; e info@al-johari.com; www.al-johari.com. Flanked by 2 golden lions, the heavily carved door of the Al Johari opened in January 2008, bringing a touch of boutique bling to Stone Town's upmarket hotel scene. The Mauritian owners have carefully refurbished the 2 old buildings which now combine to make up the hotel, & the interiors try hard to strike a balance between traditional Zanzibari influences – Omani, Swahili, Indian – & modern amenities (multi-jet jacuzzi baths to plasma TVs).

Meaning 'jewel' in Swahili, there is certainly a good degree of opulence in this property: a multi-storey cascading waterfall, show cabinets of Tanzanite & an impeccable array of antiques. Rooms are tastefully furnished with crisp white linen on beautiful Zanzibari beds, marble floors, thick Persian carpets, well-stocked minibars & large electronic safes; the en-suite rooms have massage showers (plus jacuzzis in the suites), glass sinks & organic herbal products.

There is a really lovely rooftop bar from which to sit back in antique armchairs & peruse the extensive wine list or enjoy a Cuban cigar. The décor & ambience are distinctly reminiscent of a bygone era: gentle music, Tiffany lamps, a brass sea-facing telescope, whirring fans & chivalrous staff. Adjoining the bar, in a glass AC area, is the fine dining restaurant, Fusion. Serving an extensive European menu at b/fast, lunch & dinner, the food has been very well received since opening, with meals regularly rounded off with one of the 13 whiskies in stock or a flavoured *shisha* pipe. For non-residents & guests, there is also a Kama Ayurveda Spa, run by a professional Indian therapist, offering facials, head & body massage & exfoliation treatments. Al Johari is most easily found by following the Shangani Rd to Amore Mio, then taking the signed alleyway opposite. $$$$

🏠 **Chavda Hotel** (41 rooms) ☎ 024 2232115; e chavdahotel@zanlink.com; www.chavdahotel.co.tz. Situated in Baghani St, just off Kenyatta Rd in the Shangani area, Chavda is pretty soulless in spite of it brimming with antique-style Indian furniture & Persian carpets. The generally spacious bedrooms are adequate, if uninspiring, with tiled floors, white walls & lacquered timber ceilings. Zanzibari beds, crimson chairs around an octagonal coffee table, AC, TV, mosquito nets & a good size en-suite bathroom are standard, whilst some also have a tiny concrete balcony (not big enough to sit on). Upstairs is a restaurant & a very pleasant rooftop bar, offering one of the best skyline views of St Joseph's Cathedral & the city beyond. There are 2 conference centres & free collections from the port or airport to pre-booked guests. $$$$

🏠 **The Swahili House** e reservations@ moivaro.com; www.moivaro.com. In the Ukatani area, Moivaro Lodges (behind Fumba Beach Lodge, pages 301–2) acquired what was an unloved, dilapidated hotel &, early in 2008, embarked on a serious regeneration project. They've taken a towering white house, built around a central roofed courtyard, & at the time of writing are converting it into a hotel. Given the high quality of Fumba Beach Lodge, this is an exciting move, & bodes well for the old Hotel International, so do check to see if it has reopened by the time you travel. $$$$

🏠 **Tembo Hotel** (36 rooms) ☎ 024 2233005/2069; e tembo@zitec.org; www.tembohotel.com. This hotel has a great location on Shangani Rd, just west of Forodhani Gardens, leading right down to the sea. Easily identified by its grey elephant sculpture at the entrance (*tembo* means 'elephant' in Swahili), Tembo has long been a popular mid-range option. Part of the hotel was a grand old white house

(formerly the American consulate in 1834), & there's also a more recent extension, so that it now has a new wing & old wing, both overlooking the ocean & both quite Indian in décor. The bedrooms are all off chequerboard-tiled corridors, lined with Arabesque arches & plants in colourful ceramic pots. All are en suite, including a mosaic Turkish bath, with heavily carved furniture, mosquito nets, AC, fridge, telephone & TV; most have a sea view or overlook the large courtyard swimming pool, but some don't – so choose carefully, or pay the US$10 view supplement on booking. The 2 large corner rooms are fabulous for a triple or couple wanting space, as they have huge private terraces with amazing sea views; sadly the plastic sun loungers are a little out of character.

The public spaces are good & varied at Tembo, with a notable lounge on the upper floor of the old building, boasting a huge stained-glass window which fills the room with coloured light from its bold diamond pattern, & a beachfront restaurant with neat tables on decking under a row of sweet almond trees (non-residents welcome). Whilst the hotel is on the beach & deckchairs are laid out, it's not really a beach hotel, but rather a city hotel with a seafront location. There is a reasonable amount of passing local trade on the shoreline, so expect an amount of hassle to buy cashews & sunglasses if you choose to sit out. Equally, the water will be relatively polluted this close to the harbour & city so swimming is not advisable. It's also worth noting that, as with its sister property, the Dhow Palace, the Muslim owners of Tembo do not serve any alcohol. $$$$

🏠 **Zanzibar Hotel** (15 rooms) 📱 0777 432340; e info@theafricahouse.com; www.theafricahouse-Zanzibar.com. Under the same ownership as Africa House Hotel & with a large garden plot in Stone Town, this grand hotel should be buzzing with success. But at the time of researching, its impressive public spaces, lush garden & spacious rooms were empty & its staff hard to find. Open in its present state for 2 years, the high-ceilinged rooms have been carefully furnished with antiques, island artwork & crisp, colourful linens. Mosquito nets, TV, telephone, AC & tea/coffee-making facilities are standard throughout. The Royal Deluxe rooms have king-size beds whilst the Twin Deluxe have queen-size; the latter can be found in rooms with lovely views over the fountain courtyard. The restaurant was closed in early 2008 due to a lack of guests, so anyone booking must instead walk to Africa House Hotel for b/fast (included in the room rate). There is an independently run spa, Lemon Spa, in the garden. Hopefully, good management in the future can turn this hotel into the success story it should be. $$$$

⌂ **Zanzibar Palace Hotel** (9 rooms) ☏ 024 2232230; m 0773 079222/047370; e info@zanzibarpalacehotel.com; www.zanzibarpalacehotel.com. Opened in July 2006, Zanzibar Palace Hotel has quickly gained a reputation as one of the best boutique hotels in Stone Town. Initially renovated by a dedicated Belgian couple, the hotel was taken over in early 2008 by Frans & Cootje, who hope to build on the hotel's initial success.

The hotel's interiors have a distinctly Zanzibari feel: steep staircases, a central atrium, handcrafted wooden furniture, antique Arab *objets d'art*, rich fabrics & atmospheric glass lanterns. Yet for all the historic furnishings, modern creature comforts abound:

MID RANGE $$$

⌂ **Abuso Inn** (18 rooms) ☏ 024 2235886; m 0777 425565. Set back from the Shangani Rd, almost opposite the Tembo Hotel, this convenient family-run hotel is much better than first impressions imply. Construction began on the Abuso Inn in early 2005, & 3 years later it continues, giving its entrance & reception a distinctly half-finished feel. Beyond this, however, its en-suite rooms are pretty good: polished timber floors, king-size & twin Zanzibari beds, fresh linen, lots of space & even sea views from some. Fans, AC, mosquito nets, hot water & attractive traditional Zanzibari furnishings are standard. B/fast is currently served downstairs though a rooftop restaurant is planned for the future. The spacious rooms & central location continue to make this one of the best deals in this range. $$$

⌂ **Asmini Palace** (12 rooms) m 0774 276464; e info@asminipalace.com; www.asminipalace.com. Opened in October 2007, Asmini Palace is owned by the Canadian brother-in-law of Mohammed at Ahlan Palace (see above). Located on Forodhani Rd in the Kiponda area, between Palace Restaurant (well signposted) & Kiponda Hotel, Asmini is a new white building, constructed with traditional architecture in mind: an arched entrance, central courtyard & carved timber doors, shutters & balconies from every bedroom. The staff are delightful & its rooms are clean & uncluttered, with king-size Zanzibari beds, crisp linen, a small seating area & an en-suite bathroom. AC, ceiling fan, mosquito nets, TV & fridge are provided in every room. There is a rooftop restaurant for lunch & dinner & a large b/fast area

AC throughout the public areas & bedrooms, a DVD library & in-room player & even Wi-Fi. There are 9 bedrooms, each individually named & with its own particular décor, but all beautifully finished to a high standard & boasting impressive bathrooms (the standard rooms have a shower & no bath, whereas the deluxe & suites have both). The 2 suites, Sherali & Dunia, & the deluxe room, Arabica, all on the third floor, are particularly luxurious & would make wonderfully romantic honeymoon hideaways. That said, juicy mango wedges or sugared French toast may lure you to b/fast (both continental & cooked) in the ground-floor dining room, where calming instrumental music & chatter about the day's activities set the tone. Helpful staff are on hand for travel tips, the small bar serves cold drinks throughout the day & board games are available for when you tire of city explorations or the heat. $$$$

on the ground floor. Very unusually for Zanzibar, this hotel also has a lift: it runs from the ground floor to the roof terrace — a real bonus for those with limited mobility or simply weary legs. A good-value option in this price range. $$$

⌂ **Baghani House Hotel** (7 rooms) ☏ 024 2235654; e baghani@zanzinet.com. Immediately next door to the Dhow Palace Hotel main entrance, this is a friendly place, which in mid-2008 had just 7 simple, immaculately kept rooms. However, at the time of writing, the owners (the same family have the Malindi Guesthouse) had plans to increase the size of Baghani & embark on some renovations, possibly adding balconies, upgrading facilities & enlarging some of the smaller rooms, so watch out for positive changes here. For now the spacious rooms have a pleasant décor compete with photographs of Zanzibar, comfortable beds, TV, AC & big, clean en-suite bathrooms. There's a great-value family room on the ground floor beside the entrance, which has an internal partition to separate one of the 3 beds. Rates include full b/fast served in a small open-air courtyard at the back surrounded by impressive climbers & well-kept pot plants. $$$

⌂ **Bwawani Hotel** (114 rooms) ☏ 024 2235006; m 0777 416039; e reservations@bwawani.com; www.bwawani.com. Built in 1972 on a sizeable plot on the outskirts of town, this 4-storey government-owned monolith is a drab monstrosity on the outside & abysmally dreary inside. The timber reception area sees a number of oversized presidential portraits watching over the hapless staff, whilst the adjoining lounge boasts a blaring TV broadcasting images of scantily clad women in low-budget movies. The trademark long, dark corridors exude the institutional feel of a 19th-century asylum or prison, & whilst the cool, spacious en-suite rooms are initially reasonably acceptable, a closer inspection will reveal filthy, chipped baths, dripping toilets, collapsing drawers & bedding emblazoned with marker pen stencilling of the hotel's initials (though goodness knows why you'd steal them!).

The Bwawani's 'facilities' are located in separate buildings around the grounds & include the basic Marruna Fitness Centre, the New Pemba Bar (⏱ 23.00–01.00) complete with fairy lights & year-round tinsel decorations, the 'Komba Discotheque' (⏱ 23.30–04.30 Tue–Sun) & 4 crumbling conference rooms. The Café Changu Restaurant, garishly decorated with plastic chairs, scarlet tablecloths & psychedelic flowers, produces simple meat & rice dishes 19.00–22.00 daily. There is a swimming pool but, though the hotel overlooks the creek inlet, water pollution means this is not a place for swimming in the sea.

Unverifiable rumours have long circulated that the hotel will one day be privatised & rebuilt by an international hotel chain, but for now it remains in desperate disrepair & is probably best avoided. However, the sheer number of rooms might count in its favour if you have difficulty finding any other accommodation in the high season. $$$

Clove Hotel (8 rooms) m 0777 484567; e clovehotel@zanlink.com; www.zanzibarhotel.nl. This old stalwart had become rather rundown prior to being bought, renovated & reopened by a new Dutch owner-manager, Lisette, in 2004. Since then, its service, reliability & fresh décor have transformed it into one of the best mid-range options in the city. It's well located, at the kink halfway along Hurumzi St, opposite a palm-filled café corner which lends a sense of space to Clove, in spite of the atmospheric warren of alleyways which surround it. Behind its white walls & mint-green shutters, the light lilac corridors lead to 8 en-suite rooms, each with lovely coconut wood furniture, Swahili batik bedcovers & large apricot bathrooms. There are mosquito nets & fans in every room & the beds are specifically designed for taller visitors (they're over 2m in length, unusual in Zanzibar). All except 2 of the rooms are dbls, those remaining being specifically designed for families of 4. There's a lovely, sea-view rooftop terrace — one of the city's best — for guests only. It's shady & enjoys a cool afternoon breeze which, along with its honesty bar, Wi-Fi facility & cushion-covered sofas make it a perfect hangout. $$$

Dhow Palace Hotel (28 rooms) ☏ 024 2233012; e dhowpalace@zanlink.com; www.tembohotel.com/dhowpalace.html. In the Shangani area, just off Kenyatta Rd, this is an excellent & frequently recommended hotel. It's a renovated old house built around 2 cool central courtyards, complete with a tinkling fountain & swimming pool respectively. From the blue mosaic pool & its adjacent juice bar, the distinctive harlequin stained-glass windows of the newer rooms & their balconies rise upwards. By contrast, the original rooms all access a private section of shared balcony & boast more space, & a less kitsch interior. All of the rooms are nicely furnished with Zanzibari beds, vibrantly edged mosquito nets, genuine antiques, a refreshing amount of space & an en-suite bathroom (complete with Persian baths). All mod-cons are provided: telephone, AC, fridge, cable TV & a hairdryer. The whole place is spotlessly clean, the staff are friendly & the atmosphere is very tranquil. B/fast & other meals are served in the stylised Indian restaurant overlooking the city's rooftops. It lacks only a sea-front location, although if it had this the rates would be significantly higher, so instead you get real comfort & a heat-busting pool at an excellent price. $$$

Mauwani Inn (7 rooms) ☏ 024 2238949; m 0777 475748; e reservations@ mauwaniinn.com; www.mauwaniinn.com. This relatively new hotel is situated just off Kenyatta Rd, opposite Afya Medical Centre & behind the Rendezvous Les Spices Restaurant. Mauwani, meaning 'flowers' in Swahili, offers small but very clean en-suite rooms with tiled floors, a fan, mosquito net & AC. They do free pick-ups from the port & airport, as well as a safe deposit. $$$

Mazsons Hotel (35 rooms) ☏ 024 2233062/3694; m 0741 340042; e mazsons@zanlink.com; www.mazsonshotel.com. This hotel on Kenyatta Rd in the Shangani area has an interesting history: old records show it was built in the mid 19th century by Said bin Dhanin, who is thought to have settled here about the time that Sultan Said moved his court to Zanzibar from Muscat. Ownership changed hands several times, & during the early part of the 20th century the building was a Greek-run hotel before becoming a private dwelling once again. After the revolution, the house, along with many others, fell into disrepair. Today, it is a hotel & once again beginning to look a little tired. The chilled reception area is large & dated in décor: heavily carved reception desk, chandeliers, plastic flowers & velour sofas. The slightly soulless bedrooms have white tiled floors with sage green walls & linen. Large TVs, AC, small fridges, electronic key cards & functional bathrooms feature in all. Some rooms have access to the shared balcony at the front of the hotel, overlooking the square & Kenyatta Rd. The hotel has a reasonable restaurant, Yungi Yungi, serving Swahili set menus, as well as a business centre & bureau de change. Although power supplies are pretty good on Zanzibar these days, this hotel has its own large generator in case of cuts — in fact, it's so big it supplies many surrounding buildings as well. $$$

🏠 **Shangani Hotel** (28 rooms) 📞 024 2236363; 📱 0777 411703; e info@shanganihotel.com/ shanganihotel@hotmail.com; www.shanganihotel.com. On busy Kenyatta Rd, opposite the old post office, this hotel is an adequate mid-range choice. Enter reception by passing through the tired-looking lounge & pool room, in the knowledge that the rooms are better than this first impression may give. They are little more than simple & functional, but they are all en suite, clean & uncluttered. AC, fan, fridge, telephone & satellite TV are standard, though the ambient noise level is definitely less towards the back of the hotel. B/fast & other meals are taken in the rooftop restaurant & a consistently reliable internet café is attached. $$$

🏠 **Victoria House** (9 rooms) 📞 024 2232861; e booking@victoriahotel-zanzibar.co.uk; www.victoriahotel-zanzibar.com. Next door to Beit al Amaan (House of Peace) & overlooking the northern side of Victoria Gardens, this is one of Zanzibar's original budget accommodation options. It had fallen into some disrepair but having been taken over by enthusiastic new owners in Dec 2005 & its rooms thoroughly refurbished, it's now an excellent choice in the mid-range price bracket.

Situated in a 3-storey white house, the 9 en-suite rooms vary in size from sgls to trpls, & are simple, cool & clean. Featuring a modern take on

BUDGET

🏠 **Annex II of Narrow Street Hotel** (10 rooms) 📞 024 2235659; 📱 0713 306751/0777 411063; e annextwohotel@hotmail.com; www.darsafariinn.com/annexII.asp. Between the seafront Big Tree & the market on Creek Rd, in a warren of narrow alleys, this place is something of a mission to locate. In spite of its name, it is curiously not directly connected to Narrow Street Hotel, but rather to the budget Safari Inn in Dar es Salaam. Manned by a team of laid-back, friendly locals, Annex II is a somewhat ramshackle

traditional Zanzibari beds, plenty of storage space, full-length mirrors, funky Swahili design curtains & nicely tiled bathrooms with quality, contemporary fittings, these spacious rooms are well & thoughtfully furnished. Fans & mosquito nets are standard, & a few rooms also have AC. If you have a choice, the rooms on the first floor have the same layout to those below but feel brighter & benefit from greater breeze. Buffet b/fasts are served to guests on the large balcony of the second floor; it's a great spot with lovely leafy views through tall trees to the Victoria Gardens beyond. From lunchtime (12.00–21.00), this area becomes the Bustani Restaurant (see page 148) & is open to the public. Laundry, internet (US$1/hr) services & a safe are available at reception. $$$

🏠 **Zanzibar Coffee House** (8 rooms) 📞 024 2239319; 📱 0773 061532; e coffeehouse@ zanlink.com; www.riftvalley-zanzibar.com. Housed in an 1885 Arabic home, originally built by Sir Tharia Topan, *Wazir* (high-ranking advisor) to Sultan Said Barghash & described by Stanley in *Through the Dark Continent* as 'one of the richest merchants in town', Zanzibar Coffee House is by contrast an understated, unpretentious haven. Tucked in the maze of streets behind the Creek Rd market, & with only pedestrian access, its 8 individually styled bedrooms sit above the excellent café of the same name.

Well proportioned & modestly furnished, the rooms are simple & atmospheric, with traditional Zanzibari 4-poster beds, antique dressers & glass lamps. Most are en suite, whilst a few share bathroom facilities; there are few modern trappings except AC: there are no telephones, TVs or gadgets. A stay here is in fact made all the more pleasurable for its simplicity. The gracious staff provide a very friendly service, the stunning tower-top terrace offers one of Stone Town's most appealing b/fast views, & the rates remain great value. $$$

arrangement of neat, clean en-suite rooms, at the top of some quite steep stairs (help is willingly offered to weak tourists with heavy bags). The rooms do vary considerably in size & configuration so it's worth looking at a few on arrival: Room 303 is a good choice for a trip of singletons; Room 304 is a large suite of 2 dbl beds. Perceived luxuries aren't up to much (the 5 small TVs crackle loudly & the baths are badly chipped) but the basic package is perfectly reasonable for the price. There's also a breezy rooftop terrace, where b/fast is served to the gentle tune of children playing & bicycle bells from the street below. $$

Bandari Lodge (10 rooms) ` 024 2237969; m 0777 423638; e bandarilodge@hotmail.com. Just 100m north of the port gates, Bandari's entrance is easily identified by 2 towering palm trees & a walled entrance. One of a clutch of affordable hotels in Malindi, it offers good-value, no-frills accommodation in clean, functional rooms. Zanzibari beds, indigo mosquito nets, simple furniture & fans are the norm, with 2 rooms having white, if slightly tired-looking, en-suite bathrooms. Room 8 on the second floor is a particularly spacious trpl (3 dbl beds). There's a book exchange, seemingly popular with Mills & Boon readers, & a good selection of multi-lingual magazines available. B/fast is served in the central atrium & a basic, concrete kitchen is available for guest use throughout the day. The very friendly owner is always on hand to help with Stone Town advice & onward plans. $$

Coco de Mer Hotel (13 rooms) ` 024 2230852; m 0777 433550; e cocodemer_znz@yahoo.com. Behind a striped sunshade in Shangani, off Kenyatta Rd, this is a straightforward but clean & friendly place with en-suite rooms set around an airy courtyard, decorated with potted plants. All of the rooms are different & it's well worth looking at a few on arrival. The rooms downstairs are a bit dark, but those upstairs are bright & cheerful with striking canary yellow pillows & checked blankets. All of the rooms have ceiling fans & hot-water showers; 3 have a small TV & there are plans to add AC to the downstairs rooms in 2008. The restaurant does good-value food around main meal times & there's an adjacent ground-floor bar (one of the few bespoke drinking holes in Stone Town) which serves a variety of snacks & sandwiches. Free transfers are available from the port/airport but be sure that you have a confirmed reservation at the hotel in Shangani as there have been rumours of people being taken to a less-salubrious annex. $$

Florida Guest House (6 rooms) ` 024 2233136; m 0777 421421; e floridaznz@yahoo.com. Set back slightly from Vuga Rd, near the Culture Musical Club, Florida Guest House is an avant-garde, low-budget place. The near life-size cuddly tiger which decorates the entrance offers a taste of things to come. The rooms are cramped & in some cases feature everything including the kitchen sink. Squeeze past the bed to get into the downstairs rooms & an essay in design disaster awaits: the yellow sponge-painted Louis XVI-effect chairs with green brocade covers take some beating. Add to this sound effects

from torturous dripping taps & one of the island's noisiest fans, & it's not the best value in its class. However, the manager, Fauz, is very friendly, all the rooms are en suite, with fridges, small TVs & AC, & prices are negotiable for long stays. $$

Garden Lodge (18 rooms) ` 024 2233298; e gardenlodge@zanlink.com. Situated in a white house on the busy Kaunda Rd, near Victoria Gardens & the main hospital, this place is simple but neat & very friendly. The vehicle entrance is surrounded by a small garden terrace of tropical flowers & palms, whilst the building is clad in cerise bougainvillea, making this feel like a pretty lush retreat for Zanzibar Town. Catering primarily to a middle-age clientele (40+ yrs), the en-suite rooms here all have dbl beds in twin configuration, with good-quality furniture & linen, fans, mosquito nets & reliable hot water. Upstairs rooms are brighter & airier, & try to get one at the back to avoid traffic noise disturbance. There are small balconies at the front of the hotel laid out with deckchairs & a cool first-floor lounge with crimson Zanzibari chairs — both places make good reading spots to avoid the heat of the afternoon. There is a rooftop terrace for b/fast & a few good restaurants within easy walking distance. This is a good choice for the price. Interestingly (& impressively), there is a clear note at reception stating, 'no commission paid to papaasi'. (See box, *Guides and the 'papaasi'*, page 132.) $$

Haven Lodge (9 rooms) ` 024 2235677; m 0777 437132; e thehaven@yahoo.com. This is a friendly & good-value place, in the southern part of Stone Town between Soko Mohogo St & Vuga Rd, & over the years budget travellers have written to recommend it. Curiously there is a large shark & a swordfish painted on the outside wall, so it's easy to spot the entrance when you get close. Makame, the manager, aims to offer simple but clean bedrooms & separate bathrooms, hot water, a big b/fast & as much tea & coffee as you like, & broadly he succeeds. There's a good deal of space for the price, cheerful embroidered bedspreads, fans, a generator in case of power cuts, an organised safe-deposit system, luggage storage, a kitchen for self-catering (free) & cheap transfers to the coast, boat trips & tours; they even have bikes for hire. If you do stay, be sure to visit Nyambuni Restaurant opposite for great Swahili fare. $$

Hotel Marine (24 rooms) m 0777 411102/435266; e hotelmarine@africaonline.co.tz. This stand-alone hotel is in a large, renovated (not recently) house opposite the port gates & overlooking the Mizingani Rd roundabout. Inside, a grand staircase winds around an inner courtyard to rooms on 2 upper floors. It should be impressive but instead its potential has been totally wasted, with threadbare burgundy carpets & dark-brown paint on the walls making the whole place very gloomy. The rooms are all en suite & of fair quality with dark Zanzibari beds & apparently clean linen, but they feel rundown with fans doing little more than blow the dust around. Assumed essentials, such as fridge & small TV, simply make things cramped. In addition, the general hustle of the port & the incessant din of motorbikes below make this a far from relaxing retreat. At the time of researching, we were left in no doubt that guests were a great inconvenience to the staff, which perhaps goes some way to explain why there were none. $\$\$$

🏠 **Island View Hotel** (18 rooms) ☏ 024 2234605/5222; e islandview@africamail.com/ sadrumitha@hotmail.com. About 2km south of Zanzibar Town, at Kilimani, this is a small & welcoming B&B, run by the friendly Mitha family. All rooms are spacious, clean & tidy, with dbl/twin bed, mosquito net, en-suite bathroom, fan, TV, fridge & telephone. 5 of the rooms are now available with AC too. Meals can be ordered, tea or coffee is available all day free of charge, & there's internet access. This hotel is very handy for the airport, & only a few minutes' drive from town (transport can be provided). $\$\$$

🏠 **Jambo Guesthouse** (8 rooms) ☏ 024 2233779; m 0777 496571; e jamboguest@hotmail.com. In a quiet & peaceful quarter of the Mkunazini area, 5mins from the Anglican Cathedral & opposite the pleasant outdoor Green Garden Restaurant, this straightforward little hotel has a range of room sizes, all of which share bathroom facilities. Most of the simple rooms are on the wood-panelled first floor, & all have quality coconut wood beds, neatly edged mosquito nets & ceiling fans. 2 of the rooms also have AC & this does help with the heat & humidity. Bathrooms are small & unremarkable but the water is always hot. B/fast is served beside reception & is usually accompanied by Sky News. It's a good-value budget place, offering thoughtful little extras from a free luggage store, free tea & coffee to cheap internet access, all of which have made it justifiably popular with backpackers for many years. With advance bookings, it's also possible to arrange a free pick-up from the port or airport. $\$\$$

🏠 **Karibu Inn** (25 rooms) ☏ 024 2233058; m 0777 417392; e karibuinnhotel@yahoo.com. On a narrow street, parallel with Kenyatta Rd, in the Shangani part of town, this very simple, hostel-like

place caters mainly for young travellers, budget tour groups or people on overland truck expeditions. There is a laissez-faire vibe here & consistent crowd of braided backpackers hanging around the reception & very basic lounge. Rooms are dispersed around a warren of levels & corridors; they are clean but basic & primarily sgl/dbl en suites, though dormitories are available, each of which sleeps between 4 & 7 people with sgl beds, plenty of space, ceiling fans & an en-suite bathroom. The friendly management can set you up with budget tours, & also run a well-organised safe-deposit scheme. They will not tolerate stains from henna tattoos on sheets or towels & will charge for any damage. $\$\$$

🏠 **Kiponda Hotel** (15 rooms) ☏ 024 2233052; m 0777 431665; e info@kiponda.com; www.kiponda.com. On Nyumba ya Moto St in the Kiponda area, not far from the main seafront, this is a small, quiet hotel in a building which used to house part of a sultan's harem. It has been renovated in local style & still has an original carved wooden entrance door. The Zanzibari management team, headed up by the very helpful Salma, give the place a relaxed & friendly atmosphere, & although it's a touch more expensive than the budget hotels with which it is sometimes compared, it is also a lot cleaner, quieter & much better value. The rooms are fastidiously clean, with simple furnishings & efficient fans; there is even a deep sink for washing laundry. Good b/fasts are available in the airy restaurant, complete with clear sea views from its white arches; this area mutates into a casual coffee bar from 11.00–18.00, serving cold drinks, including beer, making it a nice place to hang out in the heat of the day. The hotel has good connections with Sama Tours & the local Kenya Airways office & can help with flights & reservations. All accommodation prices are discountable for long stays & for groups, with extra reductions in low season. $\$\$$

🏠 **Malindi Guesthouse** (13 rooms) ☏ 024 2230165; e malindi@zanzinet.com. Passing through the gate from the bustling port area into a calm, private courtyard is part of what has made this place consistently popular with travellers for many years. The sound of the water splashing into the mosaic fountain, the tropical potted plants, the fine collection of island *objets d'art* & old photographs from Arab-ruled, British Colonial & early Independence years, all lend Malindi a quiet character & homely feel. In addition, the owner & predominantly female staff make a real effort to assist guests here.

The rooms are all spotlessly clean with electronic safes, efficient ceiling fans, mosquito nets & crisp white linen; some are en suite with AC & others share neat bathrooms. There is also a great room for a group of 6, with 2 good-sized bunk beds, 1 dbl & even an antique rocking crib. There are a couple of comfortable communal seating areas, where Persian carpets & low seating offer afternoon respite beneath immense ceilings & cooling fans. Alternatively the rooftop coffee house is open all day Mon–Sat, serving the usual seafood or meat with rice dishes & chilled drinks, whilst providing a hassle-free view of lively port activity.

For all this, it is important to bear in mind that this guesthouse is in an area of questionable security, especially at night. From dusk, do heed the warning signs on the gate & walk in the opposite direction to the port. $$

🏠 **Malindi Lodge** (8 rooms) ➘ 024 2232359. On Malawi Rd, close to the port gates & next to Ciné Afrique, Malindi Lodge is in a convenient location if you're arriving or departing by boat. There are just 8 AC bedrooms, 2 of which boast a fridge & en-suite shower, whilst the remaining 6 share 2 central bathrooms. Rooms are all fairly small & some do overlook the busy road below, making them a less-quiet option. However, with simple Zanzibari beds, bright turquoise linen & polished concrete floors which are consistently kept spotlessly clean, this is a good choice within its price range. B/fasts are served at the banquet table on the ground floor & offer a good time to chat to the staff about directions & onward plans. Malindi has historically also had links with Sunset Bungalows in Kendwa, on the north coast of the island, & can arrange transport there & back for US$40. On a practical note, be careful not to confuse this place with its sister outfit, Malindi Guesthouse (see previous listing). $$

🏠 **Manch Lodge** (16 rooms) ➘ 024 2231918; e kashamanchi@excite.com. A stone's throw from the Haven Hotel, this is another budget place on Vuga Rd. A friendly bunch of locals usually hang out on the veranda & lend this place its relaxed air. The interiors here are unusual: large posters showing scenes from around the world & huge maps of Canadian & British motorway networks seeming a particularly curious choice. Rooms are quite cramped with heavy brown furniture & the en suites are unventilated concrete cubes literally within the bedrooms (take a shower before bed & it won't be amorous gestures making the place steamy!). To escape the heat there's a breezy balcony on the first

floor &, unusually for Stone Town, at least a few trees to break the view. It's just about acceptable for the price but phone in advance for a free pick-up from the port, or one from the airport for US$2.50. $$

🏠 **Princess Salme Inn** (12 rooms) ➘ 024 2236588; m 0777 435303; e info@princesssalmeinn.com; www.princesssalmeinn.com. At the northern end of town, in a white building with distinctive turquoise shutters, the Princess Salme Inn is set back a little from the Mizingani Rd, beside Bandari Lodge & Warere Town House. Formerly Annex Malindi Lodge, this place had a facelift at the start of 2008 & now offers a warm welcome, clean bijou bedrooms, a continuous supply of spiced tea & an airy rooftop complete with self-catering facilities (fridge, cooker & crockery). There are pastel-shaded walls, white bedding & fluffy towels, mosquito nets over the beds & windows, & efficient fans. The majority of the rooms share 2 central bathrooms, whilst the en-suite dbl, complete with a Zanzibari bed, is best used by people who know each other well as the only divider to the bathroom is a plastic shower curtain adorned with leaping dolphins. $$

🏠 **Pyramid Hotel** (11 rooms) ➘ 024 2233000; m 0777 461451/0748 255525; e pyramidhotel@yahoo.com. On Kokoni St, between the Malindi & Kiponda areas, this old hotel is just behind the Ijumaa Mosque, a short walk back from the seafront. A budget travellers' favourite for many years, & deservedly so, it gets its name from the very steep & narrow staircases (almost ladders) that lead to the upper floors. The rooms have netting, fan & hot water, yet vary in atmosphere: some are large & bright, others small & dark, so choose carefully. The manager Ibrahim & his staff are very friendly & the rooftop restaurant does great b/fasts. Overall, it's a good budget choice, offering a free pick-up from the airport or port as well as a book-swap service. $$

🏠 **Safari Lodge** (28 rooms) ➘ 024 223 6523; m 0784 606177; e asc@raha.com/ info@safarilodgetz.com; www.safarilodgetz.com. A relatively new hotel in the Malindi quarter, Safari Lodge is a well-signed, 3-storey building with impressive carved timer balconies spanning the width of its upper floors. The spacious en-suite rooms are impressively bright & immaculately clean though somewhat sterile, in spite of the cheery red 'welcome' mats outside each room. Inside each has a large Zanzibari bed or two, AC & fan, an electronic safe & cable TV, & suites are even available for those needing more room. It has a convenient location for exploring the Old Town, a decent rooftop restaurant for skyline b/fasts & remains good value for money. $$

🏠 **St Monica's Hostel** (11 rooms) ☎ 024 2235348; e monicaszanzibar@hotmail.com; www.stmonicahostelzanzibar.s5.com. Beside the Anglican Cathedral, on Sultan Ahmed Mugheiri Rd (which everyone still calls New Mkunazini Rd), St Monica's whitewashed walls sit behind its lovely lush front garden. Built in the 1890s to house teachers, nurses & nuns working at the UMCA mission, it now offers a warm welcome to both church guests & younger backpackers.

In March 2008, under the enthusiastic management of Sula, a programme of major renovations began to rejuvenate the hostel's buildings & soft furnishings. There is a pleasant, reverential atmosphere, largely emanating from the bold architecture: cool thick walls, wide staircases, Arabesque arches, traditional wooden shutters & rooms with wide balconies overlooking the cathedral or pretty gardens of elegant palms & scarlet hibiscus. Rooms (the 5 en suites & 6 with shared bathroom facilities), are simple & very clean with new mattresses, bedding & mosquito nets for spring 2008. There is a restaurant, run by the parish's Mother's Union, offering fresh Swahili cuisine for b/fast, lunch & dinner (no alcohol); a long-standing art shop selling vibrant paintings & hand-printed T-shirts, & a new airy lounge area for games & gossip. A great-value, friendly place in this price range. (For details of the slave trade chambers here, see pages 173–5.) $$

🏠 **Warere Town House** (12 rooms) ☎ 024 2233835; m 0773 272760; e warere_townhouse@hotmail.com. Situated in a leafy corner, neighbouring the Princess Salme Inn, this 3-storey lodge has been popular for many years with travellers on a tight budget. Located in an early 20th-century homestead, it is a simple, comfortable haunt, slightly tatty around the edges, with 12 en-suite rooms offering traditional Zanzibari furnishings, *kanga* curtains & sparkling white bathrooms. 4 rooms boast breezy balconies, albeit overlooking the unattractive back of Bandari Lodge, & all guests can access the basic rooftop terrace. $$

SHOESTRING $

🏠 **Flamingo Guest House** (15 rooms) ☎ 024 2232850; m 0777 491252; e flamingoguesthouse@hotmail.com/ flamingoguesthouse@yahoo.com. In a fairly noisy area of Mkunazini St, this no-frills place has all the charm of a multi-storey car park. Past a rather sad octagonal pool behind reception, an external concrete staircase ascends to an array of en-suite (US$12pp) & shared-facilities (US$10pp) rooms. The beds are basic & all rooms have a sink & ceiling fan, though several smell of damp & the shared showers & toilets are pretty grim. Facilities include TV lounge, laundry service & sale of cold drinks. The roof terrace once had great views of the Anglican Cathedral, now it is obscured by a row of fake Paul Frank curtains & a washing line, making it a generally less than pleasant place to hang out. $

🏠 **Kokoni's Hotel** (14 rooms) PO Box 3257, Zanzibar; ☎ 024 2230239; m 0745 863817. In the Kokoni area, between Malindi St & Creek Rd, a short walk behind the Gapco petrol station, this is the former Hotel Karwan Sarai. It's a big old house with a distinctive red, wrap-around *baraza* bench outside, & a range of very basic rooms; some are large & airy with old wooden shutters leading onto a small balcony overlooking the square, while others are small & dark with no view & pretty tatty furnishings. Most rooms have en-suite shower rooms, all have good fans, & some also have TV, while the rooftop lounge has good views across Stone Town. It's a quiet place & good value, but veering towards the soulless & it can be a check-in challenge with really only Swahili spoken. $

🏠 **Mzuri Guest House** (11 rooms) PO Box 4118, Zanzibar; ☎ 024 2230463; m 0713 774261/0777 488344. In spite of its sign & location on the busy Malawi Rd, 50m or so east of the port, Mzuri's inconspicuous entrance, opposite the Passing Show Restaurant, is easily missed. Once found, head upstairs to the first-floor reception desk & all 11 rooms. Catering primarily to the low-end Tanzanian market & a few cash-strapped backpackers, Mzuri's small, en-suite bedrooms are all pretty grim: a mish-mash of patterned lino flooring with grubby, once-lemon walls & basic bathroom facilities (the hot water is switched on in the hall, so don't forget to turn it on before you shower, & hope no-one chooses to turn it off mid shampoo!). There is a TV, noisy AC unit & mini fridge in every room, though invariably the fridge doesn't work. B/fast is included in the room rate & is served on the landing at a clutch of plastic-covered tables & soft drinks are available all day at reception. $

🏠 **Narrow Street Hotel** (8 rooms) ☎ 024 2232620; e narrow22@yahoo.com. In an interesting bit of town, this old hotel is in the maze of narrow alleys off Malindi St. Renovated 5 years ago, the Zanzibari-styled rooms are all neat & tidy with carved furnishings & the option of AC (US$5/room supplement). They are quite small though, so ideally you should know your room-mate well before checking in. The en-suite bathrooms are also bijou in size but they are simple & clean & the water is always hot. The staff are a bit sleepy, but this is a fair low-budget choice for a clean bed in a central location. $

Riverman Hotel (12 rooms) ✆ 024 2233188; e rivermanhotel@hotmail.com. Located at the back of the Anglican Cathedral, this place can be difficult to find in spite of its signpost off Tharia St. Riverman is a basic guesthouse & a fair budget option (at US$20, about the cheapest dbl in Zanzibar Town). The rooms have seen better days but are just about adequate. This hotel is an agent for the TAZARA train on the Tanzanian mainland, & you can buy tickets here. $

✗ WHERE TO EAT AND DRINK

This section lists restaurants, cafés, snack bars, eating-houses and all other places that serve primarily food – or food and drink in equal measures. Bars, and other places which serve primarily drinks, are listed along with music venues in *Bars, clubs and entertainment*, pages 154–5.

Some restaurants and cafés in Zanzibar Town are simple and aimed at locals; see page 152 for these. Others are smarter and cater specifically for tourists, expatriates and more well-off residents. The following list, arranged very loosely into categories of quality and price (for codes, see page 101), cannot hope to be complete, but it indicates the type and range of places available. Nearly all those included are open in the evenings for dinner, and most also open for lunch; some are open all day. At busy times reservations may be necessary in some of the smarter restaurants.

RESTAURANTS
Gastronomic

✗ **Baharia Restaurant** Serena Hotel, Shangani Rd; ✆ 024 2233587. Not quite as flamboyant as the restaurants at the 236 Hurumzi, but this is a good-quality place nonetheless. The food is a mix of Asian, African & European. Starters like salads or mini kebabs are US$5, while main courses include curries for around US$10, fish in garlic & ginger for US$12.50, chicken in coconut for US$15, & lobster for US$25. In the coffee shop & patisserie, snacks & light meals start from around US$5, & you can have coffee & cakes for US$4. $$$$–$$$$$

✗ **Beyt al Chai** Kelele Sq, Zanzibar; m 0777 444111; e reservations@stonetowninn.com; www.stonetowninn.com. In 2007, this established little hotel opened a fabulous restaurant on its ground floor. Overlooking Kelele Sq, it serves light lunches & delicious dinners, the quality of which is fast making this one of Zanzibar Town's current culinary hot-spots. Diners are seated at neatly laid tables, amid twinkling candles & service is friendly & polite, if sometimes a little slow. Succulent prawn curries, grilled line fish & crisp vegetable accompaniments are matched with a tempting wine list & though prices may be relatively high here, the ingredients, flavours & sophisticated atmosphere combine to make it all good value for money & highly recommended. $$$$–$$$$$

✗ **Fusion** Al Johari Hotel; ✆ 024 2236779; e info@al-johari.com; www.al-johari.com. Fusion is a fine dining, glass-enclosed restaurant on the top floor of swish new boutique hotel, Al Johari. Adjoining the colonial chic bar, it serves an eclectic menu at b/fast, lunch & dinner, with tastes from Italian to Indian being equally well catered for. Delicious seafood starters are complemented with summer soups, pastas, marinated meats & totally tropical desserts, not to mention a lengthy wine list & a cocktail list which includes 4 vodkas, 7 rums & 13 whiskies! Staff are well dressed, polite & friendly, & the food has received good reviews; with the general manager's past experience in the restaurant trade, this is not a surprise. $$$$–$$$$$

✗ **Tower Top Restaurant** 236 Hurumzi, Hurumzi St; ✆ 024 2230171; m 0777 423266. Up on the roof of 236 Hurumzi (see page 135), this restaurant has a superb view, which the management modestly claims to be the 'best on the island'. The hotel is in a house built in the 19th century by Tharia Topan, financial advisor to Sultan Barghash. As the second-wealthiest man on Zanzibar at the time, he built his home as the second highest in town, lower only than the sultan's House of Wonders palace. A century later, he would doubtless be impressed that guests are still flocking to admire the view.

Meals (US$30pp) are relaxed affairs, starting with sunset drinks & cocktails, against the sound of the muezzins calling from the minarets around town. Guests sit local style on cushions & carpets, working slowly through starters & several courses of an

Arabic–Swahili meal & ending with Arabic coffee, all to the tune of the traditional musicians. Space means numbers are limited & sustained marketing & PR efforts mean reservations are essential. That said, the diners' high expectations are rarely matched these days & complaints about slapdash service & food quality are on the rise. Whilst the view is great, there are far better places in Stone Town for culinary delights. $$$$$

Creative cooking

✕ **Kidude** 236 Hurumzi; Hurumzi St; ☎ 024 2230171; m 0777 423266. Attached to the 236 Hurumzi Hotel, this place was originally set up as a ground-floor café, but it is now also a more elaborate, relaxed restaurant. The ambience is delightful; the small room has incredibly high, restored timber ceilings, wall-hangings of rich fabrics, oil paintings (for sale), brass urns, antique furniture & ornaments. During the day, light jazz plays in the background & you can enjoy great cakes & coffees, order Middle Eastern snacks from the à-la-carte menu (from around US$5) or take lunch (the US$12 fixed menu changes every day). In the evenings there's also a fixed menu (US$25), with a vast & impressive range of dishes similar to those offered

in Tower Top Restaurant (see previous listing) whilst on Fri evenings, a buffet is served (US$15). With 30mins' notice, you can even order a take-away pizza & head down to watch the sunset over the harbour. $$$$

✕ **Livingstone Beach Restaurant** m 0773 164939. Opened in August 2005, Livingstone consists of a large, uncluttered & attractively decorated dining room leading out to a private beach where you can dine with your toe trailing in the sand if you so choose. Situated opposite Zawadi Chest, the restaurant has a decidedly upmarket ambience & the (mostly seafood) menu is priced accordingly, with most main courses falling into the US$10–18 price range. $$$$

Mid range $$$

✕ **Amore Mio** Shangani Rd; ☎ 024 2233666; e e_walzl2yahoo.it. Rated by many as the best Italian eatery on the island, this long-standing, unfussy 'Cafeteria Italiano' has an attractively breezy waterfront location & offers the alternatives of eating in or outdoors. Pasta dishes & pizzas cost around US$7, sandwiches are in the US$3–4 range, & it serves a good strong coffee as well as a range of ice creams. For a late-night bite, after drinks at Africa House, it's a great choice. $$$

✕ **Bustani** (9 rooms) Victoria Rd; ☎ 024 2232861; ⊕ 12.00–last orders at 21.00 daily. On the large second-floor terrace of the refurbished Victoria House (see page 142), Bustani offers a great selection of soups, salads, grills, pizzas & curries at very reasonable prices (crab salad US$3.50; fish soup US$3.50; chicken curry US$5.50; grilled prawns US$8.50). From the rustic cane-&-skin chairs, you can gaze into the open kitchen or out into the lush tree canopy, & enjoy the shade, quiet & cooling breeze. It's easy to find, opposite the Victoria Gardens, on the left-hand side as you walk down Victoria Rd from Kaunda Rd. $$$

✕ **La Fenice** Shangani Rd; m 0777 411868; e fenice@zanzinet.com. Very near the seafront in

the Shangani area, close to the Africa House Hotel, this is a smart new place with a big open courtyard, serving Italian & Swahili food. As well as the restaurant, it's a cocktail bar & ice-cream parlour. It's not cheap but you get excellent food & a warm welcome here. Starters are US$3–4, & main courses (such as lobster risotto) are US$4–7. $$$

✕ **Mercury's Bar and Restaurant** Mizingani Rd; ☎ 024 2233076; m 0777 416666; e mercurys@ zanlink.com; ⊕ daily. Named after Zanzibar's most famous son (see box, *Freddie Mercury*, page 151), this place has a fine setting on the bay, overlooking a small beach, the bobbing fishing & pleasure boats of the new port, & the historic seafront buildings of Mizingani Rd. It's a real Stone Town institution: perennially popular & always with a relaxed, island atmosphere. Wooden tables & directors' chairs are set out on the large wooden deck under big blue sunshades & a huge almond tree (growing through the roof). You can enjoy choosing from the extensive cocktail list & a menu which unashamedly cashes in on the former Queen singer's apparent dietary preferences – Freddie's Favourite Salad (US$4) & Mercury's Special Pizza (US$6). Despite this corniness, the food is reliably good: pizzas fresh from the open oven (Margaritas from US$5 up to prawn, beef, tuna & mushroom for US$7), a mixed plate of grilled seafood (US$10), smaller dishes of octopus, grilled fish, pastas (all for around US$5) & a baffling range of cocktails around US$3–5. Happy 'hour' is 17.00–20.00, & there's live music Fri–Sun nights (19.30), ranging from traditional *bashraf* & *kidumbak* to reggae & pop. **$$$**

✗ **Monsoon Restaurant** Forodhani Gdns; m 0777 410410; e monsoon@zanzinet.com. Near the Fort & the seafront, beside the tunnel, this is a smart French-run place serving a good & interesting selection of Mediterranean & spicy Zanzibari food, accompanied by live taarab music on Wed & Sat nights. There are 2 parts to Monsoon: one is a bar, while the other is a massive open space covered in rugs & cushions. You leave your shoes at the door & lounge around kasbah-style. Thick walls & good ventilation mean it's always cool, & so are most of the clients. If you want to relax even more, with your Arabic coffee or cocktail, there is also a very pleasant & shady terrace with about 10 tables facing Forodhani Gardens. Main courses cost US$4 upwards, while 4-course dinners cost US$8–10. **$$$**

✗ **Mtoni Marine Restaurant** ℡ 024 2250117. At Mtoni Marine, just a few kilometres north of Zanzibar Town, the 3 restaurants are too far to reach by foot (& not a pleasant walk anyway) but well worth the taxi ride. The food in the main restaurant is an imaginative mix of European & Swahili techniques & ingredients, whilst the beachfront sushi bar & sports café are something of local institutions. All receive consistently good reports for being both high quality & good value. More details are given in the hotel listings: see *Chapter 7, pages 191–2*. **$$$–$$$$**

✗ **Nyumbani** Between Soko Mohogo St & Vuga Rd; e amir@artlover.com; ⏲ evenings only from 19.30. Nyumbani is similar to Sambusa Two Tables (see below), in that you eat in someone's house, although the dining room here is a bit larger. *Nyumbani* means 'at home', & it's most appropriate here, as you're welcomed into the home of Amir, a local artist, & his wife Khadija. They do the cooking, helped by Amir's sister Moulid. We think this place is wonderful, but if you need any more persuading, have a look at the visitors' book.

For US$6 you get a set menu of Swahili specialities, with soup & spicy snacks as starters, a main course with local styles of rice, fish & vegetables, & a dessert of dates, fruit & numerous sweets made from nuts, sugar & spices. (Don't forget

to check out the works of art while you're there too.) This place is opposite the Haven Hotel, in the southern part of Stone Town. You need to make arrangements by around noon if you want to eat later that day. You can also book a few days in advance. Unfortunately in the past some people have made reservations then not turned up, so Amir quite understandably, though apologetically, asks for a deposit. Reservations are most easily made by visiting the house, though you can also speak to Amir on the phone (℡ 024 2238170, *office – he has a day job!*) or leave a message at Manch Lodge (℡ 024 2231918). **$$$**

✗ **Old Fort Restaurant** Mizingani Rd; m 0744 278737/0741 630206; ⏲ for lunch & dinner 08.00–20.00 daily. Opposite the Forodhani Gardens, Zanzibar's old Arab Fort (known locally as Ngome Kongwe) has been here for centuries, but was renovated in the early 1990s. As well as a historical landmark it's now a very impressive cultural centre, with a semicircular open-air theatre, several smart souvenir shops, & this shady outdoor café-restaurant – a very good place to meet friends or take a break from sightseeing in the heat of the day, especially as it keeps unusually long hours. There's a good selection of snacks for around US$2, local dishes such as chicken & *ugali* (maize meal) or octopus & chips for around US$3, plus coffees, beers & chilled wine. Every Tue, Thu & Sat, there's an evening of entertainment (taarab music, African dance, etc) & a BBQ, which costs US$9 – you may need to book ahead. **$$$**

✗ **Pagoda Chinese Restaurant** Off Kenyatta Rd; ℡ 024 2234688; e pagoda888@hotmail.com; ⏲ for lunch & dinner 11.30–14.30 & 18.00–23.00 daily. The Pagoda, just off Kenyatta Rd near the Africa House Hotel, is run by Mr Chung, who has lived on Zanzibar for many years & used to run a diving outfit with his son George, & other members of the family. They proudly & justifiably claim to serve the only genuine Chinese food in Zanzibar. The restaurant is is highly rated, with good service, immaculate tables, nice surrounds, generous servings & excellent food. Chinese agricultural technicians from projects around the island often come here – so it must be good! Starters range from 5 spring rolls for US$1 to crispy deep-fried squid for US$1.50, & main courses include sweet & sour fish, prawns piripiri, chicken in oyster sauce & satay beef, all around US$6. Roast duck is US$9, & the menu also includes a few specialities, such as Chinese curried crab, for US$6. There are also a lot of vegetarian options, & meals include crisp, fresh vegetables specially flown in from Kenya. Rice & noodles are around US$2. $$$

X **Palace Restaurant and Internet Café** Forodhani Rd, Kiponda; m 0777 410004; ⏰ 09.00–21.00 (restaurant). Next door to the offices of the Aga Khan Foundation, the Palace Restaurant & Internet Café opened in June 2007 & is about the best signposted place in Stone Town, with A4 directions plastered to walls at nearly every alley junction. Its owner, Mr Altamimi, is a gentle, well-informed gentleman who offers fresh food & fast internet. The restaurant is in a large, open atrium with a refreshingly breezy orientation & cheerful sunshine yellow furnishings. Helpful staff serve an eclectic selection of food (lobster salad US$4; coconut noodle soup US$5; chicken masala with rice; US$6.50; beef medallions with potatoes US$7.50) & 13 excellent freshly squeezed juices (US$1.25) — try the delicious mango with ginger. Alongside the restaurant is the reliable internet café (see page 161). $$$

X **Rendezvous Les Spices** Kenyatta Rd; m 0777 410707. This French-owned restaurant, formerly known as the Maharaja, still serves what is arguably the best Indian food on the island. Easily located on Kenyatta Rd, the restaurant buzzes most evenings & the vibrant murals give the place tremendous colour & atmosphere. It's reasonably priced too, with starters around US$2–3, & main courses such as crab masala, chicken tikka, lamb biriyani or various tandooris for US$5–6. Vegetarian dishes are available, & specials, such as prawn curry, are around US$8. Following consistent fraud, credit cards are no longer accepted here. $$$

X **Sambusa Two Tables Restaurant** Victoria St; ☎ 024 2231979. Usually just called Two Tables, this place is particularly worthy of mention, because it's good & because for a long time there was nothing else

Cheap and cheerful

X **Archipelago Restaurant** ☎ 024 2235668. Opposite the National Bank of Commerce on Kenyatta Rd, this excellent first-floor restaurant has rapidly established itself as one of the most popular lunch spots in Stone Town, thanks in large part to its bright décor & elevated balcony overlooking the beach. The other chief ingredient responsible for its success is that the food — curries, fish dishes, burgers — is excellent & very reasonably priced, with most dishes falling in the US$4–5 range. The Archipelago owners are Muslim & do not serve alcohol but the fresh juices more than make up. $$

X **Camlur's** Kenyatta Rd; ☎ 024 2231919; ⏰ evenings Mon–Sat. A very long-standing favourite,

quite like it on Zanzibar. This is a small place (it really does have only 2 tables — although 1 seats about 8 people), on the balcony of a private house. It's set back off Victoria St, between the junction of Kaunda Rd & Beit al Amaan, but is clearly signposted on a roadside tree. The entrance is tucked around the back of the building, in a leafy corner past dozing cats & well-tended chickens. Food is cooked by husband-&-wife team Salim & Hidaya, with help from the rest of the family. It's important to phone or visit in the afternoon to tell Salim you'll be coming in the evening, in part because of limited space but also to allow time for food shopping & preparation. A full meal of spiced rice, curries & innumerably tasty local delicacies costs about US$10. It's highly rated by all who go here, but do pace yourself: fill up on the delicious snacks & starters & you may not do justice to the main course when it arrives! $$$

X **Sea View Indian Restaurant** Mizingani Rd; ☎ 024 2232132; ⏰ 07.00–22.00 or later. On the seafront near the People's Palace, this is one of the oldest tourist-orientated restaurants in Zanzibar Town, founded back in the 1980s & still going strong. With tables on an upstairs balcony & a beautiful view across the bay, it's ideal for b/fasts, lunches & evening meals. During the day (until 18.00) you can enjoy spicy snacks with your drinks — a plate of spring rolls, samosas & bhajis is about US$2 — plus toasted sandwiches for US$2.50, & omelette & chips from US$4. For larger lunches or evening meals the choice is very small, but the quality consistently good. Vegetarian thalis (a mixture of dishes) cost US$7.50, & fish, chicken, squid or octopus in coconut sauce with popadums, plus snacks for starter, a fruit dessert & tea or coffee costs US$7. $$$

this small & friendly place serves delicious Goan specialities, such as fish & coconut curry, starting from about US$3. (See box, *Freddie Mercury*, opposite.) $$

X **Fany's Green Restaurant** Kenyatta Rd; ☎ 024 2233918; ⏰ from 06.30. Next to the long-standing Dolphin, this relative newcomer offers a very different atmosphere, with tables inside or outside overlooking busy Kenyatta Rd. You can get b/fast (traditional English or traditional Zanzibari) here until 10.00. Lunches & dinners are mainly fish & pizza, with the main course US$3.50–4.50. $$

X **Green Garden Restaurant** Off Mkunazini St; ⏰ 11.00–22.00 daily. In the southern part of

The late Freddie Mercury, former lead singer and front man for the rock band Queen, was born on Zanzibar on 5 September 1946. His name then was Farouk Bulsara, and his father was an accountant working for the British government in the House of Wonders. His family had immigrated to Zanzibar from India but were originally of Persian extraction. When he was nine, Farouk was sent to boarding school in India, and never returned to Zanzibar. He later went to a college in London, and in the 1970s formed Queen with three other former students.

The current inhabitants of various houses around Zanzibar Town will tell visitors 'Freddie lived here'; his father moved house several times so the claims could all be genuine. Local historians confirm that the Bulsara family lived in the house now occupied by Camlur's Restaurant, and in at least one other house near the post office, either on Kenyatta Road or the small square just behind the post office.

town, opposite Jambo Guesthouse, this appropriately named restaurant is a delightfully chilled, open-air eatery, set on raised terraces under tall palms. Behind its timber wall, neat concrete paths meander between well-tended beds of hibiscus, elephant-ear grasses & flowering hedges, to shady tables & a cool *makuti*-thatched bar/lounge, complete with fans. It's a friendly, unpretentious place to catch up with life, relax or write postcards home. Food ranges from tapas-style dishes (olives & warm flatbread US$1.50) to the more substantial (king prawn fiesta US$7), with refreshing snacks (tropical fruit salad US$1.50) & local specialities (*kashata* – crushed peanut cake – with ice cream). **$$**

✗ **Radha Food House** Off Kenyatta Rd; ☎ 024 2234808. Tucked away up the narrow street which runs parallel to Kenyatta Rd near the Karibu Inn, Radha Food House is a small, simple & very reasonably priced place, proudly serving pure vegetarian Indian food. With consistently delicious food, this place is deservedly popular & at busy times it's wise to book a table in advance. A thali consisting of dal, rice, lentil & vegetable curries, okra, roti, popadum & lassi costs US$5. You can also get savoury snacks (US$1 for 4 pieces), cakes & sweets, fresh juices & beers. **$$**

Rock bottom

✗ **Buni Café** With a prime central location on Kenyatta Rd, opposite the National Bank of Commerce, this small café serves great fresh coffee along with cakes & a selection of sandwiches & other snacks for around US$2 – the raised balcony is an excellent spot for a late b/fast or light lunch. **$**

✗ **Clove Restaurant** Run by a friendly group of Swahili women, this is a nice, open-air place in a small & shady garden square opposite the Clove

✗ **Tunda Café** Hurumzi St. Beside the more locally influenced Clove Restaurant (see above), Tunda is a newcomer on the café scene, offering simple fish & salad dishes under palms & parasols. With its name meaning 'fruit' in Swahili, the fresh juices are a natural attraction here. It's a great central location & one of the few shady outdoor spots in Stone Town's maze of alleys. **$$**

✗ **Zanzibar Coffee House Café** ⊕ 08.00–17.30 daily. This friendly new café on Mkunazini St, behind the main Creek Rd market, is an excellent place to break a morning of sightseeing with a cold soda, fresh juice, milkshake or strong cup of freshly ground coffee & a light snack – the glass cabinet boasts a deliciously tempting array of fresh cakes, pies, pastries, croissants & sandwiches! Good accommodation is also available (see page 142). The café is filled with heavy wooden kitchen-style tables that are perfect for gossiping groups, as well as intimate tables for 2. Its solid, polished stone walls keep the place cool. As its name suggests, the coffee here is excellent; all of the beans are grown by the café's owners on fair-trade estates in Zanzibar & in the Southern Highlands, & there's an in-house roasting & grinding room adjoining the café. The resulting serving options are varied – from creamy cappuccinos to iced delights. **$$**

Hotel. It shares the square with another eatery, Tunda Café (see above). Their busy times seem to be b/fast & lunch, & you should check in advance if you plan on eating here in the evening. Local dishes such as meat & *ugali* (maize meal), rice & fish, or curry & chapatti cost around US$2. **$**

✗ **Passing Show Hotel** Malindi Rd; ⊕ lunchtime only. Despite the name, this is not a hotel, but a Zanzibar institution nonetheless, serving bowls of rice

& vegetable sauce or beans for around US$1, or larger plates of rice & meat or chicken for up to US$2. The food is good & the service quick. This place caters mainly for local people, although visitors are always welcomed. $

✕ **Wings Fast Food** Shangani. Opposite Tembo Hotel, this is Zanzibar's answer to KFC or McDonald's, complete with plastic tables, staff in red caps, burgers for US$2.50 & other take-away favourites. $

HOTEL RESTAURANTS Several smart hotels in Zanzibar Town, such as those at **236 Hurumzi**, **Beyt al Chai** and the **Serena**, deserve a mention in their own right, and are listed above. Among the mid-range hotels, the restaurant at **Mazsons Hotel** has good main courses in the US$4–10 range. The rooftop restaurant at the **Shangani Hotel**, on Kenyatta Road, has also been recommended, with simple main courses around US$4 and fine views. More positive comments come for the rooftop restaurant at the **Chavda Hotel**, just off Kenyatta Road, where good Indian meals are in the US$5–9 bracket. Cheaper, but very good value, the restaurant at the **Hotel Kiponda** serves speciality Zanzibari and seafood dishes for US$3–5, but you may need to order some time in advance. The restaurant at the **Coco de Mer Hotel** is friendly and offers good food: beef escalope, masala jeera and chicken Chinese are all US$4.50, and vegetarian options go for US$3.

LOCAL RESTAURANTS For a real local flavour, the **Tropicana Restaurant**, next to the High Court on Kaunda Road, caters for office workers, serving cheap meals of fish and rice for around US$1. Similar is **Café Kelele** on Shangani Road – a tiny place run by two nice old ladies. At both, only Swahili is spoken. Near the Masumo Bookshop in the Mkunazini area, just back from the market, are several local tea shops, also selling snacks and cakes, including the **Sinai Restaurant**, the **Utamanduni Restaurant**, the **SB Café**, the **Baobab Restaurant** and **Bakan's Restaurant**. There are many other, seemingly nameless, basic eating houses which you may just stumble across as you walk around the streets of Zanzibar Town. Menus are rare in these simple establishments, and some of the very small places may only have one meal available (sometimes called *chakula leo* – food of the day): you'll have to ask what they've got. If you're leaving Zanzibar by air, the airport restaurant does surprisingly good snacks and meals.

FOOD STALLS For very cheap eats, and a wonderful taste of the local atmosphere, by far the best place to eat in the evening is at the nightly food market. Traditionally held in Forodhani Gardens, on the seafront opposite the House of Wonders, the stalls have temporarily relocated to line the edge of the Old Fort's northern wall. They will remain here whilst the Forodhani is closed for renovation in 2008–09 (see *Forodhani Gardens*, page 170), and will eventually move back to a custom-built, covered hard-standing in the new gardens.

The food stalls, regardless of location, remain a gathering place for local people and tourists, and as the sun goes down, the long line of stalls fire up their braziers and hurricane lamps, and serve food such as fish and meat kebabs (*mishkaki*), grilled squid and octopus, chips, fishcakes, samosas, chapattis and 'Zanzibar pizzas' – akin to a filled savoury pancake. Or try the nutritionally challenged, *chipsi mai yai*: an omelette filled with chips, sometimes served with shredded cabbage. Most of the food is grilled on hot coals in front of you, and served on a paper plate. Prices are very reasonable, and a filling plate will cost between US$1 and US$2. You can simply stroll along the line of stalls, seeing what takes your fancy, asking the price and buying a few items at each, or get a whole plate put together at one stall. The food is invariably highly regarded but it is worth choosing from a stall doing brisk trade to ensure fresh ingredients.

Other stalls sell water, sugarcane juice, ice cream and cold drinks – look for the refreshing local pineapple drink named Zed. The sweet-toothed could seek out *haluwa*, made from tamarind, oil and sugar: it's so sweet and sticky that a little goes a long way. Coupled with the souvenir sellers touting their wares, an evening at the food stalls is often one of the cuisine highlights of a trip to Zanzibar.

MEMORIES OF THE ENGLISH CLUB

We received these reminiscences from a former member of the English Club (now the Africa House Hotel) who served in the colonial government before Zanzibar's independence:

The English Club, Zanzibar, was the oldest expatriate club in East Africa. The Rules and Regulations of 1888 – the year of its foundation – state that 'it is established for the association of an unlimited number of English Residents, together with officers of the Royal Navy stationed in these waters'. At this date the RN officers from no fewer than six warships outnumbered the other members.

By the 1950s eligibility for membership was widened to include 'any British subject or American citizen of European extraction'. Extraordinary members could also be elected from other residents such as the representatives of European trading companies. Honorary membership was extended to resident members of the Universities' Mission to Central Africa, the Catholic Mission to Zanzibar, Armed Forces officers, officers of any British Cable or Merchant Ship or Civil Aircraft, and so on. There was also reciprocity with similar clubs in Nairobi, Dar es Salaam and Mombasa, which was a bonus when travelling in East Africa.

Bedrooms were available for visitors, and for use by members when departing or arriving from home leave. A dining room provided meals for single members, if required, and was popular for entertaining. After garages were built at ground level, their roof formed an attractive terrace – which remained one of the most popular meeting spots in Zanzibar Town, especially for drinks at sunset. There was a billiard room and a quite extensive library. Sporting facilities were available at a separate site at the far end of Mnazi Mmoja Road, where tennis and golf were popular, together with squash, cricket and hockey.

In the latter years of the Club's existence, the fancy dress dance on New Year's Eve was a well-attended event. Among the other communities it was known that the *wazungu* (Europeans) would be walking through Stone Town, or arriving by car at the Club about 20.00, dressed in weird costumes, and there was always a sizeable gathering of local people to look with amusement at these strange antics.

The reader may be of the opinion that this all smacked of a monopoly of club life, but this was not so. There were Goan, Parsee, Bohora, Hindu, Ismaili, Ithnashery and other clubs, each used by a single community, whilst preserving an easy-going and relaxed contact among the various communities resident in the island.

Another place for snacks is Malawi Road in the Malindi area, in front of the old Ciné Afrique, or outside the Majestic Cinema on Vuga Road. As crowds gather for the evening films, stalls do a brisk trade in peanuts, crisps, chips, cakes, chapattis and samosas.

FOOD SHOPPING If you are self-catering, or just going on a picnic for the day, Zanzibar Town has a large market selling many types of fruit and vegetables, plus fresh fish and meat. You can also buy fresh bread in the market from the salesmen who ride in from the bakeries in the suburbs with large baskets on the backs of their bicycles. Dotted around the town are many small shops with a supply of basics, such as bread, biscuits, some fruit and vegetables, and maybe a few tinned items. As these foods are mainly for local people, prices are low. For more choice go to the 'container stores' (they're built in converted shipping containers) along Creek Road or to the shops in the street near the Ciné Afrique, where you'll find a good range of food in tins and packets, imported mainly from Kenya, but also from other parts of the Indian Ocean. Most items are reasonably priced, only slightly more than if bought in Dar or Mombasa. The best supermarket with the widest stock in Stone Town is the **Shamshuddin Cash and Carry Supermarket**, off Creek Road, near the market.

BARS, CLUBS AND ENTERTAINMENT

The number of bars in Zanzibar Town grows steadily each year as visitors continue to come in ever-increasing numbers. Some bars cater almost exclusively to tourists, others mainly to local Tanzanians who have migrated to Zanzibar from the mainland, as indigenous Zanzibaris are generally Muslim and so don't drink alcohol. Tanzanian, Kenyan, South African and a selection of international beers are usually available, as are soft drinks and a smattering of local and imported spirits. Wines are mostly South African, with international fine wines really only available at a couple of the top-end restaurants affiliated with hotels, like the Serena or Beyt al Chai. In addition, many of the larger hotels have separate bars, open to non-guests, and many of the restaurants and cafés mentioned in the section above also serve drinks.

BARS AND CLUBS

Africa House Hotel Shangani; m 0774 432340. No visit to Zanzibar is complete without a visit to the Sunset Bar at the Africa House Hotel (see pages 135–8). Since colonial days people have been meeting here for drinks as the sun sinks into the sea in front of the terrace. You can order snacks & meals (US$4–8) to enjoy on the veranda, or have something more formal upstairs in the Tradewinds Restaurant or Sunset Grill. Cocktails are de rigueur, with an extensive menu to tempt you, & especially popular among locals & the more adventurous visitors are the traditional pipes, also known as hubble-bubble pipes, water pipes or, correctly, as shisha pipes. The sun usually sets around 18.30, so try to get there in good time (say an hour before) if you want the best terrace seats.

☆ **Bwawani Disco** Bwawani Hotel. There is a disco most nights at the dire Bwawani Hotel (see pages 140–1), in a dark & equally seedy room under the swimming pool. Weekends are the most popular, entry is cheap (US$2) & evenings don't usually warm up until about midnight. If this hotel is renovated (which though talked about is not anticipated in the near future), the disco might also get a lick of paint & some decent furniture, but don't hold your breath. Or rather, do, if you visit the loos!

☆ **Dharma Lounge** Vuga Rd; ☎ 024 2233626; m 0777 416374/413031. Currently, the favourite after-dinner hangout for island expats & hip locals is the relatively new Dharma Lounge, with its well-stocked cocktail bar & invariably lively dancefloor. Under the same ownership as Mercury's on the waterfront, this is a good option for those who hit Stone Town in party spirit.

Mercury's Mizingani Rd. Along with the Africa House Hotel (see pages 135–8), Mercury's is also good for sundowners, & serves drinks & food all day & long into the evening. This place is noted for its happy hour – out of high season running generously from 17.00 to 20.00 – & its excellent range of cocktails. Ever-popular *shisha* pipes are also available. If you're here for the scenery more than the beer, in the May–Sep period the angle of the sun means the sunsets are easier to appreciate at Mercury's than at the Africa House (which is better Oct–Apr).

♀ **New Happy Bar** Shangani. Next to the Africa House Hotel, this place has a very strong local flavour, which lurches dangerously towards the dire & disreputable. Frequented mainly by off-duty hookers & tour touts rapidly spending their ill-gotten gains, the attached New Happy Lodge seems to cater for the same clientele, & is best avoided.

LIVE MUSIC There is live taarab music at the Monsoon Restaurant on Wednesday and Saturday nights. Otherwise, there is no one particular venue in Zanzibar Town for live music, but local artists – from traditional taarab to Afro-pop and rap – often perform at bars such as Mercury's or the Starehe Club. To find out what's going on, ask at your hotel or look for posters around town advertising special events. The Arab Fort is another good venue for live music – mostly traditional musicians and dancers, but sometimes contemporary performances, too. A couple of times each week a 'night at the fort' evening is organised, which includes at least two performances plus a barbecue dinner. There are often performances on other nights, too. The best thing to do is call in at the Fort during the day, and ask the staff at the desk what's happening in the evening.

CINEMAS In the 1920s, Zanzibar boasted the first cinema in east Africa, the Majestic Cinema (not to be confused with the Majestic now on Vuga Road). It was designed by the then British Resident and architect John H Sinclair, but sadly it burned down as the result of a projector fire and the island's film lovers have suffered a series of setbacks since, the most recent being the closure of the Ciné Afrique on Malawi Road and its conversion into a supermarket and offices.

Currently the only options for big-screen films are the rare showings in the atmospheric Old Fort amphitheatre (the annual Zanzibar International Film Festival showcases films here in June/July) and the very tired Majestic Cinema on Vuga Road, where Kung Fu flicks and Hindi melodramas predominate, with mainstream Hollywood movies shown only a few times a week.

There is hope that things will improve in the future though. In 2007, the Zanzibar International Film Festival (ZIFF) committee vowed to pull out the stops in seeking permission to renovate the Majestic Cinema and turning it into a decent, contemporary venue. These things can take time to materialise on Zanzibar, but ZIFF must be commended for trying.

SHOPPING

Zanzibar Town is something of an Aladdin's Cave for visiting shoppers, with a vast array of shops, large and small, catering for the ever-growing tourist influx. Even die-hard deal-hunters will be hard pushed to visit them all, and there are bound to be even more by the time you visit. A selection of both favourites and perennials are listed here, though particularly worth checking out are those mentioned in the box, *Fair-trade fashion*, pages 156–7; aside from their positive credentials, their products are without question some of the best quality and most original around.

In the larger tourist shops listed, prices are fixed and payable by Tanzanian shillings, US dollars or credit card (surcharges are usual), whilst in the market and at smaller locally run outlets, cash is necessary and bargaining is part of the experience. There are no hard and fast rules to the latter, and sensible judgement is required, but a basic rule of thumb is to start negotiations at half the asking price

In recent years, there has been a welcome trend towards training the local community, especially women, to produce high-quality, well-designed clothing and accessories. These are then sold to delighted tourists, often through hotel gift shops, whilst the individual women benefit from a new skill and a fair price for their efforts. The best of these projects and products currently available include:

MOTO Initiated in 1997 by Antje Förstle, *Moto* is an island-wide handicraft co-operative which aims to work as a competitive small industry to better develop the rural economy. Impressively, it is as environmentally responsible as it is socially aware: soil, roots and barks providing the products' striking natural dye colours and solar cookers being used exclusively in their production. The latter significantly saves on valuable natural resources, whilst educating its members about alternative energies and giving them a competitive edge on final sales. The finely made array of vibrant palm basketry (US$11 for a bag), wide-brimmed straw hats (US$17), household decorations and woven fabrics are striking and immediately appealing in both design and quality. They may be slightly more costly than some on the market, but the craftsmanship is significantly better and Moto currently operates in nine Zanzibari villages, providing an umbrella for 19 co-operatives, totalling over 300 members, all of whom benefit from the supportive structure, work ethic, shared business opportunities and established route to market, through its shops on Hurumzi Street in Stone Town and outside Jozani Forest. More details can be seen at www.solarafrica.net/moto.

MALKIA In 2003, Iben Djuraas, a Danish designer on Zanzibar, established a women's co-operative in Bwejuu, making clothing for women and children. Named Malkia, the Swahili word for 'queen', Iben's project was one of the first on the island to mix chic Scandinavian fashion design with vibrant ethnic textiles. Made entirely from Swahili *kanga* fabrics, the wrap skirts, summer dresses and tunic tops are fun and flattering attire. Training and improving the women's sewing skills, creating simple, stylish patterns and creating a route to market, Iben sought to ensure that the Malkia women learnt valuable skills and an income to better the lives of themselves and their children.

Iben no longer lives on the island, so the operations of the project have been handed over to the women whom she trained. For now, they continue to produce

and if you ultimately pay around 75% of the initial price, then it's likely both parties will walk away happy.

TOURIST SHOPS One of the best places to start any shopping trip is the **Zanzibar Gallery** on Kenyatta Road. This shop sells an excellent range of carvings, paintings, jewellery, materials, maps, clothes, rugs, postcards, antiques and real pieces of art from all over Africa. You can also buy local spices, herbs, pickles and honey, and locally made oils such as pineapple bath oil or banana-scented bubble bath – all made naturally from Zanzibar fruit. It also has a very good selection of books (see page 159). The Zanzibar Gallery is run by local photographer and publisher Javed Jafferji; his own books (signed) are also for sale here, including some beautiful large-format photo books, plus illustrated diaries and address books featuring photos from Zanzibar and Tanzania.

Another good place on Kenyatta Road is **Memories of Zanzibar**, opposite the post office. This shop sells everything from beaded flip-flops and silver bracelets to carpets and gourd-lamps, as well as a good selection of books about Zanzibar, and African music CDs. At the seafront end of the same road, is contemporary, stylish clothing at reasonable rates, and we sincerely hope that they will maintain their current quality in the years to come. Malkia purchases can be made at several hotel shops on the island, including Matemwe Beach Village and Mtoni Marine Centre, as well as at Mrembo Spa (see page 169) in Stone Town or by asking in Bwejuu village for the Malkia ladies.

SASIK Sasik, an acronym formed in part from its initiator's name (Saada Abdulla Suleiman Industry Karibuni), began in 1994 when Saada taught herself the art of appliqué and encouraged friends and family to learn too. Seeing a potential market for the colourful products they made, she applied for and received a grant from the UK-based Tanzania Gatsby Trust to set up a local women's co-operative. Initially, the funds were used to set up the simplest of workshops at the back of their current shop on Gizenga Street. Here, 12 local women were taught the fine hand-stitched technique and their distinctive Swahili-Arabic soft furnishings began to emerge. Now, 40 women are employed (there are plans to triple this in time), many earning an income for the first time and actively improving their standard of living and the education of their children. The intricate appliqué cushion covers, bedspreads and wall hangings are made on the spot and you can buy off-the-shelf or order bespoke colour schemes and designs.

UPENDO In a lovely little shop, next door to the Coco de Mer Hotel, Upendo sells the most gorgeous cotton children's clothing and some stylish ladies' summer wear! Initiated and run by Dorthe Davidsen Langås, a Danish resident on the island, Upendo operates a multi-faith sewing school and workshop on site, and seeks to empower local women through education, employment and economic independence. Every year 30 Zanzibari ladies are given vocational training to Tanzanian national diploma level, invited to seminars on business skills, and are offered interest-free loans to purchase their own sewing machines. Many go back to set up their own small businesses and ten are employed in the Stone Town workshop to make the beautifully cut, colourful clothes which are for sale in the shop. As cool, stylish, easy-to-wear outfits for travelling women and children or gifts to take home, the clothes are ideal for summer, and importantly, all of the profits are ploughed back into sustaining and developing the project. More details and the designs can be seen at www.upendomeanslove.com.

Zawadi Chest. A relative newcomer on the shopping scene, it's neatly laid out and has a particularly good display of *kikois* (see page 95), metalwork from the Dar es Salaam charity foundry, Wonder Welders, and an excellent selection of imported swimwear.

There are many more shops on Kenyatta Road and along Gizenga Street, as well as its continuations Hurumzi Street and Changa Bazaar. As well as shops, these streets are lined with pavement traders offering carvings, paintings and beaded trinkets. Most of the shops and stalls stock contemporary carvings as well as older, traditional statues and artefacts from mainland Tanzania and elsewhere in Africa. Tingatinga paintings on canvas or wooden trays, assorted gold, silver and stone jewellery, packets of spices, and mobiles made from coconut shells in the shapes of dolphins, dhows or tropical fish are readily available at every turn.

Some of the paintings and craftwork stocked in the souvenir and craft shops is bashed out and of very poor quality, but occasionally, if you search hard enough, you'll find real works of art which have been more carefully made. It's worth spending a bit more time and money (if indeed the stallholder charges more for better quality – some don't seem to) to get something that will still look good when you get it home, away from the glaring sunlight of Zanzibar which sometimes seems to cloud judgement!

Another place for good-quality crafts is **Hurumzi Art & Craft Gallery** next to the 236 Hurumzi Hotel on Hurumzi Street. The same owner has another fine shop called **Kibriti** on Gizenga Street, just off Kenyatta Road, near the post office, selling arts and crafts and a good selection of antiques and curios.

Around Zanzibar Town there are also several shops selling antiques from Arabia and India, dating from Omani and British colonial times. **Coast Antique Shop** on Gizenga Street has a particularly good selection of Zanzibar clocks. There are several more antique shops on the street between St Joseph's Cathedral and Soko Mohogo crossroads.

Other places to buy paintings and pieces of art include **Paul's Gallery** at St Monica's Hostel near the Anglican Cathedral (where you can also buy hand-painted T-shirts) and the **Tower Workshop** at the Old Fort, where the resident artists deliberately don't stock Tingatinga stuff and concentrate on watercolours and some beautiful batik-like works 'painted' with different-coloured candle wax. In the main part of the Fort is another cluster of spice and craft shops, including **Namaan Art Gallery**, which has Tingatinga works, some watercolours and some superb oil paintings. Alternatively, for original, slightly more contemporary products, **Keramica**, in the shadow of the amphitheatre is worth a look.

Outside the Fort, **Forodhani Gardens** boasted several more stalls selling carvings and jewellery – especially in the evening when nearby food stalls attract the crowds. With the gardens closed for renovations in 2008, these are more mobile, but will likely return to the new food market when Forodhani reopens. Nearby, beside the House of Wonders, Tingatinga painting salesmen hang their works on the railings, and you can also watch some of the artists (all men) working here. In the same area, local weavers (all women) make mats and baskets from grass and palm leaves. This area is also a good place to find local colourful fabrics and clothing.

Local craftwork can also be found in the **Orphanage Shop**, near the Fort. The orphanage is a large building on the main seafront road (Mizingani Road) with a tunnel passing right through the middle of it. The shop is on the side nearest the sea. Here, blind craft-workers weave a good range of baskets, rugs and other items.

On Gizenga Street, the tailor at **Mnazi Boutique** can copy any shirt, skirt or trousers you like, from material you buy in the shop or elsewhere in town. Prices start at US$10, and go up to US$25 for a complicated dress. If you prefer traditional African clothing, consider a *kanga* or a *kikoi* (see box, *Kangas and kikois*, page 95). On Kenyatta Road, the smart **One Way** boutique also sells piles and piles of T-shirts embroidered with giraffes and elephants or emblazoned with Kenyan and Tanzanian slogans and logos. If you want a T-shirt, this is the place. If not, it's a bit limited.

For postcards you can't go wrong at **Angi's Postcards & Maps**, on Mizingani Road, near the Big Tree; there's a truly massive selection here, all at good prices. Books – both coffee-table, fact and fiction – can be purchased from the well-stocked **Gallery Bookshop** on Gizenga Street, which is open from 09.00 daily, though shuts at lunchtime on a Sunday.

If a more precious purchase is what you're after, Eddy G at **Hassan Jewellers** on Mkunazini Street, close to the market, is reliable and reputable. He stocks a good range of tanzanite and will be able to supply authentication certificates showing the stone's size, cut and clarity (↘ *024 2231242*). Be aware when making your purchase that tanzanite is a soft stone which scratches easily; better to have it set as earrings or in a necklace than as a ring.

NEWSPAPER AND BOOKSHOPS Newspapers from Kenya and mainland Tanzania, some international magazines and a reasonable range of books, are available from the **Masumo Bookshop**, off Creek Road, near the market, and from some of the souvenir shops along Kenyatta Road near the old post office.

The best bookshop is the **Zanzibar Gallery** on Kenyatta Road. It has a very good selection of guidebooks and coffee-table books on Zanzibar and other parts of Africa, animal and bird field guides, maps, histories and range of general novels for those seeking some beach reading material.

FILM AND CAMERA SUPPLIES Slide and print film for cameras is available in several souvenir shops in Zanzibar Town (the ones along Kenyatta Road have the best stock). The **Shamshuddin Cash & Carry Supermarket**, near the Masumo Bookshop, also has a good stock. The best place to buy film is **Majestic Quick Foto**, on the east side of Creek Road, opposite the BP petrol station. Be sure to check the expiry dates if you buy film from more offbeat establishments.

For pictures from a different era, visit the **Capital Art Studio** on Kenyatta Road, near the Dolphin Restaurant. The shop itself gives the impression that it has been unchanged since colonial times, with a good selection of old photographic prints from the 1950s and 1960s, and a few earlier ones, all taken by the owner's father. They also sell camera film and batteries, and offer a one-day developing service.

LOCAL SERVICES

This section covers local services that visitors may require during their time in Zanzibar Town. For more general matters covering Pemba and Mafia islands, see pages 315–16 and 349–50 respectively.

AIRLINES For details of international and domestic flights to and from Zanzibar, see *Chapter 4, Getting to Zanzibar*, pages 78–80. If you do need to book or reconfirm a ticket while you are on Zanzibar, this is most easily done through one of the tour operators recommended earlier in this chapter. For further details of the airlines represented on Zanzibar, see *Chapter 5*, page 116.

✈ **Air Tanzania** Vuga Rd, near junction with Creek Rd; ✆ 024 2230213/0297; e bookings@airtanzania.com; www.airtanzania.com

✈ **Coastal Travel** Offices at Zanzibar Airport: ✆ 024 2233112; m 0713 670815/0777 414201; & Stone Town: Kelele Sq, Shangani (close to the Serena Hotel); ✆ 024 2239664; e aviation@coastal.cc/safari@coastal.cc; www.coastal.cc

✈ **Precision Air Flight Services** Kenyatta Rd (next to Mazsons Hotel); ✆ 024 2234521; e pwznz@precisionairtz.com/contactcentre@precisionairtz.com; www.precisionairtz.com

✈ **ZanAir** Offices at Zanzibar Airport: ✆ 024 232993; m 0777 413240; & Stone Town: Malawi Rd, Malindi; ✆ 024 2233670/3788; e reservations@zanair.com; www.zanair.com

BANKS AND MONEY-CHANGING Some general points on banks and change bureaux are given in *Chapter 4*, page 98.

Hard-currency cash can be changed into local currency at most banks as well as at a number of private bureaux de change dotted around the Stone Town. These days, there isn't much to choose between the rates offered by banks and the private 'forex bureaux', indeed some of the private bureaux offer an inferior rate to the banks, but you'll generally find the transaction takes a minute or two at a private bureau whereas changing money at banks often involves long queues and plenty of paperwork. Good private bureaux de change include the **Shangani Bureau de Change** (at the northern end of Kenyatta Road, near the Tembo Hotel), and

Malindi Bureau de Change (next to the ZanAir office, east of the port gates). Most large hotels will also change money, although some deal only with their own guests, and they often offer poor rates. There are also currency bureaux at the port and airport. The only place that exchanges travellers' cheques is the first-floor 'Foreign Trade Dept' at the **National Bank of Commerce** on Kenyatta Road. The rate here is pretty good and the commission (0.5%) is negligible. You can draw cash against Visa cards at the security-guarded ATM outside the same bank, but the only place where you can draw against MasterCard is at the excellent **Barclays Bank** headquarters and ATM a couple of kilometres out of town along the road towards the north coast.

Elsewhere, getting cash on a debit or credit card is virtually impossible, although most upmarket hotels will accept major credit cards.

COMMUNICATIONS

Post Some general points on postal services and costs are given in *Chapter 4*, page 108. Although letters can be sent from other post offices around Zanzibar Island, it's best to send all your mail from Zanzibar Town. The service is reliable, with letters taking about a week to ten days to reach destinations in Europe and North America (Australia takes a bit longer).

✉ **General Post Office (GPO)** ⊕ 08.00–12.30 & 14.00–16.30 Mon–Sat, 08.00–12.30 Sun. Zanzibar Town's main post office is a large building in the new part of town on the road towards the Amaani Stadium. Old Post Office ⊕ 08.00–13.00 & 14.00–16.30 Mon–Thu, 08.00–12.00 & 14.00–17.00 Fri, 09.00–12.00 Sat.

✉ **The Old Post Office** on Kenyatta Rd, in the Shangani area, is much more convenient for tourists. It's possible to buy stamps here, & this is also the place to collect letters sent by poste restante (although some items may get sent to the main post office by mistake – so make sure anyone writing to you addresses the envelope: 'Old Post Office, Kenyatta Road, Shangani').

Telephone and fax Zanzibar Town has a very wide choice of places where you can make calls or send faxes. Some are properly equipped, others are just a dusty phone in the corner of someone's shop which is nevertheless proudly touted as an 'international communication centre'.

One of the best phone centres is **Tanzanian Telecommunications** international telephone office (⊕ *08.00–21.00 daily*), next to the Old Post Office on Kenyatta Road. Calls cost US$1 for ten minutes inside Zanzibar, US$1 for three minutes elsewhere in Tanzania, US$1 for about one-and-a-half minutes to other parts of Africa, and US$2.50–3 for one minute to Europe, the USA and other international destinations. The office is large, cool and quiet, and the staff members are very friendly and helpful – so much better than some of the privately owned booths, where they put a stopwatch in your face and there's no privacy at all.

Another option for international calls is to buy a **phonecard** from the international telephone office (they are also sold at some shops and hotels) and use this in the direct-dial phone booth outside. A 150-unit card costs US$10 and gives you two minutes to Europe or the USA. A 500-unit card costs US$25. For local calls a 10-unit card is US$4, and a 100-unit card is US$8.

If the international telephone office is closed, local boys loiter by the phone booths outside with cards and will charge you per unit to use them. There's even one young entrepreneur with a mobile phone who allows international calls at negotiable rates. It makes you wonder who is really paying the bill.

At the private phone bureaux around Zanzibar Town, international calls are about the same price as those charged by the Tanzanian Telecommunications office, although a few places manage to undercut this rate, and some can be considerably more, so it's worth checking if you've got a lot of calls to make. For example, at Asko Tours, next to the Old Post Office, local calls are US$0.40 per minute, calls to Africa are US$2 per minute, and international calls cost US$4 per full minute. Opposite the international phone office a souvenir shop offers international calls to Europe for US$3 per minute. At Next Step Services on Hurumzi Street, international calls cost US$5 per minute. For cheap international calls, worth seeking out is Asad Secretarial Services, near the Clove Hotel, which offers phone calls via the internet for US$2 per minute. There's a delay of a second or two while you're speaking, but once you're used to that, it's fine.

For current codes, see box, *Zanzibar telecommunications*, page 109.

Mobile phones If you bring a mobile phone with you from home, it's emphatically worth the minor investment in a Tanzanian sim card (which costs around US$0.50 and gives you a local number) and airtime cards (available in units of TSh1,000 to 5,000). International text messages and calls out of Tanzania are seriously cheap: at the time of writing, US$1 will buy you around 20 text messages to anywhere in the world, and international calls work out at around US$2.50 for three to four minutes.

By contrast, you can expect to rack up a hefty bill using your home phone number for calls and/or messages, since in most instances these are charged at international rates out of your home country, even when you are phoning home. Sim and airtime cards can be bought at a specialist **Vodacom** outlet (there's one opposite the taxi rank on Creek Road) or at numerous other small shops displaying the ubiquitous Vodacom sticker.

Email and internet Since 2001, internet bureaux have sprung up everywhere in Zanzibar Town. Like the phone offices (indeed, many are also phone offices), some are large and air conditioned with several terminals, while others are in the corner of someone's shop and you connect to the outside world crammed between boxes of soap and tinned meat. In general, most hotels do not offer public email services, though there are increasing numbers with Wi-Fi and a pay-to-play PC.

The cost of internet use from a PC is a pretty standard US$1 per hour across town, and there are several dozen cafés to choose from. Most charge per 30-minute increment, starting at US$0.50, and if you go over this by a few seconds you'll be charged for the next 30 minutes.

Some of the more reliable and well-equipped internet cafés include:

⊟ **Asad Secretarial Services** Near the Clove Hotel is this small place with good connections, charging US$1/hr.

⊟ **Palace Internet** Part of the Palace Restaurant complex (see page 150) on Forodhani Rd, this glass, AC internet café has 20 flat-screen, up-to-date PCs from which you can surf the net (US$1/hr), print (B/W US$0.50; colour US$1), burn CDs and DVDs (US$1.50–2.50), download memory cards (US$3–4), & even laminate your favourite prints.

⊟ **Sanjay Internet Café** Just off Gizenga St, behind the House of Wonders, this small place has about 5 terminals, & normally charges US$1/hr, but sometimes offers special rates of half this price.

⊟ **Shangani Internet Café** Kenyatta Rd; ☎ 024 2232925. This is one of the best places in Zanzibar Town. It has long opening hours, fast connections, about 15 computers, a fridge full of ice cream & cold drinks, & charges US$1/hr.

⊟ **Too Short Internet** ⊕ 08.00–23.00. Opposite the National Bank of Commerce, this is centrally located with long hours, & around 8 quick machines at the standard rate of US$0.50/30mins. If you're travelling with a laptop & fancy a night in, for US$2 you can also rent DVDs here (US$10 refundable deposit).

HOSPITALS, DOCTORS AND PHARMACIES Zanzibar's main public hospital is Mnazi Mmoja General Hospital, on the south side of Stone Town. During the island's revolutionary heyday it was called the Lenin Hospital, but this title has now been dropped. Like many hospitals in developing countries, the staff are dedicated but the wards are badly underfunded, undersupplied and in very poor condition. Equally distressing is the pile of rubbish (including drip-feeds and needles) simply dumped on the beach behind the hospital.

Most tourists in need of urgent medical attention should go to one of Zanzibar's private medical clinics where the staff speak English and the service is usually better. Of course, this has to be paid for, and costs around US$50 per consultation, but all fees should be covered by your travel insurance. The medical centres also have pharmacies selling medicines and other supplies.

Private medical clinics

✚ **Zanzibar Medical and Diagnostic Centre** PO Box 1043, Zanzibar; ☎ 024 2231071, 24hr emergency m 0777 750040/413714. Just off Vuga Rd, near the Majestic Cinema, this clinic is recommended by most expatriates. It's a fully equipped facility, run to European standards, & the staff members speak several European languages.

✚ **Zanzibar Medical Group** ☎ 024 2233134. Another good-quality private clinic, on Kenyatta Rd, charging US$30 per consultation.

Serious medical emergencies In case of a real emergency, it's likely that you'll want to be flown to one of the private clinics in Dar es Salaam. The IST clinic there (m *0754 783393; www.istclinic.com*) comes highly recommended, and the The Aga Khan Hospital (☎ *+255 (0)22 2115151/53; www.agakhanhospitals.org/dar/index.asp*) is also reputed to be of a high standard. However, by the time you need one of these, you should be calling your insurance company – who will make the decisions and organise this for you.

In a case of major complications or complex surgery, it's likely that they would need to air-evacuate you to Nairobi or Johannesburg.

Other medical centres If your insurance covers only major medical problems, and you want to keep costs down for something minor, you could go to one of Zanzibar's other medical centres:

✚ **Afya Medical Hospital** ☎ 024 2231228; m 0777 411934. Off Vuga Rd at the southern end of Stone Town, Afya is large & well stocked, with friendly staff. Consultations cost US$2, blood or urine tests are available, & there's also a pharmacy.

✚ **Dr Mehta's Hospital** ☎ 024 2230194; m 0741 612889. On Vuga Rd.

✚ **Fahaud Health Centre** Near St Joseph's Cathedral, this very basic centre offers consultations for US$3 whilst a malaria blood test is US$2. Should your test prove positive, they also sell FansiDar at US$1 per tablet.

Pharmacies If you need to buy medicines, Zanzibar Town has several pharmacies stocking drugs which are mostly imported from Europe and India. Stocks are not always reliable, so if you know you're likely to need a specific drug during your visit, then it's best to bring a full supply with you. There are pharmacies near the Masumo Bookshop, next to 236 Hurumzi Hotel, and another highly recommended outfit opposite the Shamsuddin Cash & Carry Supermarket near the market (the pharmacist here is excellent if you are in need of medical advice). Straightforward medicines, toiletries and tampons are also available at the 'container stores' on Creek Road.

POLICE In case of emergency in Zanzibar Town, the main police station is in the Malindi area, on the north side of Stone Town (☎ *999 or 024 2230772*). This is also the central police station for the whole of the island. Robberies can be reported here (travel insurance companies usually require you to provide a copy of the basic report on the incident from the local police if you are making a claim), but you should not expect any real action to be taken as the police are not particularly well motivated.

Zanzibar also has a platoon of Tourist Police, supposedly to assist and protect the island's foreign visitors, although many people question their effectiveness. They are mostly seen driving around town in fancy new patrol cars, while touts continue to hassle tourists unimpeded.

SWAHILI LESSONS If you would like to learn a few words (or even more) of the local language, Kiswahili, there are options with formal classes as well as a number of local people willing to assist. For experienced teachers and structured learning, the best place to start is the **Institute of Kiswahili and Foreign Languages** (✆ 024 2230724/3337; e *takiluki@zanlink.com; www.glcom.com/hassan/takiluki.html*). Inside the State University on Vuga Road, the institute offers individual lessons and courses. Classes are normally 08.00–12.00 and cost US$4 per hour, or US$80 for a week's course. Single lessons away from the institute and longer courses, which include lodgings in the house of a teacher or local family, are also available.

SWIMMING The swimming pools at the Serena and Tembo hotels are no longer open to non-guests; however, the Dhow Palace will allow visitors to use their pool for TSh3,000 per person (approximately US$2.50). At the dismal Bwawani Hotel, swimming costs less than US$1, but the pool is at best only half full of green and slimy water, so this is not at all recommended.

If it's hot and you're desperate for some aquatic relief, Maruhubi Beach Villas, slightly out of town, allows non-residents to swim in its large beachside pool for US$5 per day; whilst children of guests at Mtoni Marine Restaurant will certainly enjoy the lush gardens and refreshing pool.

TOURIST INFORMATION The **Zanzibar Tourist Corporation (ZTC)** is the state travel service. It has offices in Livingstone House, on the northeast side of town on the main road towards Bububu, where you can make reservations for the very basic ZTC bungalows on the east coast. For general tourist enquiries, you're better off asking at the ZTC office on Creek Road, where the members of staff are a bit more helpful, and there are postcards and maps for sale.

For general information, hotel staff and some tour companies are happy to help, even if you don't end up buying a tour from them. Try **Eco+Culture**, **Sama Tours**, **Suna Tours** or **Gallery Tours**, listed in *Chapter 5*, pages 125–7. Also worth visiting is the information desk at the Arab Fort, which has details of local musical, cultural and sporting events.

For less formalised (but equally useful) information, check the noticeboard at the open-air restaurant inside the Fort. Local events are advertised here, alongside details of companies selling tours, spare seats on charter flights and local residents selling cars or motorbikes. This is also a good place to leave messages for those people you last saw in Cairo or Cape Town and are trying to contact again, as is the famous message board at the Africa House Hotel.

WHAT TO SEE AND DO

One writer has compared the old Stone Town of Zanzibar to a tropical forest where tall houses stretch to the sky instead of trees, and the sun filters through a network of overhanging balconies instead of foliage. Its labyrinth of twisting streets and alleys is a stroller's paradise, with new sights, sounds or smells to catch the imagination at every turn: massive carved doors, ancient walls, tiny

Although the narrow streets of Zanzibar are like a labyrinth, Stone Town is not very large, and getting seriously lost is unlikely. (If you don't know where you are, just keep walking and you'll soon come out onto Creek Road or one of the streets alongside the sea.) In fact, for many visitors getting lost in the maze of narrow streets and alleys is all part of the fun.

However, if your time is limited, you prefer not to become disorientated, or you want to find some specific sites of interest, it's possible to hire a knowledgeable guide from most local tour companies.

If you don't want a formal tour, but would still like to be accompanied by a local, you could engage the services of the papaasi (see box, *Guides and the 'papaasi'*, page 132), although generally they will be more interested in taking you to souvenir shops (where they might earn a commission from your purchases) than museums. It might be wiser to ask your hotel or a reputable tour company to put you in touch with someone who will happily walk with you through the streets, and show you the way if you get lost. We have heard from readers who employed a local schoolboy, who was also very happy to practise his English, and this seems an excellent idea. About US$5 (in Tanzanian shillings) for a day's work would be a suitable fee.

If you are seriously interested in the history of Zanzibar, a local artist and historian, John da Silva, is very occasionally available for private guided tours around Stone Town. John knows the history of every public building and every house (and literally every balcony and door) in the town. His rates are US$25 for a tour lasting two to three hours. You can contact John through Sama Tours (see page 126).

tempting shops with colourful wares and bustling shoppers, old men chatting on a stone bench or hunched over a traditional board game, kids with battered homemade toys, ghetto-blasters at full volume, thin cats curled in patches of sunlight, little boys hawking cashews or postcards or fresh bread, bright flowers in pots and window boxes, golden-orb spiders weaving their giant webs on a stunted tree, the sound of the muezzin calling from the mosque and the scent of cloves or ginger or lemongrass – and everywhere the echoes of Zanzibar's rich and fascinating history, the sultans, shipbuilders, explorers, slave markets, merchants and exotic spice trade.

Stone Town was originally built on a peninsula which has probably been inhabited since the first people arrived on Zanzibar (although the creek that separated its eastern edge from the rest of the island has now been reclaimed). Ras Shangani, at the western tip of the peninsula, is thought to have been the site of a fishing village for many centuries, and at least one of Zanzibar's early Swahili rulers, the Mwinyi Mkuu, had a palace here.

In the 16th century, Portuguese navigators built a church and trading station on the peninsula as it had a good harbour and was easy to defend. When the Omani Arabs began to settle on the island in the 18th century, they built a fort on the site of the church, and today's Stone Town grew up around the Fort.

Most of the houses you see today were built in the 19th century, when Zanzibar was one of the most important trading centres in the Indian Ocean region. The coralline rock of Zanzibar Island was easy to quarry for use as a construction material, so that many of the houses were built in grand style with three or four storeys. Previously most of the houses on Zanzibar had been much smaller, built of mangrove poles and palm thatch, making the fine white buildings in Stone Town even more exceptional.

Today, nearly all of these old houses are still inhabited, although many are in a very bad state of repair. The coralline rock was a good building material but it is also soft, and easily eroded if not maintained. Crumbling masonry, along with dilapidated woodwork, is sadly an all too familiar sight in Stone Town – and in some places where the surface has disintegrated it reveals the rough blocks of ancient coral beneath.

However, since the end of the 1980s and through the 1990s, several buildings in Stone Town have been renovated. The Zanzibar government, with assistance from the United Nations Centre for Human Settlements (the Habitat Fund), plans to preserve many more, eventually restoring the whole of Stone Town to something like its original magnificence. The Stone Town Conservation and Development Authority has been established to co-ordinate this work, although it is sometimes hampered by a lack of co-ordination with the local government authorities.

During the 19th century, many of Stone Town's inhabitants were wealthy Arabs and Indians. Consequently the houses were built in two main styles: the Arab style, with plain outer walls and a large front door leading to an inner courtyard; and the Indian style, with a more open façade and large balconies decorated with ornate railings and balustrades, designed to catch sea breezes and dispel the humid atmosphere.

Many of the buildings have doors with elaborately carved frames and panels, decorated with brass studs and heavy locks. The size of the door and the intricacies of its decoration were signs of the family's wealth and status. Today the Zanzibar door has become a well-recognised symbol of the town and island's historic and cultural background, and many new buildings incorporate one into their design – either a genuine one removed from an old building, or a reproduction (see box, *Zanzibar doors*, page 43).

Among the houses and tucked away in the narrow streets you will come across mosques, churches and other public buildings, almost hidden in the maze. Stone Town also has a few streets of shops, some of them still called bazaars. Some shops are very small, no more than a kiosk, with a few dusty food tins or a couple of jars of sweets on the shelf; others are larger, catering for locals and visitors, with a wider range of foods, books, fabrics, furniture and electrical goods. There are also antique and curio shops (bargain hard here!), and an increasing number of places selling a wide and inventive selection of locally produced arts and crafts, aimed specifically at the growing tourist market.

As you explore the narrow streets with all their historic links, remember that Zanzibar Town today is very much a real community, where people live and work. It is not a museum piece created for tourists. You should not enter any private house or courtyard unless expressly invited to do so, and before you peer through a window or doorway, stop and ask yourself – would you appreciate a stranger doing the same in your home? You should also show respect for local sensibilities (see *Clothing*, page 94). Mosques are not usually open to non-Muslim visitors. Taking photos of buildings is generally acceptable, but you should never photograph people without their permission (see box, *Mosques of Zanzibar Town*, page 177).

THE MARKET The market is about halfway along Creek Road and a good place to visit even if you don't want to buy anything. The long market hall is surrounded by traders selling from stalls, or with their wares simply spread out on the ground. It's a very vibrant place where everything, from fish and bread to sewing machines and secondhand car spares, is bought and sold. People bring their produce here from all over the island, and others come to buy things they can't get in their own villages. You could spot dog-eared schoolbooks, anonymous tangles of metal being soldered into usefulness, rough wooden chairs, suitcases, shoes, baskets, kitchenware, clocks and watches, CDs, mobile phones and doubtless the occasional kitchen sink. Some food displays may be best avoided by the squeamish: the massive deep-sea fish heads, jaws agape; dark haunches of beef and slabs of less identifiable meat; pearly squid tentacles; grubby recycled bottles and jars containing oil, honey, pickle and goodness knows what else ... and the inevitable accompanying buzz of flies. Don't miss the swathes of multi-patterned cotton fabrics, the fragrant spices and mound after mound of exotic fruit and vegetables – and just enjoy people-watching and being part of a Zanzibar experience which, at the time of writing, hasn't yet become touristy.

Towards the end of the 19th century, the town's marketplace was inside the Old Fort. Today's market hall was built in 1904, and some very early photographs of the market displayed in the museum show that very little has changed since then.

On occasional evenings, a public auction is held in the street behind the market where furniture, household goods, old bikes, and all sorts of junk are sold. It is very entertaining to watch, but make sure you don't bid for anything by mistake: keep your hands still!

LIVINGSTONE HOUSE On the northeast side of the town, this old building is now the main office of the Zanzibar Tourist Corporation (ZTC). It was built around 1860 for Sultan Majid (sultan from 1856 to 1870). At this time Zanzibar was used as a starting point by many of the European missionaries and pioneers who explored eastern and central Africa during the second half of the 19th century. David Livingstone, probably the most famous explorer of them all (see box, *David Livingstone*, page 174), stayed in this house before sailing to the mainland to begin his last expedition in 1866. Other explorers, such as Burton, Speke, Cameron and Stanley, also stayed here while preparing for their own expeditions. The house was later used by members of the island's Indian community, and in 1947 it was bought by the colonial government for use as a scientific laboratory for research into clove diseases. After independence and the revolution it became the Zanzibar headquarters of the Tanzania Friendship Tourist Bureau, the forerunner of today's ZTC.

THE OLD DISPENSARY Opposite the new port buildings, on Mizingani Road, this is a grand four-storey building with a set of particularly decorative balconies. It is also called the Ithnasheri Dispensary, and lettering at the top of the front wall reads 'Khoja Haji Nasser Nur Mohammed Charitable Dispensary'. It was originally built in the 1890s as a private house for a prominent Ismaili Indian merchant called Tharia Topan, who was a customs advisor to the sultans, and one of the wealthiest individuals on Zanzibar at the time. In 1899, he gave the house up to be used as a dispensary, also funding the medicine and other services. Topan also provided money (with the Aga Khan and Sultan Ali) for a non-denominational school which opened in Zanzibar in 1891. The dispensary fell into disrepair during the 1970s and 1980s, but was renovated in 1995 with funding from the Aga Khan Charitable Trust. A few years later it opened as the Stone Town Cultural Centre with a small exhibition (free) of historical photographs. The building has largely been taken over with offices now but the Aga Khan Trust for Culture is hopeful that the building will one day become the Indian Ocean Maritime Museum. We wait in anticipation for more news of this impressive building's future.

THE OLD CUSTOMS HOUSE On Mizingani Road (the main seafront), overlooking the sea, this large building has a plain façade and is fairly featureless apart from the beautiful set of carved wooden doors. These have been decorated in the Arab style with fish, lotus and anchor chain motifs. Hamoud, grandson of Sultan Said, was proclaimed sultan here in 1896. In 1995, the Customs House was renovated with funds provided by UNESCO, the United Nations' cultural organisation.

The equally large building next door to the Customs House was formerly Le Grand Hotel and then became a private house before being abandoned. A group of developers has long-term plans to convert it into a hotel once again.

THE PALACE MUSEUM (⏰ *09.00–18.00 daily; admission: adult/child US$3/1*) This is a large white building with castellated battlements situated on Mizingani Road, where the latter runs very close to the sea. Originally called the Sultan's Palace, it was built in the late 1890s for members of the sultan's family. From 1911, it was used as the Sultan of Zanzibar's official residence, but was renamed the People's Palace after the 1964 Revolution, when Sultan Jamshid was overthrown. It continued to be used as government offices until 1994 when the palace was turned into a museum dedicated to the history of the sultans of Zanzibar.

Remarkably, much of their furniture and other possessions survived the revolutionary years and can now be seen by the public for the first time. In spite of the uninspiring, dishevelled reception area, the museum itself is well organised and informative: the ground floor is dedicated to the early years of the sultanate (1828 to 1870), while the upper floors contain exhibits from the later, more affluent period of 1870 to 1896. These include thrones, banqueting tables and ceremonial furniture, and also more personal items such as beds and the sultan's personal water-closet. There is also a room devoted to Princess Salme, the daughter of Sultan Said, who eloped to Hamburg with a German merchant in 1866. It's a fascinating story, told by the princess herself in her book *Memoirs of an Arabian Princess*, which you can buy in the museum in English, French, German and Italian (see also the box, *Princess Salme*, pages 186–7). Outside in the palace garden are the graves of Sultans Said, Barghash, Majid, Khaled, Khalifa and Abdullah.

An excellent little leaflet is available containing a clear, concise historical background with plans and descriptions of all the palace rooms. Guides are also available from the ticket desk to show you around and describe the exhibits in detail; their fee is open to negotiation, but should be agreed beforehand (approximately US$5 is fair).

BEIT AL AJAIB (HOUSE OF WONDERS) (*Admission US$3; photography permitted*) This large, white building dominates the waterfront area of Zanzibar Town, and is one of its best-known landmarks. A perfect rectangle, it is one of the largest buildings on the island even today, rising over several storeys, surrounded by tiers of pillars and balconies, and topped by a large clock tower. After more than a century of use as a palace and government offices, it opened in 2002 as the Museum of History and Culture and contains some fascinating exhibits and displays. It's a pity to rush your visit: allow yourself enough time to browse.

Built in 1883 as a ceremonial palace for Sultan Barghash, Beit al Ajaib was designed by a marine engineer, hence the great use of steel pillars and girders in the construction, and located on the site of an older palace used by Queen Fatuma, the Mwinyi Mkuu (ruler of Zanzibar) in the 17th century.

In its heyday, the interior of the new palace had fine marble floors and panelled walls. It was the first building on Zanzibar to be installed with electric lighting, and one of the first in east Africa to have an electric lift – which is why, not surprisingly, the local people called it 'Beit al Ajaib', meaning 'House of Wonders'.

In 1896, the building was slightly damaged by naval bombardment during an attempted palace coup, started when Sultan Hamad died suddenly and his cousin Khaled tried to seize the throne (see box, *The shortest war in history*, page 26). From 1911, it was used as offices by the British colonial government and after the 1964

Revolution it was used by the ASP, the ruling political party of Zanzibar. In 1977, it became the headquarters of the CCM (Chama Cha Mapinduzi, the Party of the Revolution), the sole political party of Tanzania at the time. In the early 1990s, Beit al Ajaib was virtually abandoned by the government and the party and stood empty for some years, slowly falling into disrepair, despite short-lived plans, which never materialised, to turn it into a hotel.

Four years after it originally opened to the public, the museum is still under development, with about half the planned displays now completed. Those already finished cover a variety of subjects relating to Zanzibari and Swahili culture and history, including dhow-building (one of the amazing traditional 'stitched dhows' is there, its timbers literally 'sewn' together), the maritime history of the Swahili coast, and the early history of Stone Town and the Swahili trading empire of the 19th century. Further displays covering the Portuguese period, and Omani and British colonial times are planned, as is a library and conference centre. Among the many items recently transferred here from the now closed Peace Memorial Museum, although they may not yet be in their final locations, you should be able to find Dr Livingstone's medical chest, a section of track from the short-lived Zanzibar Railroad, some old bicycle lamps customised to run on coconut oil, and the old lighthouse lamp.

As well as the items on show, the House of Wonders' building itself is a fascinating exhibit, to which the museum allows public access for the first time in decades. The ground floor offers great views up through the central courtyard to the top of the building. On the next level, the floor is covered with marble tiles. On each floor are four massive carved wooden doors. On the next floor up from the exhibition room you can go out onto the upper balcony and walk all the way around the outside of the House of Wonders. Needless to say, the views over Stone Town and the bay are spectacular.

Outside the House of Wonders are two old bronze cannons which have Portuguese inscriptions. It is thought that these cannons were made in Portugal some time in the early 16th century, but the Omanis probably brought them to Zanzibar, after taking them from Persian forces who had originally captured the guns from the Portuguese in 1622.

THE ARAB FORT (*Donation on entrance; photography permitted*) The Arab Fort (also called the Old Fort, and by its local name *Ngome Kongwe*) is next to the House of Wonders. It is a large building, with high, dark-brown walls topped by castellated battlements. It was built between 1698 and 1701 by the Busaidi group of Omani Arabs, who had gained control of Zanzibar in 1698, following almost two centuries of Portuguese occupation. The Fort was used as a defence against the Portuguese and against a rival Omani group, the Mazrui, who occupied Mombasa at that time.

The Fort was constructed by the Busaidi Omani Arabs on the site of a Portuguese church which had been built between 1598 and 1612. In the main courtyard, remnants of the old church can still be seen built into the inside wall. In the 19th century, the Fort was used as a prison, and criminals were executed or punished here, at a place just outside the east wall. The Swahili word *gereza*, meaning 'prison', is thought to be derived from the Portuguese word *ireja*, meaning 'church'.

In the early 20th century, the Fort was also used as a depot for the railway line which ran from Zanzibar Town to Bububu. In 1949, it was rebuilt and the main courtyard used as a ladies' tennis club, but after the 1964 Revolution it fell into disuse.

Today, the Fort has been renovated, and is open to visitors. It is possible to reach the top of the battlements and go onto the towers on the western side. In 1994, a

(Telephone or visit to book appointments; **m** *0777 430117;* **e** *mrembozanzibar@ yahoo.co.uk)*

Recently, a number of 'spas' have sprung up around Zanzibar as the Western craze for 'wellness' treatments has descended on the island. Many are little more than a massage table, some lemongrass oil and a friendly, if untrained, local masseuse; a few, in the larger hotels, are more sophisticated and professional with Far Eastern therapists and imported lotions and potions. All can prove a thoroughly enjoyable distraction, but the most engaging and original by far is Mrembo Traditional Spa.

In an old antique store halfway along Cathedral Street, close to St Joseph's Cathedral, Mrembo is a small, wonderfully unassuming place offering the finest traditional treatments from Zanzibar and Pemba. Their flagship treatment, *Singo*, is a natural exfoliating scrub traditionally used when preparing Zanzibari girls for marriage. Prepared by hand with a pestle and mortar (*kinu*), the fresh jasmine, ylang ylang, rose petals, *mpompia* (geranium), *mrehani* (sweet basil) and *liwa* (sandalwood) combine to create the most wonderfully aromatic blend. Perfuming the skin for days after treatment and leaving it soft as silk, it's equally popular with honeymoon brides today. Whilst for men, the clove-based scrub *Vidonge* is said by Pembans to increase libido and stamina, and is even offered in souvenir packages. Hot sand massages, authentic henna painting and beauty treatments are available too, with all of the herbal products coming fresh from the owner's garden and skilfully prepared in front of you. The treatment rooms are cool and candlelit, with simple *kanga*-covered massage tables and sweet-smelling incense. There is a cold-water shower for post-scrub rinsing and a very chilled taarab music room for relaxing before and afterwards.

Although not their *raison d'être*, Mrembo is also an impressively inclusive community project. Two of the four local therapists are disabled: one deaf, Ali, and one blind, Asha. Trained in therapeutic massage by professional therapists from The African Touch (a Canadian-funded, community-based organisation in Kenya), they have both benefited enormously in confidence and social standing from their practical education and employment. Each has an able-bodied assistant at Mrembo to ease understanding, though Ali will cheerfully encourage you to try a little Kiswahili sign language, using the alphabet poster for guidance.

For a lazy afternoon of complete beauty pampering or a simple massage or manicure whilst the sun's at its peak, Mrembo Traditional Spa is a great place to while away the time with a cup of refreshing ginger tea and friendly staff. It is a true oasis of calm in the centre of Stone Town, and an experience not to be hurried.

section was turned into an open-air theatre. The development was imaginative yet sympathetic to the overall design and feel of the original building: seating is in amphitheatre style, and the Fort's outer walls and the House of Wonders form a natural backdrop. The theatre is used for performances of contemporary and traditional music, drama and dance. The Fort also houses a tourist information desk, with details on performances in the amphitheatre and other events around town, plus a selection of books for sale and a range of tour company leaflets to browse. There are also several spice and craft shops, a pleasant café, and remarkably some very clean public toilets. And don't miss the Tower Workshop in the west tower, where local artists create and display their works. (More details are given in *Shopping*, page 158.) Even if historical ruins don't interest you, the Fort is well worth a visit. With so many attractions and facilities, it's easy to spend quite a few hours here.

FORODHANI GARDENS The Forodhani Gardens (Jamituri Gardens on some maps) are between the Arab Fort and the sea, overlooked by the House of Wonders. *Forodhani* means 'customs' and this is close to the site of the original Customs House. The gardens were first laid out in 1936 to commemorate the Silver Jubilee of Sultan Khalifa (sultan from 1911 to 1960), and were called Jubilee Gardens until the 1964 Revolution. In the centre of the gardens stands a podium where the band of the sultan's army used to play for the public. Nearer the sea is a white concrete arabesque arch which was built in 1956 for the visit of Princess Margaret (sister of Queen Elizabeth II of Britain), although this was never officially used, as the princess arrived at the dhow harbour instead. She did visit the gardens, however, and planted a large tree, which can still be seen today.

Forodhani has long been a popular place for local people and visitors in the evenings, lured by the waterfront gathering of stalls serving drinks and hot snacks. Years of excessive overuse and poor maintenance had taken its toll though and for several years the 'gardens' have been a euphemism for an unattractive, parched wasteland.

Things are changing though. On 17 January 2008, the Aga Khan Trust for Culture, with approval from the Zanzibar government, finally began a major rehabilitation of the gardens. They have been in discussion about the project with the government since 2002 when the organisation first proposed comprehensive seafront rehabilitation.

Whilst few people locally seem to be aware of the exact redevelopment plans, scale models, architects' drawings, artists' impressions and clear descriptions are freely displayed in the lobby area of the Palace Museum and are worth a look. The stated aims of the project are to improve the infrastructure and to restore and preserve the civic components of the gardens, none of which has happened in the past as a result of overuse, disrepair and limited private refurbishment.

The project is due to be completed by early 2009. Although many believe this date is overoptimistic, almost everyone is agreed that the new Forodhani Gardens will be a vast improvement, which will see the introduction of wheelie bins, lighting and waste collections, a new sea wall of salvaged stone, an organised food court for the stall holders with colourful rain covers, a bandstand, a dhow-shaped adventure playground and tropical planting. We greatly look forward to visiting Forodhani on completion and, like the Aga Khan, hope that this project will prove a catalyst for urban upgrading and economic opportunity, as well as aesthetically improving the waterfront.

ST JOSEPH'S CATHOLIC CATHEDRAL This large cathedral, with prominent twin spires, is off Kenyatta Road in the Baghani part of town. Although its spires are a major landmark from a distance, the cathedral can be surprisingly hard to find in the narrow streets. It was built between 1893 and 1897 by French missionaries and local converts, who had originally founded a mission here in 1860. The plans were drawn by the same French architect who designed the cathedral in Marseilles, France. The tiles and the stained-glass windows were imported from France, and the murals on the inside walls, painted just after the cathedral was completed, also show a clear French influence. Unfortunately, some of the murals have recently been badly restored.

The cathedral is in regular use by the town's Catholic community, a mixture of Zanzibaris, Tanzanians from the mainland, Goans and Europeans. There are several masses each Sunday, and one or two on weekdays too. Outside mass times, the main cathedral doors may be locked, and entrance is via the back door reached through the courtyard of the adjoining convent.

THE HAMAMNI BATHS In the centre of Stone Town, east of St Joseph's Cathedral and northwest of Sultan Ahmed Mugheiri Road (formerly New Mkunazini Road), are the Hamamni Baths. The area is called Hamamni, which means simply 'the place of the baths' from the Arabic *hammam* (bath-house).

This was the first public bath-house in Zanzibar, commissioned by Sultan Barghash and built by an architect called Haji Gulam Hussein. It is one of the most elaborate on Zanzibar, and is constructed in the Persian style. (Such baths are found in many Arab and Islamic countries, and are commonly known by Europeans as 'Turkish baths'.) Today the baths are no longer functioning, but it is still possible to go in and look around. Inside, the bath-house is surprisingly large, with several sections including the steam room, the cool room and the cool-water pool.

The caretaker lives opposite: he will unlock the door, make a small entrance charge, give you a guided tour and sell you an informative leaflet about the baths' history and function.

TIPPU TIP'S HOUSE Tippu Tip (also spelt Tippoo Tib and Toppu Tob) was a slave trader, whose real name was Hamed bin Mohammed el Marjebi. He was born in the 1840s and began to participate in the slave trade at the age of 18. His nickname is thought to come either from a local word meaning 'to blink', as he apparently had a nervous twitch affecting his eyes, or because his eyes resembled those of a type of bird called Tippu Tib locally because it had characteristic blinking eyes.

During the mid 19th century, Tippu Tip travelled for many years across the east African mainland, trading in slaves and ivory. He also helped some of the European explorers such as Livingstone and Stanley with their supplies and route planning.

Contemporary records describe him as tall, bearded, fit and strong, with dark skin, an intelligent face and the 'air of a well-bred Arab'. He reportedly visited his concubines twice a day, and is said to have argued with missionaries that Abraham and Jacob (men of God, who appear in the Bible and the Koran) had both been slave owners themselves. Tippu Tip became very wealthy and by 1895, after many years of trading on the mainland, he owned seven plantations on Zanzibar and 10,000 slaves. He died in 1905.

The house where Tippu Tip lived is near the Africa House Hotel, behind the offices of Jasfa Tours. Until the 1960s it was a private residence, but after the revolution it was turned into a block of flats and is now occupied by several families. The house has not been maintained since its transformation, and one writer has called it 'the most magnificent squat in all of Africa'. It is not open to visitors. However, the huge carved front door (a sign of Tippu Tip's great wealth) leading into the courtyard can still be seen.

THE ANGLICAN CATHEDRAL The Cathedral Church of Christ, also called the Cathedral of the Universities' Mission to Central Africa (UMCA), is near the junction of Creek Road and Sultan Ahmed Mugheiri Road (formerly New Mkunazini Road) on the eastern side of Stone Town. It stands on the site of the slave market, used in the 18th and 19th centuries when Zanzibar was a large slaving centre.

A group of UMCA missionaries had originally come to east Africa in 1861, following the call of the explorer David Livingstone to oppose the slave trade and spread Christianity across Africa. In 1864, they settled in Zanzibar, after a number of earlier sites proved unsuccessful. When the slave market was closed by Sultan Barghash in 1873 the missionaries bought the site and almost immediately started building the cathedral. Some adjoining land was donated to the mission by a wealthy Indian merchant called Jairam Senji. Today, nothing of the old slave market remains (but see *St Monica's Hostel*, pages 173–5).

From the earliest times, slaves were one of the many 'commodities' exported from Africa to Arabia, Persia, India and beyond. In the 18th century, the demand increased considerably and Arab trading caravans from Zanzibar penetrated mainland Africa in search of suitable slaves. Various contemporary accounts describe all aspects of the trade, from the initial capture of the slaves to their sale in the infamous market of Zanzibar Town.

In the interior, the Arab traders would often take advantage of local rivalries and encourage powerful African tribes to capture their enemies and sell them into slavery. In this way, men, women and children were exchanged for beads, corn and lengths of cloth.

When the Arab traders had gathered enough slaves, sometimes up to 1,000, they returned to the coast. Although the Koran forbade cruelty to slaves, this was frequently ignored on the long journey to Zanzibar: the slaves were tied together in long lines, with heavy wooden yokes at their necks or iron chains around their ankles which remained in place day and night until they reached the coast.

The trade in slaves was closely linked to the trade in ivory: the Arab traders also bought tusks from the Africans and some of the captured slaves may have had to carry these on their heads as they marched towards the coast. If a woman carrying a baby on her back became too weak to carry both child and ivory, the child would be killed or abandoned to make the ivory load easier to carry. Any slaves unable to march were also killed and left behind for the vultures and hyenas. The passage of a slave caravan was marked by a long line of decaying corpses.

After many weeks or months of marching, the slave caravans reached the coast at ports such as Kilwa and Bagamoyo. Here, the slaves were loaded onto dhows, seldom more than 30–35m long, and taken to Zanzibar. Each dhow carried between 200 and 600 slaves, all crammed below decks on specially constructed bamboo shelves with about 1m of headroom. There was not enough room to sit, or to kneel or squat, just a crippling combination of the three. Sometimes slaves were closely packed in open boats, their bodies exposed day and night to the sea and the rain. They were thirsty, hungry and seasick and many died of exhaustion. Meals consisted of a daily handful of rice and a cup

When the first service was held in the cathedral, on Christmas Day 1877, the roof was not finished. It was finally completed in 1880. Tradition has it that the cathedral's altar stands on the site of a tree to which the slaves were tied and then whipped to show their strength and hardiness. Those who cried out the least during the whipping were considered the strongest, and sold for higher prices.

The man who was the force and inspiration behind the building of the cathedral was Bishop Edward Steere, who was Bishop of Zanzibar from 1874 to 1882. (He was also the first compiler of an English–Swahili dictionary, using the Roman alphabet; until then Swahili had been written using Arabic script.) He trained local people as masons and used coral stone and cement for building materials. Sultan Barghash is reputed to have asked Bishop Steere not to build the cathedral tower higher than the House of Wonders. When the bishop agreed, the sultan presented the cathedral with its clock. The tower was finished in 1883.

The legacy of David Livingstone lives on in the cathedral: a window is dedicated to his memory, and the church's crucifix is made from the tree that marked the place where his heart was buried at the village of Chitambo, in Zambia.

The mosaic decorations on the altar were given to the cathedral by Miss Caroline Thackeray (a cousin of the English novelist William Makepeace Thackeray), who was a teacher at the mission here from 1877 to 1902.

of stagnant water. Sanitation was non-existent and disease spread rapidly. When any illness was discovered, infected slaves were simply thrown overboard.

By the time the slaves reached Zanzibar, they were suffering from starvation and the effects of torturously cramped conditions: it was sometimes a week after landing before they could straighten their legs. The slave traders paid customs duty on all slaves who landed, so any considered too weak to live were thrown overboard as the ship approached the port. Even so, many more slaves died in the Customs House or on the streets between the port and the market.

Before being put on sale, the slaves who did survive were cleaned so that they would fetch a better price. Men and boys had their skins oiled and were given a strip of material to put around their waist. Women and girls were draped in cloth, and sometimes even adorned with necklaces, earrings and bracelets. Generous layers of henna and kohl were smeared onto their foreheads and eyebrows.

The slaves were put on sale in the market in the late afternoon. They were arranged in lines, with the youngest and smallest at the front and the tallest at the rear, and paraded through the market by their owner, who would call out the selling prices. The owner would assure potential buyers that the slaves had no defects in speech or hearing, and that there was no disease present. Buyers would examine the arms, mouths, teeth and eyes of the slaves, and the slaves were often made to walk or run, to prove they were capable of work. Once their suitability had been established, they were sold to the highest bidder.

After being sold to a new owner, slaves were either put to work in the houses and plantations of Zanzibar or else transported again, on a much longer sea voyage, to Oman or elsewhere in the Indian Ocean. However, the slaves were relatively well treated when they arrived at their new homes. They were fed, housed and clothed, and given small plots of land, with time off to tend them. Young mothers were rarely separated from their children, and good slaves were often freed after a few years. Many took paid jobs, such as gardeners and farmers, for their previous masters: some even became leaders of slave caravans or masters of slave ships.

Source: Charles Miller *The Lunatic Express* Macmillan, 1971

Behind the altar are the bishop's throne and 12 other seats for the canons. They are decorated with copper panels and show the names of several biblical figures, written in Swahili. The window behind the altar has been decorated with pictures of African saints, from Egypt, Carthage and Ethiopia.

Around the church are many plaques, dedicated to the memory of missionaries who died here, and to the sailors and airmen who were killed in action during the East Africa Campaign of World War I.

Today, services are held every Sunday (in Swahili), and an English service is held on the first Sunday of the month. The cathedral is also open to visitors.

Outside the cathedral, in a small garden next to the school, is a sculpture of four slaves chained in a pit – an understated yet powerfully emotive work of art that is well worth seeing.

During the day (except at service times) there is an entry fee of US$3, payable at a small kiosk, to the cathedral and surrounding area (which includes the slave sculpture).

ST MONICA'S HOSTEL This is an impressive old stone building in its own right. Apart from its hostel accommodation (see page 146) and its gallery and craft shop (see page 158), its basement provides one of Zanzibar's simplest, but arguably most moving and evocative, reminders of the dehumanising horrors of the slave trade.

David Livingstone is the best known of all the European explorers who travelled in 19th-century Africa, and many of his journeys began and ended in Zanzibar.

He was born on 19 March 1813 in the village of Blantyre, near Glasgow, in Scotland. In 1841, at the age of 28, he went to South Africa as a missionary doctor. There he married Mary Moffat, a missionary's daughter. On his early expeditions in southern Africa he crossed the Kalahari Desert and, in November 1855, became the first European to see Mosi oa Tunya ('the smoke that thunders'), which he renamed the Victoria Falls. Livingstone made his fourth major expedition from 1858 to 1864 in the area around the Lower Zambezi and Lake Nyasa (present-day Lake Malawi). He was accompanied by Dr John Kirk, another Scot, who joined the expedition as a medical officer and naturalist. After the expedition, in April 1864, Livingstone spent a week in Zanzibar before travelling back to Britain.

Livingstone returned to Zanzibar in January 1866 as he had been asked by the Royal Geographical Society to explore the country between Lake Nyasa and Lake Tanganyika, to solve the dispute over the location of the source of the Nile. He left for the mainland on 19 March 1866 and travelled around the southern end of Lake Nyasa.

After several years of exploring the region, during which time little news of his travels had reached the outside world, Livingstone met with journalist Henry Stanley at Ujiji on Lake Tanganyika on 10 November 1871 – the famous 'Dr Livingstone, I presume' incident (described in more detail in the box, *Henry Morton Stanley*, page 19). At this meeting, Livingstone was suffering terribly from foot ulcers, fever and dysentery, and had only a few days' supply of cotton with which to buy food. But two weeks later his strength had returned sufficiently for him to set out on a small expedition with Stanley. They explored the northern shores of Lake Tanganyika, establishing that the river Ruzizi flowed into (not out of) the lake, and could not therefore be a headwater of the Nile.

Livingstone and Stanley left Ujiji on 27 December 1871 and reached Kazeh, halfway to the coast, in February the following year. Livingstone was in good health, so Stanley continued on alone and arrived in Zanzibar in May 1872.

Livingstone stayed at Kazeh until August 1872, then set out on a short expedition around the southern shores of Lake Tanganyika. He was still looking for the source of the Nile when he became ill again with dysentery. He died at the village of Chitambo, a few miles south of Lake Bangweulu (Zambia) on 2 May 1873. Two of his loyal companions, Susi and Chumah, removed his heart and buried it under a tree at the spot where he died. They dried his body in the sun for two weeks, then carried it to Zanzibar, wrapped in bark and cloth, where it was identified by a broken bone in the left arm, once crushed in the jaws of a lion. Livingstone's body rested at the British consulate before being taken to London for burial. Stanley and Kirk were among the pall bearers at his funeral in Westminster Abbey on 18 April 1874.

The tree under which Livingstone's heart was buried eventually fell down, and a stone monument now stands in its place. However, some of the wood from the tree was made into a cross, and this now hangs in the Anglican Cathedral in Zanzibar Town.

A stone staircase leads down from the entrance hallway to what is reputed to be the dungeon where slaves were kept before being taken to market.

Try to go there with a local person or competent guide who can set the scene and recount the history while you are *in situ*. It's chilling. The dank rooms – more like tombs – are cramped and airless, with low doorways and tiny windows. Even today it's a sombre place – but imagine it crowded with slaves in their hundreds, men, women and children together, sick and exhausted after their gruelling sea voyage (see box, *The east African slave trade*, pages 172–3), crammed five deep on the narrow stone slabs and shackled with chains which still lie there today. Imagine the pain, terror, bewilderment, desolation – and death.

THE PEACE MEMORIAL MUSEUM This is at the southern end of Stone Town, near the junction of Creek Road and Kaunda Road in the area called Mnazi Mmoja. It is also known by its local title: Beit al Amaan (House of Peace). With its distinctive dome, arabesque windows and whitewashed walls, the building looks like a mosque or basilica church. It was designed by the British architect J H Sinclair, who also designed the High Court, the British residency and several other public buildings around Zanzibar Town.

'Museum' is a misnomer nowadays, as virtually all its viewable exhibits have been shifted to the rapidly developing museum in the House of Wonders and the place now serves as a library. Its well-known giant tortoises have been transferred to Prison Island.

THE ZANZIBAR ARCHIVES (⊕ *07.30–15.30 Mon–Fri, 07.30–14.00 Sat; admission free*) For real aficionados, the Zanzibar Archives (*Nyaraka za Taifa* in Swahili) contain some fascinating material. This includes many books and manuscripts in Arabic dating from the 17th century, when the Omani sultans took control of Zanzibar; consular and protectorate records from the British colonial times; papers and documents relating to the various European expeditions that started from Zanzibar in the second half of the 19th century; plus a lot of contemporary material such as stamps, newspapers, maps and photographs. If there is something of special interest, the staff on duty can help you search through the collections. If you just want to browse, there is an exhibition room where some selected items of interest are on display. The archives are situated outside the main town, about 2km along Nyerere Road from the Mnazi Mmoja Hospital, in an area called Kilimani. To get there take a *dala-dala* on Route U and ask to be dropped at Nyaraka za Taifa, or at the prison. The *dala-dala* will stop at the bottom of Kinuamiguu Hill (the only hill on this road); turn left (north) off Nyerere Road, then take the first road on the right.

More information is available from the head of the national archives, or have a look at the (not directly related) website (*www.zanzibar-archives.com*).

OTHER PLACES OF INTEREST IN ZANZIBAR TOWN Although the following places aren't major sights in themselves, you'll probably find yourself walking nearby as you visit some of the more important palaces and museums, and the following background information will be useful.

Mnazi Mmoja sports field Opposite the museum, on the other side of Creek Road, is Mnazi Mmoja sports field. (*Mnazi Mmoja* means 'one coconut tree'.) This area used to be a swamp at the end of the creek that separated the Stone Town peninsula from the rest of the island. The land was reclaimed and converted to a sports field during the colonial period, hence the English-style cricket pavilion in the corner. In the 1920s, part of the sports ground was set aside for exclusive use by members of the English Club; it contained tennis courts, a croquet lawn and the only golf course on the island. Today, Mnazi Mmoja is used mainly for football matches and, although the creek itself has been reclaimed, the sports field is still prone to flooding in the rainy season.

The road leading southeast out of the town (now called Nyerere Road) was originally built by Bishop Steere of the Universities Mission in Central Africa as a causeway across the swamp. Today it is a pleasant avenue lined with giant casuarina trees.

The People's Gardens The People's Gardens are on Kaunda Road, at the southern end of Stone Town, near the main hospital. They were originally laid out by Sultan Barghash for use by his harem. Many of the trees and bushes in the garden, including eucalyptus, coffee, tea and cocoa, were added by Sir John Kirk, the British consul on Zanzibar from 1873 to 1887. The gardens were given to the people of Zanzibar by Sultan Hamoud on the occasion of Queen Victoria's Jubilee in 1897 and they were renamed Victoria Gardens. The building in the centre of the gardens was called Victoria Hall. It was built over the baths of the harem and used as the Chamber of the Legislative Council from 1926 to 1964. After the revolution, the hall and gardens fell into disrepair. They were renovated in 1996, with help from the German government, and Victoria Hall is now rather ignominiously the offices of the Zanzibar Sewerage and Sanitation Project.

The large house opposite the gardens, on the south side of Kaunda Road, was built in 1903 as the official British Residency. After the 1964 Revolution, when the Victoria Gardens were renamed the People's Gardens, the old British Residency became the **State House** – the official residence of the president. The building next door to the State House was the embassy of the Soviet Union, but is now the offices of the Zanzibar Investment Promotions Agency (ZIPA), a government agency set up to attract foreign business capital to Zanzibar.

THE PALACES AT MIZINGANI

The Palace Museum (formerly the People's Palace, and before that the Sultan's Palace) was constructed on part of the site of an even older palace called Beit el Sahel, the House of the Coast, which was originally built for Sultan Said between 1827 and 1834. Contemporary accounts describe Beit el Sahel as a two-storey whitewashed palace, with a roof of green and red tiles, separated from the beach by a high wall, with a grove of pomegranates behind. The accounts go on to describe how Sultan Said spent three days of each week at Beit el Sahel, and the rest of the time at his country palace at Mtoni, about 5km north of Zanzibar Town. He often walked from the town to Mtoni even though his stables were full of Arabian horses. Every morning, the best horses were brought out from the stables and fastened to the seaward side of the wall with long ropes, to roam about and wade in the soft sand at low tide.

Another palace, called Beit el Hukm (the House of Government), was built later behind Beit el Sahel. Then, in 1883, Beit al Ajaib (the House of Wonders) was also built. These three adjoining palaces were connected by a series of covered ways and passages. A lighthouse in front of the palaces was nicknamed the 'Sultan's Christmas tree' by British navy officers, on account of its many rows of lamps.

Beit el Sahel, Beit el Hukm and the lighthouse were all destroyed in the bombardment of 1896 (see box, *The shortest war in history*, page 26). The palace that exists today (now the museum) was constructed partly on the site of Beit el Sahel. On the site of Beit el Hukm a private house was built, which is now the offices of Stone Town Conservation and Development Authority, easily seen between the Palace Museum and the House of Wonders, set back from the road. The building has a well-maintained garden with palm trees and shrubs. Outside the main entrance is a pair of cannons, made in Boston, Massachusetts, in 1868.

Most of Zanzibar's population is Muslim, consequently Zanzibar Town has several mosques. The oldest is the Malindi Mosque, a small, inconspicuous building near the port, with a minaret which is thought to be several hundred years old. Three of the larger mosques are in the northern part of Stone Town: the Ijumaa Mosque (Sunni); the Ithnasheri Mosque (Shia); and the Aga Khan Mosque (Ismaili). These were all built in the 19th century. Compared with the large mosques of other Islamic cities, often decorated with domes and tall minarets, the mosques of Zanzibar are relatively plain and unpretentious. However, in 1994, the Ijumaa Mosque (near the Big Tree) was completely renovated in a modern arabesque style, and the other large mosques may follow this trend.

Non-Muslims are not normally allowed to enter any mosque in Zanzibar Town although, if you have a genuine interest, a good local guide might be able to speak to the mosque's elders on your behalf and arrange an invitation. Men will find this easier than women. There are usually no restrictions on non-Muslims (men or women) visiting the area around a mosque, although photos of local people praying or simply congregating should not be taken without permission.

The Big Tree Just west of the Old Dispensary, about 100m along Mizingani Road, is a large tree originally planted by Sultan Khalifa in 1911. Known simply as the Big Tree (or in Swahili as *Mtini* – the place of the tree), it has been a major landmark for many years. It can be seen on numerous old photos and etchings of Zanzibar Town and is still clearly visible on the seafront from ships approaching the port. Today, traditional dhow builders use the tree as a shady 'roof' for their open-air workshop.

The Orphanage Next to the Fort, the road runs through a tunnel under a large building that is the island's orphanage. Built in the late 19th century, the building was used as a club for English residents until 1896, and then as an Indian school until 1950. There is a small craft shop on the ground floor opposite the gardens selling pictures and curios made by the orphans and other local artisans.

The Upimaji building Between the Orphanage and the People's Bank of Zanzibar, this building is now the Commission for Lands and Environment. In the 1860s, it was the offices and home of Heinrich Ruete, the German merchant who eloped with Princess Salme (see box, *Princess Salme*, pages 186–7).

The old British consulate This fine old house was used as the British consulate from 1841 to 1874, after which the consulate was moved to the Mambo Msiige building (see below). The first consul was Lieutenant-Colonel Atkins Hamerton, posted here to represent the interests of Britain after Sultan Said moved his capital from Oman to Zanzibar.

Later consuls here played host to several of the well-known British explorers, including Speke, Burton, Grant and Stanley (see page 19), before they set out for their expeditions on the east African mainland. In 1874, the body of David Livingstone was brought here before being taken back to Britain for burial at Westminster Abbey.

From 1874 to 1974 the building was used as offices by the trading company Smith Mackenzie, but it was taken over by the government in the late 1970s. It is still used as government offices today, and visitors are not allowed to enter, but there is not much to see on the inside; most of the building's interest lies in its grand exterior.

The Mambo Msiige building Its name meaning 'look but do not imitate', this grand house, incorporating a variety of architectural styles, overlooks the open 'square' at the far western end of Shangani Road. It was originally built around 1850 for a wealthy Arab, but the building was sold to the British Foreign Office in 1875 and used as the British consulate until 1913. From 1918 to 1924, it was used as the European hospital, after which it became government offices. Today, the Zanzibar Shipping Corporation is based here.

The Zanzibar Milestone Near the People's Gardens is this octagonal pillar, built with marble taken from the palace at Chukwani, showing the distances from Zanzibar Town to other settlements on the island. For complete accuracy, the distances were measured from this exact point. The distance to London is also shown: 8,064 miles. This is the distance by sea. (By 1870, ships between Zanzibar and London travelled via the Suez Canal. Before this all voyages were much longer, via the Cape of Good Hope.)

7

Around Zanzibar Town

All of the places listed in this chapter lie within about 20km of Zanzibar Town, the majority being really very close. Most can be reached easily from town as a day trip, whether by taxi, hired scooter, bike or a combination of foot and public transport. If you prefer not to travel independently, visits to any of the places mentioned here can also be arranged with a tour company. Some of the palaces and bath-houses mentioned in this section are included in the spice tours arranged by tour companies and independent guides. Of the places, Mbweni lies south of Zanzibar Town, whilst the palaces of Maruhubi and Mtoni, and the Persian Baths of Kidichi and Kizimbani, lie to the north.

SOUTH OF ZANZIBAR TOWN

The main attraction on the coast immediately south of Zanzibar is the Mbweni area, which lies 3km from the town centre and hosts a number of ruined and extant buildings dating to the late 19th century. There are a few hotels dotted around these southern suburbs of Zanzibar Town, and while they are not so convenient for sightseeing, shopping or visiting restaurants as their more central counterparts, they lie close to the airport, making them useful for very early departures or late arrivals. Most also run free shuttle services for guests to/from the centre. The hotels outside town are generally quieter, and many are used by people on business trips, as some government and NGO offices are also in this area.

MBWENI AND ENVIRONS The coastal area of Mbweni is almost directly south of Zanzibar Town and is a historically and botanically important area. Receiving relatively little settlement by the 7th-century Arabs, 12th-century Persians or 16th-century Portuguese, it was the site of a wealthy Omani family retreat in September 1871 when Bishop Tozer (Bishop of Zanzibar from 1863 to 1873) purchased 30 acres of land, then called Mbweni Point Shamba, for the UMCA (Universities' Mission to Central Africa). The stated intention was to create a village for freed slaves and an Anglican mission. Tozer's successor, Bishop Steere (Bishop of Zanzibar from 1874 to 1882) oversaw the building of the church and other coral-rock mission buildings in what was the first, large-scale missionary settlement in east Africa. The initial plot was extended over time to cover about 150 acres and developed to build schools, workshops, homes and a market, as well as sugar, coconut and maize plantations. Several of the buildings are still standing today and at Mbweni Ruins Hotel, and good bookshops in town, you can find an informative book called *Zanzibar: History of the Ruins at Mbweni* by Flo Liebst, which provides great insight into what's around as well as the UMCA missionaries of east Africa and a general history of Zanzibar.

Getting there and away To reach Mbweni, take the main road out of town towards the airport. Go uphill through the area called Kinuamiguu ('lift your legs')

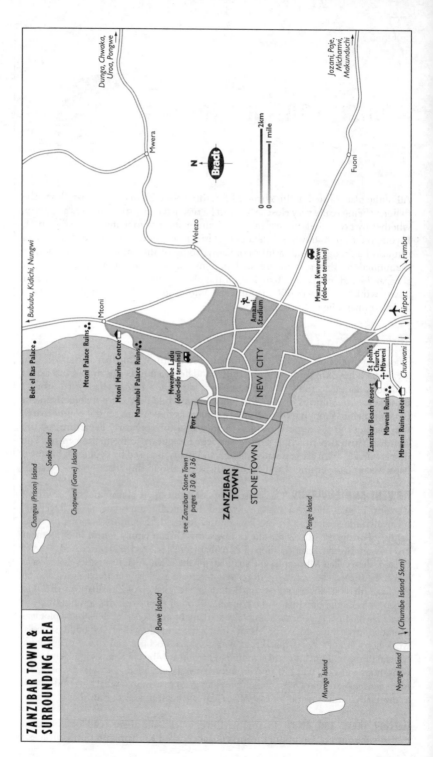

ZANZIBAR TOWN & SURROUNDING AREA

Changu (Prison) Island

Snake Island

Chapwani (Grove) Island

Bawe Island

Munogo Island

Nyange Island

(Chumbe Island 5km)

Pange Island

Bubabu, Kidichi, Nungwi

Beit el Ras Palace

Mtoni Palace Ruins

Mtoni Marine Centre

Maruhubi Palace Ruins

Mwembe Ladu
(dala-dala terminal)

Mtoni

Port

see Zanzibar Stone Town
pages 130 & 136

**ZANZIBAR
TOWN**

STONE TOWN

NEW CITY

Amaani
Stadium

Mwana Kwerekwe
(dala-dala terminal)

Welezo

Mwera

Dunga, Chwaka,
Uroa, Pongwe

Jozani, Paje,
Michamvi,
Makunduchi

Fuoni

Fumba

Airport

Chukwani

St John's
Church,
Mbweni

Zanzibar Beach Resort

Mbweni Ruins

Mbweni Ruins Hotel

N

Bradt

0   2km

0   1 mile

180

and then Mazizini. After a few kilometres, at a signpost to Mbweni and Chukwani, fork right, then after 500m turn right again onto a smaller road. Continue down this road towards the sea to reach Mbweni. *Dala-dalas* number 505 run between the town and the airport, going past the main Mbweni and Chukwani junction.

Where to stay

Mbweni Ruins Hotel (13 rooms) 024 223 5478/9; e hotel@mbweni.com; www.mbweni.com. Situated in the grounds of the Mbweni Ruins, this small hotel is widely rated as one of the best of its type in & around Zanzibar Town. The botanically named bedrooms are clean, bright & comfortable, each with a large bathroom, canopy bed, tasteful bureaux & practical additions from efficient AC to a kettle. For an especially personal touch, look carefully at the in-room artwork to discover that much of it is the handiwork of one of the owners, Flo Montgomery. Every room has a small private balcony which is a mere hop, skip, jump to the pool or beach, though Room 14, Ylang Ylang, has arguably the best view over the palm oasis to the sea beyond, & the Baobab honeymoon suite boasts its own lovely rooftop terrace.

The hotel is set in extensive well-maintained grounds with a lush botanical garden (inspired by Kirk) & nature trail through its shady terraces. From the swimming pool overlooking the beach, the new Eternal Dream Spa (www.eternaldreamspa.com) or the waterside Mangrove Bar, Mbweni is a calm, relaxing spot & a good choice for those who want to experience Stone Town but have the ability to retreat from its hustle in the heat. The food in the breezy Raintree Restaurant is made to order with fresh ingredients & it's a popular lunchtime spot for a few doting cats & visitors staying in Zanzibar Town, who have ventured out for a swim or a walk in the blossoming gardens. Lunches are US$10–20 & a full evening meal is US$10–35.

There is a free shuttle service to & from town, & transfers to/from the port or airport cost US$15 for 4 people. The ruins are open to visitors & sometimes the hotel arranges atmospheric weddings or open-air dinners amongst the pillars & arches of the school chapel. Nearby mangroves provide good birding, & the hotel has its own list of birds & butterflies seen in the grounds & further afield. The staff are keen naturalists, & can advise visitors on all aspects of local natural history. $$$$

Zanzibar Beach Resort (84 rooms) 024 2236033/44; e znzbeachresort@zanlink.com; www.zanzibarbeachresort.net. This large hotel (formerly the Fisherman's Resort & before that the Zanzibar Reef) is about 7km from Zanzibar Town & 3km from the airport, between the areas of Mazizini & Mbweni. At the time of researching, the overpowering stench of rubbish on arrival & the surly reception staff did not make for a good first impression.

The hotel is set in large, open grounds, the front section of which overlooks the sea, & has 84 en-suite rooms catering primarily for large conference groups. Accessed along neat paths lined with conical cairns, the 5 categories of room (US$20pp sea-view supplement) are all in large 2-storey chalets with whitewashed walls & thatched roofs. Inside, the en-suite rooms all have dark, heavy furniture, AC, mini fridge, TV, electronic safe & a smoke alarm. Curiously, there is pole shading above the indoor shower, sink & dressing table. The hotel has a restaurant, bar & disco, squash court, gym, swimming pool, 100-person conference room, & facilities for fishing & watersports. $$$$

What to see and do

St John's Church At the heart of Mbweni, on a small road lined with large old 'rain trees' (should you visit in a shower, you'll find the leaves all closed), is the English-style St John's Church, complete with a tower and surrounding cemetery. Nearby, is the old clergy house, which was more recently the Inn by the Sea Hotel (now closed).

St John's was opened in 1882 by UMCA missionaries and converts, and consecrated in 1904. The church has a marble altar inlaid with colourful mother-of-pearl shell and a wooden chair made for Bishop Tozer by the sailors of HMS *London*, the British naval ship famous for its slave-dhow captures. In the interesting cemetery there are also a number of very prickly cycads, naturally endemic on the east coast of Zanzibar, and thought to have been planted here by the Mbweni missionaries.

A number of descendants of freed slaves continue to live in the area and today you can visit the church and cemetery with the help of the church sexton, Peter Sudi. He is a direct descendant of John Swedi, the first African deacon of the UMCA and one of the first five slave boys to be freed and taken in by Bishop Tozer at the mission.

There are also Anglican services at 09.00 every Sunday.

St Mary's School for Girls Past St John's Church towards the sea, a dirt road leads to Mbweni Ruins Hotel, whose grounds house the remains of the St Mary's School for Girls. This Victorian school was constructed by missionaries, under the guidance of Bishops Tozer and Steere, on a property known as Mbweni Point Shamba. Constructed between 1871 and 1874, the school was a large square building, based around a central courtyard, and incorporating the old Arab house on the property into its entrance.

The school educated orphaned girls who had been freed from captured slave-dhows and the daughters of freed slaves who lived at the mission, each with their own house and small garden. Most of the girls were trained as teachers, and were taught reading, writing, arithmetic, geography and sewing. The headmistress from 1877 until 1902 was Caroline Thackeray (a cousin of the English novelist William Thackeray). In 1877, Ms Thackeray paid for the construction of an 'Industrial Wing' in which her less academically inclined pupils were given vocational training in basketry, stitching, laundry and cooking to enable them to run a home and seek employment. In 1906, the school became a convent and in 1920 the buildings were sold by the church to a consortium including the Bank of India. Over the following years, they slowly became ruins and were never used or lived in until the present time.

St Mary's also had its own chapel which, in spite of its lack of roof, is still in good condition today and makes a lovely spot for romantic dinners if you're celebrating a special occasion at the hotel.

Sir John Kirk's House Along the road which passes northwards in front of St John's Church is the house of Sir John Kirk, British consul-general in Zanzibar from 1873 to 1887. Kirk first came to Africa in the 1850s as the medical officer and naturalist on Livingstone's Zambezi expedition. As consul-general he was very active in the suppression of the slave trade and he is often regarded as the 'power behind the throne' during the rule of his close friend, Sultan Seyyid Barghash. Some historical records claim that this house was in fact a gift from Barghash, built as a country retreat for Kirk and his family when he was promoted from vice-consul to consul-general. It is certainly known that Kirk used the house frequently and that as a keen and experienced botanist, he established a large experimental garden here, which later provided the core species of all the botanical gardens of Zanzibar and mainland Tanzania. He imported many new plant species to the islands from the Royal Botanic Gardens at Kew as well as from India, the Far East and South America, and worked on improving varieties of useful and edible crops. He established spices such as nutmeg, cardamom, cinnamon, vanilla, black pepper and ginger, as well as exotic fruit trees from avocado to lychee, palms and cycads, and even rubber vines, both endemic and imported. He also planted cinchona, the source of quinine, along with other known medicinal plants. Kirk also collected trees and flowers from the mainland of Africa which formed the basis of the then standard work, *Flora of Tropical Africa*.

In 1887, Kirk left Zanzibar and sold his house to Caroline Thackeray, headmistress of the St Mary's School for Girls, and each subsequent year, she opened the impressive grounds to the public for an annual garden party.

During his lifetime, Sultan Sayyid Said (Sultan of Oman and Zanzibar from 1804–56) had three legitimate wives, or *harino* (singular *horme*). Under Islamic law, at any one time, he was allowed up to four harino.

In 1827, he married his cousin Azze binte Seif bin Ahmed, daughter of Seif bin Ahmed and grandchild of Sultan Ahmed. As in many homes today, Azze was considered to have equal status with her husband. She was reported to be strong willed and to rule the royal household with a firm hand. Apparently, no act of state was carried out without her advice and approval.

In 1847, Said married his second wife, Binte Irich Mirza, nicknamed Schesade (or Scheherazade), a beautiful, extravagant princess, and the granddaughter of the Shah of Persia. She came to Zanzibar in 1849 and Said built the baths at Kidichi for her in 1850, using stonemasons and plasterers from her homeland. Schesade had no children so Said divorced her and sent her back to Persia. By the late 1850s, Schesade had become a prominent member of the Persian army, fighting against her former husband with the hellish fury of a woman scorned!

Said's third wife was Binte Seif bin Ali, of whom little is known, but in addition to whom he is known to have possessed a great many pan-African concubines. Once these women had given birth, they were known as *sarari* (singular *surie*), immediately freed and given equal status with the legal wives.

During his lifetime, Said is credited with fathering 120 children (99 daughters and 21 sons) and when he died in 1856, he left a single widow, his first wife Azze binte Seif, and 75 sarari. Of his 120 children, only 36 were still alive: 18 sons and 18 daughters. Two of his sons, Thuwaini and Turki, became sultans of Oman; four more sons, Majid, Barghash, Khalifa and Ali, all became sultans of Zanzibar.

Although Thackeray retired as headmistress of St Mary's in 1902, she inhabited the house until her death aged 83 in 1926. She was buried in the cemetery at St John's Church and bequeathed the property to the UMCA. The house was subsequently sold to a wealthy Arab, who used it until the early 1960s. Today the property remains privately owned and not open to the public, and the gardens are somewhat wild and overgrown. Within the jungle though, Kirk's rare and exotic species stand strong.

NORTH OF ZANZIBAR TOWN

Along the coast north of Zanzibar Town, stretching over a distance of about 5km, are several palaces dating from the 19th century. Built for the various sultans who ruled Zanzibar during this period, it was commonplace for these wealthy families to retreat from the heat, smell and disease of the city in the hotter months, to less-populated corners. Some of the palaces and homes are in good condition and worth a visit; others will appeal only to keen fans of historical ruins and those with exceptionally good imaginations.

For the palaces that are open, the entrance price is very low and the ticket you buy at the first place you visit will also allow you access to many other historical sites on the same day. This includes the baths at Kidichi, the caves at Mangapwani and several other sites around the island.

The main settlement in this area, the amusingly named Bububu, is approximately 10km north of the Stone Town and is known for the attractive Fuji Beach and a number of small coastal hotels which are strung along the water's edge.

GETTING THERE AND AWAY Many of this area's historical sites are included in spice tours, and all are easily accessed with a hire car or private vehicle. On public transport, the Route 2 bus which heads north to Mangapwani village will often continue to the coast and coral cave with a little persuasion.

For Bububu, Fuji Beach and Mtoni, take *dala-dala* number 502 from Zanzibar Town, a route which can also be used for the Persian Baths at Kidichi, alighting at Bububu and continuing on foot in a westerly direction for 3km. Kidichi is also the final stop on *dala-dala* 511 and public bus Route 3.

WHAT TO SEE AND DO
Palaces
Maruhubi Palace The Maruhubi Palace is on the coast, about 4km north of Zanzibar Town. Named after the original landowner, the palace itself was built in 1882 for Sultan Barghash (sultan from 1870 to 1888) and at one time he reputedly kept 100 women here: one official wife and 99 concubines. (The sultan himself lived at the palace in Zanzibar Town.)

The palace was built with coral stone and wood, and was reported to have been one of the most ornate on the island. Large walls were built around the palace grounds, thought to have been inspired by the park walls seen by Sultan Barghash on his visit to England in 1875. Unfortunately, the palace was destroyed by a fire in 1899 and all that remains today are the great pillars, which supported the upper storey, and the Persian-style bath-house, where the separate bathrooms for the women, and the large bath for the sultan's own use, can still be seen. The original water tanks, now overgrown with water lilies, also remain

---

THE PRINCESS SALME TOUR

(Bookings must be made at least 1 day in advance: ☎ 024 2250140; m 0777 430117; e mtoni@zanzibar.cc; www.mtoni.com)

In mid 2008, the dedicated team at Mtoni Palace Conservation Project created a lovely new tour combining a number of historical palaces and traditional ceremonies, as well as an informative spice tour and delicious Swahili lunch. Escorted by a guide from the conservation project, small groups (approx four–six) are taken from the evocative ruins of Mtoni Palace, Princess Salme's birthplace, by boat to Bububu for a traditional coffee ceremony with tasty local treats (*kashata* – peanut brittle – and candy-like *halua*). After a short walk, perhaps into the grounds of Salme's cousin's home, Henrika the friendly donkey and her colourful, thatched cart transport visitors, Salme-style, to the lush Kidichi plantation area. Here, Mzee Yussuf guides a tour of his spice farm before his wife serves a deliciously fresh, homemade meal. Expect pilau rice, fish masala, roasted meats, stewed bananas, *kachumbari* salad (east African coleslaw), several vegetarian dishes and an array of tropical fruits and spice tea.

Heading back down the hillside after lunch, there are great views towards the Indian Ocean and Stone Town before the cart arrives at the Persian Baths, originally built in 1850 for Sultan Said's second wife Scheherazade. Henrika gets her break here and her two-legged cargo are whisked back to Mtoni Marine by minibus, where a chilled drink in the bar is the perfect end to the excursion.

The Princess Salme tour leaves Mtoni Marine reception at 08.00, returning at 14.00 and costs US$50 (US$5 per person supplement for fewer than three people), including all entrance fees and lunch. It's a thoroughly original and varied way to see these sites and enjoy traditional Zanzibari cuisine and US$5 of the charge is donated to the valuable work of the Mtoni Palace Conservation Project.

in the grounds. To the north of the pillars, at the back of the beach, is a small set of arches and steps; this was part of the palace's reception area. (The House of Wonders in Zanzibar Town contains a photo of the palace taken at the end of the 19th century when it was still in use.)

To reach the palace, take the main road north out of Zanzibar Town towards Bububu. Pass Livingstone House on your right and, after a few kilometres, the Maruhubi Palace is signposted on your left. *Dala-dalas* on Route B run between the town and Bububu village, past the palace entrance gate.

Beit el Mtoni or Mtoni Palace About 2km north of Maruhubi on the main road is Mtoni Palace. Built for Sultan Seyyid Said in 1828, as he moved his Empirical court from Oman to Zanzibar, it is said that the land previously belonged to Saleh bin Haramil al Abray, the Arab trader who first imported cloves to Zanzibar (see *Chapter 1*, page 12).

Mtoni, which means 'place by the river', is the oldest palace on Zanzibar and was the largest during Sultan Said's reign, being home to his first and only legitimate wife, many of his scores of secondary wives, their children and the hundreds of slaves that tended to them. It is well worth a visit, either combined with lunch at the adjoining Mtoni Marine Hotel or as part of the new Princess Salme tour (see page 184).

One of the palace's most notable residents, Princess Sayyida Salme, was one of Sultan Said's many daughters. Born at Beit el Mtoni, she became well known as the Arabian princess who fell in love with a German merchant, Rudolph Heinrich Ruete, and eloped to Hamburg, where she changed her name to Emily Ruete and converted to Christianity (see box, *Princess Salme*, pages 186–7).

In her very readable, 1888 chronicle about life on Zanzibar, *Memoirs of an Arabian Princess from Zanzibar*, Salme recalls of her paradisiacal childhood home:

> Beit il Mtoni, distant about five miles from the city of Zanzibar, lies on the sea coast, surrounded by most beautiful scenery, and quite hidden in a grove of palm and mango trees, and other gigantic specimens of tropical vegetation. The house of my birth is called 'Mtoni house', after the little river Mtoni, which rises only a few miles inland, runs through the whole palace into numerous fountains, and flows directly behind the palace walls into the splendid and animated inlet which severs the island from the African continent.

Of the building itself, she states,

> It had a large courtyard where gazelles, peacocks, ostriches and flamingos wandered around, a large bath-house at one end and the sultan's quarters at the other, where he lived with his principal wife, an Omani princess whose name was Azze.

Salme records that over 1,000 people were attached to the Sultan's court in the palace. She describes how her father, the sultan, would pace up and down on a large round tower overlooking the sea, where he could see his fleet anchored off the shore. If visitors came by boat, he would greet them on the steps of his palace as there was no landing pier, whilst Salme and the other princesses were carried out to their boats on chairs.

Sadly, she also goes on to describe her return visit to Zanzibar in 1885, after the death of Sultan Said, and the abandoned, decaying palace that she found at Mtoni. The palace was then turned into a warehouse during World War I and today only the main walls, arches, parts of the roof and bath-house remain. Yet although severely deteriorated, Mtoni Palace still offers a glimpse into the world of the Arabian royalty that once lived there. With only a little imagination and one of the conservation team guides, the impressive scale of the vast inner courtyard,

Salme was a daughter of Sultan Said. She was born at the Mtoni Palace in August 1844. Her mother was a *surie* (secondary wife) from Circassia, in southern Russia. Salme later wrote *Memoirs of an Arabian Princess*, from which we learn many interesting details about life at court and the events of the time (see *Appendix 2, Further Information*, page 378).

In her book, Salme describes her early childhood at the Mtoni Palace, where she lived until she was seven years old. Here she learnt sewing, embroidery and lace-making from her mother. She and her brothers and sisters had a private teacher and lessons were conducted in an open gallery containing just a single large mat and a Koran on a stand. The royal children were taught the Arabic alphabet, reading and a little arithmetic. The boys were also taught to write, using homemade ink, and the well-bleached shoulder blade of a camel for a slate. But Salme was rebellious and taught herself to write in secret.

Twice a day, early in the morning and in the evening, all children above five years old had riding lessons. When they had made sufficient progress, the boys received Arabian horses, while the girls received white donkeys from Muscat. When the princesses rode their donkeys to the clove plantations, slaves ran by the side of each animal with a large parasol to protect the riders from the sun. The children also learnt to swim in the sea at an early age.

Salme was given her own African slaves as personal attendants. At bedtime, one slave would massage her, while another fanned gently, until the princess fell asleep, still fully dressed. Slaves fanned the princess all night. In the morning, her slaves massaged her gently until she awoke. Her bath was filled with fresh spring water. Slaves laid out the day's clothes, on which jasmine and orange blossoms had been strewn overnight, and which were scented with amber and musk before they were worn. Windows and doors were left open throughout the year, even in colder, wetter weather when a charcoal fire was burning. The fresh air helped to disperse the strong scents. Slaves washed the linen daily. It dried in little more than half an hour, was smoothed flat (not ironed) and put away.

As a child, Salme was allowed to mix freely with boys of her own age. After she was nine years old, the only men allowed to see her were her father, close male relatives, and her slaves. She wore trousers, a shirt reaching to her ankles, and a handkerchief for the head. The shirt and trousers were always of a different pattern. On her walks, she wore a *schele*, a large shawl of black silk. When she appeared before a stranger, the law required her to be veiled; part of the face, the neck and chin, and above all, the ankles, had to be completely covered.

In October 1859, Salme became involved in family intrigue between her older brothers, Barghash and Majid. She helped Barghash escape to the Marseilles clove plantation, after his attempt to overthrow Majid failed (see box, *The Escape to Marseilles*, pages 16–17). Majid never punished Salme for her part in the plot but by siding with Barghash she lost the friendship of many of her other brothers and sisters. When she renewed her friendship with Majid, she isolated herself from her fellow conspirators.

By 1866, Salme was living in Zanzibar Town. Although 22 years old, she was still unmarried. Rejected by her family, she began socialising regularly with many of the foreigners on the island. She became friendly with a young German merchant from Hamburg, called Heinrich Ruete, who was living in a house next to hers. They began a covert relationship, speaking to each other from their balconies across the narrow street, and meeting secretly in the countryside beyond the town.

individual bathing complex and palace gardens can still be appreciated and enjoyed.

In the early 1990s, the Zanzibar Directorate of Archives, Museums and Antiquities (DAMA), in collaboration with Mtoni Marine Centre, initiated a project aimed at conserving the Mtoni Palace ruins and the surrounding gardens.

In July 1866, Salme discovered she was pregnant. Some historians have suggested that she was forced to leave Zanzibar in a hurry, as an illegitimate pregnancy would have brought disgrace to her family and the whole Busaidi dynasty and could have resulted in her death; others have described her romantic 'elopement' with Heinrich Ruete. However, an analysis by Said el-Gheithy of the Princess Salme Institute presents events in a slightly different light:

> No doubt, her pregnancy sent shock waves through her clan and threatened the position of the European traders, reliant on the goodwill of the sultan. Yet following extensive research, and through a knowledge of her personality from at least one person who knew her, it seems Salme was a very organised and stable individual, with a strength of personality which made her adverse to irrational movements. We must not overlook or underestimate her ability to choose rationally from the options available. The concept of an 'elopement' represents her as somewhat flighty. Rather, the move to Germany should be understood as a planned emigration and her departure could be described, to use a Swahili phrase, as 'leaving without saying goodbye'.

Salme left Zanzibar on a British warship, and for several months after her departure a wave of anti-European feeling spread through Zanzibar Town. Another British warship was sent to suppress any possible reprisals against Europeans. When Salme reached Aden, she stayed with some European friends, renounced Islam and was baptised into the Anglican Church, with the name Emily. In Zanzibar, Heinrich wound up his affairs, then joined Salme in Aden. They were married immediately and travelled to Heinrich's home in Hamburg.

In the following three years Salme and Heinrich had two daughters and a son. Tragically, in August 1871, Heinrich fell while jumping from a tram, and was run over; he died three days later. No longer welcome in Zanzibar, Salme remained in Germany, making one short visit to London in 1875, and two brief returns to Zanzibar in 1885 and 1888, but her attempts at reconciliation were unsuccessful. She lived in exile in Syria until 1914 and died in Germany in 1924. Among the possessions found after her death was a bag of sand from the beach at Zanzibar.

In Zanzibar Town, Princess Salme is remembered at the Palace Museum, which has a room devoted to her life and writings. This was set in place by Said el-Gheithy in collaboration with the Museums of Zanzibar. In London, the Princess Salme Institute was established in 1994 to raise awareness about the life and writings of this remarkable woman, and to promote training and research relevant to Zanzibar. The Institute is based at the Africa Centre (*38 King St, London WC2E 8JT, UK;* `\` *+44 (0)20 7240 0199;* **e** *sayyidasalme@hotmail.com*). The director of the Princess Salme Institute is Said el-Gheithy, who kindly checked the accuracy of the box text, *The Escape to Marseilles,* and provided some of the information.

For cultural events in Zanzibar, such as the Zanzibar International Film Festival (ZIFF), the Princess Salme Institute acts as a contact point in Europe. The Institute also mounts an exhibition about Princess Salme at the Festival. Additionally, the institute's modest resources keep up the enthusiasm for Salme's life and also provide practical help to academics, researchers, visitors and professionals working on or around Zanzibar. In the future, the institute hopes to establish a larger base in Zanzibar from where various projects will be administered.

Archaeological survey drawings and historical research has been commissioned and undertaken, excavations of the reservoir and impressive aqueduct in front of the palace have been completed, and substantial progress has been made in clearing the gardens, replanting original species, restoring walls using original techniques and providing visitors with some insight into the palace's history and importance. There is still a tremendous amount to be done but this work is set to continue with involvement of students from the local archives and archaeology institutes.

It is a slow, careful and expensive process, but the Mtoni Palace Conservation Project is working hard to generate the necessary funds through a number of special events and tours (see box, *The Princess Salme tour*, page 184) to fund their conservation efforts, though visitor donations are obviously welcomed. With more resources, it may just be possible to restore significant sections of Mtoni Palace and its gardens to their former splendour and to save any further dilapidation to the parts of the palace that are now beyond repair. For Zanzibaris, this is vital work to preserve a tangible memento of their past, on an island where so many historical buildings have been destroyed.

Beit el Ras Palace Further north along the coast, the construction of this palace was commissioned by Sultan Said as an 'overflow' house for his children and their servants, when Mtoni Palace became too crowded (see box, *The Wives and Children of Sultan Said*, page 183). Building started in 1847 but was not completed by the time of Said's death in 1856. Sultan Majid (Said's successor) did not continue the project and much of the stone from the palace was used during the construction of the Zanzibar railroad (described below). The remaining ruins were abandoned and finally demolished in 1947 to make room for a school and teacher-training centre. Today, the palace is within the grounds of the Nkrumah Teacher Training College (Chuo Cha Ualimu Nkrumah) and only the giant porch of the original palace remains, with high arches and steps leading up one side. Beit el Ras means 'the palace on the headland' and from the porch you get good views over this part of the coast and out towards the group of small islands off Zanzibar Town. It is reached by turning off the main road a few kilometres beyond Mtoni.

Kibweni Palace North of Beit el Ras, this 'palace' was built in Arabic style by the British authorities in 1915. In the village of Kibweni, its official title was Beit el Kassrusaada (Palace of Happiness), although this name seems to have been long forgotten. Sultan Khalifa II (sultan from 1911 to 1960) used the palace as a country residence but after the revolution it was taken over by the government and is still used as an official residence. It is not open to the public.

Chuini Palace About 10km north of Zanzibar Town, on the coast near the village of Chuini, lie the ruins of Chuini Palace. Meaning 'place of the leopard', it was built for Sultan Barghash, added to by Sultan Ali bin Said, and destroyed by fire in 1914. The ruins are on private land and cannot be visited, but there's a good fish restaurant at the nearby Hakuna Matata Beach Lodge.

The Zanzibar railroad In the early 1900s, a light railway (36-inch gauge) was built and operated by an American company. Running from a point outside the Arab Fort in Zanzibar Town, it travelled along the seafront and up the coast to the village of Bububu. Construction began in 1904 and ended in 1905, and the service was used mainly by local people, but a special first-class coach was joined to the train so that passengers from the steamers that put in to Zanzibar could get a brief glimpse of the island. The line was closed in 1928, but railway buffs can still see the remains of bridges and embankments, as today's main road between Zanzibar Town and Bububu runs parallel to the line (and in some cases over it). Bits of the original track can be seen at Bububu.

In his book *Sketches in Mafeking and East Africa* (published in 1907), Lord Robert Baden-Powell quotes from a description of the Zanzibar train by an American writer called Miss Kirkland. 'Have you ever been to Bu Bu Bu? If not, do not call yourself a travelled person,' she wrote. 'Bu Bu Bu is a settlement in a shady grove on the island of Zanzibar, and is the terminus of a new and important railroad – six and a half miles long.'

It has been suggested that the name Bububu comes from the sound made by the train's hooter, but maps dating from before the building of the railway show the village already had this title. It is more likely that the name was inspired by the sound of the freshwater springs which bubble to the surface just outside the village. Most of Zanzibar Town's water supply still comes from here.

Bububu Bububu is a small, rural village with a police station and checkpoint. The main road continues north from here towards Mahonda and Nungwi, and a new minor tar road branches off east to reach the agricultural area of Kidichi, where most visitors on spice tours arranged in Zanzibar Town are taken. If you stay on the main road for a few more kilometres, near the village of Chuini (about 10km north of Zanzibar Town) a wide dirt road forks off left, signposted to Bumbwini, and this leads to Mangapwani.

Fuji Beach Fuji Beach, near Bububu village, is a pleasant place to pause during or after some energetic sightseeing. A small dirt road leads down to the beach from near the police station in the centre of Bububu. This is the nearest beach to the town where swimming is safe and it makes a reasonable day-trip destination in its own right if you are staying in Zanzibar Town, short of time and fancy some seaside relaxing.

Local legend has it that the beach's name was due to one Mr Honda, a Japanese engineer who came to Zanzibar to build roads, but fell in love with a local girl and decided to stay. He built a 'taverna' called Fuji Beach Bar, at the time the best on the island, and the name stuck. Even though Mr Honda is no longer around, his legacy remains. The bar still sells beers and snacks, and the staff will look after your gear while you are swimming. (There have been reports of robberies here, so this is worth arranging carefully.) If you want to stay for more than a day, see the list of accommodation on pages 191–3.

Kidichi Persian Baths The Persian Baths at Kidichi lie to the northeast of Zanzibar Town, about 4km inland from the main coast road, in the island's main clove and coconut plantation area. The baths were built in 1850 for Sultan Said. He owned land in this part of the island, and he and his second wife, Binte Irich Mirza (also called Schesade, more often written Scheherazade), would come here for hunting or to oversee the work being done on their plantations. The bath-house was constructed so that they could refresh themselves after the journey from town. Schesade was a granddaughter of the Shah of Persia, so the baths were built in the Persian style, with decorative stucco work. An underground furnace kept the water warm. A small resthouse was also built nearby, but none of this remains.

Today, you can enter the bath-house, and see the changing room, bathing pool and massage tables. Unfortunately, the bath-house has not been especially well maintained over the years, and there is mould growing on much of the stucco. A colony of bats seems to have taken up residence as well. At the top of the domed ceiling is a circle of small windows: these used to be stained glass, which cast patterns of coloured light over the white walls. The conservation team from Mtoni are already looking at ways to repair and preserve the baths, and teams of specialists have been to investigate. With funding to match their care and enthusiasm, there is hope that further decay can be averted.

To reach Kidichi, continue up the main road northwards from Zanzibar Town to Bububu. At the police station, turn right onto a new tar road that leads through coconut palms and clove plantations, and past a long row of souvenir stalls selling spices and other goods. After about 4km the bath-house, a domed white building, is seen on the right, just a few metres off the dirt road. There are several more spice–souvenir stalls here, and in the surrounding area several houses where tour groups go for lunch.

Kizimbani Persian Baths Near Kidichi, these baths were also built in the Persian style for Sultan Said, at about the same time as the baths at Kidichi. They are similar in style though there is no interior decoration here. The surrounding plantations originally belonged to Saleh bin Haramil, the Arab trader who imported the first cloves to Zanzibar, but they were confiscated by Sultan Said on the grounds that Saleh was a slave smuggler (see *Chapter 1*, page 12). Today the experimental station is the island's centre for agricultural research.

To reach the baths from Kidichi, continue eastwards along the tar road. After about 2km, at a crossroads, there are roads left (north) to Mfenesini and Selem, and right (south) to Mwendo and Mwera. Go straight on, along a dirt road, passing through plantations, to reach the Kizimbani Experimental Station headquarters. The baths are on the right side of the track.

Mangapwani
Mangapwani Coral Cave Mangapwani (meaning 'Arab shore') lies on the coast, about 20km north of Zanzibar Town. The Coral Cave is a deep natural cavern in the coralline rock with a narrow entrance and a pool of fresh water at its lowest point. Water was probably collected from here by early inhabitants of this part of the island but at some time in the past vegetation grew across the entrance and the exact position of the cavern was forgotten.

Later, the area became the property of a wealthy Arab landowner called Hamed Salim el Hathy who had many slaves working on his plantations. During this time, the cavern was rediscovered by a young boy searching for a lost goat. Local people were able to use the water again, and Hamed Salim arranged for his slaves to collect the water regularly for his own use. It has been suggested by historians that the cave may have been used as a hiding place for slaves after the trade was officially abolished in 1873.

Most people come here on an organised tour, or by privately hired car or bike. Buses on Route 2 link Zanzibar Town with Mangapwani village, as do *dala-dalas* number 102, but services are not frequent. To reach the cavern from Zanzibar Town, take the main road through Bububu to Chuini, then fork left towards Bumbwini. After 6km, in Mangapwani village, fork left again and head westwards towards the coast (the Serena Restaurant and Watersports Centre, due to be the site of the new Serena Hotel, is also signposted this way). About 1km from the junction, a narrow dirt road leads off to the left (there's a small signpost). Follow this to reach the cavern. A flight of stone steps leads through the entrance down into the cave itself.

Mangapwani Slave Chamber The Mangapwani Slave Chamber is a few kilometres further up the coast from the Coral Cave. Although sometimes called the Slave Cave, it is a square-shaped cell that has been cut out of the coralline rock, with a roof on top. It was originally built for storing slaves, and its construction is attributed to one Mohammed bin Nassor Al-Alwi, an important slave trader. Boats from the mainland would unload their human cargo on the nearby beach, and the slaves would be kept here before being taken to Zanzibar Town for resale, or to plantations on the island. It is thought that some time after 1873, when Sultan Barghash signed the Anglo-Zanzibari treaty which officially abolished the slave trade, the cave was used as a place to hide slaves, as an illicit trade continued for many years.

To reach the Slave Chamber from Zanzibar Town, follow the directions to the Mangapwani Coral Cave. Instead of turning into the Coral Cave, continue on the dirt road for another 1km to reach the entrance to the Serena Restaurant and Watersports Centre. Just before you reach the Serena's 'beach club', a small dirt track branches off to the right. Follow this for 1km through palm trees and bushes to reach the Slave Chamber. With care, you can reach the steps that lead down onto the chamber floor. Nearby a small path leads to a secluded beach, separated from the main Mangapwani Beach (described below) by some coral-rock outcrops.

Mangapwani Beach Mangapwani Beach lies a few kilometres west of Mangapwani village. This has long been the planned site of a new Serena Hotel and the island's first golf club, but for now it remains the location of the accommodation-free Mangapwani Serena Beach Club. You can come here for a seafood lunch (US$30 for three courses) or something less gargantuan like lobster or prawns for US$9, or a pasta dish for US$4. There's also a nice little bar beneath the trees and a scattering of loungers on the sand. The beach is exceptionally beautiful at high tide and a great place to swim or relax. Free transfers by boat and road are arranged by the Serena Inn in Zanzibar Town (daily trips depart 10.00, return 15.00), or you can pay to travel here any time with local tour companies.

WHERE TO STAY The hotels below all lie alongside or within a few hundred metres of the main tar road between Stone Town and Bububu/Fuji Beach. They are listed in the order you would pass them coming from the direction of Zanzibar Town.

Maruhubi Beach Villas (12 rooms) m 0777 451188; e maruhubi@zanlink.com; www.maruhubibeachvillas.com, www.zanzibarmaruhubi.com. Situated close to the eponymous ruins some 3km north of Stone Town, this attractive, low-key resort is clearly signposted off the main road. It has a superb location on a sandy beach offering views back to the House of Wonders on the Zanzibar waterfront as well as to Mtoni Beach.

Accommodation is in airy & spacious semi-detached bungalows, running in a single row perpendicular to the sea. The majority are set in beautiful tropical gardens, filled with flowers, but Rooms 1–4 are set on a coral rock pier with wonderful panoramic views up & down the coast. Interiors are lovely in their simplicity with large, coconut wood Zanzibari beds, subtle apricot walls, sparkling en-suite bathrooms, AC, a fan & wide verandas, complete with mattress-covered sun loungers. The huge *makuti* Sunset Restaurant offers lunch & dinner at neat tables, around which are vibrant turquoise directors' chairs. Menu options are varied & reasonably priced – vegetarian pancake US$5; calamari tempura US$7; beef kebab US$10 – & it is licensed to serve alcohol. The new swimming pool above the beach is a big asset & non-residents are welcome to pay US$5/day to indulge. $$$–$$$$

Mtoni Marine (46 rooms) ☎ 024 2250140; m 0777 486214; e mtoni@zanzibar.cc; www.mtoni.com. Located between the palaces of Maruhubi & Mtoni, about 5mins' drive north of Zanzibar Town, Mtoni Marine is a highly recommended, friendly hotel set in exceptional, tropical gardens overlooking the bay & a large, private stretch of sandy beach.

The management style, a mix of Zanzibari & Italian, is relaxed & efficient – a perfect combination. There's a broad range of accommodation from the spacious Palm Court dbls to the new 2-bedroom family apartments, complete with kitchenette & sea-view terrace. The rooms are all cool & comfortable with high ceilings & cleverly incorporated Omani features. Each is flower-filled & tastefully decorated with beautiful colours, quality fabrics & a raft of mod-cons (AC, fans, electronic safes, minibar). Within the grounds, there are 3 restaurants, the food at which is well regarded, in particular the Zansushibar on the beach which is a draw for many from Zanzibar Town. Snacks start at US$3–5 & you can enjoy an excellent meal for US$10–20. For casual dining, there are twice-weekly buffet barbecues (US$12) & the ever-popular Mcheza Bar & Bistro serving oven-baked pizzas, sandwiches & burgers whilst broadcasting international sport to resident & tourist enthusiasts. For something more romantic, candlelit dinners & imported wines are available in the main restaurant, or there is a sunset dhow cruise for great views of Stone Town in the rosy evening light (US$15pp, including snacks & soft drinks). All-day dhow cruises are also arranged, at US$40 including lunch, drinks & snorkel gear, with discounts for hotel guests.

If you want to stay nearer your room, the hotel has a spa, pleasant swimming pool & a great playhouse/climbing frame for energetic children. The staff can also arrange tours (for something local, see box, *The Princess Salme tour*, page 184), car hire, boat trips & taxis (US$6 to Stone Town; US$15 to the airport). With lovely rooms & plenty of space at fantastic value, particularly for families or those wanting a little space for their Stone Town explorations, Mtoni continues to build on its strong reputation as a high-quality hotel. Mtoni Marine is also the official Visa International assistance agent for Zanzibar. $$$–$$$$

⌂ **Via Via** (5 rooms) m 0744 286369; e zanzibar.tanzania@viaviacafe.com. Also known as Kalinge's Garden Bungalows, after its European owner Mama Kalinge, this is an affiliate of the well-known Belgian café in Arusha. Set in a shady green oasis about 7km from Stone Town along the Bububu road, & within 5mins' walk of Fuji Beach, it's a relaxed set-up, offering uncluttered accommodation in rustic 4-bed en-suite bungalows suitable for budget travellers & families. Each room has a dbl & 2 sgl coir-rope beds, blue mosquito nets, a fan & now AC. In the large, terraced *makuti* lounge, there are comfortable chairs, a lovely coconut-wood bar & even a hutch of cute white bunnies. Facilities include free airport pick-ups & transport to & from Stone Town, as well as a home-cooked *plat du jour* for around US$5. $$

⌂ **Imani Beach Villa** (9 rooms) ☏ 024 2250050; m 0741 333731; e info@imani.it; www.imani.it. About 9km from Stone Town, Imani Beach Villa is clearly signposted off the main road. From here, a bumpy coral-rock track meanders downhill towards the sea & Imani's beachfront plot. Tucked away in a mass of cerise bougainvillea & banana trees, it is a small & delightful home-from-home hotel with 9 en-suite rooms, all featuring enormous Zanzibari beds & clean bathrooms. Centred on the villa's small, antique-filled lounge/entrance, the ocean view from the burgundy day-bed, the sound of rolling waves & the constant breeze all create a distinctly exotic air. Outside, billowing orange & monochrome fabric panels conceal a cool Arab-style bar & restaurant in the tropical garden. Meals here are at low tables sat on piles of cushions & Persian carpets & cost around US$20.

Though neat & generally well maintained, Imani was just beginning to look a little tired in 2008. However, in May, Cornish bar-manager Simon Bennett & his girlfriend Kristen took over the management, bringing a fresh approach & buckets of enthusiasm. From clearing up the beach to creating the island's most original cocktails, they have lots of plans & a hands-on attitude, so with luck Imani will be re-energised & revamped into a gem of a hidden hideaway. A taxi to/from town is around US$10 & the hotel also has bikes which are free for guest use. $$$

⌂ **Salome's Garden** (4 rooms) ☏ 024 2250050; m 0741 333731; e info@houseofwonders.com; www.houseofwonders.com. On the edge of the beach, this impressive old Omani house is set in lush gardens & surrounded by an imposing wall. Once owned by a nephew of Sultan Said, it is said that Princess Salme used to rest here on her way to the Kizimbani plantations. Its airy bedrooms are available for rent but our visit in early 2008 showed them to be distinctly unloved & very sadly falling into disrepair. The interiors were spartan with simple Zanzibari beds, Persian carpets & the odd antique mixed with uncharacteristic moulded-concrete bathrooms & a good deal of mould.

There is what should be an amazing upper terrace, perfect for relaxing & dining but the furnishings are sparse, staff mainly absent & atmosphere slightly sad. The sea views through the huge trees in the garden are nice though & the breeze always welcome. It's impossible not to think that with a little thought & attention, this could return to being a perfect place for small groups of friends & family. It was once filled with lovely old furniture to match its historical links, giving the place a really magic feel & reminding guests that to stay in such a place was a privilege. We very much hope that one day this feeling returns. The only other comment is that, like the Imani next door, the high wall around the property doesn't stop the noise of music drifting over when there's a disco (Fri–Sun), at Fuji Beach Bar a short distance along the sand. This hotel can be booked via the House of Wonders or through the contact details listed above, though our impression is that it may be set to close. $$$$

⌂ **Bububu Beach Guesthouses** (8 rooms) m 0777 422747; e kilupyomar@hotmail.com; www.bububu-zanzibar.com. Set in Bububu village, these 2

The house on Changuu Island, a short distance offshore from Zanzibar Town, once belonged to William Lloyd Mathews, a military officer and later a government official in Zanzibar in the latter part of the 19th century.

Mathews was a Welshman born in Madeira in 1850. He entered the British Navy in 1864, and from 1870 served in the slave-patrolling boats of HMS *London*. In August 1877, Mathews was seconded from the Navy and appointed to command and organise a European-style army for Sultan Barghash, who wanted to enforce his sovereignty over the interior. Until then, the sultan's army had been composed of Arabs and Persians only, but the new army contained 500 Africans, with a uniform of red caps, short black jackets and white trousers. The Arab officers wore dark-blue frock coats and trousers, with gold or silver lace, possibly modelled on uniforms of the British Royal Navy. The British government donated 500 rifles and by the beginning of the 1880s Mathews had about 1,300 men under his command.

One of the new army's first tasks was to stop the slave smuggling between Pemba and Pangani on the mainland and they were soon successful, capturing several slave smugglers and hindering the illicit trade. Mathews was released from the Navy and became Brigadier-General Mathews, commander-in-chief of Zanzibar's army.

In 1891, when a constitutional government was established in Zanzibar, Brigadier-General Mathews was appointed as His Highness's First Minister and he was awarded a knighthood on 3 March 1894. On 11 October 1901, Sir William Lloyd Mathews died in Zanzibar, of malaria, at the age of 51. He was buried with full naval and military honours in the English cemetery outside Zanzibar Town.

guesthouses are simple but clean, friendly & very relaxed. Each can sleep up to 8 persons (2 dbls; 1 quad) in adequate en-suite rooms with nets, fans & AC, & seem reasonably good value. There's a living room, dining room & kitchen. Although mainly geared to longer-stay visitors & family groups, the rooms can be rented individually, with self-catering or FB options available. Meals are available at nearby Fuji Beach (see page 189), which has a bar & restaurant.

The owner, Omar Kilupi can arrange spice tours, rental cars & motorbikes, or challenge you to a game of chess as he's one of the island's master players! There's a free transfer service to/from town twice a day or you can catch one of the frequent *dala-dalas* running between Bububu village & Zanzibar Town. From the *dala-dala* stop on the main road in Bububu village, it's a short walk down a dirt track towards the beach to reach the hotel. $$

ISLANDS NEAR ZANZIBAR TOWN

A few kilometres from Zanzibar Town are several small islands, some of which are good destinations for a relaxing day's outing. Boat trips to the islands can be arranged with a tour company, with one of the papaasi (touts) who look for business around town and along the seafront, or direct with one of the boat captains. Costs range from US$15 to US$60 for the boat, or from US$5 to US$20 per person, depending on who you deal with, the number of hours you want, the quality of the boat and whether you're prepared to share with other people or want a boat to yourself. Other factors might be lunch or snorkelling gear included in the price. You can hire a boat for yourself, or reduce costs by getting your own small group together. If you're alone, it's usually easy to link up with other travellers. Boats go across to the islands every morning from the beach by the Big Tree on Mizingani Road (the seafront), from the beach near the Tembo Hotel and the beach opposite the Africa House Hotel.

When staying on the islands overnight, check that security is provided by the hotel, and do bear in mind that these islands are isolated, without mains electricity and most of Zanzibar's boats do not have lights, making travel by sea highly treacherous after dark. There has been at least one serious 'pirate' raid on a hotel in the past, albeit some time ago now, so exercise caution after dark and consider a stay here carefully if you have small children or any existing medical conditions.

CHANGUU ISLAND Lying in the Zanzibar Channel, four miles northwest of Zanzibar Town, Changuu is a coral-rag islet, also known as Prison Island and at one time Kibandiko Island. It was originally owned by a wealthy Arab trader who used Changuu as a detention centre for disobedient slaves. After the abolition of slavery, in 1873, the island was bought by General Lloyd Mathews, commander of the sultan's army, who built a house here (see box, *William Lloyd Mathews*, page 193). In 1893, a prison (recently converted into a café, library and boutique) was built on the island but it was used instead as a quarantine station for the whole east African region. In the 1920s, passengers arriving from India had to spend between one and two weeks on Changuu before proceeding to Zanzibar Town.

Today, it is most famous for proving sanctuary to a creep of giant tortoises (*Geochelone gigantea*), descendants of four gifted from the Seychellois governor to his opposite number in Zanzibar in the 18th century. Shipped from their home on the island of Aldabra in the Seychelles, they started to breed and by 1955 there were 200 tortoises. Sadly, their numbers began to drop after independence, partly because people started to steal them to sell abroad, either as unusual pets or as food for 'exotic restaurants'. Numbering 100 in 1988, 50 in 1990 and only seven by late 1996, measures were taken to protect them and in the same year 80 hatchlings were moved to Zanzibar for protection – ironically, 40 of them still disappeared. Today the tortoises are protected in a large sanctuary compound provided by the Zanzibar government with help from the World Society for the Protection of Animals. In 2000, there were 17 adults, 50 juveniles and 90 hatchlings, all individually identified and protected by microchips injected under the skin. Since then, many more have been brought in, mostly juveniles. You can go into the sanctuary to see the tortoises close up and even feed them (they delight in fresh mango peel), but please do obey the signs and do not lift or sit on the tortoises.

Changuu Island has a small beach and there's reasonable snorkelling on the nearby reef. A secluded beach hotel has recently opened too and daily tours to see the historical ruins and tortoises are organised by many of Stone Town's operators, invariably making the 20-minute crossing by dhow under sail.

Where to stay

Changuu Private Island Paradise (27 rooms) m 0773 333241/2; e info.changuu@ privateislands-zanzibar.com; www.privateislands-zanzibar.com. Opened in 2006, the team behind Changuu Private Island Paradise has restored & converted many of the crumbling Arab & colonial buildings on the island, built 15 individual beachfront cottages, & introduced a host of guest facilities from a swimming pool to a floodlit tennis court in the forest. 'Deluxe' thatched cottages in the northwest of the island offer the most privacy & boast outdoor showers & baths, whilst the 'standard' rooms to the southwest are in the former 1931 Quarantine Area & have good views across to Stone Town's waterfront. The décor in all is bright & cheerful with vibrant coloured paint & fabrics, a good amount of space & veranda deckchairs for soaking up the sun.

There is no mains electricity on the island, & whilst there is generator power from 18.00 to 23.00, there is no AC & it's well worth remembering to take a good torch for evening beach walks. In a restored 19th-century home, Mathews' Restaurant serves extensive 4-course dinners & a good, predominantly seafood, lunch menu. There's a pleasant little beach & whilst swimming & snorkelling in the sea is possible, serious caution is advised as these are busy shipping waters. On land, guests have free run of the island whilst day visitors are confined to the ruins & tortoise sanctuary. For all the pleasures of privacy though, island life is not for those who plan on several excursions as boat transfers to Zanzibar Town soon mount up (US$60 boat/return – unless you hitch with the touring day trippers), or for those seeking lively evenings or varied entertainment. It is very quiet & isolated on the island, & worth remembering that it is not possible to return to the island after dark as few boats out of Stone Town will have lights. ♨

CHAPWANI ISLAND This is also called Grave Island as a small section of it has been used as a Christian cemetery since 1879. Most of the graves belong to British sailors who were killed fighting against Arab slave ships, including Captain Brownrigg who died with most of his men at the hands of notorious salve-trafficker, Hindi bin Hattam, as he attempted to rescue 100 slaves on board Hattam's dhow to Pemba. A number of graves belong to crew of the World War I British ship *Pegasus*, which was bombarded and sunk by the German *Königsberg* in Zanzibar Town harbour. (This latter event is described in detail in the book *Königsberg – a German East African Raider* listed in *Appendix 2*.)

There is a small beach on the island, and a lovely patch of indigenous forest, with a population of small duikers, some massive coconut crabs and a colony of fruit bats, which every evening do a few circuits of the island then zoom off to Zanzibar Town in a dark cloud. There are about 100 species of bird in the area, including a small population of black heron in the northeast, whose presence the new lodge is trying hard to encourage.

Where to stay

🛏 **Chapwani Private Island** (10 rooms) e info@ houseofwonders.com; www.chapwaniisland.com. Chapwani's original hotel ceased operating in 2003, but more recently 10 rooms in 5 small, semi-detached bungalows have opened on the sandy beach. Refurbished in mid 2005, all rooms are en suite with Zanzibari beds, mosquito nets & a timber-decked terrace, complete with a lounger & chairs. There is generator power by day but it goes off at midnight, so don't forget your torch or elect to stay here if AC is a must.

Activities are limited, but there's a nice pool tucked in the trees or, for a more natural dip, there's a tidal outlet in a coral crevasse on the northeast of the island which makes for a pleasant place to swim at high tide. At low tide, the exposed reef offers interesting exploration, with coral, starfish & barnacle-clad rock pools around the island. The environment & multi-lingual management make this a perfectly pleasant place to stay but like the other islands in the channel off Zanzibar Town, it lacks a feeling of real 'desert island' isolation from being so close to the main shipping routes, yet it doesn't benefit from the evening buzz of Stone Town. $$$$$

SNAKE ISLAND Sometimes known by its Swahili name, *Nyoka*, this is a very small island between Changuu and Chapwani islands. Tourist boats rarely land here as there is no beach and local legend claims it was once infested by snakes, which has long kept the local community away from its shores.

BAWE ISLAND About 6km due west of Zanzibar Town, Bawe is a beautiful little island with broad sandy beaches and a densely vegetated centre. In 1879, the island was given to the Eastern Telegraph Company by Sultan Barghash to be used as the operations station for the underwater telegraphic cable linking Cape Town with Zanzibar, the Seychelles and Aden in Yemen. A second line was run from Bawe Island to the External Telecommunications building in the Shangani area of Zanzibar Town. The old 'Extelcoms' building has now been converted into the Serena Inn, but the original phone line is largely redundant.

Lovely as the beach may be, it is firmly on the busy shipping route to Zanzibar Town and isn't visited as frequently as Changuu. In theory, it's possible to combine trips here with the tortoise excursions or simply arrange an out-and-back voyage with a boat captain in Zanzibar Town, though access prices do tend to be higher than those to Changuu.

Where to stay

Bawe Tropical Island (15 rooms) m 0773 333241/2; e info.bawe@privateislands-zanzibar.com; www.privateislands-zanzibar.com. The original Cable & Wireless staff posted on Bawe allegedly had regular island parties for their town-based friends & colleagues. With the arrival of this new lodge, visitors can once again retreat from the frenzy of Zanzibar Town to this pretty beach spot. 15 ochre, thatched cottages line the sand, & like its sister hotel on Changuu Island, the interior colour schemes are vibrant, the furniture solid & the en-suite bathrooms feature moulded-concrete baths. There are spacious, pole-shaded terraces & it's nice to be merely a stone's throw from the warm, shallow sea, though a good awareness of the shipping traffic is important. There is little more to do than sit on the beach, & access to Stone Town is possible only on short day trips (sea journeys in often unlit boats are dangerous after sunset), making a stay less attractive to those keen to experience Stone Town by night or the less-busy waters available elsewhere around Zanzibar. ♛

8

Northern Zanzibar

Burgeoning guesthouses, vibrant nightlife and pressure on its community and natural resources now characterise northern Zanzibar, above its pleasant, white-sand beaches, warm sea, nautical heritage and good diving opportunities. Less than two hours' drive from Stone Town on the fast tar road past increasingly rural villages, this is the heart of the island's budget tourism industry. Focused around Nungwi village on the northernmost tip, and spreading with increasing momentum toward the golden sands of Kendwa, on the northwest coast, this bustling backpacker centre initially appears to offer every component of the perfect holiday to its sun-kissed guests: cheap accommodation, fresh seafood washed down with daily cocktails, and a lovely outlook. Sadly, however, there are some serious social and environmental problems bubbling in this area and many visitors, and a good number of the foreign and local investors, appear to be blind to the spiralling situation.

It is worth contemplating some alarming statistics: in the last two years the number of places to stay in Nungwi and Kendwa has increased by 34% and 33% respectively. That may seem manageable, if it weren't for the scale of developments. Once-small backpackers' boltholes have grown from 18 to 32 rooms, mid-range hotels have added up to 77 rooms to their original 36, large scale all-inclusive resorts have bought up vast tracts of land, and virtually every beachfront plot from Ras Nungwi to Kendwa has some tourist accommodation, either operational or under construction. Every single property listed in this chapter has expanded either up or out, or is newly built, since the last edition of this book in 2006.

It is crowded and the development not always attractive: high breeze-block walls now block the once-stunning views along the northeast coast and ever-taller hotels jostle for a spot on the low coral cliffs at the seaside. It's still possible, however, to escape the 'Nungwi Strip' to seek out the quieter, more spectacular beaches of the northeast coast and Kendwa, but it's getting more challenging with every month that passes.

NUNGWI

Nungwi is traditionally the centre of Zanzibar's dhow-building industry, and, over the last decade, the coastline here has rocketed in popularity to become the island's busiest beach destination. The ramshackle fishing village has been sidelined by an ever-increasing number of guesthouses, bars, shops, restaurants and bikini-clad Europeans. Ageing hippies, cool dudes, gap-year students and bright young things escaping European city jobs are all drawn to its white sand, stage-set palm trees, turquoise sea and sparkling sunshine.

By day, the beach sees sunbathing tourists slumber, swim and indulge in lemongrass massages, whilst wandering local guys tout their 'tours' and sell a range

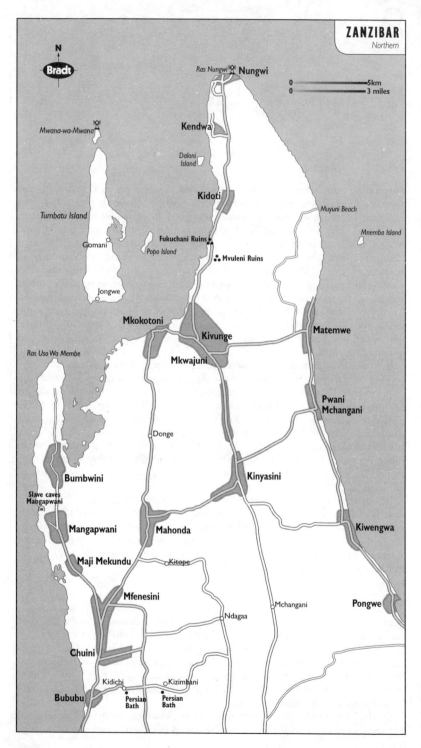

of mediocre paintings, sunglasses and replica football shirts; then, as the sun sets, the visitors arise and the whole place buzzes with party spirit. Beach bonfires blaze, cocktails flow and the music rocks till dawn; this is not a location for those seeking silence or solitude. The setting may be beautiful, but the number of people, the constant noise and the seemingly uncontrolled levels of development all take the edge off its charm.

In the two years since writing the previous edition of this guide, the number of hotel rooms in Nungwi has rocketed from 405 to 841– a staggering 108% increase! It is shocking to see and for anyone who has visited this area before, the village and beachfront are totally unrecognisable: hotels have grown into a sprawling mass in literally every direction, roads have been re-routed and costs have escalated. With the exception of the World Bank-funded tar road to Stone Town, and the police post paid for by local hoteliers, there has been no significant thought given to how the natural resources, specifically fresh water, or basic utilities will cope with this vast increase in visitor numbers. The local population is suffering the consequences, which is in danger of further alienating them from those who come to enjoy their 'island paradise'.

Ironically, given its current state, Nungwi was one of the last coastal settlements on Zanzibar to have a hotel, or any tourist facilities. For despite, or perhaps in spite of, the influx of tourists, Nungwi remains a fairly traditional, conservative place. As recently as the mid 1990s, proposals for large developments in the area were fiercely opposed by local people. Today, the proudly independent villagers give the impression that tourists are here on sufferance. However, they are not unfriendly and most visitors find that a little bit of cultural respect, politeness and a few words of Swahili go a long way. It is very important to behave and dress appropriately in the village; do follow the signs and wear modest clothing.

Some visitors, particularly backpackers, find themselves torn between either coming to Nungwi and the north coast, or going to Paje, Bwejuu and Jambiani on the east coast. For some thoughts on the differences between these two areas, see page 229.

GETTING THERE AND AWAY Nungwi can be reached by bus, tourist minibus or hired vehicle. From Zanzibar Town the main road to Nungwi goes via Mtoni, Mahonda, Kinyasini and Kivunge. There is a more scenic route directly north of Mahonda to Mkokotoni, which, once the preserve of 4x4s only, is now wonderfully accessible on the new tar road.

As you enter Nungwi, a conglomeration of signs advertising accommodation and activities marks a fork in the road and the end of the tar. Head right for Nungwi's east coast hotels and the village, or straight on for the beachfront properties of North, South and West beaches.

If you are travelling by public transport, there are daily *dala-dalas* (number 116) leaving Creek Road in Zanzibar Town for Nungwi, roughly every 30 minutes between 05.30 and 21.00. Alternatively, between 07.00 and 18.00 there are half-hourly public buses (Route 14) departing Darajani Terminal, Zanzibar Town. On arrival in Nungwi, the main stop is opposite a large football pitch inland of the village, from where it's a 15-minute walk through the village to the heart of the tourist throng. The shared tourist minibuses, a more popular option, will stop in the centre of the action, beside Amaan Bungalows. Departures south leave from the same locations.

It has also been known for onward travellers to pay local fishermen to take them by boat to their next destination, even as far as Matemwe on the northeast coast. Ask around to ensure reliability and safety, make sure people know where you're going, and do check that there's a decent motor and safety equipment (like life jackets and working radios or mobile phones) for longer trips.

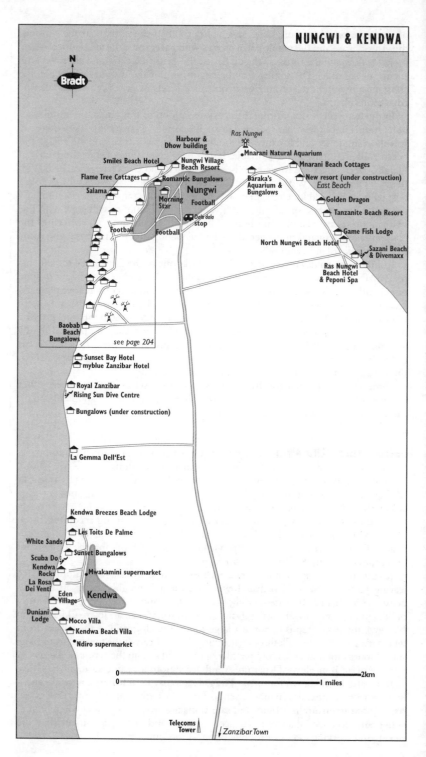

NUNGWI & KENDWA

N
Bradt

Ras Nungwi

Harbour &
Dhow building

Mnarani Natural Aquarium

Smiles Beach Hotel

Nungwi Village
Beach Resort

Mnarani Beach Cottages

Flame Tree Cottages

Romantic Bungalows

New resort (under construction)
East Beach

Salama

Baraka's
Aquarium &
Bungalows

Nungwi

Morning
Star

Golden Dragon

Football

Tanzanite Beach Resort

Dala dala
stop

Football

Football

Game Fish Lodge

North Nungwi Beach Hotel

Sazani Beach
& Divemaxx

Ras Nungwi
Beach Hotel
& Peponi Spa

Baobab
Beach
Bungalows

see page 204

Sunset Bay Hotel

myblue Zanzibar Hotel

Royal Zanzibar

Rising Sun Dive Centre

Bungalows (under construction)

La Gemma Dell'Est

Kendwa Breezes Beach Lodge

Les Toits De Palme

White Sands

Sunset Bungalows

Scuba Do

Kendwa
Rocks

Mwakamini supermarket

La Rosa
Dei Venti

Eden
Village

Kendwa

Duniani
Lodge

Mocco Villa

Kendwa Beach Villa

Ndiro supermarket

0 ————————————————— 2km
0 ————————————————— 1 miles

Telecoms
Tower

Zanzibar Town

200

GETTING AROUND Most places in and around Nungwi are within walking distance, but if you're staying on the slightly more upmarket east side of the peninsula, and fancy letting your hair down on the lively west side, the local taxi service charges US$8 each way. Ask your hotel to put you in touch with a responsible driver.

If you want to tour this part of the island, for example to visit Fukuchani and Mvuleni Ruins (see *Regional excursions*, pages 226–7), then it's possible to hire motorbikes, jeeps and bicycles. Ask your hotel or a reputable ground operator to help you arrange this.

WHERE TO STAY For simplicity, the following hotels and guesthouses are listed roughly in clockwise order, from the southwest of the peninsula, round the headland and down the eastern coast.

South Beach The road into Nungwi from Zanzibar Town reaches a fork on the village outskirts. To reach places at the southern end of the west side of the peninsula, go left here, along a dusty track, towards the sea. This area has become unofficially known as South Beach, but it's a handy name, and might just stick.

Just west of the village, South Beach is effectively the busiest beach. There is no reef in front of the shore here, so the water is deep enough for swimming, whatever the state of the tide. As the beach faces west, it is also a great spot for watching the sun go down. A number of the cheaper places to stay are located here, but more recently it has become home to the imposing, contemporary Z Hotel, so its 'budget basics' image may begin to change. Whatever the accommodation, this remains the liveliest part of Nungwi.

Royal Zanzibar (100 rooms) www.royalzanzibar.com. Set in newly planted tropical gardens & enjoying a secluded sandy cove between Nungwi & Kendwa, are the large, castellated accommodation blocks of this new 100-room resort. Opened at the end of 2008, the Royal Zanzibar is owned by the same family as Southern Palms Beach Resort in Kenya, & it will likely operate in a similar all-inclusive, entertainment-focused vein. Eating & drinking are heavily emphasised with a staggering 8 restaurants & bars, from Samaki with its oriental dining to the swim-up Upendo pool-bar. For those who want to work off the calories, there's an on-site subsidiary of the east coast's Rising Sun Dive Centre, & both residents & passers-by can organise dive excursions (other watersports equipment is for guest use only). For younger guests, the kids' club is open daily 10.00–18.00 or there are a number of swimming pools, games, racket sports & hosted activities to stay active. $$$$$

Mosquito Blue (50 rooms) e sales@ mosquitoblue.com; www.mosquitoblue.com. Under construction in mid 2008 with a planned opening in August, Mosquito Blue is the African sibling of identically named hotels in Brazil & Mexico. Promising to bring the same contemporary chic style to this 50-bed resort, it will also aim to attract a similarly young, style-conscious market from Europe.

The 2-storey, whitewashed accommodation blocks have a slightly Spanish feel & boast flat-screen satellite TVs, Wi-Fi, AC & even 'waterfall' showerheads. Yet the myriad facilities planned for the next year are designed to lure couples from their dens with a spa, gym, games room & sparkling pool. Sandwiched between the large family resorts of Royal Zanzibar & Sunset Bay, & in striking distance of many a backpacker haven, it will be interesting to see if this luxury, adult-only hotel can succeed here. Friendly owners Salvatore & Hannie are certainly brimming with the necessary enthusiasm & commitment. *US$120pp, FB*

Sunset Bay Hotel (32 rooms) m 0774 555555; e reservations@sunsetZanzibar.com/ info@bluebayZanzibar.com; www.sunsetZanzibar.com. The first foray to the north for Zanzibar's established Bluebay Group, Sunset Bay opened in December 2006. There are 32 rooms, making the hotel reasonably small by this coast's standards, divided among 8 slightly crude, 2-storey buildings (hopefully more vegetation is planned to soften them). Inside, the rooms are spacious, if soulless, with a tiled en-suite shower room, separate dressing area & balcony. There are large king-size coconut-wood beds, rich red curtains, cheap rugs on tiled floors & an array of mod-cons: cable TV, fan, AC & mini fridge. The blocks where the *makuti* roof appears to have been lifted above the outer walls, house the deluxe rooms, & this curious design is to allow for a roof terrace. Here, couples can lounge on the rooftop dbl beds, in the company of the 3 other couples sharing their block. Privacy issues aside, this vantage point affords a reasonable sea view & a good one of the antics at the neighbouring resort. For a sea view, request a room towards the front of the complex or your balcony may look at little more than the block in front. Landscaping is primarily lawn, leaving the place feeling a little stark, but there is a raised 'imported' beach above the coral cliff to ensure guests can sunbathe with their toes in the sand at any time of day, & a lovely large swimming pool.

The restaurant & bar is in a canvas-sided, *makuti* structure by the sea, & sitting on its comfy sapphire sofas, cocktail in hand, there's a distinctly tropical feel. Practise your Italian if you want to make small talk though, as 50% of the rooms are exclusively allocated to an Italian tour operator; there are also a good number of Italian staff. It is also worth knowing that without written confirmation of your reservation, gaining access to the hotel in the first place is virtually impossible, & whilst security is to be commended, surly, unhelpful gate staff are not. US$205–270/300–416 sgl/dbl, FB

🏠 **Baobab Beach Bungalows** (120 rooms) 📞 024 2236315; m 0777 416964; e baobabnungwi@ zanzinet.com/baobabnungwi@yahoo.com; www.baobabbeachbungalows.com. Having doubled in size in the last 2 years, this is now the largest establishment on this stretch of coast, though a few others are springing up in close competition. Zanzibari owned, the hotel is managed by an Egyptian tourism company, Flash International, & sold to Italians through all-inclusive operator 'Going'. If you are not Italian, the canary-yellow tarpaulin banners emblazoned with Italian slogans, the 'pasta station' in the restaurant, & Italian-speaking staff may well put you off staying here. Otherwise the location is fine, if increasingly cluttered. At the southernmost end of South Beach, Baobab does boast its own small sandy cove, albeit the rise in visitor numbers & bead-selling Maasai make it busier than ideal. Above this natural enclave, the hotel has moved sand onto the higher coral rock to create a raised 'beach', for scores of loungers & *makuti* parasols. From here, the rooms stretch back inland & are divided into 5 categories, all spotlessly clean with en-suite bathrooms, hot & cold water, ceiling fans, mosquito nets, mains electricity, UK-style 3-pin sockets & a private balcony. Compact standard rooms are set back from the sea, amid neatly manicured gardens,

but their small size makes them little more than a place to sleep. Unless your budget won't stretch the extra US$20, the best accommodation options are probably the lodges & deluxe rooms. Even if they are set far from the water's edge, these rooms benefit from a reasonable view of the sea & proximity to the central swimming pool, making them perfect for watching ocean sunsets or popping out for a midnight dip. The polygonal superior rooms at the back of the resort complex are notable for their size alone; they are furthest from everything, & have little in the way of a view. A further row of comfortable deluxe rooms does run perpendicular to the beach, & offers a little extra space along with tiled floors, AC, Zanzibari coconut-wood furniture & incongruous fluffy pink bathmats; at the same price as the superior rooms, these are a far better bet.

The new, buffet-only Baobab Restaurant serves passable Italian cuisine; although its adjacent toilets were notably smelly on our last visit. There is an Italian diving operation at the resort, Ocean Diving (www.oceandiving.it). In a beachfront centre, which arguably enjoys the resort's premium position, it is right on the edge of the coral cliff, immediately above the sea. Unlike much of this place, it is open to non-residents. *Bungalow $$$$; lodge/deluxe $$$$$*

🏠 **The Nungwi Inn Hotel** (24 rooms) 📞 024 2240091; e thenungwi_inn@hotmail.com. Nungwi Inn Hotel is unusual in that its 2 categories of room & reception are all geographically detached; its 14 sea-view rooms are right on the beach, just behind the Spanish Dancer Dive Centre, whilst its other rooms are set in gardens, without sea views, across the dirt road; & its reception is roughly between the two, at the back of the beachfront restaurant. These rooms are a good bet: bright & airy, they are spotlessly clean with starched white bedding, mosquito nets, fans (AC in some rooms), 24hr electricity, UK-style 3-pin sockets & hot water in the en-suite bathrooms. The hotel's newest rooms, scattered where there was space throughout, are neat, semi-detached thatched cottages which offer slightly more space. If a true sea view is your priority, opt for Rooms 1–5 or 7/8. The Nungwi Inn Restaurant & Bar (see page 212) is on the sand & offers nice, simple food & even the occasional beach BBQ. Rooms here can also be booked though the Spanish Dancer Dive Centre website (www.spanishdancerdivers.com). *Garden room $$; sea-view room $$$*

🏠 **Z Hotel** (35 rooms) m 0732 940303; e info@theZhotel.com/reservations@theZhotel.com;

www.thezhotel.com; closed mid-Apr–end May. The new kid on the South Beach accommodation block, Z Hotel opened its heavy designer doors in mid 2008. Z is the seaside dream of London property developers, Keith & Julian, & brings an amount of city-boy bling previously unseen on the Nungwi beach scene. Billed as 'boutique on the beach', the 35 rooms are divided into 6 levels of luxury with sophisticated interiors featuring billowing voile curtains, striking Italian wallpapers, bespoke coconut-wood beds & cool Travertine stone floors. In each, iPod docking stations, AC, plasma TVs & remote-controlled fans add a touch of technology, while White Company toiletries, complimentary flip-flops & stocked minibars complete the indulgent feel. Every room has a balcony accessed through full-height glass doors & the sea can be seen, to varying degrees, from each one; for real ocean lovers the cantilevered decks in the cottages & the third-floor jacuzzi terrace of the Z Suite are favourite lookouts. Elsewhere in the compact complex, the natural stone pool above the beach is a fine hangout, surrounded with ivory parasols & lush tropical plants, whilst the Cinnamon Bar (see page 211) & Saruche Restaurant (see pages 212–13) are already evening hot-spots.

The team at Z has tried extremely hard to raise the accommodation bar on this stretch of coast, & in many ways they have done so. They have paved the path for others, even at a much lower end of the market, to up their offering, & shown willingness to improve the general area with a smart public path running through the hotel to link West & South beaches. A great deal of money has been spent on sourcing high-end, branded fixtures, fittings & fabrics, & on trying to present a quality product. The hotel has had its issues – the salt-infused air is not kind to modern technology & the searing sun soon bleaches fabrics – so adaptations will have to be made to maintain the property to the standard at which it is being pitched. With lessons learnt & these changes made though, Z may firmly establish itself as Nungwi's chic heart. Its biggest issue for style-seekers may prove to be the less salubrious surrounding sprawl. *Superior US$280–440 dbl; deluxe US$320–480 dbl; rooftop suite US$440–600 dbl; Z Suite US$840–1,000; all rates are FB; HB is available; children 3–12yrs 50% discount*

🏠 **Safina Bungalows** (30 rooms) m 0777 415726; e newsafina@hotmail.com. Under the enthusiastic new management of Ali Omar, Safina continues to be renovated to a good standard. In spite of the lack of sea view, it's a comfortable & spotlessly clean bedtime retreat, & has benefited enormously from the main village road moving away from its front garden. The professional new reception area was completed in 2008, the staff remain as accommodating as ever & the flower-filled garden continues to flourish. All rooms now have 24hr electricity, AC, UK-style 3-pin sockets (adaptors available) & hot water in en-suite bathrooms. Dbl rooms have duvets in addition to the standard sheets, & the basket of plastic flowers in each shows care & effort, if not contemporary taste. B/fast is served upstairs in the half-finished, dbl-storey building overlooking the central garden & marooned 'Welcome Safina' dhow. If post-beach chilling on the veranda isn't enough, there is a massage room where demure Fatima offers good massages & beauty therapy. $$

🏠 **H&H Beach Bungalows** (15 rooms) ✆ 024 2250630; m 0777 416937; e info@hamimtour.com; http://hamimtour.com. Tucked behind Safina, Hamim & Hamida Abdallah's bungalows are a basic but great-value option. Dbl, twin & trpl rooms are set out around a small, sandy quad, where fruit & cooked eggs are served each morning. Rooms (US$15pp) are clean & the en-suite bathrooms have hot water & good-quality fittings. Ceiling fans, mosquito nets, 24hr electricity & UK-style 3-pin sockets are standard. Hamim is a tour operator in Stone Town, so arranging transfers & excursions can be done with ease. $$

🏠 **Amaan Bungalows** (58 rooms) ✆ 024 2240026/34; m 0777 417390; e amaannungwi@yahoo.com; www.amaanbungalows.com. Heralded by rows of fluttering international flags, Amaan Bungalows is a sprawling, whitewashed, castellated complex in the heart of Nungwi's accommodation cluster. Ever-increasing in size, the rooms are divided into 3 broad categories: deluxe, garden & sea view. The last perch on a coral-rock cliff above the sea, within easy earshot of the sound of rolling waves; the large picture windows & cantilevered decks more than justifies the upgrade cost for this category. However, all the rooms are clean & well cared for with en-suite tiled bathrooms, hot & cold water, ceiling fans (AC in deluxe & sea view), mosquito nets, mains electricity, UK-style 3-pin sockets & a private terrace throughout the complex. Most rooms can be made up for sgl to trpl occupancy, & a few are interconnecting for groups & families.

This is an ever-expanding & developing complex, popular with a young crowd seeking to be at the very centre of the action. Bordering the main footpath through town, Amaan also has a practical

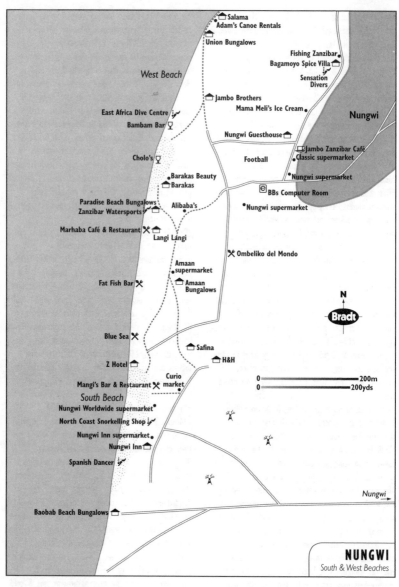

West Beach

Salama
Adam's Canoe Rentals

Union Bungalows

Fishing Zanzibar
Bagamoyo Spice Villa
Sensation Divers

Jambo Brothers
Mama Meli's Ice Cream

Nungwi

East Africa Dive Centre
Bambam Bar

Nungwi Guesthouse

Jambo Zanzibar Café
Classic supermarket

Cholo's

Football

Nungwi supermarket

Barakas Beauty
Barakas

BBs Computer Room

Paradise Beach Bungalows
Zanzibar Watersports

Alibaba's

Nungwi supermarket

Marhaba Café & Restaurant

Langi Langi

Ombeliko del Mondo

Amaan supermarket

Fat Fish Bar

Amaan Bungalows

N

Bradt

Blue Sea

Safina

H&H

Z Hotel

0 ———— 200m
0 ———— 200yds

Curio market

Mangi's Bar & Restaurant

South Beach

Nungwi Worldwide supermarket

North Coast Snorkelling Shop

Nungwi Inn supermarket

Nungwi Inn

Spanish Dancer

Nungwi

Baobab Beach Bungalows

NUNGWI
South & West Beaches

grocery shop for forgotten essentials & replenishing suncream supplies. The bureau de change inside reception will convert virtually any major currency into Tanzanian shillings, a safety deposit system is in operation (vitals sealed in brown envelopes & locked away), the internet café offers reliable PCs & internet connection, & the current manager has a travel agency in the village (Twinkling Zanzibar Tours & Travel) for arranging onward travel in mainland Tanzania. Fat Fish Restaurant & Blue Sea, immediately opposite on the seafront, are affiliated with Amaan & are good places to eat pizza & seafood, drink virtually anything & be merry at any hour of the day (HB rates include meals at either place). *Garden* $$; *deluxe* $$$; *sea view* $$$$

Langi Langi Beach Bungalows (33 rooms) ⟍ 024 2240470; e langi_langi@hotmail.com. The name Langi Langi is a Swahili derivation of ylang ylang, the perfumed Asian tree (*Cananga odorata*) planted in the hotel's lush gardens. Essential oil from the flowers is often used in the aromatherapy treatment of stress: a condition rarely encountered by holidaymakers on Zanzibar. The hotel is divided into 2 sections by the main pedestrian footpath: the 2 new 3-storey blocks on the seafront on one side & the original rooms & swimming pool in the lush garden on the other. The 19 en-suite rooms are compact & clean, each with AC, fans & constant hot water. Mosquito nets are available upon request & you can even borrow a hairdryer from reception. They are a walk from the beach, but they are of a good standard, & do sit right in the heart of Nungwi's tourist scene. Ambitious construction of this large seaside phase began in 2005 & the last rooms were only completed in early 2008. At the base, set on a large cantilevered deck over the water, is the reasonably good Marhaba Café where the food, especially curries, have made it a popular hangout for visitors & expats alike; bring your own alcohol if you wish or try one of the excellent cappuccinos. Above & beside this, are 33 rooms including the Penthouse at the top, where tunnel-vision sea views are framed by the steep *makuti* thatch. These newer rooms are large, if a little spartan, & though a great deal of money has been poured into their fixtures & fittings, the yellow marble sanitary ware &

cheap & cheerful rugs do give the impression that it was kitted out by 'Furniture Mart' in Dar. If you can live with the look, there are large dbl beds, French doors onto a sea-view balcony & plenty of mod-cons to keep you comfortable: AC, fan, fridge & shortly safes too. Aim for rooms higher up for the best views. The older garden rooms across the path, however, continue to be a terrific choice, & probably still get our vote as the rooms of choice here. In spite of being smaller, they are clean & comfortable, with AC, fan, a nice veranda & are surrounded by a totally tropical scene. The brilliant blue pool (⏱ 07.30–18.30) around which they now stand is wonderful too. Bordered by cerise bougainvillea, shady palms, comfortable loungers & neat *makuti* parasols, it's an understandably popular hangout for guests in the heat of the day or when beach hassle gets too much. The owner, Mansour Saleh Said, is clearly investing heavily in this property & is keen to see it succeed. They are friendly owners, employing only local staff, & are genuinely hospitable, & with the quality he's providing, regardless of whether the décor is to your particular taste, & facilities like the pool, this remains a great option within the price bracket. *Garden view & pool view* $$$; *sea view & penthouse* $$$$

West Beach Northwards from Paradise Beach Bungalows, still on the west side of the peninsula, is another stretch of beach which, for the purposes of this book, we'll call West Beach. The places to stay here are described south to north.

⌂ **Paradise Beach Bungalows** (18 rooms) m 0777 418860/416308; e shaabani_makame@ hotmail.com. Accessed beside the high gate at Langi Langi, Paradise Beach Bungalows no longer has any bungalows. Following redevelopment in 2004, it now offers 18 virtually identical rooms & a dormitory in a 2-storey, concrete accommodation block. Whilst the building is aesthetically challenged & the landscaping sparse bar 4 lovely coconut palms, the rooms are clean & all have fans, 24hr electricity & large, tiled en-suite bathrooms. The dorm sleeps 8 in 4 bunk beds shrouded in sapphire mosquito nets, & has its own bathroom, though the lighting & an unsightly green carpet are both poor. Equally, decent bedding has not yet reached this corner of Nungwi. That said, all rooms benefit from being positioned in front of a stepped access point to a small secluded cove: perfect for a quick dip in the heat of the afternoon sun. The affiliated sea-side restaurant serves an extensive array of pizza (US$4.50–6) & the 2008 arrival of Zanzibar Watersports (see page 217) dive & activity centre, will probably have a positive impact on the place. $$

⌂ **Baraka Beach Bungalows** (10 rooms) ☎ 024 2240412; m 0777 422910/415569; e barakabungalow@hotmail.com; http://barakabungalow.atspace.com. In the shadow of the accommodation block of Paradise Beach Bungalows, these bungalows surround a small garden beside West Beach. The en-suite rooms are dark but appear to be fairly clean & do have fans, electricity & hot water. The square interiors are simple with unpolished concrete floors & basic furniture but the bedding is cheerful & the small terraces overlooking the palms, fuchsias & hibiscus make this perfectly pleasant corner. There's a spacious sgl room available & a good trpl too. At a mere coconut's throw from the pleasant West Beach, it's also well placed for sun-worshippers. However, this proximity does also mean that the music from Cholo's (see below) is likely to prevent any sleep before dawn, at which time the villagers' radios will usually take over. For those who are up early or late, the shady, beachfront restaurant is open all hours & serves stir-fries (US$6.50), pasta (US$6), grilled seafood

(US$8) & good coconut curries (US$6–8) at inviting, scarlet-clad tables. Equally worth checking out is the adjoining Baraka Spa (see page 214). $$

🏠 **Cholo's** (3 bandas) Set at the back of a small beach, under towering *makuti* thatch, Cholo's is an idiosyncratic beach bar composed of 2 marooned dhows, suspended dugout canoes acting as seats & an array of bathroom sanitary ware serving as storage units. Immediately behind this curious establishment are 3 tiny backpacker *bandas* (or cottages). Of very basic timber & *makuti* construction, with only a cotton curtain across the entrance, these offer simply a mattress on the floor & a mosquito net. One has a light, fan & flush toilet; the others have access to a separate toilet & cold-water shower. None has any form of security. Cholo's 'Non-stop, rock it like it's hot, all-night party' attracts large numbers of locals & tourists for its cocktails & loud music, so be aware that you're unlikely to get any sleep before daybreak if you choose to stay. Anyway the only plausible reason for currently staying is so that you won't have far to stagger back from the festivities. It is possible that, along with the bar, Cholo's will change ownership in the near future & become a subsidiary of Z Hotel. If this goes ahead, a handful of bungalows are planned for the site & the facilities & price will likely rise accordingly. $

🏠 **Jambo Brothers Bungalows** (19 rooms) PO Box 1792, Zanzibar; m 0777 473901. Located immediately behind the East Africa Diving Centre, Jambo Brothers is a collection of 9 simple bungalows. The rooms are very simple with timber beds, lino floors & beach views. All have fans & mosquito nets with functional en-suite bathrooms: hot-water showers & toilets. The trpl is pretty cramped though the youthful occupants rarely seem bothered. There is no longer a bar or restaurant, the similarly named Jambo Restaurant on the beach is of no affiliation, but it's only a short walk to the clutch of eateries further south, & close enough to Cholo's to hear their Sat night festivities from the comfort of your bed. If you want to book in advance, Delene Kutz at the neighbouring dive centre (*eadc@zitec.org*) will kindly pass on any email messages & translate as necessary. $$

🏠 **Union Bungalows** (10 rooms) m 0777 454706/870345; e unionbungalow@hotmail.com; http://unionbungalow.atspace.com. A few steps along the beach from Jambo Brothers, you will come to Union Bungalows' crumbling reception building, whose foundations have been reclaimed by the sea. Check in here or at the friendly, independently run

restaurant in front of the 5 rather neat little cottages. All rooms are en suite with hot water, electricity through UK-style 3-pin sockets & mosquito nets; bed linen is colourful & *mkeke* mats adorn the concrete floors. This is certainly a budget option, but it's all perfectly acceptable. $$

🏠 **Salama** (7 rooms) m 0762 878813. Salama came under new management in August 2007, though it feels distinctly forgotten & slightly unloved. There are 7 sgl & dbl rooms with fans & mosquito nets, & all are set back from the sea in basic bungalows, with not much of a view. It's a relatively quiet corner but feels a little overpriced for the lack of common areas. The current South African managers are also running Jambo Restaurant, further round the coast. $$–$$$

🏠 **Flame Tree Cottages** (14 rooms) ☏ 024 2240100; m 0777 479429/0741 262151; e etgl@zanlink.com; www.flametreecottages.com. This fabulous little place on the edge of Nungwi village opened in mid 2004. Owned & built by a delightful Zanzibari–Scottish couple, Seif & Elizabeth, Flame Tree Cottages has a new house (including a large honeymoon/family suite on the first floor) & 11 red-roofed, whitewashed bungalows spread out in extensive gardens, beside the beach. Inside, the rooms are immaculate with lovely linen, beautifully finished wardrobes made by the local carpenters, & wide, shady verandas with white-cushioned easy & directors' chairs. There's even a thoughtfully placed mini-hose for washing the beach sand off your feet. They have electricity, UK-style 3-pin sockets, AC, fans & en-suite bathrooms with constant hot water.

Some rooms share a separate kitchenette, some have their own; they are compact but well kitted out with a hob, small oven (in some) & sink, & (for a small surcharge) the delightful head of housekeeping, Mr Salim, will supply a box of pans & crockery for anyone wishing to self-cater. That said, b/fast & snacks are served to residents on their verandas & freshly prepared lunches & dinners are also available. Chef Christopher's delicious dishes (fish goujons with tartare US$5.50; beef goulash US$8; steamed chilli crab claws US$9) make this one of Nungwi's best dining experiences, especially when enjoyed by candlelight overlooking the dhows leaving harbour.

There is a real feeling of space & peace here that is increasingly difficult to find in Nungwi; lounging around in one of many hammocks, slung between the coconut palms & casuarina trees around the garden, just reading & relaxing is lovely, & the staff are genuinely happy to help. Activities here range from lemongrass oil massage (US$12/30mins) to snorkelling trips aboard the owner's dhow. Flame Tree's website is as clear & organised as the place itself, & is well worth a look. $$$$

⌂ **Smiles Beach Hotel** (16 rooms) ℡ 024 2240472; m 0777 417676/444334; e infosmiles@ zanzinet.com; www.smilesbeachhotel.com. An architectural medley has produced Smiles' DIY Beverly-Hills-mansion appearance. Spaced in an arc around a flower-filled, semicircular garden, the 4 striking villas are resplendent in fresh pale yellow & white paint, with neatly tiled pagoda-like roofs & elaborate exterior spiral staircases. (Given that most of Nungwi's hotel builders have been unable to achieve regularly spaced steps, these spirals are a particular achievement, regardless of whether they are to your taste.)

Smiles is owned & run by Ibrahim, a smart, affable Zanzibari, whose family have owned this land for years & used it as their private beach hideaway in the days before tourism development hit this coast. Since its opening in Sep 2001, this has been one of the best-quality, quiet options in Nungwi, & is a firm favourite with passing overland groups & repeat visitors. The rooms are high quality & Indian in flavour. All are immaculate: spotlessly clean, spacious, bright & airy. Every one has a sparkling en-suite bathroom, sensibly sliding mosquito nets, high-quality security locks, AC, a telephone, an electronic safe, satellite TV & beach towels; some also have minibars. In the dbl rooms, the bed mattresses have been raised onto concrete plinths with painted moulding creating a headboard effect. The spacious trpl, which could fit 6 people, is made up with 3 large Zanzibari beds. The 'Honeymoon Sweet' [sic] features a giant corner bed as its centrepiece &, like the others, offers indulgent b/fasts in bed. For those who can drag themselves the few metres to the beach, there's an on-site restaurant (no alcohol) & regular beach BBQs. $$$–$$$$

⌂ **Nungwi Village Beach Resort** (113 rooms) ℡ 022 5503210; m 0773 606702; e relax@ nungwivillage.com; www.nungwivillage.com. Opened in 1999, this mid-range resort is set in spacious grounds on the northernmost stretch of West Beach. Over the course of 2008, the hotel tripled in size with the addition of 77 further rooms, taking it ever-closer to the dhow harbour. The style of accommodation varies tremendously between the seafront & new room blocks, though all are clean & tidy with en-suite bathrooms, AC, fans, mosquito nets & UK-style 3-pin electrical sockets. In a diagonal line towards the beach, the 20 original seafront rooms in 5, 2-storey, whitewashed houses. At the front of each level is a narrow balcony, with red concrete floors & a neat balustrade, which leads to 2 rooms. Bright, airy & spotless with high ceilings, king-size Zanzibari beds, good-quality wooden wardrobes & chests. The soft furnishings have a safari theme with herds of zebra migrating across the curtains & miscellaneous animal prints covering the lamp shades. The best are Rooms 129 to 132 for their immediate proximity to the beach & completely unobstructed views of the sea & bobbing dhows in the harbour. The 7 new blocks house 11 rooms each & will allegedly overlook a new swimming pool, though progress had stalled on completion at the time of going to press. At the other end of the beach is the restaurant, where an old dugout has been mounted on the wall & an assortment of painted fish placed in its net. The usual array of surface-level water activities is available, along with table tennis, pool & volleyball. There is a useful high-speed internet point & a satellite TV for the antisocial or sunburnt. Payment by Visa or MasterCard is preferred. $$$$

Nungwi village Away from the beaches, in Nungwi village itself, there are a number of options:

⌂ **Nungwi Guesthouse** (4 rooms) m 0777 494899; e nungwiguesthouse@yahoo.com. Located at the western edge of the village behind the nursery school, close to the football pitch & shops, Nungwi Guesthouse (formerly Ruma Guesthouse) is easily identified by the Bushman-esque paintings on its ochre walls. Owned by Rastafarian Shadrack & his English wife, Susie, this place offers very basic, en-suite rooms in a simple concrete building with a chill-out central courtyard under *makuti* thatch. There are hammocks, cushioned coir-rope sofas & a few playful kittens around, & the atmosphere is decidedly relaxed. Free-spirited backpackers are most warmly welcomed. $$

⌂ **Bagamoyo Spice Villa** (3 rooms) m 0746 442203; e sensationdivers@yahoo.com/ info@sensationdivers.com; www.sensationdivers.com. Available exclusively to Sensations Divers' clients, whose business is based within the same complex, Bagamoyo is a self-contained private house on the edge of the village. With a marked sub-aqua theme throughout, the 3 bedrooms in the main house are named after local dive sites – Leven Bank, Hunga & Kichafi. Each has 2 king-size beds, solid furniture & an en-suite bathroom. Those who haven't had enough aquatic adventure during their day can happily wallow in the deep stone bath in Leven Bank. Bagamoyo can be booked on either a FB or HB basis & has a BBQ area & fully equipped kitchen, known as Home Reef (Kitchen use supplement US$5/day). There's a large tropical garden dotted with coconut palms & cerise bougainvillea, & for rainy afternoons, a lounge area with satellite TV, internet access & some interesting books & maps. $$$

🏠 **Romantic Bungalows** (6 rooms) Opposite the main gate to Flame Tree Cottages, Romantic Bungalows opened on this small village plot in 2006. Accommodation is in whitewashed, thatched terraced rooms set around a small open courtyard where b/fast is served. The rooms are basic, with concrete floors, simple furniture, dim lighting & semi-

functioning en-suite bathrooms; b/fasts are better with fresh fruits, cooked eggs & toast on offer. This place is periodically closed, with seemingly no staff to open the gates or offer check-in assistance. $$

🏠 **Baraka's Aquarium Bunglows** (4 rooms) m 0777 422910/415569; e barakabungalow@hotmail.com; http://barakabungalow.atspace.com. Adjacent to the tidal pools at Baraka's Turtle Aquarium, there are now 2 bungalows, each housing 2 en-suite dbl rooms. The rooms are cool & spacious, with built-in moulded concrete beds, timber-framed mosquito nets, a table & chairs, & a curtain screening the toilet & shower. They are just about passable, but really not very inspiring. There are wide verandas, staggered to offer guests some privacy, & a number of free-range chickens around. There are also 4 rather sad rock pythons in a concrete cage, who for a few thousand shillings can be draped around your neck; just hope they've had their allowance of rats for the day! $$

East Beach At the tip of the Nungwi Peninsula is the lighthouse; from here, the coast curves back sharply to the south. This eastern side of the peninsula has developed significantly more slowly than the South and West beaches, but in the last two years development has started with a vengeance and every plot from Mnarani to Ras Nungwi is now under construction or operational as a hotel. It still offers some great choices of places to stay set on low cliffs of coral rock above sandy beaches, but the exclusivity is fast diminishing.

🏠 **Mnarani Beach Cottages** (37 rooms) ✆ 024 2240494; m 0777 415551; e mnarani@zanlink.com; www.lighthouseZanzibar.com. *Mnarani* means 'at or near the lighthouse' in Swahili, & aptly describes this resort's situation. Close to the northernmost tip of the island, from where it is possible to see the sun rise & set, this is a delightful place. Neat sand paths, bordered by masses of established pink hibiscus, lead between the rooms & to the beachfront bar/restaurant area. Here, overlooking a stunning stretch of beach, a new cantilevered deck area provides a perfect spot for sunbathing, sundowners or simply chilling on one of the swings. Calm & shady, this is a very relaxed & civilised place to recharge your batteries.

Rooms 1 to 8 have perfect sea views, interrupted only by an occasional coconut palm, whilst Rooms 9 to 12 are set in lush, tropical gardens close to the mosaic swimming pool. The rooms are relatively small but spotlessly clean, tastefully decorated & with good en-suite facilities. Coconut-wood furniture sits on broad terraces at the front of each one, whilst beautiful loungers & inviting rope hammocks hang between coconut palms & shady fir trees. There is even a raised, manmade beach for relaxing during

high tide. There are also 4 dbl-storey family cottages – Julie, Furaha, Huba & Maimuna – with large galleried interiors, a lounge, kitchen & useful information pack – & 2008 saw some 2- & 3-bed self-catering flats open to attract the same market. If hotel-style is your preference, the sizeable 3-storey accommodation building, Zanzibar Hse, contains 10 spacious en-suite rooms (all named after small Zanzibari islands), each filled with good-quality, coconut furniture, AC, a telephone, fridge & large, sea-view balcony (opt for the first & second floors for the finest views), complete with blue hammock. Alternatively, honeymooners on the second floor can escape up the spiral stairs to the roof terrace for some of the best panoramic views of this area; one of Mnarani's real assets is the dense vegetation that separates it from the lighthouse, for unlike any other plot on this coast, it does not feel boxed in by development.

It's possible to hire watersports equipment: hourly rental costs US$5/10 sgl/dbl kayak, US$10 surfboard & US$10 windsurfer. The lagoon immediately in front of the hotel is also a great place for kitesurfers; here the reef offers some protection, the winds are perfect, the water warm &

there's no risk of injury from the submerged canes of seaweed farmers. The bar has a cool, relaxed vibe (with handy tide timetables) & Mnarani's staff remain some of the friendliest on the north coast! *All rates are HB; FB also available.* $$$$

🏠 **Golden Dragon** 📞 024 5500590; **m** 0777 413953; **e** goldendragonlodge@yahoo.com/ info@goldendragonlodge.com; www.goldendragonlodge.com. The name & tasselled red lanterns may conjure images of late-night Chinese take-aways, but the angular accommodation blocks are more 'Mediterranean holiday apartment' in look. Unlike anything else on this stretch of coast, this place is a very curious mix. For no apparent reason, the accommodation building & huge restaurant are set way back from the beach, & orientated to look towards the breeze-block wall of the new, neighbouring Italian resort, rather than straight out to sea. The rooms, however, are spotless & spacious with nicely polished wooden beds & sliding glass doors onto wide verandas (book the first floor for better views). Mini fridges, hairdryers, AC, TV, fans & a bath are standard throughout. The food also is rumoured to be very good, with a chef from China rustling up some tasty stir-fries. There's a 30% discount for advance booking. $$$$

🏠 **Tanzanite Beach Resort** 📞 024 2240255; **m** 0777 485022; **e** info@tanzanitebeachresort.com; www.tanzanitebeachresort.com. If you can ignore the huge, rusting satellite dish at the entrance & the immature gardens, Tanzanite has a stunning ocean outlook from its raised location & clean, spacious rooms. Built in late 2005, it caters mainly to German & Italian visitors & delivers a reasonably good level of accommodation. Large rooms are in semi-detached thatched bungalows with standard dbl beds (crazy given the size of room), small fans, mosquito nets, small en-suite bathrooms & a shaded terrace. There is a restaurant (⏰ *to non-residents 12.30–22.00*) close to the rock cliff serving a fairly limited 'fish 'n' mash' menu. There is no beach immediately in front of the hotel as the coral-rock shelf extends below the property, but swimming is possible at high tide & coastal walking at low. $$$$

🏠 **Game Fish Lodge m** 0753 451919; **e** gamefish@zanlink.com. On the site of the old Mkadi Guesthouse, this small South African-owned lodge specialises in fishing trips for fellow nationals. The original guesthouse rooms remain, though they have been renovated, & sit in a terrace beside the road looking down the steep hill towards the coral-cliff edge & sparkling sea. It is a cracking view. The rooms all have pine furniture, pink appliqué

bedspreads, a cheerful *kanga*-clad coir sofa & a small en-suite bathroom; a small fan, TV, CD & DVD player are also included. Down the rocky hill, past the chicken coop, is an impressive open-sided restaurant/bar with some particularly good map murals of Zanzibar & Pemba; chill out here in a fishing-net hammock, stroke the friendly cats or have a game of pool. For ventures further afield, most guests will be heading to *El Shaddai* or *Karambisi*, the owners' boats, which are moored offshore & fully kitted out with the necessary rods & reels (see page 218). $$$$

🏠 **North Nungwi Beach Hotel** (10 rooms) **e** vugahotel@yahoo.com. Framed by the main door as you approach this hotel, the picture-perfect view of sandy paths leading down to the Indian Ocean, with cerulean waves breaking on the distant reef, is as good as it gets. Step inside, & what may once have been an idyllic retreat is now rundown & poorly managed. The main terrace of rooms by the road offers simple en-suite accommodation with ceiling fans & a broad shared veranda. In addition, there are 2 further rooms closer to the beach, beside the restaurant, which may have a better outward appearance, but are truly dismal inside: ripped mattresses, a security screen that appears to have been used as a BBQ grill in a former life, & desperately dim lighting. It is a shame that there is such an obvious lack of care & investment here, but for now this hotel's fabulous outlook is the only possible reason to stay here. $$$

🏠 **Sazani Beach Hotel** (10 rooms) 📞 024 2240014; **m** 0741 324744; **e** sazanibeach@aol.com; www.sazanibeach.com. Adjacent to Ras Nungwi Beach Hotel, Sazani Beach opened in 1997 & has been in its current form since the new millennium. Sazani gained some new American shareholders in 2008 & there are rumours of luxury renovations here but, for now, it remains part-owned & managed by an eccentric Englishman, Mike, & retains its slightly off-beat, laid-back character.

Set high up on coral rock, there are 3 en-suite rooms in the main house, 2 large rooms suitable for dbl or trpl occupancy & 4 standard dbls in semi-detached bungalows, & a beach *banda*, currently occupied by Mike but also popular with single travellers. All rooms have 24hr electricity, mosquito nets, fans, hot water, soft cotton sheets & a stunning sea view. Early-morning tea can be brought to your room, before b/fast is served on a new patio area under a trellis of passion fruit. Homemade jams & freshly brewed coffee feature alongside traditional eggs & bacon. Fish dinners are

There's ocean on both sides, but Nungwi often suffers shortages of fresh water. Nearby wells are shallow, and, as an increasing number of tourist developments tap into the natural water table, the local people justifiably fear their supply will run dry. For many existing guesthouses, the flow is already erratic, and at some larger hotels the water has to be trucked in for bathroom and kitchen use. For drinking, you can buy bottled water. Nevertheless, Nungwi is a place to seriously watch your water consumption – that is, go easy on the showers, not the rehydration!

served by the beach & over a few sundowner drinks in the sea-view bar, Mike will tell you about his passion for cricket & writing short stories.

There is an on-site dive centre, Divemaxx, but at the time of visiting no sub-aqua teaching was possible as there are no instructors on site. However, Mike is a dive master & will rent out equipment & escort group trips for experienced divers, if desired. Sazani is also a hangout for kitesurfers keen to catch the shore trade winds (up to Force 6) in the clear lagoon immediately in front of the hotel. Advice & backup can be sought from Chris, at the neighbouring Ras Nungwi Beach Hotel, even if the accommodation price there is over budget. Free internet is also available for all guests staying here: handy for anyone travelling with an overloaded memory card in their digital camera. $$$$

🏠 **Ras Nungwi Beach Hotel** (32 rooms) 📞 024 2233767/2512; e info@rasnungwi.com; www.rasnungwi.com. A perennially popular choice for high-end honeymoon couples, Ras Nungwi Beach Hotel sits on the east coast, at the southern end of Nungwi's beach. It's by far the most reliable upmarket place to stay in Nungwi & retains a calm, low-key atmosphere. Its 32 rooms are set in compact, well-tended gardens & all include quiet AC, good electronic safes & neatly tiled bathrooms. The rooms are divided into 3 classes according to their location, view & finishing touches, from the inclusion of a minibar to branded toiletries. Broadly speaking, the higher the room category, the closer it is to the sea & the more it has to offer. The 13 lodge or garden rooms sit in a row above the central area & car park, some distance from the sea. Only a couple of these have distant sea views, but each has a traditional Zanzibari bed with mosquito net, an en-suite bathroom & a veranda, & any can be made up for sgl, dbl or trpl occupancy. The 12 whitewashed rondavels of the superior chalets & 6 superior deluxe chalets all enjoy sea views, but only the latter offer dressing gowns & stereos. With

comfortable Zanzibari beds, they are very pleasant places to retreat for an indulgent afternoon siesta. In addition, set slightly away from the rondavels, the Ocean Suite operates as a private, separate villa. With 200m² of space, including a private plunge pool & sundeck, & access to a private chef, this is Ras Nungwi's premium accommodation. Alongside the large central bar & split-level dining room, there's an internet point, concealed satellite TV room & a games area with a pool table, table tennis, board games & darts, which is a popular post-dinner spot for younger visitors. In front of this area is a small, tiled, freshwater swimming pool & sundeck with paths radiating down to the beach & secluded reading areas.

There's an excellent, efficient PADI dive centre with 4 dhows & 4 permanent instructors, offering courses & recreational dives to Mnemba, the east coast & around Kendwa. Snorkelling trips, kayaking, water skiing, windsurfing & a range of other watersports are often possible with top-of-the-range equipment on site. Big-game fishing has long been one of the manager's passions & the hotel has use of 3 specialist boats through its subsidiary, Zanzibar Big Game Fishing (see page 218). For something more gentle, the Peponi Spa is a highly professional operation with superb treatments: try the Sandalwood & Sugarcane Safari Scrub (US$75/hr) or a cooling Zanzibar Sun Therapy (US$60/40mins). The exceptional food & a great wine list are highlights of any stay here. Delicious fresh, often organic, dishes are the norm. With all guests staying on a HB basis there's an extensive b/fast buffet laid out every morning, an à-la-carte lunch menu & 5-course table d'hôte dinner. Occasionally tasty seafood BBQs with Swahili cuisine classics will feature for dinner, often accompanied by some gentle live music. *Lodge US$170–195pp; superior chalet US$210–240pp; superior deluxe chalet US$250–290pp; ocean suite US$850–990pp; all rates are HB, inc activities; FB available; sgl suppt US$95/night*

✖ WHERE TO EAT Nearly all the hotels and guesthouses in Nungwi have attached restaurants, many of which are open to guests and non-guests alike (see the *Where to stay* section for more details of these). Along South Beach a number of casual restaurants, cafés and bars serve seafood dishes for around US$8, and snacks, pizza and burgers for around US$5, all washed down with fresh fruit juices, milkshakes, ubiquitous Coca-Cola and African beer, whilst Z Hotel's Saruche lords over them with its fusion feasts. Between South and West beaches, a band of more structured restaurants perch on the coral cliff above the sea. All have similar menus of fresh seafood, oven-fired pizzas and local curries, most are home to ever-hungry stray cats, and many do happy hours and backpacker meal-and-beer specials. For a more grassroots flavour, deep in the village you are likely to find cheap local fare from around US$2–3, though venues are highly changeable.

With little building regulation apparent, beachfront bars, restaurants and guesthouses tend to close and spring up again virtually overnight as land is sold on to ever-higher bidders. For many years, simply setting up a barbecue beside a few chairs, tables or logs on the sand, signalled being in business, but things are changing and more substantial restaurant structures are slowly replacing these ad hoc eateries. Here, we've listed only some of the more reliable, long-running establishments and those that are new but showing signs of staying the course, at least for a few years, but you should accept that you're quite likely to find more newcomers on arrival, and ask around for current culinary hot-spots.

✖ Bam Bam Bar At the northerly end of West Beach, Bam Bam is a dilapidated hangout for some slightly disillusioned local men & resident Rastafarians. Western tourists rarely venture inside this open-sided bar, in part because of aesthetics & in part because there is no obvious welcome; women especially may feel uncomfortable. It is open from 09.00 until the last person leaves, & judging by the state of some of the occupants, that seems to be never. There are plenty of other drinking establishments to try before this one. **$$**

✖ Blue Sea Restaurant Approached from South Beach, this is the first of this coast's clutch of raised seafront restaurants. Recommended by many for its seafood, its barbecued fish, octopus, barracuda & tuna are all popular (US$5.50–8), along with fresh fish kebabs with 'pineat butter' or hot sauce. Crab & lobster are reasonably priced at US$10 & US$19 respectively, whilst those tired of fish can sample delights from the pizza oven (US$4.50–6), or taste local curries (US$5.50–12). A high proportion of dishes boast 'Julian' vegetables. Cocktails (US$2.50–4) accompany most meals here with the 'Nungwi Mama' – dark rum, Kahlua & pineapple juice – a house special. **$$$**

✖ Cholo's Bar For all-day drinking & wild nights, Cholo's is a perennial favourite. Tucked under palms at the back of West Beach, this eccentric establishment is well known for its 24hr pumping music, cool crowd of local Rastas & backpackers, & free-flowing alcohol. The bar is a piece of living art

with dhows, motorbikes, sanitary ware & various other salvaged items used for structure & décor. Beach bonfires are a periodic evening attraction along with ad hoc BBQs & dining at upturned dhow tables. This is a place for a drink when everywhere else has shut up for the night, & you'll likely see the expat hotel staff jostling for bar space too. In the next few years, it's possible this long-standing bar will be taken over & given a facelift, but current plans will see its late-night opening & beach bar basics retained. (See page 206 for very basic accommodation here.) **$$**

✖ Cinnamon Cocktail Bar At the northern end of South Beach, on top of the coral cliff, Cinnamon is part of the new Z Hotel complex but welcomes non-residents too. With its first-floor location, overlooking the South Beach scene & sparkling sea, the young & beautiful are attracted by its trendy décor & fabulous tropical cocktails. Sipped at cushion-clad white *baraza* benches, surrounded by ever-changing mood lights & chilled tunes, this is a great pre-dinner drinks spot & is certainly Nungwi's most stylish drinking den to date. Stay for super sushi & tempting tasting platters at lunch or dinner, or just work your way through the extensive cocktail list. There is a very cool vibe here & it's the only place in town fashionable ladies won't feel out of place in high heels! **$$$**

✖ Fat Fish Restaurant & Bar Fat Fish is a wonderfully relaxed hangout. The expansive mangrove-pole terrace is cantilevered over the beach, affording diners uninterrupted views out to sea & a welcome breeze. The local fishermen's daily catch determines the extensive menu, & is served freshly grilled or in spicy curries. Sunset drinks are equally popular & there's also a satellite TV for catching up on international sporting events. $$$

✕ **Jambo Zanzibar** e june9@gmx.de; www.jambo-Zanzibar.de. Opened in January 2008, Jambo Zanzibar is a small village café run by local women under the careful guidance of German resident, Laila Nedorn. It is part of an initiative to train local women about hygiene, catering & business, to improve their family lives & give them practical skills to seek employment within the tourism sector. At Jambo Zanzibar, in the parade of shops overlooking the football field, the women bake cakes & sell their wares & drinks, as well as displaying locally made products for sale. It's not yet a glossy café but they are trying hard & the project is well worth supporting by stopping in for a shady seat, a glass of fresh juice & a tasty snack. $

✕ **Mama Meli's Ice Cream** On the village road between the main parade of shops & Bagamoyo Spice Villa, is a small ice-cream outlet known as Mama Meli's. Made by Susie of Nungwi Guesthouse, some enticing flavours are on sale: Heavenly Honey, Mango Magic & Lime Lush to name a few, & at US$1.50 they make a refreshing & affordable treat. $

✕ **Mangi's Bar & Restaurant** Sandwiched between the curio market & Z Hotel's pool, Mangi's overhangs the coral rock above South Beach. Formerly the beach-level Dolphin Restaurant, the tide washed the latter away & thus Mangi's moved to a higher level. Decked out in the same blue gingham as Nungwi Inn Restaurant, this is a relaxed hangout serving fresh juices, US$4 cocktails (*Zanzibar Mzungu* concoction of banana, rum, milk & vodka appearing popular), & snacks (samosas US$4.50; chapattis US$5; baked potatoes US$6.50). $$$

✕ **Marhaba Café & Restaurant** On Langi Langi's large cantilevered seaside deck, Marhaba is a relaxed coffee shop by day & a Swahili restaurant by night. Serving super cappuccinos & cake at b/fast & fresh curries for dinner it's a popular place & worth booking to guarantee a table for dinner. Service is friendly & menu variations always possible, whilst the breeze & rolling waves add to the relaxed, casual vibe. Dine inside amid the monochrome photos of Stone Town & antique *objets d'art*, or out on the vast timber deck. Alcohol is not sold, but beer & wine can be chilled & served if you bring your own along. Couples, families & large groups are all equally well

accommodated & personalised menus can be arranged for special occasions. $$$

✕ **Morning Star Restaurant** A very local establishment in the heart of the village, Morning Star is signposted off the main dust road through the village between the BBS Computer Room & the *dala-dala* stop. It is allegedly open daily for b/fast, lunch & dinner. However, it does seem to close regularly for 'maintenance', so best not to rely on it if you're starving. If by chance it is open though, expect a set meal of Swahili seafood dishes in a basic setting, & some curious villagers for company. Outside seems to be the hub of local bao games, so you may even be able to join the crowd for a heated match after your meal. $$

✕ **Nungwi Inn Restaurant** ⏲ from 10.00; last food orders taken 21.00. Right on South Beach, in front of the hotel with the same name, this 2006 addition to the local restaurant scene has received consistently good reviews of its simple, traditional fare. Marked out by its blue gingham-covered chairs, all sensibly under neat pole shading, guests can sink their feet in the sand, watch the beach volleyball & peruse the menu, which interestingly opens with an extensive cocktail list, perhaps indicating something about the core clientele. Order a 'Nungwi Killer' (Bacardi, vodka, Cointreau, tequila, lime & Coke!) & little is likely to be on the agenda for the afternoon, though more popular are the open-oven pizzas (US$5.50–7), burgers (US$4–7) & grilled fish (US$7–16). $$–$$$

✕ **Ombeliko del Mondo** This pleasant *cucina Italiana* is unusually located: tucked behind Amaan Bungalows, on the far side of the dusty access road, with precious little in the way of a nice view. The place was opened in 2007 by Lella, a lovely Mantovan who only speaks Italian, & the menu (in English & Italian) is full of traditional Italian delicacies: seafood antipasti, pastas, risottos & tempting *dolcis*. Good coffees are naturally available. There's an open kitchen, smart lounge & a neat restaurant area, buzzing with Mediterranean chatter, all under a huge *makuti* roof. Starters cost around US$5.50 & main courses US$5–10, & whilst quality & reviews are consistently good, portions are a little on the small side for some diners. $$$

✕ **Saruche Restaurant** The formal restaurant at Z Hotel, Saruche serves an à-la-carte menu of African–European fusion food with a heavy emphasis on local seafood. Accompanied by an international wine list, ocean views & island antiques, it's a pleasant place to dine & one of the smartest options currently in Nungwi. Peruse the menu from the lavish daybeds & couches in the lounge, then pick a table on the deck overlooking the beach or high-tide waves. There are traditional music & entertainment nights throughout the week, featuring everything from belly dancers to troops of drummers, & after-dinner nightcaps in upstairs bar Cinnamon (see above) are very much *de rigueur*. **$$$$**

SHOPPING There are several small shops in Nungwi village, where you'll find an array of cheap souvenirs, including carvings, paintings and jewellery, as well as essential items. Head inland across the football pitch behind Cholo's, and you'll first come to a neat building on your right, one half of which is the well-equipped Nungwi School computer room where email and internet services are readily available (see page 214), while the other half is Choices, a souvenir shop which also sells swimwear. A few steps further on, there is a small parade of shops. Here, the Pink Rose Salon advertises 'we prepare hair', Jambo Brother Shopping Centre offers a mixed bag of goods, an anonymous cosmetic shop does limited trade, and the **Nungwi Supermarket** is a veritable Aladdin's den of imported luxuries from toothpaste and toiletries to chocolate and Pringles.

Taking the road deeper into the village, there's another internet access point, the California Foto Store for film processing (we cannot vouch for the quality of your prints!), the New Nungwi Salon where the brave can have a bikini wax, and the local-style Jambo Mixed Shop, behind which is the Ahsanna Dispensary for villagers.

Amaan Bungalows Supermarket has a reasonable selection of knick-knacks and food/drink basics, whilst behind Paradise Beach Bungalows, Mr Alibaba and his sons, Abdul and Suleiman, sell everything from *kangas* to cold drinks, postcards and tours. The **post box** outside their shop offers a twice-daily mail collection for those all-important postcards home.

Alternatively if you just need to grab a few essentials and don't want to stray too far from sunbathing, there are now a couple of places open on South Beach. **Nungwi Inn Supermarket**, next to its namesake hotel, is very well laid out, clearly priced and stocks a good selection of snacks, drinks, toiletries and beach requisites: hats, bats and balls and sunscreen. Equally, between the curio market and North Coast Snorkelling, up some very steep and irregular coral-rock steps, **New Worldwide Supermarket** sells a similar range of goods to Nungwi Inn Supermarket, but is not nearly as nicely laid out. There's a good selection of known-brand suncreams for US$10–15 (various SPFs), a reasonable variety of US$2 alcopops and beers (Bacardi Breezer, Smirnoff Ice, Stella, Savanna Dry Cider), some warm white wine for US$8 and even some carrot cake mix. Alternatively, stay on the beach and wait for the beach traders to parade the sand with boards covered in mirrored sunglasses, beaded jewellery and cold drinks.

For artwork and souvenirs, a fairly contained **curio market** is beginning to grow on the alley running perpendicular to South Beach, between Mangi's Bar and North Coast Snorkelling. This contained and organised approach to displaying the array of colourful paintings, carvings and beadwork is to be commended, though there is still some way to go to reduce the sustained mobbing of fair-skinned passers-by.

Henna tattoos, hair-braiding and massage Temporary henna tattoos seem to be *de rigueur* in Nungwi. Painted onto your skin by friendly local ladies, as you lie under their makeshift palm shades on the beach, they seem to mark a rite of passage in the backpacker fraternity. As elsewhere on Zanzibar, the beach and bars are full of people with vaguely Arabic- or Celtic-style rings round their biceps. Many clearly believe they look cool; but be warned, the henna can badly mark bed linen, which naturally annoys the hotel owners and many will charge for stains. For all-out African beach chic, hair-braiding services are also available by the same ladies, along with basic beach massages. For a less-public massage experience, try one of the following:

Baraka Spa (*Body treatments US$20/hr; manicures US$10*) In a small, immaculate room, adjoining Baraka's Restaurant on West Beach, two very friendly therapists, Harriet and Anna, offer excellent treatments on *kanga*-covered massage tables. From deep muscle rubs to Indian head massage, foot treatments to facials, their super little business offers them all. They are both beauty trained, with Harriet previously having worked in Bluebay's commended East Coast Spa, so the standard is above that available on the beach; that said, this is not in any way a 'spa'.

Peponi Spa (*Body treatments US$50–120/40–80mins; manicures US$40/1hr; waxing & eyebrow tinting/threading US$10–35*) Set in the tropical gardens of Ras Nungwi Hotel, Peponi Spa opened in October 2007 to offer both guests and non-residents 'an array of rejuvenating, pampering and holistic treatments'. It is the area's best spa by far. Run by internationally qualified therapists and using natural oils and ingredients, treatments are carried out in calm, minimalist rooms decorated with stylish monochrome photographs, billowing linen curtains and freshly picked red hibiscus flowers. With the soothing music and intoxicating aromas of a professional spa operation, this is a wonderfully relaxing place to spend a few hours, and who could resist the hour-long Peponi Zanzibari Glow (sea salt to exfoliate; aromatic oils to nourish) to bring out their holiday tan.

Safina Massage (*Body treatments US$20/hr; manicures US$10*) In a small, neat room on the first floor of Safina Bungalows' restaurant building, gentle Fatima offers massage and beauty therapy: rarely will you see nail-care implements displayed with such care in a glass cabinet! In spite of her very limited facilities, Fatima tries hard to ensure guests relax and enjoy their treatment, and her quiet, smiling manner goes a long way to achieving her aim.

LOCAL SERVICES

Internet Several of the larger hotels have internet facilities, and a reasonable number of the smaller backpacker places will let you use an office PC to quickly check email. Amaan Bungalows has three PCs available for general use in a small internet café off reception, and there will shortly be a similar facility at Langi Langi. We would like to recommend the reliable Nungwi School IT centre as a first choice though, as income here is used to reinvest in the school's excellent computer initiative.

Founded in 2002 by Bibi Biorg, a generous 75-year-old lady who first visited Nungwi as a tourist, the **BBs Computer Room** (*⊕ 08.00–20.00 Mon–Fri & 08.30–19.30 on holidays and w/ends; rates are very low at US$0.60/30mins and US$1/hr*) was designed to offer computer lessons to all Nungwi School's pupils as well as IT training for local adults. Six years later, the classroom now has 15 computers and five Nungwi-resident teachers, who hold classes day and night on a shift basis to ensure all Form 1 and 2 pupils encounter computer technology. Adult classes are also offered to Zanzibari locals, with popular short courses teaching basic software programs helping to fund the centre's school activities (12-day MS Word course US$12.50; 15-day MS Publisher course US$15).

Four computers at the back of the class have Wi-Fi internet access and paying customers, mostly tourists, can access these at any time during opening hours, regardless of whether classes are present. Though heavily supported by pupils and parents, and proving sustainable from its commercial activities, the centre is still

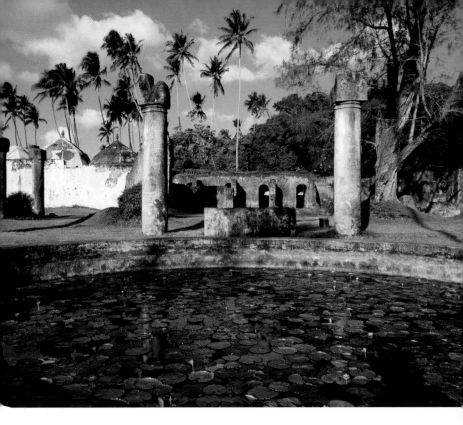

above **Maruhubi Palace** (AZ) page 184
below **Kidichi Persian Baths** (AZ) page 189

top	Flap-necked chameleon *Chamaeleo dilepis* (AZ) page 55
above left	Coconut crab *Birgus latro* (AZ) page 305
above right	Blue monkey *Cercopithecus mitis albgularis* (AZ) page 53
below	Suni antelope *Nesotragus moschatu moschatus* (CM) page 53

top left	**Nutmeg** (AZ) page 107		*above right*	**Clove bud** (TH) page 52
top right	**Cloves drying, Pemba** (TH) page 309		*below left*	**Lychee** (AZ) page 182
above left	**Pineapple** (AZ)		*below right*	**Jack fruit** (AZ) page 309

above **The rooftops of Stone Town at sunrise** (CM) page 163

below **Old Dispensary** (ED) page 166

top **Market day, Stone Town** (AZ) page 165

above **Child in Stone Town** (AZ) page 129

far right **Slavery monument** (KH) page 173

right **Children in front of traditional Zanzibar door** (AZ) page 43 top   *Dala-dala* at Jambiani post office (CM) page 276

above   Traditional fishing net, Mafia (TH)

left   Dhow building (AZ) page 45

below   Women gathering seaweed (KH) page 262

above **Tingatinga paintings and curios on sale in Nungwi** (SM) page 213

right **Climbing a coconut tree, Jambiani** (CM) page 51

below **Walking inland from Matemwe village** (CM) page 229

heavily reliant on donations and visitors' dollars, so even if a few dollars to email home is all you can manage, the cause is a good one. If you are in a position to give more support, the headmaster can be contacted on bbs@zanlink.com. The centre is clearly signposted beside the football field, on the right as you approach for the beach.

WHAT TO SEE AND DO Most visitors come to this area to relax on the beach, swim in the sea, and perhaps to party at night. For local attractions, the small turtle sanctuary and terrific local coral reefs are still a draw. If you want a more cultural experience, head down the coast to the 16th-century Swahili ruins at Fukuchani and Mvuleni, the bustling, ramshackle market at Mkokotoni, or venture across the water to Tumbatu Island.

If you want peace, quiet and fewer people, you will probably need to head to a different corner of the island; if not, then here are details of the area's main activities:

Water activities The sweeping cape on which Nungwi is sited is surrounded by sparkling, warm, turquoise seas, making it a perfect spot to engage in countless water activities. On the west side of the peninsula, especially on South Beach, locals offer simple boat rides, Mnemba picnic excursions, sunset booze cruises and snorkelling trips. Prices are all very similar; quality is variable. Listen to other travellers' advice carefully when deciding who is currently offering the best trip.

Adam's Canoe Rentals m 0754 949578. On the coastal path between Union Bungalows & Flame Tree Cottages, Adam's Canoe Rentals do exactly as you'd expect: rent canoes. Adam himself is a smart, friendly guy & his equipment is in great condition. Either hire & paddle yourself, or have Adam guide you around the coast. At US$15pp for a half day to Kendwa, it's good value, a gentle way to travel & good way to get to Kendwa's more spacious beach.
Captain Mau m 0777 415496; e mauZanzibar@yahoo.com. Next to Bam Bam Bar on West Beach, Captain Mau is a lovely local lad hiring out mask & fin sets (US$5/half day; US$10/day) & arranging local water excursions in his small wooden boat, complete with shade cloth. He will happily take visitors to Mnemba, Tumbatu & Kendwa Reef for snorkelling, but do be aware of safety considerations if you opt to go to the further destinations: he has only 1 motor & it's a long paddle back if it breaks!
Cholo Usi Snorkelling Next to Adam's Canoe Rentals, this is one of the many rent-a-mask snorkelling

outfits to have sprung up. Cholo is more expensive than his South Beach competitors at US$15/day for mask & fin hire, & the quality much the same, so use a bit of bargaining power or head to North Coast Snorkelling Shop for a bigger range.
North Coast Snorkelling Shop ⊕ 06.00–18.00. With a prime location on the coral rock above South Beach, at the entrance to the curio market, the entrepreneurial Hamadi Ali has established a small hire shop for masks, snorkels, fins & fishing rods. He buys kit from tourists in Stone Town who don't want to carry their equipment home, & rents it out here. The quality is variable but you are free to try things on & select the best for you, & there is a range of good brands available (Cressi, Mares, Tribord) as well as adult & child sizes. Rates are US$5 snorkelling kit/day; US$10 fishing rod/day. If you would like him to take you out fishing too, it's US$200 for a half day on his boat, complete with sunshade.

Diving Diving is especially popular here and many of the hotels offer dives and dive courses: you can go on the local reef, or go further afield to reefs such as Leven Bank and Mnemba. Over recent years several dive operations have come, gone or changed their name or location; at the beginning of 2008, six dive operations were in operation in Nungwi. Listed in alphabetical order, the centres are very different in feel and ethos and divers are well advised to talk seriously to the individual operators about safety and experience before signing up for courses or sub-aqua excursions.

Divemaxx ℡ 024 2240014; ✆ 0741 324744; e info@sazanibeach.com; www.sazanibeach.com. Based at Sazani Beach Hotel in Nungwi, Divemaxx does not currently have a resident dive instructor. The English lodge manager, Mike, is a dive master & will rent out equipment & escort group trips for experienced divers, but there are no scuba courses available here. *Dive packages US$40/50 Leven Bank or Mnemba sites; US$35 Mnemba snorkelling trips*

East Africa Diving & Watersport Centre ✆ 0777 416425/420588; e EADC@zitec.org; www.diving-Zanzibar.com. Owned & operated by an experienced, straight-talking German–South African couple, Michael & Delene Kutz, this is the oldest dive centre on the north coast. On the beach in front of Jambo Brothers Guesthouse, this efficient PADI 5* Gold Palm Resort offers very well-priced courses to Dive Master & a host of scuba trips. Dive sites are reached by dhow (including 2 engines for long trips) or zippy speedboat, & each boat has 2 experienced captains, with power of veto over any potentially unsafe dive. Safety appears to be taken seriously here, with all boats equipped with first aid & oxygen; dive leaders & every third diver carry inflatable marker buoys; steel tanks Bauer serviced every quarter; air quality tested annually & the whole centre actively contributing to the DAN Decompression Chamber Support scheme (anyone completing a course here is automatically fully insured for 6 days' underwater activity). Female divers also take note, the tanks here are all squat steel tanks, making them a much more comfortable shape on your back, & significantly easier to cart down the beach to the boat. Nitrox diving was introduced in 2008 to allow divers shorter surface intervals. A thankful Japanese diver created some stunning, accurate cartoon dive maps of the sites regularly visited by EADC, & these have been carefully laminated for dive briefings. Mnemba sites are visited every couple of days; Hunga is a frequent destination; Kichafi, Mbwangawa & Haji all feature on the east coast; Tumbatu is a weekly excursion & Big Wall at Mnemba is favoured over Leven Bank for safety & quality of marine life. *Dive packages US$60/110/190/400 (plus US$30 to Mnemba Atoll) for 1/2/4/10 dives; Discover Scuba US$95; Open Water US$480; Advanced US$380; Nitrox US$300*

Rising Sun Diving Centre ✆ 0777 440883–5/88; e bookings@risingsun-zanzibar.com; www.risingsun-zanzibar.com. Operating out of the all-inclusive Royal Zanzibar Hotel, this is the new north-coast sibling of Rising Sun Dive Centre (see pages 263–4) at Breezes on the Michamvi Peninsula. Opened mid 2008 along with the hotel, it offers diving & watersports to hotel guests, but only scuba courses & trips to non-residents. It is a fully accredited PADI 5* Gold Palm Resort with National Geographic Status & consistent with its sister operation has state-of-the-art technology, quality equipment & experienced staff. Safety is taken seriously with instructors being covered by DAN insurance & guests being actively encouraged to join the excellent scheme. PADI courses are taught on site whilst existing divers are taken out to less-visited local reef sites. Mnemba dives are offered on request but the focus here is on maximum underwater time & minimum transfer time. *Dive packages US$85/170/464/695 for 1/2/6/10 dives; Open Water US$672; digital photography US$386: daily equipment rental (regulator, BCD, wetsuit, mask & fins) US$39; underwater digital camera rental (inc CD of images) US$46*

Sensation Divers ✆ 0746 442203; e sensationdivers@yahoo.com/ info@sensationdivers.com; www.sensationdivers.com. Following a stint opposite Amaan Bungalows in a prime waterfront spot, Sensation is now based at Bagamoyo Spice Villa & has significantly reduced in size. As its name would suggest, the emphasis here has long been on some of the more adrenalin-influenced options for diving. They have 2 instructors, 2 dhows & a raft of underwater toys from DPV motorised scooters to underwater cameras & Nitrox tanks. The centre is PADI & SSI accredited & all boats carry life jackets, oxygen & first-aid kits as standard. Sensation is now also affiliated with game-fishing boat, *Unreel* (see Fishing Zanzibar, opposite), which is also based in the same complex. *Dive packages US$45/130/270 (plus US$30 for Mnemba); for 1/4/10 dives; Discover Scuba US$90; Open Water US$360; Dive Master US$750; Nitrox US$200; 10% discount for divers with own equipment*

Spanish Dancer Dive Centre ℡ 024 2240091; ✆ 0777 417717/430005; e spanishdancerznz@hotmail.com; www.spanishdancerdivers.com. Taking its name from both an attractive marine creature (a nudibranch – a kind of sea-slug) & its owner's nationality, Spanish Dancer has been operational since 2001. Based in an open rondavel on South Beach, Spanish Dancer is run by Anna & Gregory, their daughter Sabina & her partner Carlos, 3 of whom are dive instructors. The team regularly dives 20 sites, including Mnemba (1hr 10min by boat) & Leven Bank (divers must have a minimum of 20 logged dives to participate). Equipment & steel tanks seem in good condition, & there are 2 boats: a large one capable of carrying 25 divers, & a smaller one for 15 divers on a 2-tank trip. Oxygen & first-aid kits are standard on all boats & Anna is a doctor, which should ensure good safety standards. By rule, only the instructors carry surface marker buoys, so you may want to consider taking your own. The dive centre is PADI accredited & teaches courses in Spanish, Italian & English, & there is a live-aboard diving option on their 23m sailing boat, MS Jambo. *Dive packages US$132/226/320/475 (plus US$47 for Mnemba); for 2/4/6/10 dives; Discover Scuba US$117; Open Water US$585; Dive Master US$1,169; Course Manual US$62*

✔ **Zanzibar Watersports** ◆ 024 2233309; m 0773 165862; e info@zanzibarwatersports.com; www.zanzibarwatersports.com. With PADI 5* Gold Palm Instructor Development Centre status, offering all PADI qualifications to instructor level, Zanzibar Watersports has 2 Nungwi outlets, one at Ras Nungwi Beach Hotel for guests only, & one within the central Paradise Beach Bungalows complex, which is open to one & all. The original centre, at Ras Nungwi, offers the same high quality as the hotel in which it's based; equipment, service, safety & staff professionalism all seem top-notch here. For guests coming to learn to dive, it's worth emailing in advance; there's a home-study option which allows all the Open Water course reading & paperwork to be done before you arrive. Confined-water sessions for beginners are held in either the swimming pool or the adjacent lagoon in front of the hotel. A strict refresher policy means that all divers who have not donned scuba gear for 6 months must do a refresher course on arrival. New 3mm long & short Reef wetsuits, Aqualung masks & BCDs, Mares fins are neatly laid out pre-dive for individual collection.

Watertight pelican boxes are available for cameras. 4 permanent instructors, a dive master & 8 local boat captains & snorkel crew keep everything shipshape on board the 4 large dhows. 2 of these are capable of taking 10 divers on a 2-tank dive trip, whilst the other 2 sailing dhows are used for sunset cruises & snorkelling trips. Regular dive sites are predominantly on the west side of the island; though trips to Mnemba are also run regularly as clockwork. The 12 sites which they most frequently visit are chalked up on the centre's blackboard; they vary according to visibility & weather conditions. Trips to Leven Bank & Mnemba's Big Wall are strictly for Advanced Divers & above. Dive departure times vary by tide & sometimes depart from the village (*dala-dala* transfer) if the water in the lagoon is too shallow to allow their boat to pass through to the reef. At the new Paradise Centre, divers may not have the benefit of the swimming pool or swish surroundings, but they do benefit from reduced rates. From here, daily snorkelling & diving trips head to Mnemba, whilst divers also have a choice of 21 other local sites to choose from. 2 canopy-covered boats are on hand to accommodate a maximum of 20 persons & 4 expat PADI instructors; a local dive master & 4 boat crew are always on hand. There are also 1- & 2-man kayaks, waterskiing & wakeboarding equipment available & sunset dhow cruises for the more sedentary visitor. *Dive packages US$55/100/295/460 (plus US$65 for Mnemba) for 1/2/6/10 dives exc equipment; Refresher US$30; Open Water US$550; Advanced US$440; US$15 equipment hire (mask, fins, BCD, regulator, wetsuit); kayaks US$10pp/hr; waterskiing US$70/15mins; windsurfing US$30/hr. There's a 12% discount at Paradise branch; group deals available for 4+ persons*

Fishing

Fishing Nungwi's proximity to some of Africa's best deep-sea fishing grounds – Leven Bank and the deep Pemba Channel – offers serious anglers outstanding fishing opportunities. (For details on the fishing seasons see *Chapter 3, Natural Environment*.) In addition to the weather-beaten local dhows which plough the coastal waters, three operators currently offer game fishing in fully equipped, custom-built boats.

✦ **Fishing Zanzibar** e gerry@fishingZanzibar.com/ info@fishingZanzibar.com; www.fishingZanzibar.com. Operated by Gerry Hallam in conjunction with Sensation Divers, *Unreel* is a 30ft fly-bridge, sport-fishing boat based in Nungwi. Complete with a stand-up fishing chair, outriggers, downriggers, Shimano fishing gear (line classes 25–80lb) & a full selection of lures, it takes small charter groups (max 4 anglers) to Leven Bank & the Pemba Channel. Anglers are taken in search of black, blue & striped marlin, sailfish, yellowfin tuna, spearfish, dorado, trevally, king & queen mackerel, barracuda, & wahoo (travelling at 85km/h, these are amongst the fastest fish in the sea). Night fishing for broadbills is an option. As members of the International Game Fish Association, a catch-&-release approach to billfish &

sharks is encouraged, except when fish are injured or in the event of a possible record catch. *US$500 half day; US$800 full day, inc lunch; live-aboard US$1,000/day for 4 persons*

◢ **Game Fish Tours** m 0753 451919; e gamefish@zanlink.com. Based out of Game Fish Lodge, this new South African operation runs half-day, night fishing & 2-day Pemba tours for reef & bottom fishing. They have 2 boats: *El Shaddai* & *Karambisi*. *El Shaddai* is a 4.2m fibreglass Super Dolphin ski boat powered with 2 40HP Yamaha engines & kitted out with a fish-finder & Penn & Scarborough tackle. *Karambisi* is a Magnum 25ft game-fishing vessel powered with 2 140HP Suzuki engines & offering plenty of deck space & a harness chair for fighting fish. Focusing on the serious game-fishing market, *Karamibisi* has Shimano Tiagra 30WA, 50WA & 80WA rods & reels spooled with IGFA yellow 15kg, 24kg & 36kg fishing line, 8" Scarborough reels spooled with Berkley Whiplash Pro 37.8kg Dacron line & a selection of lures, feathers & rapalas. On a more practical note, *Karambisi* also has a toilet & sleeping facilities so is used for the multi-day Pemba trips. *US$220pp/6hr charter (max 2 persons) on El Shaddai; US$165pp/6hrs (max 3–4 persons) on Karambisi; 2-day Pemba US$550pp on Karambisi*

◢ **Zanzibar Big Game Fishing** \ 024 2233767/2512; e info@rasnungwi.com; www.rasnungwi.com. Arguably the best game-fishing operation on Zanzibar is Zanzibar Big Game Fishing (previously known as Ras Nungwi Fishing), based at Ras Nungwi Beach Hotel. They are extremely well kitted out for both professional fishermen & have-a-go holidaymakers, with 3 new professional sport-fishing boats, professional tackle & international safety equipment. *Haraka*, a 2006 model Gulfcraft Sport Fishing 35, cruising at 38 knots, is used to access distant fishing grounds, *Timim*, a custom-built Windy 24 with a fighting chair for big-game fishing, & *Suli Suli* a 24ft T-top fibreglass boat with open decks for fly fishing, are all available for guest use. On board modern, purpose-built fittings, experienced skippers & a raft of state-of-the-art technology (GPS navigational aids, colour echo-sounders & fish-finders) are utilised. A full set of tackle is provided along with Shimano, Fenwick, Harnell or KC rods & Shimano or Penn international reels, spooled with 80lb, 50lb & 30lb mono line, although clients can bring their own if preferred. Tag-&-release fishing is encouraged for all big fish unless it is the fisherman's first-ever catch, his biggest to date, or if it is likely to be an east African or All Africa record. Half-day (5hr) outings depart at either 06.30 or 13.30; whole days depart 06.30. Rates include charter of boat, skipper, bait, tackle equipment & lunch. *US$385/520 half/full day on Suli Suli; US$495/700 half/full day on Timim; US$600/900 half/full day on Haraka*

Sailing Aside from local sunset dhow trips, there are few opportunities to sail on board more modern vessels on this stretch of coast. For live-aboard 'learn-to-sail' options and simple cruising, *Julia*, listed below, is the only real option.

▲ **Dive 'n' Sail Zanzibar** m 0774 441234; e info@dive-n-sail.com/yachtjulia@hotmail.com; www.dive-n-sail.com. If sailing appeals, Dive 'n' Sail operates a lovely 50ft Admiral catamaran, *Julia*, specialising in live-aboard dive trips to Pemba & Mafia. Available for charter with its own professional skipper, chef, deckhand & optional dive instructor, the boat is fully equipped for diving & deep-sea fishing. On board are 4 en-suite, dbl cabins, a large galley & saloon area complete with stereo & DVD player, an outside deck & sunbathing trampoline over the waves. Complete with a Bauer 'Mariner' dive compressor for refilling tanks, it has 8 full sets of dive equipment, including 16 aluminium cylinders, BCDs, regulators, depth gauges, weight-belts & weights. Certified divers need carry little of their own equipment. With some notice, PADI Advanced Open Water & speciality courses can be taught on board. Dinner usually comprises the daily catch, so fishing is a frequent activity. Day or overnight trips to the reefs around Mnemba are possible, although the boat is more likely to be used by serious divers for week-long ventures to Pemba. All rates are subject to periodic change! *US$1,320/day private boat charter (1–5 persons) for min 4 days, exc dives; dives US$42/dive for first 10 dives, then US$36. US$108pp Mnemba Island snorkelling day trip (min 4 persons); US$66 dive supplement; US$480 half-day fishing*

Kitesurfing In recent years, kiting has grown in general popularity and Nungwi is no exception. Steady winds (approximately 15–20 knots) for most of the year, level beaches, warm clear water and protected, shallow lagoons make it a great place for both beginners and more experienced kitesurfers. The quiet, long, sandy beach on the eastern side of Nungwi cape allows for easy launching and landing, although, like all of Zanzibar's east coast, the tidal change is significant and this affects the exposed beach area. The fringe reef here creates a calm and sheltered lagoon which is ideal for kiting, and from May to September affords great opportunities for wave-riding and surfing. There is no seaweed farming here, and consequently no danger from concealed underwater canes.

Kite Zanzibar c/o Ras Nungwi Beach Hotel; 024 2240487/78; m 0777 415660; e chris@ kiteZanzibar.com; www.kiteZanzibar.com. Chris Goodwin of Ras Nungwi Beach Hotel is a keen kitesurfer & has a wealth of information on the local conditions. He operates a dedicated website on the kitesurfing in this area & can help secure accommodation & storage facilities for equipment. The beach in front of Sazani & Ras Nungwi Beach Hotel also benefits from proximity to the staff & boats of the latter, in the event of an emergency requiring recovery. Chris also holds the Cabrinha kite dealership for east Africa & is very helpful when it comes to buying or repairing equipment.

Dhow-building and harbour activity
As well as being a tourist destination, Nungwi is also the centre of Zanzibar's traditional dhow-building industry. A number of hardwood trees, particularly good for boats, grow in this area (or at least did grow here, until they were chopped down to make into boats). Generations of skilled craftsmen have worked on the beach outside the village, turning planks of wood into strong ocean-going vessels, using only the simplest of tools.

It is a fascinating place to see dhows in various stages of construction, but do show respect for the builders, who are generally indifferent towards visitors, and keep out of the way. Most do not like having their photos taken (ask before you use your camera), although a few have realised that being photogenic has a value, and will reasonably ask for payment.

Fishing continues to employ many local men, and it's magical to watch the local fishing boats bobbing in the sparkling waves of the morning, and then set out to sea in the late afternoon. There can be as many as 40 going out at once, their distinctive lateen sails silhouetted against the blush evening sky – it's probably been unchanged for centuries. Early in the morning, around 06.00, they return with their catch to the beach fish market. The spectacle is worth the early start, but if you don't make it, there's a smaller re-run at around 15.00 each day.

Like the east coast, Nungwi's other key marine industry centres on its seaweed. Local women tend this recently introduced crop on the flat area between the beach and the low-tide mark. The seaweed is harvested, dried in the sun and sent to Zanzibar Town for export. (For more details, see box, *Sustainable seaweed farming*, pages 262–3.)

Turtle sanctuaries
There are two neighbouring operations which allow close-up turtle viewing in Nungwi's tidal pools. Clear signposts will take you to either, but please read the descriptions of both carefully before planning a visit, as their backgrounds and motives are quite different.

Mnarani Natural Aquarium (⊕ *09.00–18.00 daily*) Hawksbill turtles have traditionally been hunted around Zanzibar for their attractive shells, and green turtles for their meat. In 1993, with encouragement and assistance from various conservation bodies and some dedicated marine biologists, the local community opened the Mnarani Natural Aquarium.

In the shadow of the lighthouse (*Mnarani* meaning 'place of the lighthouse' in Swahili), at the northernmost tip of Zanzibar Island, the aquarium was created around a large, natural, tidal pool in the coral rock behind the beach. Originally set up to rehabilitate and study turtles that had been caught in fishing nets, the aquarium project expanded to ensure that local baby turtles were also protected.

Turtles frequently nest on Nungwi Beach, and village volunteers now mark and monitor new nests. The resulting hatchlings are carried to small plastic basins and small concrete tanks at the aquarium where they remain for ten months. By this time, they have grown to 10ins and their chances of survival at sea are dramatically increased. All bar one of these turtles are then released into the sea, along with the largest turtle from the aquarium pool. The one remaining baby turtle is then added to the pool, ensuring a static population of 17 turtles.

Currently, this equates to four hawksbills (Swahili: *ng'amba*), identified by the jagged edge on their shell, sharper beak and sardine diet, and 13 seaweed-loving green turtles (Swahili: *kasakasa*). The aquarium manager, Mr Mataka Kasa, keeps a log book detailing all eggs, hatchlings and releases. On 5 June 2005, the sanctuary released its first tagged turtle, as part of a worldwide monitoring programme.

In spite of the aquarium being little more than a glorified rock pool, it's fascinating to see the turtles at close quarters. Further, the money raised secures the project's future, and goes towards local community schemes – in a bid to demonstrate the tangible value of turtle conservation to the local population. With luck, this will lessen the trade in souvenir shell products and ensure the species' survival.

On a practical note, when timing your visit, the water is clearest about two hours before high tide (Swahili: *maji kujaa*).

Baraka's Turtle Aquarium Owned by Mr Baraka, of Baraka Beach Bungalows on West Beach, this aquarium is signposted at a bend in the road, on the way to the East Beach area. It opened in direct competition with the long-established sanctuary scheme at neighbouring Mnarani Natural Aquarium. Although it has a lovely tidal pool, with a couple of large parrotfish, pretty Picasso fish, red snapper and 15 resident green turtles, all of whom appear to be healthy and well fed (for US$4.50 they practically leap out of the pool to take seaweed from your hand), this is fundamentally a business and not a conservation project. To compound this, on our most recent visit we were saddened to be told by a very friendly, if ill-informed, manager that not only could we swim with the turtles (US$6), but that if we held onto the flippers 'like a motorbike' we could ride them too. Clearly, this is a practice to be discouraged in every way and your support is probably better directed at the original rehabilitation and research scheme next door (see listing above).

Lighthouse The lighthouse at Ras Nungwi is still in operation, although it is not open to visitors. As it is a designated 'strategic point', photographing the lighthouse is officially not allowed; the marines on guard may point this out.

KENDWA

On the west coast, about 4km south of Nungwi, is the tiny village and beautiful beach of Kendwa. What a relief after the noise and crowded development of Nungwi! It's a serene place (most of the time), with some well-spaced, simple places to stay, a clutch of beach bars, a dive school, and a glorious, wide, sandy beach, which doesn't suffer the vast tidal changes of the east coast.

Until the arrival of La Gemma dell'Est in late 2005, Kendwa catered almost exclusively for backpackers and those in search of simple, low-budget escapism. Since then, yet more large resorts have been built on the coast between La Gemma and Nungwi, yet the main stretch of sand at Kendwa remains a peaceful place to chill out and has a feeling of space not found in neighbouring Nungwi. Development is coming to this part of the coast, but it is slower and the plots not so visibly cramped. Things do liven up in the evenings, with bonfires, barbecues and full-moon beach parties but apart from these, it's an absolute haven of peace. Let's hope it can stay this way.

GETTING THERE AND AWAY From Nungwi, you can simply walk along the beach at low tide. If you plan on doing this it's imperative that you are aware of tide times before setting off: with steep coral cliff bordering the beach, there is nowhere to escape the incoming tide. It is also worth noting that there have been a few incidents of robbery on the 1.5km stretch of beach between Baobab Beach Bungalows and La Gemma dell'Est, so single travellers are not advised to take this route alone.

A good option is to travel by boat or canoe from Nungwi (see *Adam's Canoe Rentals*, page 215). Several places in Kendwa run a free transfer service, or it's easy to find a local boatman who will take you for a few dollars, but do check their reliability with others first.

If you're driving, turn off the main road about 4km south of Nungwi, and follow the very rough, undulating track for about another 2km. A high-clearance vehicle is essential. The public bus (Route 14) and *dala-dalas* (number 116), from Zanzibar Town to Nungwi, will drop you off at the same junction on the tar road, leaving you to walk the final 20 minutes to the sea.

WHERE TO STAY All of Kendwa's accommodation choices are on the coast; there are no village-stay options here. For convenience, they are all listed here running from south to north (see map, *Nungwi & Kendwa*, page 200), in the order they would be approached by visitors arriving from Zanzibar Town.

Kendwa Beach Villa (7 rooms) No contact details. Neighbouring Mocco Villa on a tiny plot, this place seems to be in a perpetual state of semi-completion & is very basic indeed! Accessed up some irregular rock stairs, the spartan rooms are off a dark central corridor & boast little: unpolished concrete floors, simple beds & an adequate en-suite toilet & cold-water shower. Some rooms have a fan & all have dim electrical lighting. $$

Mocco Villa (4 rooms) No contact details. Opened in early 2007, this small, single-unit villa is in fact a collection of independent rooms. Sitting on the very edge of the coral cliff at the start of a new parade of budget development, Mocco's 4 rooms are neat & clean with en-suite showers, 4-poster beds & even a hairdryer supplied (although the plastic floor sheeting lets the place down a little). The rooms are all named after island towns, with 'Kidoti' enjoying the best sea view & commanding a consequential supplement. Since Oct 2007, there has also been an affiliate restaurant on the beach from where cocktails can be enjoyed to MTV tunes & traditional seafood specials are served at comfortable, blue cushioned coir sofas. Best to ask for Juma at the restaurant if you're interested in staying here. $$

Duniani Lodge (8 rooms) m 0754 578099; e dunianilodgekendwa@gmail.com; http://dunianikendwa.com. Formerly Malaika Bungalows, Duniani is a neat cluster of bungalows on a particularly rugged coral outcrop above an idyllic stretch of beach. Managed by friendly Bertha, the rooms are basic but light & airy with polished red concrete floors, decorative *mkeke* mats & lovely Zanzibari dbl beds with mosquito net. All the rooms have electricity, a fan & clean en-suite facilities with European flush toilet & shower. There is no restaurant as such but cooked b/fasts are served under the shady casuarinas on the beach. $$$

Eden Village (60 rooms) www.edenviaggi.it. Formerly the quiet, petite sibling of Amaan Bungalows in Nungwi, this place has now been taken over by Italian all-inclusive holidaymakers. Almost doubling in size in recent years, its 60 rooms run from the sandy beach, up the coral-rock cliff through sloping, densely planted tropical gardens to reception & the bumpy track behind the village. There are 4 categories, from the older rooms in small apricot, castellated buildings to a large 2-storey thatched block of holiday apartments & the Khartoon Villa, with those closest to the water commanding a worthwhile premium. All rooms are simply furnished & clean, with mini fridges, AC, reasonable en-suite facilities & nice extras, like swinging chairs on the beach bungalow verandas.

There is a pool & amid the hibiscus hedges, dhow sculptures & flowering oleander, neat paths run down to the sea & the large beach restaurant & bar, which serves food & drink all day under a huge *makuti* shade. Alternatively the Tutti Frutti Bistro dishes up crêpes & gelato to residents only. Although Kendwa Beach is beautiful, the small section immediately north of here is where the village fisherfolk pull ashore & park their dugouts & nets, & can get a little messy; though arguably this is far preferable to the nightly 'theatre' performed on the beach by Eden's Italian staff. $$$

🏠 **La Rosa Dei Venti** In spite of opening only in 2003, La Rosa Dei Venti began to feel decidedly tired & unkempt only a few years later. In mid 2008, it was sold to a new owner & closed for redevelopment. Coastal land is rarely left unused for long in these parts, so there will doubtless be a new hotel here by the time you visit. Please let us know if you stay in La Rosa's successor.

🏠 **Kendwa Rocks Resort** (35 rooms) m 0777 415473/5; e booking@kendwarocks.com; www.kendwarocks.com. The first property to open on this stretch of beach, Kendwa Rocks celebrated its 10th birthday in 2005. It's owned & run by Ally Kilupy, a worldly Zanzibari Rastafarian who grew up welcoming tourists at his mother's guesthouse in Stone Town before studying in Germany, taking a motorbike round Africa & living in south London. Returning to Zanzibar, Ally put his tourism skills to use & now runs a successful operation here. There are clifftop bungalows, beach bungalows, motel-style rooms & a dormitory available, & they get booked up in that order. The coral-stone bungalows on the coral cliff are all named after African countries with suitably themed interiors. All are en suite with large Zanzibari beds & a veranda; each has mains electricity with UK-style 3-pin sockets, fans & mosquito nets. Most of these rooms can be used for dbl or trpl occupancy. The new beach bungalows are spread out in a semicircle on a clean & lovely stretch of beach. They are constructed from coconut panels & *makuti*, & all now boast en-suite bathrooms, lots of lights, simple cane furniture & an inviting batik hammock on their private verandas; only a few steps from the sea, their location is excellent. Above the bungalows & beach area, towards the road, are some new 2-storey Suite Bungalows with nice sea views from the shared balcony, & a

terrace of simple, motel-style rooms. The latter are small & clean, with a neat, shared ablution block; these 15 rooms are usually used by guests arriving without a reservation, & are a good fallback in this instance. There is also an 11-bed dormitory for use by groups of off-duty VSO workers & those waiting for space elsewhere. Here, there are 2 rows of sgl, net-covered beds & a bank of lockers with a functional, if not pretty, shower & toilet block immediately behind.

On the beach, the 2-storey Mermaid Bar is the epitome of backpacker drinking dens: a hip DJ messes on decks in the corner, smiling staff in blue-branded tops stand behind a well-stocked, dhow bar festooned with laminated lists of cocktails, while batik-clad, sun-bleached blond girls recline writing diaries & drinking. That ubiquitous icon of a traveller's rebellion, Che Guevara, presides over events from a row of T-shirts pinned above the bar. This place is totally chilled, so don't expect anything to happen fast. Instead, pick one of the many green & blue hammocks which radiate from the structure, lie back & enjoy the sea views. Also on the beach, there's a genuine Finnish steam bath (US$6.50/2 persons), testament to Ally's time in Finland, and a huge, refurbished cargo ship, *Queen Jahazi* (www.jahazihouseboat.com), which now offers honeymooners an option for a seductive, all-inclusive overnight trip for US$500. For something shorter & more affordable, every evening at 16.30, the US$15 Sunset Booze Cruise departs towards Tumbatu with a dhow full of tanned travellers & jugs of island punch, whilst at full moon there's a lively beach party here where revellers can enjoy bonfires, music, acrobatic shows, fire eating, a buffet & cocktails. The ethos at The Rocks is accurately reflected by its promotional flyer: 'You've found paradise; now take time to enjoy it.' $$–$$$

🏠 **Sunset Bungalows** (56 rooms) m 0777 413818/414647; e info@sunsetkendwa.com; www.sunsetkendwa.com. A faded upturned surfboard stuck into the beach marks Sunset Bungalows' location. The board is in fact the sign for a sizeable beachside structure known as the Bikini Bar, where the staff's T-shirts proclaim 'No bikini; No party'. Here, underneath the huge *makuti* roof, circus-style swathes of blue & white fabric are draped. Outside, on wooden decking, large, white, Embassy-branded umbrellas shade diners indulging in US$6 lunches, featuring everything from fresh fish to egg & chips. On the adjacent stretch of beach, a bonfire pit is surrounded by wooden benches making it a popular after-dinner drinks spot, while the permanent volleyball net keeps the energetic entertained & the relaxed laze in the local massage tent being pampered. Set back from the sea, on the beach behind the restaurant & bar, 2 widely separated rows of bungalows have been built perpendicular to the sea. Of either timber or stone construction, these are extremely pleasant with solid furniture, bold-coloured fabrics (turquoise bed linen with white & cerise mosquito nets), white en-suite bathrooms, mains electricity, an electronic safe & AC in some. A shady terrace in front of each looks out onto white sand & feathery casuarinas. Higher up, on the coral cliff above the beach, the standard rooms (no AC) are in thatched cottages dotted around a pretty garden, overflowing with colourful hibiscus & bougainvillea. And since 2008, in a radical departure from the norm, 4 huge 'Apartment' buildings have been added at the rear. These rooms are clean & spacious with high ceilings, attractive coconut-wood furniture, built-in cushioned *baraza* benches & garden-view terraces; sadly however, their arrival has taken away a lot of the quaint beach retreat vibe the Sunset once exuded. However, the Sunset remains a reliably good choice on this stretch of beach & is remarkably convenient for divers using Scuba Do (see page 225) on the foreshore. *Cliff bungalow* $$; *beach bungalow & apt* $$$

⌂ **White Sands Beach Hotel** (32 rooms) PO Box 732, Kendwa, Zanzibar; m 0777 480987. Since 2002, there has been a fairly constant, low-level renovation & rebuilding project at White Sands. The reception & all of the accommodation is perched on a coral cliff above the beach, & is surrounded by neatly planted gardens filled with aloes, papaya & bougainvillea. The cosy standard rooms have had little more than a lick of paint since Jan took over, but they are clean & functional. The bright-red floor, neat bed, fabric-screened wardrobe, wall-mounted fan, cheerful paintings & Zanzibari concrete corner bench with cushions & table are all perfectly adequate. A little larger & with a beach-view terrace are the mid-class rooms; significantly larger in size, the king-size rooms have a large dbl bed, with plenty of room for another to be added, a bigger terrace & an en-suite bathroom. The red-painted concrete floors in these rooms are covered with dyed *makuti* mats, whilst the walls are decorated with African murals: the artwork of local talent, Moses. The mock rock art & swaying Maasai dancers may be a little crude for some but the rooms are certainly bright & individual. All have en-suite bathrooms, but the standard-class rooms do not yet have hot water. The newest rooms, built in 2007, are tucked behind the

old in whitewashed cottages with flat roofs & a tin shade over the veranda; very similar in style to Kendwa Breezes. They have large square bedrooms with huge Zanzibari beds, blue *kanga* curtains to offset the brilliant white walls & hot water en suites. None of the later rooms has a sea view which may be a negative at the price, though it's barely a stagger to the beach. There are no safes in the rooms, but a deposit box is available at reception & accessible between 07.30 and 14.00.

If you're accessing White Sands from the beach, look out for the old oil barrel suspended under a small *makuti* shade & the lodge's red & white, sun & sail logo. The drum is the restaurant's outside advertisement: 'Lobster tomorrow? Ask today! Kitchen open all day.' If you choose to book, the large circular bar & split-level restaurant is a fun hangout. Built on the beach with the sand still carpeting the floor, it has swings to rival bar stools & a sunken central lounge filled with cushion-covered coir-rope sofas. A surrounding semicircular raised platform of tables for 2 creates a feeling of enclosure, & a couple of king-size beds are laid out for those whose every effort has gone into dragging themselves away from their neighbouring lounger. *Standard & mid class* $$; *new room* $$$

⌂ **Les Toits de Palme** (10 rooms) PO Box 2728, Zanzibar; m 0777 418548. Under joint French–Zanzibari ownership, Les Toits de Palme has 6 neat, simple rooms in 3 bungalows raised above the beach on coral rock. Decorated in white & marine blue, each has a free-standing fan, a small en-suite bathroom with hot-water shower, & dbl/twin beds, curiously orientated to view the toilet rather than the sea. In addition, there are also 4 beach *bandas*, each of which has woven palm sides, a *makuti* roof & twin coir-rope beds; these are about as simple as you can get. That said, the sand is clean & soft underfoot, the bedding is fresh & the 2 shared bathrooms immediately behind have European-style flush toilets & a hot-water shower. There's generator electricity available from 18.00 to midnight, when the atmospheric light of storm lanterns takes over. $–$$

⌂ **Kendwa Breezes Beach Lodge** (16 rooms) m 0777 703999; e relax@kendwabreezes.com; www.kendwabreezes.com. Not in any way related to the more famous Breezes Beach Club on the east coast, this new hotel opened in Jan 2008 as La Gemma's southerly neighbour. Rooms are in staggered rows of whitewashed buildings with their flat roofs & decorative castellations lending the place a Moorish feel, which is said to have been inspired by Stone Town's Arab Fort. The overall design has also sought to guarantee everyone a sea view: the second row being a dbl-storey structure with bedrooms on the upper floor to look out over the rooftops in front to the sea. Rooms 1–8 in the front row enjoy a lovely ocean aspect from their verandas. Entering through the Zanzibari wooden door, the spotless bedrooms are traditional & spacious with all mod-cons inside: chunky 4-poster beds with cheerfully painted motifs, mosquito nets, free-standing fans, AC, TV, electronic safe & great en-suite bathrooms in sage tiles. The main restaurant is open-sided under high *makuti* & specialises in seafood. The laminate tables & formal, mustard-coloured dining chairs may not be to everyone's taste, in which case there's a beach bar (🕐 *10.00–18.00*) for snacks & cocktails. $$$$

🏠 **La Gemma Dell'Est** (138 rooms) 📞 024 2240087; e info.gemma@planhotel.com; www.planhotel.com. La Gemma Dell'Est opened fully in Jul 2005 at the northern end of Kendwa Beach. It's about 800m north of White Sands Beach Hotel, & barely 1.5km south of Nungwi's Baobab Beach Bungalows. It's a large hotel, managed by the Swiss-based firm PlanHotel SA, & is certainly one of the more stylish of Zanzibar's large resorts. Sensitive architecture & stunning landscaping create a feeling of tremendous space, while minimal tidal changes allow for swimming in the sea all day. The hotel's rooms have been cleverly built along the natural contours of the landscape, making them appear lower-density & fairly unobtrusive, while also allowing each one a sea-view veranda. Inside, they are contemporary & comfortable, each having a king-size bed or twin beds with mosquito net, a ceiling fan & AC, satellite TV, minibar, electronic safe, & an en-suite marble bathroom; everything you'd expect from a good, modern hotel. Thoughtfully planted screens offer privacy on each terrace & the emerald lawns & swathes of established exotic vegetation (all neatly labelled) make a beautiful foreground to the setting sun over the Indian Ocean. A walk around the sloping grounds to see the likes of lemongrass (*Cymbopogon citrates*) the size of pampas grass, the stunning russet flowers of the African tulip tree (*Spathodea campanulata*) or the crimson coral tree (*Erythrina variegate*) is highly recommended.

The beach here is wide & beautiful, with nice loungers & *makuti* umbrellas dotted around the raked sand. The enormous, floodlit swimming pool is also set right on the beach, with a children's area, jacuzzi, waterfall, & swim-up cocktail bar. There is hotel security on the beach to ensure no hassle for sunbathers yet Kendwa's clutch of beach bungalows & their associated bars & restaurants are an easy 10min walk south, past the proliferation of beach huts selling colourful local artwork. La Gemma has several bars & restaurants, from the sleek Pavilion serving tasty Mediterranean buffets to the Coral Cove alfresco pizzeria by the pool, & the intimate, à-la-carte seafood restaurant, Sea Breeze, at the end of the jetty. With the exception of the last, all food & drink is on a totally flexible, all-inclusive basis, & the Italian influence ensures that the food is invariably very good. By day, there's a PADI diving centre (run by Scuba Do, see page 225), outdoor gym, countless watersports, beach volleyball, sailing & even snorkelling over the artificial reef – created when the jetty was built – to keep everyone occupied, then the selection of optional evening entertainment kicks off with everything from quizzes to musical Swahili beach BBQs. Children are well catered for at La Gemma, with cots, highchairs & babysitting all available. The staff's attitude is extremely positive towards families, & with a children's pool, easy access to food & drink all day, a good beach with easy swimming, & on-site doctor in case of accidents, La Gemma makes for one of Zanzibar's best choices for families. ♛

✖ **WHERE TO EAT** Virtually all the hotels on Kendwa Beach have an affiliated beach bar and restaurant offering cold drinks, casual dining, and uninterrupted sea views. The menus and quality are close to identical, relying heavily on the day's catch for fresh seafood, with a number of Swahili curry and fresh pizza options. They are all open to anyone who cares to wander by and, as with many places on Zanzibar, this includes a number of friendly (and hungry) neighbourhood cats.

SHOPPING With the increase in accommodation and visitors, Kendwa now has two small, local-style 'supermarkets': **Ndiro Supermarket** on the very edge of the coral cliff at the southern end of the beach and **Mwakamini Supermarket** on the village side of Kendwa Rocks. Both sell basic supplies of tinned food, crisps, sweets and water, but little else. For **curios**, the ever-increasing span of Maasai-manned stalls on the beach bordering La Gemma offers colourful paintings, beaded jewellery and occasionally carvings. Quality varies considerably so shop around and don't be blinded by the sun into making second-rate purchases.

WHAT TO SEE AND DO Sunbathing, beach volleyball, diving and snorkelling are the main activities in Kendwa – it's a terribly laid-back beach hangout. The vast majority of the hotels and guesthouses will hire out basic snorkelling gear, organise day trips by boat to Tumbatu Island, and offer sunset dhow cruises; some will rent out kayaks too.

Watersports For fun below the water line, Kendwa's only dive operator is currently the excellent Scuba Do Diving. A second outfit, Scuba Shack, is now part of the Kendwa Rocks empire, and offers only basic snorkelling equipment and boat trips, though it may reopen as a dive centre in conjunction with one of the larger Nungwi operations.

Scuba Do Diving Stone Town; ℩ (UK) +44 (0)1326 250773; m 0777 417157/0748 415179; e info@scubado.demon.co.uk/do-scuba@scuba-do-Zanzibar.com; www.scubado.demon.co.uk/www.scuba-do-Zanzibar.com. Owned & operated by a British couple, Christian & Tammy, Scuba Do is a highly professional & well-equipped dive centre, based on the beach in front of Sunset Bungalows. The 4 permanent dive leaders take a maximum of 6 divers each to one of their repertoire of 15 reef sites, chosen according to conditions & diver experience.

Diving is done from 4 high-powered RIBs (rigid inflatable boats), allowing fast access to dive sites (Mnemba is reached in 30mins, as opposed to nearly 2hrs by dhow), & GPS navigation pinpoints precise dive entry points. There's plenty of good, new equipment – 'Buddy Explorer' BCDs (all with individual surface marker buoys), Mares regulators, masks & fins, & Reef wetsuits – & they have a code of stringent safety procedures. We were impressed to be told that all divers are issued with surface marker buoys, whilst marine radios maintain contact

INTERNATIONAL COASTAL CLEAN-UP DAY

Every September since 2005, the team at Scuba Do Diving has galvanised Kendwa into a successful beach tidy. As part of International Coastal Clean-up Day, co-ordinated by conservation foundations Project AWARE and Ocean Conservancy, the aim is to collect and prevent debris littering seaside locations and aquatic environments, thus protecting their beauty and health. In Kendwa, the initiative has been greeted enthusiastically by villagers, residents, hotel staff and even thoughtful tourists, and their efforts to make a difference are clear: Kendwa does have one of the island's cleanest beaches.

At the first beach clean-up, 82 people (75% from the local community) collected 108 bags (730kg) of rubbish, but only two years later in 2007, this had grown to 106 volunteers and a massive 1,002kg in 168 bags. Whilst this increase in litter, a manmade mix of drinks bottles, food wrappers, discarded building materials and plastic bags, is disturbing, this community's involvement to better the environment is positive.

Tammy and Christian at Scuba Do are totally committed to their community and work hard throughout the year to educate local school children and elders, as well as many hotels, about the effects of rubbish on the environment. Help their efforts by disposing of rubbish responsibly and if you're on holiday in the area in mid-September, don a pair of rubber gloves, grab a bag from the dive centre and be sure to join in the concerted clean-up campaign: snorkellers can fill crates in the shallows whilst landlubbers comb the sand. Be sure to guess the total waste weight too, and you may even win a prize at the end of the day…

between boats & base. Their on-site Bauer air compressor is regularly tested, & there's an emergency oxygen re-breather & a full medical kit. As part of this adherence to safety, Scuba Do will not take any divers underwater without proof of their qualification & insist on a US$30 PADI refresher dive with anyone who hasn't been under water for 6 months or boasts fewer than 100 logged dives. When out of the water, the team here are also involved in community work, most notably the annual beach & underwater clean-up project (see box, *International Coastal Clean-up Day*, page 225).

MKOKOTONI

On the west coast of the island, about 21km south of Nungwi, Mkokotoni is a lively fishing village. Although there's no accommodation here that we could find, it's worth a short detour to soak up some rural atmosphere and vibrant village life. The bustling market, where Tumbatuans and local Zanzibaris buy and sell all manner of fresh seafood, is crowded, noisy and full of energy. Around this, an abundance of tumbledown stalls display piles of coconuts, fruits, vegetables and spices whilst in the harbour behind, age-old techniques are used to repair and build the next generation of dhows.

In 1984, a major hoard of Chinese coins was discovered on the beach north of the village, indicating that this was once a prosperous trading port between the East, Arabia and Zanzibar, long before the arrival of the Europeans. Colonial rule brought the few grand administration buildings glimpsed along the central avenue of sweet almond trees, but today village life is still centred on simple trade with neighbours.

GETTING THERE AND AWAY Few tourists visit Mkokotoni, and those who do are usually part of a tour *en route* to Tumbatu Island. The village can be accessed on a fast tar road from both Mahonda to the south and Kivunge, to the east.

By public bus, Route 1 runs hourly from approximately 05.30 to 20.00 from Darajani Terminal in Zanzbar Town to Mkokotoni; as do frequent *dala-dalas* number 101 from Creek Road.

REGIONAL EXCURSIONS

About 12km south of Nungwi, on the main road to/from Zanzibar Town, are the ruins at Fukuchani and Mvuleni. These are the remains of large houses dating from the 16th century. They're worth a short stop if you're driving this way, and a possible excursion from Nungwi if lying on the beach gets all too much.

TUMBATU ISLAND

Tumbatu is one of the largest of Zanzibar's offshore islands, measuring about 8km long by 2–3km across. The people of the island, the Watumbatu, speak their own dialect of Swahili. They have a reputation for pride and aloofness, and are reputed not to welcome visitors on their island. The Watumbatu men are traditionally known as the best sailors on Zanzibar, or even on the whole east African coast.

On the southern end of Tumbatu Island are a group of Shirazi ruins, thought to date from the 12th century. An Arab geographer writing in the 13th century recorded that the Muslim people of Zanzibar Island were attacked (by whom is not clear) and retreated to Tumbatu Island where they were welcomed by the local inhabitants, who were also Muslim, and it is assumed that these people were responsible for the Shirazi ruins.

The ruins were probably abandoned in the early 16th century, but the Watumbatu still claim to be descended from Shirazi immigrants.

FUKUCHANI RUINS Fukuchani Ruins are on the edge of the village of the same name. Beside a large school on the western side of the road, there's a small signpost under a baobab tree which will point you in the right direction, along a track that bisects the local football pitch. The ruins are known locally as the 'Portuguese House', but although some Portuguese settlers may have built houses on Zanzibar during this period, this structure is considered by archaeologists to be of Swahili and not foreign origin. The ruins are well maintained and the surrounding land has been mostly cleared of vegetation.

Built in the 16th century, Fukuchani is a fortified dwelling that may have belonged to a wealthy merchant or farmer. It is constructed of coral bricks, with arched doorways and rectangular niches in the walls of the main room, and surrounded by a stone wall in which small holes have been inserted. It has been suggested that these are gun slits for the purposes of defence, but a more recent theory suggests they may have been to hold projecting beams which supported a raised walkway, so that anyone inside the enclosure could see over the wall. The ruins are in good condition, compared with many others on Zanzibar of a similar age, and quite impressive. Buildings of a similar style have been found at other sites along the east African coast, though – alongside the ruins at Mvuleni – Fukuchani represents the finest domestic stone house architecture of this period.

Behind the ruin, a path leads to a small beach. Across the channel you can see Tumbatu Island, with the lighthouse at its northern tip clearly visible. At the southern end of the island are the remains of a large town, dating from around the 12th century. (For more details, see box, *Tumbatu Island*, opposite.)

MVULENI RUINS Mvuleni Ruins lie just to the south of Fukuchani, on the other side of the road (east), where you'll see a small signpost. Next to a few huts and a small shop, a path leads through banana and palm plantations to reach the site. Like Fukuchani, this structure was probably once a fortified house that would have belonged to a powerful member of the community. It, too, was thought to be the work of Portuguese invaders until recent research suggested that it is more likely to be Swahili in origin. The house was once larger than the one at Fukuchani, with thicker walls, but the ruins are in poor condition, and are partly overgrown with vegetation, obscuring some of the architectural features. Substantial sections of the walls remain standing, though, complete with carved door arches, conveying something of the impressive building that this once was. One of the most interesting features of this house is the large natural cavern just northeast of the house, outside the main wall. Crystal-clear, salt water flows through the cave, collecting in a pool visible beyond an entrance fringed by vegetation: this was probably a source of water when the house was occupied.

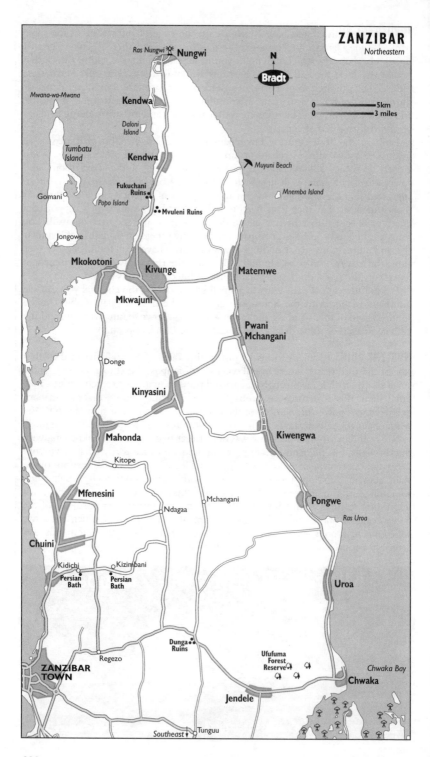

9

Northeastern Zanzibar

The east coast of Zanzibar boasts an almost continuous expanse of picture-perfect beach; it's arguably the island's greatest attraction for visitors. Stretching from Nungwi on the northernmost tip of the island to the mangrove swamps of Chwaka Bay, the superb, powder-white sand beaches of the northeastern coastline are breathtaking in length and beauty. Less than 1km offshore, waves break along the fringe reef which runs the length of the island, and the warm, turquoise waters of the Indian Ocean attract divers, swimmers and fishermen alike. Bordering the sand, an almost unbroken strip of picturesque coconut palms provides shade for traditional fishing villages and sunbathing honeymooners, and completes many people's vision of paradise.

The beaches along Zanzibar's east coast slope very little. Consequently, when the tide is out, the water retreats a long way, making swimming from the beach difficult. It does, however, allow for fascinating exploration along the top of the exposed reef. Washed-up seaweed can also be a surprise here for uninformed visitors: between December and the rains in mid-February, it's common for many of the beaches to have a band of wind-washed brown seaweed. The rest of the year, the sand remains idyllic and clear.

Compared with those found in Nungwi to the north, the accommodation choices in the northeast tend to have more space, both in their private grounds and between properties. However, most are still within an easy walking distance along the seashore, and make useful refreshment stops on long beach walks. The central stretch of the coast, around Kiwengwa, is the busiest, with its cluster of large, Italian, package-holiday resorts, but there has been less tourism development to the north or the south of this area, and it's still possible to find some lovely, individual places that seem to be virtually on their own.

Access from Zanzibar Town to the east coast is easy, on both private and public transport. However, there is currently little more than a narrow, bumpy track connecting the villages from Pongwe to Matemwe, necessitating very slow progress and either a 4x4 vehicle, or the hastening of the end for your vehicle's suspension!

MATEMWE

A long, linear village, Matemwe is the most northerly of the east coast settlements. Although less than 20km south of Nungwi, it marks the end of the coastal road heading north. It's a quintessential Swahili fishing village: little houses set among masses of elegant coconut palms with dhows and *ngalawa* (dugout canoes) bobbing in the water. The sand is so white and smooth here that the wind blows it into mounds that look like snowdrifts. A quieter section of coast, there are some great accommodation options with the added bonus of swift access to Mnemba's reefs for divers.

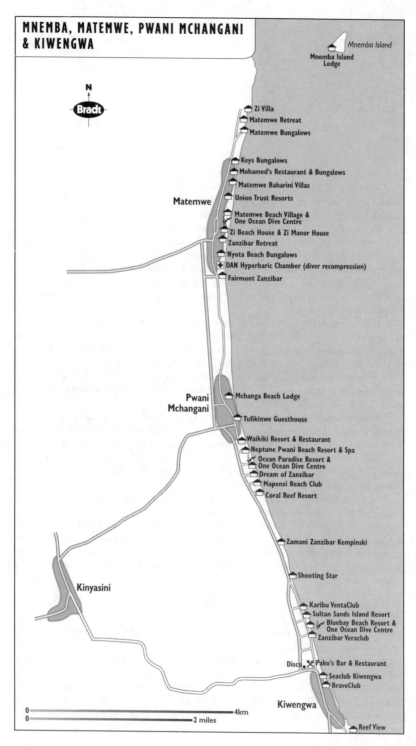

MNEMBA, MATEMWE, PWANI MCHANGANI & KIWENGWA

N
Bradt

Mnemba Island

Mnemba Island Lodge

Zi Villa
Matemwe Retreat
Matemwe Bungalows

Keys Bungalows
Mohamed's Restaurant & Bungalows
Matemwe Baharini Villas
Union Trust Resorts

Matemwe

Matemwe Beach Village & One Ocean Dive Centre
Zi Beach House & Zi Manor House
Zanzibar Retreat
Nyota Beach Bungalows
DAN Hyperbaric Chamber (diver recompression)
Fairmont Zanzibar

Pwani Mchangani

Mchanga Beach Lodge

Tufikinwe Guesthouse

Waikiki Resort & Restaurant
Neptune Pwani Beach Resort & Spa
Ocean Paradise Resort & One Ocean Dive Centre
Dream of Zanzibar
Mapenzi Beach Club
Coral Reef Resort

Zamani Zanzibar Kempinski

Shooting Star

Kinyasini

Karibu VentaClub
Sultan Sands Island Resort
Bluebay Beach Resort & One Ocean Dive Centre
Zanzibar Veraclub

Disco Pako's Bar & Restaurant
Seaclub Kiwengwa
BravoClub

Kiwengwa

0   4km
0   2 miles

Reef View

Matemwe is very much a working beach, especially close to the village centre, and this is part of its attraction for visitors looking for just a bit more than sea and sunshine. The main employment here is fishing, and the dhows and *ngalawa* go out most evenings, delivering their catch onto the beach each morning. There's also some seaweed farming here: look out for the makeshift racks of purple fronds drying in the sun. The local people are relatively friendly and don't seem to mind tourists watching the scene, but this isn't a spot to be intrusive with in-your-face photography.

Sadly, like many villages on the island, Matemwe has a litter problem. In spite of Matemwe Bungalows arranging regular rubbish collections, blue plastic bags and general household garbage can be seen caught in bushes and strewn on the ground. With continued assistance from local hotels, this will hopefully improve.

GETTING THERE AND AWAY If you are driving, there is a direct road to Matemwe from Mkwajuni, on the island's central north–south road. Alternatively, turn east after Kinyasini to Pwani Mchangani, and head north along the new tar road.

If you're staying at one of Matemwe's smarter accommodation options, transfers to/from Zanzibar Town can be arranged by them. Alternatively, a private taxi or minibus can be organised by a Zanzibar Town tour company or hotel.

By public transport, there's a frequent daily *dala-dala* service (number 118) and public bus (Route 16) from Zanzibar Town to Matemwe village, which then continues up the coast to within about 2km of Matemwe Bungalows.

WHERE TO STAY Travelling from north to south along the beach, your options for accommodation are:

Zi Villa (4 rooms) ☎ +27 (82) 8233347; m 0777 420710; e allan@starlight.co.za; www.zivilla.co.za. North of Matemwe village, in a bay called Fisherman's Cove, Zi Villa is a private villa owned & let by a South African couple. This large, well-equipped, 4-bedroomed house is an excellent base for groups who are comfortable with being relatively remote & self-sufficient. Stylish, spacious interiors, packed with interesting *objets d'art*, a rogues' gallery of Zanzibari images, all mod-cons & a superb view out to Mnemba Island are all guaranteed. The eloquent Zanzibari manager, Seif, & the housekeeping team, including a nightwatchman & resident chef, do their utmost to accommodate requests. There are 4 bedrooms, 3 dbls & a twin, 3 of which have direct access on to a large wrap-around outside deck & an en-suite bathroom. The fourth room has a separate, private bathroom. The upstairs master bedroom, or Sultan's Suite, has an enormous bed, large TV with video player, private sundeck & indoor jacuzzi. The 24hr mains electricity, hot water, AC & fans are standard throughout the house. The bright, light & airy lounge has 4 comfortable white sofas, a satellite TV & DVD player, a library of English books, & access to the pool deck through large glass French doors. Here, there's a deep swimming pool, with great sea views, & a sunbathing area of hammocks & loungers. The Fifo Bar, complete with fully stocked bar, pool table, music centre & dartboard, also accesses the deck & beach, & completes the package. *US$400/576/864, FB for 2/4/8 guests; transfers US$16pp/one-way*

Matemwe Retreat (3 rooms) m 0777 475788/0774 414834; e info@asilialodges.com/ matemwebungalows@zanzinet.com; www.matemwe.com/www.asilialodges.com. Bordering Matemwe Bungalows' main lodge to the north is its exceptional new sibling, Matemwe Retreat. Comprising just 3 imposing, castellated villas, each with private butler service, the Retreat is one of Zanzibar's most impressive & exclusive places to stay. Each of the whitewashed villas has been thoughtfully & creatively designed with strikingly unusual interiors, panoramic ocean views, a private roof terrace & highly original, locally produced furnishings. The heavy timber entrance allows access to the enormous private deck, where dbl hammocks gently sway, sofas invite siestas & a dhow-shaped peninsula table anticipates dinner *à deux*. Entering inside the French doors, the cool, calm natural feel of the beautiful bedroom & spacious bathroom are immediately relaxing. Decorated in neutral coffee & cream colours, with a mix of Swahili style & uncluttered, minimalist tendencies, thoughtful touches, luxurious linens &

modern conveniences are indicative of the attention to detail & price tag. There is a king-size bed, plenty of storage & good use of reclaimed dhow-wood throughout; AC, hairdryer, & private bar are standard. Stepping down to the large, adjoining bathroom, its twinkling Zanzibari lanterns reveal twin sinks moulded out of the wall, a circular shower (complete with star-like LED ceiling), separate toilet & a bath beside the sea-facing picture window for truly indulgent soaking. At the top of the internal spiral staircase, a door leads to the idyllic private roof terrace. A 2-tier area, half is devoted to sun worshippers & the other to a super-sized corner sofa under pole shading & vibrant bougainvillea. With an easterly outlook, the terrace catches the first rays of sunlight creeping over the horizon at dawn, making wonderful photographs & all-day sunbathing possible. There is an infinity plunge pool, complete with alcove waterfall, which offers stupendous views through the tops of coconut palms, over the coral coves & sea to Mnemba Island. Fun *objets d'art* are dotted around: a large concrete crab at the pool's edge, a life-size turtle coffee table, a metal fish candle lantern & decorative turquoise glass balls embedded in the structural detailing.

Service is top-notch with a friendly villa butler taking care of your every need without disruption or subservience. Menus are discussed daily & almost anything seasonally available is prepared on request. Food & drinks can be served anywhere: the beach, roof terrace or veranda. Retreat guests are also free to walk the neat sandy paths to Matemwe Bungalows (5mins) & have free use of all of their communal facilities, but it's important for sociable guests to realise that there are no public areas at Matemwe Retreat itself — no central lounge, bar or restaurant. This is really a place to get away from it all & chill, read & indulge in exclusive solitude. US$430–525pp, FB

⌂ **Matemwe Bungalows** (12 rooms) m 0777 414834; e info@asilialodges.com/ matemwebungalows@zanzinet.com; www.matemwe.com, www.asilialodges.com; ⏲ Jun–Mar. Just past the northern edge of Matemwe village, occupying a windswept spot beside a sweeping sandy beach, Matemwe Bungalows is a very good, smart yet informal place. Popular with well-travelled, unpretentious couples, it's relaxed & quiet. Being understated & calm, it's not really the place for families seeking action-packed adventures. Perched on the edge of a low coral cliff, lapped by the waves, each of the thatched, whitewashed cottages has a superb view across the water to

Mnemba Island. All the rooms have been upgraded into impressively stylish suites, some split-level, with private, curved verandas. Each is individual, though all are variations on a similar design, intent on providing a spacious, comfortable interior & maximising the sea view. Coconut-wood dbl beds are covered in bright appliqué throws; polished concrete floors are strewn with cheerful woven mats; & wooden lattice shutters conceal built-in wardrobe space. In the 6 suites, the spacious en-suite bathrooms have a European toilet, twin sinks, a shower & large, decadent bath, whilst those in the older style have single sinks & a large shower. Glass bottles filled with bathing condiments & tall candles are all welcome finishing touches. Constant mains electricity, UK-style 3-pin sockets, a solar-powered hot-water system, retractable mosquito nets, free-standing fan (available upon request), large Zanzibari safe box & a relaxing day-bed (sgl in the older rooms; queen-size in the new) are standard throughout the accommodation. The new rooms also feature a sunken, cushioned *baraza* which looks out through wide corner shutters to the terrace & sea beyond. On the terrace, a dbl hammock & turquoise directors' chairs make the perfect seaside retreat. The older-style rooms have a small lounge area inside, while the veranda tempts with a dbl sofa as well as a dbl hammock.

Below & behind the suites, a blush-coloured stone path meanders alongside a stream through lush tropical gardens to the swimming pools, the main dining area & onwards to the sandy beach. Significant garden developments, planting & tending frangipani, bougainvillea, sweet almonds & carpets of flowering ground cover, make this a really lovely lodge to wander around. The beach ends where Matemwe Bungalows begin, resulting in virtually no passing foot traffic from the village & very little hassle. Some locals have set up curio stalls along the beach, but few approach guests & it's relatively low-key compared with other stretches of this coast. There are 2 inviting swimming pools, 1 infinity pool atop the coral cliff with a clear view across to Mnemba Island, & another below it, connected by a gently tumbling waterfall, offering protection when the coastal wind blows. The adjacent bar is a beautifully polished old dhow, set on powdery beach sand & flanked by an impressively enormous sperm whale skeleton. Tasty buffets & plated dinners are served by friendly, uniformed staff in an open-sided dining room overlooking the end of the beach & sea. All guests stay on a FB basis &, space permitting, visitors will be welcomed for dinner with

24hrs' notice. 2 day rooms (US$50), complete with shower area, have been added so that those leaving late in the afternoon can enjoy their final hours on the beach or sunbathing by the pool.

2 dhows are based at the lodge for snorkelling & sailing excursions, escorted reef walks can be arranged at low tide (local villagers, who already work as the lodge's boatmen, are being trained to guide these), & a large wooden chess set (complete with prawns as pawns!) is set up en route to the beach. Fishing & diving trips are arranged through large activity resorts along the coast. For the more sedentary, there's in-room massage, a library, or Scrabble, Boggle, Yatzy & a host of other games. There is complimentary internet access with the facility to download digital pictures from cameras & burn them to CD or DVD: this is especially useful for post-safari guests arriving with full memory cards.

With close proximity to the local community & a desire to contribute to development, the company & guests have given time & money to supply the local villagers with fresh water, build a primary school, provide 2 deep-sea mashua dhows for fishing, assist with much-needed rubbish collections & teach English. Matemwe is one of very few lodges on the island with a staff member dedicated to community relations & development. If this appeals but something more exclusive is required, neighbouring Matemwe Retreat is the lodge's private villa alternative (see above). US$265–310pp, FB

⌂ **Keys Bungalows** (4 rooms) m 0777 411797. Behind a collapsing mkeke palm gate, Keys is a very friendly beach bar with some surprisingly nice little rooms in lush gardens of casuarinas, palms & papayas. Opened in mid 2006 by local lad Ali Dudi, this is a good option for beach-focused backpackers seeking a chilled hangout for their ocean activities. Accommodation is in individual coral-rock cottages or within a larger whitewashed building & each is small but clean & pleasant. Behind heavy Zanzibari doors, there are nicely carved dbl beds, cheerful kanga curtains, cupboards, complete with integrated safe, made from cleverly adapted ngalawa boats & wet-room-style en-suite bathrooms. Fans, mosquito nets, UK sockets, cold water & a small veranda with cane & hide chairs are all standard.

The open-sided circular bar above the beach is the centre of activity here with gentle reggae music & a sociable crowd setting the vibe. The wine may be lukewarm & from a box, but the spirits are all imported & the mood's happy. From the comfort of a Rasta-coloured hammock or bar stool it's possible to arrange snorkelling & boat trips with the local

crew, but anything more will require a trip to one of the larger resorts in the area. Meals are possible with some notice, & for now at least, Keys seems to be a good option in this price bracket. $$$

⌂ **Mohamed's Restaurant & Bungalows** (4 rooms) m 0777 431881. Follow the clear sign from the main road & you'll find these 4 small whitewashed cottages: they're hidden behind a high wall in the heart of Matemwe village. Owned & managed by Mohamed, ably assisted by his sparky girlfriend, Juliana, this compact little complex offers 2 twin & 2 trpl rooms, each with mosquito nets &, for 2008, a newly tiled en-suite bathroom with a cold-water shower & flush toilet. The rooms here are basic but fairly clean & although the beds don't always have linen, this can usually be arranged. There are sandy paths & some plants leading down to an open-sided restaurant where simple meals can be organised with a day's notice (food is bought fresh so order dinner in the morning). The beachfront location & budget continue to make this a great backpacker option. $$

⌂ **Matemwe Baharini Villas** (16 rooms) m 0777 417768/429642; e info@matemwevillas.com/ kibwenibeachvilla@zitec.org; www.matemwevillas.com. In the last couple of years, efforts have been made to improve this place, & with a good degree of success. The coral-stone paths have been levelled, the gardens slightly better tended, the rooms spruced up, a swimming pool added & available activities increased. The 2 large villas by the entrance (one 2-room, the other 4 en-suite dbls) are bright & airy, if a little soulless. They are predominantly used by families & groups, & feature an open-plan, self-catering kitchen & lounge area; electricity, hot water, fans, mosquito nets & deckchairs on the terrace all come as standard. In addition to the villas, there are 10 rooms in traditional bungalows, one of which has an interconnecting door for family use. Set back from the beach behind a garden, these are clean & tidy with a high Zanzibari dbl bed, a day-bed, mosquito net, fan, AC, emergency light, radio/clock & an en-suite shower & toilet. The mekeke & makuti ceilings are high & unusually constructed, which combined with the gauze windows allows the cooling sea breeze to circulate.

Facilities & activities here are quite limited, but there is a beachfront restaurant, drooping volleyball net, Swahili massage, & local fishing excursions on request. There is a sea view from the windows & timber louvres should the need for an afternoon siesta require blackout. For the more active, there's a raised swimming pool at the heart of the complex, surrounded by palm-strung hammocks, & a dive centre, Scuba Libre (www.scubalibrezanzibar.com), behind the large, open-sided *makuti* restaurant. For self-drivers, there is the advantage of secure parking behind the metal gate. *Villas* $$; *bungalows* $$$

⌂ **Union Trust Resorts** At the end of 2005, a smart stone wall was erected to mark a beachside plot between Matemwe Beach Village & Matemwe Baharini Villas. It has a sign reading only 'Union Trust Resorts'; on passing again in 2008, the stone wall had disappeared & a serious construction site was in its place. Les Harbottle, a hotel interior design specialist from South Africa, who is famed for the strikingly stylish, contemporary Melrose Arch Hotel in Johannesburg, is leading the design work here.

⌂ **Matemwe Beach Village** (22 rooms) \ 024 2238374; m 0777 417250; e matemwebeachvillage@zitec.org; www.matemwebeach.com; ⊕ Jun–Mar. Operating a 'no shoes, no news' policy, Matemwe Beach Village is a place to relax on the beach, read a book & indulge in the occasional dive or massage (US$15/hr). TVs & organised team games are not what this place is about: instead it is a simple, unassuming beach resort popular with European family groups & young honeymooners. The 16 compact standard rooms (2 with AC) are next to one another in a series of rows, a mere hop, skip & a jump from the beach. The interiors are simple but stylish with denim blues & lilacs giving a cool, nautical air, & thoughtful touches from hat to towels provided. With a mixture of king-size, sgl- & twin-bed combinations, all have mains electricity, fans, mosquito nets, candles & handy torches. The en-suite bathrooms are moulded concrete with hot-water showers, a toilet & sink. Outside, rattan chairs sit on a small terrace & the sound of the sea & the massage *banda* beckon. Forming a neat cul-de-sac of dbl-storey, whitewashed rondavels with steep pitched thatch are the 5 newer Shamba suites. Crossing the threshold, note the Swahili quotation inscribed above the door, '*Penzi la maana ni kuridhiana*' (The real love is to love each other), & enter the highly stylised interior of designer Ivan Sutila. Matching hats, *kangas* & beach bags greet every guest at the door. The spacious central lounge area has built-in seating filled with blue & lilac cushions, & the bedroom is airy with a large dbl bed & pastel lilac linen. The en-suite shower is a stand-alone circular feature, whilst the very separate toilet is dressed to look like a throne with swathes of blue & purple circus-style fabrics streaming up towards the roof.

On the galleried upper level, these suites have large navy mattresses covered in cushions, & a suspended dbl bed. Fun as these rooms are, their real disadvantage is that they are set at the back of the complex &, even from the upper level, their views are limited. Mains electricity, UK-style 3-pin sockets, a fan, minibar & tea/coffee-making facilities are standard throughout. The one-off Asali Suite is most frequently used by honeymooning couples keen to take advantage of its private plunge pool & dedicated chef.

The resort's raised lounge area, overlooking the beach, encourages lazy afternoons & evenings, with metres of navy mattresses covered in assorted white & turquoise cushions, low wooden tables & a welcome sea breeze. The area is thatched but the walls are made of billowing cream canvas, with ribbons of aqua & royal-blue fabric hung between the ceiling supports to create a cool, intimate den. The adjoining restaurant offers a daily, à-la-carte menu at individual tables set with neat fabric runners. New for 2008, an attractive pool area complete with pole-shaded bar & sloped loungers makes cooling low-tide dips possible, but do top up on suncream & watch children as there is no shade in this very exposed area. The lovely One Ocean PADI 5* IDC dive centre is housed behind the pool with a fun whale-tail reception & a purpose-built teaching area for dive courses; upstairs in the *makuti* thatch a DVD & TV lounge offer sports fans & sunburnt guests a shady retreat. *Standard room US$130–170 dbl; Shamba Suite US$210–250 dbl; Asali Suite US$400–450 dbl; all rates FB*

⌂ **Zi Beach House & Zi Manor House** (4 rooms each) \ +27 (11) 8075111/+27 (82) 8233347; e allan@starlight.co.za; www.zivilla.co.za. In neighbouring houses in the centre of Matemwe village, Zi Beach House & Zi Manor are recent additions to the 'Zi' property portfolio, which includes Zi Villa to the north of the village. Let mainly to groups of friends & families from South Africa, the mushroom-coloured, thatched houses can be rented for self-catering escapes or with a resident chef for those wanting a little more pampering. The house interiors are very similar in style: varnished coconut floors, family dining areas, a central bar, games facilities (pool table in Zi Manor; darts in Zi Beach), comfortable sofas for watching DVDs & neutral colour schemes sprinkled with African *objets d'art*: locally woven baskets to Congolese *kubu* cloth & tribal masks. There are 4, neatly decorated en-suite bedrooms in each house, all with fans, AC, French doors & outdoor access to the garden or an upper balcony.

The beach is immediately in front, making high-tide swimming a popular pursuit, but this is a significant seaweed farming area, so do beware not to trip over or damage the sub-aqua plantations. There is a swimming pool at each villa as well as a shared RIB (rigid inflatable boat) for fishing trips & a quad bike for beach excursions; dive centres at nearby resorts cater for underwater enthusiasts. *Zi Beach: self-catering US$128/day for 2–8 guests; Villa inc chef, FB US$320/461/691 2/4/8 guests. Zi Manor: self-catering US$128/day for 2–8 guests; Villa inc chef US$360/518/778 2/4/8 guests; 35% supplement in Aug & Dec*

⌂ **Zanzibar Retreat** (7 rooms) m 0773 079344/0753 452244; e info@zanzibarretreat.com/ inforetreat@zanzinet.com; www.zanzibarretreat.com. Behind a wall of cascading bougainvillea, immediately next door to Zi Manor, this pleasantly peaceful hotel opened in spring 2007. With just 7 rooms accessed from its broad, wrap-around veranda & a new first-floor suite, it is a small, personal place to stay & better suited to older couples seeking solitude than energetic youngsters. The main building is whitewashed & thatched with decorative Moorish arches, a shady veranda & small central courtyard from which the stairs ascend to the bar & 2-room suite. The suite has a wonderful private balcony from where it is possible to see all along the coast from Mnemba Island to Kiwengwa. The bright & airy standard rooms are on the ground floor & have polished dark timber floors, well-made louvred wardrobes, large Zanzibari beds & a dbl shower in their en-suite bathrooms. High ceilings, fans & AC ensure they are always cool, whilst minibars, Wi-Fi & satellite TV add a touch of modern convenience. Outside is a well-tended garden & an attractive view through the beachfront mangroves to the sea & bobbing *ngalawa* boats, which can be enjoyed from the restaurant over long, lingering lunches. The large pool is an asset at low tide but for those keen to hit the ocean, activities, including diving, can be arranged with the nearby (10mins) Fairmont Zanzibar or at One Ocean in Matemwe Beach Village. $$$$

⌂ **Nyota Beach Bungalows** (10 rooms) m 0777 484303/439059; e nyota@zanzinet.com; www.nyotabeachbungalows.com; ⊕ Jul–May. Opened in Dec 2004 by Italian Patrizia & Edi from Pemba, Nyota's 10 simple, stylish rooms are already receiving praise from guests. Set on a lovely stretch of beach, in the centre of Matemwe village, great care has been taken in decorating these stone-and-thatch cottages with bright fabrics, nice furniture &

natural ornaments. There are 2 new beachfront cottages, right on the sand, a selection of dbl & twin standard rooms in neat 2-storey structures & a family room for 3 people. Each room has a fan, mosquito net, mains electricity, & an en-suite bathroom with constant hot water for showers & a flush toilet. There's a small but very relaxed dbl-storey lounge & bar area overlooking the ocean, which is used by residents & guests alike. Patrizia's background in Italian restaurants ensures that the food is pretty good. Alternatively, the cushioned benches outside each room make a comfortable spot to chill, overlooking the banana & papaya trees in the garden. Diving & snorkelling trips can be arranged through one of the larger resorts nearby, & a central phone & email access are readily available. $$$

⌂ **Fairmont Zanzibar** (109 rooms) ☏ 024 2240391; e zanzibar@fairmont.com/ zan.reservations@fairmont.com; www.fairmont.com/zanzibar. The Fairmont Zanzibar opened in Jul 2007 following a US$10 million redevelopment & expansion of the old Protea beach resort. The resulting lush grounds, comfortable rooms, myriad facilities & immaculate staff have quickly made this Zanzibar's premium family resort. The 109 newly renovated rooms & suites are dotted around the vast, tropical gardens to offer a range of sizes & styles of accommodation options. Couples entering through the turquoise doors of the bijou Island Cottages will find locally sourced coconut furniture, clean crisp lines & vibrant colours touching on the island exotic. En-suite bathrooms have glass showers, modern fittings & glittering Zanzibari lamps, whilst each room has a private veranda complete with an orange *baraza* bench for early morning coffee or a shady afternoon snooze. On the rising coral rock behind, the larger cliffside rooms are popular with long-stay guests & families, who enjoy the extra space, high ceilings & sizeable deck overlooking the flower-filled gardens & swaying beachfront palms. In addition, 27 rooms have ocean outlooks with the Island Cottage sea views overlooking one of the swimming pools too, & the suites boasting baths as well as showers. Regardless of category though, the rooms are all thoughtfully designed with contemporary conveniences, Zanzibari influences & a truly tropical palette.

Outside, there are 2 lovely pools & 350m of super-soft sandy beach, where seaside activities, some with a Swahili influence, are in abundance: escorted sunrise jogging, local *ngalawa* sailing lessons, water aerobics, scavenger hunts for children, Swahili lessons

& sundown beach cricket to name but a few. With Fairmont's pedigree in large Caribbean & Hawaiian resorts, all of these are properly organised & well staffed; daily activity schedules are even placed in guest rooms at turn-down for bedtime planning of the next day's events. Divers are well catered for with an on-site dive centre & the region's only decompression chamber, whilst spa enthusiasts can visit Burahi for spice-infused scrubs & professional massage. After a hard day's sunbathing or active exertion, the glistening mosaic of Nahodha Cocktail Bar beckons. Enjoy super sundowners here before dinner at the à-la-carte restaurant (southern African game meats & local seafood) or something more casual at Tradewinds buffet & pizza parlour, where a cracking beachfront deck & stylish ivory parasols make this an equally lovely location. Fairmont Zanzibar, under the enthusiastic leadership of GM Thomas Norberg, has brought a touch of sophistication & style to the island's resort scene, which combined with its family-friendly rates make it an exceptionally good choice in this bracket. *Island Cottage US$306–540343–600 sgl/dbl; superior cliff room US$342–576/379–636 sgl/dbl; suite US$366–600/403–690 sgl/dbl; min stay 7 nights at Xmas; 4 nights at Easter; all rates HB & inc activities*

WHAT TO SEE AND DO Apart from lazing on the beach, or going for long walks along it, there are the usual diving and snorkelling possibilities which can be arranged through One Ocean:

One Ocean – Matemwe Beach Village The One Ocean Dive Centre at Matemwe Beach Village is one of the nicest centres around, & the whale-tail reception desk is bound to bring a smile to even the most nervous of waterbabies. It's a 5* PADI dive school offering a range of certification courses, Mnemba dive trips & snorkelling excursions. The staff are happy to accept referral certificates from guests who've completed dive-course classroom work before arriving in Zanzibar, or to teach from scratch in the pool & at sea. Using a purpose-built dhow, MV *Henya*, dive trips depart from Muyuni Beach (a 30min *dala-dala* ride) at 08.00 each morning. Only twice a month do high tides allow for departures from the resort's own beach. 12 divers are accompanied by 2 guides, & it is not necessary to stay at the resort to use the dive centre. *Dive packages US$134/355/513 for 2/6/10 dives; Open Water US$631; Dive Master US$947; snorkelling trips US$47*

MNEMBA ISLAND

Lying approximately 2.5km off the northeast coast of Zanzibar, Mnemba Island is a picture-perfect coral atoll. Previously uninhabited, it is now privately leased by &Beyond (formerly Conservation Corporation Africa, or CC Africa) and has become one of Africa's ultimate beach retreats.

At its centre is a tropical forest, home to nothing more dangerous than cute suni antelope, a population of cooing red-eyed doves, butterflies, an ancient well and some Ader's duiker (Africa's most endangered forest duiker with fewer than 300 remaining in the wild). The island's circular perimeter is 1.5km of soft, brilliant white coral sand: perfect for romantic evening strolls, migrating wading birds, scuttling ghost crabs and nesting turtles. In the turquoise sea around, some of east Africa's best coral reefs hide in a relatively unspoilt aquatic wonderland. There are virtually no insects on the island, making it a very low-risk malarial area.

Officially titled Mnemba Island Marine Conservation Area (MIMCA), the island is part of a coral formation supporting a staggering variety of marine life. Overfishing and general disregard for the fragility of the environment began to threaten the marine environment, but sustained lobbying by &Beyond and the government resulted in the area being declared a Marine Conservation Area in November 2002 and its future being secured.

A US$3 levy is charged on all watersports, notably snorkelling and diving, within the protected zone. This revenue is paid into a community conservation fund, the primary purpose of which is to show local fishermen and their communities the very real economic value in protecting rather than exploiting these exceptional reefs. In addition to the money generated from MIMCA park levies, the lodge and Africa Foundation (&Beyond's social development partner) have invested US$180,000 to community projects on Zanzibar close to Mnemba: building eight classrooms, a doctor's house, a windmill and ablution blocks, supporting the orphanage and assisting villagers with access to clean water.

GETTING THERE AND AWAY Guests for Mnemba Island are chauffeur-driven from the airport or Stone Town to Muyuni Beach, north of Matemwe, from where it's a 15–20-minute ski-boat ride to the island. It is not possible to visit the island unless you have a booking.

WHERE TO STAY

Mnemba Island Lodge (10 *bandas*) +27 11 8094300; e inboundsales@andbeyond.com; www.andbeyond.com; Jun–Mar. The *crème de la crème* of &Beyond's impressive portfolio, Mnemba Island Lodge is the height of rustic exclusivity: a place where the term 'barefoot luxury' is reality. Overlooking the beach from the forest's edge, its secluded, split-level *bandas* are constructed entirely of local timber & hand-woven palm fronds, beautifully finished in a herringbone pattern. These are large, airy & open-plan, & the favoured retreat of both the rich & the famous, together with a few harmless hermit crabs which periodically scuttle across the immaculate *mkeke*-mat floors. Furnished simply but tastefully, each *banda* has a huge bed & solid wooden furniture, softened with natural, ivory-coloured fabrics & plenty of forest-view windows. As a place to escape the trappings of the modern world, in-room facilities stretch only to electricity, a simple fan to enhance the sea breeze, a padlocked wooden box for valuables, a couple of cotton bathrobes & a torch to ease evening ventures to the beach or bar. A palm-covered corridor leads to a stylish timber-and-glass en-suite bathroom. The purpose of showers may be to moderate the island's freshwater consumption, but behind the stylishly curved glass-bead curtain the shower rose remains the size of a dinner plate, the pressure is high, & the desire to linger lathered becomes overwhelming.

Built-in *barazas* on the thatched beach-facing veranda are perfect for afternoon siestas & lazy b/fasts, whilst in front, private beach *salas* (shaded, open-sided beach huts) feature traditional Zanzibari loungers for leisurely hours on the beachfront. The uncluttered, indulgent luxury, peaceful isolation & stunning situation make this a blissfully romantic haven: a place to curl up & count blessings. Mnemba's cuisine is predictably excellent, with plenty of fresh seafood, fruit & vegetables, & the flexibility to cater for individual needs exceedingly well. Guests can choose what, when & where to eat at any meal, from leisurely b/fasts in bed to candlelit, lobster dinners on the beach. An engaging 'butler' is assigned to each room, & from arrival will subtly go about tailoring each guest's stay, predicting requirements, to ensure everyone is content & carefree.

An American couple, Eli & Robin, run a professional dive centre on the island &, for qualified PADI divers, up to 2 dives per day are included in the rates. PADI courses are naturally available & one-on-one tuition may be expensive but the quality instruction & warm, shallow waters in front of the lodge make for excellent training. Once divers are qualified, a number of superb dive sites are within 15mins of the lodge, from tranquil coral gardens dancing with colourful reef fish & gentle turtles to steep drop-offs: the haunt of huge, deep-water game fish. Over a delicious hot chocolate on the boat back to camp, sightings of dolphin pods are not uncommon, & even humpbacks can be spotted in season. For the non-diver, there's snorkelling, dbl kayaks, windsurfing, power kiting, sailing, & fly or deep-sea fishing. Hot stone, aromatherapy, deep tissue massage & reiki are all available, too.

In line with its environmentally aware beginnings, the lodge strives to be eco-friendly. Water is desalinated, the beaches are rid of any manmade debris, organic waste is recycled & the rest is shipped off the island. Solar power is used wherever possible, including to heat the water, & guests are encouraged to do their bit through the eco guide left in each room. The lodge is also involved in marine- & turtle-conservation projects: watch out for the beach signs heralding new hatchlings. Although children are accepted at the lodge, it's probably not the best place for them. A maximum of 2 children are allowed in the camp at any time, they aren't allowed in the bar after 18.00, & every child over 5 must have his/her own room, making it an extremely costly holiday for a 6 year old, who probably doesn't want their own room anyway! Mnemba is unquestionably expensive, but its flexibility & service levels are second to none, & its idyllic location & proximity to outstanding marine experiences are very hard to match. Payment in local or major foreign currencies; Visa & MasterCard accepted. *US$1,250 inc FB & activities (exc PADI courses).* ♛

PWANI MCHANGANI

'Pwani' means beach in Swahili and this is certainly the focus of village life. This area is particularly noted for its seaweed collection and the dramatic low tides see women and children take to the shallow water to harvest their marine quarry, which is then usually dried on the beach. The men, like most on Zanzibar's coast, concentrate on fishing, and the village boasts one of the island's main seafood markets.

Mass-market tourism is less developed than on the coastline around Kiwengwa (9km south), and Pwani Mchangani retains a more traditional air as a result. It's a sizeable village in the seaside coconut belt, where children and poultry run riot, colourful washing is strung between thatched houses, and conservative attitudes dominate.

GETTING THERE AND AWAY To go from Zanzibar Town to Pwani Mchangani on public transport, take *dala-dala* number 117 towards Kiwengwa or the 118 towards Matemwe, or local bus Routes 15 or 16. Those with a hire car approaching from the north coast or west coast should take the right turn about 1km north of Kinyasini at Kikobweni, straight into the village. The simple coastal track north and south has now been joined by a smart new tar road, making travel along the coast infinitely faster and more comfortable.

🏠 **WHERE TO STAY**

🏠 **Mchanga Beach Lodge** (8 rooms) 📱 0773 952399/569821; 📧 tradewithzanzibar@zantel.com; www.mchangabeachlodge.com. Mchanga Beach Lodge opened in mid 2008 on the site of Uzioni Beach Bungalows, a rather rundown old lodge. Totally redeveloped by a wonderfully dedicated German–American couple, Thomas & Gloria Zimmermann, Mchanga is set to be a tremendous success. Simple, stylish construction, high-quality interiors & a happy, efficient staff are testament to their concerted efforts & good natures. The location itself is stunning: on a deep, powder-sand beach between Pwani Mchangani & Matemwe, where the sparkling sea is crushed coral & urchin free, making for perfect swimming & childhood paddling. There are 8 steeply thatched, whitewashed rooms: 6 sea-view lodge rooms & 2 garden suites, the latter ideal for families with a dbl *baraza* seating area which neatly converts into an additional sleeping spot for adults or older children. These rooms also have additional outdoor terracing for private relaxation. All of the rooms, regardless of category, have an intricately carved Zanzibari 4-poster bed, covered in brilliant white soft cotton, fine wool blankets & lovely turquoise & indigo batik throws, as well as a semicircular cushion-covered *baraza* alcove & a small sand-covered terrace for morning tea. There is an en-suite toilet & shower beyond the inlaid glass arch & neat storage for clothes & belongings. Touches from light switches within mosquito nets to beach baskets brimming with towels show great attention to detail. Equally, a thoughtful mix of hand-crafted wooden shutters, electric ceiling fans, AC & traditional high-beamed ceilings all ensure the rooms remain cool & protected from the searing sun, whatever the time of day.

Outside, through the soft sand & flower-filled gardens, towards the ocean-front palm grove, there is a stunning swimming pool & open-sided *makuti* bar & restaurant. Food is a seasonal mix of Swahili specials with traditional cooking methods & tropical produce making for tasty fresh food. There are beach *bandas* & cheerfully covered coir loungers for sunbathing & snoozing, boules & board games for a bit of fun & diving can be arranged with nearby PADI centres. For many though, it will be enough to simply enjoy Mchanga's vibe & vista, for this is currently one of Zanzibar's best beach havens: delightfully simple, small & personal. $$$$–$$$$$

🏠 **Tufikinwe Guesthouse** No contact details. Right in the centre of Pwani Mchangani village, this is an exceedingly basic local guesthouse. It is owned & run by the local women's co-operative but falls into increasing disrepair every year & is regularly rented to local men. If you are keen to stay here, ask around the village for the group's representative & enquire about the current situation, but don't expect information easy to obtain. $

🏠 **Waikiki Resort & Restaurant** (8 rooms) m 0773 286881/0777 877329; e waikikigold@hotmail.it; www.waikikizanzibar.com. Opened in Apr 2007, this 8-room hotel is refreshingly small & personal! Run by an eclectic international team, Angelo, a Native American musician, & Flavio & Sarah, an Italian–English couple who are both former entertainment staff at SeaClub, the neighbouring Italian all-inclusive resort. Life here focuses on the buzzing central restaurant, where under the leafy trees & whitewashed arches, tables of chattering friends & families quaff wine & enjoy homemade Italian fare at leisurely lunches & candlelit dinners. Gentle country music plays, the multi-lingual staff whizz around checking everyone's OK & a happy, vibrant atmosphere prevails. There's a campfire for late-night lingering, a nightly band &, with a little encouragement, Angelo will even play a few tunes. In addition, once a month Flavio DJs on the beach to a large party crowd.

Accommodation is in lovely bijou rooms with Zanzibari beds (helpful for secreting luggage underneath), colourful *kanga* linen, & clean en-suite bathrooms. There is some activity equipment, including a pedalo & mountain bikes (US$8/half day), plus a small local massage zone. It is likely that Waikiki will expand in the coming year but it will probably stay pretty small, making it a good bet for somewhere fun & off-beat on this stretch of coast. *Rooms* $$$; *bungalows* $$$$

🏠 **Neptune Pwani Beach Resort & Spa** (154 rooms) 📞 024 2233449/1955; e neptunezanzibar@zanzinet.com; www.neptunehotels.com. With 4 established resorts in Mombasa, this is the Neptune Group's first departure from the Kenyan coast & already large ministerial conferences & Thomas Cook groups are regulars at the hotel. Opened in Apr 2007, Neptune Pwani is a sizeable hotel extending from the beach up along the coral cliff behind. Striking dbl-storey, mocha accommodation blocks with steep *makuti* thatch, external timber staircases are laid out in imposing rows within the lush lawns. There is little that is soft, gentle or environmentally in-keeping, rather the scale, colour & harsh geometry is quite arresting. Inside things improve: spacious bedrooms are decorated with

locally crafted furniture, crisp linen, scarlet cushions, marble & glass en-suite bathrooms & wide balconies. Satellite TV, a hairdryer, tea/coffee-making facilities, mini fridge & electronic safe are all standard.

There is an extensive network of swimming pools (the largest on the island) with a child-friendly paddling section, popular swim-up *shesha* bar & disco music throughout the day. A selection of non-motorised watersports is also available, though divers will have to make arrangements with nearby PADI centres. For relaxation, the autonomous Coconut Spa above reception is suitably sweet smelling & is staffed by 6 delightful, if homesick, Balinese ladies. Offering flower-filled baths, scrubs & professional massage & beauty therapies, this is a good place for guests & non-residents alike to break from the sun for a few hours. $$$$$

🏠 **Ocean Paradise Resort** (106 rooms) m 0777 439990–3; e info@oceanparadisezanzibar.com; www.oceanparadisezanzibar.com. Ocean Paradise is a big hit with UK honeymooners enticed to the resort by offer of a free bottle of bubbly, fruit basket & private beach dinner for newlyweds. The imposing reception is a huge semicircular area, with a high, vaulted *makuti* roof. From here, sweeping stairs curve round what is intended to be an impressive waterfall, into manicured gardens, the beautiful central pool area, & beach-level accommodation. There are 98 superior rooms & 8 junior suites, all in neat, pale yellow rondavels. The circular bedrooms are stylishly understated in neutral tones & all have mains electricity, UK-style 3-pin sockets, AC, satellite TV, a hairdryer, electronic safe & a minibar. There is even a nice laminated card of useful Swahili phrases. Each room has an en-suite bathroom with a toilet & black shower, & an outside seated terrace area accessed through French doors. The junior suite rooms are exactly the same in design as the superior, but with 2 separate rooms they are twice the size. Half of these have a king-size bed & sitting room, whilst the others have 1 king-size & a twin room, which can be used by families. Transfers around the complex by golf cart can be arranged for disabled guests.

If splashing in the tiled, seaside pool or reclining on the beach isn't stimulating enough, there's a daily schedule of hosted activities announced on a chalkboard by the pool, typically including coconut weaving, Swahili lessons & beach soccer. Alternatively, there's a One Ocean Dive Centre for scuba & snorkelling, canoeing, windsurfing, snorkelling, fishing, volleyball, table tennis, billiards &

a small fitness centre. Beach bikes can be rented (US$7.50) for outside exploration. For families, there's a children's pool & 'animators' to engage children in Butlin's-style activities; cots are available & babysitting services are provided at a standard US$5/hr. Every night musicians perform from the bridge over the pool, treating guests to traditional Swahili *ngoma* drumming or Maasai acrobatics by the Taarabu Culture group. Evening meals at the Jahazi Restaurant overlook the performers & are usually themed, with any week incorporating 'surf n' turf', Far Eastern & BBQ dinners. Non-residents are also welcome to eat here. When the cabaret entertainment is over, the Jungle Disco (Wed, Fri, Sat) & terraced Bahari Bar can get lively. *Superior* $$$$$; *junior suite* 🛥

🏠 **Dream of Zanzibar** (157 rooms) e info.dreamofzanzibar@planhotel.com. Between Mapenzi & Ocean Paradise, Swiss hotel group PlanHotel began constructing their third Zanzibari resort, Dream of Zanzibar, in early 2008. (The others being La Gemma in Kendwa, & neighbouring Mapenzi Beach Club, below.) Scheduled to open in Dec 2008, this all-inclusive property is an architectural interpretation of the grand old Arab-African palaces: whitewashed, flat-roofed buildings with shaded arcades, open terraces & palm-filled vistas. Inside, bedrooms are filled with teak furniture, natural fabrics & a raft of mod-cons: AC, satellite TV, DVD-CD player, minibar & telephones. For sea views opt for the Deluxe & Junior Suites, or one of the 3 Royal Suites for a private plunge pool. There are 3 restaurants in the grounds, the international, buffet-style Cape to Venice Brasserie, the Andiamo Pizza Co & the seafood à-la-carte Blue Vanilla, as well as a couple of cocktail & juice bars. With 2 pools, a well-equipped gym, a professional spa, games room & dive centre, activities galore are available although this is not a resort for coercive group activities. $$$$$

🏠 **Mapenzi Beach Club** (87 rooms) m 0741 325985; e gen@mapenziplanhotel.com/ planhotel@planhotel.ch; www.planhotel.com. Owned & managed by Swiss–Italian hoteliers, PlanHotel, Mapenzi is a large, comfortable resort, on a nice stretch of coast, with many facilities & activities. In spite of its size, this is a relatively serene place, catering mainly for large groups of Italian package holidaymakers. Increasingly though, British & South African families are staying here, enticed by the positive attitude towards children: easy availability of cots, highchairs & babysitting. The quiet reception area is shaded by an impressive *makuti* thatch

supported by a tremendous network of poles, & plays ethereal music to arriving guests. From here, wide corridor fingers lead to a pool table & mezzanine-level day-bed, a curio shop & stylish boutique selling pretty beaded sandals, swimwear & cotton clothing, a 'business centre' offering internet & fax services, the *makuti* massage zone & the swimming pool. Raised above the beach, the long swimming pool, with children's area & jacuzzi, is surrounded with loungers & sun umbrellas, & affords views across the entire complex. The other outside public areas are dotted with palms & largely covered in white beach sand, utilised for outdoor barbecues & impromptu football matches.

The cottages are divided into 3 categories; fundamentally these differ mainly in location. Naturally those closest to the sea fetch the premium rate. All the rooms offer 24hr mains electricity, sockets (for plugs with 3 round pins), AC, fans, mosquito nets, an internal telephone, hairdryer, electronic safe, fridge, en-suite bathroom with European toilet, bidet & shower, & a veranda. In true European-resort style, 'animators' encourage active participation in games & activities, but at least there is a Swahili influence evident in their offerings & their manner is not as intolerably coercive as at the all-inclusive Italian resorts. Tingatinga painting, village excursions & *ngoma* drumming lessons are just as likely to feature alongside archery & boules here. There's a daily fitness programme of aqua aerobics & jogging, & catamarans, bicycles, windsurfers & snorkelling equipment can be hired. Football & volleyball matches benefit from properly marked pitches, &, for waterbabes, diving is organised through One Ocean at Ocean Paradise. By night, entertainment ranges from live bands to acrobatic shows & quizzes.

Mapenzi is all inclusive & meal times & cuisine are set, though a seafood à-la-carte menu is also available. Meals are served in the spacious restaurant or new pizzeria, though Wed night sees the weekly Swahili BBQ by the pool. There are 3 bars, including 1 in the central area which opens at 22.00 for late-night revelling. Drinks are included in the room rates but long drinks are free only from 18.00 to midnight; it's a cash bar thereafter. *Garden room US$300–600 dbl; standard room US$320–620 dbl; seafront room US$340–660 dbl; all rates FB*

🏠 **Coral Reef Resort** (45 rooms) m 0777 415549; e coralreef@zanzinet.com; www.zanzibar-coralreef.com; ⊕ Jul–Apr. This was opened in 2000 by 3 Italians & virtually every guest here is a fellow compatriot. The sparse reception area is naturally raised above the beach area & decorated with simple murals showing acrobatic Maasai. It is enclosed on 3 sides, with the 4th open to reveal a fine view of the sea. From here a long central path steps down to the lovely swimming pool, complete with its own elegant palm island & sadly a roped monkey at the shower. Signs from the main path indicate the direction of various rooms, some of which are a fair stretch from the beach. The bungalow architecture is Arabic in style: brilliant white walls with arched windows & flat roofs. There are 32 standard rooms on the hillside, each either dbl or twin, plus 11 superior & seafront rooms on the beach. Every room has mains electricity, European-style 2-pin sockets, mosquito nets, & an en-suite bathroom with hot-water shower. The standard & some superior rooms have fans only, whilst 7 of the latter enjoy AC. There is an electronic safe, left-luggage facility & Wi-Fi access (US$24/week) available at reception.

This is really a resort for young couples, and while children are accepted, specific provisions & activities for them are limited. There are a number of group sporting competitions, especially volleyball, whilst a couple of canoes & snorkelling equipment are available for individual use. 'Soft animation' reduces the pressure to join in group activities. Diving can be arranged with One Ocean, at the nearby Ocean Paradise Resort, or snorkellers can hire equipment if they purchase a boat excursion. Buffets are served for every meal in the enclosed restaurant area beside the sea. Inside it is dark & smoky with the feel of a school dining hall, though outside is a very pleasant deck with large navy parasols & a lovely view along the beach through the extensive Tingatinga painting gallery. Once open-sided, this area is now behind a high wall, following a high-tide incident. It remains a pleasant spot for an evening cocktail, or as a place to relax while the high-tide waves lap below deck. $$$$–$$$$$

⌂ **Zamani Zanzibar Kempinski** (110 rooms) m 0777 444477; e sales.zanzibar@kempinski.com; www.kempinski.com. In Dec 2005, luxury hotel group Kempinski opened the stylish Zamani Zanzibar Kempinski. Set in 30 acres of immaculate landscaped gardens, the spacious guest rooms & suites are housed in contemporary coral-rock & whitewashed buildings, each with its own private terrace or balcony. Angular in design with Moorish influences evident in the carved timber balconies, patterned shutters & cool courtyards, the design is the most modern anywhere on the island; it's strikingly different from any other hotel or resort here. In addition to the standard rooms, there is a vast presidential villa & 6 smaller villas, each with a private pool. Rooms of all categories are decorated in snow white & warm natural tones, whilst the quality & number of in-room facilities reflect the resort's association with a serious European hotel group. Each offers satellite TV with movie channels, multi-lingual telephone voicemail, tea/coffee-making facilities, a minibar, an electronic safe, his & hers bathrobes, 24hr room service & even a shoe-shine facility. All the rooms have en-suite bathrooms with opaque glass doors, a contemporary free-standing bath &, in safari style, an outdoor shower in a pebbled Zen courtyard.

There are 2 restaurants: a Mediterranean buffet at Cloves Restaurant which spills out from the central glass building onto the garden patio, & a smart seafood grill, the Red Snapper, overlooking the sea. Drinks & snacks are on offer poolside & at the aptly named Zanzi Bar. For exercise & total relaxation, the Anantara Spa Zanzibar is one of the island's best well-being facilities. It is a calm, contemporary area with 6 private treatment rooms & professional Thai therapists, a large outdoor swimming pool with sundeck & pool bar, a 23m lap pool & fully equipped fitness centre. If being outside is preferable, there's a stunning swimming pool & a number of watersports are available, from surfboarding to sailing. There is no dive centre at the resort, but this is easily arranged with a neighbouring property. A stroll along the jetty offers terrific views, a cooling breeze & a touch of romance. However, the resort itself is on the edge of the coastal coral cliff so there's no real beach to speak of immediately in front of it. If it's lying on the beach you're after, then it's a golf buggy trip 1km south to the Zamani Beach Club – the resort's satellite beach bar on Kiwengwa Beach (neighbouring Shooting Star, see pages 242–3). Small conference groups are also welcomed at the resort & dedicated facilities are available: all fitted with the latest telecommunications & audio-visual equipment. ♛

WHAT TO SEE AND DO Any lodge or resort will fix you up with one or more of the ubiquitous Zanzibar Island tours (see *Chapter 5*, pages 125–7). For diving, contact the One Ocean Dive Centre at the Ocean Paradise Resort.

✔ **One Ocean – Ocean Paradise** \ 024 2238374;
m 0777 453892; e oneocean@zanlink.om;
www.zanzibaroneocean.com. The most recent of the
One Ocean dive centres, this is a professional, PADI-
accredited operation offering reliable equipment,
custom-built dive-boats, knowledgeable staff & the
usual array of certification courses. Most dive trips
are dbl dives (perhaps because of the resort's
distance from the better reefs), including a light
lunch in between, & it's possible for non-guests to
dive from here. *Dive packages US$174/489/750 for
2/6/10 dives; Open Water US$726; Dive Master
US$994; snorkelling trips US$70; underwater
camera hire US$32*

KIWENGWA

A small, traditional coastal village with a stunning beach, Kiwengwa is also the
heart of Zanzibar's package-holiday industry. A glut of exclusively Italian, large, all-
inclusive resorts cluster along the beach immediately around the village, with
several other large hotels spaced along the coast to the north. That said, with
continuous in-house entertainment and exhaustive facilities, the guests at all of
these resorts are rarely seen outside of their chosen hotel's perimeter walls, so the
area around is generally quite quiet. The contrast between the dusty Zanzibari
fishing villages and the lush, European hotel grounds is stark, and sadly the bigger
developments and their visitors have often displayed a depressing lack of
environmental and social consideration towards the local area and population.
However, there are some who have made real efforts over many years, notably
Bluebay and Shooting Star, and are good options on what is a truly beautiful beach.

GETTING THERE AND AWAY The easiest way to reach Kiwengwa from Zanzibar
Town is along the good tar road, via Mahonda and Kinyasini. The small coastal
road, both north and south, is narrow, sandy and badly maintained, so 4x4
vehicles are advisable if you choose to travel it. However, in 2006, an excellent
tar road was opened which runs north to Matemwe, parallel to the old road and
just slightly inland of it. You can come by taxi, rented car or motorbike, or
arrange a minibus through a tour company. By public transport from Zanzibar
Town, *dala-dalas* (number 117) run between 06.00 and 19.00, whilst the public
bus on Route 15 passes through the village five-times daily. The 'official' stop for
both is in the village; though for a small fee the driver may well drop off at
individual hotels. The major resorts and upmarket hotels all arrange transfers
from the airport and Stone Town.

 WHERE TO STAY Looking from north to south:

🏠 **Shooting Star** (16 rooms) m 0777 414166;
e star@zanzibar.org; www.zanzibar.org/star.
Standing on a coral cliff above the stunning
Kiwengwa Beach, Shooting Star is a firm favourite
with young, well-travelled Europeans. Built & run by
the charismatic Eliamani 'Elly' Mlang'a, a charming &
engaging Tanzanian, & his family, this small hotel is
a delightfully social place, despite the high number
of honeymooners who visit. Accommodation is
divided into 3 categories: garden rooms, sea-view
cottages & 2 new villa suites. The 3 garden rooms
border the lodge's central area & all have a
dbl/twin bed, mosquito net & en-suite bathroom.
They are small & simply furnished but light, bright
& perfectly adequate. The sea-view cottages are a
step up with lovely decorations & each offering AC,
fans, mosquito nets, en-suite bathrooms with a large
shower, & a private terrace. All have comfortable
Zanzibari beds, cool white walls, colourful Tingatinga
pictures & dyed *makuti* mats. In line with the
lodge's child-friendly attitude, 4 of these cottages
have been designed with families in mind & include
a dbl bedroom & separate twin-bedded upper room.
Until Oct 2007 these were the premier rooms at
Shooting Star, but then 2 new suites opened to
take the crown. Named after the island's trade
winds – the Kusi from the south & the Kaskazi
from the north – these separate whitewashed,
castellated villas offer luxurious accommodation &
some real privacy whilst still being very much part
of the lodge. Each suite is entered through a pair
of intricately carved Zanzibari doors flanked by

large potted palms. Inside, both temperature & style are cool: simple, high-quality finishes, antique furniture, AC & whirring ceiling fans. In the semicircular entrance hall, curved *baraza* benches are covered in a mass of white & purple cushions, Swahili-style interior-design books are piled on the coffee table, white walls are patterned with dappled light from the shutters & a dressed Zanzibari day-bed awaits tired travellers. With an adjoining shower, toilet, dressing room & kitchenette (complete with well-stocked fridge), this area is easily converted into an extra bedroom for families. Continuing up the curved staircase at the rear, the spacious master bedroom suite boasts a super-king-size Zanzibari 4-poster bed at its centre, twin *baraza* benches & a large lockable Zanzibari chest for valuables. Walls & linen are brilliant white with soft furnishing accents in indigo blue. Windows have shutters to keep out the midday sun, but when opened they afford views along the coast in both directions. There is a large en-suite shower room, separate toilet & a walk-in wardrobe in the hallway. Up a further flight of stairs, the roof terrace is the perfect place for privacy. Enjoy a sunrise coffee, stretch out on the cushioned *baraza* or indulge in a moonlit bubble bath for 2, all overlooking the island vegetation & ocean beyond. There is also a private garden on the ground floor with a small plunge pool surrounded by soft sand, coir loungers & a little bar. Tasty snacks & fruit are available & meals can be served here or at the main restaurant.

For all guests a stunning horseshoe infinity pool & sundeck in front of the main lodge area afford superb views over the ocean, barrier reef & beach below, as well as the opportunity for a cooling dip when the tide's out. Alongside, a small circular, powder-sand 'beach' area has been created, complete with coir-rope loungers & blue deckchairs. A simple shower is secreted under a nearby palm for rinsing off before heading to the bar for a refreshing pineapple juice. Dining is split among 3 adjoining areas: 2 beneath *makuti* thatch & I under date palms, but all surrounded by tropical vegetation & featuring tables laid with batik tablecloths & red hibiscus flowers in individual vases. Meals here are simple & filling, but it's the lively bar & relaxed lounge area that is the true heart of Shooting Star. Drawn to the neon fridges, the bar-flies gather nightly to laugh & chat about the day's adventures. Elly's invariably on hand to offer friendly advice & help with planning, whilst card & board games are available for those content with a bottle of wine &

a quiet seat in one of the cushioned, sweetheart booths. There is also a new Star Bar under suitably star-shaped *makuti* thatch on the beach. With the waves literally crashing underneath at high tide, this is a terrifically friendly evening hangout – especially before the famed lobster beach BBQ (an extra US$45pp).

Diving & snorkelling trips can be organised through the PADI dive centre at nearby resorts, whilst fishing trips with the locals on outboard boats will give a totally different take on life on the ocean wave. There's a central phone for guest use &, with satellite connection, fast internet access is also available. *Garden lodge US$215–245 dbl; sea-view cottage US$280–330 dbl; suite US$550–610 dbl; all rates FB; B&B and HB rates available; transfer from Zanzibar Town US$60 each way*

🏠 **Karibu VentaClub** (168 rooms) m 0777 417328; e direzione.karibu@zanzinet.com; www.ventaglio.com. One of several similar all-inclusive, all-Italian resorts on this coast, this is exclusively sold to Italians as a package holiday. All of its 168 rooms are classed as standard with little variation bar the number of beds they contain: dbls, twins, trpls & families all catered for. 2 of the sea-view rooms are completely wheelchair accessible but unfortunately there's no ramp network around the complex yet. Each room has mains electricity, a fan, AC, a reasonably sized safe, a telephone, mosquito nets, & an en-suite bathroom with hot-water shower. Local & satellite TV, internet & telephones are available centrally, along with an on-site doctor.

Group activities are encouraged here & once a week a guest football team is assembled, supporters are furnished with flags & whistles, & a match is played against another Italian resort, BravoClub. For those who want to get active without joining the team, there's canoeing, windsurfing, archery, aqua gym, volleyball, snorkelling & even yoga at sunset. Diving can be arranged through one of the neighbouring resorts. As one would expect at an Italian property, there's a very relaxed attitude towards children. Cots & highchairs are readily available & during school holidays there are separate kids' clubs. All-inclusive including charter flights & paid in advance. $$$$

🏠 **Sultan Sands Island Resort** (76 rooms) PO Box 3156, Kiwengwa, Zanzibar; m 0777 422137. On the site of a La Villa's quaint rondavel retreat, Sultan Sands is a new Moorish, hillside resort, sharing an activity centre & spa with its neighbouring, sister hotel, the Bluebay. Opened in spring 2008, the resort's 76 bijou rooms are in planted terraces above the beach with split-level interiors housing a dbl bed, sofa-bed lounge & tiled en-suite bathroom. All the rooms are single storey with very few having a sea view, but the gardens are well tended with snaking coral-stone paths to the sandy beach. In the main building, arches, courtyards, tinkling fountains & potted palms set the cool, calm tone in the reception. Beside this are the Palace Lounge & Sultan's Plate all-day restaurant, outside which the water from the pool laps gently beside the comfortable loungers. The lack of activities within the resort makes this a place to read books & soak up sunshine, not participate in volleyball tournaments, although energetic guests can venture next door to Bluebay where facilities abound.

$$$$$
⌂ **Bluebay Beach Resort** (112 rooms) ☏ 024 2240240–2; e mail@bluebayzanzibar.com; www.bluebayzanzibar.com. Set on a lush, gently sloping site, there are currently 88 rooms in Bluebay's white, thatched, 2-storey villas: 80 superior, 6 deluxe & 2 sultans – plus 2-dozen new rooms in Club 24, its superior hotel-within-hotel offering. All of the rooms in the original complex have 2 large, dark-wood 4-poster beds or 1 king-size, a dressing area, en-suite bathroom & private balcony or terrace; the garden & deluxe rooms also have a lounge area. Fans, AC, minibars, hairdryers, satellite TV, electronic safes, tea/coffee-making facilities & mosquito nets are also standard. En-suite bathrooms all have European toilets & hot-water showers, though the deluxe rooms also enjoy a sunken bath & a private outside shower. Interiors are a little tired but remain adequate, cool & spacious. Honeymooners are welcomed with arches of fresh flowers adorning their doors, & families are equally well catered for with interconnecting rooms, a children's pool, playground, the possibility of babysitting & an on-site nurse for any illness or accidents. Disabled visitors are also encouraged with 2 rooms kitted out to include a shower shelf & ramp.

There are oodles of activities from canoeing to catamaran sailing & waterskiing, a One Ocean centre on site for diving & snorkelling trips, a large freshwater swimming pool with jacuzzi, a floodlit tennis court & beach volleyball. A proper, professional spa offers Vichy treatments including a Vichy shower, massage tables with a sea view, a steam room, open-air whirlpool with loungers under shady palms, & an adjoining fitness centre. An 80-person conference room & business centre is also

available, even if all that you require is internet access. The Makuti Restaurant, Bahari Grill & Pool Bar cover everything from extensive dinners to coffees & cocktails, with the majority of guests staying here on a HB basis. For those wanting something more exclusive, Club 24 opened behind the original hotel complex in Jul 2007. Effectively functioning as an independent entity, with its own private pool & small à-la-carte restaurant, guests here enjoy fresher, larger rooms & a few more in-room amenities, but have to accept a longer walk to the beach & main resort facilities.

Bluebay is proud of being a 'Green Globe 21' organisation: companies satisfying a global benchmarking & certification programme for sustainable tourism. From its inception, it has recycled all room & laundry waste, purifying & using the water to keep its gardens green, incinerated all garden & kitchen rubbish, concealed its power generators in a soundproof structure, installed energy-efficient fittings in every room, & collected rainwater from its specially designed roofs to supplement the resort's supply. In addition, the gardens are planted only with indigenous species. *Garden room US$120–255pp; superior room US$140–290pp; Club 24 US$170–320pp; suite US$180–340pp; all rates FB; Christmas, New Year & Easter supplements US$45–50 adult/day*
⌂ **Zanzibar Veraclub** (59 rooms) �📱 0777 466233/414988/0741 320987; e veraclubznz@ zitec.org; www.veratour.it/villaggi/zanzibar/ zanzibar.html. 90% of Veraclub's all-inclusive guests come on charter flights from Italy. Whilst simply lying on the shaded loungers, beside the sea or the lovely pool, clearly holds great appeal for most, the energetic Italian & Zanzibari 'animators' are keen to encourage participation in a variety of games, competitions & shows. Countless activities are available & there are formal courses in everything from diving to windsurfing. If it all gets too much, escape the midday sun & archery tournament by heading for a massage at the beauty centre, Ibiscus, or down the new Pontile jetty. Accommodation is in traditionally built bungalows with *makuti* thatch roofs & the 59 en-suite rooms, some suitable for families, are clean & comfortable. Each has AC, a safe, & a private, polished-wood terrace with cane furniture. No rack rates available at the resort; pre-booked packages only. $$$
⌂ **Sea Club Kiwengwa** (200 rooms) 📱 0777 414351; e sckiwengwa.recep@renthotel.org. Like its neighbouring resorts, Spanish & Italian package holidaymakers throng Sea Club's lush gardens &

sandy stretch of beach. With 200 rooms divided amongst 25 villas, it's a sizeable place. Each of its en-suite rooms is decorated in pastel colours with light rattan furniture. Suitable for up to 3 adults or a family of 4, they have AC, a minibar, a safety deposit box (for which there's an extra change), telephone & a private balcony or veranda. In line with most all-inclusive resorts, there are buffets for every meal, with the welcome addition of the African Hakuna Matata Restaurant & an à-la-carte seafood establishment, Matunda. The ever-present resident entertainers run an extensive programme of daytime events & evening shows, with a dedicated children's club for those aged 4 to 12. The hotel also boasts floodlit tennis courts & a basketball court, along with the usual assortment of beach & watersports at the Blue Diving centre. $$$

⌂ **BravoClub** (107 rooms) e bckiwengwa.recep@ altamarea.it; www.bravoclub.it. Another big resort full of Mediterranean tourists. Here, even the resort signs & piped music are in Italian. With the mixture of whitewashed bungalows & dbl-storey blocks, the grounds feel quite built-up, in spite of the profusion of flowers & tropical greenery. Some rooms come with a sea view, able to accommodate 2 to 3 people each. All rooms are en suite with AC, a fridge, safe, telephone & individual terrace. The usual array of excursions & activities is available, & one of the resort's real assets is its lengthy pier, which allows easy, stepped access to swimming in the sea, even when the tide's out. By night there's a disco here, too. If you can read Italian & have good control over a computer mouse, a cartoon starfish will guide you around an interactive map of the village on the website, whilst 360° video images of your location spin in the corner. No rack rates available at the resort; pre-booked packages only. $$$

⌂ **Reef View** (12 rooms) PO Box 3215, Zanzibar; m 0777 413294. Located on a dirt road south of Kiwengwa, Reef View is owned & run by a local man, Haroub Rashid, & his English wife, Helen. Neither was around on our last visit, being replaced instead by the canine cast of *Lady & the Tramp*. The accommodation here is extremely basic, & has been falling into increasing disrepair over the last 4 years. On visiting in early 2008, we were told that renovations were underway, though sadly no change or workmen were visible. The lodge is literally right on the beach, with waves lapping only metres from some rooms, & the views along the beach & out to the headland are lovely. There's a bar & restaurant, a large library & book exchange. The 2 en-suite brick & *makuti*-thatch rooms feature a mattress on the floor under a mosquito net, a rough rack for clothes, a free-standing fan, low-voltage lights & gauze-covered windows. There are also 10 *bandas* with shared facilities. Built entirely of *makuti*, these dbl/twin rooms are dark & dingy, with only a bicycle padlock to secure the door. The shared toilets are dirty & act as a very successful nursery for mosquitoes; & the shower water is cold. This place is not recommended for children or anyone who requires basic creature comforts. For self-drivers, there are parking bays on the opposite side of the road from the lodge. Although these are neatly marked by white painted pebbles, they are outside the property gate & so relatively insecure. $$

⌂ **Land Mark Resort** Just south of Reef View, a new property was under construction in mid 2008. Little of the structures were visible on our visit, but the friendly villagers working on site were doing an excellent job of initial landscaping & had created a fine grass lawn & palm avenue approach from the new tar road. The sign read only 'Land Mark Resort', though this is likely a trading name rather than a property name, & we'd love to hear from visitors who stay at the new development when it eventually opens.

WHAT TO SEE AND DO The major resorts and hotels can fix the normal range of tourist trips and watersports, as can tour operators in Zanzibar Town. For diving, there's a One Ocean centre at the Bluebay Beach Resort.

↙ **One Ocean Bluebay** ☎ 024 2238374; m 0784 750161; e oneocean@zanlink.com; www.zanzibaroneocean.com. A well-equipped & managed One Ocean operation, this PADI 5* dive centre offers the usual array of courses & dive opportunities, including pool-based training & refresher courses. The 3 custom-built dive boats – *Manta, Greta & Winnie* – are shared with One Ocean at Ocean Paradise, & concentrate their attentions on sites around Mnemba Island. The office is open 08.00–18.00 Mon–Sat, & the helpful staff are always willing to answer questions & give underwater advice. *Dive packages US$174/489/750 for 2/6/10 dives; Open Water US$726; Dive Master US$994; snorkelling trips US$70; underwater camera hire US$32*

Northwest of the Ras Uroa headland, a series of idyllic, palm-fringed, sandy coves make up Pongwe. Bar a tiny fishing village and three small, individual accommodation options, there is very little else here: and that's its magic! Blissful beach relaxation, away from everything, is what's on offer.

GETTING THERE AND AWAY Pongwe Beach and Nature Safari Lodge can arrange minibus transfers from Stone Town, or these can be organised by local tour companies. By public transport, bus Route 6 and *dala-dala* number 209 (only 3 per day) from Stone Town travel to Pongwe, with *dala-dala* 214 to Uroa often continuing to Pongwe village: ask the individual drivers.

Self-drivers will be pleased to find that from the end of 2008, the bumpy mix of sand and coral rag which once made up the coastal road is now paralleled with a smooth, fast tar road up to Kiwengwa and beyond. A 4x4 can still negotiate the original route, but patience and a good suspension are necessary for any degree of comfort.

WHERE TO STAY

Nature Safari Lodge (10 rooms) m 0777 310604/414704; e mosses.znz@yahoo.com. This is a very rough & ready place, better suited to the self-sufficient. Surrounded by dense vegetation, on an attractive beach, are 9 mud huts, with crude, painted-brick exteriors. The marginally better rooms are those with tin roofs at the back, whilst those under *makuti* thatch are more basic. All rooms have only basic furnishings, some with thin mattresses on traditional coir-rope beds, others with better wooden ones. All are painted candy pink & have an en-suite, tiled bathroom. Security is limited to a brick that can be rested against the door. The rooms are accessed along neat, edged paths & there's a 'nature trail' from the site, along which trees have been labelled with their traditional uses. A social restaurant & bar area offer simple food & drink & it is possible to self-cater. The absent English owners allegedly plan to expand in 2009 & build 3 large 2-storey accommodation blocks, which will completely change the take-it-as-it-comes vibe & cost if the construction ever does go ahead. $$

Pongwe Beach Hotel (16 rooms) m 0784 336181/0773 169096; e info@pongwe.com; www.pongwe.com. Standing within its own quiet cove, under a shady oasis of coconut palms, this is a simple little lodge in a lovely location. In spite of its uninspiring name, it is a well-managed, good-value haven for relaxing on a beautiful beach. There are 16 airy, whitewashed bungalows, simply furnished with traditional Zanzibari beds, mosquito nets, & an en-suite bathroom with flush toilet & shower. The water here is filtered but slightly brackish, though always available hot, thanks to an immersion heater.

Dbl & trpl rooms are available, with 3 rooms capable of taking 4 beds at a squeeze. The generator electricity is time limited (meaning in-room fans will stop at 04.00) but there is emergency low-voltage bedroom lighting.

There are over 5,000 books in the library, & plenty of inviting hammocks & loungers on which to lie back & read them. For those who've done enough chilling & sunbathing, there's a kite for seaside entertainment & an array of other individual & group beach games. The barrier reef is only 15mins offshore & the resort has its own dhow for sailing, snorkelling trips (US$15, no time limit), & game or line fishing; a new Sea Fox boat is on order for faster trips to Mnemba. In 2006, a lovely new infinity pool opened on the coral rock to the north of the beach, beside the border with Nature Safari Lodge. Large enough to swim lengths with gently sloping sides, an imported beach area & decked surround, this area is a popular spot when the tide's out, if slightly exposed. Looking out to the kayakers paddling on the reef & along the sand to the Honeymoon Suite, it's a pleasant location & yellow-clad pool attendants are on hand to supply drinks & fresh fruit at 16.00.

Pongwe is especially proud of its food with tasty lunches from US$4 & varied set menus at dinner, including succulent spiced meats following the recent arrival of a professional tandoori oven. With a little notice, children are warmly welcomed, with cots & highchairs readily available & great children's discounts. $$$$

Santa Maria Coral Reef (7 rooms) m 0777 432655; e info@santamaria-zanzibar.com;

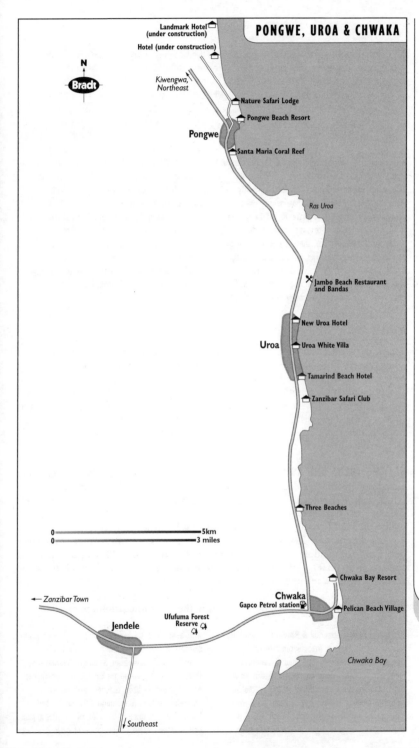

PONGWE, UROA & CHWAKA

N

Bradt

Landmark Hotel
(under construction)

Hotel (under construction)

Kiwengwa,
Northeast

Nature Safari Lodge

Pongwe Beach Resort

Pongwe

Santa Maria Coral Reef

Ras Uroa

Jambo Beach Restaurant
and Bandas

New Uroa Hotel

Uroa   Uroa White Villa

Tamarind Beach Hotel

Zanzibar Safari Club

0   5km
0   3 miles

Three Beaches

Chwaka Bay Resort

← *Zanzibar Town*

Chwaka
Gapco Petrol station

Pelican Beach Village

Jendele

Ufufuma Forest
Reserve

Chwaka Bay

↓ *Southeast*

www.santamaria-zanzibar.com. Opened in 2005 by a young local named Suleiman, this is a delightful hideaway. With no other developments currently along the beach here, & very low-density population, this really is a place to get away from it all & relax. Set in a coconut grove, in the middle of a sweeping bay, there are 3 very simple *bandas* & 3 bungalows. The *bandas* are both sgl & dbl storey, with high thatch & suspended ceilings. Rooms are basic with solid wooden beds, fresh linen, coconut-rope & timber shelves, colourful mats on the floor & block-printed buxom mermaids adorning the walls. All rooms are en suite with flush toilets & showers in neatly tiled bathrooms, & there is generator electricity from 18.00 to midnight. Lunch & dinner options are usually freshly cooked fish or chicken with rice & cost around US$6. Dhow snorkelling trips can be arranged to the reef beyond the bay, or there's a simple thatched lounge/library area for enjoying a cooling drink & a good book. $$

UROA

The small, neat village of Uroa is on the coast about halfway between Kiwengwa and Chwaka. Neat bundles of wood are piled 'jenga-style' by the roadside, quirky pedestrian crossings have been painted on the road, and village life appears active and ordered. It's a traditional, slow-paced place, centred on fishing and seaweed collection. There have been a few low-key places to stay here for many years, but 2008 saw the start of larger developments at either end of the village. We must only hope that they are sensitive to their surroundings and not the start of a flood of all-inclusive properties in the area.

GETTING THERE AND AWAY Approaching from the south on the 9km of blissfully tarred road from Chwaka, you'll pass cultivated, plantation-style fields of casuarina pines; from Kiwengwa, 11.5km to the north, there is now a fast tar road too, with the old coast track the preserve of 4x4 drivers alone. In early 2008, work began to widen the road here into a serious two-lane tar highway.

Dala-dala number 214 plies the route from Stone Town to Uroa six times a day, between 06.00 and 18.00, whilst the public bus on Route 13 adds another five services from 08.00 to 16.00. If you prefer, private minibuses and taxis can also be arranged by most reliable Zanzibar Town tour operators.

 WHERE TO STAY Going from north to south, the accommodation options here are:

Jambo Beach Restaurant & Bandas (7 rooms) No contact details. From a sizeable concrete roadside sign, advertising 'seafood, local food & continental food', a track leads down to the sea & this locally run restaurant. Once specialising in freshly cooked food, the building is now very spartan but 7 rooms have sprung up beside the quiet beach. There is 1 whitewashed bungalow right on the water's edge, with a dbl & 2 sgl beds, boasting psychedelic neon blankets, a fan, mosquito nets, & a small en-suite bathroom with flush toilet & shower. Alternatively, there are 6, tiny, round *makuti bandas* which each have 2 coir-rope beds, complete with lumpy mattresses, pillows & mosquito nets but no bed linen. In a nod towards the idea of security, a mini bolt has been fitted to the inside of each, & a large one to the outside; sadly, however, the door doesn't actually close. Outside each, perched on a minuscule curved deck, are 2 chairs. $

🏠 **New Uroa Hotel** Behind a 6ft, shell-encrusted wall, a series of large, 2-storey *makuti*-thatched accommodation blocks stretching back from the beach make up this new property. Unfinished & un-named at the time of going to press, this has all the air of a mid-range, all-inclusive resort for the European market.

🏠 **Uroa White Villa** (8 rooms) m 0741 326874/488520; e info@uroawhitevilla.com; www.uroawhitevilla.net; ⏰ May–Mar. In the centre of the low-density village, with clear signposting to help with directions, this place sits on a fairly compact, walled plot, where bright white buildings stand on 3 sides of a quadrangle, & a row of beachfront fir trees makes up the fourth. Its rooms are divided between the main villa & 2 thatched bungalows. The main villa, with its stark white blockwork walls, shiny metal window frames, tin roof & highly polished, red-painted floor, has all the character of a government administration building. The 4 rooms inside are clean & cool but, much like the exterior, entirely soulless. 2 of these rooms have en-suite bathrooms, whilst the others share facilities. There are 4 en-suite bungalow rooms. Again these are spartan in appearance with little more than a bed, small coconut-wood table, & a 'fitted' wardrobe constructed from rough timber planks, but they are clean, quiet & functional. Outside there's a terrace area with chairs. There's a central lounge in the villa, with a selection of Italian & German books, & a separate open-sided restaurant. The food here is all freshly cooked & the seafood-dominated menu is all subject to availability. Snacks will usually cost US$1–5, with à-la-carte dinners ranging up to US$12. Although the central square is rather barren, a pleasant sandy beach is literally on the doorstep. Snorkelling equipment can be hired (US$15) & fishing trips with the locals are always possible. The villagers here are very relaxed around visitors so wandering into the community is also a possibility. The capable manager, Juma, will happily help organise anything; he's friendly & helpful & speaks English & Italian with ease. $$–$$$

🏠 **Tamarind Beach Hotel** (16 rooms) m 0777 413709/411191; e tamarind@zanzinet.com; www.tamarind.nu. Owned by 3 Norwegians & 3 Zanzibari locals, Tamarind was run by a German management company from its opening in 1992 until 2000. It is now managed by the very helpful

Said Ali, & one of the Scandinavian owners, Trond. The planting is fairly minimal, which can make Tamarind feel very dry in the heat of the day, but it stands along a particularly stunning stretch of coconut-lined beach & the proximity to the turquoise sea does a lot to overcome this. There are 8 semi-detached cottages built from coral-stone blocks & cement. Each is finished with neat moulded balustrades & white arches around the porch terrace. Traditional Zanzibari doors lead into the rooms & there are external stairs leading up to a 'terrace' formed by the roof of the porch: there is only a simple, open wooden barrier along the edge making this area unsuitable for children. All 16 rooms have a dbl bed, although extra beds are easily obtained for twin or trpl occupancy. Each has mains electricity, a fan & mosquito net, plus an en-suite 'wet-room' style bathroom with flush toilet & hot-water shower. A safe deposit box is kept at reception for valuables, along with a basic first-aid kit & telephone. There's a small local TV room & a curio shop selling the usual *kangas* & carvings. The restaurant (lunch & dinner US$12pp) offers indoor dining at individual tables & fresh produce, with an emphasis on seafood, & the beach bar produces fabulous freshly squeezed juices. Children are generally welcome at the hotel, a cot is available & babysitting can be arranged with the staff, but, beyond playing in the sea & sand, activities are limited. Payment in local or major international currencies; Visa & MasterCard accepted with no surcharge. $$$

🏠 **Zanzibar Safari Club** (50 rooms) m 0777 844481; e reservations@zanzibarsafariclub.com; www.zanzibarsafariclub.com. The mock cannons resting on painted, red-brick plinths scream of the idiosyncrasies hidden behind the Safari Club's imposing gates. South of Uroa village, this is a themed, slightly kitsch, medley of Arabian & Indian styles, marketing primarily to large groups from Spain, Italy, Scandinavia & South Africa. Run by efficient, if brusque, staff, the resort has all the trappings of a large hotel (business centre, modern in-room amenities, tennis court) but the feel of a hospitality training school. In the heart of the resort, the large central pool is lovely, & surrounded by tidy rows of sun loungers, & there's an idyllic, peaceful, palm-fringed beach for those who wish to dip in the sea. The 48 standard rooms & 2 suites are a riot of colours & designs, both inside & out.

We understand that a stream of different designers came & went during the development of this resort, which explains everything. The decoration would imply that each one simply carried on from where his predecessor left off, in a style of his choosing, & regardless of what had been done before. The Disney-like bright-orange cottages with forest-green tiled roofs sit in orderly rows around the organised complex. At the entrance to each, a Zanzibari bench, covered in multi-coloured cushions, sits on a small terrace. Through the arched blue door, the décor is best described as distressed Van Gogh. Every piece of wooden furniture has been painted in bold colours & limed to reveal each brush stroke, & create an aged, beach-hut quality. Yet the rooms have all the essential hotel mod-cons: AC, a fridge, satellite TV, a hairdryer & an electronic safe. The Zanzibari beds are covered in mosquito nets trimmed with bright, patterned fabrics, & all the rooms are en suite with a flush toilet & hot shower, each with its own in-room boiler.

Reasonably sized but mediocre buffets are served in the circular, poolside Mwangaza Restaurant, or alternatively the quiet Ocean View Restaurant serves Swahili cuisine beside the beach. At the end of the jetty, which is lit like a runway by night, the Zinc Discotheque is a great place to boogie above the waves to classic disco & pop hits. Impressive, state-of-the-art sound & light systems, a good Kenyan DJ, & a free pool table for non-dancers make this an excellent, if noisy, after-dinner hangout. Even when no-one turns up, the music plays on until 02.00

every night. This hotel is very secure with a multi-gate security entry: good locks on room doors, safe deposit boxes at reception, fire alarms & extinguishers, & security guards on patrol; so much so that it can seem impossible to gain access without a written reservation! No children under 12 years are allowed. No credit cards accepted. $$$$$

⌂ **Uroa Beach Village Hotel** But for an overgrown perimeter wall, nothing remains of this once sizeable hotel. The land here has almost entirely reverted to bush. Doubtless a new property will spring up soon as Zanzibar's coastal land is being swallowed up consistently by ever-expansive development.

⌂ **Three Beaches** m 0774 281081; e info.threebeaches@yahoo.com. Between Uroa & Chwaka, the truly massive *makuti* reception of Three Beaches received its first Italian all-inclusive tour groups in Jan 2008. Under the impressive roof, there are coconut-wood bar stools at check-in, whitewashed *baraza* benches covered in Congolese cushions & piped Arabian tunes; guests are advised to enjoy their time here, for beyond the quality diminishes. The beach is not Zanzibar's finest, with seaweed strewn across its less than powdery sand & the accommodation blocks are cheaply constructed with small interiors. Each of the 40 rooms is en suite with hot water, fans & catering to dbl or trpl occupancy. There is a central sundeck & pool in a small coconut grove & a buffet restaurant. $$$

CHWAKA

Halfway down the east coast, directly due east of Zanzibar Town, Chwaka is a large fishing village overlooking a wide bay fringed with mangrove swamps. In the early 19th century, Chwaka was a major slave port, exporting human cargo across the Indian Ocean to Arabia. In more recent times, its sea breezes and lack of mosquitoes made it a popular holiday destination for British colonial administrators and affluent Zanzibari dignitaries: their grand, crumbling villas remain along the shoreline north of the village. Today, apart from some coastal researchers, there is not much in the way of facilities or activity, besides the large, lively seafood market: for the best atmosphere, arrive in the mornings when the fishing boats dock, laden with the day's catch.

Chwaka Bay itself supports the largest swathe of mangrove forest on Zanzibar and forms a significant part of the Jozani-Chwaka Bay National Park, Zanzibar's only national park. The government is currently working with international charities, like CARE International, and conservation bodies, to develop and manage the forest as a conservation area and income-generating ecotourism project. Some tours to explore the mangroves are possible, and do make an interesting diversion. There is little accommodation in Chwaka and few visitors, but it's possible to take a boat across Chwaka Bay to head further down the east coast, which may attract the adventurous.

GETTING THERE AND AWAY Chwaka can be reached by public bus (Routes 6 and 13), *dala-dala* (numbers 206 and 214), or by hired car or bike. Tourist minibuses do not usually come here, although you could privately hire one through a tour company. However you choose to travel, if you approach from the west, the smooth, tarmac road through the island's lush interior is a pleasure.

If you are heading to or from the southeast coast, and don't want to go back to Zanzibar Town in between, you can hitch a ride on an octopus-fishing boat (high tide only) across Chwaka Bay to Michamvi on the peninsula north of Bwejuu. Local people regularly travel this way, but only the occasional intrepid tourist is seen here. Boats from Michamvi come across to Chwaka's fish market most mornings, returning around noon. There are no set schedules, so you will need to ask around on the beach. A ride should cost little more than a few dollars.

WHERE TO STAY

⌂ **Chwaka Bay Resort** (30 rooms) ☐ 0774 040400; www.phoneandgo.it. North of Chwaka village on the coast road, past some near-derelict grand colonial villas, Chwaka Bay Resort has been turned into yet another all-inclusive Italian resort. Its former Swedish owners handed over their property to Euro internet operator 'Phone & Go' in 2006 & the complex is now filled with groups of 30-somethings from Rome & Milan. Little has changed in the accommodation & the 10 original whitewashed rondavels, known as bungalows, remain light, airy & spacious thanks to their 3 large windows. The simple, dark-wood furniture all matches & beds can be made up as dbls or twins. The ring mosquito nets can be tied up out of the way; there are fans, open wardrobes & sparkling en-suite bathrooms with hot water. Arguably, these rooms have more character than their newer siblings. In a bid to expand & upgrade the resort, 5 villas (each with 4 independent rooms), were built on the far side of the resort in 2002. Referred to as 'deluxe', these large en-suite rooms have AC, lockable drawers as safes, mosquito nets & constant hot water controlled by an in-room boiler. Each room has a terracotta tiled terrace or balcony with 2 coconut-wood directors' chairs, a coffee table & a view through the palm grove to the beach. The ground-floor rooms in these buildings are a mix of dbls, twins & trpls, while upstairs all the rooms have a dbl bed. All the rooms, in both categories, are raised up away from the beach.

The beach here isn't as good as many on the east coast, but boat trips to the other side of the

peninsula can be arranged, & the kidney-shaped swimming pool is pleasant enough for a cooling dip; there's also a sunken pool bar for cocktails & juices. Coir-rope loungers & striped metal deckchairs sit on the surrounding triangular tiles, some shaded by *makuti* umbrellas, & all enjoying views of the band of palms along the coast. Like a giant board game, the resort's concrete paths are seemingly colour-coded: green leads between the bungalows whilst azure blue takes you around the pool & gardens. The former décor disaster in the restaurant & lounge has thankfully been rectified & now buffet meals & drinks are enjoyed under *makuti* thatch with a more muted colour scheme. US$120 dbl, FB

⌂ **Pelican Beach Village** (16 rooms) ☐ 0777 489495/413880; e malik68@hotmail.com/ pelicanbeachvillage@hotmail.com. Opened in Sep 2005 on the outskirts of Chwaka village, Pelican Beach is a neat group of 7 large, whitewashed bungalows. Individually named after exotic spices, each houses an assortment of sgl & dbl rooms. Tiled throughout & with plenty of natural light, the interiors are bright, fresh & clean, if somewhat soulless, & with a curious number of sinks fitted in some rooms. There are neat pathways covered in pergolas of bougainvillea &, on the water's edge, a thatched bar & à-la-carte restaurant, complete with garish pink-&-yellow chequerboard flooring. There is no beach here but the lounge & games room offer pleasant views of the bobbing dugouts in Chwaka harbour & for a small fee one of the octopus fishermen will usually ferry guests to the Michamvi Peninsula beaches. $$$

UFUFUMA FOREST HABITAT

The Ufufuma Forest conservation project was set up by the people of nearby Jendele village. It aims to protect the forest habitat and to educate the villagers in sustainable use. The 102 local volunteers, led by the dedicated and charismatic Mr

Mustafa Makame, hope to make it a place for both locals and foreigners to visit, and to preserve the traditional worship of *shetani*, or spirits, which is performed here (see box, *The Shetani of Zanzibar*, pages 38–9). The forest area is at present only 1km², but the villagers are leaving the surrounding 4km² area uncultivated to allow the forest habitat to expand in size. Tiny paths, marked with periodic, mid-blue arrows, wind through thick vegetation, while underfoot a tangle of roots clings to coral rag. A visit here is not a great wildlife experience, nor is it meant to be, although you might be fortunate enough to see skittish red colobus (as we did; apparently early morning is best), island birdlife, snakes and lizards. Honey is also collected from the forest, so look out for the canopy-height hives. A few villagers act as guides, but they are not wildlife specialists and don't know a lot of the bird

MANGROVE FOREST DEPLETION

Mangroves are salt-tolerant, resilient, evergreen trees, anchored by stilt-like roots in the inter-tidal zone (eg: *Rhizophora mucronata*) or simply growing in sandy muddy bottoms (eg: *Avicennia marina*), or even perched on fossil coral pockets with minimum soil. They are found in sheltered bays and river estuaries, where the waves have only low energy levels, and are vital components of the tropical marine environment. They ensure shoreline stability by protecting soft sediment from erosion, providing nutrients for sea organisms, and offering sanctuary to migratory birds, juvenile fish, shellfish and crustaceans.

Mangroves are nevertheless one of the most threatened habitats in the world. Environmental stress from changing tides and pollution takes its toll, but increasingly it's human interference that is the primary cause of irreparable damage. On Zanzibar, this is certainly the case: many people rely on the forests for fuel (firewood and charcoal), lime burning, boat repair and dugout manufacture, as well as material for house construction. Mangrove wood is dense and, because of its tannin content, it is termite-resistant, making it preferable for house construction. Income is also generated from trading in cut wood, poles and charcoal. The absence of alternative income-generating activities means heavy dependence on mangroves.

Ominously, as the rural population continues to grow, so does the demand for this fragile resource. It is therefore critical to fully understand and address the needs of the villagers in order to have any chance of developing successful conservation initiatives.

Chwaka Bay is fringed by Unguja's largest area of mangrove forest, approximately 3,000ha and accounting for 5% of the island's total forest cover. Here, fairly dense stands of diverse mangrove species, zoned by their tolerance to the conditions of the area (eg: volume of water and salt levels), are drained by a number of lovely creeks.

Over the last 60 years, assorted management plans have been drawn up with the communities bordering the forests, in a bid to control overexploitation in the area. From issuing permits to control harvesting, imposing mangrove taxes and limiting creek access, each has successively failed to halt rapid deforestation. Ever-changing forestry policy, lack of serious patrolling, a decline in the authority of village elders to command community support, insufficient alternative income sources for villagers and minimal resources are all cited as reasons for the failure.

Conservation and development organisations continue to attempt to halt deforestation in the area, improve villager understanding of the forests' importance and lobby local and national government for support; but, without doubt, these valuable natural resources will be irretrievably ruined unless human activities are carefully controlled.

As in most African societies, many of the trees and plants found in Ufufuma Forest play an important role in the daily lives of the local population. Be it for medicinal or practical use, religious or cultural significance, the flora is fascinatingly versatile when viewed through the eyes of a resident guide. Naturally, though, we don't recommend that you attempt self-diagnosis and treatment on your journey through the vegetation. The trees below are a sample of what's to be seen and learnt. They are listed by their Swahili name, as the guides will not know them by anything else.

MCHOFU Across the island, the branches of this tree are commonly used as an all-purpose timber for firewood and furniture. Here, only its fruits are used as a cure for coughs, colds and flu.

MDAA (*Euclea natalensis*) Ufufuma's answer to Colgate: this is the local toothpaste. The villagers here chew on a piece of the tree's root to ensure a bright, white set of teeth and healthy gums. In 1991, research into this custom by the South African Medical Research Council at the University of Stellenbosch showed that oral bacterial growth was indeed suppressed by this chewing, giving the practice some scientific validity. Sadly, it also concluded that the daily exercise is too limited to have a truly beneficial effect: this is probably backed up by the smiles around you.

MKOMWE (*Caesalpinia bonducella*) Mkomwe's Latin name derives from the Arab word *bonduc*, meaning 'hazelnut'. It's easy to see why when presented with the neat spherical seed kernels (Swahili: *komwe*) from within its fruit. These are the traditional pieces used in games of bao, but the dual-purpose seeds of this tree can also be boiled with water to produce a drink for sufferers of stomach ache.

MKUYU The roots of this wild fig are boiled with water to form a drink. Given to pregnant women, the concoction is believed to have an abortive quality.

MLALANGAO Hunting for birds is a patient but ingenious process. Local men must first study the avian movements in the forest, watching flight paths and routines. To catch the birds, they cut the trunk of the *mlalangao* tree with a *panga* (long blade machete), collect the sap (Swahili: *utomvu*), and boil it to form a type of latex. Back in the forest, the chewing-gum-textured latex is smeared onto the branches where birds have been observed resting. Then the men wait … for when the birds do land, they simply stick to the latex from where they are easily collected and taken home to make soup.

MUWAVIKALI This sweet-smelling tree is boiled with water and the resulting liquid is drunk to combat symptoms of malaria.

MKAAGA Seek out the young leaves on this little bush. They'll provide you with the freshest tea!

Northeastern Zanzibar   UFUFUMA FOREST HABITAT

9

names. But they are trying to learn, and, meanwhile, they are very enthusiastic about Ufufuma's cultural importance – which is the primary reason for a visit here.

There are many underground caves hidden in the dense forest undergrowth: three are *shetani* caves being used by the local traditional healer (aka 'witch-doctor'), which tourists may also visit. It is a source of great joy and comfort to the local Zanzibari people who come to these caves to speak with the spirits. When local people are sick or troubled they come to these sites with the local traditional healer and perform rituals and recitations to cure themselves. The cave entrances are adorned with tattered strips of red and white fabric and surrounded by piles of sweet offerings, often rotting, from sugarcane to Coca-Cola. Inside, the caves are dank and spooky, with the smell of smoke from recent fires and resident colonies of bats. It's a fascinating insight into a rarely seen aspect of Zanzibari culture.

Mr Mustafa and his small team believe wholeheartedly that in protecting the forest there is potential for the local communities to benefit financially from conservation tourism; they are simply unsure how to achieve their goal. Gaining support from all of the villagers is difficult – many want the timber for firewood and rocks for building, and perceive little monetary gain from conservation. But Mr Mustafa is determined, and, whilst searching for a solution, he travels to Ufufuma from Zanzibar Town every Sunday on his moped, keen to inspire and educate the villagers about protecting the forest. He even chairs the local NGO.

Six villages in the vicinity already benefit from the income of the forest. All of the money goes directly to the community leaders, who assess their village's primary needs, be it medicine for cows, wells, or school materials, and channel the money as appropriate. If more people visit the forest, accepting that it's not a slick tourism enterprise, the village coffers will slowly increase, and in turn the communities will begin to see the benefits of preserving rather than plundering their surroundings. We wish the Ufufuma Forest conservation project every success.

ARRANGING YOUR VISIT To visit Ufufuma Forest, it is best to make contact in advance, to ensure that an English-speaking guide is available at the time of your visit (*Mr Mustafa Makame Ali;* m *+255 (0)747 491069;* e *himauje@yahoo.com*). The price of a visit is variable as a single tariff system has yet to be adopted. However, for a guided forest walk lasting a few hours, a visit to the caves, and usually a gift of fresh fruit or coconut refreshment, expect to pay US$5 per person per guide, and then volunteer to make a larger donation to the community fund. If you want to see a full *shetani* ceremony, consisting of about seven hours of singing, dancing and assorted rituals, this costs US$50 (for one or two people), and will have to be booked in advance and take place at a time convenient to the local 'doctor'. As the forest floor can be damp and rugged, be sure to take sturdy shoes, and, in the hot season, plenty of water to drink.

GETTING THERE AND AWAY To reach Ufufuma from Zanzibar Town, take the road west towards Chwaka: the forest is on the left, about 5km before Chwaka. There is currently a small, slightly rusted sign but no specific parking place, and only concealed paths lead into the forest. If you have contacted the Ufufuma volunteers in advance, then a welcoming party will likely be waiting for you. However, if your visit isn't scheduled, stop at Jendele village and ask in the market area for an official forest guide.

To reach the forest on public transport, talk to the *dala-dala* drivers heading towards Chwaka (numbers 206 or 214), and ask to be dropped in Jendele village; be aware this is a sprawling village with little tourism connection so it may not be an easy task.

DUNGA RUINS

Equidistant from Chwaka and Zanzibar Town, in the lush centre of the island, lie Dunga Ruins. Close to the modern village of Dunga, these are the remains of the palace built for King Mohammed, the Mwinyi Mkuu (great chief) of Zanzibar. Constructed between 1846 and 1856, the palace may have been built on the site of an earlier house. Prior to this, the residence of the Mwinyi Mkuu had been at Kizimkazi or Unguja Ukuu (see pages 287 and 300 respectively).

Local legend tells that when Dunga Palace was built, slaves were buried alive in the foundations, while others were killed and their blood mixed with the mortar. It was believed that this would bring strength and good fortune to the house. There may be some truth in this story as, in the 1920s, a nearby well was found to be half full of human bones. Today, in the centre of an overgrown garden, only the main walls of the palace remain, but it is still an imposing ruin and retains something of its original grandeur.

A few old passages, pillars and staircases can also be seen. The windows are empty and their decorative frames are now in the House of Wonders in Zanzibar Town, along with the Mwinyi Mkuu's sacred drums and horns. The latter were part of the royal regalia and both were kept at Dunga during King Mohammed's rule. The drums, carved from mango wood and inscribed with Arabic, were said to beat spontaneously to warn the king of impending trouble. The horns were kept in a secret hiding place, known only to the Mwinyi Mkuu. When he was near death, their location would be revealed to the heir apparent. Mohammed died in 1865 and was succeeded by his son Ahmed, but he died of smallpox in 1873, leaving no male heir. His two sisters had married into prominent families of Arab landowners, but the ruling dynasty came to an end.

A Swahili royal line is believed to have existed on Zanzibar prior to the first Shirazi immigrants arriving from Persia in the 10th century AD. Leading figures among the Shirazis are thought to have married into the family of the then Swahili ruler, as the Mwinyi Mkuu later claimed to be descended from a Shirazi prince. In the following centuries, while the island was controlled by the Portuguese, and later by the Arabs and British, a Mwinyi Mkuu continued to be regarded as the traditional leader by the people of Zanzibar.

GETTING THERE AND AWAY About 14km from Stone Town on the road to the east coast, or 30 minutes' drive inland from Chwaka, the ruins sit in the centre of the island on the southern side of the road. It is also possible to reach Dunga from the south, along the dirt track from Tunguu, on the main road to the island's southeast; a 4x4 is necessary for this route. By *dala-dala* from Zanzibar Town, it's possible to reach the ruins on the Chwaka services, numbers 206 and 214, or by public bus, Routes 4 and 6.

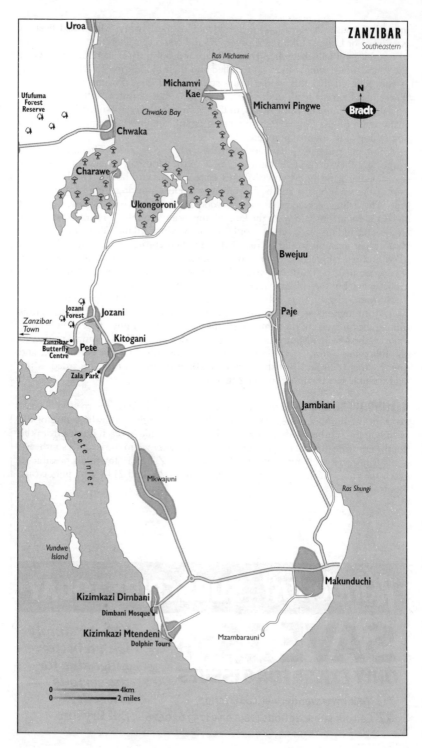

10

Southeastern Zanzibar

From the finger of the Michamvi Peninsula to the coastal curve at Makunduchi, the southeast of Zanzibar offers, in many ways, a continuation of the powder-white sandy beaches and traditional fishing villages found from Matemwe to Chwaka Bay. Certainly the environment here, with its large tidal range and fringe reef parallel to the beach, is almost exactly the same.

A decade or so ago, the area around the villages of Paje, Bwejuu and Jambiani used to be the busiest part of the east coast, especially for backpackers, as there was a good choice of cheap places to stay. However, things have changed in recent years. A scattering of mid-range and upmarket places have appeared, whilst the bulk of budget travellers have opted for livelier environs in northern Zanzibar, around the burgeoning Nungwi and Kendwa areas. (These are now much easier to access than they used to be, thanks to better tar roads.)

The end result is that southeast Zanzibar now offers some of the island's quieter beach spots with a varied choice of accommodation. The palm-fringed beaches here invariably seem wilder than their counterparts on the northeast coast, and offer fewer *makuti*-shaded cocktail bars than those of Nungwi and Kendwa. With the exception of a couple of larger all-inclusive properties, the southeast of the island is generally an area for more low-key, low-impact beach retreats.

MICHAMVI PENINSULA

Along the length of the Michamvi Peninsula's 10km east coast, the sand is the fine, powder-white stuff that 'paradise' advertising is made of, and the sea is a suitably sparkling cobalt blue. Few local people live here, concentrating instead in Bwejuu to the south or the village of Michamvi Kae, beside Chwaka Bay. Almost all of the accommodation in this area is currently high quality, and each place is individual in its style and customers. However, the number of hotels has almost doubled since 2005, and more are being built. For the immediate future, come for the pristine, palm-fringed beaches, good diving opportunities and a sense of space and hope that development stalls.

GETTING THERE AND AWAY All of the accommodation on this stretch of coast will arrange transfers, although most international guests will set this up in advance with their tour operator. For those with a hired car, north of Bwejuu there is only one road so getting lost is difficult, even if the coastal track becomes increasingly bumpy as you travel north. There is little in the way of public transport on the peninsula, but *dala-dala* number 324 from Zanzibar Town will sometimes continue from Bwejuu towards Michamvi village. If your luggage is not prohibitive, it's probably easier to cycle or embark on the long beach walk from Bwejuu.

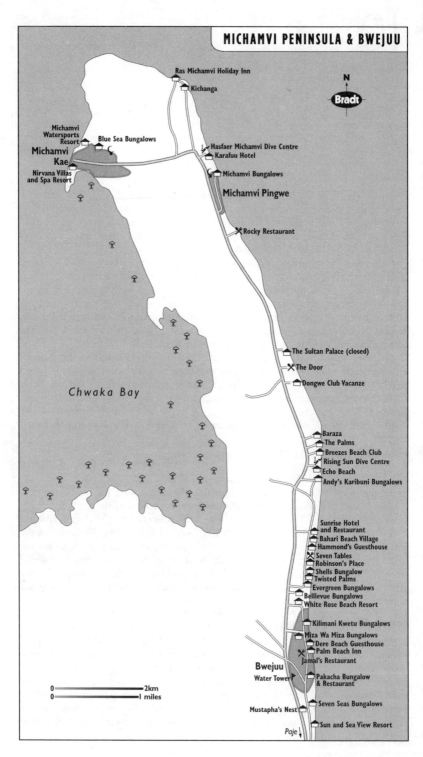

MICHAMVI PENINSULA & BWEJUU

N

Bradt

Ras Michamvi Holiday Inn

Kichanga

Michamvi
Watersports
Resort
Blue Sea Bungalows
**Michamvi
Kae**
Nirvana Villas
and Spa Resort

Hasfaer Michamvi Dive Centre
Karafuu Hotel

Michamvi Bungalows

Michamvi Pingwe

Rocky Restaurant

Chwaka Bay

The Sultan Palace (closed)
The Door
Dongwe Club Vacanze

Baraza
The Palms
Breezes Beach Club
Rising Sun Dive Centre
Echo Beach
Andy's Karibuni Bungalows

Sunrise Hotel
and Restaurant
Bahari Beach Village
Hammond's Guesthouse
Seven Tables
Robinson's Place
Shells Bungalow
Twisted Palms
Evergreen Bungalows
Belllevue Bungalows
White Rose Beach Resort

Kilimani Kwetu Bungalows
Miza Wa Miza Bungalows
Dere Beach Guesthouse
Palm Beach Inn
Jamal's Restaurant

Bwejuu
Water Tower
Pakacha Bungalow
& Restaurant

Mustapha's Nest

Seven Seas Bungalows

Sun and Sea View Resort

Paje

0 ———— 2km
0 ———— 1 miles

WHERE TO STAY This peninsula is the location for some of the island's most luxurious hotels. These are described in this section from north to south.

⌂ Michamvi Water Sports Resort (20 rooms) **m** 0777 878136/0784 758633; **e** michamvi@ yahoo.com; www.michamvi.com. The only east coast resort facing west across water, Michamvi Water Sports Resort opened in early 2007 overlooking the mirror-like Chwaka Bay. On the northern end of Michamvi Kae village, it caters mainly to young, energetic holidaymakers seeking aquatic adventure, with virtually every conceivable watersport available (for a charge) on site, from parasailing to windsurfing, & divers being collected by the Kichanga-based PADI centre.

Half of the rooms are allocated to an Italian tour operator so, like many of Zanzibar's larger resorts, there's a strong Mediterranean vibe & a number of larger groups, though bookings are still welcomed from individuals. The 20 rooms are in 6 large, 2-storey villas set out in an arc around the mosaic pool. Entering from the back, the rooms are light & spacious with thoughtful decorations made from driftwood, fishing baskets & old dhows. The en-suite bathrooms have a separate shower & concrete bath, & every room has either a private balcony or ground-floor terrace complete with hammock chair. Sunset mangrove safaris (US$20), massage (US$25/hr) & even henna tattoos (US$10/large) are on offer for those seeking more sedentary pastimes. At the time of researching in early 2008, a fairly sizeable development of circular buildings was under construction immediately next door; this will impact on the beach dynamic if ever completed. $$$$–$$$$$

⌂ Blue Sea Bungalows (3 bungalows) **m** 0777 464398. Neighbouring Michamvi Water Sports Resort to the north, Blue Sea Bungalows is a locally run establishment in the shady coconut grove above Chwaka Bay. There are just 3 bungalows here with basic facilities & no sea views. $$–$$$

⌂ Nirvana Villas & Spa Resort ✆ +27 (82) 4531044; **e** patburnell@mweb.co.za; www.patburnell.co.za. Just south of Michamvi Water Sports Resort, a large South African 'fractional ownership' (read 'timeshare') resort is potentially on the cards for Michamvi Kae. In mid 2008, developers had cleared & levelled the land with construction allegedly about to commence. If this does actually happen, Nirvana Resort is scheduled to open in Nov 2009 with a mixture of flash 2- & 4-bedroom villas & an array of activities & facilities, apparently including 2 helicopters for 'flips to other islands & Stone Town'.

⌂ Ras Michamvi Holiday Inn (15 rooms) ✆ 024 2231081; **e** info@rasmichamvi.com; www.rasmichamvi.com. Opened in Jul 2007 by Mr Suleiman of Jambo Guesthouse in Stone Town (see page 144), this impressive little resort sits high up on the coral cliffs at the very tip of the peninsula. It's in a very quiet corner of the island, so unless you have your own transport or enjoy extremely long walks, it's really quite remote; this is also its charm for the escapist. Bordered by peach & pink hibiscus bushes, the paths around the complex are all on slightly raised boardwalks with *makuti* thatch & neatly planted macramé hanging baskets. These neat walkways take guests to surprisingly nice rooms with tiled floors, quality Zanzibari beds & large, blue en-suite bathrooms. There are some rooms classed as 'disabled-friendly' with ramp entrances & walk-in showers, though the beds remain fairly high to be practical to those who are truly wheelchair-bound. There is an impressive semicircular restaurant offering fabulous reef panoramas & glimpses into the open kitchen. Outside this, steep steps lead down the cliff to a small private cove, where the sand is at its deepest & best in Jun/Jul. $$$

⌂ Kichanga (23 rooms) **m** 0773 175124/193775; **e** info@athomehotels.com; www.athomehotels.com. Opened in Dec 2005, on the northernmost tip of the Michamvi Peninsula, Kichanga is an attractive clifftop lodge above a lovely sandy cove. Its 23 cottages are of stone-and-thatch or rustic timber construction & in staggered rows to give a mix of beach-facing & garden outlooks. Interiors are a little sparse, especially in the family rooms, & slightly tired, but they do all benefit from large wooden terraces for enjoying the cool afternoon breeze or absorbing sea view. Mosquito nets, fans, safes & en-suite bathrooms are standard throughout. In the main building, there's an internet point, telephone facilities, local tailor (US$15/top), a lounge bar & an Italian-influenced buffet restaurant (tomato & mozzarella chapatti; pasta stations, etc).

Watersports are well catered for with the Israeli-run Hasfaer Michamvi Dive Centre on site, organised snorkelling trips, canoe rental & boat trips; even beach towels are provided. The cove geography means that very few non-residents come even close to the beach, & children are pretty safe from wandering too far. The sand here migrates, & is at its best from Aug to Dec; the beach gets progressively rockier as the *Kaskazi* wind blows.

There is a swimming pool popular with young families, a massage *banda* for local treatments (US$25/hr) & a pool bar for midday drinks and snacks. $$$–$$$$$

Karafuu Hotel & Beach Resort (89 rooms)
m 0777 413647/8; e karafuuhotel@zanzinet.com; www.karafuuhotel.com. Karafuu is the friendly & stylish place one would normally expect from an Italian-owned resort. Beautifully carved chaises longues sit on polished granite floors in reception, antique clocks adorn the walls, cosmopolitan young couples sip margaritas around the swim-up pool bar, & all around an air of cool confidence & sophistication pervades. Its 89 en-suite rooms are all terrific: smart & newly painted. They're divided into 3 categories, based solely on proximity to the beach, with only the junior suite having a sea view. The rooms all have big beds with neat wrought-iron seats at the end of each, a day-bed, fan, AC, minibar, telephone & spacious en-suite bathroom. Outside each, a wide terrace with tasteful wooden furniture looks out on to gardens filled with beautiful white lilies & coconut palms: a perfect place to catch the evening breeze. Children are warmly welcomed & well catered for. There's a children's playground, sectioned-off baby area within the main swimming pool, & the general manager's own child's nanny is available for reliable babysitting. For older children & the young at heart, there's a large, brightly coloured diving & watersports base beside the pool: the Kaskazi Sports Centre (see *What to do and see*, page 264). $$$$–

Michamvi Bungalows No contact details. At the northern end of Michamvi Pingwe village, overlooking the *mkadi* palms, beach & emerald waters below, these 2 russet rock bungalows are pretty basic with dbl beds, a cold-water en-suite shower & small private terrace. The manager, Mr Ilyas, is very accommodating & the small octagonal restaurant, decorated with shell mobiles & psychedelic flowers, serves fresh fish to order. There were a reasonable number of villagers touting for trade on the beach during our last visit, most likely heading to the larger neighbouring resort, Karafuu, but otherwise this is really a simple place to get away from it all. $$

The Sultan Palace High on a coral cliff, at the northern end of a pristine beach, the Sultan Palace was a sedate, elegant lodge, with beautiful rooms, a sociable bar & a welcome feeling of space. Sadly, it closed in 2006 & is currently sitting empty. We await news of its new owners & eventual reopening, perhaps with the welcome addition of a swimming pool.

Dongwe Club Vacanze (76 rooms) ✆ 024 2240251/2; e book@dongweclub.co.tz; www.dongweclub.co.tz. If the name Club Vacanze doesn't give away this resort's origins, entering the vast *makuti* structure of the rectangular reception area will. Noticeboards in Italian display the 'Dongwe Club Programma', listing numerous timed activities throughout the day. At the time of researching, an exuberant Italian could be heard over the tannoy cheering on a kayak-racing competition in the nautilus-shaped pool. This is an all-action, family-friendly, unquestionably Mediterranean, holiday spot. Mountain biking & beach volleyball are available on the beach, whilst diving, snorkelling & countless other watersports are arranged for the seafaring.

A DVD 'cinema' offers an escape from the sun. Aside from the emphasis on activities, this is a smart complex. Luxurious red & white fabrics cover the traditional Zanzibari beds standing on the cool tiled floor of the reception; welcome drinks are enjoyed on groups of green-cushioned, wooden sofas looking out across the resort's gardens; walking around the resort it is impossible not to notice the beautifully tended walkways & carefully planted kitchen garden borders. There are 76 rooms, of which 4 are suites. The spacious standards have good-quality, solid-wood furniture with huge wardrobes & cheerful turquoise soft furnishings. Each has a twin/dbl bed with mosquito nets, AC, a minibar, safe, telephone, hairdryer &, naturally in a resort of this size, 24hr electricity & hot water. Close by, but perpendicular to, the beach, the suites are accessed along neat paths lined with bougainvillea being trained into low colourful hedges. Surrounded by established hibiscus bushes & with inviting rocking chairs on their terraces, these are tastefully decorated bungalows. The cream & orange interior includes a large bedroom with a huge bed & satellite TV, a separate lounge & a bathroom. The only (debatable) negative is the red light chosen to light the jacuzzi room. The main all-inclusive restaurant offers international food with an Italian twist & usually hosts a weekly Swahili theme night, whilst the addition of the Pontile Jetty in 2006 allows for over-water dining. Soft drinks & beer are included in the rates. $$$$$–

Baraza (30 rooms) e info@ baraza-zanzibar.com; www.baraza-zanzibar.com. Opened in Dec 2008, Baraza is the youngest sibling of Palms & Breezes. Offering an all-inclusive option at a similar high level to The Palms, Baraza promises to be a more child-friendly luxury hotel. With strong Omani influences in its architecture, ornate gardens, & plunge pools in every room, its aim is clearly at affluent families who are not interested in the island's activity-focused mega-resorts. Villas are divided into categories based on their proximity to the sea & size, yet with all being spacious & well kitted out. Given the success of its sister hotels & the affiliation with the respected Rising Sun Dive Centre, we anticipate Baraza being a high-quality, slick operation. *Villas: ocean view (1 bed) US$730; ocean front (1 bed) US$780; sultan's sea-facing (2 bed) US$790; all rates FB*

🏠 **The Palms** (6 rooms) m 0774 440882; e info@palms-Zanzibar.com; www.palms-zanzibar.com. Immediately adjacent to Breezes & owned by the same family, The Palms is significantly more exclusive & expensive. With just 6 large, luxurious villas, Palms attracts young, affluent, honeymooners lured by image & intimacy. This is certainly a small, stylish option, but although the resort area is private, it's important to remember that it sits immediately next door to a family-friendly, 70-room resort, & everyone shares the same beach: romantic dinners for 2 on the sand may be subject to intrusion. Palms set out to achieve 'understated elegance', & this has broadly been achieved. The colonnaded Plantation House is the main resort building, housing its bar/lounge, dining room & mezzanine library. Here, antique cabinets, carved dark-wood sofas & natural palm mats rest on highly polished floors, while heavy old-fashioned fans spin in the high *makuti* thatch. The cappuccino & cream cushions, billowing organza curtains & afternoon tea on the deck complete the colonial feel. At the ocean end of the building, tarnished mirrors & candles fill a dining room set with ever-changing colours of linen, sparkling crystal glasses & simple flower arrangements. Individually named after exotic spices, the whitewashed villas sport shaggy thatch roofs & a large curved front terrace. Through the wide French doors, there is a lounge area with picture windows revealing the bedroom beyond. Decorated in chocolate brown, cream & apricot, with Arabian brass lanterns & wooden furniture, the huge rooms are classically elegant but feature all mod-cons: AC, minibar, safe, satellite TV & DVD player. There's an en-suite bathroom with a bath & even a private outdoor plunge pool. The villas share a small, split-level, tiled swimming pool, & each is also allocated a private *banda* overlooking the beach. *Makuti* shades draped with panels of indigo fabric make these a good place to escape the heat of the day & survey the beach beyond. For most activities, head to the bigger facilities at neighbouring Breezes, though Palms does have a tiny spa, The Sanctuary. *US$642–770pp dbl; all rates FB min age 16*

🏠 **Breezes Beach Club & Spa** (70 rooms) m 0774 440883–5; e info@breezes-zanzibar.com; www.breezes-zanzibar.com. A perennial favourite with honeymooners & families, Breezes is a large, efficient, family-run beach resort. Amid extensive, colourful gardens, there are 70 rooms in whitewashed villas virtually identical in size & interior, decorated in muted neutral colours, & with all the amenities of a good hotel. The rooms are comfortably furnished with large beds, & all have AC, en-suite bathroom, hairdryer, safe, fridge, & sofa-bed, but deliberately no telephones & TVs. The suite & deluxe categories are closer to the sea, & are upstairs & downstairs respectively. The suite also features a walk-in dressing room, slightly larger bathroom & wrap-around balcony with sun loungers. There is a large swimming pool at the centre of the resort, surrounded by verdant green grass, & a great stretch of sandy beach. Tall palms & *makuti* umbrellas offer shade at both, & wooden loungers are comfortable for reading & relaxing.

The Rising Sun Dive Centre is based between the beach & pool. Independently owned & run, it's a fully kitted-out, friendly PADI dive centre. Watersports from windsurfing to pedalos are easily arranged here, alongside an array of dive courses & trips (see pages 263–4). Or escape the sun to watch one of the DVDs available, or play pool, darts, cards or one of the board games. The Frangipani Spa is another great retreat: modern treatment rooms, a calm candlelit relaxation room, a deep private jacuzzi, a steam room, a new hair salon, & a team of Thai & Balinese professional masseuses ensure you leave purified & pampered. Entertaining, & appropriate, treatments, including the 'Kili Foot Treatment' & the 'Après Safari Treatment', allude to most guests' pre-beach trip on the mainland. For indulgent couples, there's an enchanting private spa for 2. The yoga studio (which had a genuine yogi when we last visited), fitness centre & floodlit tennis court complete the spiritual & physical well-being offered.

There's a baffling number of restaurants: the Salama Dining Room for b/fast & the evening table d'hôte, Breakers on the beach for those in need of lunchtime sustenance or the intimate Sultan's Table offering Indian cuisine in a wood-panelled tower filled with red velvet cushions & brass lanterns. For private dining *à deux* the carved beach hut, The Tides, comes complete with its own chandelier &

SUSTAINABLE SEAWEED FARMING

Seaweed has been harvested by coastal dwellers for centuries. This practice led to the export of red seaweed from Zanzibar to Europe in the 1950s, and continued until the wild stocks became exhausted. However, in the late 1980s, several development organisations and private companies began working with Zanzibar's north and east coastal communities to develop and promote the commercial cultivation of seaweed. This later expanded to the rest of the island, neighbouring Pemba Island and more recently on the mainland coast.

Providing initial funding, seedlings and technical skills, the aim is to encourage sustainable resource management, an essential prerequisite for long-term economic growth and employment, particularly for women. It is estimated that 30,000 people are currently engaged in seaweed farming, providing a much-needed household income for many coastal workers. The revenue from this trade is also a great foreign-exchange earner for Zanzibar's economy.

Seaweed is used commercially as a source of carrageenan, a natural gelling agent produced from it by alkaline extraction. Used in the manufacture of toothpaste, cosmetics, medicine and also as a thickening agent in many food products, particularly some which are milk-based, this is a valuable, natural product.

With real market demand, several species of seaweed are now farmed, though the most common are the reliable, profitable strains of *Kappaphyicus alvarezii* (*cottonii*), *Eucheuma denticulatum* (*spinosum*) and *Kappaphycus striatum*. By hammering stakes into the sandy inter-tidal zone, and stretching lines of coir rope or nylon monoline a foot above the seabed, cultivation lines are prepared and small seaweed stems are attached. Each plot can have up to 50 rows of strings 30cm apart, each line carrying ten to 15 cuttings. The seaweed grows at a rate of 7% per day, increasing to tenfold its original weight in a fortnight. This rapid growth allows farmers to harvest their crop every six weeks; a total of 697kg of seaweed is harvested annually per farmer, earning them an average US$100 per annum.

The seaweed is then dried in the sun for a few days, bagged, and sold to seaweed brokers who transport it to Zanzibar Town and onwards to Europe. Replanting of seedlings can be done immediately, using fragments from the old crop, ensuring sustained

staff. Note that dinner at the smaller restaurants is charged as an extra, & not included in the HB rates. For a cocktail & bar snack, the shady Pool Bar is a fun spot, with soft sand on the floor, coir-rope sofas & smiling staff in funky indigo-blue batik shirts. By night, the sophisticated & atmospheric

Baraza Bar is a cool drinking den. Shrouded in biscuit & ivory silk, it offers whisky, liqueurs & cigars. Beach weddings, which must be arranged in advance, are increasingly popular. An altar shaded by fresh palm fronds & white bougainvillea will be erected for such ceremonies. $$$$$—🍽

✕ WHERE TO EAT

✕ **Rocky Restaurant** m 0777 840724/490681. Probably the most remarkable location of any Zanzibar restaurant, Rocky Restaurant is perched on top of a marooned, seriously undercut coral-rock outcrop, just off the shore of the Michamvi Peninsula. Accessed by wandering across the sand at low tide, or by boat or breaststroke at high tide, the local team in this dilapidated building, with its cheery yellow window frames (no glass) & sea-life murals, serve up a simple 'catch of the day' menu. It's very basic, quirky & often empty, but the views are terrific, the staff friendly & the experience

unique. Calling in advance is probably a good idea if you're coming from afar. $$$
✕ **The Door** m 0777 414962; ⏱ for lunch & dinner daily. Accessed from the beach, you'll find The Door on top of the coral cliff above the Rafiki shop; from the tar road, it's signed down a bumpy track. Owned by Jamal of his namesake restaurant in Bwejuu village, this is a good place for fresh seafood, though book in advance for dinner. It's a sizeable shady restaurant with a friendly staff & a great outlook over the waving palm fronds to the Blue Lagoon (the only place where swimming is

farming and income. The Tanzania Coastal Management Partnership hopes that the country's export will increase to more than 8,000 tons in the very near future: in 2007, 7,000 tons were exported.

In 2006, a group of female seaweed farmers in the northern Zanzibar village of Kidoti began learning how to further increase their income by making finished products out of seaweed. Known as *Tusife Moyo* (translation: 'we should not lose heart'), they are part of the Zanzibar Seaweed Cluster Initiative who are adopting new methods of farming seaweed, such as deep-water floating lines, promoting working together with neighbouring villages and the invention and production of seaweed products. Aided by the Small & Medium Enterprises Competitiveness Facility and the Tanzania Commission for Science and Technology, the Kidoti women have recently acquired the necessary machinery to manufacture seaweed soap (they also make soaps infused with aromatic spices). The first 600 bars of seaweed soap were produced in March 2008, packaged neatly in specially created seaweed boxes and distributed for sale. Spurred on by their success, the Zanzibar Seaweed Cluster Initiative has already embarked on diverse product trials from seaweed biscuits to shampoo. Their commitment and the determination of the women is deeply impressive.

The personal income generated from seaweed farming and its products has helped significantly to improve many villagers' standard of living. In many parts of Africa, farming has been traditionally regarded as women's work, and this remains the case with seaweed farming on Zanzibar. Consequently, much of the money earned stays in the hands of these rural women, who would not normally have their own source of income. The advent of seaweed and the more recent development of seaweed product manufacture have resulted in many having a degree of freedom and empowerment previously impossible. Money is often used for school fees, house improvements, kitchenware or even luxuries like radios and cassette players. The villagers of Paje have collectively built two day-care centres for their children with their profits. Thus, sustained trade in these fast-growing marine algae and related products may just be a viable way out of poverty for many Zanzibari families.

possible in this area of coast at low tide). After some fried squid with lemon rice (US$6.50) or a divine 2-person whole grilled lobster (US$40), leave your things behind the bar & take a cooling dip or snorkel. $$$–$$$$$

WHAT TO SEE AND DO With many of the hotels on this stretch offering a gamut of activities in idyllic grounds, few visitors need step outside their own resort in search of entertainment. Divers, however, may need to head to a neighbouring property for use of a dive centre. Although these are aimed mostly at hotel guests, it's commonplace for visitors to arrange dives in this manner, and any hotel will be able to assist. Excluding the one at the Italian-speaking, all-inclusive Club Vacanze, the dive schools on the peninsula follow.

Rising Sun Dive Centre m 0777 440883–5/88; e bookings@risingsun-zanzibar.com; www.risingsun-zanzibar.com. This smart, efficient company is based on the edge of the beach at Breezes Beach Club, but is independently owned & operated. The enthusiastic English manager, Paul Shepherd, is a great east coast fan with a passion for underwater photography. The scuba kit here is regularly updated & always in excellent condition, all Rising Sun instructors & clients are also covered by DAN (Divers Alert Network) insurance, but for those travelling throughout the continent, they recommend all divers take out insurance online with DAN Europe (www.daneurope.org). The dive school is geared to taking both beginners & experienced divers looking for PADI speciality courses. Using GPS

& echosounder technology, several brand-new sites have been discovered, & the team are always keen to show experienced divers underwater treasures rarely visited by other companies. Rising Sun is also the only PADI National Geographic Dive Centre in east Africa & regularly works with Sea Sense, a Dar-based charity supporting dugongs & turtles. New in 2007, the watersports centre has expanded the activity offering beyond snorkelling safaris (US$15/25 child/adult) & fishing trips to include skippered boat rental, speedboat trips to the mangrove forests & daily kitesurfing lessons (wind dependent). Payment is accepted only in cash or by travellers' cheque. *Dive packages US$85/170/464/695 for 1/2/6/10 dives; Open Water US$672; Digital photography US$386; daily equipment rental (regulator, BCD, wet suit, mask & fins) US$39; underwater digital camera rental (inc CD of images) US$46*

✓ **Karafuu Dive Centre** m 0777 415447; www.dive.karafuuzanzibar.com. Formerly Kaskazi Sports Centre, the Karafuu Hotel has now taken over the management of this dive & watersports centre which sits within the hotel grounds. It has all the latest branded equipment, as well as welcoming divers who bring their own, & offers everything from PADI dive to windsurf courses, kitesurfing, canoeing & mountain biking. *Diving US$60/100 sgl/dbl; dive packages US$220/310/590 for 4/6/12 dives; Open Water US$500; windsurf hire US$30/70 for 1/3hrs; kitesurfing US$190 for 6hrs*

✓ **Hasfaer Michamvi Dive Centre** m 0773 209676; e michamvidiving@hotmail.com. Owned by the same Italians as Kichanga, in whose grounds it's based, Hasfaer is a small PADI centre with only 1 instructor, currently an Israeli gentleman, & 1 boat (so hope there are no problems). Dives mainly take place within the reef at Michamvi.

BWEJUU

Bwejuu is about 4km north of Paje. Sitting just back from the beach, the village itself is a dense network of dusty alleys and cramped houses, interspersed with towering palm trees. Bwejuu is currently experiencing alarming population growth which, combined with the increase in tourism on the coast, is putting great pressure on the resources here. Given the fact that 83% of the children here failed even the basic school exam in 2007, the village's problems sadly look set to increase.

The local people do some fishing and the women make coir rope from coconut husks (see page 284), but seaweed farming is the major industry and Bwejuu retains a very traditional atmosphere.

North of the village, towards Michamvi, it is still a quiet area, excellent for escapism, where there are plenty of places to enjoy just the sound of the waves and the wind rustling in the trees. Like the rest of the east coast, the tide goes out for miles, and so long as you're not hankering after a cool dip, there's a great feeling of space. There are still a few huts and houses dotted among the palms, but generally speaking the local population thins out and, in their place, you'll find a wide choice of places to stay from all-inclusive resorts to upmarket boutique hotels and simple bungalows. The beach to the north is truly beautiful, and the water its customary deep turquoise, making this an ideal place to relax for anything from a day to a week.

With the arrival of the tar road up the centre of the peninsula, a great deal of the tourist traffic has withdrawn from the winding village paths, making things a lot more pleasant for both the residents and drivers, neither of whom appreciated the resulting dust or track corrugations. However, there have been reliable reports of an increase in threatening snatch-and-grab crime on the isolated tracks from beach accommodation to the bus stops on the main road. A few pairs of women have been targeted on this walk, and single travellers (especially women) are naturally now advised to be careful, and ideally to avoid unknown, remote routes. These are undoubtedly disturbing occurrences, but for now at least the assailants seem more interested in stealing bags than causing physical harm.

GETTING THERE AND AWAY From the roundabout at Paje, connecting the island's main east–west artery to the south east's new tar road, self-drivers should turn north on the well-signposted road towards Michamvi. This fast, smooth road now runs all the way to Pingwe, where a reasonable gravel road continues west to Michamvi Kae. Most of the beach hotels have clear signs marking the relevant turning off the tar road, and we have marked those present in mid 2008 on the area map. Tracks spring up as quickly as new hotels though, so do be aware that more of these less-official routes will appear by the time you travel. If you are keen to head into the centre of the village, follow signs to Palm Beach Inn. This will take you along the old coastal road: a narrow, bumpy, dusty track that wanders between village huts and palm trees. It's not for faint-hearted drivers: children and chickens regularly dart across the road, and navigation through Bwejuu village's dusty tracks is tricky and often without room for a three-point turn! If you're on foot or bicycle, hit the beach and enjoy the sea breeze as you travel.

Dala-dala number 324 leaves Zanzibar Town for Paje three times a day, and often travels onwards to Bwejuu: check with the individual drivers as some will turn south at Paje for Jambiani.

From Bwejuu and the beaches north, adventurous travellers heading to the north of the island can opt to hitch a lift with the octopus fishermen across the bay from Michamvi Kae to Chwaka. This is a fun way to avoid back-tracking round the hinterland, but agree costs clearly in advance and don't chance it if you can't swim.

WHERE TO STAY Bwejuu has something to cater to almost every taste and budget. The accommodation options below have been divided between those in the immediate vicinity of the village, and those strung out along the coast to the north of the main settlement. The pick of the bunch, offering great value for money in their class, is Bellevue Bungalows for its laid-back vibe, food and cheery bungalows; Robinson's Place for its character and eco-credentials, Andy's Karibuni Bungalows for peace and escapism, and Echo Beach for raising the bar on all fronts in Bwejuu.

Bwejuu Village

Sun and Sea View Resort (10 rooms) m 0773 168839; e info@sunandseaviewresort.com; www.sunandseaviewresort.com. Covering a large, open plot beside the beach, this is a quiet corner. At the end of the entrance path, a rough-hewn, pink coral-stone building houses the reception & restaurant area. It's a relaxed place with cheerful African music playing at the bar & neat tables set with green tablecloths & fresh bougainvillea in vases. The large whitewashed rondavels contain 2 independent en-suite rooms. Simple & clean, they have white tiled floors, fresh linen on the beds, nets, mains electricity with UK-style 3-pin sockets &, curiously, a free-standing fan mounted to the ceiling. A desk & wicker-style chair covered in hide completes the look. Unusually for many budget rooms, there's plenty of natural light from 3 large windows, & a bath as well as a shower in the en-suite bathroom. The hospitable owner is often around the property & his thoughts about the island, its people & politics are enlightening; with time he can also arrange village tours covering the school, clinic & local occupations. As there is no gate to the property,

self-drivers may prefer to opt for a more physically secure option, but otherwise this is a reasonable budget choice. $$

Mustapha's Nest (7 rooms) 024 2240069; e mustaphas@africamail.com; www.fatflatfish.co.uk/mustaphas. Set back from the beach, across the sandy road, Mustapha's Nest is long established as a totally chilled, slightly eccentric hangout. Its name bears reference to both its Rastafarian owner, Mustapha, & the site's overwhelming population of bright yellow weaver birds. Carefully constructed nests belonging to the latter drip from every available branch & these chirping little birds have become so iconic that they now adorn the signpost & staff T-shirts. Set around a neat, sandy circle (complete with bonfire & miscellaneous pieces of coir rope & wood furniture) are 6 small, uniquely decorated *bandas*, 2 of which share a bathroom. An additional room is set further back beside the beehive (honey available on request). Inside, the white adobe walls are decorated with brightly painted patterns or pictures, & colourful *kangas* are used to cover the solid beds & as curtains. The floors &

surfaces of the en-suite bathroom are a mosaic of different tile sizes, shapes & colours, with miscellaneous plants sprouting from soil-filled bottles & deliberately placed holes in the floor – a crude, back-to-nature feel that will not suit everyone. The 2-storey bar & restaurant area is as laid-back as the reggae tunes it plays, & is repeatedly praised for its food. *Camping* $; *rooms* $$

🏠 **Seven Seas Bungalows** (9 rooms) PO Box 2330, Zanzibar. Once acceptable, this place is now in some disrepair. Local people are still willing to rent out rooms, but they are increasingly basic. Seven Seas' only asset is its location right on the beach, although not a particularly pleasant bit of it.

🏠 **Pakacha Bungalow and Restaurant** (2 rooms) ℡ 024 2234158; m 0777 484811; e pakacharestaurant@gmail.com. Opened in late 2007, Pakacha is a small village restaurant & solitary bungalow run by friendly Bwejuu resident, Ali Chamnda. Built on family land amid the palms, the accommodation comprises 2 spacious, if spartan, rooms, each with twin dbl beds & an en-suite cold-water shower. 1 room has AC & a mini fridge whilst the other has a large ceiling fan. There is a very basic 'relaxing area' upstairs with some less than stylish armchairs & a few concrete planters, but there is a pleasant sea view through the trees. The adjacent *makuti* restaurant serves big b/fasts of fruit & Spanish omelette, & Swahili dinners (octopus in coconut cream (US$5.50); whole crab (US$7.50); grilled fish (US$6)). Rates reduce by half in low season. $$

🏠 **Palm Beach Inn** (14 rooms) ℡ 024 2240221; m 0777 410070/411155/0773 414666; e mahfudh28@hotmail.com. In the heart of Bwejuu, sandwiched between the dusty village track & the beach, Palm Beach Inn sits behind a high, secure gate. Opened in 1990 by Niala Jadawi, a local girl & influential former MP, this is a real hotch-potch of a place. The management makes an admirable effort to employ Bwejuu residents, particularly single mothers & the disadvantaged. The key employees are friendly & helpful, but there are also a high number of women wandering around – gardening, cleaning, or seemingly just ambling through – which adds to the distinctly local feel of the place. Separate cottages as well as rooms in a central building house 8 dbls, 2 twins, 1 trpl & 2 family rooms. Each is individually named after a marine animal or fish & doors are marked with carefully hand-painted signs of the corresponding creature. All the rooms have 24hr mains electricity, sockets with a universal adaptor, mosquito nets over the beds, fans & efficient AC, a fridge & an en-suite toilet with a hot-water shower. Wooden boxes, painted with red & yellow flames, tidy fire extinguishers neatly away outside each room. Kamilo's suite, with its sea view & tiny lounge area, is viewed as the best room, but this depends upon your taste. Its interior has the décor of a budget Indian restaurant: heavy claret & gold sofas, a large brass, mock-Victorian kettle on the dresser, plastic beaded curtains separating the wardrobe area, floral velour-covered chairs, a large clock, & curiously, a Constable-esque picture of haystacks in Kent. If you enjoy minimalist design, don't stay here! The nicest room is the newest, named after Abdi Karume. Situated under the sun terrace, it's a compact space but the simple white linen & clean blue bathroom make this a more aesthetically appealing retreat.

The split-level, circular dining room is capable of seating 40, & there are easy chairs in a lounge area where games & cards are available. Although there are windows facing the sea, the restaurant is enclosed on all sides to give shelter from the evening wind. Most guests stay here on a B&B basis, but other basic meals are available: the staple fish, vegetable & rice dishes of the island (special fried prawns with rice & vegetables US$10). There is a large menu but, as is often the case, it's invariably only the 'specials' menu that shows what's available that day. Order food as early as possible to increase chances of it being available, & accept that service is slow. There's a well-stocked bar of beer & spirits to ease the wait.

The nursery planting is striking all around this little complex: low timber trellis fencing is adorned with white bottles, each sprouting young climbing plants. Clearly the aim is to create lush hedging; it has a long way to grow. The rest of the area is divided into beds filled with miscellaneous cacti, frangipani & large-leafed climbers. The gardens are also home to 2 very old caged tortoises, a sizeable pigeon coop, & a few wooden tables with blue & yellow wrought-iron chairs. Like the bottled plants, Palm Beach has the general appearance of trying to cram too much into too small an area, making it feel cluttered & a little oppressive. Although it's located beside the ocean, there is a fence between the lodge area & the beach. Loungers are above the beach, not on it, & the staff are keen to warn guests not to take valuables onto the beach. As well as potential issues of theft, the beach immediately outside the property is strewn with sharp coral rock, & litter caused by its proximity to dense village settlement. Think twice about a night-time stroll on the beach too, as high-speed motorbikes are known to bypass the bumpy village lanes, by taking to the sand. $$$

⌂ **Dere Beach Guesthouse** PO Box 278, Bwejuu; m 0777 864818471840. Once a reasonable backpacker haunt, this place has now completely degenerated. In the centre of the village, the beach immediately in front of the guesthouse is covered in litter, far from the east coast's pristine image, & the whole place has a generally unkempt look & unpleasant air. The en-suite rooms are grubby & basic with saggy mattresses, plastic chairs & ripped lino flooring. It is hard to do anything other than recommend not staying here. $$

⌂ **Miza Wa Miza Bungalows** (14 rooms) m 0777 871751; e ibrahim@kunst-gsund.at; www.kunst-gsund-sein.at. Opened in 2005 by Rastafarian artist

North of Bwejuu village
⌂ **Kilimani Kwetu Restaurant & Bungalows** (4 rooms) ☎ 024 2240235; m 0777 465243 (Wadi)/0777 214133 (Clemens); e info@kilimani.de; www.kilimani.de. Opened in 1994 as a partnership between 5 Germans, led by Dirk Rabien, & the village of Bwejuu, Kilimani Kwetu is rooted in community development. Built by local people from local materials, on a gentle hill to the north of the village overlooking the sea, this is a relaxed, hassle-free spot, with a positive impact on those who live in the area. Wadi & a delightfully friendly local team manage Kilimani Kwetu & are happy to help any visitors. There are 4 rooms — 2 dbls & 2 twins — in 2 white, thatched bungalows. Surrounded by palms & sweet almond trees, the rooms are basic if a little uninspiring, with newly painted concrete walls. They have simple furniture, 2 deckchairs, mosquito nets with inside fan, & en-suite bathrooms with a cold-water shower & clean squat, flush toilet (these may ultimately be changed to Western sit-on style). Electricity is available & there's a traditional well on site. The neat restaurant serves fresh fish & vegetarian dishes on request, & b/fast boasts homemade tropical fruit jams & locally produced honey. Take any one of several zigzag paths, 50m to the sea, & there's a private beach area for guests, with makuti umbrellas, deckchairs & a new beach bar.

Development projects centred on Kilimani Kwetu have successfully financed the construction of an adult education centre & library in the past & it remains a place for visitors keen to immerse themselves in local life. $$

⌂ **White Rose Beach Resort** (49 rooms) m 0777 469824; e whiteroseznz@yahoo.com;

Ibrahim & his Austrian wife, Miza Wa Miza is an off-beat place brimming with character. The highly individual rooms are found in a collection of thatched, wattle-and-daub houses varying in size & design, & surrounded by sandy paths & lush tropical plants. Coconut House (complete with an actual palm growing through the centre) & Africa House are self-contained en-suite dbls, whilst the largest building, Mauerhub, has 4 rooms & 2 shared bathrooms. The rooms are all individually decorated by Ibrahim, in an array of media from mosaic to paint, & each contains a Zanzibari bed, mosquito net & fan. The décor will not be to everyone's taste but the place is clean & the staff pleasant. The on-site 'Bantu Restaurant' serves up African cooking in a circular rondavel & art courses are often available. $$

www.whiterosezanzibar.com. White Rose Beach Resort reopened in 2006 after a complete refurbishment, & by early 2008, Italian package holiday operator, Viaggiland, was its sole booking agent, the place had magnified in size & efforts were underway to modernise the room interiors. It is possible that independent travellers will soon be welcome to stay again, so it's worth contacting the lodge directly close to the time of travel. Rising from the beach up the hill behind, there are 33 garden rooms set on the slope above the coconut line, still with great sea views, & 16 beach rooms, surrounding the new swimming pool. The white stone garden bungalows are all the same basic design with wide verandas, spacious bedrooms & en-suite bathrooms, whilst the new pool-side rooms are in 2-storey, whitewashed terraces with small individual balconies. It's a peaceful place with pleasant landscaping, including sapling sweet almonds & poinsettia, several makuti sun umbrellas & coir-rope chairs dotted around. The restaurant, beach bar, shop & massage room provide guest diversions & there's a secure parking area making this a great option for self-drivers. Sea view US$134–236pp; garden US$87–189pp; all rates FB

⌂ **Bellevue Bungalows** (6 rooms) m 0777 209576; e bellevuezanzibar@gmail.com; www.bellevuezanzibar.com. On the top of a high rise of coral rock, this is a thoroughly relaxed, gentle place offering one of the best budget deals on the island. In recent years Bellevue has flourished & since the arrival of a young Dutch couple, Melanie & Dim, in Dec 2007, it has taken on a new energy. Building on the good work in recent years to establish pretty gardens, they have transformed the restaurant, lounge & rooms with vibrant co-ordinated colours & original solutions to storage & lighting. Working closely with the charming local owners, Mussa & Chulla, the place has retained its homely, relaxed vibe but benefited greatly from its stylish facelift. The 6 clean, spacious dbl rooms are in 3 thatched bungalows & have good en-suite bathrooms, matching linen & towels, fishing basket shelves & even bedside reading lights. Each room has a sunrise terrace, with clever *kanga* woven coir dividers to create privacy. The raised level allows for a great outlook (though a villa is currently under construction which may part-obscure this) & a cooling breeze. Chef Chulla, who has appeared on Dutch TV in 2008, makes terrific tapas as well as a variety of fresh European & Swahili cuisine (US$5–7). Scrumptious b/fasts of spice-infused juices, fresh bread, pancakes, locally produced honey & homemade jams are a great start to the day too. With a 5min walk down to the beach & Dim's kitesurfing school (see page 276) in Paje open to all, the focus is on traditional seaside activities & the chance to chill under the storm lanterns with a cold beer in the evening. The team here is all justifiably proud of its achievements, & at this price their success is virtually guaranteed. $$$

⌂ **Evergreen Bungalows** (14 rooms) ☏ 024 2240273; e zanzievergreen@yahoo.com; www.evergreen-bungalows.com. There are 14 rooms in 2-storey beach bungalows: those upstairs are in the apex of the *makuti* thatch & are accessed by steep steps at the front of the chalets. The older of these rooms are extremely simple, with no real windows upstairs, though the open-weave palm mesh does allow some light & air to penetrate, but plans are afoot make some changes. Downstairs, the rooms are much lighter & better, with solid walls, simple wooden furniture, clean bedding, mosquito nets & a cold-water en-suite bathroom. There are 2 new, much improved, *makuti* bungalows on the beach – in these the lower circular rooms are spacious & original, with large coconut-wood beds, pale bedding, Maasai blankets & moulded concrete en-suite bathrooms concealed behind batik curtains. Above them, high-ceilinged, airy rooms in the *makuti* roof offer lovely views & a welcome sea breeze. There is no mains electricity, but some solar-powered lighting is provided at night. The central bar & restaurant is airy & spacious, & snacks & meals are available throughout the day, served under a striking red snapper light (chapatti US$2.50; avocado salad US$4). African Blue Divers (US$45/dive) is based here & run by the German owners; though it is not a PADI-registered operation & at the time of researching was lamentably unaware of the location of the island's only decompression chamber. $$$

⌂ **Twisted Palms** (12 rooms) m 0777 4249913; e info@twistedpalms.net; www.twistedpalms.net. Locally managed by a friendly team, this former backpacker stronghold is now distinctly tired & dreary. 6 dbl rooms sit in stone-and-thatch bungalows on the beach, 1 has taken the place of the former first-floor restaurant, & another 5 rooms (2 trpls & 3 dbls) are set back on a small hill. The rooms now have a fan, mosquito net, electricity & en-suite bathrooms with European flush toilets & cold-water showers. The restaurant, opened in 2005, sits on stilts above the sea & there is a daily set menu &, in theory, alternatives may be possible with enough notice. There is no safe deposit, the first-aid kit is lost & the fire extinguisher is kept down the road in the village, so this is probably not the place for those who are very safety conscious. $$

⌂ **Shells Bungalow** (10 rooms) PO Box 4666; m 0787 400772. There are 6 bungalows here named after Tanzanian places – Serengeti to Kilimanjaro – as well as 4 rooms in the neighbouring villa available from Sep–Jan. Although the bungalows are a little rough on the outside, each is in fact large & clean, with a big dbl bed, some basic furniture & an adequate en-suite bathroom with flush toilet & cold-water shower. Hand-painted flowers around the windows & Tingatinga pictures show thoughtful decorating attempts, & a generator providing electricity at night does make getting around easier. There's a good stretch of white-sand beach here, where hammocks under shady palms & no hassle make for a relaxed atmosphere. There's an extensive menu but don't be fooled as only fish & vegetables are actually available, & it's probably best to order in the morning if you want to eat dinner. $$

⌂ **Robinson's Place** (5 rooms) m 0777 413479; e robinsonsplace@hotmail.com; www.robinsonsplace.com; ⏲ Jun–Mar. This is a delightfully off-beat family home set in lovely mature gardens, beside a superb beach. To Ann & Ahmed, the fascinating European–Zanzibari couple who own & run the place, being here is about a particular lifestyle choice rather than business, hence you can expect a very friendly welcome, a gentle & relaxed pace, but none of the trappings of a commercial lodge. Robinson's does its best to be fairly self-sufficient – keeping chickens across the road & growing tropical fruit. Simple meals are served either under the trees or on rugs & cushions on the floor in the main lounge area. There is no electricity, though plans are afoot to harness wind power, so all cooking is done on open fires. In an effort to conserve wood, the only hot meal of the day is dinner (US$8). For lunch, guests often wander along the beach to Sunrise or Breezes where for a fee they can also enjoy a dip in their pools.

Robinson's rooms cater for a maximum of 12 people so advance booking is invariably necessary. All rooms are very different in style & are divided amongst 2 small houses & a Robinson-Crusoe-esque, 2-storey treehouse. The master bedroom in the main house is a huge room with a dbl & a ¾ bed, bright fabrics, & vases filled with flowers. It is the only room with an en-suite bathroom, & this is spotless. Attached, but not interconnected, the main house 'guest bedroom' is a small but pretty room with a ¾ bed, a day-bed & vibrant orange linen. The proximity & contained feel of these 2 rooms make the house perfect for a family with older children. House Bondeni, literally meaning 'house in the corner', is a lovely, airy, 'L'-shaped room with white walls, cheerful *kangas* on both the European & Zanzibari dbl beds, & brightly coloured, woven palm mats on the floor. The *pièce de résistance* is Robinson's House, newly renovated in 2008, a rough-hewn, wattle-and-daub, 2-storey affair under a large tree on the edge of the beach. Upstairs is a basic but fun 'honeymoon suite' from where, under a lovely mangrove & *makuti* roof, the dbl bed looks out through the shell mobiles & trees to the ocean beyond. Downstairs is a small, clean sgl room with its own sea view. All rooms, except the master, share immaculate bathroom facilities. There are 2 cold-water showers & 2 toilets, each separated by stylish cream curtains, & a large open-ended central area with mirrors & sinks. These are cleaner & more pleasant than many of the en-suite facilities offered by Zanzibar's more mid-range properties; certainly the best 'shared facilities' that we've ever seen in Africa! Several resident dogs roam the property as effective security guards. Min 2-night stay. $$

⌂ **Hammond's Guesthouse** (4 rooms) In an increasingly dilapidated house by the beach, there is an assortment of sgl & dbl rooms; some en suite, some with shared facilities. At the time of visiting, Hammond's had ceased to take guests, though this may change in the future. In any case, there are plenty more pleasant & reliable options in the area. $$

⌂ **Bahari Beach Village** (6 rooms) m 0784 619579; e shafeefznz71@hotmail.com; www.bahari-becah-village.com. Opened in 2003, Bahari is now being managed by a local couple, Shareef & Fatima. There are 4 neat rooms in 2 bungalows, each with dbl bed, en-suite facilities & good sea views, plus a sgl & a dbl room inside the main house. There's no electricity or hot water, but the latter can be arranged if needed. The simple hexagonal bar/restaurant area opens onto a pleasant beach area which slopes down to the sea. There's a selection of good rope hammocks from which to enjoy unobstructed ocean & a varied Swahili menu. $$

⌂ **Sunrise Hotel and Restaurant** (13 rooms) ☎ 024 2240270; m 0777 415240; e sunrise@zanlink.com; www.sunrise-zanzibar.com; ⊕ Jun–Apr. Opened on 1 Jan 1994 by a Belgian chef, Georges Noël, Sunrise has been a popular, laid-back hangout over the years & until recently this hotel offered excellent-value accommodation on a good stretch of beach & fabulous food. Sadly, standards of service have slipped, & reliable reports are increasingly less than glowing. There are 8 bungalows facing the sea & 5 standard rooms in a row at the back of the main building. None is fancy but they are clean, en-suite & reasonably priced. Both the standard rooms & bungalows are available with Zanzibari beds or European twin/dbls; additional sgl beds are available for families using the bungalows. All the en-suite bathrooms have hot-water showers & there's 24hr national-grid electricity, AC, fan & mosquito nets in the bedrooms. There is a backup generator & emergency security lanterns in case of power failure; a safe is available at reception for valuables. The water is from a neighbouring well but free bottled water is provided. The food is tasty, though the canary-yellow humpback bridge to the dining room & shallow canal beneath are tired & dated these days.

There is a fairly large sheltered swimming pool, bikes to rent, local massage for US$10/hr & internet access. Diving & snorkelling excursions can easily be arranged through Karafuu Hotel or Breezes Beach Club, the latter only a 20min stroll along the beach. 10% surcharge credit cards; 5% surcharge travellers' cheques. $$$

⌂ **Andy's Karibuni Bungalows & Romantic Garden** (2 rooms) m 0748 430942; e romantic-garden@web.de/nussera@web.de; www.eastzanzibar.com. Away from the village, this tranquil place is owned & run by a well-travelled German-Hungarian, Andrea, with help from a friendly team of locals & 7 obedient dogs. There is currently only 1 bungalow here, divided into 2 independent en-suite dbl rooms. These are light, bright & airy with neatly painted ceiling beams, sparkling terracotta floor tiles, & cheerful orange café curtains.

Each room has a large, low, king-size bed, shrouded in a powder-blue mosquito net, & with spotless en-suite toilet & cold-water shower. Woven tabletops make great book rests, while coat stands act as space-saving wardrobes. Outside, a small terrace area looks over the pretty, shaded gardens towards the beach. Beautiful bougainvillea, hibiscus & other tropical plants surround the compound, attracting small birds & butterflies, & creating a pleasantly green setting. Andy's is a place to relax by the beach, read, walk & enjoy the peaceful setting; don't come here for a multitude of activities. There is a generator for electricity, though it is only occasionally used to power lights in the evening. The casual restaurant offers local produce, best ordered in advance, cooked simply but well. Payment preferred in US$. $$$

🏠 **Echo Beach Hotel** (11 rooms) m 0773 593260/593286; e echobeachhotel@hotmail.com; www.echobeachhotel.com. In 2007, British expats Sue & Andrew Page swapped life at their quaint B&B in the Loire Valley to create Echo Beach. Opened in Oct of the same year, this small, friendly lodge has high aspirations & is receiving some admirable reviews. 5 small detached cottages & 2 dbl-storey houses are arranged in an arc behind the inviting kidney-shaped swimming pool, & mid-2008 saw the addition of 2 cottages at the rear of the property, offering more privacy & a day bed in the loft. Almost every room has a sea view from the day bed on its private terrace, & each is attractively screened with billowing fabric panels in a rainbow of colours, giving this lodge an original take on the Zanzibari norm. Room interiors vary slightly from each other, though all are similar in style: a 4-poster dbl bed swathed in a mosquito net, African bedside lamps, carved wardrobes, highly polished floors, good AC, ceiling fans & open, en-suite bathrooms with huge walk-in showers. The large open-sided lounge/dining room is sited under high *makuti* thatch with gleaming aqua tiles on the floor; it's a little spartan & glossy but the food is consistently very good (Andrew is a chef) & the pre-dinner bar chatter makes it a cheerful hangout. It looks out towards the sea through a coconut grove, & the lovely stretch of beach is a stone's throw away.

Echo Beach is more about relaxing than action: read by the pool, siesta in a hammock, snack on tasty treats. That said, Rising Sun Dive Centre at Breezes is a 10min beach walk & can arrange any number of water-based activities for the restless. Children are welcome to stay at the discretion of the management, so advise at time of booking. *All rates are HB, inc a 3-course à-la-carte dinner.* $$$$$

✕ **WHERE TO EAT** Nearly all of the hotels cater for guests and non-residents alike (see individual listings). In addition, there are a few small shops and local-style eating houses in the village itself, and increasingly a few locally run Swahili restaurants catering specifically to visitors.

✕ **Jamal's Restaurant** Immediately opposite Palm Beach Inn, this has been recommended by several travellers. In spite of a sign implying that it's operational from 07.00 to midnight, Jamal's opening is erratic at best & seemingly only in high season. No-one was around during our lunchtime visit, so visitors keen for some good Swahili fare should probably head instead to Jamal's more substantial establishment, The Door, at the northern end of the Michamvi Peninsula. $$–$$$

✕ **Sunrise Restaurant** Sunrise Hotel; ✆ 024 2240270; m 0777 415240; e sunrise@zanlink.com; www.sunrise-Zanzibar.com; ⏱ 07.30–09.30 b/fast, 12.00–14.30 lunch, 19.00–22.00 dinner (last orders 21.00); non-residents welcome. French classics at the long-established Belgian-run Sunrise mix with local flavours. Excellent crab pancakes are crisp on the outside & succulent inside; tasty *poisson cru* uses bluefin tuna; large juicy tiger prawns feature in Swahili-influenced curries; & the Belgian chocolate mousse is fabulous! The hotel may be getting increasingly mixed reviews, but for now at least the food remains good. The waiters are polite, the tables neatly laid & it is an easy walk along the beach from many of the hotels in the area. $$$–$$$$

✕ **Seven Tables** m 0777 866096. Neighbouring Hammond's Guesthouse to the south, on the site of the old Gomani Bungalows, Seven Tables opened in 2008 to offer simple Swahili cuisine. It is best to order well in advance to guarantee food being available. Some construction is still underway at the time of writing so feedback from more recent diners would be very welcome. $$$

WHAT TO SEE AND DO Most visitors to this area are kept occupied by resort activities and sun-worshipping. If you're staying somewhere small or simply fancy

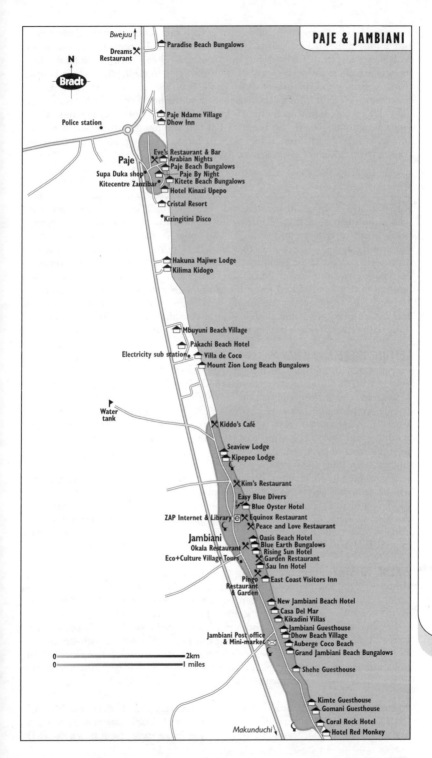

PAJE & JAMBIANI

Bwejuu ↑

Dreams ✕ Restaurant

Paradise Beach Bungalows

N

Bradt

Police station

Paje Ndame Village
Dhow Inn

Paje

Supa Duka shop
Kitecentre Zanzibar

Eve's Restaurant & Bar
Arabian Nights
Paje Beach Bungalows
Paje By Night
Kitete Beach Bungalows
Hotel Kinazi Upepo

Cristal Resort

Kizingitini Disco

Hakuna Majiwe Lodge
Kilima Kidogo

Mbuyuni Beach Village

Pakachi Beach Hotel

Electricity sub station
Villa de Coco
Mount Zion Long Beach Bungalows

Water tank

Kiddo's Café

Seaview Lodge
Kipepeo Lodge

Kim's Restaurant

Easy Blue Divers
Blue Oyster Hotel

ZAP Internet & Library
Equinox Restaurant
Peace and Love Restaurant

Jambiani

Okala Restaurant
Eco+Culture Village Tours

Oasis Beach Hotel
Blue Earth Bungalows
Rising Sun Hotel
Garden Restaurant
Sau Inn Hotel

Pingo Restaurant & Garden
East Coast Visitors Inn

New Jambiani Beach Hotel
Casa Del Mar
Kikadini Villas
Jambiani Guesthouse
Dhow Beach Village
Auberge Coco Beach
Grand Jambiani Beach Bungalows

Jambiani Post office & Mini-market

Shehe Guesthouse

0 ————— 2km
0 ————— 1 miles

Kimte Guesthouse
Gomani Guesthouse
Coral Rock Hotel
Hotel Red Monkey

Makunduchi ↘

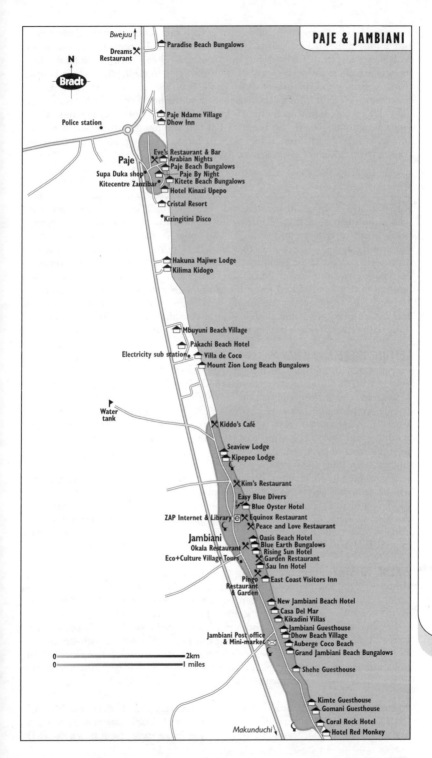

a change, you can explore the offshore reef with snorkelling gear hired from Palm Beach Inn, in the village (around US$4 per day for mask, snorkel and flippers), or, with better kit, from Rising Sun Dive Centre, at Breezes. At low tide, the long inter-tidal walk to the ocean is a rewarding excursion in itself, but be sure to top up the suncream and drink lots of water on the way. You can also hire bikes (US$5) or scooters (US$40) from local villagers, with a little help from your hotel, and ride a few kilometres north up the beach to the 'lagoon' at Dongwe, in front of The Door Restaurant, where the break in the reef means it's possible to swim and snorkel off the beach even at low tide. (If hiring a scooter, see *Chapter 5*, *Hired vehicles*, page 119, and *Driving licences*, pages 122–3.)

PAJE

Paje is a small fishing village, straggled along the coast; it's centred on the point where the main road from Zanzibar Town joins the new tar coast road, which heads north to Bwejuu and south to Makunduchi. Its location at this junction makes it the easiest place on the coast to reach by public transport and contributed to its early success as the backpackers' choice location. With the rise in Nungwi's dominance over the livelier side of the budget scene, the percentage of travellers heading to Paje has reduced (even if real numbers probably continue to rise). By and large, the area surrounding the village remains a quiet spot for an idyllic beach break. Genuine interaction with the local community is virtually non-existent here, with only the beach traders mixing with the tourists.

GETTING THERE AND AWAY To reach Paje, the main tar road from Zanzibar Town leads through Tunguu, Jozani and Kitogani before reaching the coast. From Paje, a new tar road then leads north to Bwejuu and Michamvi, while another heads south to Jambiani and Makunduchi, in the far southeast corner of the island.

Paje can be reached by public transport (*dala-dala* number 324 or bus Route 9), tourist minibus or self-drive rental car, motorbike or bicycle. If you want to go north beyond Bwejuu or south past Jambiani, there's no regular public transport, so you'll need to have your own wheels, be willing to hitch on a local *ngarawa*, or enjoy a really long, hot walk.

If you come to the Bwejuu–Paje–Jambiani area by tourist minibus, many drivers will be keen to take you to the hotels and lodges where they expect to be paid a good commission, often regardless of your own requests. (Read our comments in the box in *Chapter 6*, *Guides and the 'papaasi'*, page 132.) If you take a minibus from Zanzibar Town, then we strongly advise that you agree precisely where you want to go before departing, and preferably have a reservation in advance.

WHERE TO STAY There are several places to stay in Paje, most of them closely clustered at the southern edge of the village. All the accommodation here is small scale, individual and relatively cheap; most places are owner-run. Not all hotels are on the beach though, so choose carefully if it's a sea view you're after.

Beside the main group of guesthouses is a private house, locally known as 'Paje Palace'. Ignore the aesthetic damage that this pink-and-mint monstrosity may do to your architectural sensibilities, and be grateful that it has brought floodlighting to its immediate surroundings, including the beach, as it is generally felt to have increased security here in the evening.

Paradise Beach Bungalows (10 rooms) ℡ 024 2231387; m 0777 414129; e paradisebb@zanlink.com/saori@cats-net.com; www.geocities.jp/paradisebeachbungalows/. Follow the track opposite Dreams Restaurant on the tar road to reach this long-standing budget favourite. Opened 13 years ago by a gentle, diminutive Japanese lady, Saori Miura, who abandoned her high-powered communications job to travel in east Africa, learn Swahili & avoid the corporate rat race, this is a cheap beach retreat offering basic facilities & great sushi. There are 10 rooms, 3 of which were added in 2005 as larger, dbl storey options. The original rooms are in semi-detached cottages with 2 ¾-size traditional Zanzibari beds with mosquito nets. Some of these have interconnecting doors for groups of friends or families. The en-suite bathrooms are basic concrete rooms with squat toilets & cold-water showers. Hot water can be boiled on request though this does take some time (we're still waiting!). The new chalets are a better bet with a simple but spacious, ground-floor bedroom with a dbl & a ¾-length bed, neat coconut-wood shelves & a Zanzibari chest for storing valuables. The en-suite pink bathroom has a European toilet & shower, while outside, polished coconut-wood stairs lead from the veranda to a pleasant, private roof terrace with a picnic table, chairs, washing line & view into the surrounding palms & frangipani trees. There is now electricity here with low-level lights helping significantly at night & storm lanterns still used for atmosphere; power cuts are frequent though so a good torch is essential.

The split-level central restaurant houses 7 wooden tables, neatly covered in blue batik tablecloths adorned with white giraffes & glasses of fresh flowers, some simple dining chairs & a small multi-lingual library. The evenings see guests come here to read, play cards, chat & eat, all sheltered from the sea breeze by retractable wooden shutters. The home-cooked food is all good quality, especially the Japanese options of fresh sushi & tempura, but supplies are limited so order dinner well in advance to ensure your choice is available, & check Saori is around if you're coming for the sushi. B/fasts are simple affairs of fruit, fresh bread & a selection of local preserves. Next to the restaurant, a 2-storey, hexagonal lounge area offers cushioned seating, good sea views & some shade during the heat of the afternoon. There is also a new bar behind the restaurant which is well stocked with imported alcohol & CDs. In spite of its very basic amenities, Paradise's quiet location, Japanese food & inexpensive rates do mean that it can get very busy, so advance booking is advisable. It is also worth being aware that there are a number of seemingly docile-looking dogs dozing around the gardens — their bite is stronger than their bark! Local or major international currencies accepted. No credit cards; travellers' cheques 7% surcharge. $$

⌂ **Paje Ndame Village** (28 rooms) m 0777 865501; e booking@ndame.info; www.ndame.info. Managed by a pleasant Swedish couple, Lisbeth & Jan Kastner, since 2004, Paje Ndame caters mainly to Scandinavian families (large family rooms available) & is consequently at its busiest during the Nordic school holidays in Jul & Dec. Rooms in 2-storey villas or neat whitewashed bungalows are all light & bright & clean with chequerboard lino flooring, tiled en-suite bathrooms with a shower & toilet, & either a shared semicircular balcony with a good sea view or a garden terrace. Each is named alphabetically after a car manufacturer, with Buick & Honda being particularly spacious sgls. All rooms have mains electricity (through sockets with 3 round pins — adaptors available), fans, mosquito nets & bedside lights.

The resort sits along a lovely long stretch of beach on which guests laze, enjoy one of Flora's African massages & watch the world go by. There's a pleasant seafront restaurant, a curio shop with a reasonable selection of colourful local paintings, a new circular beach bar for sundowners & a popular beach volleyball court. Activities are relatively limited but the youthful crowd seems happy playing cards, snorkelling from a local *ngarawa*, renting bicycles & embarking on 'romantic moonrise tours'. Child & student reductions available. $$$

⌂ **Dhow Inn** (5 rooms) m 0773 215929/0786 266941; e info@dhowinn.com; www.dhowinn.com. Opened in Nov 2007, this is the newest of Paje's accommodation options, neighbouring Paje Ndame to the south. Its 3 Dutch owners are on site & keen to warmly welcome guests & live up to their 'come as a guest, leave as family' motto. Currently there are just 5 small en-suite rooms here, though plans will slowly extend this to 15 by 2009. Hot water, fans, mosquito nets & even Wi-Fi are standard. Set 40m back from the water's edge, the rooms don't have a sea view but the atmospheric 2-storey bar-restaurant does. There is a flexible dining programme with Full Moon pool parties & regular poolside BBQs, for those who simply don't want to leave the water's edge. It's also worth noting that if you can't get a room, non-guests are welcome to use the swimming pool at a bargain rate of US$4/day — perfect for cooling dips when the tide is out & temperatures are searing. $$$$

⌂ **Arabian Nights** (11 rooms) ☎ 024 2240190; m 0777 854041; e anights@ zanzibararabiannights.com/anights-arabian@ hotmail.com; www.Zanzibararabiannights.com. Tucked down a narrow alley to the beach beside Kitete

Beach Bungalows, Arabian Nights is one of Paje's more mid-range, sedate options. Its 11 rooms are in yellow coral-rock cottages with neat thatched roofs. Some surround the large, private pool & 2 suites face directly onto the beach with a private plunge pool. Inside, all have cool, very spacious bedrooms, lockable walk-in wardrobes & tiled en-suites; TV & AC are added extras. There is a small souvenir shop & 2 PCs for internet use (no memory card downloading); the upstairs Swahili restaurant is open to all & the efficient on-site PADI dive school has classrooms for courses & a resident team of 2 instructors & a dive master (see page 276).
$$$$

🏠 **Kitete Beach Bungalows** (21 rooms) ☎ 024 2240226; m 0773 444737/074373; e reservations@kitetebeach.com/ kitetebeach@hotmail.com; www.kitetebeach.com. Owned & run by a kind, smart Zanzibari lady, Elhaam, Kitete has moved on from being just an old villa offering basic rooms. Guests are still welcome at the original house opposite Paje By Night, known as Kitete Cottage, with its bright entrance & 6 simple rooms, but walk a little further along the beach & you'll reach Kitete's 4 new, blush-pink villas. Here, 15 immaculate rooms are cool, modern & offer much better facilities. The downstairs rooms all have a dbl & sgl bed, whilst the upper floor has only dbl rooms. Sunny yellow interiors, mains electricity, 2 fans, mosquito nets, serious burglar bars & a small outside terrace/balcony feature in all. The rooms are spotlessly clean, with crisp linen, neatly folded towels, modern clip-on bedside lights & a comprehensive guest information sheet. There is also a lovely family villa with 3 cheerfully decorated bedrooms, 1 en-suite bathroom & 1 shared, & a central dining area. New for 2007, funky Le Galawa Restaurant occupies the prime spot next to the beach, & offers stunning views along the sand from its first-floor location. The good Kenyan chef serves up traditional Swahili dishes (US$5.50–12) alongside specials such as lobster thermidor (US$30), whilst upbeat African tunes keep the holiday vibe alive. There are evening cocktails & *shesha* pipes on offer, & at full moon a lovely beach braai. $$$

🏠 **Paje By Night or PBN Bizzare Hotel** (23 rooms) m 0777 460710; e info@pajebynight.net; www.pajebynight.net. Opened in 1984, this is a totally unpretentious joint where jovial Italian manager Marco warmly welcomes 'the young & the not so young any more'. The row of hammocks at the entrance hint at the pervading mood before you even get inside, for this is a slightly hippy, take-it-

as-it-comes place. Come here for the relaxed vibe & social atmosphere rather than for chic style, modern facilities or endless activities. Set 50m back from the beach, & without a sea view, the hub of PBN is the bar. Chunky coconut-wood sofas are dotted all around, as are moulded concrete tables & chairs, & tall plastic sunflowers. Tiger-stripe faux-fur chairs & white shell chandeliers furnish the adjoining *makuti* TV lounge, which plays satellite international news & sport virtually all day. An open-sided *makuti* structure, screened with panels of pastel fabrics, is used as a simple massage area, whilst the neighbouring rondavel with its spider's-web rope pattern across the window frames is a quiet reading spot. A nice curio shop (closed Wed) & a games area are all in a shaded garden building.

The food quality is good with a definite Italian bent: fresh pasta & pizza are always available. Spur-of-the-moment lunches are occasionally prepared by Marco himself who will knock up some great homemade ravioli if the mood takes him. Seafood & Swahili BBQs are a weekly occurrence whilst the social cocktail bar is open 24hrs. Herbs & vegetables that aren't bought from local spice farms can be spotted around the gardens: tomatoes, peppers, lemongrass & very hot chillies. Amusingly, 80% of the papaya crop is used as Marco's 'miracle cure' for sunburn.

The gardens attract a number of small birds & butterflies &, for 1 month a year, Marco guarantees that twittering yellow weaver birds 'have a big party in the eucalyptus tree'. Around the garden area are 10 spacious standard rooms each with a dbl/twin bed, & 11 king-size rooms. The latter refer to the larger size of the room not the bed, for only 9 of the rooms have a king-size bed while the other 2 are trpls. All of the rooms now have hot water from small Chinese electric boilers. There is mains electricity available throughout the complex, & every room has polished concrete floors with colourful mats, cheerful batik pictures, lockable wardrobes, a fan, & a clean, tiled en-suite bathroom. Room 1 is a newly decorated family bungalow with 2 bedrooms, a shared bathroom & spacious entrance hall. Each of the bedrooms has 2 sgl beds with mosquito nets, primary coloured walls, vibrant curtains, a small desk, wardrobe & ceiling fan. Designed & proudly built by Marco, the 2-storey 'jungle bungalows' are very rustic. Within the downstairs coral-stone walls are twin beds & a small, hot-water bathroom; fumble upstairs in the dark & there's an additional dbl bed in the *makuti* roof space. Although a baby's cot was once borrowed from the village for a visiting child, the basic facilities & party spirit here are not really conducive to holidaying with infants. Primary guest activities seem to be sleeping & sunbathing on the beach by day, then chilling over cocktails & fresh juices before building up to serious parties by night. On a practical note, there's free internet access, a safety deposit box in the office, night-time security & a doctor in the village. Local & major currencies accepted. Visa, MasterCard & Amex all subject to 5% surcharge. $$$

Paje Beach Bungalows (20 rooms) m 0777 461917; e pajebeach@hotmail.com; www.pajebeachbungalows.com. Opposite Paje By Night, but better located in a beachfront plot, is Paje Beach Bungalows. The 20 rooms, predominantly twin bedded, are arranged around a central quad of red & cream hexagonal tiles. The gardens are slowly maturing & the rooms are simple but functional with clean en-suite bathrooms, mains electricity, UK-style 3-pin sockets, hot water & ceiling fans. The new, open-sided restaurant is right on the beach to enjoy a cooling breeze & great sea views. Minimal activities are arranged here, but it's right on the beach for swimming & sunbathing, & there's a dive centre only a few mins away. $$$

Hotel Kinazi Upepo (7 rooms) m 0777 875515; e info@cristalresort.com; www.kinazi.com. In a shady grove of beachside coconut palms, Kinazi Upepo has recently been leased to the couple running Cristal Resort next door. In early 2008, it had 6 simple, thatched bungalows remaining from its previous incarnation, 3 new timber cabins (very similar to those at Cristal) & a room of moulded concrete with Moroccan interior, known as the Blue Lagoon Room. All of the rooms are now en suite with hot water, fans & mosquito nets. It is possible that more accommodation will be built here in the coming year. There's a recently refurbished, rustic beach bar, popular with locals, serving the usual array of cocktails & fresh juices, & a restaurant serving open-oven pizzas. Hammocks & loungers seem to be enough to occupy the guests here, & on a beautiful stretch of beach it's easy to see why. $$$

Cristal Resort (18 rooms) m 0777 875515; e info@cristalresort.net; www.cristalresort.net. Just south of Paje village, a substantial magnolia wall surrounds Cristal Resort's sizeable beachfront plot. Opened in 2006, this French–American owned place has received mixed reviews, perhaps because its marketing imagery sets expectations too high. That said, it's clear that a great deal of thought is going into producing neat accommodation & a pleasant environment, & aspirations to improve & expand are evident. There are 2 room types: 5 rather

uninspiring 'deluxe' cubes with thatched roofs & glass windows, & 13 timber 'Ecologic' cabins. The latter have more character by far & are dotted around the beach, not stood in an orderly row, though they miss out on the AC & bath. Interiors in both are colour co-ordinated & the safari-tent layout of the eco-cabins with the bathroom concealed behind the coral-rock headboard is particularly nice. There's a good-size swimming pool & an impressive dhow cocktail bar in the lounge behind; it's just a shame the overhead electricity cables break the view between them & the sea. New for 2008, there is a small souvenir shop & dive centre on site, Peponi, run by Italian Rasta, Franco, though it is not PADI licensed for those who want to take courses. $$$$

Hakuna Majiwe Lodge (20 rooms) m 0777 454505; e booking@hakunamajiwe.net; www.hakunamajiwe.net. Situated about 2km south of central Paje, & now accessed from the main tar road to Jambiani, Italian-owned Hakuna Majiwe opened in late 2004 to rave reviews. Meaning 'a place without stones', a reference to the wide sandy beach & expansive inter-tidal flats here, it certainly has a lovely beach position & the benefit of relative isolation. The large, en-suite beach bungalows are very nice indeed, with colour co-ordinated fabrics, varnished floorboards, fluffy towels, fans & impressive 4-poster beds. Wide individual decks have inviting swinging beds & a cushioned bench, whilst loungers are tucked amid the low beach vegetation to provide some privacy. There is a huge (slightly lacking in atmosphere) open-sided *makuti* restaurant & *baraza* lounge; a swimming pool set back from the beach & 2 on-site tailors running up made-to-measure beachwear from *kanga* fabric (www.mago-eastafrica.com). Sadly, we have heard allegations of staff being mistreated here; so in spite of the location & facilities, we must refrain from a wholehearted recommendation until we've been able to learn the truth behind these allegations. $$$$–$$$$$

Kilima Kidogo (5 rooms) ☎ +27 (84) 225 5500; m 0777 460079; e status@lantic.net/ dina.evans1@yahoo.com; www.kilimakidogo.co.za. Hakuna Majiwe's southern neighbour, Kilima Kidogo is essentially a fully staffed villa, though rooms can be booked individually. Owned by South African twins, Dina & Joey, it's very much their home from home & retains that relaxed, comfortable feel throughout. With 4 en-suite bedrooms in the main villa & a small gateside cottage in the bougainvillea-filled garden, it represents very good value for groups looking for quality accommodation & beachfront privacy. Under high *makuti* thatch, the central villa area has a pool table, beautifully set table beside the open kitchen & a small lounge full of games, jigsaws & books to while away lazy afternoons; bedrooms are tastefully furnished with rustic beds, fluffy pillows, quality linen & colourful scatter cushions. There is AC, fans & an electronic safe as well as open wardrobes & shuttered windows. There is a licensed bar & small restaurant under *makuti* on the beach, & a flat roof overlooking the sea for sunrise sea views. For 2008/09, a swimming pool is planned, which will be a welcome addition with the tidal extremes of this coast. 'Mr Nice' is the friendly on-site manager who can turn his hand to island tours & catering, though booking is best arranged through South Africa. $$$

✕ WHERE TO EAT All of the hotels above welcome non-guests to eat and drink. For some local flavour, try **Kizingitini Disco**. Just south of Cristal Resorts, this gated complex is a large local disco with music, dancing and food available, along with an amount of sculpture and paintings for sale to visitors.

WHAT TO SEE AND DO The primary activities in Paje are sunbathing on the beautiful beach and swimming in the sparkling sea. If staring out at the waves breaking along the fringe reef pricks your curiosity, there is a good dive school in the vicinity for underwater adventures, or the new Dutch-run kitesurfing school is already a success with lessons daily. And for those tired of the salt and sand, Dhow Inn's new pool is open to non-residents for a small fee.

✈ Paje Dive Centre ☎ 024 2240190/91; 📱 0777 416614; ✉ paje@pajedivecentre.com; www.pajedivecentre.com. Based within Arabian Nights (see pages 273–4), & with the same owner, Paje Dive Centre is an efficient PADI dive school which has large classrooms, a swimming pool for course work & a resident team of 2 experienced instructors & a dive master. Their reception bears the hallmarks of a reputable, safety-conscious operation with clear certification from DAN & PADI on display, a clear dive-briefing board & some enticing underwater photography. *Sgl/dbl dive US$50/80; sail boat snorkelling US$15; lagoon snorkelling trip US$20*

✈ Kite Centre Zanzibar ✉ kitecentrezanzibar@ gmail.com; www.kitecentrezanzibar.com; ⏱ seasonally mid-Dec–mid-Mar & Jul–Sep. Owned & operated by Dim of Bellevue Bungalows in Bwejuu, this a new activity outfit in Paje & the only dedicated centre to the sport on the island. It offers high-quality, branded kit, lessons & courses, experienced instructors & a thoroughly exhilarating seaside diversion. The courses are open to all abilities (you do need to be able to swim though), but if you are a novice to the sport, take along a T-shirt, plenty of sunscreen & a sense of humour! *Beginner course (3x1hr) US$140; advanced US$62/hr; board & kite rental US$70/2hrs, US$130/day, US$463/wk*

If you fancy something less watery, there is an old mausoleum nearby: a low rectangular edifice with a castellated wall, inset with antique plates and dishes. This design is thought to have originated in Persia, and may indicate that this part of the island was settled by Shirazi immigrants prior to the western side of the island, near present-day Zanzibar Town. Ask one of the local villagers to escort you for a small fee.

JAMBIANI

Straddling the provinces of Kibigija and Kikadini, Jambiani village is a sprawling, linear coastal village. Beginning a few kilometres south of Paje, it spreads for about 6km down the coast towards Ras Shungi. With around 6,000 permanent residents, of whom 50% are children, Jambiani has a relatively low population density. It benefits from having nursery, primary and secondary schools and a medical centre. All warmly welcome visitors to donate money to improve facilities; indeed the nursery was built entirely by money raised by the local village NGO, not by the

The Jambiani Marine and Beach Conservation (JAMABECO) organisation was founded in Jambiani village in 2001, receiving official recognition in February 2005. It aims to eradicate beach pollution and destruction in the area by providing villagers of all ages with environmental education. It hopes ultimately to improve villagers' incomes by promoting sustainable, long-term use of the local marine resources.

Jambiani village life revolves around the sea – fishing, seaweed farming, coir-rope manufacture and beach tourism – so the quality of the sea life and coastal environment has the ability to impact directly upon the vast majority of villagers. Well-managed resource use and protection is important in maintaining and developing all of these industries and incomes.

The 30 JAMABECO committee members operate a year-round education programme to advocate environmental conservation, plant trees along the beaches and regularly patrol and clean the beaches and village, removing the broken glass, bottles, batteries, iron materials and huge number of plastic bags that litter many of Zanzibar's coastal villages. Since 2003, they have also organised annual clean-up days to mark International Environment Day on 25 June. In addition, it looks like they will also follow Scuba Do Kendwa's lead and participate in September's annual International Coastal Clean-up Day.

With support and sustained education, we must hope that their efforts pay off in Jambiani, and that the message spreads to other coastal settlements. Without question, there is already significantly less litter here than in most of Zanzibar's other villages.

More information is available from Abdu M Vuai or Abdul Simai (e *jamabeco@yahoo.co.uk*). To visit the organisation in Jambiani, ask for directions to the JAMABECO office or head to Okala Restaurant.

government. There are several basic food stores, a local craft shop (selling delicious natural honey), a friendly post office and a bakery.

The village's name comes from the Arabic word *jambiya*: a dagger with a markedly curved blade. Local legend holds that early settlers found such a knife here; proof that others had been in the area before them. It now offers a wide choice of places to stay and emits an active community spirit. On a village tour with the local Eco+Culture team (see page 285), Jambiani is probably the best place on the island to gain genuine insights into Zanzibari village life and enjoy rewarding community interaction.

The beach is wide with powder-white sand and turquoise sea, and is the hub of daily life: work, rest and play. For visitors it's a place to catch some sun and explore the fascinating tidal flats; for children it's a place to cool down, run and play football; for local men it's a launch for their picturesque *ngalawas*, and for the large number of seaweed-farming women it's a valuable natural asset. The beach is kept clean thanks to two dedicated community organisations who arrange litter collections and local environmental education, and the sand is simply never as busy as the northern beaches of Nungwi and Kendwa.

GETTING THERE AND AWAY For the last year, the new paved road has made travel to and from Jambiani a pleasure compared to the past! The road runs inland of the village with a number of well-signposted turns to various coastal lodges. The old uneven, meandering 'highway' through the village remains, though quieter, and it is no longer possible to travel all the way to Paje along the coast, as a wall has been erected on the northern boundary of Mount Zion Long Beach Bungalows.

Southeastern Zanzibar **JAMBIANI**

10

It's possible to reach Jambiani by private vehicle or tourist minibus. In addition, *dala-dala* number 309 runs from Zanzibar Town about five times a day, and the public bus Route 9 to Paje sometimes continues as far as Jambiani: it's important to check each individual bus's destination though. It's also worth noting that most public transport heads only as far south as Auberge Coco Beach. To get to the more southerly resorts, you will have to either make a special plan with the driver, walk, or wait for one of the few daily *dala-dalas* that continue on to Makunduchi.

At the southern end of Jambiani village, the beach fizzles out and low coral cliffs, covered in vegetation, come right down to the sea. The dirt road heads inland past the Hotel Red Monkey to meet with the main road for the final 10km to Makunduchi. There are no hotels along this stretch of road, and public transport is extremely limited. If you want to keep heading south to Makunduchi, you may be lucky and find a lift on one of the occasional vehicles on the main road, otherwise, if you decide to walk, it takes a very hot three to four hours.

WHERE TO STAY Until the recent arrival of Kikadini Villas, nothing on this stretch of coast qualified as upmarket. However, Kikadini does now offer some of the island's finest accommodation, and in doing so has certainly raised the bar for standards in this part of Zanzibar. Of the mid-range options, Blue Oyster and Casa del Mar are ahead of the pack, with Hotel Red Monkey at the far south of town, probably being the best of the budget-choice places to stay. The places below are listed from north to south, though development seems to be constant, so expect a few more names by the time you arrive.

Mbuyuni Beach Village (16 rooms) 024 2240149; m 0777 843622; e mbuyunibeachvillage@yahoo.co.uk/ uhurul3@hotmail.com; www.mbuyuni.com. Opened in Dec 2007, Mbuyuni is 200m north of Pakachi & currently reached on the bumpy coastal track, though there are plans to build a road directly into the hotel from the tar road, & this may be completed by the time you travel. Accessed from the beach road, you will first pass the restaurant, about 50m south of the accommodation, sitting atop the coral cliff. Decorated with paintings of dancers & fish, the à-la-carte cuisine is both Swahili & international, ranging from US$3.50 for salads to US$20 for lobster, & there's a lengthy cocktail menu (try a Zanzibar Pirate: local gin & Cointreau with lime, orange & passion juice). The 'village' itself has 2 rows of whitewashed, thatched bungalows running perpendicular to the sea, with established flowerbeds & wide sandy paths. The rooms are simple with tiled floors, white walls & technicolour sheets. Painted dancers decorate the walls, there is a hat stand, fan, mosquito net & en-suite shower; some of the rooms also have a mini fridge. $$

Pakachi Beach Hotel (8 rooms) m 0777 423331; e pakachi@hotmail.com; www.pakachi.com. Appropriately, *pakachi* means border, for this pleasant little hotel is situated on the coral rock roughly halfway between the centres of Paje &

Jambiani. The local Zanzibari manager, Mo, his Norwegian wife & Scottish business partner have created a friendly, rustic haven. The 6 pale yellow, thatched bungalows are set amid flower-filled gardens of lilies, palms, hibiscus & papaya trees. Inside, the rooms are nice, simple & spotlessly clean, with Zanzibari beds, crisp linen, sky-blue curtains, large ceiling fans & en-suite bathrooms. There is also a 2-bedroom family house available. On the other side of the bumpy road, the bar/restaurant sits on top of the coral rock overlooking the sea. The coastline is very rocky at this point, so it's not always ideal for shore swimming, but there is a range of boats & good-quality kayaks to paddle around & the inter-tidal zone makes for fascinating beachcombing at low tide. The chef, Salome, rustles up both local & international dishes, with recommendations coming in for his pizzas. $$

Villa de Coco (11 rooms) m 0777 844413; e villadecoco@hotmail.com. Beside the electrical substation, about 400m off the tar road south of Paje, Villa de Coco is an Italian-run lodge, currently catering to fellow citizens on all-inclusive package holidays with the Italian operator, Phone & Go. That said, if there's space outside high season, the friendly owner, Marco, will happily accept ad-hoc visitors. The majority of the rooms are in 3 rows of en-suite coconut-wood bungalows amid lush gardens; inside they are small but neat with attractive coconut floorboards, clean beds, fans, open wardrobes & a small terrace. There are also 2 separate rooms, set back across the dusty car park in a new 2-storey villa, which also houses the massage room &, unusually, an inflatable jacuzzi (US$12/30mins). The *makuti*-thatched restaurant allows diners to eat pasta beneath the setting sun of the Serengeti mural, whilst the chill-out lounge by the beach is a great place to relax. Early 2008 saw the construction of a swimming pool which will doubtless be a great asset at low tide. $$$

🏠 **Mount Zion Long Beach Bungalows** (13 rooms) m 0777 439001/439034/0713 061900; e znzmountzion@hotmail.com/ znzmountzion@yahoo.se; www.mountzion-zanzibar.com. Mount Zion is the most northerly of Jambiani's resorts, situated along the village road just before you reach the newly constructed brick wall that now stops traffic continuing to Paje along the coast. The 9 coral-rock bungalows sit amid overgrown gardens & offer moderately clean, sparsely furnished en-suite accommodation with ceiling fans & Heath Robinson-style mosquito nets. There are also 2 pagoda-like *makuti* structures on the beach, which contain a total of 4 *banda* rooms & a small shared WC/shower. These are very basic with coir-rope beds & little else inside. The varnished palm-frond door offers limited security so guests are advised to secure any valuables elsewhere. The buzzing beach bar is adorned with Rasta Revolution posters & seems to be the preferred hangout for a good number of local Rastafarians too. Mount Zion is an adequate establishment & in a reasonably attractive situation, but the rather gloomy bungalows & rickety *bandas* remain overpriced. *Banda* $$; *bungalow* $$$

🏠 **Seaview Lodge** No contact details. Neighbouring Kipepeo Lodge, Seaview opened its restaurant & 4 small, square bungalows in Oct 2006. There is nothing fancy here but the local owners are trying hard to offer clean, simple accommodation, if a little overpriced. Decorated with painted sealife outside, the bungalows have low dbl beds, starched linen, built-in wardrobes, en-suite showers, a portable TV & small fan as standard. There are a few loungers in front of each, & even a beach shower for rinsing off salt water (but bear in mind the water immediately in front of the lodge is predominantly used for seaweed farming so you'll have to wade out quite far for a dip in the sea). The beach restaurant is open for lunch & dinner, with market availability determining the menu, & it's a casual spot to watch the local beach activity. $$$

🏠 **Kipepeo Lodge** (5 rooms) ☎ +44 (0)208 1239180; m 0777 457733; e maha@ kipepeo.it/kimsamour@yahoo.com; www.kipepeo.it. Jointly owned by local lad Kim, from Kim's Restaurant (see page 283), & an Italian businessman, Kipepeo Lodge is a newly opened, villa-style accommodation option in the village. The main lodge building, with its central open-plan kitchen & lounge, is really better geared towards a family or group of friends sharing, though rooms can, in theory, be booked individually. There are 5 irregularly shaped bedrooms (1 en suite), 2 bathrooms & an individual 2-person bungalow which can be rented separately (though be aware pool use is not always possible if you do). The rooms are cool, aided in part by a particularly high *makuti* roof in the communal areas & ceiling fans elsewhere, though the bedroom décor is a little more dark & cramped than ideal. Outside, there's a raised jacuzzi pool for refreshing dips, inviting palm-slung hammocks & a raft of sun loungers on some carefully raked sand above the beach. Discounts on rates of up to 30% are available in Apr, May, Jun & Nov; & negotiations are possible for exclusive use of the main house. $$$

🏠 **Blue Oyster Hotel** (19 rooms) ☎ 024 2240163; m 0748 432911; e blueoysterhotel@gmx.de; www.zanzibar.de. In lovely gardens of oleander & hibiscus, Blue Oyster remains one of the friendliest, most cared for & best-value hotels in its range. The main 2-storey building has ground-floor rooms around a rear palm courtyard & a wonderfully breezy first-floor restaurant, from which the wide veranda overlooking the ocean encourages leisurely lunches & relaxed afternoons reading & painting (watercolours available on request). Further accommodation is available in a trio of smaller 2-storey buildings, all of which come with en-suite facilities & balconies. There is a lovely raised stretch of sand in front of the hotel, which has been laid with loungers, shaded by *makuti* parasols & softened with tropical planting — a perfect sunbathing spot, especially if you also opt for one of Zena's coconut-oil massages (US$15). With friendly staff, clean rooms, good beds, running water & electricity, & an attractive location, this is a fine deal for the price. In the restaurant, snacks & sandwiches cost around US$3, delicious salads US$4 or pizzas & good evening meals like coconut-infused octopus with rice around US$5. $$$

🏠 **Oasis Beach Hotel** (6 rooms) ☎ 024 2240259; m 0777 858720. This rather rundown resort lies about 750m south of the Blue Oyster, just along the beach. The en-suite rooms with free-standing fan are literally 20m from the beach, but the luxury ends there; inside, ripped plastic sheeting on the floor & nowhere to attach the shower head show a lack of care & thought. In early 2008, a bar & new restaurant were under construction though we have little faith that the rooms or service will improve to match. $$

⌂ **Blue Earth Bungalows** PO Box 574, Zanzibar; ☏ 024 2240351; m 0777 486225/846597. Just north of the Rising Sun Hotel, Blue Earth Bungalows are relatively new. They were closed at the time of researching this edition, but may well have opened by the time you travel. Any news from travellers who stay would be most welcome.

⌂ **Rising Sun Hotel** (6 rooms) PO Box 20, Jambiani, Zanzibar; m 0777 497488. Next to the new primary healthcare unit, about 50m south of the Oasis Beach & similar in price & standard. Behind a white wall, & well signposted, the 6 en-suite rooms are in very basic bungalows. The rooms are quite dark, in part because of the timber-clad ceilings, the fans have only 2 out of 3 prongs & the mattresses have seen better days. It's a rather cramped set-up & can really only be recommended if other resorts & hotels are full. $$

⌂ **The Sau Inn Hotel** (39 rooms) ☏ 024 2240169; e sauinn@zanlink.com. Once the smartest hotel in Jambiani, the long-serving Sau Inn is beginning to show its age: faded interiors, dusty corridors, a lifeless restaurant & disinterested management. The 2-storey thatched buildings are surrounded by lush, established gardens. Inside, rooms are simply furnished by largely clean Zanzibari beds, free-standing fans & tiled bathrooms; the first-floor rooms have a little more space & newer mattresses. The 'Elegance Pool' has a defunct-looking swim-up bar & is surrounded by a low wall (just high enough to trip over) & some particularly tasteless swan planters. However, it is a welcome relief in the afternoon heat, when the tide is out. There is a narrow strip of manufactured 'beach' too, just wide enough for the hotel's loungers & parasols, which overlooks the actual beach & sea beyond. For diving trips there is an on-site dive centre, Sau Inn Diving Centre, although it was not staffed at the time of researching, & is not PADI accredited. The hotel is used by some tour groups which often results in a lively atmosphere. $$$

⌂ **East Coast Visitors Inn** (28 rooms) ☏ 024 2240150; m 0777 438640/417312; e visitorsinn@zitec.org; www.visitorsinn-zanzibar.com. Situated about 150m south of the Sau Inn along the village main street, past the health centre & the school, this is

quite large for a budget place, in spite of the recent closure of the guesthouse. Reception is tucked under the 'Karibuni' arch & is a popular spot for locals to watch TV, while the rooms are in en-suite white bungalows above the beach. The rooms are a little rundown with saggy mattresses & plastic mats on the concrete floors, & some have a dining-table too! Alternatively, meals are available in the cheerfully painted Visitor's Palate restaurant for around US$5. There is a nice stretch of beach here & shade to be had under the casuarina trees. $$$

⌂ **New Jambiani Beach Hotel** No contact details. Owned & run by a German woman, Marlies Lehmann, Jambiani Beach Hotel first opened in 1987 as a joint venture with her Zanzibari husband. Following their separation & contentious land division, the place fell into disrepair & closed. However, in early 2008, Marlies began a rebuilding programme, hence the addition of 'New' to the hotel name. The 6 resulting bungalows, currently sitting amid the crumbling ruins of the old ones, are solid, clean & functional with rustic beds, a small lounge area, spotless bathrooms, free-standing fans & a terrace. The gardens are non-existent at present, though planting is planned, & there is a beach restaurant, popular with local lads. At the time of our visit, the atmosphere was slightly uneasy, so time will tell if this reincarnated lodge survives. $$

⌂ **Casa Del Mar** (12 rooms) m 0777 455446; e infocasa-delmar@hotmail.com; www.casa-delmar-zanzibar.com; lodge ⊕ Jun–Mar. Opened in 2005, this is among the more aesthetically pleasing beach lodges in this part of Zanzibar, consisting of 12 rooms in 2 thatched dbl-storey houses, made almost entirely of organic material. It's owned & managed by a young, gentle Palestinian couple, with impressive enthusiasm, skill & environmental awareness. All of the unique lodge furniture & *objets d'art* were made on site & every palm uprooted during its construction has been successfully replanted. Community relations are very strong, with the vast majority of the staff (14 out of 17) being Jambiani residents & the school & clinic receiving regular support. These credentials aside, the accommodation & friendly vibe are good reasons to stay too.

The 6 ground-floor rooms are en-suite dbls with a mosquito net, fan & balcony overlooking the gardens, while the first-floor suites are dbl storey with a downstairs lounge (or children's room) & balcony, & a galleried bedroom high in the *makuti* thatch. The circular restaurant is in a cool, shady spot with colourful cushions, tropical planting & good food; there's a detailed notice board of local

activities & island excursions & the lodge has its own boat for snorkelling trips (US$15pp/day). $$
🏠 **Casa Villa** (2 rooms) m 0777 455446; e infocasa-delmar@hotmail.com; www.casa-delmar-zanzibar.com. Opened in Jul 2008, Casa Villa is an offshoot of Casa del Mar (see above). It has 3 dbl bedrooms (1 en suite), a large kitchen, bar & lounge, huge first-floor terrace for seaview sundowners. Excursions & activities can be arranged at Casa del Mar Hotel, about 15mins on foot through the village, whilst the villa has its own housekeeper, waiter & security guard, as well as a dedicated chef to rustle up super Swahili feasts: any stay here is on a FB basis. $$
🏠 **Kikadini Villas** e reservations@ kikadinivillas.com; www. escape-zanzibar.com. On a large beachfront plot in the centre of the village, the 4 (soon to be 5) unique villas that make up Kikadini are unparalleled on the island. Stylishly designed, owned & managed by a lovely Norwegian couple, Sylvia & Torgeir Barner, Kikadini is in essence a boutique hotel: striking architecture, delicious food, attentive staff & tremendous individuality. Each of the beach-facing villas is architecturally different, from 3-bedroomed Villa Palm with its Moorish feel, seductive roof terrace & inner courtyard to the privacy of Villas Maroc & Pwani & homely feel of the original villa, Kikadini. The interiors feature eclectic *objets d'art* & huge Zanzibari oil paintings alongside soft linens, comfortable furniture & cool en-suite bathrooms. All the rooms have electricity, fans, small fridges & plenty of space, with Wi-Fi, bottled mineral water & beach towels provided as standard. All bar 1 of the rooms has a fabulous ocean view & there are terrific roof terraces for shady lunches & stunning stargazing. There is a swimming pool planned, & as the new planting matures to soften the sandy garden, this will only serve to extend Kikadini's position as the best accommodation in the area. In a bid to maintain a quiet, calm haven for other guests, children under 10 cannot stay unless a villa is exclusively booked. All rates are HB, which is a great deal given the high quality of the food! Kikadini's villas are excellent value, with good prices for exclusive use, making it a highly recommended base for exploring Jambiani village & the southeast coast. $$$$$
🏠 **Jambiani Guesthouse** (5 rooms) m 0773 147812; e anne@zanzibar-guesthouse.com; martin@zanzibar-guesthouse.com; www.zanzibar-guesthouse.com. Built in 2006, Jambiani Guesthouse is in the coconut line immediately above the beach in the southern end of the village. It's a small,

whitewashed, thatched building, clearly signposted off the main village road, best booked by a group of friends or a family. It's a simple villa with 5 clean dbl rooms (1 en suite), 2 shared bathrooms, a small kitchen-lounge & a veranda overlooking the sandy beach & ocean. The local caretaker, Dudde, lives on site & can help with local tours &, if necessary, catering. The weekly rates are not really discounted, but you can check availability online. $$
🏠 **Dhow Beach Village** (6 rooms) m 0777 417763; e dhowbeachvillage@yahoo.com/ info@dhowbeachvillage.com; www.dhowbeachvillage.com. Set in the coconut line above the beach, Dhow Beach Village opened in 2006 & is a good option in this price range. Set in 2 neat rows, the en-suite rooms are small but stylishly simple, with coconut-wood furniture, retractable mosquito nets, nicely striped bedding, batik curtains, a small ceiling fan & a little outside terrace. The tiled bathrooms are clean & have constant hot water for post-beach (or party!) showers. The quite attractive 'Spicy Restaurant' at the centre of the small complex is lined with billowing hessian, & serves both Swahili & European cuisine favourites, & there's an octagonal bar, Day n Nite, on the beach. Popular for 'cockatails', the bar is also the focus for the regular beach parties (18.00–06.00 in high season Sat & at full moon) when camp fires & the tunes of DJ Kweli attract locals & budget travellers alike. Pricing of rooms is dependent on size, not location, with Room 3 on the beach being arguably the best but not the most expensive. Room rate discounts of up to 50% are available in low season. $$
🏠 **Auberge Coco Beach** (5 rooms) m 0777 413125; e cocobeach@zitec.org. This long-standing small lodge offers clean, simple en-suite dbl rooms. White bedding, blue towels with matching curtains, fans, sparkling bathrooms & a small terrace leading onto a shady garden of coconut palms & sweet almond trees. It's a calm, quiet spot. Several travellers over the years have recommended the restaurant here, which has an extensive menu, & a past affiliation with the French cuisine of Stone Town's (now sadly closed) Fisherman Restaurant giving it good credentials. Decked out in shipping memorabilia from buoys to turtle shells, there is no mistaking the seafood emphasis of the catering here (smoked sailfish US$2.50 starter; jumbo prawn masala US$14 main). Visa & MasterCard accepted with 5% surcharge. $$
🏠 **Grand Jambiani Beach Bungalows** (8 rooms) m 0773 048894/148013; e grandbungalows@ gmail.com; www.accommodationzanzibar.com.

Immediately next door to **Auberge Coco Beach**, Grand Jambiani opened its doors in 2006 to offer simple, hospitable family-run accommodation. The 8 basic & clean en-suite rooms, the tidy flowerbeds & small restaurant are well tended by Rashid & his family, & it is clear that they are trying hard to offer guests a positive stay. Fans, mosquito nets & hot water are standard inside the rooms & shaded deckchairs dot the outside area. Guests can dine under the huge beachfront sweet almond tree, take a fishing trip on the local *ngalawa* or simply talk to the team to get an insight into local life. Be aware that the end, 'Honey Moon' room is on the first floor & accessed by a steep pole ladder which requires careful climbing. $$

🏠 **Shehe Bungalows** (21 rooms) ☎ 024 2240149; m 0777 843622; e shehebungalows@hotmail.com; www.shehebungalows.co.uk. Along the beach, about 1km south of the centre of Jambiani, Shehe was one of the first backpacker refuges in the village & has been operating for over a decade. Popular on the budget-travel trail for many years, it has now lost much of its once-legendary laid-back air & buzz of activity, as it falls into an ever-increasing state of disrepair. The accommodation is divided between a short terrace of beachfront rooms & a larger complex of small bungalows. The former are in pretty poor shape outside – rusted burglar bars & gates – though slightly better inside with clean Zanzibari beds & cold-water en-suite bathrooms. In the main complex, further south along the beach, past the Coffee Pot Café & a private house, there are a good number of whitewashed, en-suite bungalows, of varying ages & comfort. The newest of the rooms are set around a sandy courtyard towards the back. Given the geographical separation of Shehe's accommodation, you may have to ask around a little to find someone who can help you view rooms or check-in. There is around a US$5 discount on rates from Mar to Jun. $$

🏠 **Kimte Guesthouse** (7 rooms) ☎ 024 2240212; m 0777 430992; e kimte@lycos.com. Straddling the road, about 500m beyond Shehe, at the quieter end of the village, this Rasta-managed lodge offers a warm welcome & its ever-popular bar boasts a good location on a great stretch of beach. The rooms are all within a sgl-storey white house, with orange windows & a tin roof, on the right of the road as you head south of the village centre. Inside it's cool but otherwise rather basic, with corridor walls adorned with vast murals & en-suite rooms & a 7-bed dormitory (US$15pp) housing little more than ceiling fans & beds. With such limited in-room

facilities & little sign of general upkeep, the rooms are probably a touch overpriced. $$

🏠 **Gomani Guesthouse** (13 rooms) ☎ 024 2240154; m 0777 455957. 200m further south of the Kimte, this is a clean & friendly place with a memorable location on a low coral cliff offering excellent views over the ocean. The simple rooms with fan, net & bathroom are good value for what they offer. $$

🏠 **Coral Rock Hotel** (8 rooms; 1 villa) ☎ 024 2240154; e coraltrees@yahoo.co.uk; www.coralrockhotelzanzibar.com. Behind a new wall & large gate towards the southern end of Jambiani, Coral Rock began a process of relatively recent redevelopment. A South African–Zanzibari partnership, the hotel lives up to its name, with the bungalows, pool & restaurant all perched along the rocks above the beach. Divided among 4 whitewashed, thatched bungalows, the 8 standard rooms are clean & simple, with low beds, local paintings for decoration, mosquito nets, AC & en-suite shower rooms. There is a small red concrete terrace in front of each with a few deckchairs to admire the sea view. There is also a 5-bedroom house behind the bar, which can be taken exclusively by families. The Rocky Bar at the end of the complex offers terrific views of the craggy, notch-cut headlands to the south, & the extensive seaweed farming in front of the hotel. It's a funky hangout for sundowners with a nice vibe & chilled music. At the time of our visit in early 2008, Coral Rock was a mixture of new contemporary features (the triangular infinity pool & sun terraces) & crumbling remnants, like the broken paths. With luck the necessary upgrades will be made, & it'll make its mark as one of the better mid-budget options in Jambiani. $$$

🏠 **Hotel Red Monkey** (9 rooms) m 0777 497736; e soloman@sansibarulaub.de/ marketing@rundfluege-online.de; www.rundfluege-online.de. This is the most southerly lodge in Jambiani, about 2km from the centre, on an increasingly bumpy track. It is also set on the low coral cliffs, & named after the Kirk's red colobus monkeys that live in the adjacent forest & pass through the grounds most days. Everything is clean & tidy, there's a nice view of the beach (which is reached by a short flight of steps), & the German–Zanzibari staff are very friendly. The rooms, complete with timber beds, large ceiling fan, mosquito nets & high-pressure en-suite showers (some also have mini fridges), are extremely clean & represent one of the better budget deals in this part of Zanzibar. There are a few raised flowerbeds & palms, & up in the restaurant area on the coral cliff, a skilful chef prepares fresh fish & other good meals for about US$4. $$

✘ WHERE TO EAT Virtually all of the places to stay listed above have affiliated restaurants, most of which serve a fairly standard range of seafood and island curries. Casa del Mar and The Blue Oyster are both recommended for food, with the restaurant at Auberge Coco Beach still going strong, in spite of its affiliated French cuisine outpost in Stone Town closing down. Kikadini Villas currently serves guests only, but should this change in the future, their food is really excellent. Good-quality meals at any of these, naturally with a seafood emphasis, cost US$5–10, drinks, snacks and lunches are also readily available, and if your taste buds get the better of your wallet, you can often pay with a credit card.

Unusually for a Zanzibari village, there are also some really very good local-style restaurants which, with a bit of notice, will prepare an excellent medley of island dishes for you to sample (talk to them in the morning if you want to eat that afternoon or evening). Kim's and Okala, listed below, warrant special mention – don't be discouraged by the ramshackle exteriors and sand floors; the food really is very tasty!

If you just want supplies, there are a number of small local shops. The **Jambiani Post Office & Mini Market** on the main village road, near the Auberge Coco Beach, doesn't quite warrant its prominent signposting throughout the village, but it does supplement the usual local fare with a selection of tinned foods and a few imported goodies (sweets and potato crisps), as well as selling stamps.

✘ Kiddo's Café Tucked off the main road through the village between Seaview Lodge & Mount Zion, or accessed from the beach, this is an understated, calm café where gourmet fruit juice concoctions are mixed by the dreadlocked, cool dude after whom the bar takes its name. It's a place to retreat, order a cafetiere of fresh coffee or something exotic (Kiddo's Mix of pineapple, passion & mango juices with coconut milk & ginger is divine!), grab a paperback from the recycled dhow bookshelf (an eclectic mix from Nick Hornby to Louis de Bernières is available), kick back & relax in the treehouse-like upper bar or under the sail-cloth shade in the sand garden below. **$$**

✘ Kim's Restaurant Owned by a charming local entrepreneur, Kim, this simple, shaded restaurant is the realisation of a childhood dream. Opened in 2006, his place serves authentic, Zanzibari cuisine for lunch & dinner (best ordered in advance), all freshly prepared by Kim & his mother. The spicy fish samosas (US$2.50), fish soup (US$2.50) & coconut-crusted fish with mango chutney (US$5) are particularly tasty. The small palm-clad shack & sand on the floor that make up the restaurant only add to the local flavour, & this is one of a few reliably good village dining options in Jambiani. Kim's is located between Kipepeo Lodge & Blue Oyster Hotel. **$$**

✘ Equinox Restaurant Owned by a local Rastafarian, known as Captain Cook, Equinox is tucked behind a woven makuti fence, behind the Zanzibar Action Project buildings. Follow the neat blue signs & you'll

find it with ease. Originally opened in 2006, Equinox's suffered a major setback following a fire, but with great determination on the part of its young, entrepreneurial owner, it has been rebuilt for 2008. It's a very basic, casual place, doubtless influenced by Cook's own friendly, informal manner. With a flag-flying rondavel bar & outdoor seating, it's primarily a place to chill out & chat in the village. There is some simple cooking equipment & if you're keen to eat (fish in masala US$5; grilled octopus US$5.50), Captain Cook will proudly read the glowing multi-national reviews in his little red guest book. **$$**

✘ Okala Restaurant m 0777 430519. In a small, unremarkable makuti building, just up from the beach (between the Rising Sun & Oasis Beach hotels), Okala's food far exceeds any expectations arising from its architecture! Run by a small co-operative of Jambiani families, the Zanzibari food here is really excellent by any standards, making the restaurant well worth a visit. The woven makuti walls, sand floor & crude shell mobiles may discourage some from entering, but we highly recommend that you do. With some notice, the team here can prepare a fabulous meze of Swahili curries, grilled seafood & tasty vegetable accompaniments. Filling up on fresh coconut rice, wilted spinach with lime & rich tomato fish curry is a real Zanzibari treat. Individual dishes, such as grilled octopus or fish, are US$4–5, with special items, like the amazing (and enormous!) coconut-crusted jumbo prawns costing US$11. If you like what you taste,

COIR-ROPE PRODUCTION

The fruit of the evocative coconut palm does not look as many imagine: it has a smooth, leathery, green skin. The brown nuts sold in supermarkets worldwide are simply the central element of the fruit. Between the well-known shiny shell and green exterior is a coarse fibrous husk known as coir; it is from this that rope is made.

The patient process begins when the husk is separated from the nut. The fibres are then buried in the sandy inter-tidal zone and covered with a cairn of coral rock. Over the coming six to ten months, micro-organisms in the surrounding sand cause the husk tissues to begin biodegrading, in a process known as retting, loosening the fibre strands. The remains are then uncovered, beaten and sun-dried. When dry and clean, the long fibres are simply rubbed together to form strands which can be twined to the required thickness of rope.

According to the Royal Botanical Gardens at Kew, the total of world coir-fibre production is about 250,000 tonnes, with over 50% of the coir fibre produced annually consumed in its countries of origin. This bears out on Zanzibar where the relatively waterproof nature of the coir and its resistance to saltwater damage make it an invaluable material for boat rigging, fishing nets and seaweed-farming lines. As a tourist, you are likely to benefit from its more recent application in the manufacture of sun loungers, hammocks and the beds used by budget hotels.

the Okala team can also offer short courses in Zanzibari cooking. The team here are also closely involved with JAMABECO (see box, *Jambiani Marine and Beach Conservation*, page 277) & several community projects, so ask them if you're interested in what's happening, or arrange to end your Eco+Culture village tour (see page 285) with a deliciously satisfying lunch. $$

✘ **Garden Restaurant** Follow the yellow sign from Sau Inn or access this place from the beach; either way it's very clearly marked. With lovely sea views from its beachfront plot, Garden Restaurant is breezy & popular with friendly staff & a mixture of both Zanzibari & European menu options available. $$

✘ **Pingo Restaurant & Gallery** m 0777 496645. Just south of Sau Inn, with its clear, colourful sign, Pingo is a popular local hangout serving simple, authentic local fare & cold beers. There is an adjoining neat shop selling carvings & paintings. $$

LOCAL SERVICES

Bureau de change If you need money, there's a bureau de change at the East Coast Visitors Inn, or Auberge Coco Beach might be able to give you cash back from a bank card (although you'll need to have a meal at the restaurant first).

Internet In 2006, a UK-based NGO, **Zanzibar Action Project**, opened a village library in Jambiani. This white bungalow, surrounded by a neat pole fence and cerise bougainvillea, is just alongside the main village road between the Rising Sun and Blue Oyster hotels, and offers a free book loan service to villagers. Books are in Swahili and English, with donations of more always welcome. There is also an internet terminal here, charging US$2.50 per 30 minutes, and with all of the money being redirected into worthy village projects.

WHAT TO SEE AND DO As with most of Zanzibar's coastal villages, the main focus of the tourist agenda is swimming and sunbathing. Diving and snorkelling can be arranged through local dive centres and the Sau Inn continues to allow non-residents to use its swimming pool for US$3 per person per day. But if you want a change from the beach and water, Jambiani has a number of good options, most especially its excellent Eco+Culture village tour which is probably the island's best insight into genuine rural life.

Eco+Culture Jambiani Cultural Tours ✆ 024 2233731; m 0777 410873; e ecoculturetours@gmail.com/ hajihafidh@yahoo.co.uk/kassimmande@hotmail.com; www.ecoculture-zanzibar.org. Meet in the small, signposted *makuti* hut under a grove of coconuts in the centre of the village (opposite the school), or be collected on foot from your hotel for these well-run, enlightening community-focused walks. Organised & guided by resident Kassim Mande (m 0777 469118) & his colleagues, a percentage of your fee goes directly towards community development initiatives, a direct result of the organisation's original NGO status. Depending on your enthusiasm & heat tolerance, the tours last anything from a few hours to the best part of a day & take in many aspects of everyday life. Spend time helping the women make coconut paste, reciting the alphabet in unison at the efficient kindergarten & meeting the *mganga*

(traditional healer). Kassim's presence, reputation within the community & ability to translate allow for genuine interaction with the Jambiani residents & a thoroughly engaging time. The trip can also be arranged in advance from Eco+Culture's Stone Town office on Hurumzi St (see page 125).

Do be aware that of late there are a few villagers operating apparently copycat walks. It is well worth taking the time to seek out Kassim or the Eco+Culture office, not only for his knowledge & friendliness, but also to be sure that your money is going to be directed back into vital village projects from the kindergarten to the planned handicraft shop for the women's co-operative.

Jambiani Wellness Centre e habszanzibar@yahoo.ca; www.handsacrossborderssociety.org; ⏰ 09.00–14.00 Mon/Tue & Thu/Fri. Opened in 2003 by a joint Canadian–Zanzibari NGO, Hands Across Borders, the

THE MWAKA KOGWA FESTIVAL AT MAKUNDUCHI

If you happen to be visiting Zanzibar during the last week of July, try to reach Makunduchi. Every year there's a large festival here called the Mwaka Kogwa when local people come from all over the island for a great get-together of singing, dancing, drumming, making new friends and meeting old ones. It's no problem for tourists to see the festival, and when it's taking place several of the tour companies listed in *Chapter 5* (see pages 125–7) run day trips to the village.

The festival is also called Mwaka Nairuz and it originates from Persia, marking the start of the New Year in the Shirazi calendar (for more details on the Shirazis in Zanzibar, see *Chapter 1, History*, page 5) and involves several rituals, including a mock fight where men from different parts of the village beat each other with banana stems. It is believed that this fight gives each combatant a chance to vent his feelings, and in this way the disagreements and arguments of the past year are exorcised so that the New Year can be started peacefully. (Although this is a mock fight, it can still get pretty serious. Fortunately the men are only fighting with banana stems – they used to do it with real clubs and cudgels!)

While the men are beating each other, the women have a far more genteel way of celebrating: dressed in their finest clothes, they parade around the village singing about love, families and village life.

The next stage of the festival is the ritual burning of a traditional hut, which has been built especially for the purpose. A local healer goes inside before the fire is lit and runs out again when the hut is burning strongly. It is thought that the burning of the hut symbolises the passing of the old year and also ensures that, during the coming year, should any house in the village catch fire its inhabitants will escape unharmed.

After the fighting and the hut-burning, a large feast is held with all the villagers bringing food and eating together. People from other parts of Zanzibar are welcomed, as a local tradition holds that any villager without a guest must be unhappy.

After the eating, the music starts – traditional *ngomas* and *taarab* (see *Music and dance*, pages 37–42), but these days may include some more modern amplified sounds as well. The locals dance into the night, and die-hard party animals move on to the beach to continue singing and dancing until dawn.

Jambiani Wellness Centre primarily offers chiropractic treatment, homeopathic remedies & other therapy free of charge to the local community. Tourists are welcome to visit for massage, acupuncture, breema or homeopathic treatments. A donation of at least US$15 is asked in lieu of a fee. The charitable work of the group now extends well beyond the clinic boundaries, with current community projects including a vocational school to educate adults about tourism & starting up a business.

Kumbi Cavern About two hours' walk outside Jambiani is a large underground cavern called Kumbi, which contains a natural spring. According to local legend, it was lived in at one time but today it is a traditional shrine and local people go there to pray and make offerings. You'll need a local guide to show you the way and it's an interesting trip; even if the cave doesn't leave you in awe, the walk is pleasant. Around the village, you can also see several old tombs decorated with plates and dishes, similar to the mausoleum at Paje.

MAKUNDUCHI

The ill-defined settlement of Makunduchi lies at the southeastern end of Zanzibar Island, and is divided into two distinct parts. On the coast is the small fishing village of 'old' Makunduchi, with some local huts and houses, a few holiday cottages, and a small beach from where you can sometimes spot dolphins. Then, about 2km inland is 'Makunduchi New Town', complete with one main road, some dusty side-streets, a bank, post and telephone office, police station, small shop and a few incongruous blocks of austere flats, built as part of a 1970s' East German aid scheme.

With the exception of July's Mwaka Kogwa Festival (see box, *The Mwaka Kogwa Festival at Makunduchi*, page 285), Makunduchi hardly receives any visitors. It is significantly quieter than Bwejuu or Jambiani – not that they are particularly noisy – and its community focuses on seaweed farming and fishing, not tourism.

GETTING THERE AND AWAY From Zanzibar Town, Makunduchi can be reached by public bus (Route 10), *dala-dala* (number 310), or by rented car, scooter or bike. There are no tourist minibuses working regularly on this route, although you could always hire one for exclusive use through a tour company. You can also reach Makunduchi from Jambiani; see *Getting there and away*, page 278.

✗ WHERE TO STAY Accommodation in Makunduchi is extremely limited and from the extremes of the tourism spectrum – a very basic government-run bungalow, which is often closed, and a full-on Italian activity resort.

🏠 **La Madrugada Beach Resort** (30 rooms) ☎ 024 224038; e contact@lamadrugada-resort.com; www.lamadrugada-resort.com. The only large resort in the southeast, La Madrugada Beach Resort is a noisy complex full of Italian & Spanish groups, mainly on all-inclusive packages through Italian operator Viaggiland. The 10, 2-storey whitewashed buildings surround 2 pools, 1 freshwater & 1 saltwater, but each emblazoned with the hotel name in mosaic. There are 3 rooms per building with the upper level accommodating the large suites, & standard dbl rooms, complete with small terrace, downstairs. There are several restaurant & bar areas & a discotheque for those who haven't heard enough pumping music during their time round the pool. There's an amount of coercion to participate in group activities or en-masse minibus tours to the island's attractions, so this probably isn't the right place for non-Italian couples, or anyone looking for peace & privacy. $$$$$

🏠 **ZTC Bungalow** The ZTC bungalow is in the old village, but it seems to be almost permanently closed. In theory, if you really wanted to stay here, you could make enquiries at the ZTC office in Zanzibar Town. $$

11

Southwestern Zanzibar

For most of Zanzibar's overseas visitors, the island's southwest corner holds little more than day-trip opportunities to see dolphins from Kizimkazi and troops of red colobus monkeys in Jozani Forest. Yet some of the best marine, animal and historical conservation projects on the island lie on the coast between Chukwani, 10km south of Stone Town, and the ruins at Unguju Ukuu, and on the coral reefs of Chumbe Island and the Menai Bay Conservation Area. Few people stay in this area, in part because accommodation options are limited, with most opting instead for the endless beaches of the east coast or the buzz of Zanzibar Stone Town. Away from the main tourist attractions, the villagers in these parts rarely encounter many visitors, and their welcome is one of genuine friendliness and interest. It's a refreshing contrast to the more crowded and visitor-centric feeling taking over significant parts of the island's north and east coasts.

KIZIMKAZI

The village of Kizimkazi lies at the southwestern tip of the island, about 12km west of Makunduchi. In a beautiful bay, it is one of the island's oldest settlements, being the former home of the Mwinyi Mkuu (the traditional ruler of Zanzibar). It is steeped in history, though there is little evidence of this today.

Kizimkazi has a sizeable population, a school, a dispensary, a reasonable selection of places to stay, and a burgeoning tourist industry based on dolphin-watching. Bottlenose and humpback dolphins are regularly seen off the coast here and Kizimkazi has become the major launch point for boats taking visitors out on viewing trips.

Technically, Kizimkazi consists of two villages: Kizimkazi Mkunguni and Kizimkazi Dimbani. Most boats go out to see the dolphins from the larger of the two, Kizimkazi Mkunguni, and this is generally just called Kizimkazi. As an increasing number of tourists have arrived over the last few years, so an increasing number of 'guides', touts and hustlers have taken to the streets as well – sadly some of them can be quite aggressive, rude and generally unpleasant. If you're driving, watch out for the squad that wait for custom on the roadside by the entrance to the village.

Kizimkazi Dimbani is 2km north along the coast from 'main' Kizimkazi (3km by road); it is smaller, much quieter and arguably prettier, and a few boats do depart from here as well. There are far fewer touts, probably because it's mainly groups who come here, and only one place to stay, the rather nice Karamba resort above the harbour. Dimbani is also the site of east Africa's oldest mosque.

GETTING THERE AND AWAY Most people come to Kizimkazi by tourist minibus or as part of a day tour; the alternative is to come by hired car, scooter or bike. To reach Kizimkazi Dimbani, turn off the main road between Zanzibar Town and

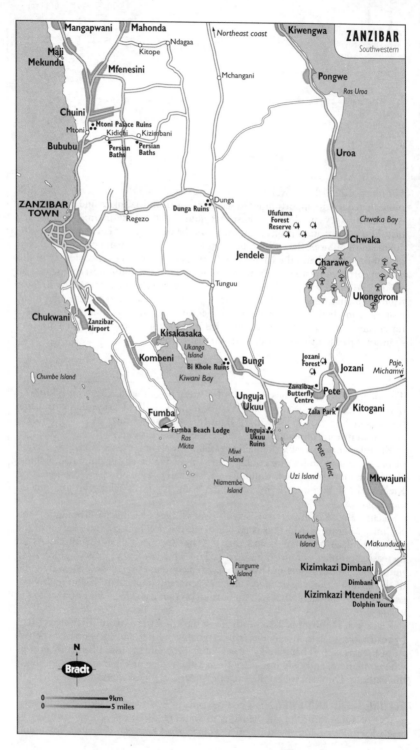

ZANZIBAR
Southwestern

Mangapwani   Mahonda   Kiwengwa

                        Ndagaa
Maji   Kitope
Mekundu
        Mfenesini   Northeast coast

                                Mchangani   Pongwe

                                                Ras Uroa
Chuini
        Mtoni Palace Ruins
Mtoni   Kididhi   Kizimbani   Uroa
Bububu   Persian   Persian
            Baths   Baths

                                Dunga   Chwaka Bay
                    Dunga Ruins
ZANZIBAR   Chwaka
TOWN   Regezo   Ufufuma
                                Forest
                                Reserve
                            Jendele   Charawe

                        Tunguu   Ukongoroni

Chukwani   Kisakasaka
        Zanzibar
        Airport   Jozani
            Kombeni   Ukanga   Forest   Paje,
                        Island   Jozani   Michamvi
Chumbe Island   Bi Khole Ruins Bungi
                    Kiwani Bay   Zanzibar   Pete
                            Unguja   Butterfly
                            Ukuu   Centre
Fumba   Zala Park   Kitogani
        Fumba Beach Lodge   Unguja
        Ras   Ukuu Ruins
        Mkita   Miwi
                    Island
                                            Mkwajuni
                Niamembe   Uzi Island
                Island
                                Pete Inlet

                                Vundwe
                                Island   Makunduchi

                Pungume   Kizimkazi Dimbani
                Island
                                        Dimbani
                            Kizimkazi Mtendeni
                                        Dolphin Tours

N

Bradt

0   9km
0   5 miles

Makunduchi at Kufile junction and follow this road to a fork, heavily adorned with miscellaneous accommodation and tour signs. Here, right goes to Kizimkazi Dimbani and the ancient Shirazi mosque; left goes to the main part of Kizimkazi (Kizimkazi Mkunguni).

It is also possible to get here independently from Zanzibar Town on one of the five daily *dala-dalas* (number 326), by public bus or tourist minibus. Some buses (Route 10) running between Zanzibar Town and Makunduchi stop in Kizimkazi Mkunguni, but if this cannot be arranged, get off the bus at Kufile junction and walk the tar road, predominantly downhill, to Kizimkazi Dimbani (3km) or Kizimkazi Mkunguni (6km).

WHERE TO STAY
Kizimkazi Dimbani

Karamba (14 rooms) m 0773 166406; e karamba@zanlink.com; www.karambaresort.com. This attractive clifftop lodge started life as a large restaurant, aimed almost exclusively at dolphin-viewing tour groups from town & coast hotels. Since Jul 2007 though, the dedicated new managers have transformed the smart, en-suite bungalows into one of this coast's most appealing places to stay. In spite of their linear layout, the rooms all have individual interiors thoughtfully decorated in nautical blues & whites with a splash of sunshine yellow in the luxury rooms. Some boast outdoor circular baths,

whilst others have blissful open-air showers hewn in coral rock. There's a sea view from every veranda though the harbour vista from the cushioned lounge/restaurant is arguably the finest of them all. Here, fresh sushi (US$20 sharing platter) & tapas dishes (US$3–6 each) are served at solid tables or casually round the dhow bar. Then, once the tour groups head home in the afternoon & real peace & quiet returns, cocktails overlooking the sunset dhow activity makes for a quintessentially Zanzibari experience. Yoga, reiki & Ayurvedic therapies are also available. *Standard* $$$; *lux* $$$$

Kizimkazi Mkunguni

Unguja Lodge (11 rooms) m 0774 477477/857234; e info@ungujalodge.com; www.ungujaresort.com. Unguja Lodge opened in Dec 2006 & is already offering accommodation & service which is up with the best on the island. Owned & managed by a friendly, unpretentious Dutch couple, Ralph & Elies, it is a small, quiet place with striking accommodation. The rooms (8 with sea views) are enormous & unusual, & are dotted around the dense gardens between a few large baobabs. Under vast, steep *makuti* roofs, the sinuous interior walls conceal a cushioned lounge, shower room, mezzanine seating area & a fully enclosed bedroom. The 3 'baobab villas' have a small plunge pool, whilst 7 'sea-view villas' & the new 3-bed family villa have direct views over the coral cliff to the ocean below. The furniture is island-produced from coconut wood, & the artwork contemporary. The main restaurant & bar area is a similar mix of modern & traditional – curved white walls, low-hanging *makuti* thatch & terraces of square tables with white directors' chairs. Punched brass lanterns cast a patterned glow at night, wall-mounted basketry adds colour & 3 large spinning fans enhance the sea breeze. Buffet meals are served 3 times a day, with social, pre-dinner drinks at the bar from around 18.30. By day, there

is a lovely swimming pool surrounded by bougainvillea, hibiscus & fan palms to one side & wide *makuti* umbrellas & timber loungers on deck to the other. Alternatively, the crushed-shell beach is a pleasant alternative.

There is a lovely, purpose-built PADI dive centre, currently being run by One Ocean though the owners are keen divers themselves. Shore diving is possible, with good sightings of lionfish & even seahorses being reported on the closest reef (70m away), though most people choose to boat-dive. Dive courses are run, with other water-based activities from dhow cruises to dolphin-viewing also being organised here. There is also a village tour, escorted by one of the local staff, costing US$5, all of which is donated to vital village projects. *Sea-view villa US$175–255pp; baobab villa US$175–245pp; all rates HB; children 2–18yrs, 50–75% reduction*

Kizimkazi Beach Village (8 rooms) m 0773 309628. Just before the village dispensary, this is an extremely basic option & one of the cheapest in town. All 8 rooms are in a single rectangular building on the coral cliff above the sea. They are tiny in size with beds, mosquito nets & no other facilities; grim, cold-water bathrooms harbour a thriving mosquito colony at the end of the corridor. There has been little redecoration or maintenance in the recent past, & any changes in the foreseeable future seem unlikely. The small *makuti* restaurant is a popular hangout for local lads selling dolphin tours. $

⌂ **Swahili Beach Resort** (19 rooms) ☎ 024 2240491; e info@swahilibeachresort.com/ annaswahilibeachresort@gmail.com; www.swahilibeachresort.com. At the far side of Kizimkazi Mkunguni village, Swahili Beach Resort opened its very high gates in 2007. Inside, guests are welcomed into a large, castellated reception area, from where views extend to the swimming pool & sea beyond. Spacious rooms come in 3 categories, all in sgl-storey, lemon-painted coral bungalows except the 4 dbl-storey 'cabanas'. Each is named in Kiswahili after a marine creature & there is a fan, AC, mini fridge, TV & broad terracotta-tiled terrace as standard. The bedroom interiors are perfectly fine, if a little dated in décor, & the en-suite bathrooms spotless & brilliant white.

There is a central, mosaic tiled pool, including a small children's pool, & an on-site PADI dive centre, Kizimkazi Divers (e kizimkazidivers@hotmail.com), which, like the resort, shares the same owners as Arabian Nights in Paje (see pages 273–4). Local tours by dhow & speedboat are possible, kayaks can be hired & there's the usual array of island excursions offered. *Superior room US$120/160 sgl/dbl; cabana US$140/180 sgl/dbl; sand room US$170/210 sgl/dbl; US$10–20 high-season supplement; all rates are FB; HB is available*

⌂ **Kumi Na Mbili Centre** (3 rooms) m 0777 841252; e info@d-t-p-ev.de; www.zanzibar-tourism.org. Close to the 'big baobab', this village development centre is a collaborative venture between the Hamburg-based NGO, German–Tanzanian Partnership, & the local women's group, Tufahamiane. It's a neat white building, with an attractive small garden & seeks to offer services to both the local community & tourists. Accommodation is in 3 simple, clean en-suite rooms with fans & mosquito nets, & there's an affiliated bakery & juice bar for b/fasts & snacks. There is a small internet café equipped with

3 PCs (US$0.50/30mins), a printer & photocopier (mainly used by local teachers); bicycles are available for rent & tours to local sites can be arranged with Mudi. Local crafts are sold in the shop, & like everything here, the proceeds go directly to the women's group & local school. For those keen to offset their carbon footprint, the centre also runs a 'plant a palm' initiative. At US$3/tree, the centre will supply the sprouting nut & villagers will show you where to start digging. A little Kiswahili will really help if you're interested in getting involved: *Ninaomba kupanda mnazi moja/tatu/kumi* means, 'I would like to plant 1/3/10 palm trees'. $–$$

⌂ **Coral Reef Bungalows** (6 rooms) m 0757 781558; e coralreefbungalows@gmail.com. New South African management took over this sleepy lodge in Jun 2007, & in spite of plans to expand, the property remains a small, simple place with spotless rooms & a cracking view across the dhow harbour from its *makuti* restaurant. Accommodation is in whitewashed bungalows & each room is tiled in white with a large Zanzibari dbl bed, en-suite bathroom featuring a wet-room style shower, & has AC & permanent hot water. It's very relaxed here, though proximity to the busy harbour makes it less than ideal for sunbathing. $$

⌂ **Dolphin View Village** (9 rooms) m 0777 863421. Situated about 500m further along from the Coral Reef Bungalows, Dolphin View is the most southerly of Kizimkazi's accommodation options. Owned by Jan & Lisbeth of Paje Ndame (see page 273), & with a similar Scandinavian following, this place is now under the careful management of a very smart, imposing Maasai called Freddy. The neat semi-detached bungalows house a mixture of dbl & family en-suite rooms; all are simple & functional with small fans, *mkeke* mats, reading lamps & small terraces. Thoughtful additions like a terrace foot-bath for washing off beach sand & a mop for post-shower cleaning are surprisingly handy. Rooms come in a variety of sizes so do look around if there's a choice available when you arrive. The staff are very friendly but the lodge's finest feature remains its small secluded beach, in a cove between 2 coral-rock outcrops. $$$

✗ **WHERE TO EAT** In the main part of Kizimkazi, near where the boats are launched, is the Jichane Restaurant, serving mainly lunches for the tour groups from Zanzibar Town.

In Kizimkazi Dimbani, there are two places – both geared mainly around feeding large groups. Karamba is mentioned above, and serves fresh sushi, pasta and traditional Swahili seafood dishes from around US$6. **Cabs Restaurant** (m *0777 415554*), on the opposite side of the harbour mouth, has meals like chicken and chips or grilled seafood for around US$5. This place also has a fleet of boats for dolphin-viewing. It caters mainly for large groups from the all-inclusive east coast resorts, but it's reckoned by local operators to be one of the safest and best-organised outfits based here, so may be a good bet if you don't arrive with a trip pre-booked.

WHAT TO SEE AND DO The main reason people visit Kizimkazi is to see the dolphins, but if you're keen on history you might also want to stop off at the ancient Shirazi mosque in Kizimkazi Dimbani.

Kizimkazi Mosque Hidden behind its new plain walls and protective corrugated-iron roof, the mosque at Kizimkazi Dimbani is believed to be the oldest Islamic building on the east African coast. The floriate Kufic inscription to the left of the *mihrab* (the interior niche indicating the direction of Mecca) dates the original mosque construction to AD1107 and identifies it as the work of Persian settlers, working under the orders of Sheikh Said bin Abi Amran Mfaume al Hassan bin Muhammad. The silver pillars on either side of the niche are decorated with pounded mullet shells from the island of Mafia, and the two decorative clocks, which show Swahili time (six hours' different from European time), were presented by local dignitaries. However, though the fine-quality coral detailing and columns date from this time, most of the building actually dates from an 18th-century reconstruction, attested to by a further inscription, to the right of the *mihrab*. The more recent additions of electrical sockets and flex have not been installed with a comparable degree of style or decoration.

Outside the mosque are some old tombs, a few decorated with pillars and one covered by a small *makuti* roof. The pieces of cloth tied to the edge of the tomb are prayer flags. The raised aqueduct which carried water from the well to the basin where hands and feet were washed is no longer used: running water is piped straight into a more recently built ablution area at the back of the mosque.

Archaeological evidence suggests that when the mosque was built Kizimkazi was a large walled city. Tradition holds that it was founded and ruled by a king, Kizi, and that the architect of the mosque itself was called Kazi. Legend has it that when the city was once attacked by invaders, Kizi prayed for divine intervention and the enemies were driven away by a swarm of bees. Later the enemies returned, but this time Kizi evaded them by disappearing into a cave on the shore. The cave entrance closed behind him and the enemies were thwarted once again.

Today, very little of the old city remains, but non-Muslims, both men and women, are welcome to visit the mosque and its surrounding tombs. It's normally locked, and you'll probably have to find the caretaker with the key (he lives nearby, but is usually under the trees near the beach a few hundred metres further down the road). Show respect by removing your shoes and covering bare arms and legs (this part of the island is very traditional so, out of politeness, your arms and legs should be covered anyway – see *Clothing*, page 94). On leaving you'll be shown the collection box and be able to make a donation.

Dolphin tours Most visitors come on all-inclusive 'dolphin tours' which include road transport, the boat, snorkelling gear and lunch. If you don't take an all-in tour, or want to spend the night at Kizimkazi, you can make your own way here, then hire a boat on the spot or arrange to join a group.

Generally, dolphin-viewing trips last for about two to three hours – usually enough time to locate the dolphins – although some captains trim the time down to about 90 minutes. Sometimes tourists become bored if they don't get quick and easy sightings, and decide to go back even sooner.

11

THE KIZIMKAZI DOLPHINS

The shallow coastal waters around Kizimkazi have been favoured by dolphins for many years (quite possibly for millennia) because the area offers a reliable food supply and is a good place to nurse calves or simply to rest and socialise. Two species of dolphin are resident all year round: the Indo-Pacific bottlenose dolphin (*Tursiops aduncus*) and the Indo-Pacific humpback dolphin (*Sousa chinensis*). The bottlenose dolphin is more sociable, and more readily observed, whereas the humpback dolphin is a shyer creature.

Studies conducted have revealed that there are about 150 bottlenose and 60 humpback dolphins inhabiting the area. A catalogue of all the individual dolphins has been compiled based on the shape, nicks and marks of their dorsal fins and most of the animals have been given names. (Look closely if you see the dolphins and you'll notice that they all look different.)

Tourists first started coming to see dolphins at Kizimkazi in the early 1990s. The continued presence of these popular creatures has attracted growing numbers of visitors, such that tourism has now created new job opportunities for the local villagers. Contrary to the practices of other fishing communities in the Indian Ocean, the fishermen of Kizimkazi are very protective of the dolphins and no longer hunt them, seeing instead the economic rewards from conservation.

In 1997, villagers from Kizimkazi also helped to arrest dynamite fishermen from Dar es Salaam, knowing their methods destroyed the coral reefs and important habitats for the dolphins. Today, other fishing methods, such as drift nets, pose the greatest threat to the dolphins as they are liable to get tangled up in the nets and drown.

Over the years there have been a number of studies carried out at Kizimkazi, to monitor the interaction between dolphins and tourists. It's widely believed that the overall effect is detrimental. However, on a positive note, in 2005, all the stakeholders involved in dolphin tourism formed an association, the Kizimkazi Dolphin Tourism Operators Association (KIDOTOA), and they are working towards getting a management plan in place. Training courses have also been initiated where boat operators are taught how to conduct their tourism activities in a responsible, sustainable way. Further, a system of certifying those who have taken the course is also being considered.

On the whole, the creation of KIDOTOA is very promising for the conservation and management of both the dolphins and the tourism. It is still early days and many boats continue to compete for the best views of the dolphins. But it is now up to everyone to make sure that this new strategy is put in practice. As a tourist you should ask for a copy of the existing dolphin tourism guidelines (see box, *Dolphin-watching guidelines*, opposite) and ask the boat operators to follow them strictly. This should minimise the impact on the dolphins and ensure that they remain in the area for many years to come.

This section is based on information from the Marine Mammal Education & Research group at the Institute of Marine Sciences, Zanzibar, and Dr Per Berggren, Department of Zoology, Stockholm University, Sweden.

Dolphin tours are often promoted in a misleading light. It is important to realise that sightings cannot be guaranteed, and swimming with the dolphins is a rare occurrence. This is not a Florida-style dolphinarium; these are wild animals and their whereabouts cannot be predicted. It is they who choose to interact with people, not the other way around.

Observing dolphins in their natural environment, as with any other animals, requires time and patience. Shouting and excessive movement will not encourage them to approach your boat. Be satisfied with passive observation – do not force the boat-driver to chase the dolphins, cross their path, or approach too close, especially when they are resting. If you decide to swim, slip quietly into the water and avoid splashing. Never jump in. Stay close to the boat and let the dolphins come to you instead of you trying to catch up with them. You could try attempting to excite their curiosity by diving frequently and swimming below the surface, maintaining your arms alongside your body to imitate their own streamlined shape.

In reality, unless you charter your own boat and go out early in the morning, so as not to be disturbed, you're unlikely to be able to put any of these theories into practice. On some days it's not unusual to see 20 or more boats, carrying at least ten people each, all chasing the dolphins and desperate for a sighting. When the dolphins are seen, big groups of people jumping in do little to entice them any closer. One visitor commented: 'it's billed as "swimming with dolphins" but it's actually "jumping into the water a long way from the dolphins"'; another called it a 'shambolic turkey-hunt'.

It's little wonder that the dolphins are beginning to head for somewhere more peaceful. In recent years, the number of sightings has definitely gone down. They used to be almost guaranteed, but it's not unusual now for groups to return without having seen a single dolphin. Sadly, as the disturbances from too many boats and people increasingly outweigh the benefits of food and shelter, this trend is likely to continue, with fewer and fewer dolphins appearing in Kizimkazi's waters in the future.

When to visit The best time of year to see the dolphins is between October and February. From June to September, the southerly winds can make the seas rough, while during the rainy season (March to May) conditions in the boat can be

DOLPHIN-WATCHING GUIDELINES

Kizimkazi is one of very few places where wild dolphins can be admired in their natural habitat. The following guidelines minimise the disturbance to the dolphins while allowing tourists to make the most of the experience. By following these, and encouraging your boat-driver to do likewise, it is possible that tourists may continue to enjoy dolphin-watching for the foreseeable future.

GUIDELINES FOR BOATS
- Drive the boat slowly with a steady speed; do not rev the engine and avoid going in and out of gear
- Approach the dolphin group from the side or from behind; never head-on
- Do not chase the dolphins; let them come to the boat
- Always make sure the dolphins have a clear escape route
- Never be more than two boats on one group of dolphins
- Never approach a mother and calf
- Never stay longer than 30 minutes with the same group of dolphins
- Dolphins slapping their tails at the surface, making coughing sounds, leaping or turning away from the boat, indicate that they are disturbed: leave them alone and look for other animals

GUIDELINES FOR SWIMMERS
- Enter the water as quietly as possible; do not jump or dive in
- Stay close to the boat and hold on to the rail or to lines alongside
- Do not swim after or chase the dolphins; let them come to you

11

unpleasant. However, out at sea you're likely to get wet anyway. You should also protect yourself against the sun.

Organised tours Most people who visit Kizimkazi come on a fully organised tour. These are easily arranged before you arrive, in Zanzibar Town, or by one of the hotels elsewhere on Zanzibar. Costs for these tours vary between US$25 and US$100 per person from Zanzibar Town, including transport to/from Kizimkazi, the boat, all snorkelling gear and lunch.

These prices vary considerably depending on the season, the quality of the vehicle, the standard of driver and guide, the number of passengers, and whether you want a private tour or are happy to share with others. Obviously they also depend upon where you are coming from: if you're taking a day trip from Zanzibar Town, then it's going to be cheaper than driving here from Nungwi.

Private boat charter Excursions can be arranged with local fishermen through any of the guesthouses and restaurants in Kizimkazi Mkunguni and Kizimkazi Dimbani. (The latter is more group orientated; it might be harder finding spare seats here unless you can muster a group together.) Traditional wooden fishing boats are most commonly used, although several fishermen have upgraded to modern fibreglass boats. Chartering a boat costs about US$30–35 for the whole boat. If you're in a small group, you can of course share these costs, although you'll probably find that for groups of five or six the price for a boat may go up to about US$40, or you'll be charged US$10–12 per person. You can also hire snorkels, masks and flippers (around US$2–5 per person) from the souvenir stalls beside Jichane Restaurant. This is essential if you want to get in the water and observe the dolphins below the surface – which is highly recommended. As competition between the boatmen is stiff, some include free snorkel gear in the price of the boat, so it's always worth asking about this.

JOZANI-CHWAKA BAY NATIONAL PARK

Roughly halfway between Zanzibar Town and the broad beaches of the southeast coast is a lush area of protected forest reserve, the Jozani-Chwaka Bay National Park, and small, rural villages lining the road. It's a gentle part of the island, with little development and some of Zanzibar's best opportunities for viewing land animals. The communities here are increasingly involved in a number of conservation projects and even though the forest is an ever-popular, sometimes busy, destination for visitors, the neat boardwalks, diversity of dense vegetation and terrestrial mammals make for a great escape from the sun loungers and souvenir stalls of the rest of the island. For smaller-scale insect and reptile encounters, the new Butterfly Centre and Zala Park (see page 298) are worthy add-ons to a trip in the area.

Jozani-Chwaka Bay National Park (⊕ 07.30–17.00 daily; admission US$8) incorporates the largest area of mature indigenous forest remaining on Zanzibar, although today it is only a tiny remnant of the forest that once covered much of the island. It stands on the isthmus of low-lying land which links the northern and southern parts of the island, to the south of Chwaka Bay. The water table is very high and the area is prone to flooding in the rainy season, giving rise to this unique 'swamp-forest' environment. The large moisture-loving trees, the stands of palm and fern, and the high water table and humid air give the forest a cool, 'tropical' feel.

Historically, local people have cut trees and harvested other forest products for many centuries, but commercial use started in the 1930s when the forest was bought by an Arab landowner and a sawmill was built here. In the late 1940s, the

Jozani Forest asks all visitors to observe the following rules. They apply to watching primates anywhere in Zanzibar, or elsewhere in Africa:

- You must be accompanied by an official guide.
- Do not approach monkeys closer than 3m, and preferably remain at a distance of 5m. This is for your own safety – the monkeys are wild animals and can bite or pass diseases to you.
- Do not invite any interaction with the monkeys or try to feed them. If they come close, avoid eye contact and move away. Do not make noises to attract their attention.
- You are one of the major threats to the monkeys, as primates are susceptible to human diseases. Do not visit the monkeys if you are suffering from any illness, particularly a cold or flu.
- Observe the speed limits if driving through Jozani, and ask your driver to slow down if you're in a minibus. Even though speed-humps have been introduced, monkeys are regularly killed by cars.

forest came under the control of the colonial government and some replanting took place. Jozani has been protected since 1952 and, as the forest areas in other parts of the island have been cleared, much of the island's wildlife has congregated here. The forest was declared a nature reserve in the 1960s, but despite this the trees and animals were inadequately protected. Local people cut wood for building and fuel, and some animals were hunted for food or because they could damage crops in nearby fields.

Nevertheless, Jozani Forest retained much of its original natural character and now forms the core of the island's first national park, Jozani-Chwaka Bay National Park. Developed from a partnership between the Zanzibar government's Commission for Natural Resources and the charity CARE International, with funding from various sources including the government of Austria, the Ford Foundation and the Global Environment Facility, the park now has clear targets to protect natural resources and improve conditions for local people and wildlife in the area.

WHEN TO VISIT Keen naturalists who want to watch wildlife undisturbed, or those who just like a bit of peace and quiet, should try to visit the reserve either very early or in the early afternoon, as most groups come at about 09.00–10.00 on their way to the coast, or 15.00–16.00 on their way back. The monkeys and birds seem subdued in the midday heat, so from about 14.00–15.00 seems to be the best time for watching their behaviour.

GETTING THERE AND AWAY The entrance to Jozani Forest Reserve is on the main road between Zanzibar Town and the southern part of the east coast, north of the village of Pete. You can visit at most times of the year, but in the rainy season the water table rises considerably and the forest paths can be under more than 1m of water. The reserve is clearly signposted, and entrance costs US$8, inclusive of the services of a guide and the mangrove boardwalk.

Many tour companies include Jozani on their east-coast tours or dolphin tours, but you can easily get here by frequent public bus (Routes 9, 10 or 13), *dala-dala* (numbers 309, 310, 324 or 326), hired bike or car. Alternatively, take a tourist minibus heading for the east coast, and alight here. This road is well used by tourist

11

minibuses and other traffic throughout the day, so after your visit to the forest you could flag down a vehicle and continue to the coast or return to Zanzibar Town.

GETTING AROUND THE FOREST A network of nature trails has been established. The main one takes about an hour to follow at a leisurely pace, with numbered points of interest which relate to a well-written information sheet which you can buy for a nominal cost at the reception desk. There are also several shorter loops. Some other information leaflets and species lists are also available, and there are a few very good display boards and other exhibits.

As you walk around the nature trails, it's possible to see lots of birds and probably a few colobus and Sykes monkeys, but these animals are shy, and will leap through the trees as soon as they hear people approaching. On the south side of the main road live two groups of monkeys who are more used to humans and with a guide you can come and watch these at close quarters. This is ideal animal viewing – the monkeys are aware of your presence but not disturbed. They are not tame at all, and don't come close, but just get on with their usual feeding, playing, grooming or resting. As the colobus monkeys look so cute, some visitors have been tempted to try to stroke them or give sweets to them. This is bad for the monkeys, but can be bad for tourists too – several people have been given a nasty nip or scratch. (See box, *Rules for responsible monkey-watching*, page 295, for the rules to follow, and look but don't touch.)

South of the forest, a long thin creek juts in from the sea, and is lined with mangrove trees. A fascinating boardwalk has been constructed, the only one of its type in east Africa, so you can easily and harmlessly go deep into the mangrove to experience this unique ecosystem. This is also a community project, and revenue from visitors coming to the boardwalk helps fund local development projects.

JOZANI'S FLORA Several distinct habitats exist within Jozani's borders – evergreen bushland to the west; dense groundwater forest of laurel wood (*Callophyllum inophyllum*), screw palm (*Pandanus rabaiensis*) and untidy oil palms (*Elaeis guineensis*) in its heart; thickets of flowering *Macphersonia gracilis*, cloves (*Eugenia*), and cabbage trees (*Cussonia zimmermannii*) to the north; and mangrove forest forming the eastern border along Chwaka Bay, dominated by the common red mangrove (*Rhizophora mucronata*), yellow mangrove (*Ceriops tagal*) and grey mangrove (*Avicennia marina*).

Other trees in the reserve include moisture-loving palms (five species, of which three are true palms), figs (two species) and red mahogany, plus some introduced species such as Sydney blue gum. Red mahogany (*Khaya nyasica*) was formerly regarded as an introduced exotic, but the weight of evidence is that it is native or anciently naturalised; this tree is found on other Indian Ocean islands and, like the mangrove, its seeds can float and survive in sea water. Although the size of the trees in Jozani is impressive, few trees become truly huge as the soils are too shallow to allow deep roots to penetrate, and they get blown over by strong monsoon winds. With several diverse habitat types, each brings its associated and equally varied wildlife to the reserve.

JOZANI'S MAMMALS Several rare and endemic animal species occur in Jozani, making it a major attraction for wildlife fans. Even if you've got only a passing interest, a visit can be fascinating. The main reason most visitors come here is to see some of the resident red colobus monkeys – their full name is Zanzibar red colobus or Kirk's red colobus (*Procolobus kirkii*); their local name is *kima punga* meaning 'poison monkey' – which are unique to the Zanzibar archipelago. Many wildlife fans rate the red colobus of Jozani as one of the best

Kirk's red colobus (*Procolobus kirkii*) are named after Sir John Kirk, the 19th-century British consul-general in Zanzibar, who first identified these attractive island primates. They are endemic to the archipelago and one of Africa's rarest monkeys. Easily identified by their reddish coat, pale underside, small dark faces framed with tufts of long white hairs, and distinctive pink lips and nose, the monkeys are a wildlife highlight for many visitors to Zanzibar.

Kirk's red colobus live in gregarious troops of five–50 individuals, headed by a dominant male and comprising his harem of loyal females and several young (single births occur year round). They spend most of the day hanging out in the forest canopy, sunbathing, grooming and occasionally breaking away in small numbers to forage for tasty leaves, flowers and fruit. Their arboreal hideouts can make them hard to spot, but a roadside band at the entrance to Jozani-Chwaka Bay National Park allow for close observation and photography.

Timber felling, population expansion and a rise in agriculture have resulted in the rapid destruction of the tropical evergreen forests in which the Kirk's red colobus live, thus dramatically reducing population numbers. Researchers estimate that around 2,700 of these monkeys currently exist, a fact verified by their classification as 'endangered' on the IUCN Red List (2004) and their inclusion in Appendix II of CITES.

Human behaviour has undoubtedly caused the decline in Kirk's red colobus population numbers, yet now tourism may help to save the species. With national park status now protecting their habitat in Jozani Forest, and visitor numbers increasing, the local communities are beginning to benefit from the tangible economic rewards (see box, *Jozani Community Fund*, page 298) that come from preserving these striking monkeys. If this continues, the future survival of the species should be secured.

monkey-viewing experiences in Africa. Nowhere else can you get so close to a monkey in the wild that is not aggressive or likely to bite, as well as being attractive, endearing and very rare.

Brochures produced in the mid 1990s said there were 1,500 individual colobus monkeys in Zanzibar, but this was an estimate, and more accurate surveys in 1997 put the figure at around 2,700. The red colobus population of Jozani is growing, which is partly a result of conservation efforts. However, recent research shows that this is most likely caused by monkeys fleeing ongoing destruction of the small patches of forest elsewhere on the island into the safety of the Jozani area, rather than their numbers increasing as the result of breeding. Researchers think that Zanzibar's total population of red colobus is probably stable, but emphasise that habitat destruction is still a major threat.

Other residents of Jozani include a population of blue or Sykes monkey (*Cercopithecus mitis albgularis*), which you are also quite likely to see. The forest is also home to Ader's duiker (*Cephalophus adersi*), a species of small antelope found only on Zanzibar and some parts of the Kenyan coast, and suni (*Nesotragus moschatu moschatus*), another antelope which is even smaller than the duiker, but both of these are extremely shy and unlikely to be seen. The Ader's duiker is virtually extinct in Kenya now and is one of the two rarest antelopes in the world. Its only chance of survival is on Unguja. Its population is between 400 and 1,000 and efforts have been underway over recent years to ensure its survival, including protecting Jozani, working with local communities to establish sanctuaries and the proposed translocation of some individuals to Chumbe Island.

There are even reports of leopards (*Pathera pardus adersi*) in Jozani. If present they would be a local subspecies, smaller than the mainland version, although the veracity of these claims is very questionable. (For more details of wildlife in Jozani and Zanzibar, see *Wildlife*, pages 296–8.)

JOZANI'S BIRDS Jozani has a fairly good bird population, with over 40 species recorded, although many of the forest birds are shy and therefore hard to spot. Species occurring here include Kenya crested guineafowl (*Guttera pucherani*), emerald-spotted wood dove (*Turtur chalcospilos*), little greenbul (*Andropadus virens*), sombre greenbul (*Andropadus importunus*), cardinal woodpecker (*Dendropicos fuscescens*), red-capped robin-chat (*Cossypha natalensis*), dark-backed weaver (*Ploceus bicolour*), golden weaver (*Ploceus xanthops*), olive sunbird (*Nectarinia olivacea*) and crowned hornbill (*Tockus alboterminatus*). An interesting speciality is an endemic race of Fischer's turaco (*Turaco fischeri*), which is slightly larger than the mainland race, with blue-purple on the wings instead of green. In the mangroves you'll see various kingfishers, including the localised mangrove kingfisher (*Halcyon senegaloides*), sunbirds and coucals.

If you're especially keen on birds, it is well worth engaging the services of a bird guide. Jozani has two bird specialists on the staff: Ali Addurahim is an ecologist and chief bird guide; Ali Khamis Mohammed was trained by the other Ali, and also knows his stuff. They have a bird checklist and a copy of the big fat *Zimmerman Birds of Kenya and Northern Tanzania* book, which includes most species which occur on Zanzibar.

OTHER PLACES TO VISIT

Zanzibar Butterfly Centre (e *mail@zanzibarbutterflies.com; www.zanzibarbutterflies.com;* ⊕ *09.00–17.00 daily; admission US$4pp*) Opened in Pete in January 2008, the Zanzibar Butterfly Centre (ZBC) aims to show visitors the forest's fluttering friends close up as well as generating an income for local villagers and preserving the forest. Local villagers around Jozani-Chwaka Bay National Park are being encouraged to protect the surrounding vegetation in an unusual initiative which has them trained to sustainably farm native butterflies. Participants (currently 26 farmers) are taught to identify butterfly species, gently capture female butterflies, net small areas for breeding, harvest eggs, plant appropriate caterpillar fodder and ultimately collect the resulting pupae for breeding the next generation and sale back to the centre. The pupae are then sold on to overseas zoos and live exhibits or displayed for visitors here in the large, netted tropical garden. Here, 200–300 colourful butterflies can be seen in the enclosure, making for a fascinating diversion and one of Africa's largest butterfly exhibits. There are good guides and clear informative signs to explain the project and butterfly lifecycle, and experienced photographers can also get some wonderful shots. The income generated from visitors to ZBC is channelled back into further funding local conservation and poverty-alleviation projects, whilst the message is made clear to the communities that protecting the natural habitat of these insects provides much-needed income. The centre is a fun, worthwhile 30min stop, and its location, just outside Jozani Reserve, makes it a convenient addition to a forest trip.

Zanzibar Land Animals Park (m *0741 329357;* e *mohdayoub@hotmail.com;* ⊙ *08.00–17.30 daily; admission US$5 adults; children free*) The Zanzibar Land Animals Park (ZALA for short) is in the village of Muungoni, just south of Kitogani, where the main road from Zanzibar Town divides into roads towards Paje and Makunduchi.

At first glance it's just a zoo, with various pens and compounds to hold the animals (mostly reptiles). However, this private project, run by the tireless and enthusiastic Mohammed Ayoub, has a more important purpose. It's primarily an education centre for groups of Zanzibari schoolchildren to come and learn about their island's natural heritage.

For tourists this is one of the few places on Zanzibar where you can observe snakes and lizards at close quarters; the chameleons are particularly endearing. Also look out for the geometric tortoises which are not native, but were brought to the park by customs officials who confiscated them at the airport from a smuggler of exotic pets. There are a few other species on display, most notably the small group of tree hyrax who spend some time in their pen and some time in the nearby forest. These part-time zoo animals come back mostly at feeding time, then seem quite content to rest or play in their pen before returning to the trees at nightfall.

Zala Park is only about 3km down the road from Jozani Forest Reserve, and can be combined with a visit there. If you have an overwhelming interest in wildlife, conservation or education, it is sometimes possible to stay in the small one-roomed guesthouse, although this is often used by visiting volunteers. Mohammed plans a nature trail in the nearby forest and mangrove stands, and can organise guided walks if you are interested in seeing more of this area; ideally, this should be arranged in advance.

Zanzibar Heritage Conservation Park This rather grand-sounding place is actually a fairly low-key project run by some local people. Located to the north of the main road from Zanzibar Town to the east coast, west of the village of Tunguu, the park has some game birds on display (which are not that interesting), and a vast garden (which is more interesting) full of spices, herbs, fruit trees and medicinal plants. Everything is labelled, and sometimes a guide is available to show you round and explain the uses of the different plants. There's a small entry charge and it might be worth visiting on the way to Jozani Forest.

UNGUJA UKUU AND BI KHOLE RUINS

For keen fans of history and archaeology, there are two places of interest in the southwest of the island. Both are just off the main road between Zanzibar Town and Jozani Forest, Paje and Kizimkazi, so make convenient stop-offs *en route* to there or the southwest coasts. There is now also an excellent full-day dhow trip in the Menai Bay Conservation Area which launches from Unguja Ukuu (see page 300) and is run by ethical local operator Eco+Culture (see page 303).

WHERE TO STAY

⌂ **Menai Bay Beach Bungalows** (10 rooms)
m 0777 411753; www.menaibaybungalows.com. Set beneath the palms along an impossibly beautiful

crescent beach at Unguja Ukuu, 5 whitewashed bungalows offered idyllic, if simple, island solitude. The place closed in 2008, and has allegedly been sold to an Italian, but it's possible that it will reopen again soon in some form so do check if you're planning on being in the area. The rooms were simply furnished with basic facilities &, being within the protected Menai Bay Conservation Area, trips to the nearby mangrove forests & uninhabited, outlying islands could be easily arranged. We hope something suitably small scale and environmentally aware is planned for this site.

WHAT TO SEE AND DO

Unguja Ukuu This is the site of the oldest known settlement on Zanzibar, dating from the end of the 8th century AD. It was believed to have been founded by early Shirazi immigrants from Persia, but recent archaeological evidence from here and other sites on the east coast of Africa suggests that it was Swahili in origin. Research at Unguja Ukuu is still taking place and more evidence may yet come to light.

Unguja is the local name for Zanzibar Island today, and Ukuu means 'great'. It is believed that the settlement may have been quite large, but was probably abandoned in the 10th century when the local Muslim population came under attack. An Arab geographer, writing in the 13th century, recorded that the people of 'Lenguja' had taken refuge from their enemies on the island of Tumbatu, off the northwest shore of Zanzibar Island (see box, *Tumbatu Island*, page 226).

Despite this site's fascinating history, today there is very little remaining that would be of any interest to anyone except the keenest archaeologist – just some shallow earth pits and the remnants of a few crumbling walls.

Getting there and away To reach this site, you need to pass through the modern village of Unguja Ukuu, reached by turning south off the main road between Zanzibar Town and the southern part of the east coast, at a junction about halfway between the villages of Tunguu and Pete. South of the village, a small track branches off the dirt road that leads to Uzi Island (reached by tidal causeway); follow this to reach the remains of old Unguja Ukuu. If you don't have a car, *dala-dala* number 308 takes passengers to Unguja Ukuu from Zanzibar Town as does the public bus on Route 8.

Bi Khole Ruins Situated about 20km to the southeast of Zanzibar Town, the Bi Khole Ruins are the remains of a large house dating from the 19th century. Khole was a daughter of Sultan Said ('*Bi*' is a title meaning 'lady') who came to Zanzibar in the 1840s, after Said moved his court and capital from Oman. With her sister, Salme, she helped their brother, Barghash, escape after his plans to seize the throne from Majid were discovered (see the *History* and *Economy* sections, pages 16–17).

Khole had this house built for her to use as a private residence away from the town; she is recorded as being a keen hunter and a lover of beautiful things. The house had a Persian bath-house where she could relax after travelling or hunting, and was surrounded by a garden decorated with flowering trees and fountains. The house was used until the 1920s but is now ruined, with only the main walls standing, often overgrown,

The main front door has collapsed into a pile of rubble but this is still the way into the ruin. Directly in front of the door is a wide pillar, designed so that any visitor coming to the door would not be able to see into the inner courtyard, in case Khole or other ladies of the court were unveiled. In this room are alcoves and niches with arabesque arches, although the windows are rectangular. With some imagination, it's possible to see what an impressive house this once was.

Getting there and away The Bi Khole Ruins lie a few kilometres to the west of the main road from Zanzibar Town to the southern part of the east coast, about 6km south of the village of Tunguu. The road passes down a splendid boulevard of gnarled old mango trees, supposed to have been planted for Khole (although they may date from before this period): about halfway along is the track to the ruins. If you're travelling on public transport, take any of the buses (Routes 9, 10 or 13) or *dala-dalas* (numbers 309, 310, 324 or 326) heading to the southeast and ask the driver to tell you when to alight.

FUMBA AND MENAI BAY

At the far end of the island's southwestern peninsula, on an increasingly rutted coral road 15km from Zanzibar Town, is the peaceful village of Fumba. It's a quiet, scenic place and very few tourists ever come here, which gives it a good deal of its charm. There is only one upmarket lodge offering accommodation, but day trips to the marine conservation area of Menai Bay are run by two reputable operators (Safari Blue and Eco+Culture – see page 303), so even if you can't stay, it's still possible to get a taste for this beautiful corner. From the beach south of the village, local fishermen take their *ngalawa* outriggers and dhows to the islands and fishing grounds beyond, and here too is the departure point for one of the boat trips. It's truly stunning in the surrounding waters but if you also want to get a deeper insight into the community, ask around for a local villager called Issa Kibwana, who conducts small tours of the nearby fruit and spice plantations, or arrange a meeting with him through Sama Tours (see page 126).

GETTING THERE AND AWAY To get here, take the road from Zanzibar Town towards the airport, then fork left (east) down a main road just after a petrol station. This will lead you northeast, before turning east and heading south, along the airport runway's eastern boundary fence. Leaving the airport behind you, you'll continue southeast along a bumpy, but picturesque, tree-lined road.

After around 5km there is a right turn from the main road, signposted to the Menai Bay Conservation Area. You can continue straight on or turn right to get to Fumba, as these roads join up at the rocky, southern end of the peninsula. Alternatively, if you don't have your own transport, take one of the four daily local buses (Route 7) from Zanzibar Town.

WHERE TO STAY

Fumba Beach Lodge (26 rooms) m 0777 860504/878025; e reservations@ fumbabeachlodge.co.tz/info@fumbabeachlodge.co.tz; www.fumbabeachlodge.com. Built on 40 acres of private land, including 3 separate sandy coves, Fumba Beach Lodge opened its doors in Jun 2005 after only 8 months of construction. Just half an hour from the airport, & currently the only upmarket lodge in the WWF's Menai Bay Conservation Area, this is unquestionably one of the islands most stylish places to stay. Designed & built by Edwin van Zwam, a Dutchman with a solid African background, Fumba was created in line with contemporary, upmarket safari camps, & they've done a superb job. The result is a fabulously original place that oozes style & has been beautifully crafted with clean, crisp lines & bold colour. There are 20 well-spaced, deluxe rooms with canopied dbl beds, mains electricity, en-suite showers, fans & a sea view; 3 can become family rooms using inter-connecting doors. There are also 6 special suites with huge dbl beds, fabulous sunshine-yellow details, beautifully carved, built-in wooden wardrobes with safes, & tremendous views. Beautiful finishing touches abound, from sweet-smelling cinnamon sticks on the desk to a lovely, natural mobile above the bath, complete with sand dollars, corals & sun-bleached shells. There's a stylish outside shower & a magnificent dbl bath with a view. Large, shuttered terrace doors open onto a private deck & the beach beyond, or there's a delightful rooftop terrace with views out to Kwale Island. 2 of these suites are built on the edge of a low coral cliff, around a beautiful baobab tree, into which an additional large outdoor bath has been set.

Beside the large, infinity swimming pool is a comfortable cushioned lounge & a sophisticated, open-sided restaurant, specialising in seafood, though

Tremendous effort is being made by the government, research institutions and NGOs to increase the returns from seaweed production (see box, *Sustainable seaweed farming*, pages 262–3). At the beginning of 2006, a pilot scheme began to integrate seaweed and shellfish farming. Funded and supported by the Institute of Marine Sciences in Dar es Salaam, Woods Hole Oceanographic Institute in Massachusetts and the McKnight Foundation, the scheme aims to maximise workers' time by engaging them in the farming of both seaweed and shellfish, particularly oysters. Some 200 women from Fumba, Bweleo, Nyamanzi and Unguja Ukuu are already involved in the project and it's hoped that the benefits of a dual income will considerably improve their independence and standard of living. If the scheme proves successful, it is probably a model that can be transferred to other island communities.

To complement this work, the Institute of Marine Science is also working with the Western Indian Ocean Marine Sciences Association (WIOMSA), the Coastal Resource Center (CRC) at the University of Rhode Island and USAID on a programme called Sustainable Coastal Communities and Ecosystems (SUCCESS). Operating as a local NGO, they aim to promote the inclusion of shellfish on tourist hotel menus so as to increase its overall consumption. It is hoped that this raised demand for shellfish will drive market prices up, and ultimately improve the incomes of the shellfish collectors and farmers.

The SUCCESS programme has successfully developed a floating line system for seaweed farming and adapted it to shellfish and mabe pearl farming. (A mabe pearl is a hemispherical pearl which has grown against the inside of an oyster's shell, rather than in its tissues.) The pearl farming, which started in 2006, had the first crop of 28 mabe pearls from 25 animals in November 2007. The mabe pearls were subsequently sold, with 19 of these being bought by a US company for US$2,000. The company donated three resulting necklaces back for the project's first Zanzibar pearl auction in February 2008. These pieces, together with the remaining raw mabe pearls earned the group of seven (three men and four women) a further US$1,000 at auction, and clearly shows the tremendous success for the aptly named project. There are currently an estimated 400 animals implanted for mabe pearls at different stages of development and this is set to be a potentially significant marine crop.

The group have also been trained on other aspects of entrepreneurship including pearl and shell polishing, making ornaments, packaging and marketing, as well as running co-operatives. Three of these people, all women, have become so successful that they are earning approximately US$170 per month out of the part-time activity. This is significant: a low-ranking government officer will earn US$70 per month, and 50% of the island population is still on the US$1 per day poverty line. The group, together with the seaweed soap manufacturers of Kidoti (see page 263), have been successfully selling their merchandise to tourists and residents and we very much hope that the opportunity and their entrepreneurial skills can be passed on to other coastal communities within the archipelago.

candlelit meals are often enjoyed on the beach. Nearby, the outside bar, 'Dhow FumBar', constructed from an old dhow, is a stunning spot for sundowners or a pre-dinner aperitif. The new multi-storey tropical spa is in an ingenious open-air treehouse, complete with 'rooftop' jacuzzi & excellent therapists. For more active excursions, there's an on-site dive centre & some truly wonderful day trips to Menai's idyllic islands. $$$$$—♨

WHAT TO SEE AND DO The Menai Bay Conservation Area has a number of picturesque, uninhabited islands and sandbanks to explore as well as some fascinating marine life, and it's well worth taking one of the full-day sailing and snorkelling excursions, either through Fumba Beach Lodge, if you're a guest, or with one of the two operators running trips: Safari Blue departing from the Fumba Peninsula, or Eco+Culture departing from Unguja Ukuu.

Some shade is available on these boats and beaches, but remember to apply sunscreen and preferably wear a T-shirt for protection when snorkelling. Towels and waterproof shoes are also recommended as you'll most likely have to wade out to the boat across coral rock.

Eco+Culture (✆ *024 2233731;* m *0777 410873;* e *ecoculture@gmx.net, www.ecoculture-zanzibar.org*) This socially and environmentally aware tour operator (see page 125) runs a fabulous full-day Menai Bay excursion: the Unguja Ukuu Boat Trip. Departing from its namesake village, Unguja Ukuu, on a traditional dhow, small groups are taken past rich mangrove forests to the pristine beaches of Miwi, Nianembe or Kwale islands and accessible sandbanks. Snorkelling kit is provided and the shallow reefs around the bay and islands provide excellent opportunities to spot an array of brightly coloured marine fish and corals. After a good amount of time to mess around in the water, a delicious barbecue lunch is prepared on the beach, which invariably features a selection of tasty freshly caught fish, Swahili side dishes and tropical fruits. On all trips, there is an English-speaking guide alongside the two crew and local chef, all of whom are happy to answer questions and talk about the surroundings and traditions of the area – top culinary tips are available from the chef if you're keen to impress your friends back home. Life jackets, a small first-aid kit and outboard motor are also kept on board the dhow for emergencies.

Eco+Culture have a firm policy on limiting numbers on their trips with the express aim of protecting the environment and making the trip more enjoyable for their guests. There is a maximum of eight people per dhow and only 12 guests (in two boats) are ever taken out at the same time. This is a real pleasure and one of the main differentiators of this trip over its competitor. *The trip leaves Stone Town at 08.00, returning at 17.00; US$50pp for 4 persons, dropping to US$30pp for groups of 8*

Safari Blue (m *0777 423162;* e *adventure@zanlink.com; www.safariblue.net*) Safari Blue has been operating in Zanzibar since 1996 and many of the local crew have worked with the company since its inception. The trips are made on board locally made, traditional sailing dhows 8–10m in length, which have been kitted out with Yamaha outboard engines, marine VHF radios, life jackets, sunshades, boarding ladders, first-aid kits, fire blankets, and waterproof bags for cameras and valuables. Public liability and marine insurance complete the adherence to safety.

The trip pauses at a few of the bay's islands and sandbanks for exploration, a tasty lunch and relaxation, in between guided snorkelling forays in the turquoise waters and hopeful spotting for humpback and bottlenose dolphins.

The first stop of the day is usually Kwale sandbank, an idyllic spot for gentle snorkelling and sipping fresh coconut milk. Sailing on further, barbecued seafood lunches await on Kwale Island, where tamarind trees offer a shady spot to enjoy a cold beer, or to sample fresh calamari, lobster and fish (vegetarian/non-fish options must be ordered in advance). It's worth noting that there's also a field toilet on the island. A visit to a mangrove lagoon, where swimming is possible during high tide, a walk across the island, and a chance to try your hand at sailing a *ngalawa* follow, before the dhow's lanteen sail is hoisted and the boat heads back to Fumba.

There is an element of forward thinking needed for this trip. Fumba Beach is a remote beach with no formal changing facilities, so it's best to wear swimwear under your clothes.

11

The experience has been recommended by many travellers in the past, although there have been an increasing number of complaints about the sheer volume of people on the trips, and the number of boats being taken out. In some ways, perhaps Safari Blue has started to become a victim of its own success. *The trip leaves from close to Fumba Beach at 09.00, returning about 18.00; US$45 adult, US$22 child aged 6–14 years; children under 6 years free; transfers from Stone Town to Fumba cost an additional US$50/vehicle*

CHUKWANI

The small village of Chukwani, to the south of Zanzibar Town, is about 5km beyond Ras Mbweni. Southwest of the village, on the coast, is the Chukwani Palace. It was built by Sultan Barghash in 1872 and used mainly as a place to recuperate after illness, as the air here was supposed to be particularly healthy. The palace was built as a smaller version of the House of Wonders, without the tower. During the reign of Sultan Ali bin Hamoud (sultan from 1902 to 1911) the palace was used by government officers.

Today, most of the palace has been demolished, leaving only the bath-house. The new buildings around the ruins are used by the army, so visitors are not allowed to enter, but you can get a good view from the air if you fly out of Zanzibar as the palace lies only a few kilometres southwest of the airport.

✕ WHERE TO STAY

🏠 **Coconut Beach Inn** (6 rooms) 📞 024 2235897; 📱 0742 740030; e coconutbeachinn@ hotmail.com. This quiet & simple place is about 9km south of Zanzibar Town, on the road towards Chukwani, about 4km from where the road to Mbweni turns off the main airport road. The owner-managers are relaxed & friendly & the setting is perfect. 6 little cottages surround a swimming pool overlooking the beach, with views straight out to Chumbe Island. Evening meals (lots of seafood, around US$6) & lunches are available. $$

🏠 **Mawimbini Club Village** (85 rooms) 📞 024 2231163. Near the village of Chuini, about 20km outside Stone Town, this is an international-style resort complex, part of the Italian VentaClub chain, catering almost exclusively for fly-in package tourists. The hotel consists of bungalows set in a large garden around a central area with a swimming pool, restaurant & bar. A theatre has regular dancing & cabaret shows. To stay here, it is perhaps easier to make arrangements through one of the tour companies in Zanzibar Town. $$$$

CHUMBE ISLAND

Chumbe lies about 10km south of Zanzibar Town, and is one of the largest of the offshore islands in this area. The coral reef surrounding Chumbe Island is in very good condition because until recently the island was inside a military area and public access was not allowed. Consequently, it has not been damaged by high volumes of tourists, transfer boats, or destructive fishing techniques employed by local fishermen. The reef on the western side of Chumbe Island was officially gazetted a Marine National Park (the first in Tanzania) in 1994, and the island has since been declared a Forest Reserve. Together, the island and reef are known as Chumbe Island Nature Reserve or Chumbe Island Coral Park (CHICOP).

CHICOP's own information states: 'Chumbe Island is a rare example of a still pristine coral island ecosystem in an otherwise heavily over-fished and overexploited area. It includes a reef sanctuary and a forest and bird sanctuary of exceptional biodiversity.' This has been verified by various global conservation and scientific bodies, including IUCN, WWF and UNESCO. A specialist from the Australian Institute of Marine Sciences called Chumbe 'one of the most spectacular coral gardens to be found anywhere in the world'.

Common on Chumbe Island, yet endangered elsewhere in the south Pacific and Indian Ocean, the rare and remarkable 'coconut crab' (*Birgus latro*) is the world's largest land invertebrate.

A member of the *Coenobitidae* family, it is one of only a few hermit crabs that is wholly adapted to spending most of its life away from the sea. In some areas coconut crabs are known to move several kilometres inland; however, they do begin life in the sea, with the female depositing hatched eggs in the water as planktonic larvae (*zoea*). Over a matter of a few weeks, the larvae develop claws to become *megalopa*, and sink to the seabed as tiny crabs, in search of a protective shell. They retain these shells when they reach land, discarding them only when their carapace is fully hardened. Unlike other hermit crabs, these creatures develop a dual-purpose shell over their abdomen, similar in appearance to a lobster. This guards against water loss and saves on 'house-hunting'. And without the need to fit inside abandoned shells, the coconut crab is free to grow indefinitely, accounting for its serious size (adults have been recorded with a 3ft leg span!).

Nocturnal by nature, the crabs scavenge and feed on decaying vegetation, fruit, small animals and, naturally, coconuts. Although adept at climbing palms to reach the coconuts, these crabs do not actually have any special adaptations for scaling tree trunks. The crab will use its powerful claws to heave itself up to the coconut, snip it off the palm using its sharp pincers, descend the tree backwards (facing up), gather its prize and feast. With its razor-sharp claws, the crab attacks the coconut, ripping away the husk, cracking its shiny nut and devouring the flesh inside.

The coconut crab is listed on the IUCN endangered species list, with no record of the number in existence. Habitat destruction, human hunting and introduced predators continue to threaten their global survival. Happily, Chumbe Island reports a healthy population and is working to gain international support for the protection of this amazing species. Guided by one of the island's staff, you are likely to be able to watch them forage by night (especially in the salubrious surroundings of the camp's compost heap!) – but keep still and quiet; the crabs have poor eyesight and so detect predators and threats by vibrations.

Over 400 species of fish have been identified in the marine park and other marine wildlife frequently seen includes turtles, dolphins, and seasonally even the great humpback whale. On the island, 60 species of bird have been recorded, including breeding pairs of the rare roseate tern (*Sterna dougallii*). The island is also home to various lizards and a population of rare giant coconut crabs (*Birgus latro*) – see box, *Coconut crabs*, above. Six Ader's duiker (*Cephalophus adersi*), an endangered small antelope whose range is restricted to a handful of coastal forests in and around Zanzibar, were reintroduced to Chumbe Island in 1999 and 2000, and the small population is reproducing and appears to be thriving in the dry and rough coral-rag forest on the island.

Buildings of historical and cultural interest on Chumbe include a lighthouse built by the British in 1904 (still clearly visible from ships approaching Zanzibar from Dar es Salaam). The lighthouse is still functioning but is now also used as an observation tower with a spectacular view of the island and the marine park. There is also an old mosque built in an Indian style unique to Tanzania which is still frequently used by the local Muslim staff. A cottage originally built for the lighthouse keepers has been converted into a visitor information centre, including an education room for local schoolchildren who are brought here by the Chumbe management and other conservation organisations to learn about local environmental issues.

Tourism is being developed on Chumbe in a very sensitive manner. Former fishermen have been employed as park rangers on the island. They have been trained by CHICOP and now take the visitors on guided walks along trails in the dense forest and along the inter-tidal flat around the island at low tide. The most popular excursion on the island is the guided snorkelling tour to the protected reef, where the tourists will learn more about the delicate coral reef ecosystem. Profits from tourists visiting the island are channelled back into local education and conservation projects.

Chumbe Island's unique situation has been recognised by an almost unparalleled string of awards for its responsible approach to tourism, and its ecologically sensitive approach to the environment. Meanwhile Chumbe seems effortlessly to combine a tourist attraction with a centre for ongoing education projects for the local people. It is an exceptional place.

For tourists, day trips to the island are available (these cost US$80 including all transfers, snorkelling equipment, guides and lunch) when the island isn't full, but visitors are encouraged to spend at least one night here – and two or three would be perfect.

WHERE TO STAY

Chumbe Island Lodge (7 rooms) ✆ 024 231040; ☎ 0777 413582; e chumbe@zitec.org; www.chumbeisland.com; ⏲ mid-Jun–mid-Apr. Run as part of the Chumbe Island Coral Park (CHICOP), this superb, trail-blazing lodge is an example of truly eco-friendly accommodation. Its 7 bungalows are simple but clean, very comfortable, ingeniously designed & genuinely ecologically sensitive. Each dbl bungalow has 2 storeys & they are all made mostly from local materials using traditional construction techniques, & yet employing cutting-edge eco-architectural systems. Downstairs there's an open-fronted lounge terrace, complete with dbl sea-view hammock, animal mosaics inlaid in the floor, & a bathroom at the rear. Upstairs, the bedroom comprises a comfortable mattress laid on the floor, shrouded in a mosquito net, & a stunning view through the ocean or stars, for the triangular front wall can be entirely lowered using a pulley system. The chalets are completely self-sufficient with solar panels to provide electricity, funnel-shaped roofs to catch, filter & store rainwater (there is no good groundwater on the island), & even 'compost toilets' to avoid septic tanks & the pollutants they often produce. Used water from the showers goes onto flowerbeds where specially chosen plants absorb nutrients before the water drains into the ground. This accommodation is unique in Zanzibar, & very unusual in the whole of Africa. The central area is a huge, star-shaped *makuti* structure – perfect for catching the sea breeze in the heat of the day. Simple, fresh meals & drinks are served on the terrace (on the sounding of a large gong), & there's a lovely upper deck of hammocks & chairs for chilling & counting blessings. The reference library & education centre are also here. Activities are all escorted & focus on learning about the surrounding environment & ecology. They include snorkelling (scuba diving is prohibited) on the nearby reefs; forest walks along the nature trail; & walks across the inter-tidal zone, with its plethora of rock pools. The coconut crab is a nocturnal creature & seldom seen in daylight, but if you ask the staff to take you into the woodland at dusk or after dark, you are virtually guaranteed to see several!

The lodge is a private company with not-for-profit aims & ploughs its proceeds back into great community education & conservation initiatives, making it not only a stunning holiday spot, but a cause worthy of great support. *US$280/500 sgl/dbl, FB inc soft drinks, guides, transfers & all activities; reduced rates Oct–mid-Dec & Mar–mid-Apr*

12

Pemba

Pemba Island lies about 80km to the northeast of Zanzibar Island (Unguja), and about the same distance from the Tanzanian mainland, directly east of the port of Tanga. Smaller than Zanzibar Island, at just 67km long, it covers an area of 985km² and has a more undulating landscape, even though its highest point is only about 95m above sea level. But one of the first things that most strikes the visitor is how green it is. More densely vegetated than Zanzibar (with both natural forest and plantation), Pemba has always been seen as a more fertile place. The early Arab sailors called it *El Huthera*, meaning 'The Green'. Today, as always, far more cloves are grown here than on Zanzibar Island.

With 362,168 inhabitants at the last census, in 2002, Pemba is – like Zanzibar Island – one of the most densely populated areas of Tanzania, although this is no urban jungle. Most of the population live in traditional square houses, with a wooden frame and mud walls, the thatched roofs occasionally upgraded to corrugated iron. The largest town on Pemba is Chake Chake, the island's capital and administrative centre, about halfway down the western side of the island. The island's other main towns are Wete, in the northern part of the island, and Mkoani, in the south, which is the main port.

As in Zanzibar as a whole, the people are predominantly Muslim. Right across the island, women wear the veil, most in bright colours but some in sombre black, while schoolgirls look immaculate in the uniform dark skirts and cream veils. Typically it's a subsistence economy, with cloves the only real revenue earner, and few jobs available, so the nascent tourist industry brings much-needed employment. Although English is spoken in the larger hotels, and by most of those who regularly come into contact with tourists, few villagers speak anything other than Swahili, so it's advisable to learn at least a few words of the language.

HIGHLIGHTS

For today's visitor, Pemba's greatest attractions include long, empty beaches, some excellent diving and snorkelling, particularly around Misali Island, and the unspoilt forest reserve at Ngezi. There are several small historical sites which, although not 'must sees', certainly repay a visit if you use just a little imagination. Perhaps more important, though, with relatively few visitors, and little in the way of tourist facilities, Pemba is still a place where travel for its own sake (by car, bus, bike or on foot) remains a prime reason for visiting.

NATURAL HISTORY AND ENVIRONMENT

Verdant and very fertile, Pemba was once densely forested, although all that remains now is Ngezi Forest, on the northwestern tip of the island. Nevertheless, numerous spice and fruit trees dominate the rest of the landscape. Cloves represent

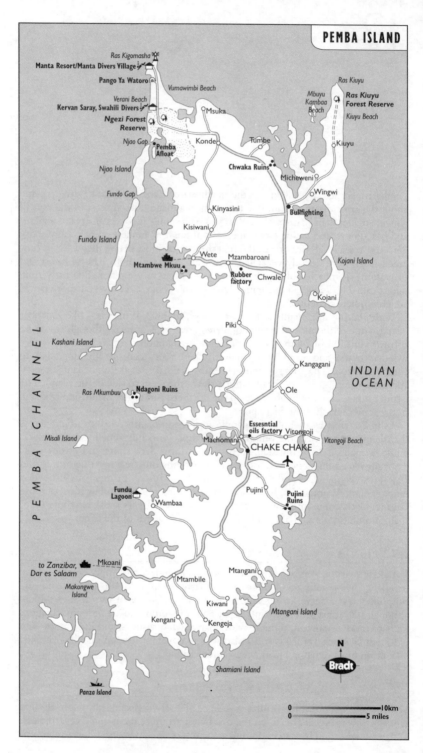

PEMBA ISLAND

Ras Kigomasha
Manta Resort/Manta Divers Village
Pango Ya Watoro
Verani Beach
Kervan Saray, Swahili Divers
Ngezi Forest Reserve
Njao Gap
Pemba Afloat
Njao Island
Fundo Gap
Fundo Island

Vumawimbi Beach
Msuka
Konde
Tumbe
Chwaka Ruins

Ras Kiuyu
Mbuyu Kambaa Beach
Ras Kiuyu Forest Reserve
Kiuyu Beach
Kiuyu
Micheweni
Wingwi

Kinyasini
Bullfighting
Kisiwani

Kashani Island

Wete
Mzambaroani
Mtambwe Mkuu
Rubber factory
Chwale
Kojani Island
Kojani

Piki

Kangagani

P E M B A   C H A N N E L

Ras Mkumbuu
Ndagoni Ruins

Misali Island

Ole

INDIAN OCEAN

Essesntial oils factory
Machomani
Vitongoji
CHAKE CHAKE
Vitongoji Beach

Fundu Lagoon
Wambaa

Pujini
Pujini Ruins

to Zanzibar,
Dar es Salaam
Mkoani

Makongwe Island

Mtambile
Mtangani

Kiwani
Kengani
Kengeja
Mtangani Island

N

Shamiani Island

Bradt

Panza Island

0   10km
0   5 miles

308

For the people of east Africa, the island of Pemba is particularly known as a centre for traditional medicine and witchcraft. The British writer Evelyn Waugh, in his classic travel book *Remote People* (1931), described Pemba as a centre of 'black art' learning, and went on to record how

> ... novices would come from as far as the great lakes [of central Africa] to graduate there. Even from Haiti, it is said, witchdoctors will come to probe the deepest mysteries of voodoo. Nowadays everything is kept hidden from the Europeans, and even those who have spent most of their lives in the country have only now and then discovered hints of the wide, infinitely ramified cult which still flourishes below the surface.

Sixty years later, little had changed. A 1995 travel story in a British newspaper reported that the village of Vitongoji, in the centre of the island, was 'the capital of Pemban sorcery ... a place of dark secrets. Some years ago a witchdoctor was arrested for eating children in the course of his duties.' This report may have been tongue-in-cheek, but it's an inescapable fact that local people seeking cures for spiritual or physical afflictions still come to the local doctors of Pemba from Zanzibar Island, mainland Tanzania, Kenya, and even as far as Uganda and Congo.

As a visitor to Pemba from the West, you shouldn't expect to be taken to see any cures or ceremonies. This type of thing is strictly for the locals. Even the most innocent of questions about witchcraft from tourists here will be met with nothing more than embarrassed smiles or polite denials. (For more details on traditional religion and witchcraft, see pages 38–9.)

the biggest cash crop, with Pemba responsible for the vast majority of cloves exported from Zanzibar, and sales monopolised by the government (see box, *Cloves*, page 52). For several months each year, cloves are left to dry in the sun on mats by the side of the road. Consumption of almost all other fruit and spices, however, is restricted to domestic use. Mango, banana, avocado, coconut, citrus fruits, pineapple and papaya grow almost side by side with less familiar fruits: breadfruit, custardfruit, plantain, tamarind, bungo and jack fruit – this last a huge and hard sponge-looking thing that yields an improbably sweet flesh. Spices such as ginger, vanilla, cinnamon and pepper also grow in abundance.

Of the three primates that inhabit the island, the most visible is the Pemba vervet monkey (*tumbili au kima*, *Cercopithecus aethiops nesiotes*), while the small-eared galago or bushbaby (*komba*, *Otolemur garnettii garnettii*) is more likely to be heard than seen, its human-sounding cry disturbing many an otherwise peaceful night. A small population of Kirk's red colobus is also present in Ngezi Forest. Relatively easy to spot is the Pemba flying fox (*popo wa Pemba*, *Pteropus voeltzkowi*), a large fruit bat which is the only fully endemic mammal on Pemba, and is classified as a globally endangered species. Its name comes from its orange fur and dog-like snout and ears. This animal seeks out the high canopies of undisturbed forest with a ready supply of fruit and tree blossoms. Pemba flying foxes roost throughout Pemba, particularly along the west coast and on islands off the west coast, but are readily seen at Ngezi Forest where the forest rangers monitor their whereabouts, and at Kidike. They feed on soft fruits and weigh up to 1.5kg. Local people consider their flesh a delicacy, tasting like an oily chicken.

The Zanzibar tree hyrax (*pelele*, *Dendrohyrax validus neumannii*) is present not only at Ngezi but also on Njao and Fundo islands, whereas the rare and threatened Pemba blue duiker (*paa wa Pemba*, *Cephalophus monticola pembae*) and marsh mongoose (*chonjwe*, *Atilax paludinosus rubescens*) are to be found only in Ngezi Forest.

Bird species on the island include three endemics: the russet or Pemba scops owl, which is fairly common in the clove plantations and at Ngezi, the Pemba white-eye and the Pemba violet-breasted sunbird. A number of sub-endemic species include the Pemba green pigeon, the African paradise flycatcher and the Pemba African goshawk. Without doubt, the best place to see birds on Pemba is in the Ngezi Forest. (For more details, see pages 333–4.)

GETTING THERE AND AWAY

TO/FROM THE MAINLAND

By air Daily services between Dar es Salaam and Pemba are run by ZanAir and Coastal Aviation (for contact details, see page 116), although all flights go via Zanzibar, and some may involve a change of plane. The duration of the flight is just over an hour. At the time of research, **ZanAir** operates two daily flights between Dar es Salaam and Pemba: 09.00 from Dar via Zanzibar, arriving Pemba at 10.15, and a direct service, departing Dar at 13.45 and arriving in Pemba at 14.30. This route is US$240 return, including tax.

Coastal Aviation operates one daily flight from Dar to Pemba, which travels via Zanzibar then onwards to Tanga on the Tanzanian mainland. Flights depart Dar at 14.00, Zanzibar at 14.30, and arrive on Pemba at 15.05. The one-way fare from Dar is US$110 and from Zanzibar US$90. The onward 20-minute flight to Tanga leaves Pemba at 15.15, and costs US$70. For return journeys, the flight leaves Pemba at 16.35, arriving in Zanzibar at 17.05, and landing back in Dar at 17.35. Fares are the same as for the outbound trip.

If you're coming from any other part of Tanzania or Kenya and want a direct flight, your only option is to charter a plane. In Dar, Nairobi or Mombasa, a travel agent will be able to help you. Spare seats on charter flights are sometimes sold to individuals. Once again, the best thing to do is contact a travel agent, who will probably phone the airport or one of the local charter companies to see if anything is going your way.

On leaving Pemba, don't forget that there is a US$6 departure tax (made up of US$5 'safety' tax, and a further US$1 airport tax), and be prepared to hand this over in cash. The modern terminal has few facilities – just a small bar serving drinks and a couple of toilets.

By sea For some time, the only scheduled ship from the mainland to Pemba has been the *Sepideh*, which plies daily between Dar and Zanzibar Island, continuing on to Pemba (Mkoani) three times a week. The fare between Dar and Pemba is US$44. Recently, however, a newer service on board the *Sea Express II* has started up on the same route, with similar timing and a fare of US$45. In addition, the *Aziza* operates a weekly service connecting Tanga with Zanzibar Island and Wete on Pemba. (For details of all these, see *To/from Zanzibar Island*, below.)

In theory, there is a weekly service on the *New Happy* between Tanga and Wete, leaving Wete on Sundays at 09.00 and returning on Tuesday mornings. In practice, though, this service is none too reliable; for the current state of play, and for details of any other boats on this route, contact the tourist office in Chake Chake.

Similarly, you can in theory reach Pemba by dhow from Tanga or from Mombasa, in Kenya, although police at the port are unwilling to let tourists board, with good reason – the safety record on these boats is pretty dire (see page 117), and it's worth remembering, too, that services are irregular and far from idyllic. Most dhows from Tanga or Mombasa go to Wete, but a few go to Mkoani.

Immigration formalities Whichever type of boat you use to reach Pemba from the mainland (Kenya or Tanzania), you need to show your passport to the immigration officials at the port. This is a very relaxed and low-key affair. So low key in fact that sometimes the office is empty, and you have to go to the police station in town to present your credentials, or get redirected to wherever the immigration staff might be.

TO/FROM ZANZIBAR ISLAND

By air Scheduled flights run by ZanAir and Coastal Aviation between Pemba and Dar es Salaam (see above) touch down in Zanzibar Island in both directions. On all flights, the one-way fare for non-residents is about US$115, plus the departure tax of US$5.

Your other option for reaching Pemba from Zanzibar Island is to fly with one of the local air-charter companies based in Zanzibar Town. If you can get a group together and charter a whole plane, it can sometimes be cheaper per person than buying a ticket on a regular flight. Alternatively, these companies will often sell spare seats on charter flights to Pemba. In high season there are flights at least every other day, so it's worth contacting the companies direct, or getting a travel agency to do it for you, to see if there's anything going. (For contact details, see *Chapter 5, Scheduled flights*, pages 115–16.)

To book scheduled or charter flights to the mainland from Pemba, contact Pemba Aviation & Airport Services (the Coastal agent) opposite the National Microfinance Bank in Chake Chake, or the ZanAir agent on the other side of the road. Alternatively you can phone the airport control tower (✆ *024 2452238*) and enquire yourself. This is a fairly standard procedure – the charter companies often tell the tower if they're looking for passengers to fill spare seats.

By sea Nearly all passenger ships, and some cargo ships, coming into Pemba arrive at the town of Mkoani (at the southern end of Pemba Island), while it's mostly cargo ships and dhows that go to/from Wete (at the northern end of Pemba Island). Very few ships or dhows, other than local fishing boats, go to/from Chake Chake. (In fact the old harbour of Chake Chake is silted up and only canoes can get here; the town's port is now at Wesha, about 10km west along the coast.) Schedules given below were correct at the time of research, but are notoriously unreliable and subject to change.

For more details on buying tickets to Pemba on one of the ships listed below, see *Chapter 5, Passenger ships and ferries*, pages 117–18. To buy tickets on Pemba, contact the relevant local agent in Chake Chake, Mkoani or Wete (see pages 321–2, 325 and 329).

🚢 **MV Sepideh** Operated by Mega Speed Liners, the *Sepideh* runs between Dar es Salaam & Zanzibar Island once a day, with a 2hr crossing to Pemba (Mkoani) Mon–Thu & Sat. On Mon, Thu & Sat, the ferry starts its circuit in Dar es Salaam at 07.15, arriving in Zanzibar around 09.00, before heading on to Pemba at 09.30. The boat then returns from Pemba to Zanzibar at 12.30, & back to Dar at 16.00. On Tue, Wed & Sun, it departs Dar for Zanzibar at 07.30 & returns at 16.00; Pemba boats depart Zanzibar at 10.00 & return at 12.30 on these days. *Fares: Pemba–Dar US$79 one-way; Pemba–Zanzibar US$44*

🚢 **Aziza** This leisurely weekly service connects Pemba (Wete) with Zanzibar Island & Tanga. It leaves Zanzibar on Fri at 22.00, arriving 06.00 in Wete; departs Wete for Tanga Sun 10.00, taking 4hrs, returning Tue at 10.00 to arrive in Wete at 14.00, & finally leaves Wete for Zanzibar on Wed at 06.30, arriving 14.30. *Fares: US$20 one-way, inc port tax*

🚢 **Mapinduzi** Between Zanzibar Island & Pemba, this old government-run Zanzibar Shipping Corporation vessel plies between Zanzibar Town & Mkoani, carrying both cargo & passengers; in season, the smell of cloves being loaded on board is highly pervasive. Departs Zanzibar Island on Mon & Fri at 22.00, returning from Pemba on Tue & Sat at around 10.00, with the journey taking about 6hrs. *Fares: one-way on deck US$15; cabin bed: second class US$20; first class US$25*

🚢 **Serengeti** Much more reliable than the old ZSC vessel is the passenger ship *Serengeti*, operated by Azam Marine Ltd. The 6–8hr crossing between Zanzibar Town & Mkoani runs 3 times a week (currently Tue, Thu & Sat), returning the following day. *Fares: one-way US$20*

🚢 **Sea Express II** This new speedboat owned by Fast Ferries Ltd commenced operations between Dar, Zanzibar & Mkoani on Pemba in 2005. At the time of writing, Fast Ferries were departing Zanzibar at midday for the 3hr crossing to Pemba on Mon, Wed & Sat; for the return Pemba to Zanzibar boats were departing at 08.30 on Thu. Journeys from Dar to Zanzibar depart 07.30 & 09.00, arriving 2–3hrs later. *Fares: one-way fare non-residents Zanzibar–Pemba US$45; Dar–Pemba US$65*

Most of Pemba's **dhow** traffic goes to/from Tanga on the mainland, and only occasionally do dhows go between Zanzibar Town and Pemba. Of those that do, most land at Mkoani. Although it is illegal in Tanzania for tourists to travel by dhow, and not especially safe, some intrepid travellers still report finding captains willing to take them on board. If you're determined to consider this, see *Chapter 5*, page 117.

GETTING AROUND

Pemba's road system was given a boost in 2005 with the completion of the tarred road across the island from Mkoani to Konde, paid for by the World Bank. North of Konde, and elsewhere, however, most of the roads are pretty poor, with access to some of the outlying villages requiring 4x4 vehicles, particularly in the rainy season. From Chake Chake to Wete, a bumpy alternative to the main road is the 'old' – and more direct – road via Mzambaroani, which goes through some beautiful scenery. Timewise, though, the new road is considerably quicker, despite the apparent diversion.

Options for getting around on Pemba are limited, although public transport allows independent travellers to see at least some parts of the island. To get further afield independently you'll have to hire a bike, motorbike, car or boat. It is also possible to arrange a car with driver, or an organised excursion, through hotels and guesthouses, a local tour company, or direct with the drivers.

For many travellers, the easiest way to set up an excursion or a tour of the island is to contact a driver, either direct (see below) or through your hotel or guesthouse. Alternatively, there are a number of companies in Chake Chake and Wete that can organise this for you (see pages 321–2 and 329).

TAXIS AND CAR HIRE It's pretty straightforward to rent a car with a driver for around US$70 a day, including petrol, depending on the distance you want to travel. Most of the hotels can organise this for you, as can tour companies. Alternatively, try contacting one of the following, both of whom offer tours to various places of interest around the island. They are reliable, interesting guides, and both speak excellent English:

🚗 **Said Mohammed** m 0777 430201. Known to everyone as Saidi. Offers city tours, spice tours, transport to the north & east (inc 4x4 by arrangement), & visits to all Pemba's places of interest.

🚗 **Suleiman Seif** m 0777 431793. The driver for Fundu Lagoon also offers a range of tours. He is a mine of information & is particularly knowledgeable about the island's spice & fruit trees.

In Chake Chake, vehicles and drivers wait for business outside the ZTC Hotel. In Mkoani and Wete they can be found near the market. Rates vary according to the vehicle: pick-ups, saloon cars, minibuses, Land Rovers and small Suzuki 'jeeps' are often available. Rates are also negotiable and should be discussed fully (and agreed) in advance. To give you an idea, a trip from Chake Chake to Wete or Mkoani costs about US$45 return. If you're planning a tour, a newish vehicle covering a round trip from Chake to Wete, Ngezi Forest and The Manta Resort and back would cost about US$70. All rates include petrol. Whatever you hire, part payment in advance is usually required, and the first stop is likely to be the petrol station.

Although in theory it's possible to self drive, in practice this is less easy to set up. Some of the tour companies may be able to help, or perhaps North Lodge in Wete (see page 328), though unless you strike lucky you'll need to speak Swahili. Do check the insurance details, and see pages 118–19 and 122–3 for further information.

MOTORBIKE AND BICYCLE HIRE There is no official establishment in Pemba for hiring bikes, although it's perfectly possible to hire both motorbikes and pedal bikes in each of the four main towns. The system seems to involve simply finding somebody who is not using their bike and doesn't mind making some extra shillings lending it out to tourists. Rates start at about US$4 per day for a bicycle, and US$22 for a motorbike. Be warned, however: motorbikes or scooters – locally known as *piki piki* – can be extremely dangerous, both on pot-holed side roads and on the main north–south road, where erratic driving, sharp bends and numerous chickens or goats are just some of the hazards. If you're determined to go this route, remember that you probably won't be insured. Check that your vehicle is in reasonable condition, particularly the tyres and the rims, and don't even consider it if you've no previous motorbike experience.

Alternatively, you can sometimes arrange to hire a bike or motorbike through your hotel. Tell the staff what you want to do, and they may well know someone who can help you out – prices will be the same as mentioned above. Both Sharook Guesthouse and North Lodge in Wete rent out bikes for around US$5 a day. For details, see page 329.

BUS, MINIBUS AND DALA-DALA Pemba's main form of transport is by *dala-dala* (see pages 120–2). Pemba used to be served by quaint old buses (actually converted trucks with wooden benches and canopies on the back), but these days they've been replaced by more modern *dala-dalas* (converted pick-ups) or the occasional minibus. Routes and numbers are listed below. On the main routes, of which the number 606 seems to have the most frequent service, there are several buses each day (at least one an hour after 06.00, or after 04.00 during Ramadan), but on the minor routes buses might operate only a few times – or just once – per day, and that'll be in the morning. Services to/from Mkoani are tied in closely with ship (especially the *Sepideh*) arrival and departure times. In fact, it seems that Pemba Island's entire public transport system revolves around ship timetables. The fare on the longer routes (eg: Chake Chake to Mkoani) is about US$1. For shorter trips it's half that. The most useful routes for visitors are as follows, though it's worth noting that *dala-dalas* will stop to collect or drop off passengers at any point along their route:

Route

602	Chake Chake to Konde
603	Chake Chake to Mkoani
606	Chake Chake to Wete
305	Chake Chake to Wesha (Chake's port)
316	Chake Chake to Vitongoji (5km east of Chake Chake)

319	Chake Chake to Pujini
330	Chake Chake to Wambaa
10	Wete to Wingwi/Micheweni
24	Wete to Konde

Other buses connect Chake Chake and, to a lesser extent, Wete with outlying villages. There will be a station manager at the bus depot in each town so check with him for details.

BOAT HIRE Aside from booking through one of the hotels, there's no organised means of getting from Pemba across to the individual islands, although it's worth asking any of the tour operators in case they can help. Alternatively, some of the local fishermen are prepared to carry passengers for a fee, which is fine for short distances, but do remember that the longer crossings – especially to Misali Island – could take a considerable period of time, and be pretty uncomfortable, especially in rough seas.

 ## ACCOMMODATION

Pemba has a very small number of places to stay compared with Zanzibar Island, from rock-bottom basic hotels and small local guesthouses through to a good backpackers-cum-dive lodge. More exclusively, the coastal areas boast just one mid-range hotel and a highly exclusive tourist hideaway. While rumours of further options have been mooted for some time, little has changed in recent years. For divers, though, there is the added bonus of a permanently moored live-aboard, as well as a number of more conventional live-aboards (see page 318).

As on Zanzibar Island, all accommodation on Pemba must officially be paid for with hard currency: cash US dollars are preferred, and anything else (pounds, euros) may not be accepted, unless otherwise quoted. If you have only Tanzanian shillings, these are usually accepted at the current rate of exchange. Breakfast is normally included in the room price unless stated otherwise. Other meals are payable in Tanzanian shillings. Also as on Zanzibar Island, during quiet times many of the lodges and guesthouses on Pemba lower their rates. Even if reductions aren't advertised, it's often worth asking about this. At the cheaper places, rates are often negotiable at any time of year.

 ## FOOD AND DRINK

All the hotels on Pemba serve food, although at the cheaper places it has to be ordered, even by residents – sometimes quite a long time in advance. Additionally,

ELECTRICITY ON PEMBA

Power cuts are more frequent on Pemba than they are on Zanzibar Island, and last much longer. According to one local, the power cuts out every third day, and sometimes is unavailable for two or three weeks when the generators run out of fuel and more has to be ordered. Despite plenty of rumours to the contrary, plans to improve reliability have yet to materialise.

Although the power is more reliable at night, some hotels have their own generators. Nevertheless, it's worth bearing in mind when choosing a room that having an electric fan or air conditioning is not nearly as important as having some sort of natural breeze.

the island's main towns have simple restaurants where you can get local dishes, and Chake Chake has a couple of places with more elaborate options. Alongside the basics, featuring varying combinations of chicken, fish, chips and rice, many of the restaurants sell Indian-influenced dishes such as pilau and biryani.

Roadside stalls proliferate during market hours, most selling variations on meat kebabs (*mishkaki*) and omelettes. For a nutritious and cheap meal, try *chipsi mai yai* – an omelette filled with chips, sometimes served with shredded cabbage, for around US$0.50. On the drinks front, it's easy enough to get branded fizzy drinks such as Coke and Fanta, but more refreshing is the local pineapple soft drink, brand-named Zed. And if you fancy a snack (or a simple souvenir), seek out the tamarind sweetmeat sold in small, hand-woven palm-leaf baskets. Called *haluwa*, it's made from oil and sugar, costs just a few shillings, and is so sweet that one packet will happily serve a whole group. Open it with caution, though – *haluwa* is very sticky. The best on the island is said to come from Wete.

For lunches or picnics, you can buy fruit at the markets and roadside stalls in Chake Chake, Mkoani, Wete or Konde. You can also buy bread – either from the occasional stall, or from men on bikes with baskets of fresh loaves on the back. Shops in the towns sell a reasonable range of food in tins and packets, imported from the mainland or elsewhere in the Indian Ocean, but in the smaller villages this kind of stuff is more difficult to find.

LOCAL SERVICES

BANKS AND BUREAUX DE CHANGE Banking is limited to Chake Chake, which has branches of the People's Bank of Zanzibar and the National Microfinance Bank (⏱ 08.30–15.00 Mon–Fri, to 12.30 Sat). The banks will change money, but expect a wait of 30 minutes or so, and be advised that US dollars are best. Travellers' cheques are another story though and are likely to be refused. Financially, you may do slightly better at a bureau de change. The only one on Pemba is at the Zanzibar Tourist Corporation (see page 322), but be warned: it takes only US dollars cash and tends to run out of shillings. An alternative is to ask at a local shop or seek advice from staff at your hotel who may be able to direct you to a local trader who could change cash dollars, though naturally rates may well be higher than at the banks. If you're travelling to Pemba from Dar es Salaam or Zanzibar, you'd be well advised to change money at one of the bureaux de change at the airport or in town before travelling to Pemba.

CINEMA Chake Chake's cinema, located on the main road coming into the town from the south, offers a nightly diet of Hindi melodrama and cheap action movies, with Hollywood films once a week or so. There's more of the same at Wete's inappropriately named Novelty Cinema.

COMMUNICATIONS Although there are communications centres in each of the main towns, the introduction of yellow public phone booths has made these somewhat redundant for the visitor. Phones take TTCL phonecards which cost US$10 and are available from the Tanzanian Telecommunications office and numerous other outlets – just look for the TTCL sign outside. International calls cost US$1.50 a minute. For more general information on telephone services into and out of Zanzibar, see pages 108–9.

There are post offices in Chake, Wete and Mkoani and Konde (*usually* ⏱ 08.00–13.00 & 14.00–16.00 Mon–Thu, 08.00–12.00 & 14.00–17.00 Fri), but public email services are confined to the internet bureaux in Chake Chake (see page 322).

HOSPITALS AND PHARMACIES The island's main hospital in Mkoani is a modern place, built with overseas aid. Although it is staffed by dedicated Chinese and Tanzanian doctors, the hospital suffers from shortages of drugs and other essential supplies. There's also a smaller hospital in Chake Chake, which has Western doctors and the island's only obstetrics unit, while X-ray facilities are based at the hospital in Wete, near the ferry port.

There are several pharmacies, including near the hospital in Chake Chake (close to the museum), where reportedly most things are available – if you know what you're looking for, that is.

TOURIST INFORMATION The Pemba office of the Zanzibar Tourist Corporation (ZTC), the state travel service, is in Chake Chake. The manager and members of staff are helpful, and happy to give advice and information about the area, within reason. For their range of services, see page 322.

ACTIVITIES

DIVING Recreational diving off Pemba is for the most part confined to the Pemba Channel on the more sheltered west of the island. Misali Island in particular provides a wonderful array of corals and fish life. Unlike the reefs around Zanzibar Island, many of the reefs off Pemba fall away into steep walls, offering opportunities for some exciting drift dives and the chance to see creatures such as the spotted eagle ray, with its 3m wingspan. Despite Pemba's undoubted reputation for the big pelagics, such as barracuda, trevally, giant groupers and the endangered Napoleon wrasse, sightings of shark are extremely rare on the west of the island, and even to the south. If it's sharks that you're after, you need to dive on the east of the island, where the steep walls and fast currents attract hammerheads. Discuss the options with one of the live-aboard outfits (see page 318), some of whom will visit the east of the island if sea conditions are favourable.

Most of the operators use either speedboats or motorised dhows to get to the dive sites. While the former are undoubtedly faster, there's a lot to be said for the leisurely pace of a dhow, giving the opportunity to take in the beauty of the islands or to watch large teams of fishermen working with their nets from narrow wooden boats. On the way to the dive sites, particularly further north, you may be joined by schools of common or spinner dolphins, just tagging along for the ride.

Diving on Pemba, as on Zanzibar Island, is good all year round, with visibility ranging from 10m to 30m or even more. Between December and March, the water is warm – around 30°C, but even quite early in the season the water temperature is a reasonable 25°C or so, and most operators have good wetsuits if you didn't bring anything suitable. (For more details, see box, *Zanzibar diving and fishing seasons*, page 106.) Visibility, current and thus the choice of dive sites is strongly affected by the state of the tide: not just the level, but also whether it is spring or neap. Be guided by your dive instructor on this – it's important. On almost all boats, entry is a backward roll into the water.

Dive sites Although much of the reef around Pemba was adversely affected by the El Niño of 1998 (see page 63), and the situation hasn't been improved by dynamite fishing (which sadly continues, despite being illegal), the diver is still spoilt for choice. Dive sites on Pemba tend to have been given different names by the individual dive outfits, so the following is an overview of what to expect.

Particularly popular is the protected area to the west of **Misali Island** (see pages 326–7), with its calm waters and spectacular coral gardens, where most (but not all) of the dives are suitable for novice or relatively inexperienced divers. Improbable giant clams hug the reef, as do numerous smaller creatures such as the exquisitely coloured nudibranchs: keep an eye out especially for the 30cm Spanish dancer. At one dive site to the northwest of the island, though, currents can be strong, so this is more suitable for advanced divers with considerable experience. The rewards can be great, however, with eagle rays and some of the big pelagics.

Dives around the southwestern tip of Pemba are for the most part in the vicinity of **Panza Island**, and are normally recommended for advanced divers. Sites here are relatively spread out, with 'blue dives' offering good opportunities to see pelagics. There's also the wreck of a 1950s' freighter in 12m of water.

North of Misali, some excellent sites around **Ovinje Gap**, **Fundo Gap** and **Njao Gap** with their steep walls are usually better explored by more advanced divers with plenty of experience, able to cope with strong and sometimes unpredictable currents. Diving through the 'gaps' between the islands can be seriously exciting, earning plenty of comparison with fairground rides and express trains. Even the more leisurely drift dives may not be suitable for a just-certified novice, so do be sure to tell your dive leader if you have any doubts. **Manta Point**, just off Fundo Gap, is a great circular dive, as its name would suggest, with huge mushroom and cabbage corals; even if you don't get to see the manta ray, there are plenty of ocean-going fish in the vicinity, and all sorts of nudibranchs. Out of the currents, gentler dives offer plenty to see, while sheltered lagoons to the east of the islands are good locations to learn to dive and hone your skills. North of Njao Gap, however, the quality of the reef is poor, and dive operators rarely visit.

Dive companies There are currently three dive operators in Pemba, each linked to one of the island's resorts and with its own style. Be sure to check out what is available and choose the right operator for you. Equipment is available to hire from all companies, with standards generally pretty high. All offer PADI-certified courses, including the popular Discover Scuba and Open Water. Night dives can usually be organised with advance notice. For those interested in underwater photography, cameras can be rented from Manta Resort for US$25 per dive, or from Swahili Divers, who run photography courses.

On a practical note, some of the operators do not carry water on their boats, so check this before you leave and take your own if necessary, particularly in hot weather. For other practical advice, see pages 104–5.

For comparison purposes, prices below have been given for a single or two-tank dive, and the PADI Open Water course. Inevitably, though, options vary considerably, and many other courses are offered, so do check these out.

⚓ **Fundu Lagoon** ✆ 024 2232926; m 0777 438668; e fundu@africaonline.co.tz; www.fundulagoon.com. Dive 710, the professional yet friendly dive centre at Fundu Lagoon (see pages 325–6), is a PADI 5* Gold Palm operation, & is exclusive to the resort's guests. Its location, just 20mins or so by speedboat from the dive sites of Misali Island, makes it possible to leave at a civilised hour for the morning dive & be back in time for lunch. A more leisurely day allows for 2 dives, with a picnic lunch on the island. *Dive at Misali US$70/140 sgl/dbl (further afield additional US$15 per dive); Open Water US$620*

⚓ **Swahili Divers** m 0773 176737/8; e resort@kayakpemba.com; www.swahilidivers.com. The longest-established dive operator on Pemba is a relaxed & friendly outfit run by Raf Jah, who has lived & dived in Pemba for 10 years. The company, which was the first on the island to attain PADI 5* status, has recently moved from Chake Chake to its new base at Kervan Saray Beach (see page 332) in the northwest, near Ngezi Forest. From here, Raf or his crew take divers all over the central & northern dive sites of the island in fast RIBs or traditional dhows, with the nearest dive sites just a 4-min journey. There are 2-tank dives every morning (departing 09.00; returning 13.30), with afternoon dives at 14.30, each taking a maximum of 5 divers. Night dives are available for very experienced divers who bring their own equipment & torches, although equipment is otherwise available to rent. Snorkelling is also on offer, as are sunset cruises. *Dive US$ 80/130/160 sgl/dbl/tpl; Open Water US$450, or US$650 for individual tuition.*

The Manta Resort & Divers Village www.themantadiversvillage.com. On the northwestern tip of the island, Manta Resort & its neighbouring, dive-only sibling, Manta Divers Village (see page 333) run an efficient dive school with good access to most of Pemba's west-coast dive sites. *Dive US$50/100 sgl/dbl*

Live-aboards Three live-aboards that cover the area around Pemba, the *Aristos*, the *Jambo* and the *Kisiwani*, run one-week trips out of Kenya. Alternatively, there's the unique experience of a live-aboard that's firmly anchored in calm waters: the Floating Beach Resort, which falls somewhere between a live-aboard and a floating hotel. For details of dive operators who include live-aboards in their itineraries, see page 77.

SY Aristos +254 (0)720 441487/(0)733 825718/(0)723 110031; e info@divingsailing.com; operates Sep–Apr. This 17m ketch operates diving & sailing trips out of Kalifi in Kenya. Owned by a former British army officer, Tony Allport, & his Kenyan-born wife, Ali, it regularly visits Pemba & Zanzibar Island, & sometimes Mafia Island. Deep-sea fishing are also on the agenda. Max 6 passengers. *7-night cruise about US$1,800 FB, inc unlimited diving; check website for special offers; courses & equipment extra, by arrangement*

Floating Beach Resort m 0777414177; e info@floatingbeach.com; www.floatingbeach.com. Book through Italian agents such as Albatros (www.albatros.com) or Viaggiland (www.viaggiland.it). On Pemba, the booking office is in Mkoani, just as you leave the port. The Italian-owned & run 32m *Relax* forms the basis of a floating hotel, moored off the south coast near Mkoani. Once a hydrofoil, it now features 15 en-suite dbl rooms with fans, a

restaurant & bar, with a second, 18m vessel alongside housing the kitchen & dive centre. Smaller boats take guests diving or over to the beach to relax or explore further afield. *Rates on application*

SY Jambo www.oneearthsafaris.com. Under the same ownership as The Manta Resort, the twin-masted 23m *Jambo* operates out of Shimoni. Impressive under full sail, the boat cruises down the west coast of Pemba, sometimes as far as Ras Nungwi at the northern tip of Zanzibar, with 6 nights on board & the last on land. 5 AC cabins; 2 tender boats. *$1850pp sharing FB, inc land transfers, 3 dives a day & night dives; dive equipment & some drinks extra; charters available for groups of 5 or more*

MV Kisiwani Book through one of the specialist dive operators (see page 77). Also based at Shimoni, the 22m motor yacht *Kisiwani* cruises the waters of Pemba for a week at a time. 6 AC cabins. *Around US$1,550/£850pp per week FB, inc diving, tanks & weights*

SNORKELLING While there is no shortage of places to swim and snorkel off Pemba, most are viable only at high water. One of the best places for snorkelling lies in front of the visitor centre on Misali Island, where – in just a few feet of water, and regardless of the tide – countless fish and other underwater life can be seen in almost perfect visibility. As you drift through the water, keep an eye out among many others for unicornfish, sea goldies, cleaner wrasse, deep red and blue parrotfish, and the startling Moorish idol. Giant clams hug the reef, and sea cucumbers edge along the sandy bottom; you may even spot a grouper. Other possibilities include areas around the sandbanks that dry out at low tide along the west coast. Snorkelling trips can be organised through all the hotels and lodges; expect to pay US$20–40, depending on the distance to the site.

FISHING AND OTHER WATERSPORTS

Fishing The waters of the Pemba Channel are well known for their abundance of fish, including blue marlin, sailfish, barracuda, trevally, mahi mahi, rainbow runner and kingfish. Fishing is offered by Kervan Saray Lodge from a 7m Yamaha vessel, kitted out with electronics and echo sounder, and sometimes ranging as far as 8km offshore. This is suitable for two serious fishermen, or three if they know each other. Trolling, fly fishing, spinning gear and vertical jigging rods are all available for rent. (US$200 pp a day, plus fuel and lures; equipment hire US$40 pp per day). Three-hour fishing trips can also be arranged for their own guests with Fundu Lagoon on their 10m catamaran, the *Solkattan* (US$85 per person for two–four people). At the other end of the scale, The Manta Resort offers three days of game fishing for up to four people at US$2,100–2,300, depending on the season, including lunch, beer and soft drinks. All conventional gear from 6lb to 80lb is provided, but guests should bring their own fly-fishing and spinning equipment. Rather more accessible is a three–four-hour trip at US$150. While you could try asking around in the harbours at Wete, Wesha or Mkoani, there are few fishermen nowadays who are prepared to take visitors on board. Add to this the fact that the boats are small, and that safety records are none too great, and you'd do better to stick to one of the established operators.

Kayaking and sailing All the larger tourist lodges and hotels have kayaks, with guided trips offered by Fundu Lagoon for their guests. The Manta Resort charges US$25 for up to two hours, or US$40 for half a day. At Swahili Divers, marine anthropologist Cisca Jah runs kayak tours under the name Kasa Kayaking. A half-day guided mangrove tour with snacks and support boat costs US$59. Sailing, too, is available, either in traditional *mashuas*, or – in the case of Fundu Lagoon – in the *Solkattan*. For contact details, see *Diving*, pages 317–18.

CHAKE CHAKE

Chake Chake is the largest town on Pemba, just over halfway down the western side of the island. The island's capital and administrative centre, it forms the hub of the bus and *dala-dala* network. Although Chake Chake has been settled for as long as Zanzibar Town, it has never achieved the same degree of importance, and thus has little in the way of grand palaces or the winding narrow streets of the old Stone Town, although part of the Omani Fort, near the hospital, has recently been opened to the public as a museum.

When the first edition of this guide was researched in the early 1990s, Chake Chake – and Pemba itself – was a real sleepy backwater. Today, it's a bustling community with more than a hint of modernity: there are a couple of video-rental shops, and many of the tin-roofed houses have sprouted satellite dishes. In other ways, though, it's still very quiet and traditional, with ox-carts still trundling up the high street (although there are even more scooters). The market, around the bus station, is lively, and the old port, down the hill from the town centre, is also worth a walk. Down the back streets, particularly on the road opposite the market, are countless shops selling everything from foodstuffs and car parts to plastic mops and all types of clothing. In tiny booths tailors will knock you up a suit or skirt on an ancient treadle sewing machine. The whole place is more peaceful than Zanzibar Town, with a laid-back atmosphere, and tourists get no hassle at all, so it's great just to stroll around.

WHERE TO STAY Chake Chake's renowned Old Mission Lodge, for years the home of Swahili Divers and a first-rate hangout for laid-back scuba enthusiasts, closed its doors when owners Raf and Cisca Jah moved their operation north to Kervan Saray Beach (see page 332), leaving something of an accommodation vacuum. Fortunately there are a couple of decent and central alternatives, though you'd have to be pretty desperate to stay at the government-run Chake Chake Hotel (024 2454301; $), where the bathrooms don't look as though they've been touched for years. And the rundown GT Hotel looked even worse when we visited.

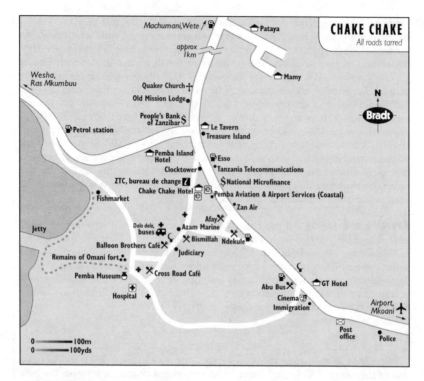

CHAKE CHAKE
All roads tarred

Machumani, Wete / Pataya

approx 1km

Wesha, Ras Mkumbuu

Mamy

Quaker Church
Old Mission Lodge

People's Bank of Zanzibar

Petrol station

Le Tavern
Treasure Island

Pemba Island Hotel

Esso
Clocktower
Tanzania Telecommunications

ZTC, bureau de change
National Microfinance

Chake Chake Hotel
Pemba Aviation & Airport Services (Coastal)

Fishmarket

Zan Air

Afay
Azam Marine

Dala dala, buses

Bismillah
Ndekule

Jetty

Balloon Brothers Café

Judiciary

Remains of Omani fort

Pemba Museum

Cross Road Café

Hospital

Abu Bus

Cinema
Immigration

GT Hotel

Airport, Mkoani

Post office

Police

0 ———— 100m
0 ———— 100yds

⌂ **Pemba Island Hotel** (15 rooms) ☏ 024 2452215; e islandhotelpembaevergreen@hotmail.com. This relatively new hotel run by strict Muslims is a welcoming & pleasant place to stay in the centre of town. Painted white with bright pink decorative tiles, it's easy to spot just down the hill from the People's Bank of Zanzibar. En-suite rooms have dbl beds (even the 'singles') with AC/fans, nets, TV & fridge. In keeping with the hotel's Muslim ethos, no alcohol is permitted on the premises, & a marriage certificate is required for a couple to share a room. Rooftop restaurant. $$$

⌂ **Hotel Le Tavern** (9 rooms) ☏ 024 2452660. On the main street, between the Chake Chake Hotel & the Old Mission Lodge, above a small row of shops. (If you're asking for directions, forget French; it's pronounced 'Lay' Tavern.) Clean, en-suite rooms with sgl beds have mosquito nets & fans. *Meals to order around US$5.* $$

Just north of the town, a handful of small guesthouses with basic but clean rooms have sprung up at lower prices:

⌂ **Venus Lodge** ᴍ 0777 475164. Just beyond the village of Machumani, about 3km north of Chake Chake on the main road towards Wete, Venus Lodge is reached easily on a number 606 *dala-dala* from the centre of town. Reopened in 2005, it's simple & looks reasonably clean, although when we visited there was no-one available to show us round. Prices are unlikely to have changed much in the last few years. *Meals on request.* $$

⌂ **Mamy Hotel** (4 rooms) ᴍ 0777 432789. This new, whitewashed building with wooden louvred shutters is tucked away in the back streets north of Chake Chake, close to Pataya Lodge. Here, too, rooms have fans & bed nets. *Dinner on request.* $

⌂ **Pataya Lodge** (6 rooms) ᴍ 0777 852970. This simple local guesthouse is fine if you want a feel of suburban living, Pemba-style. Rooms, 1 en suite, have mosquito nets & ceiling fans. To get there, head north out of town, then take the first major right turn you come to – look out for the big white wall with railings on the top. Pataya Lodge is signposted on your left, about 20m from the junction. *Meals US$4pp, with advance notice.* $

WHERE TO EAT AND DRINK All the hotels and guesthouses listed above will serve meals to non-residents, although normally food has to be ordered several hours in advance. Elsewhere, most of the town's street restaurants open from approximately 07.00 until 15.00, when the market closes.

There's also no shortage of street stalls around the market or on the main road near Le Tavern selling simple hot food during these hours, with *chipsi mai yai* at US$0.50, beans and rice for around US$1, or chicken and rice at US$2.50. In the same area around the road junction, more small stalls open up in the evening, selling food such as fried fish and chapattis.

Abu Bus Opposite the cinema, & open from 19.30, this place serving street food comes highly recommended. Try the *rojo* (a sauce made of green mango) with *mishkaki* for less than US$1, & there's fruit juice & chapattis as well. Despite the inevitable queue, it's worth the wait. **$**

Afay Restaurant Popular with local people, the more central Afay is often open till around 22.00, depending on trade & whether there's any food left. Serves good tea; pleasant service. **$**

Balloon Brothers Café Close to the market, there's quite a choice of snacks here — samosas, cake, popcorn, & *chiahoro* (like Bombay mix), as well as more substantial dishes such as *mishkaki*, or *chipsi kasava*. **$**

Bismillah This is one of the better small places around the market, & good for a no-frills lunch. **$$**

Chake Chake Hotel The government hotel has a restaurant serving b/fast, lunch & evening meals, with advance notice only, until 22.00, costing around US$6. The hotel also doubles as the town 'pub', with a bar at the front that serves beer (usually cold). Stocks are decidedly erratic, but it remains one of the very few places in this predominantly Muslim community to sell alcohol. **$$$**

Cross Road Café Also near the market, & well frequented with traders, this café serves a range of local dishes. **$$–$$$**

Ndekule Restaurant Set among the shops in the town centre, this is a good, local-style place, clean & tidy with wipe-clean plastic tables. There's usually only a few choices, such as chicken & chips or fish & rice (or vice versa) for about US$0.50. If you stroll in at lunchtime you should find something ready. **$$**

Pemba Island Hotel 07.00–10.00 & 19.00–22.00. A large TV dominates this hotel's pleasant rooftop restaurant, which boasts views across the town to the trees beyond. For evening meals, you'll need to order ahead. Food available includes egetable dishes (mashed potato US$2) as well as curries at US$4–6. Soft drinks only. **$$–$$$.**

TRAVEL AND TOUR COMPANIES

The tourist who arrives in Chake Chake in the hope of organising something on the fly could well be disappointed, since the town is less geared to visitors than in the past.

Azam Marine Down the hill from the Chake Chake Hotel, next to the market, this is the main agent for the *Serengeti*. (For the *Aziza*, the agent is in a general trading shop opposite the Chake Chake Hotel.)

Coastal Travels Ltd 024 2452162; m 0777 420702; m (Airport) 0777 418343; 07.30–17.00. This helpful bureau, almost opposite the National Microfinance Bank, is set up to handle bookings of Coastal Aviation flights between Pemba & Zanzibar, Tanga & Dar.

Modern Travelling Agency On the other side of the main street behind the Chake Chake Hotel, this is the main agent for the *Sepideh* ship to/from Zanzibar & Dar.

Treasure Island Travel & Tours 024 2452045; m 0777 862131/437397; e treasurecompany2005@yahoo.com. Next to Le Tavern, this company offers a range of tours at prices that vary according to the number of passengers. A full-day trip to Ngezi Forest & Vumawimbi Beach, for example, would cost US$70 for 1 person, dropping to US$25pp with 6 passengers. Prices include all entry fees & a light lunch. Other tours (prices shown are also for 6 people sharing or per person) include boat trips to Shamiani Island (US$70–20), tours of Chake Chake & Wete, bullfights (US$100–40), Pemba traditional dancing (US$100–40), & the Pemba flying fox. On a practical note, the company can organise motorbike & bicycle hire, & will book both accommodation & flights.

ZanAir 024 2454990. The booking office for ZanAir flights is just down the hill from the National Microfinance Bank.

Zanzibar Tourist Corporation 07.00–15.30 Mon–Fri. The state travel service, widely known as ZTC, runs

trips for a minimum of 4 people to Ngezi Forest (US$30pp), Misali Island (US$35pp) & spice tours (US$25pp), including entrance fees, lunch & soft drinks. They can also book train & ferry tickets (including the Sepideh), & change money.

SHOPPING Chake Chake's market is in the centre of town, around the bus station. In the narrow streets leading away from the market, small shops sell an almost infinite variety of goods. If you're craving *mzungu* ('white person's') food, look no further than the Why Not shop at the northern end of town, opposite the Old Mission Lodge, where the likes of chocolate, cereal, biscuits, cheese triangles, and even Pringles may be in stock, as well as good fruit juice for US$0.50.

OTHER PRACTICALITIES

Post and internet The post office is on the way into town from Mkoani, on the left-hand side. For internet users, Chake Chake's Adult Training Centre (① 07.30–22.00; TSh1,000/hr), opposite the National Microfinance Bank, has five computers. In front of the Chake Chake Hotel, the ZCF internet café (① 07.00–21.00; TSh1,000/hr), with several computers, is located on an upper storey, up a flight of outside steps. Set up by the Zanzibar Children's Fund, it is run as a fundraising venture by the Muslim community in order to help children in orphanages in the fight against HIV/AIDS. Note that in both places you are expected to remove your shoes before entering.

WHAT TO SEE AND DO Chake Chake itself has a dusty charm that repays a walk through its small market and around its narrow streets and alleys crowded with shops selling a wide range of goods. Definitely worth a visit is the new **Pemba Museum** (① 08.30–16.30 Mon–Fri, 09.00–16.00 Sat/Sun; admission US$2), opened in 2005. Located in part of the town's 18th-century Arab Fort, it retains the original wooden door, but other features were lost during restoration, and the cannons at the entrance came from Wete. Exhibits are clearly laid out on five broad themes, covering every aspect of Pemba's history, economy and culture. Of particular interest are the display on the ruins of Pemba, and the room on the island's maritime history and boatbuilding, complete with a model of a *mtepe* – a boat made of coconut rope, with sticks for nails and a sail of palm leaves, that was in use until the 1930s; the original is in the House of Wonders in Zanzibar Town. In addition to exhibitions on politics, fishing and farming, and a jailhouse (the fort was at one time Pemba's prison), there is also a considerable amount of space devoted to Swahili society. Several rooms are set out like the interior of a Swahili house, complete with relevant furniture and implements for cooking, while related displays focus on individual aspects of Swahili culture, from initiation and burial rituals to the use of herbal plants and traditional musical instruments. In the final archives room, researchers will delight in papers that have been painstakingly boxed and labelled.

Visitors to the museum will be accompanied around the exhibitions by a guide. Ask for Hamis Ali Juma, who speaks English and is particularly knowledgeable.

AROUND CHAKE CHAKE While most places in Pemba are within easy reach of Chake Chake, there are a few places of interest that are particularly well placed for those staying in the town. Of these, the easiest to get to is the flying fox centre at Kidike (see below). It is also possible to visit the **essential oils factory**

(*admission TSh2,000*). To get there, head north out of Chake Chake to the village of Machomani, then turn right towards Vitongoji; it's a ten–15-minute drive from the town centre, or you could take the number 316 *dala-dala*. Oils are extracted from a variety of plants – cloves, of course, but others include citronella and eucalyptus. Interestingly, spent cloves are used to power the burners. You could combine this with a trip to Vitongoji Beach, another 10km or so to the east.

There are also a couple of archaeological sites relatively close to the town that give a glimpse into Pemba's past and provide a great reason for a day out in the country. The route to Pujini Ruins, for example, goes through scenic fields and farmland and a few small villages, while a visit to Ras Mkumbuu usually involves a beautiful boat ride down the bay, and a walk through a grove of massive palms.

Kidike Home to more than half of Pemba's flying foxes, Kidike (⊕ *08.00–18.00 daily; admission US$3.50*) is a shared initiative between villagers and the government. Located about 7km north of Chake Chake, it is clearly signposted from the main road. Several tour operators run trips here, and individual drivers charge around US$25 from Chake Chake, including entrance. Alternatively you can take a *dala-dala* from Chake Chake, then walk the 45 minutes or so along the 3.5km track to the reserve.

Pujini Ruins The Pujini Ruins, the remains of a fortified palace built around the 15th century by Swahili people, lie about 10km to the southeast of Chake Chake, near the village of Pujini. Locally the place is called Mkame Ndume, meaning 'milker of men', derived from the name of a reputedly despotic king who ordered the palace walls to be built by local inhabitants who were forced to carry large stones while shuffling on their buttocks.

Today, the ruins of the palace cover an area of about 1.5ha, and the remains of the defensive ramparts and surrounding ditches can still be seen, although much of the area is overgrown. The ditch was once connected to the sea by a 1km-long channel. Inside the walls, a team of archaeologists working here since the mid 1990s have found remnants of three large buildings, and an underground shrine with plaster bas reliefs on the walls, and several other features. It is also possible to see some wide stairways that presumably allowed access to the defensive ramparts, the remains of a walkway that joined the town to the shore, and the site of the well. Legend tells of a wall that was built across the well so that the ruler's two wives, who lived in separate parts of the palace, would never meet if they came to get water at the same time.

The ramparts are the most interesting feature of the Pujini Ruins, in that they can be seen and appreciated by any visitor, and also because there is nothing else like them at any other Swahili site along the east African coast. They were built when the Swahili civilisation was at its zenith (see *History*, pages 5–6), and when the presence of Portuguese ships in the area posed a very real threat. It seems, however, that the walls may not have been strong enough to withstand the invaders: some Portuguese records dating from the 1520s mention the sacking of a fortified 'treasury' on the east coast of Pemba.

Archaeological evidence suggests that, although the palace may have fallen on hard times after this invasion, it remained occupied (or was possibly re-occupied) and only finally abandoned in the 19th century. Remains of other buildings, including a mosque, have been found in the area around the palace, suggesting that it did not stand alone, and that a town or larger settlement also existed here – possibly for many centuries.

Getting there You can walk the 8km or so from Chake Chake to the Pujini Ruins and back in a day, or take bus Route 319 as far as Pujini village, but it is easier to travel by hired bike or car. To get there, leave Chake Chake on the road south, and turn left onto a dirt road just after the tar road turns off to the airport. Follow the dirt road to a fork near a small dispensary, where you go left. At the next junction, go right to reach a flat grassy area which is usually wet. The ruins are amongst the trees and bushes on the far side of the grassy area. (If you get lost, ask for directions to Mkame Ndume.)

Ras Mkumbuu Ruins The headland of Ras Mkumbuu is at the end of a long peninsula about 14km to the west of Chake Chake. The relatively well-preserved ruins are at the tip of the peninsula and also seem to be called Ndagoni (although Mkumbuu and Ndagoni may have been different places). This is the site of a Swahili settlement, thought to have been one of the largest towns on the coast (and in east Africa) during the 11th century. It is also considered to be the site of the earlier port of Qanbalu, where Omani sailors traded in slaves and timber.

Today, the remains of a large, 13th-century mosque can still be seen here, although this is becoming very overgrown, and also several 14th-century pillar tombs, graves with a tall 'chimney' at one end, used to mark the burial place of prominent Muslims. Pillar tombs are found in other parts of east Africa and are held to be one of the most distinctive forms of monument built by the Swahili people. The tombs here are in poor condition, although an inscription on one states that they were restored in 1916.

Getting there and away The easiest and most enjoyable way to reach the ruins is by hired boat, or on an organised tour – which may also visit Misali Island on the same day. Near the ruins is a small fishing village, and to reach the mosque and tombs you walk through maize fields and a plantation of tall palms with smooth white trunks. A road from Chake Chake leads westwards along the peninsula towards Ras Mkumbuu, but it becomes impassable and turns into a track for the final 5km, which is negotiable only on foot or by bike.

SOUTH OF CHAKE CHAKE

The main road from Chake Chake south to Mkoani follows a winding route through hilly terrain clothed by an abundance of fruit trees, interspersed by villages at every turn. Bananas grow freely, with jack fruit, passion fruit, breadfruit, mango and papaya all very much in evidence. In season, cloves lie drying on mats by the side of the road, their scent pervading the air. Look out in particular for the trees to the east of the road that are home to the Pemba flying fox.

MKOANI Mkoani is the smallest of Pemba's three main towns, but the passenger boat services linking it to Zanzibar Town and the mainland make the port the busiest and most important on the island. Any time a boat is docking or leaving there's a buzz in the air, and perhaps the opportunity to watch boats being loaded with cloves for Zanzibar, but for the rest of the time Mkoani is very quiet and sleepy. Although a few businesses are located near the port, and the market is just along the coast, the main town of Mkoani is up the hill towards Chake Chake. A footpath leads up some steps from opposite the port towards the town, cutting out the bends in the road and bringing you out by the old petrol station.

 Where to stay For some visitors, Mkoani remains the main gateway to Pemba, and a couple of local guesthouses cater for this, but the closure of some in recent years reflects the increasing reliance by visitors on air travel.

🏠 **Jondeni Guesthouse** (8 rooms) 📞 024 2456042;
e pembablue@hotmail.com. By far the best place
to stay in Mkoani itself, Jondeni is to the north of
town, a dusty 10–15min walk uphill from the port.
The clean, white-painted bungalow is set in lush
gardens, complete with hammock, & the friendly staff
make staying here a pleasure. Clean, simple rooms —
some en suite — have fans & mosquito nets. Drinks
& meals (around US$5) are available, taken on the

shady terrace overlooking the sea — a perfect place
for whiling away a hot afternoon. If you're feeling
more active, the guesthouse can also arrange
snorkelling, sailing & fishing trips, & island tours.
$-$$

🏠 **Mkoani Hotel** This ZTC-run hotel is a clone of
the ZTC Hotel in Chake Chake, with the same prices,
& is equally uninspiring. $$

✗ **Where to eat** Apart from the hotels above, both of which serve food (the Jondeni
is by far the better bet), places to eat in Mkoani are very limited. There's a small
restaurant close to the hospital, at the eastern end of town, but that's pretty well it.
A couple of stalls sell fruit, sweets and biscuits for the passing boat-passenger trade.

Travel agents and tour companies Almost next to the quay, Mkoani's port office
is open from 08.00 to 15.30 daily. Tickets can be bought here for the *Mapinduzi*,
Serengeti and *Sepideh* ferries that run between Pemba and Zanzibar Island (see pages
311–12).

Other practicalities Aside from the hospital, towards the eastern end of town,
Mkoani has very little to offer the visitor. A couple of communications centres lie
on the road near the port, but more usefully there's a yellow telephone kiosk by the
port office. In the centre of Mkoani, close to the Mkoani Hotel, is the post office,
and there's a small shop in the hotel's car park selling groceries and general stores.

WAMBAA The small village of Wambaa is to the north of Mkoani. Nearby is the
long and idyllic Wambaa Beach, facing southwest overlooking Mkoani Bay and out
towards the Pemba Channel. At its northern end lies Pemba's most exclusive hotel,
Fundu Lagoon.

🏠 **Where to stay**

🏠 **Fundu Lagoon** (16 rooms) reservations 📞 024
2232926; hotel m 0777 438668; e info@
fundulagoon.com; www.fundulagoon.com;

🕓 mid-Jun–mid-Apr. It's not difficult to see why
young honeymooners flock to this secluded, lodge-
style place tucked away 15mins by boat from

Mkoani. Combining the flexibility of a hotel with the individuality of a smaller lodge, it's a relaxed hideaway on the beach with attentive service, & a lively atmosphere of bright young things. Linked to the central area by sandy walkways, tented rooms nestle among the trees to form the core of each carefully designed, thatched bungalow. Inside are polished wooden floors, furniture of wicker & wood, & a ceiling fan above the bed. At the back, a small en-suite bathroom showcases the hotel's own range of handmade aromatherapy toiletries (available to purchase from the shop). Each bungalow has its own veranda, facing out to sea. Suites expand on the theme to offer a private plunge pool, & — in superior suites — a 2-storey lounge area to sit & watch the birds with a cool drink or simply to chill.

The restaurant serves 3-course meals with 3 or 4 options for each course; fish dishes are a speciality. The tables are individual, some overlooking the beach, while less formal bites may be taken in the breezy jetty bar, a perfect spot to watch the sun go down (eased by the availability of a free 'cocktail of the evening'!). There are also regular BBQ & Swahili nights.

When it comes to activities, snorkelling, kayaking & fishing are on offer, as well as a fully equipped dive centre (see page 317). Rather less strenuous are sunset dhow cruises, boat trips to Misali Island & poolside loungers with panoramic ocean views. Off the water, there's a popular treatment room with a wide range of massages & beauty treatments at US$15–80, & a games room with satellite TV. Excursions to the village of Wambaa can be arranged with members of the resort's staff, as can hair braiding.

Fundu Lagoon's marketing & prices are glossy & top-notch. The reality is quite a pleasant beachside lodge that's often top of young honeymooners' lists, whilst rather further down the pecking order for the well travelled. Researchers for this book & holidaymakers have consistently disagreed over the general quality of the finishing & food (one noted 'first-class — some of the best fish I've ever had', whilst another regarded the food as 'mediocre & way below the standard expected for a lodge of this cost level'). *Ocean view US$305–370pp; beachside US$330–405pp; suite US$425–485pp; superior suite US$530–610pp; sgl supplement US$135–220/night; all rates FB & inc canoe use and a dhow sunset cruise; airport transfer US$40pp*

MISALI ISLAND Misali (also spelt Mesali) Island lies to the west of Chake Chake Town, an easy boat ride from Chake Chake or Mkoani. Surrounded by a coral reef, it's a popular destination for tourists, with some idyllic beaches, good swimming (it's one of the few places in Pemba where you can swim at high or low tide), and even better snorkelling, with clear shallow water, and a good display of corals. It's also a favourite spot for divers.

The island is covered in forest, with a mix of evergreen and deciduous species, and most notably many large baobabs. Vervet monkeys cavort among the branches, peering down at visitors. Birds to be spotted here include red-eyed dove, mangrove kingfisher, paradise flycatcher, Pemba white-eye and Pemba sunbird. Fischer's turaco has also been recorded. An increasing number of green sea turtles are successfully nesting on the beach on the western side of the island, with hawksbill turtles also present.

Locally, Misali has 'holy island' status. When the Prophet Hadhara found himself without a prayer mat, it is said that he made use instead of the teardrop-shaped island which faces Mecca; the word *msala* means 'prayer mat'. The strong Islamic environmental stewardship ethic is being used to support management and environmental education, and the island was a 'sacred gift for a living planet' from the Islamic faith as part of a millennium celebration organised by WWF in 2000.

The notorious pirate Captain Kidd is reputed to have had a hideout on the island in the 17th century, and even to have buried treasure here. Today, the island and the surrounding reef are incorporated in the Misali Island Marine Conservation Area, under the auspices of the Misali Island Management Committee. Formed as a partnership between the Zanzibar government, the local fishermen's association and the Misali Island Conservation Association (MICA), with support from CARE International, the committee is dominated by fishermen, while the rangers are employed by MICA. It's not entirely satisfactory, with considerable concerns locally about infringements of the no-take zone to the west of the island, and armed soldiers have recently been introduced to support the rangers. Almost two-thirds of the revenue from visitors goes towards managing the island, with the rest earmarked for community development. Conservation measures involve the input of local fishermen, who can continue working here in a managed environment. As just one example of how the scheme is working, local fishermen are prevented from camping on the beach itself (they camp among the trees), so as not to disturb turtles nesting. Additionally, the nests are monitored and protected, along with the rest of the island, by the rangers.

Just 1.4km long, and covering a total area of 90ha, the island consists of 15,000-year-old uplifted coral, with a surrounding coral reef to a maximum depth of 64m. Mangroves fringe much of the island, making a fascinating place for snorkelling during spring high tides. A series of walking trails has been established through the forest, where there are three caves that are considered sacred. In time of need, local people would come to one of the caves with a witchdoctor to pray for help, making payment in the form of a chicken, a goat or even a cow. It takes about 2.5 hours to walk round the island (at low tide only), taking in an inter-tidal trail to the west of the island. At the landing point for visitors, there is a shaded information centre, with benches for picnics, and displays on what to see with a good map showing the various trails. On the beach in front, a few sun beds have been set out, but banish all thoughts of commercialism – it remains a tranquil spot visited by just a few people at any one time.

Getting there Misali Island can be reached by hired boat from Chake Chake or Mkoani (see the *Boat hire* and *Travel and tour companies* sections on pages 314 and 321–2 respectively). There are also organised excursions run by various local tour operators, as well as by individual hotels for their guests. In addition, a few of the dive centres based in the northern part of Zanzibar Island run trips here. The island is also visited by groups from passing cruise ships and live-aboards.

Some unlicensed fishing boats run to the island, but few have lifejackets or back-up engines. One that does is the *Victoria*, owned by Captain Hamoud, who can be found at Chake Chake's port area of Wesha.

SHAMIANI ISLAND Shamiani Island, also called Kiweni Island, is a remote and beautiful spot east of Mkoani, just 100m or so off the far southeastern tip of Pemba Island. Until recently Shamiani has been a deserted island accessible only to the very determined. Getting there involved taking some form of transport from Chake Chake to the village of Kengeja, reached by branching off the main Mkoani to Chake Chake road at Mtambile. From the small beach south of Kengeja, you have to sail across to Shamiani. Now that is all set to change with the development of a new, eco-friendly lodge on the island, finally settling the rumours that have flowed for many years.

Where to stay

Pemba Lodge ✆ 024 2240494;
e mnarani@zanlink.com; www.pembalodge.com.
Currently under construction, Pemba Lodge is the vision of Nassor Ali, owner of the popular Mnarani Beach Cottages (see page 208). Focused clearly on those seeking both privacy and R&R, it will incorporate thatched bungalows with en-suite bathrooms to be constructed on raised platforms, all set along the beach. The lodge is being designed to create minimum environmental impact. Features include not just solar-powered lighting & hot water, & composting eco toilets, but also a design that will harness the breeze that blows from the Pemba Channel, thus obviating the necessity for energy-guzzling AC. No opening date has been set, but at the time of writing it was estimated to be towards the end of 2009.

The second-largest town on Pemba, Wete is at the head of a large inlet on the west coast, in the northern part of the island. Spread out down a long central street, it's quieter than Chake Chake, with more ox-carts and fewer mopeds. For most travellers Wete is a good base for exploring northern Pemba: from here Tumbe, the Chwaka Ruins, Konde and Ngezi Forest can all be easily reached.

Wete has a large harbour, mainly used by cargo ships and dhows. It can sometimes be busy here, with vessels from Tanga offloading cement or timber, and loading up with cloves, coconuts or other Pemban commodities. Local ferries also sail across the inlet to Mtambwe Island, where you can get to the ruins of Mtambwe Mkuu, and to Fundo Island.

GETTING THERE AND AWAY North of Chake Chake, the dense vegetation of the south gives way to open pasture and scrubland. The new main road bypasses Wete entirely as it hugs the eastern side of the island, but it is still the quickest route between the two towns. The turn-off to Wete is about 20km from Chake Chake at the village of Chwale. From here it's a reasonable road to Mzambaroani, past the rubber plantation where what look like old flannels are hung out on racks to dry in the sun, before winding the last few kilometres to Wete.

WHERE TO STAY

Bomani Guesthouse (8 rooms) ☏ 024 2454384. Rather less attractive than the nearby Sharook (see below), but on the same street, the Bomani is owned by the port authorities in Wete, & is fairly basic. $

North Lodge (4 rooms) m 0777 427459. Not far from the ZTC Hotel, behind a block of flats on the other side of the road, this converted house has basic rooms of sometimes dubious cleanliness, with fans & nets; 2 are en suite. The owner, Mr Abouey, is something of a Mr Fixit, prepared to arrange tours, & cars or bikes for rent. *Dinner on request* TSh4,000. $

Sharook Guesthouse (5 rooms) ☏ 024 2454386. Wete's best accommodation bet is in the lower part of town, on a quiet side street near the market & bus station. It's a small, clean, family-run place with a peaceful & friendly atmosphere. With its own generator, the guesthouse offers constant running water & functioning TV. Dinner, with local dishes, must be ordered well in advance. Bike hire (US$5 per day) can be arranged, as can a range of tours around the island. *Dinner US$5.* $

Wete Government Hotel (6 rooms) ☏ 024 2454301. This is the third in the series of cloned ZTC-run hotels on Pemba, & its en-suite rooms afford no pleasant surprises. $

WHERE TO EAT

All the hotels and guesthouses serve food with advance notice, and Wete also has a choice of local eating houses, most open until the last buses have left at 16.00. Several are located to the west of town, close to the port and bus station. Of these, the best is **Green Garden Refreshments**, a pleasant open-air café. Omelette and chips or beans and rice are less than US$1, and other meals, based on beef and chicken, are also available. It's open all day, but not always at weekends. Opposite the market and bus station, **Laki Sipesa** (which means '100,000 has no value') serves pilau rice and meat, plus bread, chapattis and tea, while next door is the similar **Ramsally Restaurant**. There's also a good bakery next to the market.

Further up the main street away from the port is the **Salim Café**, a large place with loud TV popular with locals, who recommend the biryani and pilau at TSh1,500 each. Unusually, it's open all day, 07.00–22.00. Up towards the ZTC Hotel, a number of small local cafés vie with street stalls selling the usual range of fare, including – we've heard – very good octopus and chapattis, with sugarcane juice to drink at TSh100.

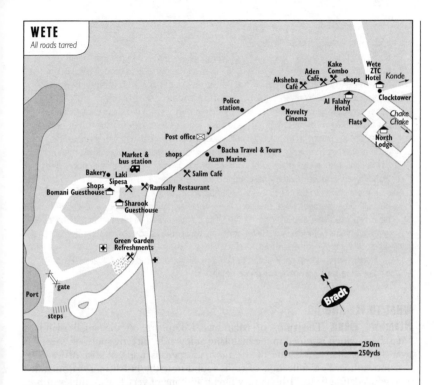

WETE
All roads tarred

Konde
Wete ZTC Hotel
Kake Combo shops
Clocktower
Aden Café
Chake Chake
Aksheba Café
Al Falahy Hotel
Police station
Novelty Cinema
Flats
North Lodge
Post office
Bacha Travel & Tours
shops
Azam Marine
Market & bus station
Salim Café
Bakery
Laki Sipesa
Shops
Ramsally Restaurant
Bomani Guesthouse
Sharook Guesthouse
Green Garden Refreshments
Port
gate
steps

N

0 — 250m
0 — 250yds

TRAVEL AND TOUR COMPANIES

Azam Marine Opposite the post office. Sells tickets for the *Serengeti* boat.
Bachaa Travel & Tours m 0777 423429/427658; e samhamx@yahoo.com; ⏰ 07.30–15.00. Opposite the post office, Bachaa handles everything from tourist information, tickets & accommodation reservations to various tours. Sole agent for Fast Ferries' *SES II* ferry, it also handles tickets for the

Aziza. Various trips include visits to Ngezi Forest (US$110 for 1–3 people; US$150 4–9, including fees & lunch, or US$85/115 without lunch).
Raha Travel Agency On the main street, sells tickets for the *Sepideh* (although this ship goes to/from Mkoani).
ZSC office Opposite Green Garden Refreshments. Sells tickets for the *Mapinduzi*.

For additional services, including organised tours, try the Sharook Guesthouse or North Lodge (see *Where to stay*, opposite). **Sharook Guesthouse** offers a good range of tours: a boat ride to Mtambwe Mkuu Ruins costs US$5 per person; a minibus to Ngezi Forest costs US$35. Highly recommended all-day trips to Fundo Island cost US$30 for the whole motorboat (seating up to ten) or US$27 for a dhow; or you can go to Misali Island for US$70.

CAR AND BIKE RENTAL If you want to reach the places of interest around Wete independently, North Lodge (see *Where to stay*, opposite) can arrange small Suzuki 'jeeps' for US$50 per day, motorbikes for US$20 per day, and bikes for US$5 per day. The Sharook, too, can hire out bikes for the same price.

OTHER PRACTICALITIES The **post office** (⏰ 08.00–13.00 & 14.00–16.00 Mon–Thu, 08.00–12.00 & 14.00–17.00 Fri) is on the right of the main street about halfway towards the port. The so-called Novelty Cinema, on the left nearer the entrance to the town, opens in the evenings, with an entrance fee of TSh600.

Somewhat surprisingly, the island of Pemba is a place where you might see bullfighting in Iberian style. The origins of this sport are uncertain although it is thought to have been introduced here by the Portuguese during the 16th century. Bullfights take place close to Wingwi, in the northeast of the island, during holiday times, mostly between August and November, after the harvest and before the short rains, but also between December and February after the short rains. Local 'matadors' put on a brave display, posing in front of the bull, goading him into a charge and then standing aside at the last moment, much to the appreciation of watching villagers. At the end of the fight, the bull is not killed but praised by the fighter, and sometimes decorated with flowers and leaves, then paraded around the village.

If you happen to be in Pemba when a bullfight is planned, it's worth going to see, but, although sometimes it can be a lively and fascinating spectacle, a few visitors have reported that in reality some bullfights can be fairly uneventful, and seem to involve a group of local wide-boys annoying an apathetic cow by beating her with sticks, while the local girls shriek loudly.

Exactly when a bullfight is about to take place is hard to find out. Ask at your hotel or a reliable tour company for more details.

WHAT TO SEE AND DO

Mtambwe Mkuu The ruins of Mtambwe Mkuu are on the small island of Mtambwe, which is joined to the mainland at low tide, directly south of Wete. For over 1,000 years, it was one of the most prosperous ports of east Africa. The 'Mtambwe hoard', a collection of coins found near the beach in 1984, included gold coins dating from 11th-century Egypt, and one of very few examples of pre-colonial minted silver currency anywhere in east Africa. Despite its rich past, there's little to see at Mtambwe Mkuu these days, although a trip there from Wete is a very pleasant way to pass the day.

Getting there and away From Wete harbour you go by small dhow or canoe to Mtambwe village, then walk south, west and north around a creek and through mangrove swamps to reach the ruins. Apparently, when the water is high, you can get cut off at the ruins, or be forced to wade back to Mtambwe village through the mangroves, so careful checking of the tides is recommended. Sharook Guesthouse in Wete can arrange tours or give you advice.

NORTH OF WETE

Although there are more direct routes from Wete to the north of the island, it is quicker to head east to Chwale, then take the main tarred road north. This also has the advantage of passing close to many of Pemba's places of interest, so makes for an interesting journey in its own right.

From Chwale, the landscape is mainly farmland, dotted with coconut palms as it heads up the east coast. Just before the turn-off to Micheweni, in an area generally known as Wingwi, is a rather unprepossessing stretch of green which, come the end of the year and at times of government celebration, plays host to the island's bullfights (see box, *Bullfighting on Pemba*, above).

KIUYU PENINSULA To the east of the main north–south road, a narrow isthmus separates the rest of Pemba from the Kiuyu Peninsula. A rough road, north of the 'bullring', leads to the village of Micheweni (about 5km), which has a school, a hospital and a few shops, but no place to stay. (Confusingly, Micheweni is also sometimes called Wingwi, the name not only of the area but also of another village a few kilometres to the south.) The road deteriorates from here passing through the village of Kiuyu, and becoming a deep-red dirt track, reminiscent of mainland Africa, before it reaches **Ras Kiuyu Forest Reserve**, almost at the tip of the peninsula. It's a remote and somewhat inaccessible place, smaller than the forest at Ngezi (see pages 333–4) and with a less impressive range of vegetation and wildlife. Nevertheless, it has been highly recommended as a day trip from Wete or even Chake Chake, as much for the interesting journey through the fields and villages as for the forest itself. The unspoilt Kiuyu Beach, to the east of the forest, is an added attraction.

Getting there and away By public transport, you can catch an early *dala-dala* from Wete to Micheweni. From here, it's a 5km walk to the village of Kiuyu and another 5km into the forest itself. About 3km beyond Kiuyu village, a narrow track branches right (east) to Kiuyu Beach. Nearby, another track branches left to another small beach on the west of the peninsula called Mbuyu Kambaa. The only alternative is to hire a driver with a 4x4, since the road beyond Micheweni is unsuitable for other vehicles.

CHWAKA RUINS Continuing north from the bullring, near the coast, are the ruins of the town of Chwaka. Dating from as early as the 9th century, the town was active as a port in the 15th century, probably linked to a network of villages trading with the east African coast and beyond. The ruins are sometimes referred to as Harouni, a reflection of the town's association with a local king called Harouni, who was the son of Mkama Ndume, builder of Pujini (see pages 323–4).

The most easily recognised buildings are two small mosques, standing well apart. The larger and better-preserved Friday mosque is also the site of the king's tomb. Local legend has it that the two mosques were built because the king's two wives were constantly at loggerheads, and that the town was eventually destroyed by the second wife's family.

There are also remains of houses and tombs. Nearby stood another group of tombs and an 18th-century fort built by the Mazrui group of Omanis, and on the other side of the road are some more remains called Old Tumbe. As with most of Pemba's ruins, don't go expecting a major archaeological find, but it's an interesting place and offers free rein to the imagination.

Getting there and away Chwaka is signposted to the east of the main road between Wete and Tumbe, just north of where it crosses a swampy area on an embankment with metal crash barriers on either side. The ten-minute walk takes you through cassava fields and past lofty palms, with a splendid view over the bay towards Micheweni as you approach the ruins themselves.

TUMBE The village of Tumbe, not far from the Chwaka Ruins, has the largest fish market on Pemba. Particularly busy in the mornings, it attracts people from all over the island to buy fish, which they carry away in plaited baskets strapped to the back of bicycles. It's an interesting place for visitors to watch the boats come in with fish of all sizes to be offered for sale.

Tumbe lies off the main tar road about 5km east of Konde, and can be reached by bus or bike from Wete, or with a hired car. A *dala-dala* stops at the junction, from where it's a pleasant walk through the long, narrow village to the coast; by car, it's about a ten-minute drive from the main road.

KONDE Near the end of the tarred road, the small town of Konde is also the end of the road for the *dala-dala* network, and the last place to stock up for a picnic before venturing further north to Ngezi Forest and Vumawimbi Beach. Men on bicycles weave up and down the dusty main street, with palm-leaf baskets strapped to the back laden with produce. During market hours, until 14.00, fruit stalls line the road, and there's a bakery selling fresh bread. There's also a restaurant where dishes such as pilau and *chipsi maiyai* can be bought for around TSh550. And for those with a sweet tooth, Konde is said to be the only place on Pemba where fresh ice cream is sold.

NGEZI PENINSULA

The Ngezi Peninsula is the northernmost point on Pemba, jutting out from the northwestern corner of the island. Beyond Konde, a significant area is taken up by Ngezi Forest, the last remains of a huge tract of indigenous forest which used to cover much of Pemba.

Curving round the eastern side of the peninsula is **Vumawimbi Beach**, one of the most beautiful on Pemba, with miles of dazzling white sand flanked by pristine forest. Here and there fishermen sit and mend their nets, watching over their *ngalawas* as they wait for the tide, and occasionally an ox-cart rolls along the sand. Rumours have abounded for years about the construction of a hotel, but for now the beach remains remote and unspoilt. You can walk there across the fields from Ngezi Forest or The Manta Resort, or go with a driver.

The west of the peninsula is flanked by the long expanse of **Verani Beach** with, at its northern end, a place called **Pango Ya Watoro** ('the cave of the fugitives'). At low tide, sandbanks dry out offshore, and boat trips from the nearby Manta Resort Lodge take visitors out with a picnic to swim and snorkel. It's possible to walk along the beach to the **lighthouse** near Ras Kigomasha, but only at low tide, so do check carefully before setting out; there's an alternative route through the fields if the water is up. Built by the British in the 1800s, the lighthouse offers some outstanding views out to sea and across the lush green landscape of northern Pemba. It costs US$2 per person to climb the 95 narrow steps to the top – just ask at the house nearby for the lighthouse keeper.

GETTING THERE AND AWAY You can get from Wete as far as Konde by *dala-dala*, but from there you'll have to walk the 5km along the road, bordered by farmland, to the Ngezi Forest entrance gate. If you make an early start this walk is a nice part of the day out. Alternatively, and especially if you want to go on to one of the beaches, you'll need to hire a car from Wete or Chake, for which you can expect to pay US$40–70 for the day, or travel as part of an organised tour (see pages 329 and 321–2 respectively). Beyond the entrance gate to Ngezi Forest the road is rough, and to get to the beach is sandy too, so unless it's dry a high-clearance 4x4 is recommended.

 WHERE TO STAY It's possible to visit the forest and beaches around Ngezi for the day, and stay overnight in Wete or Chake Chake. Alternatively, there are a few more upmarket places to stay nearby:

Kervan Saray Beach m 0773 176737/8, 0784 394980; e resort@kayakpemba.com; www.kervansaraybeach.com. The first hotel to open on Pemba since the millennium, Kervan Saray Beach is Swahili Divers' new home. Owned & managed by Turkish adventurer Raf Jah & his Dutch anthropologist wife, Cisca, this is a simple & unpretentious affair. Located in the far northwest of the island, close to the small village of Makangale, Kervan Saray's thatched, whitewashed cottages are just above a sand and rock beach that is excellent for swimming at high tide. The outgoing tide can leave 100m of reef exposed at low tide, which makes for great beachcombing.

Inside each room, there's a dbl & sgl bed, both complete with mosquito nets, an en-suite bathroom & even an African-style solar-heated outdoor shower (the water is cool if the sun isn't out). There is generator power 18.00–06.00 for light, but laptops & cameras can be charged in the office at other times. Everything is simple. Don't come expecting luxuries; come instead for the informal friendliness of the place, & perhaps the marine adventure.

The lodge boasts a PADI 5* Resort Dive Centre with a team who are experienced in the surrounding reefs & sometimes challenging waters (see Swahili Divers, page 317). Snorkellers, sunbathers & cruisers are more than welcome to hop on board, too. Birdwatching tours can be arranged to see Pemba's 4 endemic species: the Pemba white eye, Pemba scops owl, Pemba green pigeon and Pemba sunbird. Trips are free for guests who prebook as birders, but park fees are payable extra (see below). Kayaking, fishing, local hikes & trips to the Ngezi Forest are also on offer.

Aside from making sure everyone has a good time, the lodge is trying hard to maintain a low carbon footprint & to work with the local community. In addition to employment & donations of expertise & practical help, the lodge has a programme to enhance the lives of the local villagers. $$$–$$$$

🏠 **The Manta Resort** (10 rooms) www.themantaresort.com; ☉ Aug–May. Overlooking the northern end of Verani Beach, in a truly stunning location, The Manta Resort was originally built as a dedicated diving place offering simple but good accommodation & service. Recently however, it has been renovated as a smarter beach resort catering to divers & landlubbers alike. Spacious, individual sea-front villas are built up on stilts with an open front

to catch the sea breeze, affording a panoramic view across the Pemba Channel. With AC, a big dbl bed, small lounge area & en-suite bathroom, these are the resort's premium rooms. The garden rooms set behind the chalets are less open, with views across the gardens. They are cool inside though, with all-white interiors, AC & rustic 4-poster beds. A central area serves as dining room, bar, lounge & lobby, with a big terrace looking out to sea & steps leading down to a powder-sand beach, with a newly built 2-tiered beach bar. For entertainment & relaxation, there is a pool for swimming & diving lessons, a TV, a pool table by the cocktail bar & a small selection of books to browse.

Aside from watersports, guests benefit from a location that boasts a wide range of birdlife & some interesting walks to the lighthouse, Vumawimbi Beach & Ngezi Forest (5km). Other options include kayaking, boat trips & fishing (advance notice required for big-game fishing), as well as village tours, & massages in the Peponi Spa. An on-site shop sells the basics & internet access is available. *Sea-front villa US$310–345 pp; garden room US$199–234pp; all rates FB; airport transfer US$48pp; transfers also possible from Shimoni in Kenya (min 2 people) by speedboat (90mins) or MS Jambo (3hrs)*

🏠 **The Manta Divers Village** (10 private chalets) www.themantadiversvillage.com. A dedicated dive resort, this has the benefit of using its sister property's upmarket facilities at Manta Resort, whilst maintaining a more low-key feel & cheaper rates. New for 2008, the en-suite palm-thatched chalets are dotted around the gardens, overlooking the Pemba Channel. They are rustic in appearance & décor with wooden floors, king-size beds, & en-suite bathrooms as standard. *US$151–186pp, FB; airport transfer US$48pp*

NGEZI FOREST RESERVE (☉ 07.30–15.30 daily; admission short tour US$5 pp, longer tour or birdwatching US$10; transit fee US$2; night walks by prior arrangement) This reserve is virtually all that remains of a vast area of indigenous forest that used to cover much of the island. One of the highlights of Pemba, especially if you have an interest in wildlife, it offers the opportunity to discover Pemba as it once was. It's advisable not to arrive too early because mosquitoes remain active in the morning. A 2km nature trail takes in sections of moist forest, and several large ponds. A guided walk with the rangers takes about an hour, and is a must if you want to have a brief insight into the forest's different habitats and to spot some of the animals and birds that live among the trees. Tips are negotiable, but it's reasonable to give around US$5 for a small group. Birdwatching trips can be organised, too, as can walks in the late evening, or at night, when you have a much better chance of seeing the Pemba flying fox and the russet scops owl. To set up a trip of this ilk, contact the rangers' office in advance, during opening hours.

History Historically, the forest was used by local people, as it provided timber, fuelwood, edible plants, medicinal plants, and material for baskets and ropes, but at the same time areas of forest were being cleared for small-scale agriculture, and since the early 19th century for large plantations – especially for cloves. Although the first forest inventory was carried out in the 1920s, it wasn't until 30 years later that the reserve was established. Even then, a commercial sawmill owned by one Vi Arnjosh continued to extract timber until the mid 1960s, when the government officially took control. The rude hut in which he lived and the rusting remnants of his sawmill can be seen on the nature trail.

Through the 1970s and 1980s Ngezi was virtually ignored by the government, while encroachment and overuse by local people endangered the forest and its wildlife. Then, in 1995, funds were received from the Forest and Park Service of Finland, and a management plan was drawn up to preserve the remaining forest by strengthening conservation efforts and improving management. In this way, people from the ten villages within the reserve could still utilise the forest, but at a sustainable rate, and wildlife could also benefit. It is hoped that the forest can be developed to attract tourists as a way of raising revenue – which would in turn ensure its future protection.

Ecology The reserve covers just 1,476ha but the variety of soil types has resulted in a wide range of vegetation. Dominant are 943ha of tropical moist forest, which once covered most of the island. Found mainly in the central and eastern parts of the reserve (the part most easily reached by visitors) it has some trees reaching over 40m in height – most notably the *Odyendea zimmermanii*, known locally as *mbanko*. Also to be found is the endemic Pemba palm *(mpapindi, Dypsis pembanus)*, an ornamental tree whose red seeds are attractive to birds.

Other vegetation types include swamp forest, coastal thicket, heathland, pockets of mangroves and palms, and raffia stands. The mix is unique in east Africa, with several species more usually found in lowland mountain regions, as well as those more often found in coastal areas, plus eastern Indian and Malagasy species, and even a southeast Asian wild banana. There are also several introduced tree species.

The forest is home to several animal species, most notably the Pemba flying fox. Other animals found in Ngezi include the Pemba vervet monkey, the greater bushbaby, Zanzibar tree hyrax *(pelele, Dendrohyrax validus neumannii)*, blue duiker *(paa wa pemba)* and marsh mongoose *(chonjwe, Atilax paludinosus)*. A band of wild European pigs, descended from domestic animals introduced by the Portuguese centuries ago, also lives in the forest. As most people on Pemba are Muslims and abstain from pork, these animals are not hunted.

For birdwatchers, Ngezi Forest is undoubtedly the best place on Pemba, with all the endemics and sub-endemics present here. Visitors could also see palm-nut vultures, crowned hornbills, red-billed hornbills, and kingfishers, as well as turacos and starlings. (For more details, see *Chapter 3, Natural environment*, page 60.)

13

Mafia Archipelago

While Zanzibar is entrenched as probably the most popular ocean resort in east Africa, the small archipelago around Mafia Island, 160km to its south, remains virtually unknown. Poor communications with the mainland and a rather unfortunate name have not served Mafia well, but a growing trickle of visitors over recent years has been unanimous in singing the island's praises. A few interesting Swahili ruins notwithstanding, Mafia lacks for an equivalent to Zanzibar's atmospheric Stone Town, so that it cannot be recommended as an alternative destination for those whose primary interest in Tanzania's islands is cultural or historical.

By contrast, the combination of a clutch of small, high-quality lodges, offshore diving and snorkelling that ranks with the very best in the Indian Ocean, and a conspicuous absence of hassle and crime, make it the ideal destination for those seeking an exclusive but low-key Indian Ocean retreat. Paradoxically, perhaps, Mafia also has considerable potential for budget travellers seeking a truly off-the-beaten-track and adventurous experience.

The Mafia Archipelago, which lies in the Indian Ocean some 20km east of the Rufiji River Delta in central Tanzania, probably became isolated from the mainland some 20,000 years ago. The archipelago consists of about 15 sandstone and coral-rag islands and numerous smaller atolls and sandbars, none of which reaches an elevation above 80m, and all but two of which are little more than 1km² in extent. The central island, known today as Mafia (though it seems that this name applied to the archipelago rather than any specific island prior to the 20th century), is by far the largest, approximately 50km long by 15km across. The second-largest island is Juani, about 8km long and up to 4km wide, which lies to the southeast of the main island and was the centre of local political activity in medieval times. Sandwiched between these two larger islands, the tiny Chole Island superseded Juani as the local centre of trade in the Omani era.

The archipelago's estimated population of nearly 41,000 lives in rustic fishing communities and farming villages dotted all over Mafia and the smaller islands, although many of the islands are theoretically uninhabited. The largest town and

WHAT'S IN A NAME?

There are a number of suggestions for the source of the archipelago's name, but it isn't derived from the Sicilian crime syndicate. It may have origins in the Arabic word *Morfiyeh* meaning 'group', describing the archipelago of Mafia, or be named after the Ma'afir, an Arab tribe from Merku (Mocha) in present-day Yemen. An unlikely suggestion is that the name derives from the Arabic *mafi* meaning 'waste' or 'rubbish', or perhaps from the Swahili *mahali pa afya* meaning 'a healthy place to live'. The authors would be grateful for any further suggestions!

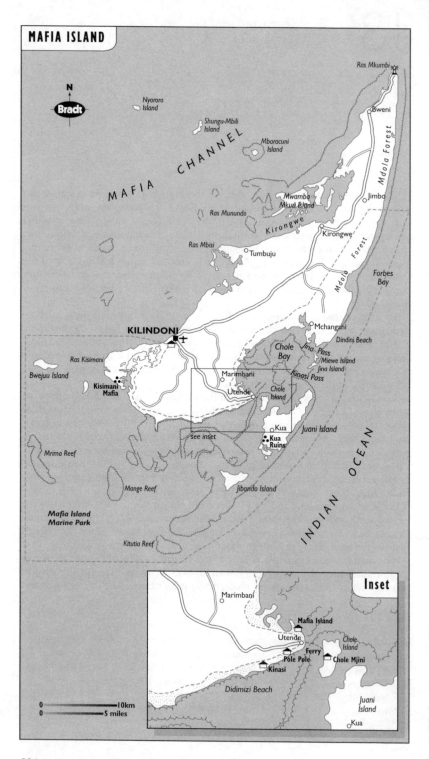

MAFIA ISLAND

N

Bradt

Nyororo Island

Shungu-Mbili Island

Mbaracuni Island

MAFIA CHANNEL

Mwamba Mkuti Island

Ras Munundo

Kirongwe

Kirongwe

Ras Mbisi

Tumbuju

Mdola Forest

Mdola Forest

Jimba

Bweni

Ras Mkumbi

Forbes Bay

KILINDONI

Mchangani

Dindini Beach

Ras Kisimani

Chole Bay

Jina Pass

Miewe Island

Jina Island

Bwejuu Island

Kisimani Mafia

Marimbani

Utende

Kinasi Pass

Chole Island

Kua

Kua Ruins

Juani Island

see inset

INDIAN OCEAN

Mrima Reef

Mange Reef

Jibondo Island

Mafia Island Marine Park

Kitutia Reef

Inset

Marimbani

Mafia Island

Utende

Chole Island

Ferry

Pole Pole

Chole Mjini

Kinasi

Didimizi Beach

Juani Island

Kua

0 ——— 10km
0 ——— 5 miles

port on Mafia Island is Kilindoni in the southeast, the site of the airstrip, and the main landing point for dhows from the mainland. Although several local guesthouses can be found in Kilindoni, the centre of upmarket tourist development is Chole Bay on the southeastern side of the island. Three established tourist lodges lie within 1km of each other near the village of Utende, roughly 10km from Kilindoni by road, with a fourth situated on Chole Island within the bay. Utende is the only area other than Kilindoni that has electricity.

HISTORY

Little is known about the early history of the Mafia Archipelago, but presumably it has been settled for millennia, and it may well have participated in the ancient coastal trade with Arabia. The eminent archaeologist Neville Chittick regarded Mafia as a strong candidate for the 'low and wooded' island of Menouthesias, described in the 1st-century *Periplus of the Erythrian Sea* as being two days' sail or 300 *stadia* (roughly 50km) from the river port of Rhapta (which, according to this theory, was situated in the Rufiji Delta). Although the anonymous writer of the *Periplus* also mentions the sewn boats and hollowed-out tree canoes that are still used widely on Mafia today (as they are elsewhere on the coast), several other aspects of the description count against Mafia. Two days rather exaggerates the sailing distance from the island to the Rufiji Delta; furthermore, either the *Periplus* was mistaken in its assertion that there are 'no wild beasts except crocodiles' on Menouthesias, or the crocs have subsequently vanished and the island's few hippos are a later arrival.

The earliest known settlement on the archipelago, Kisimani Mafia, was situated at Ras Kisimani in the far southwest of the main island. Archaeological evidence suggests that this town, which covered about three acres, was founded in the 11th century, possibly by a favoured son of the Sultan of Kilwa. Several coins minted at Kilwa have been unearthed at the site, as have coins from China, Mongolia, India and Arabia, all minted prior to 1340. A second important town, Kua, was probably founded in the 13th century, again as a dependency of Kilwa, and it must surely have usurped Kisimani as the islands' political and economic hub soon after that. In its prime, Kua was probably the second-largest city along what is now the southern coast of Tanzania, boasting seven mosques as well as a double-storey palace and numerous stone homesteads spread over an area of more than 30 acres.

Following the Portuguese occupation of the coast, Kua was chosen as the site of a Portuguese trade agency in 1515, when a fortified blockhouse was built at the town. The name Mafia (more accurately Morfiyeh) was well established by this time, and the islands are marked as such on the earliest Portuguese naval charts. Several explanations have been put forward for the origin of this name (see box above). Because the archipelago lies 20km offshore, Mafia attracted a large influx of refugees from the mainland during the cannibalistic Zimba raids that dealt the final deathblow to so many coastal settlements during the late 16th century.

Control of Mafia changed hands frequently in the 17th century as Portugal's fortunes declined. An Omani naval raid in 1670 effectively terminated the Portuguese presence on the Mafia islands, and by 1598 the entire east African coast north of modern-day Mozambique was under Omani control. Little is known about events on the islands over the next two centuries. In about 1829, however, the archipelago was attacked by the cannibalistic Sakalafa of Madagascar, who succeeded in wreaking havoc at Kua, one of the few coastal towns left untouched by their Zomba forbears 250 years earlier. Kisimani, though also attacked by the Malagasy, stumbled on into the 1870s, when a devastating cyclone dealt it a final deathblow, but Kua was abandoned to go to ruin.

One reason why Kua was not resettled after 1820 is that a new seat of the Sultanate of Zanzibar had been founded on the north end of Chole Island barely ten years earlier. Known as Chole Mjini (Chole Town), this settlement was also attacked by the Sakalafa, but it was soon rebuilt to emerge as the most important town on the islands. Chole became the established home of a number of wealthy Omani traders and slave owners, while the main island of Mafia, known at the time as Chole Shamba (Chole Farm), was occupied by newly established coconut plantations and the slaves who worked on them. Although Chole was not so directly involved in the slave trade as Pangani, Bagamoyo or Kilwa Kivinje, it was an important stopover for slave ships heading between Kilwa and Zanzibar, and the ruined mansions that survive today indicate that it was a very wealthy settlement indeed.

Mafia was part of the Zanzibar Sultanate throughout the Omani era, and it should have remained a part of Zanzibar in the colonial era, according to a treaty that placed it under British protectorateship along with Zanzibar and Pemba islands. However, in the complex Anglo–German treaty of 1890, Mafia was ceded to Germany in exchange for a part of what is now Malawi, and it has been administered as part of mainland Tanzania ever since. In 1892, Germany sent a local administrator to Chole, who constructed the two-storey Customs House that can still be seen on the beach today.

In 1913, Germany relocated its administration from Chole to the deeper harbour at Kilindoni on the main island. Two years later, Mafia was the first part of German East Africa to be captured by British forces. The island was subsequently used as the base for a series of aerial assaults on the German cruiser *Königsberg* which, having evaded capture in the Rufiji Delta, was finally sunk on 11 August 1915. A six-cent German Tanganyika Territory stamp overprinted 'Mafia' by the British and listed at £9,000 in the Stanley Gibbons catalogue makes philatelists one of the few groups of people aware of the existence of the islands.

ECONOMY

Coconuts were the main source of income for the islands until the 1970s, when the price of coconut products dropped, and the fishing industry grew in importance. Cultivated since the 19th century, coconuts remain a secure income source and, although the trees are still climbed by hand, some 30 tonnes are exported to Dar daily in dhows. Coconut products have a number of local uses: leaves are used for roofing, coconut coir makes doormats and ropes, and even the ribs are used to make fishing traps and brooms. The wood can also be used to make furniture.

Other produce grown on Mafia is used for subsistence farming, particularly the primary crop, cassava. Rice, sweet potato, maize, pumpkin, okra, banana, pineapple, lime, mango and tomato are also seen growing on the islands, some of which are exported to Dar. Cashew nuts are either sold locally or exported, and the cashew fruit is used to make local beer. At subsistence level, mushrooms, raffia fibre, medicinal plants and game (monkey, bush pig and duiker) play an important role. Mangrove trees provide many raw materials; their wood is used for building poles, and boatbuilding and repair. Dead mangrove branches are used for firewood; leaves, bark and fruit are all used for medicines and colour dyes. Firewood is collected to burn coral rag for lime, and also for charcoal, which is sold to locals, hotels, and at Kilindoni, as well as exported.

The sea is vital to the livelihood of many of Mafia's inhabitants. Seaweed farming exists on a small-scale basis, used for export and for processing food additives. It is grown on lines attached to wooden stakes across the seabed of shallow lagoons, and is dried on palm leaves. Traditionally the inter-tidal area has been the women's domain, where they fish for octopus at spring tide. In the 1990s, however, men too began collecting octopus on the inter-tidal flats, as fish catches were declining yet prices increasing. Now 60% of octopus is caught by men, often through free-diving. Sea cucumbers are harvested for export to Zanzibar or Dar, then out to the Far East. Fish is also exported. Chole and Jibonde were well known for their boatbuilding in the past, but this now is in decline. You can still see people working in the shipyards, but more of the work is now repairing smaller dhows rather than building large cargo-carrying boats.

RELIGION AND CULTURE

The majority of the islanders are Muslim, but there are also many Christians. Voodoo manifests itself in ritual dances linked to the lunar cycle. While traditionally reserved, the islanders are tolerant of visitors provided they dress discreetly and behave in a manner becoming to local customs. Mafia women wear the colourful patterned *kanga* of the Swahili coast (see box, *Kangas and kikois*, page 95), and on weekends and religious holidays men exchange Western dress for the long, white *kanzu*. Older folk who remember the British era can speak some English, as can staff working at the tourist lodges, but it can help to know a little Swahili when talking to other islanders.

A word of caution: Mafia is a conservative society, and the passing visitor is unlikely to be asked for handouts. Children who beg from tourists are quickly reprimanded by their elders. Please make sure that you, and your travelling companions, keep it this way. (For further information, see page 110.)

NATURAL ENVIRONMENT

VEGETATION Natural vegetation on Mafia ranges from tidal mangrove thickets (eight species of mangrove grow here), marshland, heath and scrubby coastal moorlands to palm-wooded grassland and lowland rainforest, although the evergreen forest was cleared for coconut plantations in the 1980s. Baobabs are prominent along with the native Albinza. A patch of coastal high forest, the Chunguruma Forest, is a dense tree canopy interlaced with lianas and having an abundant floor covering of ferns.

WILDLIFE

Mammals A large, reed-lined lake in central Mafia, probably a relic lagoon dating from when the island was joined to the mainland, harbours about 20 hippo that were washed out to sea during flooding in the Rufiji River system. Unpopular with locals, they eat from the rice farms at night and can cause considerable damage, but are hard to see. Other island fauna includes a colony of flying foxes (the lesser Cormoran fruit bat), while bush pigs are found in Mdola Forest and Juani Island. The pigs eat the cassava from farms on Juani, so are a menace to farmers, who try to trap the pigs where possible.

Mdola Forest stretches along the east coast of Mafia Island for about 30km, from Bweni to Chole Bay, and has a high level of diversity, as well as a number of endemic species, such as the blue duiker, a subspecies endemic to Pemba and Mafia. Other fauna includes at least one bushbaby species, the genet, and the black-and-rufous elephant shrew. Monkeys (Sykes's and vervet) and squirrels were introduced for the pot by the Portuguese.

Reptiles and insects The leaf-litter toad has been recorded in Mdola Forest, and may be endemic to Mafia; the writhing gecko is found both in Mdola Forest and on the Tanzanian mainland. The monitor lizard is known locally as *kenge*.

13

Butterflies (there are five endemics) are best seen in the wet season, particularly around Ras Mbizi and mangroves, which flower during the rains.

Birds More than 120 species of birds have been recorded on Mafia, including five different types of sunbird. The island is of particular interest for its concentrations of resident and migrant shorebirds, which have breeding grounds in northern Europe but come to Mafia from October to March for the nearby mangrove estuaries, where they feed on the mudflats. Waders include ringed plover, crab plover, grey plover, Mongolian plover, great sandplover, curlew, whimbrel and turnstone, and the island is also a nesting area for fish eagles and open-billed storks.

Marine life Of far greater ecological importance than Mafia's terrestrial habitats is the immensely rich marine environment, which provides some of the finest snorkelling and diving sites in the Indian Ocean. It may be surprising that the biodiversity of the Rufiji–Mafia complex has global significance, and of 21 sites in east Africa has been described as having 'one of the world's most interesting and diverse ecosystems'. The coral-reef habitats around Mafia have a diversity of species rivalled only by rainforests, with at least 380 species of fish and 48 of coral. The beds of seagrass (12 species of which are found here, the only flowering plants to have colonised the sea) and the deep open waters support some of the planet's most endangered marine life.

Four species of turtles live in Mafia's waters, and two of these use Mafia as a nesting ground. The hawksbill (*Cretmochelys imbricata*), lays eggs between December and January; the green turtle (*Chelonia mydas*), between April and June. The east African coast is one of the last strongholds for the critically endangered dugong (*Dugong dugon*), and during the 1960s and 1970s these gentle seacows were regularly caught in the shark nets of Mafia's fishermen. Despite two separate sightings in 1999, there are fears that the dugong may now be extinct from Mafia's waters.

The lowland coastal forest of the eastern seaboard has been 'recognised as a critical site for biodiversity', and the inter-tidal flats are important for octopus, while in the open sea marine mammals like the humpback whale give birth and nurse their young in east Africa's warm waters. Sadly the demand for shark-fin soup in the Far East is one contributor to diminished populations of shark along the coastline. The large pelagics such as marlin, billfish and tuna also inhabit the deeper sea.

Oceanographers often talk of the Rufiji River Delta–Mafia–Kilwa area being one extended ecosystem. It's particularly exciting that a coelacanth was caught here in 2003. Archaeologists have found fossils of this very rare, bony fish which date back to the era of the dinosaurs, and today's specimens are almost identical.

From October to April, whalesharks are seen in the area. Chole Mjini on Chole Island is the headquarters for the newly formed Mafia Island Whaleshark Conservation Project and during the season offers regular dhow excursions for guests to visit these gentle giants.

CLIMATE

The Mafia Archipelago experiences a tropical climate tempered by ocean breezes. Rainfall averaging 2,000mm a year occurs mainly between April and May, although November can also be wet. February and March are hot and humid, while a strong southerly wind, the kusi, blows during July. The best holiday period is from June until mid-October, when the islands enjoy blue skies with temperatures kept pleasant by light coastal breezes. The water temperature varies from 24°C to 31°C while the air temperature rarely exceeds 33°C or drops below 20°C.

Over the past 2,000 years, turtle-shell, mangrove poles and seashells have been part of east Africa's trade to Arabia. By the 1960s, however, it had become clear that natural resources were not coping with human progress. In Tanzania, dried and salted fish, exported to the mainland, contributes more to the national protein consumption than meat and poultry combined. Dynamite fishing became very popular on Tanzania's coast, despite the destruction that it causes to fish populations and to coral. Small-mesh, beach-seine nets were catching all sizes of fish, again damaging populations. In some areas the only source of building materials has been coral, used as bricks and in the production of lime: this was the second-largest industry on Mafia at one time. Mangrove wood is very hard, insect-resistant, and makes excellent building material, so vast areas were cleared to provide timber, fuelwood, farmland and salt-pans for salt production.

In the 1970s, four islands were declared marine reserves to slow the damage, but in the absence of facilities to police the park, fishermen ignored the rules and continued as usual. By 1995, it was clear that conservation had become an urgent priority, so the following year a partnership of investors, communities and the government set up the Board of Trustees of Marine Parks and Reserves of Tanzania, and on 6 September 1996, an area of Mafia extending across 822km² was gazetted as Tanzania's first marine park, to protect the ecosystems as well as the future livelihood of coastal people. The park embraces most of the southern and eastern shore of Mafia, including Chole Bay and associated reefs, a number of isolated atolls to the south of the main island, and the reefs enclosing Juani, Jibondo and Bwejuu islands.

The marine park now owns six boats and has one full-time park warden. The park authorities are aiming to co-operate and collaborate with local residents, using community-based projects to dispel conflict between groups. If the islands are to be protected, the success of the marine park is imperative. Mangroves trap river sediments that would be otherwise washed out to sea and, along with coral reefs, protect the shoreline from the erosion of rising sea levels. The natural forest shields the island's crops from storm damage from the ocean, and a healthy ecosystem helps in the recovery from natural disasters such as cyclones, hurricanes and floods. Significantly, wetlands have also been shown to provide clean water, perhaps the most significant issue in terms of sustainable development of the islands.

For further details, contact the warden-in-charge, Mr George Msumi, Mafia Island Marine Park (✆ 023 2402690; e mimpMafia@raha.com).

GETTING THERE AND AWAY

BY AIR The most efficient way of getting to Mafia is by light aircraft (Cessna Caravan or AIRVAN) with either Tropical Air or Kinasi who jointly operate a morning service from Zanzibar via Dar es Salaam to Mafia, or with Coastal Travel, who run two scheduled flights from Dar es Salaam every day, costing US$110 for a single flight: the first leaves at 15.00, arriving in Mafia at 15.30, and the second at 17.00, arriving at 17.30. This is perfectly timed so that the sun sets behind the Rufiji Delta as you fly in. If one of these flights is not running, you can sometimes persuade Coastal to fly by paying for a minimum of two passengers. Coastal also fly from Kilwa via Songo Songo to Mafia daily (departing 06.15; arriving 06.50) for US$110 one-way and Zanzibar to Mafia daily, usually via Dar (14.00–15.30), costing US$145 single.

If you are staying at Kinasi Lodge for three nights or more, ASF Kinasi can fly you one-way to/from Mafia from Dar for US$110, to/from Zanzibar to Mafia for

US$140 or to/from the Selous Game Reserve (see pages 359–66) for US$190. They try to be as accommodating as possible for their guests, looking after bags, etc, but these flights are ad hoc, and therefore not scheduled. If you're not staying at Kinasi, it's worth giving them a call anyway as it's the same rate for non-guests if there's space on a flight already running. It is possible that at the end of 2008, Kinasi will operate twice-daily flights from Dar to Mafia.

You can also charter planes to Mafia from a range of companies in Dar es Salaam and Zanzibar, with the cost of a small aircraft from Coastal, Tropical or Kinasi costing around US$500.

The flightpath to Mafia is within sight of the Rufiji River Delta, at 40km^2 the largest delta in east Africa with the region's greatest concentration of mangroves. The dhows look tiny as they go about their fishing unfeasibly far from shore. With a new 1.9km runway in place, arrival on Mafia is not the bumpy ride it once was.

Note that an airport departure tax of US$5 per person, which includes a US$1 'safety fee', is payable in cash on leaving Mafia.

Airline operators

✈ **Coastal Aviation** 107 Upanga Rd, Dar es Salaam or Dar Airport; ☏ 022 2117959 (HQ)/022 2842700/1 (Dar Airport)/024 2233112, m 0713 670815 (Zanzibar Airport); e safari@coastal.cc; www.coastal.cc

✈ **Kinasi** m 0777 474911/0773 719719 (Dar Airport); e kinasilodge@mafiaisland.com
✈ **Tropical Air** Zanzibar; ☏ 024 2232511 (HQ); m 0773 511679 (Zanzibar Airport)/0773 618367 (Dar Airport); e reservations@tropicalair.co.tz; www.tropicalair.co.tz

Mafia Airport Mafia's small airport (⊕ *around 08.00–18.30, unless there's an early-morning flight*) is situated on the edge of the main town of Kilindoni, a 15km drive from Utende, where the tourist lodges are located. It's Mafia's centre of communication for visitors, and even if visitors arrive on Mafia by boat they tend to be directed the 1km from the harbour to the airport.

Currently, the airport has a simple waiting room with wooden benches and basic toilets but a new terminal is promised following the addition of a decent runway in 2007. At the Chole Interbureau Change (⊕ *08.00–17.00*), you can change limited amounts of currency at market rates, as well as US dollar, euro and sterling travellers' cheques, but it's probably best not to rely on this tiny exchange for all your financial needs on Mafia. There is a branch of the National Microfinance Bank in Kilindoni and lodges will take credit cards, but it's still wise to bring an amount of cash with you.

Visitors holding a hotel reservation will be met at the airport for their transfer. If you don't have a reservation, most of the lodges have representatives who speak English, and can radio the lodges to organise your accommodation. They can also help individual travellers to find a Land-Rover taxi, costing US$25 to Utende one-way; note that you'll cross the border into the marine park *en route*, so have the fee (US$10 per person per day) for the requisite number of days ready in US dollars cash, and remember to keep your receipt as proof of payment when you leave the island.

BY BOAT The options for budget travellers who wish to visit Mafia are limited to boats that connect Kilindoni to the mainland. Many of these dhows are uncomfortable and crowded and the trip can take anything from ten to 24 hours. The safety record is none too inspiring; sailing dhows have a reputation for hitting reefs, as these are very dangerous waters that require an experienced captain. If you want to take a boat, make sure you check that they're properly licensed to carry passengers or vehicles, and at least that they have marine radios and life jackets.

For the incorrigible, a tide table is incorporated in the free booklet, the *Dar Guide*, available from bars and hotels in Dar es Salaam. This is invaluable when trying to organise a boat trip to Mafia, as the boats have to arrive at high tide, and often leave on a high tide, too. There are, though, plans to build a jetty in Kilindoni, which would mean that boats no longer have to restrict their arrival to high tide. This should lead to a much more regular service in the future.

The closest mainland port to Mafia is Kisiju, 30km from Dar, and 45km southeast of Mkuranga on the Kilwa road. From the Kariakoo bus depot in Dar, you take a bus to Kisiju and then a dhow to Mafia. Another possibility from Dar es Salaam is via Kimbiji, easily reached by catching the motor ferry from the city centre to Kigomboni (boats leave every ten minutes or so and take five minutes) then a *dala-dala* direct to Kimbiji (about one hour). There are also dhows connecting Mafia to Kilwa Kivinje.

GETTING AROUND

The island infrastructure is basic. Hardly any villages are connected to mains water or electricity and at the time of writing there are no tarmac roads. Throughout the island the best you'll find is a bouncy sandy track. Vehicles are few, mainly Land-Rover pick-ups and 4x4s belonging to the hotels and other organisations. Most local people use bicycles to get around, although this is quite hard work on the sandy roads. Bicycles can be rented by arrangement with the Hotel Lizu in Kilindoni, or from any of the lodges.

A minibus runs every three hours or so between Kilindoni and Utende charging around US$1 one way. It seats a minimum of 12, and has no fixed timetable – it departs when it's full. There are also two *dala-dalas*, one at Kilindoni and one at Utende, and these pick people up along the way. They're not the most comfortable way of getting around, but are a good way of meeting local people and really getting to understand life on Mafia. Hitchhiking is an accepted means of getting about, but it usually entails a long wait. Islanders also use *jahazis*, widely referred to in English as dhows, to commute between Kilindoni and outlying villages on Mafia, and for inter-island travel.

Maps of Mafia can be obtained from Mafia Island Tours at Mafia Island Lodge for US$5.50.

WHERE TO STAY

Mafia isn't really the place for easy backpacking, but budget travellers who do come here may stop in Kilindoni itself. Meanwhile, the majority of Mafia's (very few) tourists head straight though town and over to one of three or four more upmarket small lodges on Chole Bay.

CHOLE BAY Chole's three upmarket lodges – Pole Pole, Kinasi and Chole Mjini – are all totally different in style and approach, and each has its advocates to claim that it is 'the best'. The truth is that they're all very good, given their different styles – and all offer really very good value for money given their relative isolation, and the quality of the marine experience to be had here. The trick is to choose the one that's right for you.

Mafia Lodge doesn't reach the standards of the other three, but you won't find a better-value spot for a quiet retreat with access to great diving.

Pole Pole (7 bungalows) ✆ 022 2601530; e info@polepole.com; www.polepole.com. Pole Pole, meaning 'slowly, slowly' in Swahili, is a superb destination for relaxation. This Italian-managed lodge is designed to be fairly luxurious whilst still a little rustic, & smart without being pretentious. Set in a garden of coconut palms, & connected by pathways of the softest sand, Pole Pole has a small beach in front of it, perhaps 100m wide, with mangroves on either side. A path through the mangroves leads in a short walk of a few minutes to Kinasi Lodge (if you turn right) or to Mafia Island Lodge (if you turn left).

Pole Pole's large bungalows, built almost entirely from organic materials, have modern en-suite bathrooms, including twin washbasins, showers, a bidet & a flush toilet. The bedroom has a polished wooden floor, some stylishly simple furniture, a ceiling fan & 24hr electricity; dbl or twin beds which are surrounded by a walk-in mosquito net. Large double-doors lead onto a very wide, shaded veranda overlooking the sea below, complete with some relaxing day-beds & chairs. In keeping with its chill-out vibe, Pole Pole operates a strict mobile phone policy with guests requested to keep phones on silent mode & only make calls from within their rooms.

Typical Italian 4-course dinners are served at private tables in the restaurant. Starters are usually light, eg: crab salad, followed by a sizeable pasta course (or soup), a main dish (typically seafood with simple vegetables) followed by dessert. Swahili dinners are offered once a week or on request if guests wish. Service is attentive & helpful, & there are also 2 good local masseuses to relax your muscles after a hard day's exertions.

Pole Pole has no swimming pool, but snorkelling, diving, game fishing & other excursions are offered. 1 dhow trip — usually including some snorkelling & perhaps a picnic lunch — is normally offered every day on a complimentary basis, if guests wish to join in. Between Oct & Mar the lodge also operates trips to see (and on occasion swim with) the migratory whalesharks.

If you're looking for somewhere small, comfortable & fairly remote with great diving & snorkelling, & involving very low-key excursions, then Pole Pole offers very good value indeed. *US$286/220pp sgl/dbl, US$325/250 Aug & Christmas period, inc dinner (early-morning tea & 3 meals), airport transfers, laundry, tea, coffee & bottled water, snorkelling & excursions in Chole Bay; all rates FB; diving US$40/70 sgl/dbl; equipment US$20 per day*

⌂ **Kinasi Lodge** (14 bungalows) m 0777 418256, operations m 0741 242977; e kinasi@ intafrica.com; www.mafiaisland.com; ⏱ Jun–end Mar. A 5min walk along the beach from Pole Pole brings you to the more formal Kinasi Lodge. This Indian Ocean hideaway is named for the indigo pass through the outer reef that leads into Chole Bay. Set on a steeply sloping site, Kinasi has quite large, landscaped grounds of lawns studded with coconut palms, which slope steeply down to a small sandy beach and the ocean. Either side of the beach, which perhaps extends for 100m, are mangroves — through which weaves the short sandy path to Pole Pole.

Inset into the lawns, about halfway up, is a swimming pool area, complete with poolside bar & grill. Dotted around are 14 solid, self-contained bungalows with *makuti* roofs & stone verandas complete with armchairs & addictive hammocks. Inside, Zanzibar-style dbl beds are enveloped in vast mosquito nets, & each has an en-suite bathroom, including a washbasin, shower & flush toilet. Throughout the hotel great attention has been paid to soft furnishings.

The lodge's multi-level, open-sided bar & lounge area contains a top-notch reference library, book-swap service & comfortable long couches & armchairs. The adjacent dining area serves an eclectic fusion menu & themed dinners ranging from a seafood fondue to poolside Swahili nights. A separate grill & pizza kitchen have also been installed for more casual dining. Meals can be either in a group or individually, & there's a well-stocked walk-in wine cellar & cocktail bar for pre-dinner wine tastings & canapés.

Kinasi has its own fully equipped watersports & PADI dive centre beside the beach, & the resident instructor can arrange dives in & around Chole Bay, as well as snorkelling trips, windsurfing, kayaking & game fishing. An 'activity manager' in the lodge organises the various excursions (at additional cost), which include the usual range of dhow trips, village visits, & 4x4 excursions across the island, plus the unique option of borrowing mountain bikes to explore local villages. The lodge has also constructed a 2hr nature trail for birdwatching along the coastal flats, which are rich in waders, & through patches of coastal scrub that harbour sunbirds, tinker-birds & bee-eaters. To complement these activities, the Isis Spa was constructed in 2006. With 3 treatment rooms & 2 charming professional Thai therapists, massage, aromatherapy treatment & beauty care are now available to guests from any of the Mafia lodges. *Garden room US$223–270/US$215–270 sgl/dbl; seafront room US$286–350/US$246–302 sgl/dbl; family room (4 persons) US$580–731; all rates FB; Mafia Airport transfer US$24pp one-way*

🏠 **Chole Mjini Lodge** (6 treehouses, I chalet) m 0748 520799; e 2chole@bushmail.net. This fabulously original lodge, situated on the northern side of Chole Island, consists mostly of large, wooden treehouse-style bedrooms perched high in the baobabs, amongst the crumbling 19th-century ruins of Chole Mjini. The owners, Jean & Anne de Villiers, who live on site, stress that they are emphatically not catering for people seeking Sheraton-style luxury or a conventional beach retreat – there is no electricity for starters (lighting is by paraffin lamps at night, so bring a good torch!), & the waterfront in front of the lodge is overgrown with mangroves. Nevertheless this must rank as one of the most original & aesthetically pleasing lodges on the east African coast. It's also an atmospheric base for exploring Chole Island & the surrounding waters. Lunch is usually served at group tables in a family atmosphere, with fresh seafood & vegetable dishes in a mixture of African & European styles, usually with tasty sauces. B/fast & dinner are served at individual tables dotted around the garden, jetty or ruins. 6 of the bedrooms at Chole Mjini stand high on stilted platforms; 3 are in or beside their own huge baobab tree. Each is made almost entirely of wood, thatch & local materials by the local people of Chole – & the sheer quality of the carpentry says much for the islanders' reputation for building fine dhows. All the rooms are slightly different, but climb the stairs & inside you'll generally find a large dbl bed surrounded by a walk-in mosquito net, billowing fabrics, an open wardrobe & dressing area & a large, padlocked wooden box for your valuables. Most also have an upper floor, with relaxing day-beds. Each of these treehouse rooms has private ablutions – but all are separate & down on the ground. The sit-down toilet is a long-drop, using ash to keep it dry & composting; they rank as one of the cleanest long-drops in Africa! Enclosed from view behind a circular bamboo enclosure, the large open-air showers use an 'Intermediate Technology'-type of design to heat the water. You light a small metal cup of paraffin, push it under a hollow waterpipe, & turn on the tap. Remarkably, these usually supply a very good, hot shower. Chole Mjini has just I, more conventional chalet which is on the ground level, next to the lodge's main lounge/dining area. This is very open-plan, with walls open to the breeze, & has a huge bed, a conventional en-suite flush toilet (the only one on the island) & large sunken bath. It's not quite as romantic as the treehouses, but might be just the place if stairs to the toilet don't appeal. Finally, a recent addition to the lodge's range of accommodation is a converted wooden dhow, allowing guests to spend a night or 2 on the water or fly-camping on a secluded beach. In keeping with the eco-friendly ethos, a community fee is included in the rates.

The owners & their dive instructor have more than 50 years' experience of diving Mafia between them, can instruct in English, Italian, French or German, & know the dive sites intimately. Jean is also a research biologist who teaches coral-reef ecology to US college students twice a year, & can teach short PADI courses on this, & fish identification, on request. He has a fully equipped dive centre here, making Chole Mjini an excellent lodge both for experienced divers seeking adventure, & those learning to dive, or for finding out more about the marine environment.

There is no pool here, or any beach to lie on. However, there are organised walks, snorkel trips & excursions to nearby sandbars to entertain non-divers. (There are usually I or 2 complimentary trips organised every day.)

Chole Mjini can be either totally magical or quite uncomfortable. It's owned & run by a couple who have put their heart & soul into the lodge, & in helping the surrounding community to develop. Visitors need to accept the lodge, & its team, as they find them; & then a really enjoyable stay is almost guaranteed. *US$180–342/360–540 sgl/dbl, FB inc US$10 village levy & daily activity; No children under 2 years of age; Mafia Airport transfers US$30/vehicle; diving US$40 /dive; scuba equipment US$15/day*

🏠 **Mafia Island Lodge** (40 rooms) m 0786 303049; e info@mafialodge.com; www.mafialodge.com. This very simple lodge, built by the government in 1971, is situated on one of the island's few open, palm-lined beaches; it's next to Pole Pole & about 10mins' walk from Kinasi Lodge, directly opposite the ruins of Chole Mjini on Chole Island. The lodge consists of 40 reasonable, box-like rooms, with a mix of standard & superior rooms available for couples, friends & families. The rooms have recently undergone a much-needed refurbishment but have retained their terracotta tiled floors & French windows facing the sea. There's AC & en-suite bathrooms with 24hr hot water as standard, & despite the uninspiring interiors & rather featureless lawn, it's a reliable, functional place offering access to Mafia's superb diving at bargain-basement rates.

The bar/restaurant is a large & fairly pleasant spot, with a large airy terrace facing the ocean for the seafood-inspired menu. Myriad games are available & there is a small shop which contains a few essentials, from toothpaste to tampons. There's also an internet access point costing US$5/hr, a pool table & equipment for beach volleyball.

Mafia's only real tour company, Mafia Island Tours, is based here, & makes an obvious choice from which to book dives & excursions if you're not staying at one of the upmarket lodges.

For example, a short hop to Chole Island for a village tour, including a visit to the flying foxes, costs US$10pp; & a half-day trip to the Kua Ruins & Channel, or Jibondo Island, costs US$25pp. A longer snorkelling trip with a picnic lunch to Marimbani or Kitutia costs US$35/45pp; & a full-day excursion to Ras Mkumbi or Bwejuu Island costs US$50/60pp. *Diving US$40/70 sgl/dbl dive; equipment US$20/day.* $$$$

KILINDONI The guesthouses in town are all pretty basic, with little to draw travellers to them; even Mafia Pwani Camp has relatively little to recommend it.

⌂ **Mafia Pwani Camp** (4 *bandas*, camping) ✆ 023 2402244; m 0745 696067; e carpho2003@ yahoo.co.uk. Outside central Kilindoni, a 15min walk from the airport, this camp is also known as Sunset Resort Camp. It's owned by one of the directors of Pole Pole, & is one of the only basic lodges that offers a relaxing atmosphere. It's also an excellent area for spotting the rufous elephant shrew, as well as vervet monkeys. To get there, turn right out of the airport, follow the road round to the right, & take the first left by the concrete wall. By the time you read this, the entrance should be here (currently it's behind the hospital: follow the sand road through the chicken wire). The camp is in a beautiful area overlooking the sea, & has considerable potential. Its individual *bandas* (3 twin, 1 dbl) are sizeable & clean, with nets on windows & beds & 24hr electricity; a laundry service is available. Despite the good standard of building, facilities are very basic, with no running water; buckets of water are provided in the shared bathroom facilities, & this can be heated on request. If you follow the steep pathway down to the beach, you'll come to the campsite (US$7). There are plans to build a platform, bar & lounge area. $$

⌂ **Classic Visitor's House** (7 rooms) m 0746 749176. The signpost to this local guesthouse is quite unhelpful. To get there from the Sports Bar on your left, take the first right, then left – it's behind the white wall. From the mosque on your right, take the first left at Sofia Soft Drinks, walk to the end of the road, then it's on your left. The owner speaks English, so the manager (who doesn't) will call him if needed. This is a very basic but pleasant

guesthouse, with mosquito nets on the windows & the beds, & ceiling fans (24hr electricity). Existing rooms share 2 squat toilets with a tap & bucket, & 2 sporadically functioning showers. There are also 3 newer en-suite twin rooms with similarly basic interiors. There is no restaurant here but a laundry service is offered. $

⌂ **Harbour View Lodge** (10 rooms) m 0745 360314. Owned by an ex-MP, this lodge is right on the seafront: an interesting location as you have to walk through the timber yard to get here & the lodge itself overlooks the fishing boats. There is a large bar area with music & a dancefloor, with small tables outside so you can sip your drinks by a view of the harbour. This is a good basic lodge with fans & AC, nets on the windows (not on the beds), & 24hr electricity. En-suite rooms have a shower, washbasin & flushing toilet, & hot water can be boiled for you. There's also a lockable cupboard. Harbour View also has a little restaurant with a fan. $

⌂ **New Lizu Hotel** (5 rooms) Bookings c/o Post office, Mafia; ✆ 023 2402683. This is the most comfortable of 4 guesthouses in the centre of Kilindoni. Used by local traders, it is a 1min walk from the market, & 10mins from the dhow landing jetty. With 24hr electricity, mosquito nets & fans, it is fairly clean but extremely basic. All but 1 room (a sgl) share washing facilities, with water very limited (depending on who else is using it!). Toilets are flushed with a bucket; hot water can be boiled on request. The hotel also offers a laundry service, a stationery shop, a phone & a tailoring school. A simple bar/restaurant with fan sells beer, sodas & rice & seafood meals. $

Camping There is a campsite at Mafia Pwani (see above). Otherwise, check with the marine park authorities before camping independently, as it's not legal to camp in Tanzania unless you're in a specified area. Don't take any chances.

DIVING *With Jean de Villiers*

Many people visit Mafia purely for its diving, which is often considered the best anywhere in east Africa. It's easy to dive two sites outside the bay on a single outing; the trip out and back can also be great for fishing, sunbathing, sailing and dolphin-spotting. The marine park off Chole Bay is home to 48 species of coral, including giant table corals, delicate sea fans, whip corals and huge stands of blue- and pink-tipped staghorn coral.

As well as the spectacular variety of reef fish there are turtles and large predatory fish such as grouper, Napoleon wrasse and barracuda. Manta rays and several species of shark are encountered in Kinasi Pass. November to January is best for black-tip and white-tip reef sharks. The corals of Chole Bay, in the heart of the marine park, have recovered dramatically from damage caused by El Niño (of 1997–98) and the destructive fishing practices used before the establishment of the park.

Almost all Mafia's best diving is in depths of less than 30m. Between June and September you can dive only within Chole Bay, albeit in almost any weather. For the more challenging dives outside the bay, you have to wait until the calmer conditions in mid-September. Outside the bay the average size of the fish is bigger, and you've a good chance of seeing a 2–3m grouper; these are friendly and let you come quite close. Visibility from June to September tends to be 10–15m, whereas in October to February it can be 25m. Mafia is good for beginner divers, as it's very safe inside the bay. However, diving outside the bay on an outgoing tide can be extremely dangerous, with strong currents that can sweep you out to sea: in this position, if you miss your rendezvous with a boat, the next stop is Mogadishu.

When diving in the open ocean, divers are advised always to carry two means of signalling: one audible (a whistle or air horn) and one visible (an inflatable surface marker, a flare, strobe light or mirror). In addition, always wear a full wetsuit as protection against exposure, and drink water before commencing a dive. Don't take any risks or push the safety boundary while diving here; it's a long way to the nearest decompression chamber in Nairobi. Note that you can't buy diving insurance in Tanzania – you must have this before you travel.

All of the lodges on Mafia offer diving excursions as well as full PADI courses. Chole Mjini, Pole Pole, Kinasi and Mafia Island lodges all offer specialist diving courses with every conceivable type of dive site – reefs and bommies, channels, walls, caves, drift, ocean and night dives. All these are accessible in a day, while diving safaris catering for 12 people can be arranged to destinations further afield such as Ras Mkumbi, Forbes Bay southeast of Mafia, and the spectacular reef complex around the Songo Songo Islands, which lie about 80km south of Mafia and about 50km north of Kilwa.

Diving and snorkelling sites in Mafia Marine Park

There are at least half a dozen more scuba-diving sites in the park and numerous snorkelling sites. Wherever possible, names given are those used by local fishermen.

The first three sites are relatively close together and can be reached on a stronger drift dive starting near the Pinnacle in Kinasi Pass. These sites sometimes suffer from being in the mouth of a bay in that the visibility can be poor for a few days after stormy periods at sea and when tidal currents are very strong at full moon or new moon.

Kinasi Pass: South Wall *Dive depth: max 27m. Recommended for experienced divers or beginners under professional supervision. Justifiably Mafia's most* famous dive site, this has it all: wall with caverns, big critters & spectacular corals. At times huge volumes of water flow through the pass, creating an exhilarating drift dive, or dive at slack water to enjoy the 30m wall & its resident potato cod & giant grouper. Schools of snappers & sweetlips are often here, as are their predators: barracuda, giant trevally, jacks, cobia, wahoo & kingfish. Rays & morays are common, with whalesharks, eagle rays & manta rays seasonal visitors (late Dec–Mar is best). Finish the dive in a splendid coral garden, & maybe catch up with a Napoleon wrasse or a feeding turtle.

Utumbi (or Kinasi Wall) *Dive depth: 5–25m. Recommended experience: all certified divers. (Outstanding snorkelling site nearby, mainly at low tide.)* If you don't tackle the pass right off then this is the must-do dive in Mafia. About 300m before the pass, inside the bay, is a truly gorgeous reef: the ease of access & safe, sheltered location & the obliging currents all add up to a world-class dive. The corals rapidly change from soft corals (gorgonians & whip corals at the pass end), to more & more hard corals, until finally you find yourself in shallow gardens of tabular & staghorn acropora & gold-hued fire coral. The fish fauna is mostly typical reef inhabitants, with a huge variety of multi-coloured wrasses, parrotfish, damsels, surgeons, triggerfish & anthiases. Big wahoo & barracuda cruise off reef, & 2–3ft greasy cod & malabar grouper are abundant.

Kinasi Pass – Pinnacle *Dive depth: max 29m. Recommended for experienced divers or beginners under professional supervision.* In the entrance of the bay, 50m north of Kinasi Wall, this pinnacle rises sharply to within 8m of the surface, usually surrounded by a school or two of sweetlips or trevally & their attendant predators. When the visibility is good, this is the most likely place within the bay to meet a bull shark (or zambezi). We also occasionally come across a 3m guitar fish (shark that is half ray, with a flat, triangular head) & a huge, mottled green-black giant grouper accompanied by a bevy of attendant yellow-and-black-striped pilotfish. It's an excellent site at slack water.

Dindini or Shangani Wall *Dive depth: max 24m. Recommended for experienced divers only.* Dindini is only accessible seasonally: it's directly in front of surf-pounded cliffs. There are a lot of fish: big fish, small fish, sharks, rays & also turtles. In periods of good visibility, usually Nov–Mar, this is one of the better places in Mafia to see sharks (usually reef sharks). It's also good for large groupers &, very occasionally, big-game fish like tuna, sailfish & marlin. The wall has many caverns & U-shaped tunnels, & some deep, unexplored caves where there is the occasional appearance of a big shark or other large creature. The dive ends on the top of the wall, with really spectacular powder blue, purple & pink alcyonaria soft corals teeming with fish, especially red-toothed triggerfish, & a variety of surgeons.

Mlila or Jina Wall *Dive depth: max 24m. Recommended for experienced divers or beginners under professional supervision.* Seasickness can be a problem. Less than a mile away, the wall has formed a slight fold close to the cliffs. It starts out quite mediocre but rapidly changes as you get where fishing boats seldom penetrate. In the pocket there are more grouper than you'll probably ever see. There are also lots of other fish around & this is likely to be your best chance of seeing big Napoleons or getting close to a feeding turtle. At the base of the wall is a lot of coral, with many holes to investigate; look out for lobster & small stingrays as well as giant & ribbon-tailed rays.

Milimani – 'mountain tops' in Swahili *Dive depth: max 20m. Recommended experience: all skill levels; often used for courses & Discover Scuba experiences.* The most often-requested repeat dive in the park. This is a long reef inside the bay, characterised by spectacular coral turrets rising above corals to form mini mountains & alleys. A gentle entrance in just 6m of water over pure white sand makes this the easiest dive in the park, & the diversity of the coral is phenomenal: the topology of the reef is stunning & it just goes on & on. As you explore the twisting, turning reef interspersed with mounds of coral teeming with fish you may become so absorbed that you suddenly find you're in 20m with a towering reef above. A small gap in the reef is an excellent place to view planktivores, usually swarms of counter-shaded fusiliers & schools of unicorns but occasionally (in the right season) a cruising manta, accompanied by a flotilla of remoras & pilotfish. You can end the dive by climbing over the reef crest to look for turtles or to join the millions of kasmira & blackspot snappers in the very shallow water among the magnificent fire corals.

Miewe Shoulder – the 'Washing Machine' *Dive depth: max 25m. Recommended experience: in slack water possible for all levels.* In deep water just outside the bay during spring tides, 2hrs before high tide, this is almost white-water diving & only for experienced & advanced divers who can control their buoyancy instinctively & know how to surf currents without fear of injury. Outside the bay, this is a sloping fringing reef north of the pass, with a fabulous diversity of fish, corals & topology. The reef is teeming with fish but you can't stop because the relentless current drags you over the top. The trick is to then drop down into one of the many deeper pools that lie just behind the jagged reef crest for a 'rinse & spin' cycle & watch the fish rush in & out. When you have been thoroughly wrung out you leave this lunar landscape of craters & spires & head south, across the current as much as possible, & will soon drift along the drop-off through Kinasi Pass for a very satisfying & relaxed end to an awesome experience.

Mkadini *Dive depth: max 25m. Recommended experience: all skill levels.* Outside the bay, off Miewe Island, there is a short vertical step in shallow water (12–14m max). This flattens out into a deeper shallow-sloping reef. There are many alcyonaria soft corals & diverse hard corals, lots of turtles (green & hawksbill), diverse groupers (backsaddled, lyretail, greasy cod, potato cod), schools of batfish & a good chance to see white-tip reef sharks & dolphins.

Juani Reef *Dive depth: max 30m. Recommended for experienced divers or beginners under professional supervision.* Outside the bay, a sloping fringing reef south of the pass extends for 12km. This is a good place to see turtles (green & hawksbill), guitar fish & white-tips, as well as stunning alcyonaria soft corals.

Mange Reef *Dive depth: max 24m. Recommended experience: all skill levels.* 12 nautical miles south-southeast of Chole Island, this is another beautiful coral-encrusted sandbar, once feared by local fishermen because of the many sharks. There is a good variety of reef fish & this is easily combined with Kitutia (see below) for an excellent day trip.

Chole Wall *Dive depth: max 16m. Recommended experience: all certified divers; good training site.* Reef inside the bay; gentle slope. About 1km in length with lots of coral & reef fishes. A grand skin-diving site when the weather is calm.

Musambiji *Dive depth: max 16m. Recommended experience: Open Water or equivalent; good training site.* This is a submerged island inside the bay, with diverse walls & sloping fringing coral reefs. It would be better if it were deeper & didn't suffer from poor visibility so often; but it can be a great snorkelling site.

Kitutia *Dive depth: max 20m. Recommended experience: all skill levels.* Once a fantastic dive site, Kitutia was badly degraded by El Niño some years ago, although it's recovering rapidly & regaining much of its former glory. It is a spectacular sandbar encrusted with corals, ideal for a day of mellow dives, snorkelling & swimming. Combined with a picnic & a fabulous sail home, it's the perfect day.

AROUND MAFIA ISLAND

Although Mafia is predominantly visited for its waters, many choose to explore the islands, and see some of Mafia beyond the marine park. It's easiest to arrange this through one of the lodges. For a good English-speaking guide, ask for either Moussa from Chole Mjini or Ali from Pole Pole. To go it alone, you could either hire a bike, or negotiate a price with the 4x4 drivers parked in Kilindoni to take you on an excursion.

KILINDONI All arrivals on Mafia pass through Kilindoni, the main town as well as the island's airport and sea port, but few visitors venture into Kilindoni for any length of time. New by east African standards, the town was established by the Germans in 1913 on discovering that Chole Island lacked a deep-water anchorage. While it has none of the Arab architecture of Stone Town on Zanzibar, its coral and lime-mortar shop-houses with quaint signs and rusting corrugated-iron roofs exude an ambience of old Indian Ocean days.

At first, Kilindoni appears to have all the accoutrements of a small town: a district hospital, school (complete with science laboratories), police station, bank, post office, airport, mosque and churches. Then suddenly the sandy road opens into a square full of clothes for sale, music and activity. There are stands selling mobile phone chargers (continental two-pins), an unexpected but necessary slice of modern Africa.

Peaceful rather than bustling, the **market** is the centre of local life. Tomatoes, chillies, potatoes, onions, limes, dried prawns, bananas, cassava and whatever the trader can get his hands on are arranged in little piles. A large amount of food here

13

is from Dar, grown elsewhere on the Tanzanian mainland. Spices are from Zanzibar, naturally, all wrapped up in little plastic packets. Baobab seeds for kids to chew are sold in piles and the fish stalls are pungently gathered together a little further off. Other stalls sell pottery, *kangas* and secondhand clothes, and if you're brave enough to buy a homemade snorkelling/diving mask, ingeniously made of pieces of metal stapled to thick black rubber, it'll set you back US$2.50.

A number of small **shops** are of interest to the visitor: the **Dubay Store**, next to Mapozi Haircutting Salon, sells cold Cokes and Fantas for US$0.50. For items such as sausage, orange juice, Sprite, water, chocolate, toilet paper, washing power and toothpaste, try **Mwishehe Shopping Centre**. On the road to the harbour (Bandani Road), by the little roundabout, you'll find **WTC** selling drinks, ice cream and chocolate, chicken and chips. **Kisoma Store** sells basic stationery; its proudly advertised 'computer' doesn't have internet access, but you can print from it at TSh800 per sheet. Make a right turn from the petrol and diesel pumps (opposite the 4x4 parking area), and you'll find **Fantastic Hair Cutting** which can cut different grades using a proper shaver for US$2 a haircut, and US$1 for a wet shave.

There are more stores on the road descending to the dhow landing. The **Market General Supply Store** and the **Peace and Love** sell soft drinks, and off the main square, Utende Road has a rather vulgar monument presented by the fish factory. On the left is a grey weather-beaten **mosque** and further along the Roman Catholic **church**, one of at least six churches.

The **landing** in Kilindoni usually has 15–20 *jahazis* moored on the beach. Whether unloading fish or mending their nets, the fishermen object strongly to being photographed, as do the people frying cassava chips and cooking octopus on small stoves under the trees.

✗ Where to eat With a burst of modernity, Kilindoni has recently gained the **Mafia Sports Bar**, complete with flat-screen TV and satellite. This big orange building is slap-bang in the middle of the town, providing a bar and restaurant for tourists and locals alike, and is part owned by Kinasi Lodge. A more African establishment, the tiny **Royal Pub Mafia**, may be rather surprised by visitors, but sells local beers: Kilimanjaro, Tusker, Serengeti, Bin Bingwa for US$1, and Konyagi (a local firewater with rather descriptive flames on the bottle) for US$2.50. This local bar also sells food: chips are US$0.50, egg and chips US$1, and a beef kebab US$1.50.

Other practicalities A bank and a post office are located on the airport road. The bank is the National Microfinance Bank (⏰ *08.30–15.00 Mon–Fri, 08.30–12.30 Sat*). The post office (⏰ *08.00–13.00 & 14.00–16.30 Mon–Fri, closed Sat*) is just past the bank, but be aware that your letter may take months to leave Mafia. A better option may be to ask your lodge to post your letters in Dar es Salaam.

NORTH OF KILINDONI One of the few places that travellers visit on Mafia is the lighthouse at Ras Mkumbi, via the charming village of Bweni. This is approximately 47km north of Kilindoni, and the drive there, over bouncy sand roads that follow or run parallel to the west coast of Mafia, takes about two hours direct, or all day if you want to include swimming and a picnic. Note, though, that while there are some stunning white-sand beaches along this coast, with excellent swimming opportunities, the sea on this side of the island is largely devoid of the underwater attractions around Chole Bay to the east. The excursion is best organised through one of the lodges; you'll find an English-speaking guide is invaluable. Alternatively, a full-day excursion to Ras Mkumbi with Mafia Island Tours costs US$50 per person. Bring everything you are likely to need from your hotel, not forgetting clothes to cover knees and shoulders, suncream, and insect repellent in case you return after dark.

Driving through Mafia is a good way of seeing the island, and finding out about everyday life here. As you drive through the villages, you'll see crops of mangoes, pineapples, bananas, cassava and cashew nuts, as well as sweet potatoes, which grow after the rainy season. About 8km from Kilindoni is a picturesque swamp covered in mauve lotus. Small tilapia and catfish dart among the reeds. Further on, the old agricultural village of **Kirongwe**, with a tradition of making clay pots, counts a score of houses, a handful of shops and a market selling the usual dried octopus, bananas and coconuts. Beyond here the countryside is intensively cultivated with beans, pigeon pea and cassava, and – rather less attractive – numerous indications of slash-and-burn agriculture. Sykes's and vervet monkeys raiding the crops flee at the sound of any vehicle.

The north of Mafia is markedly different from the wetter southern part of the island, which is dominated by vast coconut plantations. After **Jimbo**, where you may see local blacksmiths working by the side of the road, the landscape suddenly becomes more undulating open grassland with outcrops of mia'a or palm, and baobabs similar to those on the mainland coastal plain. Birdlife is plentiful with bee-eaters and lilac-breasted rollers flashing amongst the trees and large flocks of guinea fowl scuttling off the road. While only about 30m above sea level, it is noticeably cooler here than on the coast.

Bweni village, built behind 2km of glistening white-sand beach, seems a likely spot for future tourism development. Its traditional Swahili-style houses of coral and lime plaster are dotted among slender coconut palms. You need to stop to collect the lighthouse key from a keeper in the village, and will be soon surrounded by excited and curious children, delighted at the chance to shout *Mzungu!* at the unexpected visitor. Their behaviour is polite, however, and their fascination mixed with a fear of the unknown. Bweni women are experts at weaving striped prayer mats from the palms on the plateau, and you only need to show interest for items to be shyly produced. The larger mats are 2.5m by 1.5m, and cost around US$4; smaller oval mats go for US$3.

The **lighthouse** at **Ras Mkumbi** is a 3km drive on a good stretch of road from Bweni. Built on coral rag on the northern tip of Mafia, it is worth climbing the 15m up to the top of the red-and-white structure for a spectacular view of the Mafia Channel lying between the archipelago and the mainland. The stretch of deep-blue water is reputed to offer some of the best big-game fishing in east Africa. This working lighthouse also has concrete outbuildings, now owned by Pole Pole, who organise trips to the area. One of the buildings has basic rooms with mosquito nets around basic beds, and flushing toilets. At present it is used for overnight fishing trips but is being developed into a small guesthouse.

The grassy area in front of the lighthouse leads towards a rocky beach which repays half an hour or so of exploration at low tide. Black kites swoop low over the cliffs, while further out fishermen search for octopus in their race against the tide. It's possible to rent a bike from the village, or to go on a forest walk to see birds and monkeys. Snorkelling, fishing and diving trips can also be organised in this area.

KISIMANI MAFIA Kisimani (Kiswahili for 'the place of the well') lies on Ras Kisimani, at the south end of the island 30 minutes' drive from Kilindoni, or a two-hour boat trip. The town was an important centre during the Shirazi domination of Kilwa between the 12th and 14th centuries (see page 337). The hands of the sultan's chief mason were cut off after he built the palace, so that he could never repeat the task. The story goes on to claim that this was why a few months later Kisimani was inundated by the sea. There is little left of the submerged medieval settlement, but you can see the well for which it is named on the beach. Wandering about, you might find a few coins and pottery shards.

The shady coconut palms are a nice spot for a picnic, and there's a lovely white beach with good birding and snorkelling, but bring everything you want to eat or drink.

UTENDE The three main tourist lodges on Mafia Island all lie along the beach below this small village, at the end of the 15km road west from Kilindoni. Many of Utende's inhabitants are Makonde people from the mainland, who keep their fishing boats in Chole Bay. One or two shop-houses sell strings of dried octopus and fish. Like everywhere else on Mafia, the village is quite safe to explore, being only ten minutes' walk from any of the hotels. The beach in front of Utende (close to Mafia Island Lodge) is where local dhows leave for Chole Island every 30 minutes or so, costing US$0.50 on a local ferry one-way. Alternatively, it'll cost around US$10 to hire a boat.

Schools here are developing with aid from the lodges. A new primary school is being built on the site of the old school, offering Standards 1–6, and nursery education for 31 pupils. Since 2000, this has been financed by Pole Pole. The government then helped them to build another school building for seven–14 year olds. Utende also has a couple of small shops, and you'll notice a number of buildings made with cement blocks and corrugated iron. Although not as picturesque, cement blocks are relatively cheap and an easy material for building, while corrugated-iron roofs last longer than a palm-leaf roof, which has to be replaced every three years or so.

OTHER EXCURSIONS Most other villages on Mafia are inaccessible by road and, like the offshore islands, may be visited only by boat. Given advance warning, the lodges can usually arrange trips to visit them.

However, the most popular excursions are probably those to isolated sandbars. You'll sail to these from your lodge, and then the boat crew will set up some shade on the beach, and cook lunch over a barbecue. Meanwhile, you can relax, sunbathe, swim and snorkel with nothing around you except miles and miles of deep blue ocean. Trips like these are included by some of the lodges, which others will charge you extra, depending on the destination (US$40–60 per person per trip is typical).

Destinations for excursions include Chole, Juani and Jibondo islands, described in the following pages, and several smaller spots including:

Mchangani Village is the end of an interesting excursion winding for nearly 3km up a creek on the north side of Chole Bay. Sykes's monkeys can be seen in the mangrove forests and fish eagles are commonly observed. The village lies on the east bank of the creek, and takes about an hour to reach. Depart only on a high tide. If you would rather walk, it takes 90 minutes over sand and rock.

Dindini Beach is likewise accessible only at high tide. It faces the ocean from Mafia Island just north of Chole Bay, and from December to February can see big waves. Behind the beach is a large, sea-fed rock pool, which contains a variety of marine life. There are also low sand dunes and interesting vegetation on the coral rag.

Didimizi Beach is the lovely white-sand beach seen from Chole Bay, around 4km from the main tourist lodges, or a 45-minute walk. You could arrange for a vehicle going to Kilindoni to drop you at the turn-off and walk back, not forgetting to take refreshments and a hat. Alternatively a short trip by dhow brings you straight to the beach dotted with little pyramids of sand caused by the white ghost crabs that scuttle around – they'll be all you share the sandbar with.

Bwejuu Island, off Ras Kisimani to the west of Mafia, has its own small village and makes a good day trip. Located between the Rufiji River Delta and Mafia's main island, it offers good snorkelling at Mange Reef, as well as diving and fishing. You can also camp on Bwejuu Island for a few nights. Further afield, the Rufiji River is close enough for trips which can go all the way to the Selous Game Reserve.

Ras Mbisi, only 90 minutes by road from Kilindoni, has an ideal beach for picnics, swimming and snorkelling.

Mbaracuni Island, lying 12km northwest of Mafia, can be visited by arrangement. Uninhabited, quiet and said to be very beautiful, it is used by fishing dhows. This is a good place to see black kites and occasionally two or three fish eagles.

Miewe is another small, uninhabited island, used by fishermen to clean and dry fish, and can be visited for picnics, as can the sandbank of **Marimbani**. If you're interested in sailing a little further, and for a good chance of seeing dolphins, you can take a day excursion to the island of **Kitutia**. After a couple of hours under sail, you'll be rewarded by some stunning snorkelling on a reef which surrounds a pure-white sandbank. This is all covered by the sea at high tide, so the trip needs to be timed carefully.

CHOLE ISLAND

Chole is the lush, tropical island lying to the west of Kinasi Pass. With the adjacent islands of Juani and Jibondo, it forms a barrier between Mafia and the open ocean. The shallow reef in front is rich in soft corals, sea anemones and sponges, and, sloping to 15m, it is a good spot to practise drift diving. The bay itself is ideal for sailing and windsurfing. The town of Chole Mjini was the main urban centre on the archipelago for much of the 19th century, the home of wealthy merchants whose plantations lay on the main island of Mafia (see *History*, page 339, and box, *Recollections of Chole*, page 354). Ruins dating from this era include a reasonably preserved German Customs House on the waterfront, and several more ruined mansions dating to the Omani era. A path behind the new market leading to the village brings you to a prison, whose broken cells are invaded by tangled tree roots. Farther along and also in ruins is a Hindu temple.

Hanging upside down in a nearby baobab is a colony of fruit bats of the same family as the Comoros Islands' lesser flying fox (*Pteropus seychellenis comorensis*), found in the Comoros, the Seychelles and Mafia, but nowhere on mainland Africa. Each evening the bats fly across Chole Bay to feed on the cashew-nut and mango trees of Mafia, as well as marula fruit, figs and mangrove flowers. Like the Comoros bats they dip over the surface of the water – an action which scientists believe may be an attempt to rid themselves of parasites. A more enchanting local explanation claims 'they are washing before evening prayers'. Bats are nocturnal, so it's imperative for the continuation of the Chole colony that visitors allow them to sleep in the day, ensuring that neither they nor their guide throw stones at them, or shake their tree, just to wake them up and take photos of the bats in flight. Remember that it is a bat sanctuary.

Chole's population was estimated at 5,000 during the early years of German rule, but today it is no more than 1,000. The islanders cultivate smallholdings of cassava, beans, mangoes, paw-paw, citrus (including very sweet oranges) and

Factual histories of the east African coast tend to focus on the activities of the ruling classes – whether indigenous, Arabic or European – largely because such accounts are drawn from historical sources written by the powerful, and archaeological excavations of their mosques and palaces. The following quotes provide a rather different perspective, though it should be borne in mind that they are not first-hand accounts, but traditions passed from one generation to the next.

The woman quoted is the late Bi Hadija Mahommedi Bacha of Chole Island, and her stories are reproduced from the *Chole Handbook* (available from any of the lodge gift shops on Mafia) with the kind permission of its editors Chris Walley and Dudley Iles.

The wife of an Arab slave owner said, 'I don't understand how a child lies in the womb', so [her husband] cut open a pregnant slave woman to show his wife how the foetus lay inside. That young woman was cut open like a piece of dried fish so they could see how the child lay inside the womb of its mother ... Next the wife asks the slave master, 'When a monkey is shot what happens?' So a person is found to climb up a tree, like that baobab over there. He sends a gun over there, he shoots, Pow! Down falls a human being. That slave master was called Masinda; he was the owner of Kaziwa ... He was harsh! If you did anything at all, you would be made to climb a tree and shot – boom! – with a gun. You would fall down like an animal. You would already be dead and then you would be thrown away.

[Under the Germans,] if someone did something wrong, that person would be hanged at the Boma there on the beach, near the Casuarina tree at the spot along the beach where people today like to sit. It was an open spot and a box would be placed below and the person's neck would be placed in a rope. It was the Germans who arranged to use the place in this manner, and indeed they were the ones who did the hanging.

passion fruit. Encouraged by the lodges, these smallholdings have flourished and produce is now exported to Mafia, with the oranges also making their way to the mainland. Most of the menfolk fish, while many of the women are engaged in catching octopus beyond the mangroves at low tide. Winding past traditional houses, the path brings you to a beach where fishermen can be seen mending nets, or making sails and coconut-coir ropes. Chole was once a centre of boatbuilding, and boats are still repaired and occasionally built on the island. The boatyard is indicated on the circular walk available from Chole Mjini, about half an hour from the lodge.

The Norwegian Women's Front and Chole Mjini Lodge have been instrumental in much of Chole's development. They have funded the building of a hospital and a free clinic for the under fives, a kindergarten, a market, and the Society for Women's Development (which runs savings and loan schemes). They have also helped to set up a school, so that children no longer have to walk across to Juani Island at low tide, and a learning centre to help educate adults.

GETTING THERE AND AWAY The lodges at Utende operate boat trips to Chole, or you can visit it independently from Mafia, or on a 'bat and village tour' with Mafia Island Tours (US$10). A dhow dubbed the 'Chole taxi' leaves the beach in front of Mafia Island Lodge throughout the day – last sailing at 16.00 – a crossing of ten to 15 minutes depending on the wind and tide, for a cost of TSh500 one-way. It is also possible to charter a local boat across for a fee of about US$10. If you plan to stay more than a few hours on the island it is advisable to bring a picnic and refreshments from your hotel, and note that you'll have to wade a short distance from the boat. Make sure that you're wearing shoes, as there are stingrays in this area.

There is no motorised transport on Chole Island. In the early 1990s there was only one bike, which now hangs from the rafters of Chole Mjini; today there are 150. Neither are there any budget hotels; the only place to stay is Chole Mjini Lodge (see *Where to stay*, page 345), which does not cater to passing custom or serve meals to non-residents.

JUANI ISLAND

The boat trip from Mafia to Juani, site of the ruined city of Kua, takes about ten minutes longer than the one to Chole, but the island can be approached only at high tide. The landing, in a small bay sheltered by dense mangroves, is covered in thousands of opened oyster-shells, so remember to wear good shoes, as you'll have to wade to shore. Seafood is the staple diet on Juani, but, unlike Chole, Juani has no well water, and locals practise rain-dependent cultivation.

Beneath three big baobabs near the landing, your shoes crunch on the rocky paths of a buried civilisation. Bits of blue-and-white Shirazi pottery suggest trade links with China are embedded in the dirt. In the past, people from the mainland came to Juani to bathe in a seawater cave reputed to have curative properties for rheumatism. It is a long, difficult walk across to the ocean side, where there are also said to be three turtle-nesting beaches. The Kua Channel slices a tiny chunk off Juani as it opens into Chole Bay. It makes a superb picnic excursion with birdwatching and swimming. A friendly grouper lives in one of the rock pools at the southern end.

The ruined city of **Kua** (see *History*, page 337), spread across 15 acres on the west coast of Juani, was the Shirazi capital of Mafia. It was one of the few east African ports to be continuously inhabited from medieval times into the early 19th century, when it was sacked by raiders from Madagascar. A trail hacked out of the undergrowth leads up to a large building shedding masonry: the former palace, still

---

KUA'S REVENGE

The political relationship between Kisimani and Kua is unclear, but an intriguing if unverifiable oral tradition recounted by T M Revington in an essay in *Tanganyika Notes & Records* suggests that it was not always amicable:

The people of Ras Kisimani constructed a ship, and when it was finished and still on the stocks, they made a feast to which they invited the people of Kua. From amongst the guests they took by force several children, laid them on the sand, and launched the ship over their bodies. When the Kua people heard what had been done at Ras Kisimani, they were infuriated and thought out a scheme of revenge. Seven or eight years later, when they thought that the incident had been forgotten, an invitation was sent to the inhabitants of Ras Kisimani to attend a wedding at Kua. When the guests arrived in the evening they were ushered to a room that had been especially prepared beneath a house; the hosts one by one left their guests on the excuse of inquiring into the food, until only an old man remained to entertain them. This he did so well that the doors were bricked up without the guests perceiving it. The bodies are there to this day

So, too, is the sealed-off basement in which the bodies lie, according to the site's caretaker, who claims that it is situated below the ruins in front of his hut!

revered locally as a 'spirit place' where offerings such as bits of glass are left. The ruins here have been defeated by the powerful strangler figs that dominate a number of the walls, and the tomb of the sultan himself has been destroyed by a tree growing in its centre. The path passes other ruined edifices, including two 14th-century mosques and a series of tombs.

The buildings are made from coral rock and lime cement, which does not survive well in this sea air. Looking at cracks in the walls you wonder how long they will remain standing, with the occasional monkey as the only inhabitant. If you see the caretaker, he expects and deserves a small gratuity; ask him to show you the foundations of the house referred to in the box *Kua's revenge*, page 355.

You depart on a beautiful sail home between the islands, watched by the scores of ibis on the mangroves. There is a guide and map of the ruins, as well as the report on its archaeology, in the library at Kinasi Lodge.

JIBONDO ISLAND

Jibondo is a long, low-lying island another 20-minute sail from Juani. This traditional village community is rather different from the rest of Mafia, and the atmosphere is somehow more charged than in other villages. Coming ashore, a big jahazi dhow is one of the first things you see. Built 15 years ago, it has never been launched and is subsequently something of a museum piece, but the old men sitting under the quinine tree nearby have already learned its value to tourism, wanting to charge US$1 for a photo. Behind the boat is a rather plain white mosque, built in 1979.

Some of its furniture was taken from the queen's palace in the ruins at Kua, and it's worth wandering around the back to see the carved wooden door from Kua (by contrast, the window frames were made of wood from India). This is all set off by the pungent smell from the row of long-drop loos that literally drop into the sea. Jibondo does not have a fresh water supply, so the islanders depend on rain which is collected in a primitive concrete catchment area.

The rainwater lasts only three months after the rains; after this, the islanders have to go to Mafia with drums to collect water. Jibondo people are well known as shipbuilders and, as on Chole, use only traditional tools. Even the nails are handmade and the holes are plugged with local kapok and shark fat. Local women play a prominent role in trading as well as fishing. They also sail boats, which is unusual in African society, and are more affable and confident than women elsewhere. Jibondo people also collect and dry seaweed to export.

Another unusual aspect of Jibondo is that cultivation is carried out at one end of the island while the people live in an urban community at the other. The village, which consists of traditional Swahili-style houses with *makuti* roofs, is laid out in a grid pattern. As on Chole and Juani, there is no transport other than boats which shelter on the western side of the narrow neck of the island.

The island has one school, easily identified by the football field in front. If the tide is good for fishing, the children – encouraged by their parents – go straight out on the water, ignoring lessons. In a year, only one child is likely to leave the island and go to secondary school on Mafia. There are, however, three *madrasas* on the island, where there is a strong Muslim faith. There are no other social services, and only a basic shop. On the other side of the island is Flamingo Beach, which makes an interesting two-hour trek. The village trail and sailing dhow with Mafia Island Tours costs US$25.

14

Southern Tanzania Safaris

with Philip Briggs

In recent years, there has been increasing interest in the national parks and reserves of southern Tanzania – especially the Selous and Ruaha, and to a lesser extent Saadani. For decades these areas have been overshadowed by their more famous northern counterparts (Lake Manyara, Ngorongoro Crater and the Serengeti), but today the secret is out, and southern Tanzania is a favourite amongst safari aficionados as well as first-time visitors who are put off by the crowds which so often mar the northern parks.

Zanzibar is barely 200km from the Selous, the largest of all Tanzania's (and indeed Africa's) game reserves, making it easily accessible by air. Ruaha is further – about 400km from Zanzibar – while Saadani is just a 25km hop away, directly across the channel separating Unguja (Zanzibar Island) from the mainland.

Gradually a 'southern circuit' has developed, with many individuals and small groups flying to Selous (and sometimes also Ruaha) before finishing their trip with time on the islands. These flight links are now daily, even to Ruaha, making this an increasingly straightforward option. If you want to include the parks of southern Tanzania in your travels, then this chapter aims to help you plan your trip, and enjoy it to the full.

OVERVIEW OF YOUR TRIP

It's often difficult for first-time visitors to decide which reserves to visit – so an overview here might help.

If you're planning on a beach-and-safari trip then first be mindful that safari time will usually cost much more than beach time; it's often double the nightly cost. For example, an uncomplicated safari lodge will easily cost US$300 per person per night, whilst you'll have to try hard to find luxurious beach lodges at more than US$150 each per night. (The reason for this is partly that most safari lodges include a full day of activities and all your meals, whereas a beach lodge often provides only a room and breakfast; and partly because the logistics at most safari lodges are that much more expensive.)

With this in mind, consider how long you want to spend on each part of your trip. A 50/50 split (a week on safari and a week by the beach) is typical for a two-week trip, but this depends on your priorities and budget.

If you decide on five nights or less on safari, then our advice is probably to stick to Selous – and spend all your time there. If you decide on eight nights or more on safari, then you should consider combining time in Selous with time in Ruaha – as then the extra cost of flying between the parks is worth it for the change in scenery and environment. If you decide on six or seven nights on safari, then it's less clear if Ruaha is worth the extra travelling or not; you need to think about it.

Finally, if you're really looking for just two or three days of safari, perhaps beside a beach where you can lie back and forget safari activities completely if

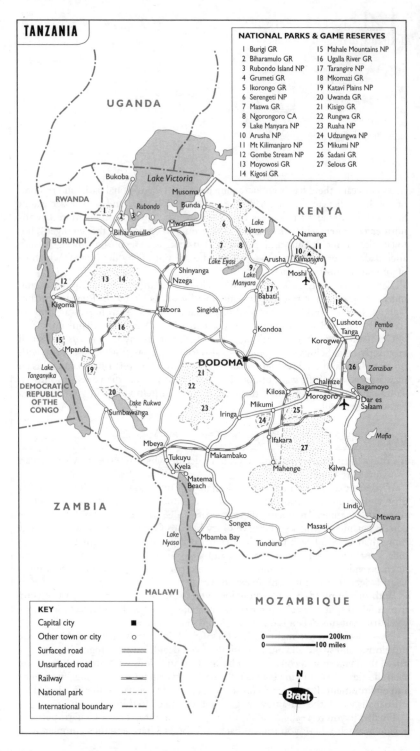

TANZANIA

NATIONAL PARKS & GAME RESERVES

1	Burigi GR	15	Mahale Mountains NP
2	Biharamulo GR	16	Ugalla River GR
3	Rubondo Island NP	17	Tarangire NP
4	Grumeti GR	18	Mkomazi GR
5	Ikorongo GR	19	Katavi Plains NP
6	Serengeti NP	20	Uwanda GR
7	Maswa GR	21	Kisigo GR
8	Ngorongoro CA	22	Rungwa GR
9	Lake Manyara NP	23	Ruaha NP
10	Arusha NP	24	Udzungwa NP
11	Mt Kilimanjaro NP	25	Mikumi NP
12	Gombe Stream NP	26	Sadani GR
13	Moyowosi GR	27	Selous GR
14	Kigosi GR		

UGANDA

Bukoba
Lake Victoria
Musoma
Rubondo
Bunda
Mwanza

RWANDA
KENYA
BURUNDI
Biharamullo
Lake Natron
Namanga
Lake Eyasi
Arusha
Kilimanjaro
Moshi
Shinyanga
Lake Manyara
Nzega
Babati
Lushoto
Tanga
Pemba

Kigoma
Tabora
Singida
Kondoa
Korogwe

Mpanda
DODOMA
Zanzibar
Chalinze
Bagamoyo
DEMOCRATIC
REPUBLIC
OF THE
CONGO
Lake Rukwa
Kilosa
Morogoro
Dar es
Salaam
Sumbawanga
Iringa
Mikumi
Mafia
Ifakara
Mbeya
Makambako
Mahenge
Kilwa
Tukuyu
Kyela
Matema
Beach
Lake Tanganyika

ZAMBIA
Lindi
Mtwara
Songea
Masasi
Lake Nyasa
Mbamba Bay
Tunduru

MALAWI
MOZAMBIQUE

KEY

Capital city	■
Other town or city	o
Surfaced road	
Unsurfaced road	
Railway	
National park	
International boundary	

0 ———— 200km
0 ———— 100 miles

N

Bradt

you wish, then consider Saadani. This small, coastal park allows you the flexibility to do just that.

SELOUS GAME RESERVE

Covering more than 45,000km², the Selous (pronounced 'Seloo') is Africa's single largest game reserve, three times larger than the Serengeti, more than twice the size of South Africa's Kruger National Park, and roughly 50% bigger than either Belgium or Swaziland. It is, furthermore, the core sanctuary within the greater Selous-Niassa ecosystem, which extends over 155,000km² of practically uninhabited wilderness in southern Tanzania and northern Mozambique – the largest chunk of comparably untrammelled bush left in Africa.

The claim that the Selous lies at the core of the greatest surviving African wilderness is supported by the prodigiously large mammal populations protected within the reserve and the greater ecosystem. The elephant herd of 65,000 represents more than half of the Tanzanian population, and 5–10% of the African total. The buffalo, estimated at 120,000–150,000, and the reserve's 40,000 hippo and 4,000 lion are probably the largest such populations on the continent. The Selous also harbours an estimated 100,000 wildebeest, 35,000 zebra, 25,000 impala and significant herds of greater kudu, hartebeest and eland. It is also one of the most important sanctuaries in Africa for the endangered black rhinoceros, African wild dog, and sable and puku antelope.

BACKGROUND INFORMATION That the Selous ranks as one of east Africa's most alluring and satisfying safari destinations is not in dispute. However, given that much of the publicity surrounding the Selous bangs on and on about its vast area, prospective visitors should be aware that the extent of the reserve is in practice something of a red herring. The Selous is divided into two disproportionate parts by the Rufiji, Tanzania's largest river, which together with the great Ruaha, a major tributary, runs through the reserve from west to east. About 90% of the Selous lies to the south of the river and has been divided into a number of privately leased hunting concessions, all of which are off-limits to casual tourism. A proportion of the northern sector has also been set aside for hunting concessions. The remainder – no more than 5% of the reserve's total area – forms what, to all intents and purposes, is the Selous Photographic Reserve. The lodges (and most activities for visitors) are actually concentrated within an area of about 1,000km² immediately north of the Rufiji.

Fortunately, this photographic part of the Selous is wonderfully atmospheric, a dense tract of wild miombo woodland abutting the meandering Rufiji River, and an associated labyrinth of five pretty lakes connected to each other and the river by numerous narrow streams. Arriving by light aircraft, as most visitors do, it is exhilarating to sweep above the palm-fringed channels teeming with hippo and waterfowl, the swampy islets where immense herds of elephant and giraffe graze alongside each other, and exposed sandbanks where antelope drink and all manner of shorebirds scurry about.

No less exciting are the boat excursions along the Rufiji, which generally culminate with a brilliant red sun setting behind the tall borassus palms and baobabs that line the wide sandy watercourse. Gulp-inducing dentist's-eye views of the Selous's trademark gigantic crocs can pretty much be guaranteed from the boat, as can conferences of grunting, harrumphing hippo – and you'd be unlucky not to be entertained by herds of elephant, buffalo or giraffe shuffling down to drink.

The most memorable aspect of the boat trips, however, is the profuse birdlife. Characteristic waterbirds along this stretch of the Rufiji include yellow-billed

SELOUS GAME RESERVE

Tourist sector

N

Bradt

Kisaki, Dar es Salaam

Matembwe entrance gate

Fuga Halt Railway station

Sable Mountain Lodge

Beho Beho Campsite

Beho Beho

Beho Beho Hills

Selous' Grave

Hot Springs

Lake Tagalala

Lake Manze Camp

Lake Manze

Mbuyu Camp

Lake Nzelokela

Selous Safari Camp

Lake Siwandu

Selous Impala Camp

Lake Mzizmia

Mtemere entrance gate

Ndouli Camp

Rufiji River Camp

Selous Mbega Camp

Mwasene

Mloka

Rufiji

Dar es Salaam, Kilwa

Lake Tagalala Campsite

Sand Rivers Selous

Rufiji

Selous Wildlife Lodge

Mivumo River Lodge

Stiegler's Gorge

0   15km

0   10 miles

stork, white-crowned and spur-winged plovers, various small waders, pied and malachite kingfishers, and African skimmer. Pairs of fish eagle and palmnut vulture perch high on the borassus palms, seasonal breeding colonies of carmine and white-throated bee-eater swirl around the mud cliffs that hem in some stretches of the river, and pairs of trumpeter hornbill and purple-crested turaco flap between the riparian trees. Worth looking out for among a catalogue of egrets and herons is the Malagasy squacco heron, a regular winter visitor, while the elusive Pel's fishing owl often emerges at dusk to hawk above the water.

Game drives along the network of rough roads to the north of the Rufiji are reliably rewarding, especially towards the end of the dry season, when large mammals concentrate around the five lakes. More frequently seen ungulates include impala, common waterbuck, bushbuck, white-bearded wildebeest, eland, greater kudu, buffalo and common zebra.

The northern sector of the park has been dubbed 'Giraffic Park', with some justification, as herds exceeding 50 individuals come down to drink in the heat of the afternoon. Giraffes seem exceedingly common here, which is odd as they are entirely absent south of the Rufiji. The river also forms a natural barrier between the ranges of the distinctive white-bearded and Niassa races of wildebeest. The endangered African wild dog is commonly observed, as is the spotted hyena, while leopards are common but elusive, but cheetah have not been recorded in this part of the reserve for about 20 years.

Much in evidence are Selous's lions, with two or three different prides' territories converging on each of the five large lakes. The lions typically have darker coats and less hirsute manes than their counterparts elsewhere in east Africa. During the dry season, the lions of Selous evidently rely on an unusual opportunistic diurnal hunting strategy, rarely straying far from the lakes, where they rest up in the shade to wait for whatever ungulate happens to venture within pouncing distance on its way to drink.

While the marketing line of 'only five small camps in a 50,000km² wilderness' does rather overstate the exclusivity of the Selous experience, it is true that a mere 5,000 foreigners annually – about 1% of tourist arrivals to Tanzania – ever make it to this excellent reserve. Particularly if you are based at one of the western lodges – Beho Beho, Sand Rivers and Sable Mountain – it is still possible to undertake a game drive in the Selous without coming across another vehicle.

Whereas the national parks of northern Tanzania are dominated by large impersonal hotels that evidently aim to shut out the bush the moment you enter them, the Selous boasts a select handful of low-key, eco-friendly, thatch-and-canvas lodges whose combined bed capacity amounts to little more than 100 visitors. Furthermore, because the Selous is a game reserve and not subject to the regulations that govern Tanzania's national parks, visitors are offered a more primal and integrated bush experience than the usual repetitive regime of one game drive after another. In addition to boat trips, all lodges offer guided game walks, which come with a real likelihood of encountering elephant or buffalo – even lion – on foot. Better still are the overnight fly-camping excursions offered by some of the camps, which entail sleeping beneath a glorified mosquito net in the middle of the bush. It's thrilling stuff!

Note that the roads within the Selous become impassable after heavy rain. Hence camps here close towards the end of the wet season, in April, and reopen in July.

Entrance fees In July 2008, the entrance fees saw a massive increase, and more than doubled overnight. An entrance fee of US$75 per person per day is now charged (US$50 for park fees and a new US$25 conservation charge). This is payable in hard currency. On most organised trips this will be included in the overall price, but it's worth checking this when booking.

Further information Two useful booklets are *Selous Game Reserve: A Guide to the Northern Section* and the glossier *Selous: Africa's Largest & Wildest Game Reserve*. Most lodges stock both and they are similar textually. For details on the man behind the park's name, read *The Life of Frederick Courtney Selous* by J G Millais, published by Gallery Publications and available in Zanzibar.

GETTING THERE AND AWAY Many tour operators, both overseas and in Tanzania, offer a variety of trips to the Selous. These usually include flights to/from the reserve, accommodation and activities. Most use frequent daily flights between Dar es Salaam and Selous operated by Coastal Airlines and ZanAir. These generally connect very easily to/from Zanzibar. Some of the Coastal flights continue (daily from 2006) to connect with flights to/from Ruaha. Once inside the parks, these flights will all stop at any of the camp airstrips by prior arrangement.

If you are travelling in mainland Tanzania it's perfectly possible to reach the Selous by road, although that's generally more costly than flying. For full details of these options, *Tanzania: The Bradt Travel Guide* by Philip Briggs is, of course, highly recommended.

WHERE TO STAY Over the last few years, accommodation options in Selous have increased significantly, although the sheer size of the park still ensures privacy in the majority of areas. Of the 14 camps listed below, 11 are within the park boundaries and levels of service and experience are almost invariably high.

Beho Beho Camp (8 units) ☎ 022 2600352–4/(UK) +44 (0)20 8750 5655; e reservations@behobeho.com; www.behobeho.com. Beho Beho's site was used for a safari camp as early as 1972; one of the first such sites in the Selous. It still has an unusual location for this park, high on a hill in an area dotted with baobabs. In 2004, it was virtually rebuilt & completely refurbished, & is now widely regarded as the best lodge in the Selous. Accommodation is in one of 8 very large & attractively decorated en-suite *bandas* built of local stone on the footslopes of the Beho Beho Hills, on the west side of northern Selous. All have large bathrooms with great outdoor showers, flush toilets & dual washbasins. The bedrooms have canopied king-size beds, ceiling fans & 24hr electricity (UK-style 3-pin plugs). All are slightly different, & each has a separate area that is partly lounge, partly veranda. This lies under a high thatched roof, with almost a whole wall open at the front. The elegant dining area serves very high-quality food, with everyone usually sitting around the same table – even if the location of the table varies. Afterwards there are vast sofas to relax in around the bar area, & a full-size slate-bedded billiards table to keep the restless entertained. Slightly down the slope, the swimming pool & its sundeck also command a spectacular view. Beho Beho is the only lodge within Selous set away from the river, but a permanent pool in the valley below supports a resident pod of hippos & attracts plenty of game & birdlife. Although very comfortable, what has really gained such a top reputation for the camp is the quality & enthusiasm of its guiding team.

Sean Lues & Sacha Toronyi are both Zimbabwean & trained there under what was certainly Africa's best system of safari guide accreditation; Sean even becoming a guide trainer. They offer a depth of knowledge & guiding experience that's very hard to match in the reserve. Being in a relatively remote area of the park, you'll find few other visitors in Beho Beho's vicinity. The camp's activities include 4x4 game drives, boat trips on Lake Tagalala, & particularly good walking safaris. (It's not unknown for morning activities to last for 5 or 6hrs if you are enthusiastic & energetic!) Nearby sites of interest include some World War I trenches (complete with scattered artefacts), the grave of Frederick Courtney Selous & a group of hot springs set in a patch of riparian woodland. Beho Beho also offers super-luxurious 'bush nights' – with a small fly-camp set up for just 2–4 guests. At a high cost, this must rate as some of Africa's most exclusive, & expensive, camping! As a relatively new camp which rapidly gained revered status, Beho Beho has raised its rates substantially since opening in 2005 (around 25% a year) & they may well continue to rise. It is expensive, but the camp is certainly the best in Selous & arguably one of the best camps in Tanzania. The camp actively prefers guests to book through an operator rather than directly, & you will almost certainly get a better rate by doing so. *US$900–1,025pp sharing, FB inc drinks & all activities but exc park fees; 'Bush nights' extra US$350pp, on top of normal room cost*

🏠 **Lake Manze Camp** (12 tents) ✆ 022 2452005/6; e reservations@adventurecamps.co.tz; www.adventurecamps.co.tz. Opened in Jul 2007, Lake Manze Camp is part of the highly regarded Adventure Camps circuit, joining sister-properties Selous Impala Camp & Mdonya Old River Camp in Ruaha National Park. Distinct from many of the other camps in the park, Lake Manze is about being in the wilderness & enjoying bush simplicity: paraffin lanterns replace electricity, bathrooms are open air & there is fireside dining under the stars. Dotted under borassus palm trees, the tents are spacious & surrounded with gauze windows to allow for long views & a cooling breeze, furnishings are simple but high-quality wrought-iron & canvas furniture, & there is an en-suite bathroom complete with hot shower & flush toilet. Perhaps the greatest asset of the tents is their shady stone veranda, from where their slightly raised position affords good views across the lake, floodplain & passing wildlife. Activities are varied with 4x4 safari drives, boat safaris & morning walks all available, & with the good reputation & standards of its sister-camps firmly set, it's likely Lake Manze will become an increasingly popular choice in the Selous. *US$235/360 sgl/dbl, FB for drive-in clients (no activities); US$345/580 inc FB & activities*

🄌 **Lake Tagalala & Beho Beho campsites** These little-used official campsites have no facilities worth talking about, but they both boast a great setting & bush feel. *Camping US$10pp*

🏠 **Mbuyu Tented Camp** (20 rooms) This attractively located camp lies on the shore of Lake Nzelakela, & its lounge & dining area are built around a large baobab tree. An attractive feature is the stilted hide overlooking the lake, which is visited by numerous animals. The camp had fallen into some disrepair though & has been closed for some time. In spite of long-running rumours that it will reopen under new ownership & with new facilities, this had still not materialised at the time of writing this edition.

🏠 **Mivumo River Lodge** (12 rooms) ✆ + 255 22 260 2888; e reservations@mivumoriverlodge.com; www.malalaluxurylodges.com. This brand-new lodge in the Stiegler's Gorge area is the more upmarket of 2 opened in September 2008 by Malala Luxury Lodges. Set along the river, its suites — all with AC & en-suite bathroom with both a free-standing tub & an outdoor shower — are designed for both privacy and luxury. Guests can laze in their own plunge pool, or take in the latest news on satellite TV in the lounge with a drink from the minibar. The river view is shared by a central lounge, library & dining area, as well as an extensive pool. *US$720–860pp sharing FB, inc local drinks, activities & laundry, exc park fees; children over 6 welcome*

🏠 **Ndovu Campsite** (5 units) m 0744 782378; e hkibola@yahoo.co.uk. This new budget camp, situated outside the reserve boundaries between Mbega Camp & the Mtemere Gate, consists of 5 dbl standing tents with thatched roofs, as well as a campsite, all of which use common toilets & showers. A restaurant is periodically operational but is best not relied on — bring your own food to be sure of eating. Though the camp caters primarily to self-drive visitors, boat trips are offered at US$35pp. *Camping US$10pp. Tents* 💲

🏠 **Rufiji River Camp** (20 rooms) ✆ 022 2128663; m 0744 267706; e fox@tanzaniasafaris.info. One of the first lodges to be established in the Selous, the ever popular & reasonably priced Rufiji River Camp is situated at the eastern extremity of the photographic northern area of the reserve, overlooking an atmospheric stretch of the Rufiji River alive with hippos & crocs & regularly visited by elephants. The camp is frequently visited by monkeys & numerous birds, & occasionally by more exciting large mammals. Rufiji River consists of 20 en-suite standing tents, shaded by thatch, spaced along the river in a lush stretch of woodland. The interiors have traditionally been pleasant but simply furnished, with dbl/twin beds & an en-suite bathroom, each with a flush toilet & solar-heated shower. In mid 2008, Foxes Safari Camps, who also own Ruaha River Lodge, took over this camp from its laid-back Italian owner-manager. They plan to introduce larger tents & upgrade the interiors, so Rufiji's informal & unpretentious atmosphere may change in the future.

Rufiji River Camp has traditionally offered an excellent range of boat & foot activities, as well as half-day game drives encompassing the 3 nearby lakes, full-day excursions further afield & overnight fly-camping. The guides are generally experienced Tanzanians, most of whom have been guiding here for many years; many have worked as game scouts before joining the lodge. For guests who don't want to venture far, there's a swimming pool for in-camp relaxation. *US$365/530 sgl/dbl, FB, inc activities & park fees*

⌂ **Sable Mountain Lodge** (13 rooms) ☏ 022 2110507; 📱 0713 323318; 📧 info@ selouslodge.com; www.selouslodge.com. Situated 1km outside the park's western park boundary near the Matambwe Gate, Sable Mountain Lodge is situated among the small Mua Hills, offering views into the surrounding dense brachystegia forest. The accommodation consists of 8 fairly simple stone cottages & 3 more luxurious tented *bandas*. In addition, there are 2 open-fronted honeymoon tents each with a small, private plunge pool overlooking a lush green valley. All the rooms have en-suite hot shower & toilet, mosquito nets over the beds & 24hr solar electricity. Sable Mountain has 2 dining areas, one on each side of the lodge, with good views & varied international cuisine. There's a spring-water swimming pool & a sun lounging area, & for the more energetic, activities include 4x4 safaris in the park, walks & boat trips. The tireless can go on all-day trips, with a picnic lunch & a boat trip on Lake Tagalala. The surrounding woodland is very thick, & guided walks offer the opportunity to see forest-associated species such as blue monkey, black-and-white colobus & the amazing chequered elephant shrew, as well as a host of forest birds including the exquisite Livingstone's turaco, a variety of hornbills & the vociferous forest weaver. Between Dec & May, sable antelope move into the area. Game drives concentrate on the plains north of the main cluster of lodges, which can be very worthwhile seasonally, with very few other vehicles around. Fly-camping on high wooden platforms is also available, as are river trips during the wet season on the lushly forested Mbega River. Sable Mountain is very close to the train station at Kisaki, on the TAZARA line between Dar & Zambia. In the past there have been attempts to start a luxury train service; when successful, Sable Mountain will be an obvious first-stop for visitors to the reserve, but sadly, this rail service seems doomed. It is one of very few camps which can be arranged on a FB basis, without activities – so is ideal for those on a tighter budget who just want to do nothing for a few days! *US$200/290 sgl/dbl; US$380/580 sgl/dbl inc activities; all rates FB*

⌂ **Sand Rivers Selous** (8 rooms) ☏ 022 2865156; 📧 info@nomad.co.tz; www.sandrivers.com. Set above a wide, sandy bend in the Rufiji River, Sand Rivers Selous has been regarded as the top camp in the Selous for many years, & still puts up very stiff competition to Beho Beho. Sand Rivers' pedigree is top-notch, it's run by Nomad Tanzania & is the sister-camp of Chada Katavi, in Katavi National Park, & Greystoke Mahale, in Mahale Mountains National Park – both of which are top camps & names to conjure with in the safari world. Like Beho Beho, Sand Rivers is situated in an isolated area of the Selous, the wild southwest of the photographic section of the reserve, which is visited by vehicles from the other lodges infrequently. It is another very comfortable lodge with a large, open-fronted, thatched *boma* dotted with large sofas sporting sumptuous heavy-cotton cushions, but in contrast Sand Rivers stands on a wide curve of the Rufiji River; being able to watch the life of the river adds greatly to the special feel of the lodge. For those who need to be closer still to the water, there is a stylish curved swimming pool under a large baobab tree. Meals are high quality & eaten either together around a large table, or separately if guests prefer. Recently renovated, the lodge's 8 stone-and-thatch cottages are large & elegant with large dbl/twin beds, walk-in mosquito nets, an en-suite bathroom with flush toilet, shower & wash basin & a private balcony. There are 5 standard rooms, 2 suites (with small plunge pool & separate lounge area) & The Rhino House – a private 'honeymoon cottage' offering private dining & game drives. All the rooms are open fronted, & raised up to look out over the river.

Sand Rivers' activities focus on 4x4 game drives (the plains around nearby Lake Tagalala are one obvious goal); boat trips along the river & up through the impressive Stiegler's Gorge; & walking safaris. The standard of guiding is exceptionally high & the camp is very proud of its Tanzanian guides, some of whom have been there for many years. Sand Rivers also run very popular fly-camping trips, whereby a couple of guests sleep out on a dry riverbed with their guide – usually having had a lovely meal under the stars, complete with table-linen, crystal glasses & some fine food. Usually these are run for 1 or 2 nights as part of a longer stay at the lodge, although they do offer 5-night set walking trails (on fixed dates throughout the year) for die-hard walking-safari addicts. *Standard room from US$620pp, FB*

⌂ **Selous Impala Camp** (8 units) ☏ 022 2452005/6; 📧 reservations@adventurecamps.co.tz; www.adventurecamps.co.tz. Set up by its owner Gillie

Zanacchi in 2004, this unpretentiously tasteful new camp boasts a magnificent location on a wooded stretch of the Rufiji. It's relatively small, with just 8 Meru-style tents, built on wooden platforms with a private balcony. These are very comfortably furnished, in an 'old Africa' style. There is a family option here, with 2 full-size tents sharing 1 platform allowing parents with younger children to have their own space but remain within easy access of their children. The camp also uses Maasai guards to escort guests to their rooms at night. Impala has one of the most scenic locations in the park & its thatched lounge & communal deck looks out over the river to mountains, although one's gaze is usually drawn back to the Rufiji River by the elephants & other wildlife which visit it. Activities are fairly flexible, including game drives & boat trips, & the camp has a lovely swimming pool – allowing you to look out over the river & to the hills while you're in the pool. Impala is a very welcome addition to the Selous: a good camp that doesn't charge top prices. Over recent years this camp has consistently strengthened its reputation to become a firm favourite. It has high standards of service, a great team & excellent prices, & though it isn't as luxurious as Selous Safari Camp & Sand Rivers, it's stylish enough & tremendously good value. This has made it justifiably popular & you need to book a fair bit in advance to stay here now. In combination with its sister-camps in Selous (Lake Manze Camp) & Ruaha (the rather more spartan Mdonya Old River Camp), safaris are varied & particularly excellent value. *US$450/760 sgl/dbl for drive-in clients (no activities); US$515/890 sgl/dbl inc activities; all rates FB*

🏠 **Selous Mbega Camp** (13 rooms) ☎ 022 2650250/1; e info@baobabvillage.com; www.selous-mbega-camp.com/www.baobabvillage.com. This small German-owned camp lies on the banks of the Rufiji immediately east of the park boundary some 5.5km outside Mtemere Gate. Most of the en-suite tents are set in the riparian woodland overlooking the river, but 2 stand alongside a small waterhole. Game drives, guided walks, & boat trips can be arranged at US$40/80pp half-day/full-day excursion, plus park fees. Substantial discounts are offered to backpackers who are prepared to take the 7–9hr bus (US$8.50) from Dar es Salaam to the village of Mloka, about 4km from the camp (a free transfer is provided); these rates will not be offered to anyone who has not travelled on the bus. $$$$$

🏠 **Selous Safari Camp** (13 rooms) ☎ 022 2128485; m 0748 953551; e info@selous.com; www.selous.com. This plush camp is set back slightly

from the shores of Lake Siwandu. Approaching across the lake, all you see of the camp over the treetops are the tall apexes of the main *bandas*, which have been built on stilts. The camp has recently been divided into a main camp with 9 rooms, known as 'Selous Safari Camp', & a smaller section with just 4 rooms called 'Selous Private Camp'. Both provide accommodation in raised, spacious en-suite tents, which are set far apart from each other & have fans, open-air showers & a private deck. The main camp's lounge & dining area is a fabulous stilted treehouse lit at night by dozens of gas lamps. The main camp has a separate swimming pool. The private camp's tents are in essence identical to the main camp, though they are more luxuriously appointed & as a group have their own dining area on decking near the swimming pool. Private camp is booked on an exclusive-use basis only. Game drives, boat trips, guided walks & fly-camping are all offered here – although the camp is geared more for driving & boating than it is for walking. When last visited, activities commenced quite late in the morning, at 08.00; perfect for honeymooners who want a long lie-in & a safari. More recently we understand that they're starting these earlier, if requested. In short, Selous Safari Camp is a very high-quality, professional operation that pays great attention to detail – especially where comfort & food are concerned. *US$525/700 sgl/dbl main camp; US$600/800 sgl/dbl private camp inc 2 activities daily; all rates FB & exc park fees; drinks usually inc at the private camp; charged as extra at the main camp*

🏠 **Selous Retreat** (12 rooms) ☎ (Switzerland) +41 79 444 03 28; e retreat@bluewin.ch; www.retreatsafaris.co.tz. In 2008, in a remote northern section of the park, the strikingly stylish Selous Retreat opened. Architecturally impressive, its ochre walls, Omani arches, stunning pool deck & impressive array of African *objets d'art* are testament to its Swiss owners' attention to detail & high standards. Accommodation is divided between the main clay 'fort', 6 hillside tents, 4 riverfront suites (complete with waterside plunge pools & viewing decks), & a honeymoon hideaway boasting a private chef, guide, butler & pool. The tents, raised on teak decks, are spacious & well furnished & all have inviting outdoor baths to complement the en-suite facilities. In the public areas, there are lovely shaded lounge areas & the lodge also has a well-equipped, professionally run outdoor spa on the riverbank. With an array of traditional massage & holistic treatments available, this is a great place to relax in the heat of the day.

Food is served in the main restaurant overlooking the infinity pool & river or, for romantics, atop one of the 2 towers for panoramic views. Cocktails & sundowners' spots are equally varied, with bars both riverside & raised on the hillside.

If you can drag yourself away from the obvious comfort of the lodge, activities are varied: game drives, river cruises, guided walking & fishing trips. Open 4x4 vehicles & aluminium boats are used for these, with experienced Tanzanian guides escorting all trips. A particularly nice touch is that guests staying for 4 days plus are offered a fly-camping trip at no extra cost. It is likely that Selous Retreat will attract a growing following in the coming years

as its style is so unusual & service ambitions are high. *From US$500pp, FB & 2 activities/day*

🏠 **Selous Wildlife Lodge** (12 tents) 📞 + 255 22 260 2888; e reservations@selouswildlifelodge.com; www.malalaluxurylodges.com. The second of Malala Luxury Lodges' new offerings, opened in Sep 2008, lies on the Simbazi River, a tributary of the Rufiji. Each of the individual tents, sheltered under grass thatch, has its own en-suite bathroom. Central to the lodge is a natural waterhole, overlooked by the dining area and lounge. There's also a viewing deck & an infinity swimming pool. *US$540–610 pp sharing, FB, inc activities, local drinks & laundry, but exc park fees*

RUAHA NATIONAL PARK

Tanzania's second-largest national park extends over 10,300km² of wooded hills and open plains to the west of Iringa, and it lies at the core of a greater ecosystem that is five-times larger, embracing six other protected areas including the contiguous Rungwa and Kizigo game reserves. Ruaha is widely regarded by Tanzania's safari cognoscenti to be the country's best-kept game-viewing secret, and it has unquestionably retained a compelling wilderness character that is increasingly savoury when compared with the package safaris and 100-room game lodges common in the parks of northern Tanzania.

BACKGROUND INFORMATION The dominant geographical feature of the park is the Great Ruaha River, which follows the southeast boundary for 160km, and is known to the local Hehe people as the Lyambangori (Ruaha being a corruption of the Hehe word *luhava*, which simply means 'river'). Only the small part of the park around the river is developed for tourism, with just five small lodges currently operating. Its limited 400km road circuit sees relatively few visitors and has a reassuringly untrammelled mood.

Ruaha has a hot and rather dry climate, with an average annual rainfall of around 500mm falling almost exclusively between October and May, and peaking in February and March. Daytime temperatures in excess of 40°C are regularly recorded, particularly over October and November before the rains break, but a very low humidity level makes this less noticeable than might be expected, and it cools down reliably at night. The best game viewing is generally from May to November, but the bush is greener and prettier from January to June, and birding peaks during the European winter months of December to April. The vegetation of Ruaha is transitional to southern miombo and eastern savanna biomes, and a wide variety of habitats are protected within the park, including riparian forest along the watercourses, swamps, grassland and acacia woodland. The dominant vegetation type is brachystegia woodland and several areas of the park support an impressive number of large baobab trees.

The floral variety of Ruaha is mirrored by the variety of wildlife likely to be seen over the course of a few days on safari. The most common ungulates, not unusually, are the widespread impala, waterbuck, bushbuck, buffalo, zebra and giraffe, all of which are likely to be encountered several times on any given game drive. The park lies at the most southerly extent of the range of several east African ungulate species, including lesser kudu and Grant's gazelle. Yet it also harbours a number of antelope that are rare or absent in northern Tanzania, most visibly the

RUAHA NP & SITES AROUND IRINGA

splendid greater kudu – some of the most handsomely horned males you'll come across anywhere in Africa – but also the more elusive roan and sable antelope. The elephant population is the largest of any Tanzanian national park, despite heavy losses due to poaching in the 1980s, with some 12,000 elephants migrating through the greater Ruaha ecosystem. The most impressive pair of tusks weighed in the 20th century – combined weight 201kg – were from an individual shot in Ruaha in the 1970s, but the poaching of the recent past means you're unlikely to see anything comparable these days.

Ruaha is an excellent park for predators. Lions are not only numerous and very habituated to vehicles, but the prides tend to be unusually large, often numbering more than 20 individuals. The park also boasts a justified reputation for good leopard sightings, and, while it's not as reliable as the Seronera Valley in the Serengeti, leopard are usually seen every few days and they are less skittish than in many game reserves. Cheetah, resident on the open plains, are quite often encountered in the Lundu area – known locally as the mini Serengeti – northeast of the Mwagusi River. More than 100 African wild dogs are thought to be resident in the greater Ruaha ecosystem. Wild dogs are known to have very wide ranges, and their movements are often difficult to predict, but one pack of about 40 individuals regularly moves into the Mwagusi area, generally hanging around for a few days before wandering elsewhere for a couple of weeks. Visitors who particularly want to see wild dogs should try to visit in June or July, when they are normally denning, and are thus easier to locate than at other times of year. Black-backed jackal and spotted hyena are both very common and easily seen, and the rarer striped hyena, though seldom observed, is found here at the southern limit of its range.

With 450 species recorded, Ruaha also offers some excellent birding, once again with an interesting mix of southern and northern species. Of particular note are substantial and visible populations of black-collared lovebird and ashy starlings, Tanzanian endemics associated with the Maasai Steppes, found here at the southern extreme of their distribution. By contrast, this is perhaps the only savanna reserve in east Africa where the crested barbet – a colourful yellow-and-black bird whose loud sustained trilling is a characteristic sound of the southern African bush – replaces the red-and-yellow barbet. Ruaha is also the type locality for the recently described Tanzanian red-billed hornbill (*Tockus ruahae*), a Tanzanian endemic that is very common within its restricted range. Raptors are well represented, with bateleur and fish eagle probably the most visible large birds of prey, and the localised Eleanora's falcon quite common in December and January. The watercourses support the usual waterbirds.

Ruaha is best visited between July and November, when animals concentrate around the river. Internal roads may be impassable during the rainy season (December to May).

National park fees An entrance fee of US$20 per person per night must be paid in hard currency. On most organised tours this will be included, but it's worth checking this when booking.

Further information The *Ruaha* booklet, published in 2000 by the African Publishing Group, is normally available at the lodges, and contains useful maps, animal descriptions and checklists, and details of where to look for localised species. The older 64-page booklet *Ruaha National Park* is just as useful, and cheaper, assuming that you can locate a copy!

GETTING THERE AND AWAY The most straightforward way to reach Ruaha from Zanzibar is by Coastal Aviation's daily scheduled flights via Dar es Salaam, which also serve the Selous Game Reserve. Typically these cost about US$300 per person one-way between Selous and Ruaha, or US$330 per person one-way between Dar and Ruaha.

As with the Selous, if you are travelling in mainland Tanzania you can reach Ruaha by air from Dar es Salaam, without going to Zanzibar. It's also possible to get there by road, although this is usually at least a two-day trip; for more details see *Tanzania: The Bradt Travel Guide* by Philip Briggs.

WHERE TO STAY

Jongomero Tented Camp (8 tents) ✆ 022 2128485; m 0748 953551; e info@selous.com; www.selous.com. Sister-camp of Selous Safari Camp in the Selous, this is the most overtly luxurious of the lodges in Ruaha, & the only one with a swimming pool. Jongomero consists of 8 spacious tented rooms with private balconies carved into the dense riverine woodland bordering the eponymous seasonal river. It's about 500m upstream of its confluence with the Ruaha, where a semi-permanent pool hosts a resident pod of around 50 hippos. Jongomero has a very isolated feel, situated 60km southwest of the entrance gate, & the little-used road running back towards the entrance gate often yields good elephant & buffalo sightings. The area to the south of camp functions much as a private game reserve, because so few other vehicles head this way, but this area borders a hunting concession & so the wildlife tends to be rather skittish. The birdlife within camp can be excellent, with Livingstone's turaco topping the gaudiness stakes, while the localised Bohm's spinetail can be distinguished from the other swifts & swallows that soar above the camp by its distinctive bat-like fluttering. Walking safaris & fly-camping now complement the existing game drives. The catering is to an exceptionally high standard, but, unlike several other lodges in this price range elsewhere in Tanzania, drinks are not included. *US$495/660 sgl/dbl, FB & inc all activities*

Mwagusi Safari Camp (13 tents) ✆ (UK) 07525 170940/07901 904562; e oeas.co@btinternet.com. This small & exclusive tented camp, situated on the north bank of the seasonal Mwagusi River, is one of the most alluring lodges anywhere in east Africa, immensely comfortable, yet with a real bush atmosphere. The accommodation, strung along the riparian woodland fringing the river, consists of spacious walk-in tents, enclosed in a wood, thatch & reed shelter, each of which has a vast shower & toilet area, & a private balcony. Because the lodge is owner-managed, the service is top-notch & includes some great touches – most memorably, starlit bush dinners around a campfire in a clearing above the camp or in the riverbed. Game viewing from the

camp is superb, with elephant & greater kudu regularly putting in an appearance, & plenty of birds hopping around the trees. Wild dog are regularly sighted in the area, several lion prides are resident, & the closest game-viewing circuits are situated far enough from the larger Ruaha River Lodge & park headquarters to let you feel you have the whole park to yourself. Game walks with an armed ranger are also offered, with a good chance of encountering elephants & other large animals on foot, & it is best to book these in advance. For early risers, Mwagusi also runs free early-morning bird walks around the camp, a lovely way to start the day. *US$390/450 sgl/dbl inc all activities, meals & park fees; drinks are extra; US$25/group plus US$10pp for ranger-guided walks*

Ruaha River Lodge (28 rooms) ✆ (UK) 01452 862288/022 2862357; m 0784 237422/0713 237422; e fox@safaricamps.info; www.tanzaniasafaris.info. This wonderfully scenic & comfortable camp is the oldest in Ruaha, situated on a rocky hillside above a set of rapids on the Ruaha River some 15km from the entrance gate. Game viewing is excellent from the camp, with rock hyrax scuttling around everywhere, hippos resident in the river, elephant passing through regularly, & many other animals coming down to drink. Accommodation, in fixed tents or unpretentious stone cottages, was rebuilt in 2007 to refresh & enlarge the rooms. The interiors remain simple but each has a dbl & a sgl bed & a comfortable lounge area. Ruaha River Lodge is actually divided into 2 camps of 14 rooms each, both of which have their own restaurant & bar. *US$295/540 sgl/dbl inc all activities, meals & park fees; drinks are extra*

Mdonyo Old River Camp (11 tents) ✆ 022 245 2005/6; e reservations@adventurecamps.co.tz; www.adventurecamps.co.tz. Like its sister-camp, Selous Impala Camp, Mdonyo Old River Camp was set up with help from Coastal Aviation in 2002. It stands on the wooded banks of the 'old' Mdonyo River, which has not flowed in earnest since a newer path was carved by the river a couple of decades back. Comfortable rather than luxurious, the en-suite standing tents all have a private balcony, while the culinary emphasis is on tasty home-style cooking eaten beneath the stars. Mdonyo Old River makes no apologies for being a fairly simple camp; it's aiming for a fairly elemental experience of Africa, & not for the comforts & fripperies that so many camps seem to have been striving for in recent years. Isolated though it may be, the camp offers good access to the superb Mwagusi Sand River game-viewing circuit. The old riverbed is an important wildlife passage, & plenty of animals pass through camp daily, most profusely impala, warthog & giraffe, but also the occasional lion or elephant, while the helpful staff will gladly show you nocturnal visitors such as honey badger, genet & bushpig. The birding is also superb, with the likes of purple-crested turaco, bearded woodpecker, crested barbet, black-necked weaver, orange-breasted bush-shrike & green-winged pytilia among the colourful & conspicuous residents. US$235/360 sgl/dbl for drive-in clients (no activities); US$345/580 inc activities; all rates FB

🔺 **Tandala Camp** (11 units) e tandala@ iwayafrica.com/tandalacamp@yahoo.com. Situated some 12km outside Ruaha's entrance gate along the Tungamalenga road, this new lodge overlooks a seasonal sand river in private conservancy buffering the national park. Accommodation is in straightforward but comfortable en-suite tents set on a stilted wooden base, while facilities include an attractive *makuti* restaurant & bar area alongside a small swimming pool. The greater kudu for which the camp is named is evidently quite common in the surrounding woodland, while a waterhole fringing the camp attracts a steady stream of wildlife in the dry season, including elephants on most days. US$175pp/dbl; US$255pp/dbl & activities (inc full-day game drive); all rates FB; park game drives US$60/80pp half day/full day, inc park entrance fees

🔺 **Ruaha Hilltop Lodge** (15 rooms) m 0784 726709/0754 489375; e ruahahilltoplodge@ yahoo.com; www.ruahahilltoplodge.com. Situated on the steep slope of Ideremle Mountain, some 15km from the park entrance gate along the Tungamalenga road, this is another new good-value lodge, with accommodation in a simple en-suite thatched *banda* with hot water, solar power (19.00–22.00) & a private balcony. There's a great panoramic view from the restaurant/bar area, & the management can arrange transfers from Iringa as well as game drives into the park, visits to Hehe & Maasai villages & hiking to Ideremle Volcanic Caves. US$80pp/dbl, FB

🔺 **Msembe Camp** (11 rooms) PO Box 369, Iringa, Tanzania; no telephone. This national park camp near the headquarters lies close to the river & some extensive open plains teeming with game. The accommodation isn't up to much – prefabricated en-suite dbl & family *bandas* that look like they must get seriously hot during the middle of the day – but it's the cheapest on offer within the park. Bedding, firewood & water are provided, & drinks can be bought at the nearby staff bar, but all food must be brought with you. $

🔺 **Tungamalenga Lodge and Campsite** (12 rooms) m 0744 983519/0745 469504; e tungcamp@yahoo.com; www.ruahatungacamp.com. This new camp & curio shop is situated in the eponymous village about 27km before the park entrance gate on the left fork coming from Iringa. The small en-suite *bandas*, each with 2 beds & netting, would seem rather overpriced were it not for their proximity to the park. Camping, with access to a clean shower & toilet & a self-catering area, costs US$10pp. Meals are available by arrangement & there's an on-site carving workshop. US$45, FB

SAADANI NATIONAL PARK

Protected as a game reserve since 1969 and recently gazetted as a national park, Saadani is the only wildlife sanctuary in east Africa with an Indian Ocean beachfront. The original 200km² game reserve, centred on the small but ancient fishing village of Saadani, was expanded to cover 500km² in 1996, and it is likely to redouble in area with the proposed incorporation of a tract of former ranchland. As recently as ten years ago, despite its proximity to Dar es Salaam, Saadani was among the most obscure and inaccessible conservation areas in east Africa, lacking tourist facilities in any form. Inadequate protection and resultant poaching also meant that wildlife had been severely depleted, to the extent that Saadani's status as a game reserve seemed all but nominal. In recent years, however, Saadani has received renewed attention from conservationists and tourists alike. A top-notch private tented camp has been established, access has improved, there's been a concerted clampdown on poaching and an attempt to integrate adjacent villages into the conservation effort that was initiated by the Department of Wildlife with assistance from Germany's GTZ agency in 1998.

Viewed purely as a wildlife destination, Saadani cannot yet bear comparison to Tanzania's finest – though if present trends continue, it may well be up with them ten years hence. But even as things stand, Saadani is a thoroughly worthwhile and enjoyable retreat, allowing visitors to combine the hedonistic pleasures of a perfect sandy beach with guided bush walks, game drives, and boat trips up the Wami River. It is also the closest national park to Zanzibar – 15 minutes away by air, with scheduled flights likely to be introduced in the near future.

The park has an excellent website for information, camps and current fees (*www.saadanipark.org*).

BACKGROUND INFORMATION Inland of its 20km coastline, Saadani supports a park-like cover of open grassland interspersed with stands of acacia trees and knotted coastal thicket. Along the coast, palm-lined beaches are separated by extensive mangrove stands, while the major watercourses are fringed by lush riparian woodland. The park supports a wide range of ungulates, with game densities generally highest in January and February, and from June to August, when the plains near the lodge hold more water. At all times of year, however, you can be reasonably confident of encountering giraffe, buffalo, warthog, common waterbuck, reedbuck, hartebeest and wildebeest, along with troops of yellow baboon and vervet monkey. Something of a Saadani special, likely to be seen a few times on any game drive, is the red duiker, a diminutive, beautiful and normally very shy antelope of coastal scrub and forest. Quite common, but less easily seen, are greater kudu and eland. Saadani also harbours a small population of Roosevelt's sable, an endangered race that also occurs in the Selous Game Reserve.

The elephant population, though small, is on the increase, and herds of up to 30 are sighted with increasing frequency. Lion are also making something of a comeback; leopard, spotted hyena and black-backed jackal are also around, along with the usual small nocturnal predators. In addition to game drives, guided walks offer a good chance of seeing various antelope and representatives of Saadani's rich variety of woodland birds. Hippo and crocodile are normally encountered on river trips, along with a good selection of marine and riverine birds. The beaches in and around Saadani form one of the last major breeding sites for green turtles on mainland Tanzania.

The lodge – and effectively the park – is often forced to close over April and May when the black cotton soil roads tend to become waterlogged.

Entrance fees Entrance to the game reserve costs US$20 per person per 24 hours, with vehicles being charged an additional US$30.

GETTING THERE AND AWAY No scheduled flight currently lands at Saadani airstrip but air charters can be arranged in Zanzibar through reliable tour operators or agents, or through the lodges listed below. The lodges also operate road transfers to/from Dar es Salaam, so you could fly between Zanzibar and Dar and go the rest of the way to Saadani by road.

WHERE TO STAY
Upmarket
Saadani Safari Camp ☎ 022 2773294; **m** 0713 555678; **e** info@saadanilodge.com; www.saadanilodge.com. This small & intimate tented

camp, which runs attractively along a palm-fringed beach about 1km north of Saadani village, has undergone a major facelift over the last couple of years, most notably with the addition of a swimming pool & the luxurious Siri Suite. Accommodation is in comfortable framed canvas tents with a *makuti* roof, en-suite facilities, solar electricity & twin or dbl bed, as well as a second netted bed on the balcony should you want to sleep outside. The open wooden bar & dining area is very peaceful, while a treehouse overlooks a waterhole regularly visited by waterbuck, bushbuck, buffalo & various waterbirds — & very occasionally by lion & elephant. Activities include game drives, guided walks with a ranger, & boat trips on the river. *US$285/480 sgl/dbl & 1 activity/day; a honeymoon rate of US$300pp inc private dinner & wine; all rates FB*

🏠 **Tent With A View** (9 rooms) 📞 022 2110507; 📱 0741 323318; e tentview@cats-net.com; www.saadani.com. This is another small camp, built a couple of years ago along a pretty beach about 30km north of Saadani village near Mkwaja, an area regarded to be the best in the park for elephant sightings. The camp consists of 9 standing tents on stilted wooden platforms spaced out in the coastal scrub immediately behind the beach. Built predominantly using local materials, from elephant-felled palms to old dhows, the interiors are simple but clean & bright in sapphire & white. There is solar power for lights & hot water. It offers a similar range of guided activities to Saadani Safari Camp, while several short self-guided walking trails emanate from the camp, & you can canoe in the nearby Mafuwe Creek. *Luxury tent US$275/390 sgl/dbl exc activities; honeymoon suite US$590 dbl; all rates FB; game drive & boat safari (full day) US$90pp/min 2; game drive (half day) US$40pp; walking safari US$40pp*

Budget

🏠 **Saadani Resthouse** No contact details. Though somewhat rundown, this 10-room government resthouse situated on the beach some 500m north of Saadani Safari Camp is by far the most affordable option in the park. Bookings are seldom necessary & although camping is permitted, it costs the same as a room. §

Appendix 1

LANGUAGE with thanks to Said el-Gheithy

PRONUNCIATION Pronunciation of Swahili is generally straightforward: every syllable is sounded and there are no 'silent endings'. In longer words the stress is on the penultimate syllable. The most confusing feature for learners is that many words have a prefix and suffix which change according to subject and tense. However, when speaking, beginners can ignore these additions, and still be understood.

Of course, the best way to learn is to listen to the people around you. For more detailed information, use a phrasebook (see *Appendix 2*, page 380), or visit the Institute of Kiswahili and Foreign Languages (see page 163).

USEFUL SWAHILI WORDS AND PHRASES The following basics are necessarily very simplified, and may not be grammatically correct, but by using them you will be understood in most situations. Many Zanzibaris will be delighted to hear a visitor using a few Swahili words – even if they are mispronounced or put in the wrong order!

Introductions and greetings Introductions and salutations are very important in Swahili culture, particularly when speaking to adults or people older than yourself, even if the age difference is slight. (Children are not usually greeted by adults outside their family.)

The most common forms of address are the traditional Muslim greetings (in Arabic), regardless of the religion of the people being greeted, each with its own response:

Salama aleikum	Peace be with you
Aleikum salam	And peace be with you (response)

You can also use the following greetings when addressing older people:

Sblakheri	Good morning
Msalkheri	Good afternoon/evening
Shkamoo	(a general greeting which can be used at any time of day)
Marahaba	(response to '*shkamoo*')
Habari zako or *hujambo*	How are you?
Al humdul allah	Everything is well (response: literally 'Thanks be to Allah')

For people of the same age, and especially for friends, you can use *Habari*, which means 'Hello' (also meaning 'How are you?', literally 'what news?'). The reply might be *Al humdul allah*, or the more casual *Nzuri* ('good'), *Nzuri sana* ('very good') or *Safi* ('fine'). In areas where Swahili is not spoken as a first language the reply is often *Mzuri*, with an 'M', rather than 'Nzuri'. *Habari* can also be used for 'Excuse me' (when attracting somebody's attention), but it is still considered impolite to simply say '*Habari*' ('hello') to someone older than you.

Mambo is an even more casual way of greeting friends, meaning 'how's it going?' The response is *Poa* (something along the lines of 'neat', 'cool' or 'dandy').

Although *Jambo* also means 'Hello', Zanzibaris never use this word speaking to each other, and it tends only to be used by Zanzibaris talking to tourists. (In the same way, the oft-quoted 'Hakuna matata' – 'no problem' – is mock-Swahili-for-tourists imported from Kenya, and not used by Zanzibaris. If you want to express this idea, a more correct alternative would be 'Hamna neno' or 'Haidhuru'.)

Children in Zanzibar greet adults with *Chechei*, usually followed by the title of the adult. The response is the same.

Even when speaking in English a Swahili acquaintance will ask 'How are you?', 'How are things today?', 'How is your husband/wife/friend?' You should do the same. Launching straight into any subject without the opening questions is rude. Traditional Zanzibaris expect women to be less forward than men, although in areas used to tourists this does not apply.

Hodi means 'Hello, anyone at home, can I come in?' used when knocking on somebody's door. *Karibu* is the response, meaning 'welcome' (literally 'come near').

You may hear the word *mzungu* ('white person') directed to you, particularly by children, but it is not disrespectful.

The basics

Goodbye	*Kwaheri*
Welcome	*Karibu*
Please	*Tafadali*
Thank you (very much)	*Asante (sana)*
yes	*ndiyo*
no	*hapana*

Conversation starters and enders

What is your name?	*Jina lako nani?*
My name is Chris	*Jina langu Chris*
Where are you from?	*Unatoka wapi?*
I am from …	*Mimi ninatoka …*
	(the *mimi* is often dropped)
Where do you live?	*Unakaa wapi?*
Where are you staying? (ie: locally)	*Umefikia wapi?*
I am sorry, I don't understand	*Samahani sifahamu*
I don't speak Swahili	*Sijui Kiswahili*
I speak a very little Swahili	*Nazungumza Kiswahili kidogo tu*

Other useful words and phrases

OK (agreement)	*sawa*
sorry (condolences)	*pole* (not used for apologies)
where?	*wapi?*
what	*nini*
here	*hapa*
there	*hapo*
there is	*ipo*
is there…?	*iko…?*
there isn't…	*hakuna…*
how much?	*bei gani?* (literally 'what price?')
how many shillings?	*shillingi ngapi?*
I want to go to Bububu	*Nataka kwenda Bububu*
Where is the bus for Makunduchi?	*Liko wapi basi la Makunduchi?*

Where is the ruin?		Liko wapi gofu?	
I am ill		Mimi mgonjwa	
Where is the hospital?		Iko wapi hospitali?	
Where is the doctor?		Yuko wapi daktari?	
I am lost		Nimepotea	

left	kushoto	tomorrow	kesho
right	kulia	yesterday	jana
straight on	moja kwa moja	bank	benki
near	karibu	shop	duka
far	mbali	market	soko
today	leo	café, eating-house	hoteli ya chakula

Food and drink

beef	nyama ya ngombe	water	maji
chicken	kuku	tea	chai
eggs	yai	coffee	kahawa
fish	samaki	milk	maziwa
potato	viazi	sugar	sukari
rice	mchele		

The word *soda* means any fizzy drink in a bottle. In the smarter hotels in Zanzibar Town, if you want soda water try asking for a club soda.

Numbers

1	moja	21	ishirini na moja
2	mbili	30	thelathini
3	tatu	40	arobaini
4	nne	50	hamsini
5	tano	60	sitini
6	sita	70	sabini
7	saba	80	themanini
8	nane	90	tisini
9	tisa	100	mia
10	kumi	101	mia na moja
11	kumi na moja	102	mia na mbili
12	kumi na mbili	200	mia mbili
20	ishirini	300	mia tatu

Time Swahili time starts at 00.00, the hour of sunrise, which is at 06.00 in Western time.

What time is it?	Saa ngapi?
07.00	saa moja (literally one o'clock)
08.00	saa mbili
noon	saa sita
13.00	saa saba

When finding out about bus or boat departures, check if the time you've been told is Swahili time or Western time. This can be complicated further by some buses leaving outlying villages very early in the morning.

Appendix 2

FURTHER INFORMATION
BOOKS
History and background

General histories of Africa The following books are general histories of Africa or the east African region, which include sections on Zanzibar. Some are old and now long out of print, but make interesting reading if you can find them – try a specialist historical bookshop. Pakenham's classic history of Africa from the 1870s onwards is particularly compulsive, and often reprinted in paperback. Taylor's book about the European settlers who 'stayed on' in east Africa after the countries gained independence, looks at the colonial past in the present context, and neatly combines history with contemporary travel writing.

Coupland, R *The Exploitation of East Africa 1856–1890: The Slave Trade and the Scramble* Faber, London, 1939
Davidson, B *The Story of Africa* London, 1984
Freeman-Grenville, G S P *The East African Coast: Select Documents* Oxford University Press, 2nd edn, 1975
A History of East Africa Oxford University Press, London, 1963
Pakenham, T *The Scramble for Africa* Weidenfeld and Nicolson, London, 1991
Prestage, E *Portuguese Pioneers* A & C Black, London, 1933
Taylor S *Livingstone's Tribe* HarperCollins, London, 1999

Early histories of Zanzibar The next six books cover Zanzibar specifically, but they are old guidebooks and histories from British colonial days. Most are out of print, though a local Zanzibar publisher, Gallery Publications, has reprinted some of the titles.

Brode, H *Tippu Tip: His Career in Zanzibar and Central Africa* Gallery Publications, Zanzibar, 2002. This is a reprint of the original 1903 study of the career of Tippu Tip, Zanzibar's most famous (or infamous) trader. A fascinating and highly readable account of life on Zanzibar and the east African mainland over a century ago.
Gray, J *History of Zanzibar from the Middle Ages to 1856* Oxford University Press, London, 1962
Ingrams, W H *Zanzibar: Its History and People* Witherby, London, 1931
Lyne, R N *Zanzibar in Contemporary Times* Darf, London, 1905. Reprinted 1987
Ommanney, F D *Isle of Cloves* Longman, London, 1957
Pearce, Major F B *Zanzibar: The Island Metropolis of Eastern Africa* Fisher Unwin, London, 1920

General histories of Zanzibar and the Indian Ocean

Hall, R *Empires of the Monsoon* HarperCollins, London, 1999. A fascinating history of the lands around the Indian Ocean, including good sections on Zanzibar.
Hamilton, G, *In the Wake of da Gama* Abacus, London, 1951
Hamilton, G, *Princes of Zinj* Hutchinson, London, 1957. Comprehensive and accessible historical accounts, with an emphasis on readability, sometimes at the expense of accuracy.

Modern histories of Zanzibar

Nurse, D and Spear, T *The Swahili: Reconstructing the History and Language of an African Society* The Ethnohistory Series, University of Pennsylvania Press, Philadelphia, 1985. This is an excellent, short, readable book which argues convincingly that the Swahili culture is more of an African (and less an Arab) phenomenon than previously thought. Highly recommended.

Horton, M C 'The Swahili Corridor'. This article was published in *Scientific American* 255(9) 86–93 (1987). Horton has been one of the most influential archaeologists to work on the east African coast, and has done excavations and surveys on Pemba and Unguja (Zanzibar Island). This is an excellent short piece that touches on some of the Mediterranean connections with east Africa.

Mapuri, O *The 1964 Revolution* (published 1996). This short, locally published book is a concise history of Zanzibari politics, covering the period from 1964 up to the 1995 elections.

These three books are modern, post-revolution, textbook-style histories:

Martin, E B *Zanzibar: Tradition and Revolution* Hamish Hamilton, London, 1978
Sheriff, A *Slaves, Spices and Ivory in Zanzibar* James Currey, London, 1987
Sheriff, A, and Ferguson E D *Zanzibar under Colonial Rule* James Currey, London, 1991

Zanzibar and Oman Four modern and very detailed books, with specific reference to the Oman-Zanzibar link:

Al-Maamiry, A H *Oman and East Africa* Lancers Books, New Delhi, 1979
Al-Maamiry, A H *Omani Sultans in Zanzibar* Lancers Books, New Delhi, 1988
Bennett, N R *A History of the Arab State of Zanzibar* Methuen, London, 1978
Bhacker, M R *Trade and Empire in Muscat and Zanzibar* Routledge, London, 1992

Railways and ships

Hill, M H *The Permanent Way* East African Literature Bureau, Nairobi, 1949 and Miller, C *The Lunatic Express* Macmillan, Ballantine Books, Random House, 1971. These two books are histories of the East African railways, both with good sections on Zanzibar.

Patience K *Zanzibar and the Bububu Railway* (published by the author, 1995). A fascinating little booklet about the only railway on Zanzibar, which existed at the beginning of the 20th century.

Patience K *Zanzibar and the Loss of HMS Pegasus* (published by the author, 1995) and Patience K, *Zanzibar and the Shortest War in History* (published by the author, 1994). Two excellent booklets written and published by Zanzibar historian Kevin Patience. Well researched, they describe in full events which might otherwise be confined to the footnotes of history. The gunship *Pegasus* was sunk during World War I and this book also contains background information on British naval ships in east Africa, while *Shortest War* describes the 1896 bombardment of the sultan's palace, with several fascinating archive photos.

Patience K *Königsberg – A German East African Raider* (published by the author, 1997). The *Königsberg* was the German gunboat which sunk the British *Pegasus,* fully described in an earlier book by the same author. This painstakingly researched book covers historical events before and after the *Pegasus* incident, including the *Königsberg*'s final sinking by another British ship in the Rufiji Delta, southwest of Zanzibar. The chapter describing the present-day position of the *Königsberg*'s relics scattered all over East Africa is particularly interesting.

Architecture and history

Mwalim, M A *Doors of Zanzibar* Gallery Publications, Zanzibar, 2002. Using hundreds of photographs by Uwe Rau, this fascinating book catalogues the unique doors which have become an icon of Zanzibar Stone Town, and covers the various Indian, Arabic and Swahili influences.

Pitcher, G and Jafferji, J *Zanzibar Style* Gallery Publications, Zanzibar, 2001. This celebration of Zanzibari architecture is listed under *Large-format photo books*.

Siravo, F, and Bianca, S *A Plan for the Historic Stone Town* Gallery Publications in association with the Aga Khan Trust for Culture, Zanzibar, 1997. A large and detailed discussion document, full of fascinating photos, plans and drawings, which analyses the current situation then proposes a major and systematic plan for the repair, preservation and conservation of the many old buildings in Stone Town. This is a vital reference for anyone interested in the history and architecture of Zanzibar.

Sheriff, Prof A *Zanzibar Stone Town: An Architectural Exploration* Gallery Publications, Zanzibar, 1998. With skilful photographs by Javed Jafferji and illuminating text by a leading Zanzibar historian, this handy little pocket-sized book is an ideal guide and companion for your strolls around the narrow streets of Stone Town. Highly recommended.

Sheriff, Prof A *The History and Conservation of Zanzibar Stone Town* (published by James Currey). This book is part of Currey's Eastern African Studies series, and although quite academic in tone, it has a lot of useful information for anyone keen on the history of Zanzibari architecture.

Princess Salme

Ruete, E (born Salme binte Said Al-Busaidi), *Memoirs of an Arabian Princess from Zanzibar* Gallery Publications, Zanzibar, 1998. This book is a translation of *Memoiren einer Arabischen Prinzessin*, which was first published in 1888. It was also reprinted by Markus Wiener Publishing (New York, 1989), but the latest translation is now easily available in Zanzibar bookshops. It is a very readable first-hand account by a unique figure in the history of Zanzibar, providing a good overview of the period and several fascinating personal insights. Highly recommended.

Ruete, E (born Salme binte Said Al-Busaidi), *An Arabian Princess Between Two Worlds: Memoirs, Letters, Sequels to the Memoirs*, ed E Van Donzel, (E J Brill Publishing, Leiden, Netherlands, 1993). Volume 3 in a series on Arab History and Culture. This is a very detailed and comprehensive account of Salme's life in Zanzibar, Germany and Syria. Includes a biography of her son, Said-Rudolph Ruete. Expensive and hard to obtain.

Travel and exploration

Batchelor, J and J *In Stanley's Footsteps* Blandford Press, London, 1990, and Wilson, C, and Irwin, A, *In Quest of Livingstone* House of Lochar, Scotland, 1999. Two books in which British couples follow the routes of the great explorers in Africa. Livingstone started many of his travels in Zanzibar. The Batchelors mount a full expedition, while Colum Wilson and Aisling Irwin trace Livingstone's final journey through Tanzania and Zambia at a more grassroots level.

Burton, Richard Francis *Zanzibar: City, Island and Coast* London, 1872. Many early European explorers in Africa mentioned Zanzibar in their journals, but Burton, perhaps the most 'colourful' of them all, is the only one to write a specific book on Zanzibar. Although published first over a century ago, reprints are sometimes available.

Hugon, A *The Exploration of Africa* New Horizons, Thames and Hudson, 1999. This is a fascinating and beautifully illustrated little book, with good coverage on the journeys of Livingstone, Stanley and others in east Africa.

Moorehead, A *The White Nile* Hamish Hamilton, London, 1960. A classic book on the history of European exploration in the east African region. Often reprinted. Readable and recommended.

Mountfield, D *A History of African Exploration* Domus Books/Hamlyn, London, 1976 and Richards, C, and Place, J *East African Explorers* Oxford University Press, London, 1960. Two books on exploration in Africa, although both out of print and hard to find, including some mentions of Zanzibar where many journeys began and ended.

Royal Geographical Society (ed John Keay), *History of World Exploration* Paul Hamlyn, Reed International, London, 1991. Includes sections on the exploration of east Africa.

Teal, J *Livingstone* Putnam, New York, 1973. A fine biography of the great explorer.

Waugh, E *Remote People* Duckworth, 1931, republished 1985 by Penguin Books, UK, as part of their 20th Century Classics series. Waugh travelled to many parts of Africa, including Zanzibar, as a newspaper correspondent, and his dry observations are as engaging today as they were when first written.

Large-format photo books

Jafferji, J, and Rees Jones B *Images of Zanzibar* HSP Publications, London, 1996. Much of east Africa has been covered by publishers of lavishly illustrated 'coffee-table' books, but until recently Zanzibar seems to have escaped their notice. Local photographer Javed Jafferji has made up for this with a portfolio of his finest work, showing rich colours and an eye for detail perfectly capturing the spirit of the islands.

Jafferji, J, Jafferji, Z and Waterman, P *A Taste of Zanzibar: Chakula Kizuri* Gallery Publications, Zanzibar, 2001. Not hungry? You will be if you read this bountiful cookbook which celebrates (and helps you create) Zanzibar's delicious cuisine, enhanced with 250 mouthwatering colour photos.

Pitcher, G and Jafferji, J *Zanzibar Style* Gallery Publications, Zanzibar, 2001. This sumptuous and stimulating book combines evocative photos by Javed Jafferji and text by Gemma Pitcher to explore the themes that have inspired Zanzibar's unique architecture and interior design – from Europe, Oman and India, as well as of course the natural forms of Africa – and also covers related aspects such as crafts, textiles and furniture. Listed by *The Times* as one of the 'Top 20 travel books for Christmas' 2001.

Sheriff, A *Zanzibar – Romance of the Ages* HSP Publications, London, 1996. Accomplished photographer Javed Jafferji compiled this fascinating collection of archive photos from the late 19th and early 20th centuries – the text and captions were provided by Abdul Sheriff, Professor of History at the University of Dar es Salaam and Principal Curator of the Zanzibar Museums.

Fiction and autobiography

Bateman, G *Zanzibar Tales* Gallery Publications, Zanzibar, 2002. Another reprint from the industrious Gallery house; a collection of amusing (and sometimes confusing) Zanzibari folktales originally recorded and translated into English by George Bateman almost a century ago, and enhanced by lively illustrations by Walter Bobbett.

Haji, M M *Sowing The Wind* Gallery Publications, Zanzibar, 2002. This autobiographical novel explores life and politics on the islands of Zanzibar during the turbulent years which led to independence in 1963, and the revolution which followed.

Kaye, M M *Death in Zanzibar* Penguin, London, 1984 – first published as *The House of Shadows*, Longman 1959 and Kaye, M M, *Trade Wind* Longman, 1963, Penguin, 1982. Two historical romantic novels set in Zanzibar. *Death in Zanzibar* is also published with two other M M Kaye *Death in…* stories in a larger book called the *House of Shade*.

Field guides
Mammals and birds

Kingdon, J *The Kingdon Fieldguide to African Mammals* Academic Press, USA and UK, 1997. For animals on Zanzibar, a field guide to the more common species of east Africa is of limited use. However, Kingdon's book is by far the best, as it covers every species in Africa in detail, including those on Zanzibar, with excellent illustrations and background notes.

van Perlo, B *Illustrated Checklist of the Birds of Eastern Africa* Harper Collins, London, 1996 and Williams, J, and Arlott, N *A Field Guide to the Birds of East Africa* Collins, London. For birds, the field guide you choose is determined by your level of interest. Of the books listed above, the van Perlo *Illustrated Checklist* is complete, with illustrations of every bird occurring in Africa, including those on Zanzibar, while the classic Williams & Arlott also has fairly good coverage. The large and comprehensive *Birds of Kenya & Northern Tanzania* by Zimmerman is used by keen birders, and it includes most species which occur on Zanzibar, but it's quite heavy to carry around.

Marine wildlife

Richmond, M (ed), *A Guide to the Seashores of Eastern Africa and the Western Indian Ocean Islands* Sida/SAREC, 1997. This excellent book contains around 450 pages, including over 150 of colour illustrations. More than 1,600 species of marine plants and animals are illustrated, plus notes on geology, climate, ecology and human activities. This is an essential tool for scientists, and a useful handbook for all visitors to the region. Proceeds from the sales of this book are put towards marine education purposes in the region, administered by the SEA Trust. Although hard to find overseas (only specialist stores stock it), this book is readily available in Zanzibar from all good bookshops.

Forstle, A, and Vierkotter, R *Marine Green Book* Green Ocean, Zanzibar, 1997. This handy little pocket encyclopaedia covers everything you need to know about marine life (from algae to zooxanthellae) and marine activities (from anchor damage to the Zanzibar Sea Turtle Project) in and around the Zanzibar archipelago. It also covers snorkelling, diving, coral reefs, fish and marine habitats. It is available in Zanzibar bookshops at a very reasonable price, and all proceeds go to fund environmental education projects.

Manuals, guidebooks and phrasebooks

Bogaert, P *The Krazy Kanga Book* Gallery Publications, Zanzibar, 2002. An offbeat 'adult' study of the *kanga* or 'wrap', the ubiquitous and vital garment for the women of east Africa.

Briggs, Philip *Tanzania: The Bradt Travel Guide* Bradt Travel Guides, 6th edn 2009. The most comprehensive guide to Tanzania, ideal both for those heading off the beaten track and travellers visiting the country's major attractions.

Dawood, R *How to Stay Healthy Abroad* Oxford University Press

Leonard, R *Swahili Phrasebook* Lonely Planet

Hatt, J *The Tropical Traveller* Pan

Koornhof, A *Dive Sites of Kenya & Tanzania, including Zanzibar, Pemba & Mafia* New Holland

Rattray, Gordon *Access Africa: Safaris for People with Limited Mobility* Bradt Travel Guides, 2009. Covers everything relevant to planning a safari in Africa for those with limited mobility, including transport, accommodation, and access to restaurants and national parks.

Wilson-Howarth, Jane, and Ellis, Dr Matthew *Your Child Abroad: A Travel Health Guide* Bradt Travel Guides 2004, with updates on www.bradtguides.com

Wilson-Howarth, Jane and Levene, Betty *Bugs, Bites and Bowels* Cadogan, UK, 2006

BOOKSHOPS

The Travel Bookshop 13 Blenheim Cres, London W11 2EE, UK; ☏ 020 7229 5260; www.thetravelbookshop.co.uk. Stocks guidebooks, phrasebooks, history, fiction, maps, and anything else to do with travel publications. They can source old and out-of-print books, and operate a worldwide mail-order service.

Risborough Books 81 Manor Park Av, Princes Risborough, Bucks HP27 9AR, UK; ☏ 01844 343165. Specialises in second-hand books on east Africa, and offers mail order only. Contact them by post (no fax or email) for a list.

WEBSITES If you've got access to the internet, you can get further information on Zanzibar from the following websites. Most have links to other useful relevant sites.

Africa Confidential (*www.africa-confidential.com*) gives the inside story on political events across Africa, including Tanzania and Zanzibar.

Africa Travel Association (*www.africa-ata.org*) has close links with the US-based *Africa Travel* magazine and is an interesting source of information on the whole continent.

African Travel and Tourism Association (*www.atta.co.uk*) represents many tour operators covering Africa, and is an excellent directory of useful contacts.

Internet Living Swahili Dictionary (*www.yale.edu/swahili*) is a very handy on-line Swahili–English dictionary, with links to other Swahili-related sites.

The Hunger Site (*www.thehungersite.com*) is not directly related to Zanzibar, but if you visit this site (no more than once per day) and click on a 'donate' button, the site's sponsors will give two *free* cups of food to a developing country.

Zanzibar Travel Network, also called **Zanzibar Net** (*www.zanzibar.net*) has sections on history, diving, touring, beaches, history, travel tips and so on. It also has a good selection of links to other sites which cover Zanzibar.

Zanzibar.org (*www.zanzibar.org*) is a gateway site with pages on several hotels in Zanzibar Town and around Zanzibar Island, plus coverage of various aspects of Zanzibar such as culture, history and wildlife.

Sites for general news and information

www.allafrica.com Huge pan-African news site with vast amounts of topical content.

www.theexpress.com/ Weekly newspaper based in Dar es Salaam.

www.tanserve.com Interesting and slightly off-beat Dar-based portal with a mix of news and information.

www-sul.stanford.edu/depts/ssrg/africa/tanzan.html Extensive listing of links for Tanzania and Zanzibar.

www.zanzibarwatch.org/ Human rights organisation listing abuses in the run-up to recent elections.

www.zanzibargovernment.org/ Official site of the government of Zanzibar.

http://home.globalfrontiers.com/Zanzibar/sights_to_see_in_zanzibar.htm Historical site on Zanzibar, with pictures and illustrations.

www.africa.upenn.edu/Country_Specific/Tanzania.html University of Pennsylvania African studies course – links pages.

www.zanzibar-travel-guide.com Online site where you'll find much of the text of this guide, plus many additional useful links.

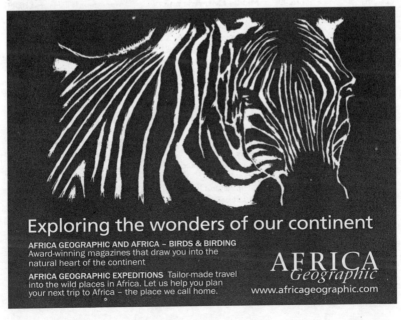

Bradt Travel Guides

Africa

Africa Overland	£15.99
Algeria	£15.99
Benin	£14.99
Botswana: Okavango, Chobe, Northern Kalahari	£15.99
Burkina Faso	£14.99
Cameroon	£15.99
Cape Verde Islands	£14.99
Congo	£15.99
Eritrea	£15.99
Ethiopia	£15.99
Gambia, The	£13.99
Ghana	£15.99
Johannesburg	£6.99
Madagascar	£15.99
Malawi	£13.99
Mali	£13.95
Mauritius, Rodrigues & Réunion	£13.99
Mozambique	£13.99
Namibia	£15.99
Niger	£14.99
Nigeria	£17.99
Rwanda	£14.99
São Tomé & Principe	£14.99
Seychelles	£14.99
Sudan	£13.95
Tanzania, Northern	£13.99
Tanzania	£16.99
Uganda	£15.99
Zambia	£17.99
Zanzibar	£14.99

Britain and Europe

Albania	£15.99
Armenia, Nagorno Karabagh	£14.99
Azores	£13.99
Baltic Cities	£14.99
Belarus	£14.99
Belgrade	£6.99
Bosnia & Herzegovina	£13.99
Bratislava	£9.99
Budapest	£9.99
Bulgaria	£13.99
Cork	£6.99
Croatia	£13.99
Cyprus see North Cyprus	
Czech Republic	£13.99
Dresden	£7.99
Dubrovnik	£6.99
Estonia	£13.99
Faroe Islands	£15.99
Georgia	£14.99

Helsinki	£7.99
Hungary	£14.99
Iceland	£14.99
Kosovo	£14.99
Lapland	£13.99
Latvia	£13.99
Lille	£6.99
Lithuania	£14.99
Ljubljana	£7.99
Luxembourg	£13.99
Macedonia	£14.99
Montenegro	£14.99
North Cyprus	£12.99
Paris, Lille & Brussels	£11.95
Riga	£6.99
River Thames, In the Footsteps of the Famous	£10.95
Serbia	£14.99
Slovakia	£14.99
Slovenia	£13.99
Spitsbergen	£14.99
Switzerland: Rail, Road, Lake	£13.99
Tallinn	£6.99
Transylvania	£14.99
Ukraine	£14.99
Vilnius	£6.99
Zagreb	£6.99

Middle East, Asia and Australasia

China: Yunnan Province	£13.99
Great Wall of China	£13.99
Iran	£14.99
Iraq: Then & Now	£15.99
Israel	£15.99
Kazakhstan	£15.99
Kyrgyzstan	£15.99
Maldives	£15.99
Mongolia	£16.99
North Korea	£14.99
Oman	£13.99
Shangri-La: A Travel Guide to the Himalayan Dream	£14.99
Sri Lanka	£15.99
Syria	£14.99
Tibet	£13.99
Turkmenistan	£14.99
Yemen	£14.99

The Americas and the Caribbean

Amazon, The	£14.99
Argentina	£15.99

Bolivia	£14.99
Cayman Islands	£14.99
Chile	£16.95
Colombia	£16.99
Costa Rica	£13.99
Dominica	£14.99
Falkland Islands	£13.95
Grenada, Carriacou & Petite Martinique	£14.99
Guyana	£14.99
Panama	£13.95
Peru & Bolivia: The Bradt Trekking Guide	£12.95
St Helena	£14.99
Turks & Caicos Islands	£14.99
USA by Rail	£14.99

Wildlife

100 Animals to See Before They Die	£16.99
Antarctica: Guide to the Wildlife	£15.99
Arctic: Guide to the Wildlife	£15.99
Central & Eastern European Wildlife	£15.99
Chinese Wildlife	£16.99
East African Wildlife	£19.99
Galápagos Wildlife	£15.99
Madagascar Wildlife	£16.99
New Zealand Wildlife	£14.99
North Atlantic Wildlife	£16.99
Peruvian Wildlife	£15.99
Southern African Wildlife	£18.95
Sri Lankan Wildlife	£15.99
Wildlife and Conservation Volunteering: The Complete Guide	£13.99

Eccentric Guides

Eccentric Australia	£12.99
Eccentric Britain	£13.99
Eccentric California	£13.99
Eccentric Cambridge	£6.99
Eccentric Edinburgh	£5.95
Eccentric France	£12.95
Eccentric London	£13.99

Others

Your Child Abroad: A Travel Health Guide	£10.95
Something Different for the Weekend	£9.99

CLAIM YOUR HALF-PRICE BRADT GUIDE!

Order Form

To order your half-price copy of a Bradt guide, and to enter our prize draw to win £100, please fill in the order form below and send it to Bradt Travel Guides by post, fax or email.

Please send me one copy of the following guide at half the UK retail price

Title	Retail price	Half price
. . .	. . . .	. . . .	. . . .

Please send the following additional guides at full UK retail price

No	Title	Retail price	Total
. . .	. . . .	. . . .	. . . .
. . .	. . . .	. . . .	. . . .
. . .	. . . .	. . . .	. . . .

Sub total . . . .
Post & packing . . . .
(£2 per book UK; £4 per book Europe; £6 per book rest of world)
Total . . . .

Name . . . .

Address . . . .

Tel . . . .   Email . . . .

☐ I enclose a cheque for £ . . . . made payable to Bradt Travel Guides Ltd

☐ I would like to pay by credit card. Number: . . . .

Expiry date: . . . / . . .   3-digit security code (on reverse of card) . . . . .

Issue no (debit cards only) . . . . .

☐ Please add my name to your catalogue mailing list.

☐ I would be happy for you to use my name and comments in Bradt marketing material.

Send your order on this form, with the completed questionnaire, to:

Bradt Travel Guides ZAN7
23 High Street, Chalfont St Peter, Bucks SL9 9QE
☎ +44 (0)1753 893444   f +44 (0)1753 892333
e info@bradtguides.com   www.bradtguides.com

Index

Page numbers in **bold** indicate major entries; those in *italic* indicate maps